LONGSTREET HIGHROAD GUIDE

TO THE

OREGON CASCADES

BY TERRY W. SHEELY

LONGSTREET
Atlanta, Georgia

Published by
LONGSTREET PRESS, INC.
2140 Newmarket Parkway
Suite 122
Marietta, Georgia 30067

Great efforts have been made to make the information in this book as accurate as possible. However, over time trails are rerouted and signs and landmarks may change. If you find a change has occurred to a trail in the book, please let us know so we can correct future editions. *A word of caution:* Outdoor recreation by its nature is potentially hazardous. All participants in such activities must assume all responsibility for their own actions and safety. The scope of this book does not cover all potential hazards and risks involved in outdoor recreation activities.

Printed by RR Donnelley & Sons, Harrisonburg, VA

1st printing 2000

Library of Congress Catalog Number 99-068570

ISBN: 1-56352-538-0

Book editing, design, and cartography by Lenz Design & Communications, Inc., Decatur, Georgia.
www.lenzdesign.org

Cover illustration by R. Swain Gifford, *Picturesque America*, 1872

Cover design by Richard J. Lenz, Decatur, Georgia

Illustrations by Danny Woodard, Loganville, Georgia

Photographs: Pages 1, 17, 33, 93, 171, 211, and 315 by Terry Sheely. Pages 133, 257, and 289 courtesy of Oregon State Parks.

The mountains of the Pacific Northwest are tangled, wild, remote, and high. They have the roar of torrents and avalanches in their throats.

Rock cliffs such as Kloochman rise as straight in the air as the Washington Monument and two or three times as high. Snow-capped peaks with aprons of eternal glaciers command the skyline—giant sentinels 11,000, 12,000, 14,000 feet high, such as Hood, Adams and Rainier.

There are no slow-moving, sluggish rivers in these mountains. The streams run clear, cold, and fast.

There are remote valleys and canyons where man has never been. The meadows and lakes are not placid, idyllic spots. The sternness of the mountains has been imparted to them. There are cougar to scout the camp at night. Deer and elk bed down in stands of mountain ash, snowbrush, and mountain-mahogany. Bears patrol streams looking for salmon.

Trails may climb 4,000 feet or more in two miles. In 20 miles of travel one may gain, then lose, then gain and lose once more, several thousand feet of elevation. The blights of forest fires, overgrazing, avalanches, and excessive lumbering have touched parts of this vast domain. But civilization has left the total scene in strange degree alone.

These tangled masses of thickets, ridges, cliffs, and peaks are a vast wilderness area. Here man can find deep solitude, and under conditions of grandeur that are startling he can come to know both himself and God.

—From *Of Men And Mountains*, Supreme Court Justice William O. Douglas, 1950

Contents

Oregon
Portland
Salem
Eugene
Roseburg
Grants Pass
Medford
Ashland
Klamath Falls
Bend
Madras
Cascade Lakes National Scenic Byway
84
30
5
26
197
97
216
22
226
20
126
242
58
138
230
62
140
66

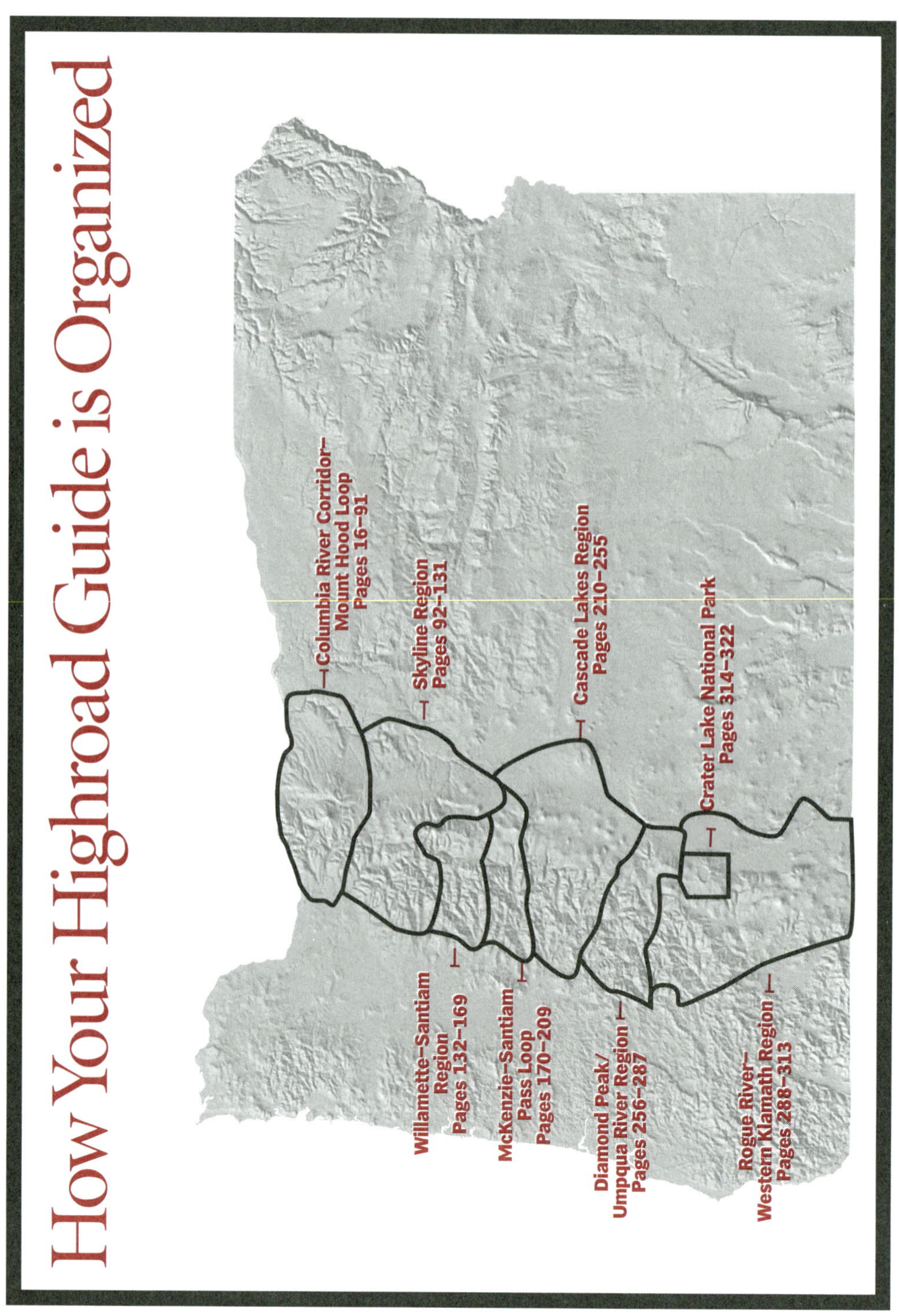
How Your Highroad Guide is Organized
Columbia River Corridor–Mount Hood Loop Pages 16–91
Skyline Region Pages 92–131
Cascade Lakes Region Pages 210–255
Crater Lake National Park Pages 314–322
Willamette–Santiam Region Pages 132–169
McKenzie–Santiam Pass Loop Pages 170–209
Diamond Peak/ Umpqua River Region Pages 256–287
Rogue River–Western Klamath Region Pages 288–313

How To Use Your Longstreet Highroad Guide

The *Longstreet Highroad Guide to the Oregon Cascades* includes a wealth of detailed information about the best of what the Oregon Cascades have to offer, including hiking, camping, fishing, scenic driving, biking, and canoeing. The Longstreet Highroad Guide also presents information on the natural history of the mountains, plus interesting facts about Cascades flora and fauna, giving the reader a starting point to learn more about what makes these mountains so special.

The book is divided into eight major sections, beginning in northern Oregon and ending at the state's southern border with California. There is also an introduction to the natural history of the Oregon Cascades.

The maps in the book are keyed by figure numbers and referenced in the text. These maps are intended to help orient both casual and expert mountain enthusiasts. Below is a legend to explain symbols used on the maps. Remember that hiking trails frequently change as they fall into disuse or new trails are created. Serious hikers may want to purchase additional maps from the U.S. Geological Service before they set out on a long hike. Sources are listed on the maps.

A word of caution: The mountains can be dangerous. Weather can change suddenly, rocks can be slippery, and wild animals can act in unexpected ways. Use common sense when in the mountains so all your memories will be happy ones.

Legend

Amphitheater
Parking
Telephone
Information
Picnicking
Dumping Station
Swimming
Fishing
Interpretive Trail
Camping
Bathroom
Wheelchair Accessible
First Aid Station
Picnic Shelter
Horse Trail
Horse Stable
Shower
Biking
Comfort/Rest Station
Cross-Country Ski Trail
Snowmobile Trail
Park Boundary
Special Areas
Town or City
Physiographic Region/ Misc. Boundary
Appalachian Trail
Regular Trail
State Boundary
70 Interstate
522 U.S. Route
643 State Highway
SR2010 State Route
T470 Township Road

Preface

The Cascade Range is the youngest range of volcanic mountains in the contiguous United States. It forms a wall of mile-high peaks for more than 600 miles from British Columbia south into northern California. The separation is more political than geological, however, because on both ends of the Cascades, there is a continuation of other mountain ranges: British Columbia's Coast Range and California's Sierra Nevada.

The wall is a formidable blockade that protects the entire west side of the continent from Mexico to Alaska, a glacier-encrusted buffer against the massive winter storms pounding inland from the Pacific Ocean. Pushed by warm, nearly tropical winds, the storms arrive low and heavy with water vapor. They lift above the coast line, sweep across the low-elevation coastal ridges and bank against the West Slopes of the range. For nine months the West Slopes catch the seemingly endless string of storms as they arrive almost back-to-back and milk the clouds of water vapor. In contrast, just a few miles east of this greenery, behind the protection of the Cascade shield, the East Slopes are semiarid, nearly desert in areas. Within 40 miles there is a five foot difference in the amount of annual rainfall.

Between these amazingly different zones is still another climate—an alpine area that follows the summit line of the mountains around young volcanoes, past lava flows so vast they disappear into the horizon, and so infertile that nothing grows there. Small ribs of roads lead away from the spine to lakes—some of which rank high in the world for clarity, depth, and purity—to the edges of canyons and the beginning of steelhead and salmon rivers, and to places where snow lies deep under the trees for 10 months of the year. The Oregon Cascade Range creates three distinctive climates in the space of about 75 east to west miles. On the West is a temperate rain forest, at the highest peaks are arctic-like environments, and the East Slopes qualify as semiarid.

ELK

(*Cervus elaphus*)

Also called "wapiti" — the Indian word for "white" — referring to the light color of the animal's rump, elk herds are distributed through mountain forests and valleys in the West.

In Oregon, the Cascades are a softer, rounder link in the overall range. Only a few peaks thrust dramatically into the sky, glistening white with glacial ice, deeply etched with scree slides, moraines, and avalanche chutes. Such dramatic mountains are common in the North Cascades of Washington and the Sierra Nevada in California. This gentleness, however, in no way lessens the quality, complexity, diversity, and drop-dead beauty of Oregon's tallest major range. The range fairly bulges with superlatives, and is a source of intrigue for geologists, historians, and recreationists. The deepest lake in North America. The second purest lake in the world. The biggest that, the heaviest this, the oldest...superlatives are marked everywhere. The lack of a ragged, jagged skyline, in fact, is a plus for travelers who enjoy adventuring in the high country. The wide, rounded backbone of the Oregon Cascades has allowed the construction of north-south roads that run the length of almost the entire range. The existence of north-south running roads may not seem so earthshaking in the context of lowland travel, but at the top of the Cascades, it's positively unique. Only Oregon's Cascades have a system of public roads, some paved, that trace the summit crest for hundreds of miles, winding through beautiful wooded wild country, and bringing—for better or worse—many high country features within reach of roads. The roads feature views and natural features that in other areas are enjoyed only by those who can walk to them.

BELTED KINGFISHER
(*Ceryle alcyon*)

The intent of this book is to serve as an introductory guide to the amazing complexities and diversities of the geology, history, and recreational opportunities in the Oregon Cascade Range. The landscapes described in these pages are etched with tumbling clear rivers, ridges, valleys, gorges, volcanoes, and strikingly contrasting climates. The content is necessarily broad in scope, but if it provides a single answer to a single question before that question is asked, its purpose will be accomplished. When you explore this region, take a second to examine the intricately layered composition of a pine cone, stir the duff with your foot, breathe deeply, move close enough to a waterfall to mist your face, walk in the tracks of an elk, and try to comprehend the years that have brushed a chunk of lava or rotting log.

The *Highroad Guide to the Oregon Cascades* is organized to begin on the north edge, where the range was abruptly cleaved by the most devastating floods in the history of the world, where streams now spill into emptiness, and where yellow lichens cling to angular cliffs of columnar basalt looming high above the Columbia River. It ends in the red dirt and ponderosa pines just above the California border, where Klamaths and Modoc Indians were hunting when Mount Mazama erupted. Adventure well.

—Terry W. Sheely

Acknowledgments

Compiling and fact-checking the enormous amount of information required to research and write a book on a subject as sweeping and complex as the Oregon Cascades requires the cooperation and assistance of hundreds of good people. Without these folks, this project would have been impossible, and I am forever grateful for their above-and-beyond work ethic, resourceful initiatives, and amazingly cheerful attitudes. So here's to the following people:

Natalie, who drove while I rode shotgun and wrote feverishly in a laptop computer, often beneath a pile of maps, pamphlets, guides, books, and camera gear. Within the first 20 miles she mastered the ability to power reverse along the shoulder against traffic, to give me the perfect camera angle, time to read a signboard, or to puzzle out a collection of high road signposts, animal tracks, or an odd-looking rock. Marge McDonald of Longstreet Press, a powerfully cheerful motivator who initially brought me to this assignment. Richard Lenz and Pam Holliday, editors at Lenz Design and Communications, for their tolerance, patience, and editing skills. Kara Wiergacz for her many hours spent checking facts in the book and for her editing assistance. Chip Evans for his skill and dedication in making the best maps possible. The following were exceptionally helpful in providing reference material in their areas of expertise, pointing me in the right direction, filling in the gaps, and proudly showing me the resources of their regions. Gregg B. Morgan, outdoor recreation planner, Roseburg Office of the Bureau of Land Management. Bob Ballou, executive director, Pacific Crest Trail Association. Dan Haas, U.S. Park Service, Seattle office. Steven Brutscher, Rivers Program team leader for Oregon Parks Department.

Sheela McLean, Public Affairs Office, U.S. Forest Service, Region 6, Portland; Geoff Hill, publisher of Fishing Central Oregon, and Maddy Sheehan, publisher of Fishing In Oregon, for the research and detail on fishing lakes in the Cascades. Trish Hogervorst, public affairs office of the BLM, Salem District Office for information on the Sandy River Gorge, Wildwood, Elk Camp and the undiscovered Molalla River camps and climbs. Joanne Holland-Bak, assistant director of tourism, Lane County convention and visitors association. She provided the most comprehensive and extensive materials of

MOUNTAIN LION
(*Felis concolor*)

anyone. Christina Lilienthal, Forest Lands and Scenic Byways coordinator for the Winema National Forest, excellent local information on Region 8, and the Volcanic Legacy Scenic Byway. Patsy McMillan, director, Klamath County Department of Tourism. (Saint) Joyce Thomas and Executive Director Diane McKeel, Troutdale Area Chamber of Commerce. They provided a wealth of energetic help on Columbia River Gorge, where to stay, and good places to dine. Jim and Marianne Parker, volunteer hosts at Clackamas Lake Historic Ranger Station. From Marietta, Georgia, Jim and Marianne were into their sixth year volunteering in the mountains south of US 26 and I suspect they know this region better than most residents. Great insights into history, without which I would never have unraveled the name source for Blue Box Pass. Jeree L. Mills, information assistant at Mount Hood National Forest in Sandy, whose enthusiasm for her forest's attractions is so contagious every traveler should stop in and see Sandy. Roger A. Perkins, for sharing our campfire at Sagandraga Campground on the Middle Fork of the Willamette, and filling us in on local insights, history, geographical interest, steering us to "the world's best water" at Indigo Springs, and sharing his sense of tradition from Westfir to the Willamette. Jean Thompson, communications manager, Oregon Parks and Wildlife, for digging deep in state files for background and camping information on Oregon's state parks. And thanks to Tami Edmunds, ODFW Willamette Fish Hatchery, who so generously followed up on my request for information and contacts at this exceptional facility. Special thanks to the following people for reviewing parts of the manuscript for factual accuracy: Sue Baker, Ray Crist, Linda DeLaRosa, Mike Ferris, Gene Flint, Terri Gates, Bruce Haynes, Frank Howard, Sherri Jensen, Doug Jones, Janet Kirsch, Marv Lang, Patty Ann Monze, Ron Murphy, Steve Otoupalik, Pat Pilcher, Rowena Ponce, Larry Reed, Jeanie Sheehan, Kent Taylor, John Wallig, and Sheryl Walters.

—Terry W. Sheely

Fig. 3: Oregon Physiographic Regions

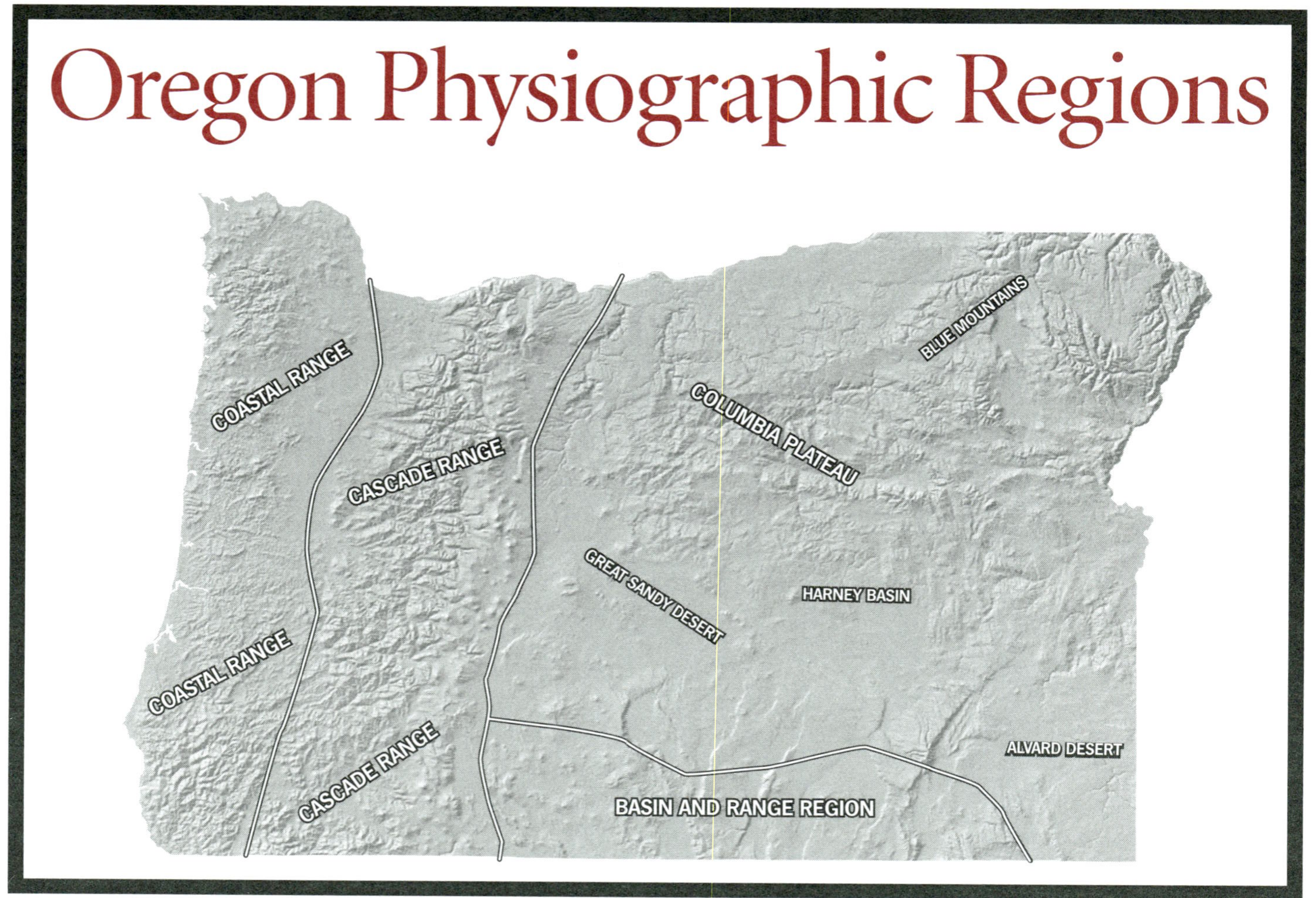

The Natural History of Oregon's Cascades

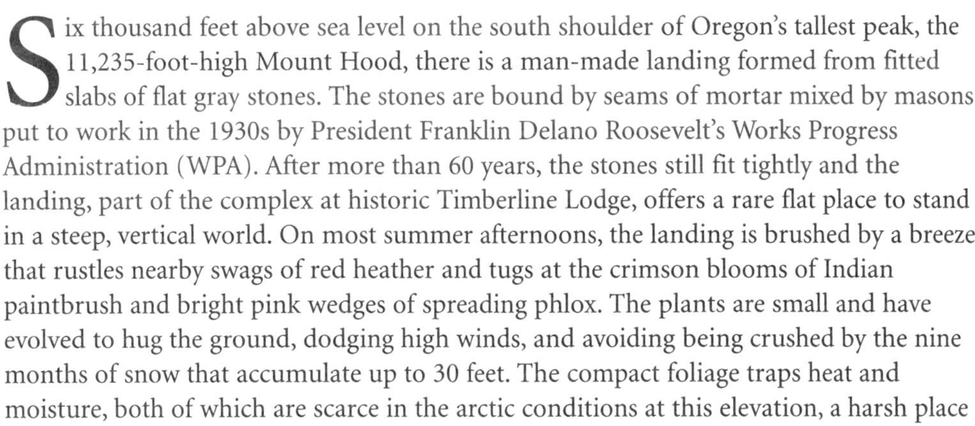

Six thousand feet above sea level on the south shoulder of Oregon's tallest peak, the 11,235-foot-high Mount Hood, there is a man-made landing formed from fitted slabs of flat gray stones. The stones are bound by seams of mortar mixed by masons put to work in the 1930s by President Franklin Delano Roosevelt's Works Progress Administration (WPA). After more than 60 years, the stones still fit tightly and the landing, part of the complex at historic Timberline Lodge, offers a rare flat place to stand in a steep, vertical world. On most summer afternoons, the landing is brushed by a breeze that rustles nearby swags of red heather and tugs at the crimson blooms of Indian paintbrush and bright pink wedges of spreading phlox. The plants are small and have evolved to hug the ground, dodging high winds, and avoiding being crushed by the nine months of snow that accumulate up to 30 feet. The compact foliage traps heat and moisture, both of which are scarce in the arctic conditions at this elevation, a harsh place

[*Above:* The east side of Mount Hood seen from a wheat field south of Dufur across Badger Creek Wilderness.]

Geologic Time Scale

Era	System & Period	Series & Epoch	Some Distinctive Features	Years Before Present
CENOZOIC	Quaternary	Recent	Modern man.	11,000
		Pleistocene	Early man; northern glaciation.	1/2 to 2 million
	Tertiary	Pliocene	Large carnivores.	13 + 1 million
		Miocene	First abundant grazing mammals.	25 + 1 million
		Oligocene	Large running mammals.	36 + 2 million
		Eocene	Many modern types of mammals.	58 + 2 million
		Paleocene	First placental mammals.	63 + 2 million
MESOZOIC	Cretaceous		First flowering plants; climax of dinosaurs and ammonites, followed by Cretaceous-Tertiary extinction.	135 + 5 million
	Jurassic		First birds, first mammals dinosaurs and ammonites abundant.	181 + 5 million
	Triassic		First dinosaurs. Abundant cycads and conifers.	230 + 10 million
PALEOZOIC	Permian		Extinction of most kinds of marine animals, including trilobites. Southern glaciation.	280 + 10 million
	Carboniferous	Pennsylvanian	Great coal forests, conifers. First reptiles.	310 + 10 million
		Mississippian	Sharks and amphibians abundant. Large and numerous scale trees and seed ferns.	345 + 10 million
	Devonian		First amphibians; ammonites; fishes abundant.	405 + 10 million
	Silurian		First terrestrial plants and animals.	425 + 10 million
	Ordovician		First fishes; invertebrates dominant.	500 + 10 million
	Cambrian		First abundant record of marine life; trilobites dominant.	600 + 50 million
	Precambrian		Fossils extremely rare, consisting of primitive aquatic plants. Evidence of glaciation. Oldest dated algae, over 2,600 million years; oldest dated meteorites 4,500 million years.	

where every mammal, plant, and rock is a testimonial to survival of the fittest.

The breeze stirs a light gray swirl of microscopic particles, the dust of eroding pumice and andesite lavas. The dust of these metamorphic rocks is a reminder that Oregon's tallest mountain, a glacier-encrusted beauty that dominates a hundred miles of awe-inspiring landscapes and attracts recreationists like moths to a flame, is a volcano that may or may not be dead. The fumaroles that warm the steep ground, belch gases and vent sulfur-smelling steam into the clear icy air at Crater Rock, near the summit, are pipelines to the earth's molten core.

The landing is a testament to the tenacity and set-jawed perseverance that Oregonians have applied to building a little stone platform in this high thin air; a man-made flyspeck in a spectacular and entirely uncontrollable natural environment. For the last 10,000 years, humans have been bent on leaving permanent footprints in the natural history of this restless mountain range, and the mountains have resisted magnificently.

While it may not seem so in this era of environmental concern, man's best and worst—dams, clear-cuts, burns, plows, pollution, explosions, tunnels, scrapes, and drainage—are minor when measured against natural forces so overwhelming that in a blink of an eye they reshape miles of thick rock, collapse mountains, reroute waterways, and incinerate forests. Every year, it seems, the mountains remind us of humanity's fragility. Earthquakes, forest fires, landslides, avalanches: These are memos from the Cascades explaining why a civilization that has learned to live in space, walk on the moon, and turn salty oceans into fresh drinking water has been unable to overwhelm these mountains with technology. At best, our inroads are to temporary outposts where we are allowed seasonal visitations. The Cascade Range is young, 50 million years old compared with the Rockies at 100 million years, and the ancient Appalachian Mountains at 250 million years. Human history is barely 13,000 years old

The Cascades, in fact, are still enduring growing pains. Their growth is unpredictable and never takes into account world-class winter ski areas, timber cuts, reservoir dams, hiking trails, campgrounds, luxury resorts, highways, spotted owls, llama ranches, endangered species, mines, old-growth groves or yurts. The WPA landing is chiseled into the steeply angled mountainside in a zone known as timberline, a natural vegetative demarcation line that appears on all of Oregon's highest peaks. By definition, timberline is the highest elevation at which trees will grow, which in the Oregon Cascades is a wavering striation between elevations of 6,000 and 7,000 feet. No single environmental factor determines the elevation of timberline. It changes from mountain to mountain, evolving through a combination of growing seasons, winds, snow depth and freezing temperatures. It is always, however, marked by an abrupt change in vegetation.

When viewed from a distance, timberline resembles a collar that divides the dark shadow of dense conifers that carpet mid and lower slopes from an ascot of alpine meadows usually leading to steep scree slides, ragged rock pinnacles, and clusters of icy, crevasse-scarred glaciers left over from the last Ice Age. At the top are summits encased in permanent snow.

The collar appears below the treeless summits on all of Oregon's highest peaks. Mountains lower than 6,000 feet are nearly always cloaked from creek bottom to summit in trees, usually Douglas firs, Western hemlocks, cedars, tamaracks, Ponderosas, and sugar pines.

The trees at the very edge of timberline are wind-bent conifers, mostly tough little subalpine firs, white bark pines, and mountain hemlocks. These timberline trees are called *krummholz,* a German word for elfin timber or crooked wood; a fitting description for these dwarfed and twisted trees, which—while rarely more than a few inches in diameter—are often hundreds of years old. The wood is incredibly dense and hard enough to blunt an ax stroke.

Amazingly, just a few hundred feet below the krummholz zone, inside the protective shield of the collective forests, conifer trees grow as straight as telephone poles. They are sometimes more than 100 feet tall and grow in groves as thick as dog hair, watered by rain and snowfalls that are measured in increments of feet. In the sweeping overview from the WPA landing, which is just above timberline, these towering trees seem to form a thick carpet molded to the irregular lumps and folds of the Oregon mountains. The carpet rolls toward the horizon in great purple-hued waves. The intensity of the color spectrum fades as the distance increases. Each rounded wave of mountaintops is dramatically lighter in color than the wave before it, fading finally into a pastel without definition that makes it impossible to distinguish land from air.

There is an illusion, from this viewpoint, that the Oregon Cascade Range is eternal, a topographical solidarity too immense and too grand to be anything less than forever.

The truth, however, is that history in the Oregon mountains—measured in the context of North American natural history, let alone the earth's—is only in its first chapters. It is a growing, straining, grinding work much closer to its beginning than its end. This range was still sea floor when the mountains in Virginia and North Carolina were already 200 million years old. Human history in Oregon's Cascades is downright infantile, less than 13,000 years old, according to the best estimates. Oregon historical writer Terence O'Donnell colorfully describes the incursion as "a noisy pageant—laughter, gunfire, war whoops, the intoning of sermons, a politician's blast, the cries of love and pain, ironshod wheels on cobblestones, all in all a terrible racket."

The mountain range didn't even have an official name until 1841 when the Wilkes Expedition chartered it as the Cascade Range, a name often used by Scottish botanist David Douglas, who cataloged and named most of the plant life in the Northwest, including the stately Douglas fir (*Pseudotsuga menziesii*), which was adopted in 1939 as Oregon's state tree. To put the newness of this region into historical perspective, realize that by the time the Cascade Range was officially named, wagon loads of settlers were already headed west from St. Louis on the Oregon Trail, Abraham Lincoln had served nine years in the Indiana legislature, the electric telegraph was humming, and General Santa Ana's troops had stormed inside The Alamo.

The geological history of the region is just as young. The last major eruption of Mount Hood occurred in 1790. The towering white pyramidal peak was still rumbling and steaming in 1805 when Lewis and Clark's Corps of Discovery camped along the Columbia River in the shadow of the mountain's northern slopes, and Oregon pioneers reported the volcano belching fire and smoke in September of 1859. It still infrequently quivers beneath the thousands of recreationists who hike, ski, camp, and sight-see on its massive flanks.

Far from being eternal and permanent, the entire 309 miles of the Oregon Cascade Range is riding the uplift of the North American Plate northwest as it is pushed up and out by the force of the Juan de Fuca Plate (floor of the Pacific Ocean), which is sliding eastward underneath the North American Plate. The trip, so far, has taken 400 million years and is the reason that tropical saltwater seas no longer lap at the coast of Idaho.

Even the land is transitory and far from ancient. Less than 40 million years ago, salt water in the Pacific Ocean lapped at what are now the western foothills of the Cascade Range and filled the 50-mile-wide trough of the Willamette River Valley. That valley now forms the west edge of the Cascade Range and houses the population, industrial, and governmental centers of the state.

Reminders of the youth of Oregon's mountains are scattered throughout the range. Sixteen major hot springs bubble to the surface from steam vents; hardened lava flows still too sterile to support vegetation extend for miles below cinder mounds that gushed molten rocks so recently that present-day Indian tribes recorded the events.

Anthropologists are confident that the Oregon Cascades were among the last areas on earth to be inhabited by humans. Man arrived in the region that is now Oregon between 7,000 and 13,000 years ago, near the end of the most recent Ice Age. According to state historians, the first people originated in Mongolia and migrated to Oregon through Siberia and Alaska. They are the genetic ancestors of today's Bannock, Chinook, Klamath, Modoc, and Nez Perce tribes. They crossed by an Alaskan land bridge—and possibly by boat. Settlement appears to have first occurred in the interior, later along the Columbia River and finally on the coast. The second incursion of discovers didn't begin until the mid-1500s when Spanish ships sailed north as far as Oregon's southern coast. It was another 300 years, about the mid-1800s, before settlers with European ancestries established permanent settlements at the edges of the Oregon Cascades.

The Mountains Begin

The topographical scar of the Cascade Range is actually two overlapping volcanic mountain ranges. The first range, which geologists distinguish as the Western Cascades, erupted into existence during the Eocene period 40 to 50 million years ago, a volcanic upheaval that created land from sea floor. The second and younger range, known as the High Cascades, began to evolve during the Oligocene and early Miocene periods about 20 million years ago. Volcanoes born during that event continue to evolve today and include the highest mountains in the range. Most peaks in the High Cascades stand in a ragged row on the east side of the range, and what's left of the Western Cascades are now known as the foothills along the middle and lower West Slope.

The overlapping formation of two mountain ranges is a huge headache for geologists, archeologists, and historical geographers. Efforts to accurately document the region's prehistoric roots are frustrated and often less than precise because much of the Western Cascades—and their history—was burned or buried beneath thousands of feet of basalt, rhyolite and andesite lavas and sediments from ash flows, mud slides, pyroclastics and pumice deposits. The overlay filled in the valleys and smothered the peaks of the Western Cascades during the dome-building formation of the younger High Cascades. That layer has since hardened into a dense mass that shields whatever historical secrets the land may offer. And there are many.

One of the biggest secrets that geologists would like to uncover is how a hundred miles of the southern Oregon Cascade Range broke off and moved 60 miles west to become an offshore island. The mountains, now called the Klamath Range, apparently separated from the southern Cascade Range near the California border during the earliest formative periods of the Western Cascades and existed for several million years as an offshore island. That explains why there are sea shells in stone quarries in Medford.

The roaming mountain range is one of the Oregon Cascades' most intriguing unanswered mysteries. Geologists David Alt and Don Hyndman wrote: "It is really quite unusual for a segment of a developing coastal range to detach itself from the continent and move offshore. We can't explain why, or how, but there is no doubt that it indeed happened."

Eventually the developing Western landmass filled the 60-mile-wide gap, displaced the sea water, and rejoined the Klamath Range to the continent's western shore. This time, however, the Klamath Mountains were aligned with the Coast Range mountains.

After the topographical indignation of being topped and buried beneath the debris from younger upstarts, the remnants of the once-proud peaks of the Western Cascades—some estimated to have been more than 5 miles high— were then ground off by Ice Age glaciers, and smoothed in the northern regions by walls of water from the over 100 floods that followed the collapse of ice dams that impounded Lake Missoula 15,000 years ago. The impact of the Lake Missoula floods on the topography of Oregon's northern Cascades is almost as great as the volcanoes that created the range.

The prehistoric lake was immense. Scientists compare it in size with a Great Lake. It spread across 3,000 square miles east of the Rocky Mountains. The natural dam that held back the impounded water was a 2,500-foot-high wall of icebergs that had broken away from the Cordilleran ice sheet on its southern descent from Canada. The bergs floated downstream along the course of the Clark Fork River as far west as a narrow mountain valley where the river was squeezed into a pass through the mountains.

Massive chunks of ice wedged into the jam, piling into a dam almost half-a-mile high. When the water reached a depth of 2,000 feet, the dam broke, unleashing a wall of water shot through with jagged chunks of ice, building-size boulders, and mountains of gravel. The effect was equal to pulling the trigger on a hydraulic sand blaster with a muzzle the size of a mountain aimed across eastern and central Washington directly at the Cascade

Mountains. The wall of water was still 1,000 feet high when it slammed into the eastern foothills of the Cascades at the place where the Columbia River had breached the mountains en route to the ocean. The impact scoured out a 2,000-foot-deep gorge where the Columbia River divided the Oregon and Washington Cascades (now Oregon's greatest natural attraction) and formed the north wall of the Oregon Cascades. The flood waters continued raging west from the gorge beyond the Cascades. They continued to roll for roughly 50 to 75 miles until hitting the east wall of Coast Range Mountains. Rebuffed, the flood water surged back to the east, and spilled south into the Willamette Valley, which became a monstrous swirling backwater eddy. Rocks and sediment suspended in the flood ground away at the already battered face of the Western Cascades that follows the east side of the valley. Incredibly, this earth-shaping event is believed to have been repeated dozens of times. Scientists now estimate that ice dams formed and broke another 50 to 100 times during the retreat of the Cordilleran ice sheet.

Between Spokane, Washington, and Eugene, Oregon, which is near the head of the Willamette Valley, the path of the flood is marked with boulders, some 10 feet across, called "erratics." Erratics were trapped in ice and randomly dropped out of the flood as the ice melted and the velocity of the water subsided. In a strange twist, one of the erratics is a 4,814 pound meteorite, the largest ever found in the United States. Even more amazing, the meteorite was found south of Portland near the small town of West Linn, Oregon, yet it hit the earth in British Columbia. Geologists believe the meteorite was encased in an ice berg, drifted south on the Cordilleran ice sheet, and was carried west across two states on the Missoula floods before coming to rest below the foothills of the Western Cascades.

The magnitude of the Missoula floods, larger than any flood ever documented in the world, was so inconceivable that the event escaped scientific recognition until J. Harlan Bretz, a stubborn geology professor at the Universities of Washington and Chicago, pieced together a geologic puzzle of seemingly unrelated deposits between Idaho's Lake Pend Oreille and the Willamette Valley. Lacking precedent of an event anywhere near this scale, the scientific community required years of amassing overwhelming evidence before it accepted Bretz's Missoula floods explanation.

From this monstrous beginning on its northern border, the Oregon Cascade Range runs almost directly north-south through the west central part of the state. The crest averages about 5,000 feet above sea level although nine peaks, all part of the High Cascades reach beyond 9,000 feet. For two-thirds of the route, the Cascades are the high ground between two vast river systems, both of which drain north into the Columbia River.

West slope water funnels into the Willamette River, which enters the Columbia River at Portland. East Slope waters drain into the Deschutes River, which joins the Columbia just east of The Dalles. The remaining southern third of the range feeds into the Klamath River on the east and Rogue and Umpqua River on the west. All three of these rivers flow west and empty directly into the Pacific Ocean near the Oregon/California border. All four rivers, and their many clear-water tributaries, are major spawning waters for anadromous steelhead, cutthroat trout, and runs of Pacific salmon.

The Oregon Cascade Range is a continuation of a ragged row of volcanic-origin mountains that extends thousands of miles beyond the state line. The Cascades continue north through Washington, becoming British Columbia's Coast Range. In California, Oregon's mountains join the Sierra Nevada. On a global scale, the Oregon Cascades are an active link in the Pacific Rim Ring Of Fire, a chain of active and dormant volcanoes that runs the length of the continental coast. Two of the most violent links in that ring are within sight of the Oregon border. The 1980 eruption of Mount St. Helens in Washington and the 1914 eruption of California's Mount Lassen are two of the greatest volcanic upheavals ever recorded in the contiguous United States. Except for an occasional quake, rock fall, tremor, or steam vent, Oregon's volcanoes have been inactive for at least 200 years.

Most volcanologists, that peculiar breed of geologist who finds it reasonable to walk to a crater's rim and stare into molten magma, are unwilling to guess which Oregon volcano will erupt next. Their best guess is that it will be one of the pristine glaciated peaks in the vicinity of the Three Sisters, or possibly Mount Hood.

What they are willing to predict is that there will be future eruptions and they will occur in the High Cascades. The High Cascades are a belt of upper Miocene to quaternary volcanic rocks that form a broad platform of chiefly basalt and basaltic andesite volcanoes.

The combination of lavas and pyroclastic sediments found in this range give some clues to the complexity of the geology here. The major quaternary volcanic centers along this northern platform are Mount Hood, Mount Jefferson, Three Sisters, Broken Top, and Crater Lake the caldera of Mount Mazama. Newberry volcano, at the east edge of the High Cascades, is also a quaternary volcanic center.

The central High Cascade Range is chiefly a Pleistocene volcanic platform of overlapping basalt and basaltic andesite lava flows 4,000 feet thick and 20 to 30 miles wide. The platform is composed of dozens of dead volcanoes. Most were active only briefly and produced small cinder cones. Few are distinguishable to anyone other than geologists. A typical shield volcano is a low, broad breastwork of light-colored, basaltic andesite with a cinder cone core that has been plugged. One of the best examples is the squat form of Belknap Crater on McKenzie Pass summit. Some basaltic andesite volcanoes, however, reach 10,000 feet in height and may have a shield base 10 miles wide. Oregon examples include The Husband, North Sister, Mount Washington, and Three-Fingered Jack.

The adjoined Three Sister Mountains, which some argue are the prettiest of Oregon's peaks, are each of a different volcanic composition. Stately South Sister volcano, the highest of the snowcapped sisterhood visible northwest of Bend, is chiefly andesite with minor dacite and rhyodacite. Broken Top just east of South Sister is basaltic andesite. Middle Sister is basalt with minor basaltic andesite, andesite, dacite, and rhyodacite. South of Mount Jefferson to Santiam Pass, the High Cascades make up a broad ridge composed of several shield volcanoes and numerous cinder cones. Most visible summits mark either relatively young vents or deeply eroded vent complexes. The youngest peaks are within the Mount Jefferson Wilderness Area in Willamette National Forest.

Southwest of Sisters, McKenzie Pass (open only during the summer) is in the center of a massive lava flow, the most spectacular flow accessible by road anywhere in Oregon. Basalt and andesite lavas form at least four volcanoes converged on this spot, leaving miles of broken lava barren of plant life. Radiocarbon tests indicate the last of these flows, from Yapoah Crater, happened less than 400 years ago.

Evidence of the central Cascades' recent volcanic history is everywhere along the mountain roads. Boulders of brown, red, and black lava litter the forests and meadows between the cross-Cascade highways of US 20 and OR 140, and stockpiles of ground pumice are stored beside major highways. In the winter, the pumice will be scattered on the icy roads to provide tire traction. Many road cuts, especially from the crest eastward, pass between walls of angled columnar basalt.

The East Slope of the High Cascades is also defined by volcanic geology. While the west slopes face the ocean, the east slopes face the deserts and arid plateaus of eastern Oregon. Remnants of the pyroclastic eruptions, lava flows, fault lines, earthquakes, and Ice Age glaciers that formed the East Slope country from 6,000 to 75 million years ago stand out in stark topographical detail against the often treeless, sometimes barren background.

Between the Columbia River and Bend, US 97 is built on the Columbia Plateau, which amounts to a sea of hardened basalt, much of it deposited during the Pliocene era between 3 and 10 million years ago. Near Willowdale, the geological jigsaw left behind huge deposits of "thundereggs." In 1965, these distinctive agates became Oregon's state stone (*see* Thundereggs, page 244). Tuff rocks have been unearthed near Shaniko that contain 34-million-year-old fossil nuts. Just north of Willowdale, US 97 crosses a distinctive flat-topped ridge that is the remnant of a10-foot-deep flow of 5-million-year-old basalt. In uncultivated areas between The Dalles and Shaniko, you may see "mima mounds," which are mysterious humps two- to three-feet-high and 10 feet across. These forms have been attributed to just about every natural event from Ice Age freezes to prehistoric ant hills, yet they remain a mystery. Oregon's largest lava-oriented geologic features are south of Bend. Amateur rock hounds and professional geologists love the monstrous cataclysmic events that took place here. From 6,000 to millions of years ago, the apron at the bottom of the East Slope between Bend and Klamath Falls was a seething low-elevation site of the same volcanic events that created the glacier-streaked volcanoes that jut like icy pyramids above the nearby Cascade Range.

The events left behind miles of slab and cinder lava rock, exploded and imploded craters, cinder cones, and lava buttes. Newberry National Volcanic Monument, just south of Bend, offers visitors close-up looks at vents and craters and unusual geologic formations such as Lava Island Falls, Obsidian Flow, Lava Cast Forest, and Lava River Cave. There are places along the shore of Paulina Lake inside Newberry Crater where you can create a private hot springs by scraping a shallow depression into the sand and gravel and letting it fill with naturally warmed water. The resort can tell you how to get there, and rent you a boat. In Klamath Falls, the earth's hot core remains so close to the surface that some homes and businesses are heated with hot water and steam from taps driven into shallow wells. According to geologists, old lake beds have formed a thin but watertight lid over a mass of molten rocks, so near the surface that it's economically feasible to tap the steam that develops beneath the lid. What look like overhanging cliffs above the west side of Upper Klamath Lake are actually young fault scarps created by recent shifts in the earth's crust. Klamath Falls is on shaky ground, and quakes and tremors, while startling, are never unexpected.

A Trio of Climates

For 50 million years, the string of mile-high Cascade mountains has divided Oregon into three extreme weather zones creating three equally distinctive flora and fauna regions. The explanation is that Oregon's weather nearly always develops over the Pacific Ocean and moves inland in a series of fronts. From November through March, most of these weather systems develop in an area known as the Aleutian Low above the Gulf of Alaska.

Weather systems pushed out of the Aleutian Low travel in counter-clockwise directions, spinning far to the south. While over water, the clouds continue to collect moisture from the ocean. Eventually they head inland arriving from the southwest, low and heavy with water vapor. According to most measurements, these winter fronts deliver up to 85 percent of the rain and snow that falls on the West Slope every year. Pushed by onshore winds, the marine air moves inland across the lower Coast Range mountains until stopped by the 5,000 foot wall of Cascade Mountains. It's common for these clouds to bank up against the mountains, and as the air ascends the mountain range and the clouds cool to a saturation point, the water vapor turns into snow at the higher elevations, and rain below 2,000 feet. It falls in prodigious amounts.

This marine effect inundates the West Slope. Measurements taken at Larch Mountain at the western threshold of the Columbia River Gorge consistently show more than 200 inches of rain each year. Cascades Locks, at sea level near the center of the Cascades, averages 72 inches per year. At the higher elevations, the moisture falls as freezing rain or snow and accumulations of snow from 20 to 30 feet are common. Driving across mountain passes in the heart of winter means mandatory tire chains and traveling through miles of road wedged between overwhelming walls of snow.

There are two primary benefits to so much precipitation: green landscapes and ski areas open 11 months of the year. Along with the water vapor, the marine effect brings in air warmed in southern climes. This blesses western Oregon with an unusually mild temperature range for northerly regions between 42 and 45 degrees latitude. The long growing season created by the mild temperatures and the abundant rainfall produce lush, jungle-like groves of towering deciduous and conifer trees, 30 types of ferns, 400 varieties of wildflowers, understories of wild rhododendron tangles, thick mosses, 200 species of mushrooms, and hundreds of clear, cold year-round trout streams.

Portland, at the base of the mountains, records more than 300 days a year with above-freezing temperatures. Summer high temperatures in the Western Cascades, measured in Fahrenheit, usually range from the high 60s into the 70s, only occasionally reaching into the 80s. Winter lows rarely dip below freezing and are often in the mid-40 degree

Fahrenheit range below 1,500 feet elevation. Snow is rare below 500 feet, but every winter sees a few days of sea-level white. The moderate winter temperatures and marine effect produce a wet, heavy snow in the foothills.

Oregonians like to say if you don't like this season, head for the mountains, there's another one up there. While lawn mowers hum and the Willamette Valley edges into summer, the higher foothills of the Western Cascades will be showing the first skunk cabbage and trillium blooms of spring. At 5,000 feet, the national forests will still be locked in late winter with freezing nights and snow drifts. In late fall, thermal inversions produce the opposite effect: mountain passes basking in Indian summer sun, and 60-degree days, while the lower hills are 20 degrees colder and shrouded in cold fog or drizzle.The crest of the Cascades has an alpine climate, with less rain, more sun, drier snows and much more severe temperature extremes. Below-zero temperatures are often recorded at the highest winter ski areas, but it's far more likely for daytime winter temperatures to register in the 20s. Snow falls every month on higher peaks, and occasionally at highway pass elevations. Winter snows don't begin to accumulate, however, until November and continue to stack up into April. March is notorious for heavy snowfalls and avalanches. In May and June you can expect to see drifts of old snow on north slopes and in heavily shaded forests above 4,500 feet elevation. During heavy snow years, some seasonal mountain passes remain closed well into July. By July and August, daytime high temperatures are in the 60s and low 70s, and all but the very highest lakes are ice-free.

As you travel south along the backbone of the Cascades, the amount of annual snowfall shrinks, and mean temperatures climb. Mount Bachelor, near Bend, collects 300 inches of new snow every year. Mount Shasta, just south of the Oregon border, gets about 50 inches. The temperature difference in the south is not as dramatic as the snowfall, but simultaneous temperatures registered at 5,000 feet near Mount Hood and just again north of the California border are about 10 degrees Fahrenheit higher in the south.

The contrast is even more dramatic on the east slopes of the range. The lush rain forest conditions on the west side are replaced on the east slopes by a semiarid desert-like environment. Instead of soggy mosses and clusters of ferns, the land grows sagebrush and arrowleaf balsamroot, plants common to high desert areas.

The difference between east and west is rainfall. Most water vapor is milked from eastward moving clouds while they're banked against the western slopes of the Cascade. By the time these marine clouds have dropped enough moisture to lighten and rise above the mountains, little is left to water the east slopes. It's called a rain shadow, and the impact is dramatic.

The front range along the East Slope forms a 300-mile-long shield, which protects the west side from the central basin's searing summer winds and soaring temperatures, and winter's brittle freezes. Instead of 300 inches of annual precipitation, East Slope tourism promoters brag of 300 days of sunshine. And The Dalles at the eastern edge of the Columbia Gorge records about 12 inches of rain a year—60 inches less than Cascade Locks just 40 miles west. East slope woodlands are open. Underbrush is usually thin, and many creeks run dry by midsummer. Summer high temperatures on these sun-kissed slopes often edge into the 90s and low 100s. Winters are cold. January air temperatures average 15 to 25 degrees at night, rising to 35 during the day, and it's not unusual for temperatures to fall below zero several times each winter. East slope residents hide from the sun and pray for rain. West slope residents plead for sun and pray for the rain to stop. Like the old-timers said, if you don't like the season, go for a drive, there's another one down the road.

Lakes and Rivers

Oregon's Cascade Range, as the name implies, gushes with water. From bone-cold springs trickling down stairsteps of mossy rocks to world-famous wild and scenic romps and giant lakes, including the second purest lake in the world, Oregon's Cascade Range is crowded with water.

Every ravine on the West Slope contains a stream, or at the least, a trickle of seep water that leads to a named creek, then a river, eventually reaching the wide Willamette and Columbia rivers. East slope creeks are fewer and many are dry by August, but the major drainages are world-class fisheries, with major recreation appeal and industrial credentials. The Deschutes River, like its western counterpart the Willamette, collects runoff from the northern two-thirds of the Cascades and flows north into the Columbia River. South of Crater Lake, the east side of the range drains into Klamath River, which wraps around the southern end of the Oregon Range and flows west to the ocean.

Oregon State University has counted more than 6,000 standing water environments in Oregon, including 1,400 named lakes and hundreds of unnamed lakes, ponds, marshes and sloughs. More than half lie in volcanic or glacial depressions near the summit of the Cascade Range. Counted among the notable is Crater Lake, which fills the collapsed caldera of Mount Mazama, and at 1,932 feet is the deepest lake in the United States. This spectacular water is the centerpiece of Oregon's only national park. Near Santiam Pass, Waldo Lake's 10 square miles of cobalt-blue water rank second in purity only to Siberia's Lake Baikal, which at 2,400 feet is the world's deepest lake.

For the most part, surface water in Oregon's mountain lakes is of good quality and is low in mineral content. Hundreds of natural lakes in national forests and Bureau of Land Management lands are inaccessible except to hikers and horseback riders, and display little evidence of manmade pollutants. Most streams and rivers are cold, clear, and fast-dropping freestone flows that support little plant life and offer little in the way of nutrients. Much of the fish life is anadromous, scampering out to sea to mature and requiring little from these fast flows except clean water in which to be spawned and spawn. Most of the Western Cascades consist of steep east-west ridges between gorges eroded out by major rivers, including the Clackamas, Santiam, McKenzie, Willamette, Umpqua, and Rogue. Each of these rivers is closely shadowed by cross-Cascade state or federal highways. Campgrounds, parks, and recreation areas are plentiful.

The High Cascades drain east, carrying snow melt down troughs carved by the

Metolius, Williams, White, upper Deschutes, and Klamath rivers. All or portions of 20 of these rivers, more than any other state, have been selected as national wild and scenic waterways,

WESTERN REDCEDAR (*Thuja plicata*)

Wildlife

When the first inhabitants arrived during the Pleistocene and Holocene eras, Oregon was a land of giant bison, mammoth, mastodon, wild horses, camels, giant bear, giant ground sloth, and other oversized fauna.

Today, the largest animal supported by these mountains is the Yellowstone elk (*Cervus elaphus*) which stand about 5-feet-high at the shoulder and commonly weigh 350 to 700 pounds. Three-hundred-pound black bears are substituted for giant bears, and wild camels have been replaced by black-tailed and mule deer.

Biologists estimate that about 120 species of birds and 75 species of mammals live in these mountains, including most of North America's glamour species: mountain lion, deer, elk, black bear, beaver, pronghorn, bighorn sheep, coyotes, fishers, otters, marmots, pikas and beaver.

There are no grizzly bears, moose, caribou, mountain goats or wolves, and the only white-tailed deer are a few Columbian white-tailed, a rare subspecies of the widespread *Odocoileu virginianus,* found at the edge of the western foothills near Roseburg.

Mountain species are surprisingly healthy, especially considering that many of the lowland species are in trouble from pollution, habitat destruction, human encroachment, and over-harvesting. Anadromous salmon and steelhead are in the most trouble, primarily because of commercial overharvesting and habitat destruction.

Reductions in the timber harvest, especially of old-growth Douglas firs, cedar, and Western hemlock, appears to have headed off problems in the high mountains associated with habitat loss.

Deer are the most common hoofed mammal in the range. Mule deer (*Odocoileus hemionus*) and a slightly smaller cousin the Columbian black-tailed (*Odocoileus hemionus columbianus*) share the mountains from the Columbia River to California. Mule deer live almost exclusively on the East Slope. Blacktails are the West Slope deer, but it's not unusual to find them low on east-facing slopes, and cross-breeding with mule deer is fairly common in the eastern range. Restrictions on hunting have seen a surge in cougar, bear, and coyote numbers in most areas, and conflicts between these predators and man is increasing annually.

After the pesticide scourge of the 1950s and '60s, golden and bald eagles are again fairly common, soaring on updrafts or watching for prey from the top of snags. There are

Fig. 5: National Forests of Oregon

more golden eagles in the open east side than in the thick timber on west slopes. Bald eagles are usually found near larger lakes and rivers on both sides.

The country's greatest concentration of nesting ospreys is at Crane Prairie Reservoir, southwest of Bend. Dozens of the big fish hawks live and nest in the snags of a vast flooded forest. The lake, one of Oregon's premier sport-fishing reservoirs, is a fertile feeding ground. There is an observation area. Bring binoculars.

Public Lands

Most of the Oregon Cascade Range is owned by the federal government and open to the public. The state of Oregon operates several quality parks at large reservoirs and lakes popular with recreationists. The Oregon Fish and Wildlife Department manages fishing and hunting on both federal and state land, but its property ownership is limited to small plots set aside for deer and elk winter feeding stations, boat access to lakes and rivers, and dozens of fish hatcheries. The U.S. Forest Service Region 6 office in Portland is the primary land holder in the mountains, managing 15.5 million acres, six national forests, 35 wilderness areas, and the Columbia Gorge National Scenic Area, the only one of its kind in the country.

In recent years, new timber harvesting restraints on Forest Service land have reduced the agency's emphasis on managing for logging, and redirected it at developing recreational opportunities. The change in direction has had a positive impact on Oregon's Cascade Range, opening trail systems, improving campgrounds, and improving information services. The change has also, however, brought use fees and contract vendors to the forests. The national forests are contiguous from the north to the south borders in the Cascades, and include Mount Hood, Willamette, Umpqua, Rogue River, Winema, and Deschutes National Forests. Traveling on the Forest Service road that forms the backbone of the Oregon Cascades, it is next to impossible not to be in a national forest. Roughly 11,000 miles of trail are maintained for hikers, bikers, and horseback riders, snowmobiles, cross-country skiers, and snowshoers. Hundreds of Forest Service campgrounds are operated during summer in the Oregon Cascades.

Most of the Forest Service holdings are on the timbered upper slopes and high-mountain alpine areas. The lower foothills, 15.7 million acres at least, are managed by nine district offices of the Bureau of Land Management.

Columbia R. Corr./ Mt. Hood Loop

The Columbia River Corridor measures more than 80 miles long, 2 miles wide, and one mile deep.

7 Columbia River Gorge
8 Hatfield Wilderness Area
9 Hood River Area
10 Mount Hood Area
11 The Dalles
12 Dufur Area
13 Sandy River Gorge Area
14 Salmon–Huckleberry Wilderness
15 Lost Lake Area

Columbia River Corridor/ Mount Hood Loop

In the extreme northern reach of Oregon's Cascade Range the topography dovetails, each remarkable geologic and physiographic region overlaying the next in a line that connects the highest point in the state to a sea-level passage.

The landscape ranges from lush rain forests to semiarid deserts, massive alpine glaciers to sea-level riverbanks thick with deep moss, ancient trees, and Ice Age scars. The region is encircled by a chain of highways known as the Mount Hood Loop, possibly the most diverse loop drive in America.

On the wet west side, the loop spills eastward from the urban metropolis of Portland. On the dry eastern side is the historic city of The Dalles, where the region's pioneer heritage and Oregon Trail history are depicted in colorful two-story murals on brick and block buildings.

The northern leg of the loop follows either Interstate 84 or historic US 30 into the

[*Above:* The east face of Mount Hood]

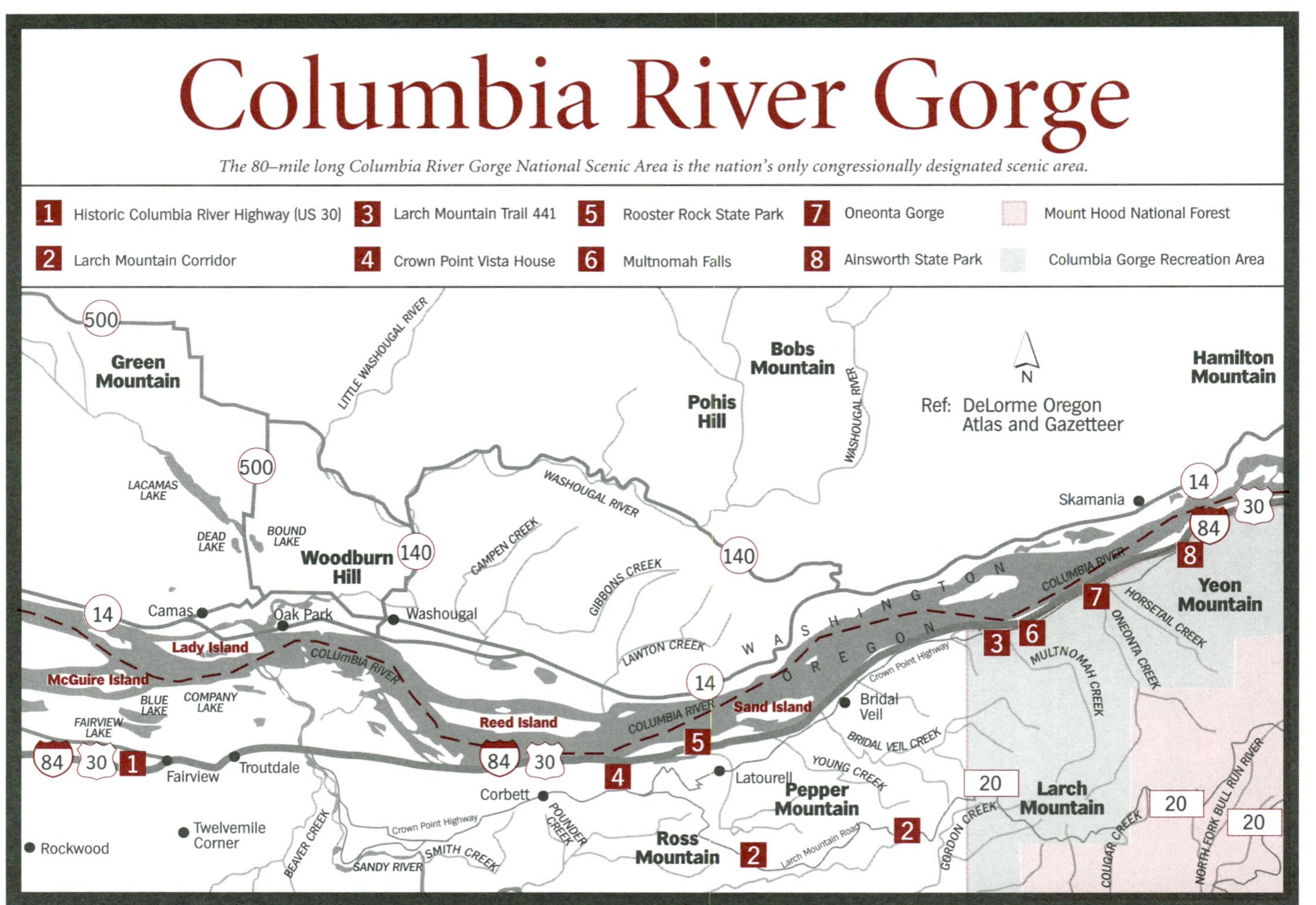
Columbia River Gorge
The 80–mile long Columbia River Gorge National Scenic Area is the nation's only congressionally designated scenic area.
1 Historic Columbia River Highway (US 30)
2 Larch Mountain Corridor
3 Larch Mountain Trail 441
4 Crown Point Vista House
5 Rooster Rock State Park
6 Multnomah Falls
7 Oneonta Gorge
8 Ainsworth State Park
Mount Hood National Forest
Columbia Gorge Recreation Area
N
Ref: DeLorme Oregon Atlas and Gazetteer
Green Mountain
Woodburn Hill
Pohis Hill
Bobs Mountain
Hamilton Mountain
Yeon Mountain
Larch Mountain
Pepper Mountain
Ross Mountain
LITTLE WASHOUGAL RIVER
WASHOUGAL RIVER
CAMPEN CREEK
GIBBONS CREEK
LAWTON CREEK
LACAMAS LAKE
DEAD LAKE
BOUND LAKE
BLUE LAKE
COMPANY LAKE
FAIRVIEW LAKE
Camas
Oak Park
Washougal
Skamania
WASHINGTON
OREGON
COLUMBIA RIVER
Lady Island
McGuire Island
Reed Island
Sand Island
Fairview
Troutdale
Corbett
Latourell
Bridal Veil
Twelvemile Corner
Rockwood
Crown Point Highway
Larch Mountain Road
BEAVER CREEK
SANDY RIVER
SMITH CREEK
POUNDER CREEK
YOUNG CREEK
BRIDAL VEIL CREEK
GORDON CREEK
MULTNOMAH CREEK
ONEONTA CREEK
HORSETAIL CREEK
COUGAR CREEK
NORTH FORK BULL RUN RIVER
500
140
14
84
30
20

Columbia River corridor through an 80-mile lava-rock gorge so exquisite that it has been singled out for national acclaim as America's only congressionally designated national scenic area. The southern link, US 26, ties the arid, open eastern slopes of the Cascade Range to the lush, dense rain forests on the western slopes. About 50 miles east of Portland, the highway climbs onto the south shoulder of volcanic Mount Hood, which at 11,240-feet is the highest summit in the state and the starting point for people visiting many of Oregon's most popular year-round recreation areas.

The destinations and sights connected by the paved legs, graveled spurs, forest trails, and waterways of the Mount Hood Loop are superlative. Most of Mount Hood National Forest lies within the loop, including three designated wilderness areas. This loop also encompasses America's only national scenic area, its first designated scenic highway, its greatest concentration of tall waterfalls, the last leg of the famous Oregon Trail, the geological scars of the continent's most devastating floods, the only sea-level pass through the northern Cascades, the glacial pyramid of Mount Hood with its clutch of ski areas, and a handful of national historic landmarks, including the 1930s-era Timberline Lodge, where the U.S. Olympic ski team trains year round.

The loop drive leads to wildflower nature areas, cathedral-like groves of old-growth conifers, arguably the world's wind-surfing mecca, waters with prehistoric white sturgeon that grow to 12 feet long, four rivers federally designated as wild and scenic, a valley that bulges with fruit orchards, and ultramodern interpretive centers overflowing with the region's history.

The loop route can be driven in as little as five hours, without stops, but even a quick trip with just a few key stops to appreciate a view, snap a shutter, and open a picnic basket will require most of a long summer day. The trip can be stretched into weeks of exploration, education, and adventure.

Columbia River Corridor

The northern brink of the Oregon Cascade Range is a titanic east-west breach through a range of volcanic north-south mountains, scoured down to sea level by an Ice Age catastrophe so unlikely that for centuries it escaped the wildest scientific imaginations.

From the air, the breach looks like a Homeric 80-mile-long furrow plowed diagonally across the mountain range through 4,000 feet of hardened black basalt. At the bottom of the furrow, shining like a broad silver ribbon, flows the Columbia, the largest river draining into the Pacific Ocean from the Western Hemisphere. The river is the only sea-level connection between the seared-tan desertscape of central Oregon and the dense green drizzle of rain forests that blanket western slopes.

The gorge is a unique and a strikingly clear line dividing the Oregon Cascades from the northern continuation.

Two highways pass through the gorge on the Oregon side: four-lane Interstate 84, and America's first official scenic highway, US 30. Choosing between the routes is a choice between the work of twenty-first century transportation engineers and the European-educated artisans of 1913.

Travelers find the gorge to be a curious mélange of topographic phenomena, cataclysmic geological history, and adrenaline-snapping recreation, with a history of eccentric philanthropy, and containing some of the finest destination lodges in the Northwest.

The diversities and contrasts along the river are as common as the shadow patches of bigleaf maples (*Acer macrophylla*) flitting on the corridor pavement below black-green walls of volcanic mountains. The drive is brightened by plants found nowhere else and unusual wildlife. It is cooled in the mists of dozens of waterfalls and energized by world-famous recreation.

This sea-level crossing of the Cascade Range is the only nonmountain pass through the Cascades and the Coast Range mountains between Canada and California. The gorge divides the Cascade Mountains of Washington from those of Oregon. Its measurements are massive: more than 80 miles long, up to 2 miles wide, and 1 mile deep.

Below the cliffs, the Columbia River rumbles on a course that was scoured through the mountains by the most cataclysmic chain of floods in continental history—the Bretz Floods.

One hundred and ninety times larger than any flood in earth's history, the waters ripped through the mountains along the Ice Age course of the Columbia. The explosive torrent of water and loose rock gouged out the gorge that in 1986 became America's only national scenic area. The designation infuriated prodevelopment factions, creating a controversy that may be part of the reason why a second national scenic area has yet to be designated in the United States.

The cataclysmic Bretz Floods forever changed the Northwest landscape 15,000 years ago when impounded water exploded toward the sea in a mountain-size wall unleashed by the collapse of Lake Missoula, an Ice Age lake comparable in size with the Great Lakes of the Midwest.

Lake Missoula was an impoundment growing behind a massive ice lobe that plugged the natural outlet of the Clark Fork Valley near northern Idaho's Lake Pend Oreille. Lake Missoula grew to more than 3,000 square miles, with 500 cubic miles of water, enough to fill both Erie and Ontario Great Lakes. As the depth at the dam neared 2,000 feet, the ice plug collapsed, unleashing a 1,200-foot wall of water, icebergs, and house-size rocks. The awesome violence roared toward the Pacific Ocean at a rate of 9.5 cubic miles per hour for 40 hours.

When the water slammed into the eastern edge of the Cascades near The Dalles, Oregon, the devastating wall was 1,000 feet high. It was still 700 feet high when it reached the west side of the range.

Scientists now estimate the hydraulic energy concentrated into this relatively small river valley was equal to 10 times the combined flows of all of the world's rivers, and 70 times the flow of the Amazon River. Evidence of the floods is still visible on the walls of the gorge.

The force eroded mountains into raw cliff faces. Hundreds of ruptured creeks gushed into emptiness, creating dozens of waterfalls and a fine gorge mist that now transforms shafts of sunlight into flickering rainbows.

Geologists believe that up to 100 floods scoured the gorge during the next 3,000 years as succeeding ice plugs impounded and collapsed. Filled with seething rock sediment, the floods chewed into the mountains, driving the floor of the river deeper into the 3-million-year-old basaltic lava bed.

Today, a drive through the Columbia River Gorge is a pastoral adventure, yet the scenery reveals more than a pretty face and a footnote to a violent creation. How much more depends on which route is taken.

The here-to-there route is Interstate 84, Oregon's primary east-west shipping and travel freeway. The interstate hugs the south riverbank, carrying 65-mph traffic with multiple lane efficiency. There are numerous exits and easy access from the freeway to most gorge attractions, a concession to tourism, which is a major economic factor throughout Oregon.

The leisurely alternative is Historic Columbia River Highway US 30, the first scenic highway in the United States and one of Oregon's 12 designated scenic byways. Construction started in 1913 and the highway was dedicated by President Woodrow Wilson in 1916. US 30 is a narrow, winding, two-lane strip of old blacktop that clings to the steep, misty, green folds of the hillsides above the interstate as if it were thrown there.

The narrow turn-of-the-century highway, which the *London News* dubbed "The King Of Roads," was designed and built with European craftsmanship in the mold of Charlemagne's Rhine Valley marvel. It is one of the few routes in America deliberately built to agree with the scenery. The scenic route slides past deep green forests thick with carpets of rich moss, delicate ferns, and wildflowers as well as dozens of waterfalls, scenic overlooks, and trailheads.

WESTERN GRAY SQUIRREL
(*Sciurus griseus*)
Active all year, this squirrel buries food and steals birdseed to eat in the winter.

FORGET-ME-NOT
(Myosotis scorpioides)

The two highways run parallel through the gorge corridor, and either will serve as a northern travel link in a loop route that encircles Mount Hood with the greater Portland area.

Promoted as the Mount Hood Loop, the route follows the Columbia Gorge Scenic Corridor to OR 35, then leads south into the mountains along the tumbling East Fork of Hood River. The loop connects with US 26 on the glacial white shoulders of Oregon's tallest peak, Mount Hood (elevation 11,235 feet). To complete the loop and return to Portland, turn west at the OR 35/US 26 junction and swing sharply downhill past summer hiking and winter skiing areas along steep rhododendron-flowered *(Rhododendron macrophyllum)* slopes in the headwaters of the Sandy River.

By turning east at the US 26 junction, travelers can connect with several routes along the backbone of the Cascades or slowly descend from alpine through picket-fence forests of towering ponderosa pine into the open, arid sagebrush breaks of the Deschutes River and US 97.

In both directions there are numerous side-trip routes that lead to an almost endless succession of recreation, camping, lakes, river, trails, scenery, remarkably diverse physiographic regions, and nineteenth-century history,

Eastern roads wind along hillsides through semiarid country splattered with the contrasting colors of golden irrigated grain fields, green fruit orchards, blocks of large ranches, and seemingly endless tracts of harsh scab lands. The eastern slopes withstand extreme seasonal temperatures. There are treeless plateaus, shale-rock coulees, blowing sand, and the sharp scent of sagebrush.

The dramatic transition between east and west can be measured in rainfall inches. On the dry eastern side of the gorge, near The Dalles, annual precipitation is as little as 12 inches. Just 60 miles west, 75 inches of precipitation, mostly rain, falls on Bonneville Dam. The wall of the Cascade Range holds back the low rain clouds moving inland from the Pacific until most of their moisture content falls. Lightened of moisture, the clouds rise and slide over the mountains, creating what is known as a rain shadow over the eastern slope. In this rain shadow, the climate is semiarid, near-desert in the extreme.

Western routes squeeze between river valley walls of lush Oregon green. These roads are frequently washed by Pacific squalls that pile against the mountains, dumping equatorial rains that feed dense vegetation, towering trees that were old before Columbus was born, quick creeks, and plunging waterfalls. In the foothills, the roads slide through cathedral-like groves of ancient conifers and canopies of bigleaf maple. Roads pass glacial snow fields, scrabbled tiers of shattered lava, plunging cliffs and gushing waterfalls, and meadows of wildflowers where the snow can pile 30 feet deep and last seven months.

Weather swings are notoriously extreme, ranging from sudden winter ice storms that make interstate traffic slide to stops that can linger for days before a thaw. In summer, blistering heat is frequently blasted across the landscape by 70 mph winds so hot that plant leaves dehydrate and wilt on the stalk.

Powerful winds rip the river into whitecaps that stand 15 feet high, and attract wind-surfers from around the world. The winds that are created by the convergence of cool marine air from the west colliding with hot desert air pushing in from the east occur most frequently during the summer. Then the gorge becomes the home of an international community of hundreds of wind-surfers. Their electric-colored sails and acrobatic boards zing through the whitecaps, and their tents and RVs often crowd public and private campsites.

COLUMBIA RIVER GORGE NATIONAL SCENIC AREA

[Fig. 7, Fig. 9(8)] All of the Columbia River corridor lies within the 295,500-acre, 80-mile-long Columbia River Gorge National Scenic Area, the nation's only congressionally designated scenic area.

The gorge drew international recognition in 1986 when President Ronald Reagan signed the congressional act to create the scenic area, the first ever aimed at specifically preserving scenic, cultural, recreational, and natural resources. The boundaries of the scenic area run along both the Oregon and Washington shorelines, and frequently extend uphill to include specific nearby resources.

Conserving such a vast natural area in the gorge continues to be a source of controversy, especially between conservationists and prodevelopment factions. The National Scenic Area Act is not as preservation-oriented as acts establishing wilderness areas and national parks. Instead, it allows for the existing rural and scenic characteristics to be retained and, at the same time, encourages compatible growth and development within existing urban areas.

The scenery hip-hops from pastoral to powerful. World-famous wind-surfing and fishing begin at the edge of the roadway, and intriguing evidence of small-town entrepreneurship is everywhere. Baskets thick with sweet-smelling flowers splash swatches of blues, greens, yellows, and reds across the walls of mom-and-pop stores with gas pumps in front, a satellite dish on the roof, and Douglas fir needles in the gravel dust of the driveway.

The western boundary of the scenic area begins near Troutdale in the lush green of foothills, quarter horse pastures, wood lots, and moss-green ranches. The eastern threshold is a wind-chapped sage hill in the treeless near-desert a few miles down river from the US 97 bridge at Biggs.

In between are native petroglyphs, historic lodges, dozens of waterfalls (including 620-foot Multnomah Falls—Oregon's tallest and the fourth highest in the U.S.), monumental hydro-power dams, shipping locks, sternwheeler boats, blocks of columnar basalt, a few inactive volcanoes, mountainsides that glow with wildflowers, sturgeon that grow to 12 feet long, and misty cool gorge hiking trails.

Forest Service Trail 400 is the only east-west hiking trail across the face of the gorge on the Oregon side. It parallels the Historical Columbia River Highway for 35.5 miles, generally riding a little higher on the hillside and out of sight of the highway.

Because the trail is less than 500 feet above sea level, snow is rarely a problem. In this area, winter snow rarely drops below elevations of 1,000 feet, and then only temporarily. The dirt and duff surface is passable year-round to those using nonmotorized transportation, such as bicyclists, hikers, and horseback riders. Trail 400 passes all of the gorge's prominent natural attractions, including the concentration of tall waterfalls, and is the main arterial access for north-south trails leading up the walls, ridges, and gorges within the scenic area. Trail 400 is accessible from every parking lot and pullover along the scenic highway.

Outdoor recreation is a way of life in the gorge and a coveted industry in an area where the economy is struggling to make the transition from traditional logging and commercial fishing to tourism. More than 4 million visitors explore the gorge every year, and 84 percent of them, according to the Oregon Tourism Department, engage in some sort of outdoor activity.

The most popular activity is hiking the hundreds of miles of postcard-quality trails, most rated easy to moderate. Fishing the Columbia River is a major attraction for sportsmen who like the challenge of giant white sturgeon, chinook and coho salmon, steelhead trout, walleye, shad, and smallmouth bass. There are few opportunities for hunting in the gorge, although on the plateaus above the breaks of the gorge black-tailed deer (*Odocoileus hemionus*), black bear (*Ursus americanus*), cougar (*Felis concolor*), and ruffed grouse (*Bonasa umbellus*) are hunted September through November. Ducks and geese are hunted in the river sloughs, and from blinds on islands, from November through mid-January.

The winds that howl through the climatic convergence zones in the scenic area create huge waves on the Columbia River and have earned the gorge international acclaim as the universal capital of wind-surfing. Surfers from around the world pile into the gorge to challenge the high winds of summer, and their colorful sails can be seen zipping and flipping across the river whenever there is a good breeze.

Opportunities for camping, wildlife viewing, boating, whitewater running, rock climbing, mushrooming, and outdoor photography are unlimited.

Directions: I-84 follows the scenic area through the Columbia River Gorge east from Portland or west from The Dalles. US 30 parallels the interstate in places and offers a more leisurely, scenic, and historic route. WA Hwy 14 provides access on the north shore.

Activities: Camping, hiking, fishing, boating, wind-surfing, trail bicycling, seasonal

BLACK BEAR
(*Ursus americanus*)
The black bear in the Western United States is black to cinnamon color with a white blaze on its chest.

hunting and wildlife viewing, wildflower areas, photography, and scenic highway touring.

Facilities: Scenic area interpretive and discovery centers are located at Multnomah Falls, The Dalles, and on the north bank of the Columbia at Stevenson, Washington. From I-84, cross the river into Washington at Cascade Locks on The Bridge Of The Gods at Exit 44. Three state parks, four Forest Service sites, and numerous private campgrounds are available for tent and RV travelers. There is an extensive visitor center, fish hatchery, sturgeon pool, and flower garden complex at Bonneville Lock and Dam. There are public boat ramps at Rooster Rock State Park, Corbett, Bonneville Dam, Cascade Locks, Hood River, and The Dalles.

Dates: The scenic area is open year-round, and state parks and national forest campgrounds are open from May through Sept. The river-elevation hiking trails west of Hood River are snow-free for most of the winter. All north-south trails, however, have steep gradients and are usually snowbound above 2,000 feet from Nov. to mid-May.

Fees: There is a charge for Forest Service trail usc passcs required on seven trail systems in the Oregon Columbia River Gorge National Scenic Area. Fee trails are Wahclella Falls Trail 436, Larch Mountain Trail 441, Wyeth Trail 411, Eagle Creek Trail 440, Herman Creek Trail 406, and Bridge Of The Gods. Passes are available on an annual or one-day basis and a single pass is valid at all sites.

Fees are also charged for winter parking in designated snow parks, for state park camping, and for admission to the interpretive centers at Stevenson, Washington, and The Dalles. Trail and snow park passes can be bought at all forest service offices, and at most gorge businesses that cater to recreationists. State park and interpretive center admission fees are collected on site.

Closest town: Troutdale is at the western end of the scenic area and The Dalles is at the eastern end. Hood River is about midway through the scenic area, and is where OR 35 northbound crosses the Columbia River into Washington. Southbound, OR 35 connects with US 26 on the southeast side of Mount Hood.

For more information: Columbia River Gorge National Scenic Area Headquarters, 902 Wasco Avenue, Suite 200, Hood River, OR 97031. Phone (541) 386-2333. Web site: www.FS.Fed.US/R6/Columbia.

HISTORIC COLUMBIA RIVER HIGHWAY (US 30)

[Fig. 7(1)] This picturesque and internationally acclaimed highway originally stretched 74 miles between the Sandy River at Troutdale and Chenoweth Creek Bridge at The Dalles.

It was built in two sections. The first section was completed between Troutdale and Hood River in 1915. After its June 7, 1916 dedication, the Columbia Gorge Scenic Highway US 30 was described by *Sunset Magazine* as "one of the most noted scenic automobile boulevards of the world," and proclaimed in Europe by England's *London News* as "The King of Roads." The second leg was built from 1918 to 1922, and extended the highway from Hood River east to The Dalles. When the gorge segment was tied into an existing section of US 30 that went west from Portland to the ocean, the result was 202 miles of paved highway, and the first Northwest highway to be entirely paved. Half a century later, US 30 was honored as America's first designated scenic highway.

Today, roughly 57 miles of the original highway dedicated by President Woodrow Wilson remain driveable. Sections of this historic roadway were destroyed when Interstate 84 was constructed in the 50s. Fragments have fallen away, and some of the tunnels have been collapsed for rock fall control. Ornate stone archway railings are moss-encrusted and show weathering cracks, and only three of the original concrete mileposts exist.

Financed by famed Seattle philanthropist and engineer Sam Hill, the road featured elaborate ornamentation, including stone benches at overlooks, mortarless masonry, Florentine viaducts, arched railings, and carved tunnels. The narrow highway passes the greatest concentration of tall waterfalls in North America, Miocene lava formations, gorges dripping with ferns and mosses, tumbling streams, and towering old-growth conifers.

This two-lane road continues to reflect the original dream of engineer Sam Lancaster to build a great boulevard in harmony with the landscape. "Not one tree felled, not one fern crushed unnecessarily," Lancaster ordered in 1913. He designed the road to ride high on the side of the mountains to provide sweeping views and to gently follow the curves of the landscape. He based the design on the great mountain roads of Europe and hired skilled Italian-American stonemasons to create the walls and observation areas. Their craftsmanship on the road is commonly referred to as a "poem in stone," according to Oregon historian Richard Ross.

Directions: The historic scenic route is accessible from nearly all of the I-84 exits through the scenic area. The western access is through Troutdale at the Sandy River bridge. The western driveable section is between exits 17 and 35 on I-84. The eastern access is on the western side of The Dalles fronting the Columbia Gorge Discovery Center. Use I-84 Exit 82. The center section of the old highway between Ainsworth State

Park and Mosier is not passable. In Fall of 1999, the abandoned section was rebuilt into a hiking, biking, wheelchair trail. You can drive around the vacated section by detouring onto I-84, and then reconnecting at Exits 35 or 76.

Activities: Scenic drive with historic stops, overlooks and access to day-use picnic areas, waterfalls, and hiking trails. Summer camping at Ainsworth State Park. Lofty overlooks, two dozen waterfalls, and old-growth conifers provide great photographic opportunities.

Facilities: Vista House interpretive and historic site at Crown Point State Park, Multnomah Falls Lodge and Forest Service interpretive center, and Tom McCall Wild-flower Area on Rowena Plateau. Benson State Park, a small day-use area at I-84's Exit 30, has a boat ramp to the Columbia River and a pair of fishing ponds. Both Wahkeen and Benson lakes are suitable for small boats and canoes. Try your luck casting a worm and bobber for panfish.

Dates: US 30 is open and maintained year-round.

Fees: There is a charge for camping and for parking at the most heavily used trail-heads.

Closest town: The west end of the highway through the gorge is in Troutdale. The Dalles is on the east end. The highway is no longer usable through Hood River, however this I-84 town has full services in the central gorge area.

For more information: Troutdale Chamber of Commerce, PO Box 245, Troutdale, OR 97060. Phone (503) 669-7473, or Columbia River Gorge National Scenic Area, 902 Wasco Avenue, Suite 200, Hood River, OR 97031. Phone (541) 386-2333.

LARCH MOUNTAIN CORRIDOR

[Fig. 7(2)] It's 0.1 mile from Chanticleer Point to Larch Mountain Road and the first major side trip if you are eastbound on the north leg of the Mount Hood loop route. This paved corridor is 14.3 miles long and ends in a shaded forest service picnic area at the 4,050-foot summit of Larch Mountain. From the picnic area parking lot a paved path leads 0.3 mile to Sherrard Point in the caldera of an extinct volcano.

Visible 7 miles to the east is the Hatfield Wilderness Area of the Mount Hood National Forest. This 39,000-acre wilderness is only 30 miles from the state's largest population center yet is one of the least visited areas of the Mount Hood National Forest.

The view from Sherrard's Point is volcanic: 46 miles north is 8,363-foot Mount St. Helens, at 97 miles is 14,411-foot Mount Rainier, and 54 miles away is 12,307-foot Mount Adams. Southeast is 11,239-foot Mount Hood and 62 miles into the distance is 10,497-foot Mount Jefferson.

The path to the point is wheelchair accessible except for the last 100 feet, where 126 steps climb steeply to the lofty observation area. Very little of this sweeping view can be seen without climbing the stairway.

Ironically, not a single western larch tree (*Larix occidentalis*) grows on Larch Mountain. The paved two-lane corridor is maintained as a scenic green space by Metro Regional Parks, and it winds steadily uphill from the Historic Columbia River Highway to the summit through groves of second-growth Douglas fir (*Pseudotsuga menziesii*) and western hemlock (*Tsuga heterophylla*).

After the first frost of fall, this roadside explodes with red swatches of mountain ash (*Sorbus sitchensis*) berries, the twined branches and radiant scarlet leaves of vine maple (*Acer circinatum*), thick clusters of red elderberries (*Sambucus racemosa*), and the electric orange-red of frosted sumac (*Rhus glabra*) leaves.

In summer, the brushy shoulder of the corridor seems to be quilted with wildflowers, among them purple and pink foxglove (*Digitalis purpuraea*), American vetch (*Vicia americana*), perennial pea (*Lathyrus latifolius*), salmonberry (*Rubus spectabilis*), goldenrod (*Solidago canadensis*), pearly everlasting (*Anaphalis margaritacea*), pink swatches of fireweed (*Epilobium angustifolium*), and banks of Oregon's state plant, Oregon grape (*Berberis nervosa*).

The table-size stump remains of old-growth timber are visible in the forest along the upper 10 miles of the drive. Look carefully at these mossy-green stumps and you can see where loggers long ago cut springboard notches just above the root balls. Springboards were short, stout planks that timber fallers wedged into the notches and stood on, in order to cut above the root systems of these ancient giants.

Directions: Larch Mountain Corridor Road intersects with US 30 about 4 miles east of Troutdale between Chanticleer Point and Crown Point. It's 14.3 miles to the end of the corridor at the top of Larch Mountain, elevation 4,050 feet.

Activities: Picnicking, hiking, views of five Washington and Oregon volcanoes.

Facilities: At the summit of Larch Mountain are picnic tables, drinking water, restrooms, trailheads for hikers, and a large parking lot adequate for motor home turnarounds. A signboard describes the system of trails, including Trail 441, which lead away from the parking lot.

Dates: Closed during times of heavy snow.

Fees: Trail park pass required.

Closest town: Corbett, 2.5 miles west.

For more information: Columbia River Gorge National Scenic Area Headquarters, 902 Wasco Avenue, Suite 200, Hood River, OR 97031. Phone (541) 386-2333.

LARCH MOUNTAIN TRAIL 441

[Fig. 7(3)] From the parking lot and picnic area this trail (*see* page 18) descends steadily for 6.8 miles, sometimes through groves of old-growth hemlock, western red cedar, Noble fir, and Douglas fir that grow to 6 feet in diameter. The trail ends 3,900 feet lower at Multnomah Falls, adjacent to I-84. Much of the hiking route is beneath a conifer canopy along Multnomah Creek, which drops through multiple small waterfalls. Several species of fern and clover-shaped oxalis (*Oxalis oregana*) grow on the forest floor.

Directions: Drive 6.5 miles east from Troutdale on US 30, turning southeast onto Larch Mountain Corridor and continuing 14.3 miles to the trailhead in a parking lot at the end of the road.

Trail: 6.8 miles one-way. There are several intersecting and side trails that loop into this system.

Elevation: The trailhead at the summit of Larch Mountain is at 4,050 feet with an elevation change of approximately 3,900 feet to the base of Multnomah Falls, which is about 150 feet above sea level.

Degree of difficulty: Strenuous. Steep. Many hikers arrange for a shuttle vehicle to drop them off at the top for a one-way hike downhill to Multnomah Falls. No commercial shuttle service is available.

Surface: Natural duff.

CROWN POINT VISTA HOUSE

[Fig. 7(4)] East of the Larch Mountain Corridor turnoff, the Columbia Gorge Scenic Highway slides into the first of dozens of tight turns that cling to the undulating contours of the hillside. Less than 0.5 mile east of the turnoff, the highway breaks from the trees onto a breathtaking aerie known as Crown Point. The striking limestone-walled dome of Vista House, a national historic landmark, sits like a copper jewel atop Crown Point. The two-story, octagonal building is on the outer edge of a bluff overlooking a 733-foot drop to the river. The scenic highway encircles the promontory in a horseshoe-shaped switchback, where the roadbed was blasted and dug into the rock wall.

Crown Point is a remnant of a large Miocene basalt flow. It falls steeply away on three sides. The lofty 30-mile views of the Columbia Gorge Scenic Area and the Washington shoreline are unparalleled. The overlook provides a commanding view and so embodies the spirit of the scenic highway that it was chosen as the site of the highway's June 6, 1916 dedication.

Two years later the construction of Vista House was completed on the point. Now it is the centerpiece for 307-acre Crown Point State Park, and the unofficial sentinel of the western gorge. Opened in 1918 as the most glorious rest stop in America, Vista House was designed and built by European masters of stone and mason. The design is a German version of Art Nouveau, and the European-style dry masonry foundation was laid by Italian masons.

Tokeen Alaskan Marble is used for the floors and stairs of the rotunda and basement wainscoting. The light cream and pink walls of the rotunda interior are Kasota Limestone. A hand-carved drinking fountain on the rotunda floor still satisfies thirsty travelers. The interior and the supporting ribs are painted to simulate marble and bronze. The exterior is faced with light gray sandstone and the roof, originally a matte-glazed green tile, is now copper. On the national register of historic places, Vista House is still considered the grandest structure in the gorge.

Directions: Follow US 30 east from Troutdale or west from Multnomah Falls. It's about 7 miles either way to Vista House.

Activities: 30-mile view of the Columbia River Gorge, picnicking, historical information.

Facilities: An information kiosk and pioneer-era interpretive center, paintings, museum pieces, and artifacts are inside the rotunda.

Dates: The rotunda is open daily, Apr. to Oct. Exterior walkways and viewpoints are open year-round. There are picnic tables and restrooms.

Fees: There is no charge, but there is a donation box.

Closest town: Corbett, 3 miles west.

For more information: Oregon Parks Department, 1115 Commercial Street NE Salem, OR 97301-1002. Phone (800) 551-6949 or (503) 695-2233.

ROOSTER ROCK STATE PARK

[Fig. 7(5)] Located directly below Vista House, Rooster Rock State Park is wedged onto a cool strip of grass and tree groves between the Columbia River and I-84 at Exit 25. This is one of Oregon's largest day-use only areas. There is no camping. Located only 22 miles east of Portland, Rooster Rock is a popular weekend picnic and recreation destination for metro residents. On weekdays and during nonsummer seasons, however, the park is never crowded. This is a big park, with lots of tables and plenty of run-and-play room. A daily use fee is charged year-round.

The park features large rolling grass and woodlands with 3.2 miles of easy, near-level, wheelchair-accessible hiking path, picnic tables and shelters, a protected Columbia River boat ramp with loading docks, river and slough fishing areas, and a large sandy swimming beach on the Columbia. A clothing-optional beach is at the extreme east end of the park about 0.5 mile from the picnic area. The area is well screened from the main park by distance and thick brush.

The park's namesake rock is a basalt tower more than 100 feet high that splintered away from the face of Crown Point about 20 million years ago and slid into its present location. The rock scar is visible on the cliff above. There is no trail to the vertical column, which is located at the edge of a lagoon between the interstate and the picnic grounds. Technical climbing is permitted with advance reservations.

Directions: The park is at I-84 Exit 25.

Activities: Visitors are limited to day use only, with no overnight camping permitted. The park offers a large Columbia River swimming area, trail walks with interpretive exhibits, technical rock climbing, picnicking, fishing, boating, and wind-surfing.

Facilities: There are picnic tables and grills, shelter houses, boat ramps and moorage dock, nature trails, interpretive exhibits, swimming beaches, and a trail system.

Dates: Open year-round.

Fees: There is a charge for vehicle access.

Closest town: Troutdale, 6.5 miles west.

For more information: Rooster Rock State Park, PO Box 100, Corbett, OR 97019. Phone (503) 695-2261. Write Oregon State Parks and Recreation Department, 1115 Commercial Street NE, Salem, OR 97310-1001.

MULTNOMAH FALLS

[Fig. 7(6)] The greatest concentration of tall waterfalls in the United States can be found plunging down the south wall of the Columbia River gorge above the Historic Columbia Scenic Highway. Within 11 miles there are 24 named waterfalls, and 16 of them cascade at least 100 feet. The waterfalls spray across lava rock, splattering lichen-yellowed rock faces, and gush over black lips of basalt. All totaled, there are 77 waterfalls on the Oregon side.

Multnomah Falls is the highest and most commercialized. The 620-foot, two-tier plunge in Multnomah Creek is the second highest year-round waterfall in the United States and Oregon's number one natural tourist attraction. The creek collects near the 4,000-foot level of Larch Mountain and drops over four major falls en route to the Columbia River.

Clustered near the base are a 1925-era cedar and rock destination lodge and restaurant, a year-round U.S. Forest Service information center that is open daily, gift shops, and trailheads for some of the gorge's most popular trails.

The thick whitewater falls in a narrow stream that spritzes where it touches the dark, mossy walls of volcanic rock, explodes into misty rainbows, and roars with a power that shakes the ground beneath observation platforms.

This is one of the best places in the gorge to see geological formations that were exposed by the Lake Missoula Floods. The scars of five separate volcanic flows of Yakima basalt are visible in the cliff face.

A 0.25-mile paved path climbs uphill from the information center beside the falls. Between the upper and lower tiers of the falls, the path crosses the plunge pool on arched Benson Bridge. Here, hikers get a chance for a cool misting and a spectacular close-up view of both upper and lower falls. The paved path becomes unpaved Larch Mountain Trail 441 to the top of Larch Mountain, elevation 4,055 feet.

US 30 runs east and west from Multnomah Falls and offers a delightful fern-hemmed alternative to the straight-line expediency of I-84.

Directions: From I-84 either east or west bound, use Exit 31, which is 30 miles east of Portland. The freeway exit leads into a parking lot. Another parking area is adjacent to historic US 30 in front of the lodge. Both lots are free.

Activities: Hiking, photography, interpretive walks.

Facilities: Multnomah Falls Lodge and the interpretive center are open daily under supervision of the Forest Service. The lodge offers a gift shop, restaurant, snack bar, and lodging; reservations are advised.

Dates: Open year-round.

Fees: None.

Closest town: Troutdale, 15 miles west.

For more information: Multnomah Falls Lodge, Box 367, Troutdale, OR 97060. Phone (503) 695-2376. Columbia Gorge National Scenic Area, 902 Wasco Avenue, Hood River, OR 97031. Phone (541) 386-2333.

ONEONTA GORGE

[Fig. 7(7)] Two miles east of Multnomah Falls on US 30 is a narrow pullover parking area where badly marked Oneonta Trail 424 leads into Oneonta Gorge, a cleft between cool walls of dark lava rock. The wet emerald walls evoke a cathedral-like atmosphere, with gossamer drapes of hanging mosses, drooping sheaves of ferns, and more than 50 species of wildflowers and flowering shrubs. It's a favorite haunt of nature photographers, botanists, and summer travelers looking for a cool, primitive spot.

At the back of the gorge are two waterfalls in Oneonta Creek. The first is a 75-foot horsetail plunge called Lower Oneonta Falls. Above that is Triple Falls, a 135-foot segmented drop.

Along Oneonta Trail 424 are remnants of stonework from one of the highway's original bridges and the rubble-filled remains of a 1914 tunnel now bypassed. The walls of the gorge are scarred with gaping holes left by the decomposition of 25-million-year-old fossilized tree trunks. The botanical area supports endemic hybrid plants and dozens of temperate ferns, mosses, hepaticas, and lichens.

Directions: From the east, take I-84 to Exit 35. Exit on Columbia River Scenic Highway and follow to the trailhead. The trail follows Oneonta Creek south from the trailhead. Beyond Oneonta Gorge, Trail 424 intersects with Trail 425, which connects with the trail systems leading to Horsetail Creek, Sherrard's Point on Larch Mountain, and Multnomah Falls. From the west, take Columbia River Scenic Highway.

Activities: Hiking, waterfall scenery.

Facilities: None.

Dates: Open year-round, and is snow free Apr. through Nov.

Closest town: Cascade Locks, 10 miles east.

For more information: Columbia River Gorge National Scenic Area, Waucoma Center, 902 Wasco Avenue, Suite 200, Hood River, OR 97031. Phone (541) 386-2333.

Trail: 7.7 miles through a narrow gorge botanical area.

Elevation: Change of about 4,000 feet elevation. The high point is at 4,056 feet.

Degree of difficulty: Strenuous uphill hike south from US 30 trailhead, but the return trip is downhill and rated moderate.

Surface: Natural duff.

AINSWORTH STATE PARK

[Fig. 7(8)] This park is the major state campground in the heart of the western Columbia Gorge. Its secluded, heavily wooded sites are popular bases for hikers, bikers, and gorge travelers.

Directions: Follow historic highway US 30 for 22 miles east of Troutdale, or use I-84 Exit 35. The campground is at the exit.

Facilities: 45 campsites with full hookups, and 4 walk-in tent sites. RVs to 60 feet, dump station, picnic area with tables and grills, restrooms, drinking water, hiking trails. There is a resident campground manager.

Dates: Open Apr.-Nov., depending on weather.

Fees: There are charges for camping and day-use picnic area.

Closest town: Cascade Locks is about 9 miles east.

For more information: Ainsworth State Park, PO Box 100, Corbett, OR 97019. Phone the park at (503) 695-2301. Oregon State Parks, 1115 Commercial Street NE, Salem, OR 97310-1001.

BONNEVILLE DAM

[Fig. 8(1)] Massive Bonneville Dam is the first Columbia River impoundment above the Pacific Ocean, and it is the largest manmade attraction in the gorge. It was built between 1933 and 1937, and was the first concrete barrier across the Columbia River. Now listed on the National Historic Register, the dam generates 1 million kilowatts of hydroelectricity that powers 500,000 homes.

The landscaped site has evolved with tourism in mind. It is co-managed by the U.S. Army Corps of Engineers, Bonneville Power Administration, and Oregon Fish and Wildlife Department. Access roads and walkways wind through floral gardens, past picnic areas, visitor centers, gift shops, navigation locks, and a state fish hatchery.

Rose gardens and ornamental trees mix with live displays of Columbia River fish, including a 9-foot, 10-inch, 400-pound white sturgeon (*Acipenser transmontanus*) named Herman. The glass-walled sturgeon habitat center offers gorge travelers a rare chance for an underwater close-up of these strange, diamond-plated, boneless fish. Herman is 60 years old, middle-aged by sturgeon standards, and was caught in 1998 near Troutdale.

White sturgeon are the premier game fish of the gorge. They date back to the era of dinosaurs, and grow to more than 12 feet long, and several hundred pounds. It's common to see these huge fish free jumping a body length and more above the water in the frothy white rip lines below the spillways. When an angler hooks a 6- to 12-footer, the peaceful scene erupts into pandemonium.

On the Washington side, underwater viewing windows are cut into the wall of the dam's fish ladder, used by millions of Columbia River fish. During spawning runs visitors get an eye-to-eye view of Columbia River anadromous fish as they migrate toward upstream spawning areas.

Bonneville Dam.

The best time to see American shad (*Alosa sapidissima*) is May through June; steelhead trout (*Oncorhynchus mykiss*), July through August; chinook salmon (*Oncorhynchus tshawytscha*), April through September; sockeye salmon (*Oncorhynchus nerka*), July. All year the ladder is used by lamprey (*Entosphenus *tridentatus*), and nonanadromous fish such as suckers, northern pikeminnows (*Ptychocheilus oregonensis*), and mountain whitefish (*Prospoium willamsoni*).

Fishing guides for sturgeon, salmon, steelhead, and shad can be contacted through The Fishery by phoning (541) 374-8577. A free Oregon boat launch ramp is downstream of the Bonneville hatchery near the mouth of Tanner Creek.

Directions: I-84 Exit 40. Turn north into the Bonneville complex or south to Tanner Creek Trail 431. There is no access to the complex on the Washington side from the Oregon complex. To tour the Washington turbine room and underwater fish ladder viewing chamber, continue east to I-84 Exit 44, cross the Columbia River on the Bridge of the Gods (toll charged), and return west 2 miles on WA 14 to the visitors center.

Dates: Open daily except Thanksgiving, Christmas, and New Year's days.

Activities: Self-guided tours of the dam, powerhouse, navigation locks, and hatchery, plus fishing, boating, and picnicking. Tanner Creek Trail 431 begins south of Exit 40, and it is an easy 0.5-mile walk up Tanner Creek past a narrow 30-foot creek falls to Wahelella Falls, which thunders through a basalt cleft, plunges 25 feet into a pool, reforms into a misty veil, and cascades another 70 feet.

Facilities: Oregon-side dam and locks visitor centers, restrooms, fish hatchery, boat launch, sturgeon viewing habitat, landscaped picnic areas, gift shop, surfaced pathways, and Tanner Creek Trail 431.

Fees: None.

Closest town: Cascade Locks, 4 miles east.

For more information: Bonneville Lock and Dam Visitor Center, U. S. Army Corps of Engineers, Bonneville Lock and Dam, OR 97014-0150. Phone (541) 374-8820.

EAGLE CREEK

[Fig. 8] Eagle Creek is one of the most intriguing and heavily used natural areas in the gorge. There is spectacular hiking on Eagle Creek Trail 440, a waterfall complex, and two campgrounds. At the state-operated Cascade Fish Hatchery, in late summer and fall, there is a mix of mature adult salmon returning from the ocean ready to spawn, and cigar-long smolts, or young salmon, being readied for release to the sea.

Built in 1916, the Eagle Creek Campground was the first U.S. Forest Service campgrounds in the country. The campsites and a popular picnic area sit on a bluff at the mouth of Eagle Creek, overlooking the Columbia River. Eagle Creek Trail 440 is chiseled into the cliffs above the creek and climbs 3,600 feet through a visual wonderland of a dozen waterfalls, rock formations, towering cedar and fir trees, hanging gardens, and glades glowing with the pink, purple, and white blooms of Dutchman's breeches (*Dicentra cucullaria*), wild ginger (*Asarum caudatum*), and western trillium (*Trillium ovatum*). Within 0.25 mile of the picnic area the trail runs through the Troutdale lava formations, where sharp-eyed geology buffs will see petrified wood frozen into the edges of the lava.

In spring and summer, Eagle Creek visitors can see many uncommon varieties of wildflowers. Included are red monkey flowers (*Mimulus lewisil*), yellow balsamroot (*Balsamorrhiza sagitatta*), red columbine (*Aquilegia formosa*), skyrocket phlox (*Gilia aggregata*), purple lupine (*Lupinus latifolius*), and scarlet common paintbrush (*Castilleja minata*). At the higher elevations inside the wilderness area are wild rhododendrons and stands of huge old-growth Douglas fir. Firs that survived a 1910 fire now measure up to 8 feet in diameter. The Hatfield Wilderness boundary is 4.8 miles south of the Exit 41 trailhead.

Directions: At I-84 Exit 41 about 1 mile east of Bonneville Dam.

Activities: Hiking, camping, hatchery and waterfall viewing.

Facilities: Campgrounds, trail, hatchery.

Dates: Open year-round, but upper elevations are often snowbound from Dec. through Apr.

Fees: There is a charge for a trail park pass.

Closest town: Cascade Locks, 2.75 miles east.

For more information: Columbia River Gorge National Scenic Area, 907 Wasco, Hood River, OR 97031. Phone (541) 386-2333.

EAGLE CREEK TRAIL 440

[Fig. 8(2)] This exceptionally popular, often congested trail ends at Wahtum Lake 13.3 miles inside the Hatfield Wilderness Area of Mount Hood National Forest.

Summer and fall are the most popular times to hike this trail. The upper elevations are snow-covered from November to late June. The first tent site along the trail is Tenas Camp, 3.7 miles from the trailhead. The heaviest used site is at 7.5 Mile Camp.

The trail was built in 1915. It is wide, well maintained and climbs at a moderate rate. It is, however, hazardous for unrestrained children because of the cliffside drop-offs along much of the route. Handrails offer a thin guard in extreme areas, but this is not a trail for anyone with a fear of heights. Occasionally the trail is blocked by avalanches of rock and tree debris.

Three waterfalls stand out from the dozen or so along the trail. Metalko Falls, a 150-foot plunge, is 1.5 miles up the trail. At 2.1 miles, a side trail drops down to creek level and Punch Bowl Falls. At 3.3 miles, hikers cross a 25-foot-long bridge above a 125-foot-deep gorge. Six miles from the trailhead, the trail's surface turns into columnar basalt forming uneven stepping stones leading into a 30-foot-long tunnel blasted through solid rock. Outside the tunnel wall is the thundering cascade of 100-foot-high Tunnel Falls.

Trail: 13.3 miles, one way.

Elevation: Trailhead is at 110 feet, rising to 3,360 feet.

Degree of difficulty: Moderate, strenuous in places with catwalk sections across cliff facings that may prove daunting for those with a fear of heights.

Surface: Dirt and rock.

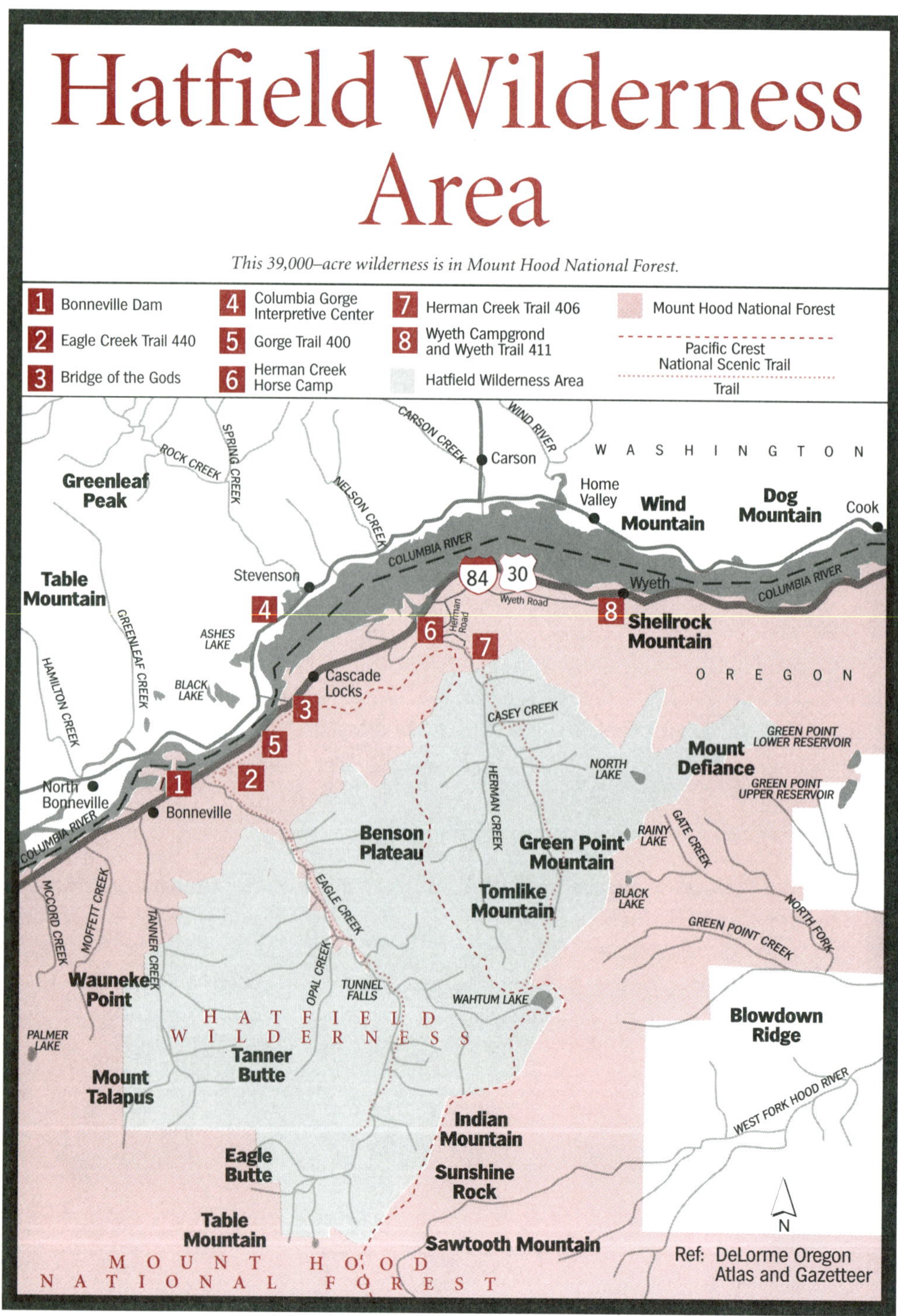
Hatfield Wilderness Area
This 39,000–acre wilderness is in Mount Hood National Forest.
1 Bonneville Dam
2 Eagle Creek Trail 440
3 Bridge of the Gods
4 Columbia Gorge Interpretive Center
5 Gorge Trail 400
6 Herman Creek Horse Camp
7 Herman Creek Trail 406
8 Wyeth Campgrond and Wyeth Trail 411
Hatfield Wilderness Area
Mount Hood National Forest
Pacific Crest National Scenic Trail
Trail
WASHINGTON
OREGON
Greenleaf Peak
Table Mountain
Stevenson
Carson
Home Valley
Wind Mountain
Dog Mountain
Cook
Wyeth
Shellrock Mountain
Cascade Locks
North Bonneville
Bonneville
Mount Defiance
Benson Plateau
Green Point Mountain
Tomlike Mountain
Wauneka Point
Mount Talapus
Tanner Butte
Eagle Butte
Table Mountain
Indian Mountain
Sunshine Rock
Sawtooth Mountain
Blowdown Ridge
HATFIELD WILDERNESS
MOUNT HOOD NATIONAL FOREST
Ref: DeLorme Oregon Atlas and Gazetteer

HATFIELD WILDERNESS AREA

[Fig. 8] The landscape in Oregon's most northerly wilderness area is steep. Rugged slopes rise to uneven wooded plateaus. The Hatfield Wilderness Area consists of 39,000 acres in the Mount Hood National Forest.

The land is characterized by spectacular basalt cliffs, rocky slopes, and outcroppings. The main drainages, Tanner, Eagle, and Herman creeks, are sharp green creases between heavily wooded mountains. The creeks flow north into the Columbia. The trout fishing opportunity in these shallow, fast-dropping streams is minimal.

Scenic forest walk-in camping areas are at Wyeast, Blue Grouse Falls, 7.5 Mile Camp, and Wahtum Lake on Waucoma Ridge, just inside the eastern boundary of the wilderness area. At Wahtum Lake, Eagle Creek Trail 440 merges with PCT 2000. Wahtum Lake's 57 acres make it the second largest lake north of Mount Hood. Depths plunge to 180 feet and give the water a dark blue look that invites fishing for colorful green, orange, and blue brook trout (*Salvelinus fontinalis*).

On older maps, this wilderness may still bear the original name Columbia Wilderness Area.

Directions: Located in the north region of the forest, the wilderness area is accessible via hiking trails at US 30, Cascade Locks, and Forest Service Road 13, southwest of Hood River. Three of the most popular gorge trailheads are Eagle Creek Trail 440, Herman Creek Trail 447, and the Pacific Crest National Scenic Trail 2,000 at Cascade Locks.

Activities: Summer hiking, backpacking, camping, and trout fishing. Fall deer, elk, black bear, and grouse hunting. All mechanical vehicles, including mountain bikes, are prohibited.

Facilities: 200 miles of maintained trails and mountains where elevations range from 1,200 to 4,600 feet.

Dates: Open year-round. Most upper-elevation trails are snow-covered until May.

Fees: There is a charge for trail park passes at all trails entering the Hatfield Wilderness.

Closest town: Cascade Locks, about 2 miles north of the wilderness boundary.

For more information: Hood River Ranger District, 6780 Highway 35, Parkdale, OR 97041. Phone (541) 352-6002.

CASCADE LOCKS

[Fig. 8] The small riverside settlement of Cascade Locks, population 900, is an understated concentration of attractions and recreation opportunities that once gave rise to historical events and Indian legends.

The inoperative locks are the historical focal point for 23-acre Marine Park, which includes a covered pavilion, picnic area, boat ramp, marina, campground, playground, museum, and visitors center. The museum, built in 1905 to house lock workers, features a life-size replica of a 30-foot-high commercial fish wheel. During peak migrations these wheels, now outlawed, caught more than 2,500 salmon a day. The museum is crammed with Oregon Trail artifacts, and features an 1860 locomotive, the first built on the West Coast.

The locks are one of two National Historic Sites in Cascade Locks. Built in 1896 to allow boats and ships to bypass The Great Falls of the Columbia, the locks became obsolete in 1937 when water rising behind Bonneville Dam submerged the falls.

Today the locks are used mostly by sport and tribal fishermen trying for salmon and steelhead, which take refuge in the quiet waters of the locks during their July to September migration to spawning areas. Tribal commercial fishermen occasionally dip net chinook salmon in the channel.

A historically interesting waterfront jaunt follows a paved pathway onto a footbridge that crosses the lock channel to wooded Thunder Island. One of the local legends details how explorer Meriwether Lewis, while camping here, nearly lost his pet Newfoundland dog to an Indian's stew pot. The dog was returned, but according to history, Lewis' wrath was ignited and the intervention of three armed men from the Corps of Discovery was required.

The white-and-red triple-deck sternwheeler, *Columbia Gorge,* embarks on daily river excursions from the last week in June until the first weekend in October. The paddle wheeler docks at the marina visitor center. For sternwheeler information call (541) 374-8427.

Cascade Locks is a favorite jumping-off spot for hikers backpacking south into the Oregon Cascades on PCT 2000, and hikers going east or west on Columbia Gorge Trail 400. The PCT trailhead is on the approach to Bridge Of The Gods. Hikers find Columbia Gorge Trail 400 at the end of Moody Street.

Directions: I-84 Exit 44.

Activities: River boating, fishing, picnicking, paddle boat river cruises, and hiking.

Facilities: Marine park, boat launch and harbor, museum of Columbia River artifacts and history, trailheads to PCT 2000 and Columbia Gorge Trail 400, full traveler services. Campers will find 40 tent and RV sites up to 35 feet long at Marine Park Campground (541) 374-8619), which are available year-round with a daily fee. There is a central water supply, hot showers, RV dump station, but no hook-ups. Full-service RV sites are available at KOA and other private RV parks in Cascade Locks.

Dates: The park and marina are open year-round. The stern wheeler is in port during summer months only.

Fees: There is a charge for museum admission, stern wheeler tour, camping, and boat moorage.

For more information: Cascade Locks Marine Park Visitor Center, PO Box 307, Cascade Locks, OR 97014. Phone (541) 374-8619.

BRIDGE OF THE GODS

[Fig. 8(3)] Cascade Locks's other National Historic Site and its most prominent architectural feature is the cantilever ironwork of The Bridge Of The Gods. The narrow toll bridge spans 1,858-feet of the Columbia River 135 feet above the water between Oregon's I-84 and Washington's State Highway 14. It's located at the west end of town. Use I-84 Exit 44.

Bridge Of The Gods draws its colorful name from an Indian legend and a natural rock bridge that formed at this site about 1,000 years ago when a wall on Table Mountain is believed to have collapsed into the river from the Washington side. There's no trace of that bridge now, but the story has spawned some of the gorge's most colorful legends, and assorted explanations for the area's volcano and earthquake legacies.

There are several variations of the Legend of Bridge Of The Gods. One of the most popular is recounted in a brochure at the Cascade Locks visitor center:

"Manito, the Great Spirit, placed Loo-Wit, the wise old woman, on the bridge as its guardian, and sent to earth the great snow mountains, which were really his sons: Multnomah, the warrior; Klickitat (Mount Adams), the totem-maker; and Wyeast (Mount Hood), the singer. All was peace and happiness until beautiful Squaw Mountain moved into a small valley between Klickitat and Wyeast. This was the Evil One's opportunity, for a rivalry soon sprang up between the brothers for the affections of Squaw Mountain.

"Though beautiful Squaw Mountain grew to love Wyeast, she thought it great fun to flirt with his big, good-natured brother Klickitat, and soon the brothers began quarreling. At first they argued, growled, and grumbled at each other.

"They stomped their feet and spat ashes and fire in the air and belched forth great clouds of black smoke so that the sun was hidden. Each hurled white-hot rocks setting fire to the forests and driving the people into hiding.

"Finally, they threw so many stones onto the Bridge of The Gods and shook the earth so hard that the bridge broke in the middle and fell into the river.

"Upon hearing of this, the Great Spirit was angry and he, too, shook the foundations of the earth. Klickitat, who was the larger of the two mountains, won the fight , and Wyeast admitted defeat, giving over all claims to beautiful Squaw Mountain. Loving Wyeast as she did, this was a severe blow to Squaw Mountain. Though she dutifully went over and took her place by the side of Klickitat, her heart was broken. In a short time, she fell at Klickitat's feet and sank into a deep sleep, from which she has never awakened. She is now known as the Sleeping Beauty and lies where she fell, just west of Mount Adams.

"Klickitat truly loved Squaw Mountain and her fate caused him such grief that he dropped his head in shame and has never raised it. During the war between the brothers, Loo-Wit, who was very old and homely, tried to stop the fight. When she failed, she stayed at her post, although badly burned by the fires.

"When the bridge fell, Loo-Wit fell with it, but the Great Spirit, hearing of her faithfulness, promised to grant her one wish. She asked to be young and beautiful once more, and when her wish was granted she took her place among the great snow mountains. Today, she is known as Mount Saint Helens, the youngest mountain in the Cascades."

COLUMBIA GORGE INTERPRETIVE CENTER

[Fig. 8(4)] Two major sources for gorge information are located at Stevenson, Washington, across the Columbia River from Cascade Locks. Cross to the north side of the river on the Bridge of The Gods, I-84 Exit 44, and turn east on WA 14 for about 2 miles to the Columbia Gorge Interpretive Center.

Features include a 37-foot-high replica of a nineteenth-century fish wheel, restored sawmill equipment, a theater re-creation of the cataclysmic formation of the gorge, an exhibit on the cultural diversity of gorge inhabitants, a model of the water route followed by Lewis and Clark, and artifact collections.

The Forest Service has a staffed informational kiosk in the lobby of Skamania Lodge, which is about 0.2 mile beyond the interpretive center on Rock Creek Drive. The kiosk is stocked with a full range of recreational maps, informational pamphlets, and books about the gorge.

Directions: I-84 to Exit 44 Cascade Locks. Cross the toll Bridge of the Gods, and turn east on OR 14 to Rock Creek Drive. Turn north on Rock Creek Drive to the interpretive center. The Forest Service information center is another 0.2 mile on Rock Creek Drive, inside Skamania Lodge.

Dates: Open daily except Thanksgiving, Christmas, and New Year's Day.

Fees: There is a charge for admission to the interpretive center, but not to the Forest Service information kiosk at Skamania Lodge.

For more information: Columbia Gorge Interpretive Center, 990 SW Rock Creek Drive, Stevenson, WA 98648. Phone (509) 427-8211.

COLUMBIA RIVER GORGE TRAIL 400

[Fig. 8(5)] Columbia River Gorge Trail 400 parallels US 30 on a year-round, low-elevation, east-west route dug into the mountainside below the high basalt cliffs of the Columbia Gorge. The grade varies only 240 feet and the trail is nearly flat in most places. Talus slope crossings can, however, be a challenge.

The 35.5-mile route can be divided into segments, round-trips, or a one-way trip. Several of the more popular segment rides include a 3-mile route between Dodson at I-84 Exit 35 and the junction of Nesmith Point Trail 428. Another popular ride is the 4.6 miles between Nesmith Point at McCord Creek and Eagle Creek Recreation Area.

MOUNTAIN HEMLOCK

(Tsuga mertensiana)

Growing in the shade of other trees, hemlocks reach maturity producing a dense shade that few other tree species can survive under.

One of the best river views from Columbia River Gorge Trail 400 is east of Eagle Creek Recreation Area at I-84 Exit 41. Take the 1.8-mile Wauna Trail 402 to a place under overhead power lines where there's a marked viewpoint. After reaching the viewpoint, many bicyclists and hikers return to Gorge Trail 400 for the 2.4-mile ride or hike between Eagle Creek Recreation Area and the river community of

Cascades Locks at I-84 Exit 44. The trail is closed to motorized vehicles.

Directions: The west end of Trail 400 is in Benson State Park. Use I-84 Exit 30. The east end continues from the end of Moody Street in Cascade Locks. Use I-84 Exit 44. On the trail between these two points are dozens of access spots leading from US 30. Some are marked and some are no more than packed dirt trails leading uphill from a roadside pullover.

Facilities: Food, lodging, and trail information at Multnomah Falls Lodge, I-84 Exit 31, and Cascade Locks, I-84 Exit 44. Many of the waterfall viewpoints adjacent to the trail also have picnic tables.

Dates: Year-round, rarely snow-covered.

For more information: Columbia River Gorge National Scenic Area, 902 Wasco Avenue, Suite 200, Hood River, OR 97031. Phone (541) 386-2333.

Trail: 35.5 miles paralleling US 30.

Elevation: Approximately river level, with 240 feet of change.

Degree of difficulty: Easy.

Surface: Natural.

HERMAN CREEK HORSE CAMP AND TRAIL

[Fig. 8(6)] Herman Creek Horse Camp is just far enough off the interstate corridor to provide a quiet stop for lunch, a scenic hike break, or an overnight camp out. The area is designed for recreationists riding and packing with horses, but it is open for general camping and primitive picnicking.

Directions: From the westbound lanes of I-84 use Exit 47. Eastbound travelers must continue to Exit 44 and backtrack 2 miles east through Cascade Locks.

Facilities: 7 tent and RV sites, well water, tables, and restrooms. There is a trailhead for Herman Creek Trail 406, which follows Woolly Horn Ridge into the Hatfield Wilderness Area to Wahtum Lake. This is one of the most popular horse routes into the wilderness.

Dates: Open year-round.

Fees: There is a charge for camping.

Closest town: Cascades Locks, 2 miles west.

For more information: Columbia River Gorge National Scenic Area, 907 Wasco, Hood River, OR 97031. Phone (541) 386-2333.

HERMAN CREEK TRAIL 406

[Fig. 8(7)] Begins at Herman Creek Horse Camp and follows a creek bottom below Woolly Horn Ridge, paralleling PCT 2000, through Hatfield Wilderness Area to Wahtum Lake. Several small waterfalls tumble into the creek.

Trail: 11.2 miles one way.

Elevation: Trailhead elevation is 1,000 feet, and the high point is 3,732 feet at Wahtum Lake.

Degree of difficulty: Moderate, strenuous in places.

Fees: There is a charge for a trail park pass.

Surface: Dirt.

WYETH CAMPGROUND AND WYETH TRAIL 411

[Fig. 8(8)] One mile southeast of Wyeth Campground, Shellrock Mountain, an inactive volcano, juts above the conifers on the south side of I-84.

Shellrock Mountain is considered by geologists to be the topographical sister volcano to Wind Mountain, which rises across the Columbia River on the Washington shore at the community of Home Valley.

The diorite rocks at the base of the Shellrock Mountain sometimes sparkle with crystals of plagioclase feldspar. Look carefully toward the prominent bulge that is Benson Point, and you can make out a brush line that reveals the perilous route of a pioneer wagon road, used from 1872 through 1876, built to connect The Dalles and Sandy.

Four miles south of Shellrock Mountain is the 4,736-foot summit of Green Point Mountain, the highest point in the gorge. The summit can be reached from Wyeth Campground by hiking Wyeth Trail 411 south and connecting with one of two summit routes: Forest Service Trail 423 winds past North Lake, and Forest Service Trail 418 follows Green Point Ridge. Either route is a lung-stretching 7-plus miles of switchbacks with a 3,900-foot elevation gain. The trail is closed to motorized vehicles.

Wyeth Campground makes an excellent base for exploring this area of the Columbia Gorge.

Directions: I-84 Exit 51 about 4 miles east of Herman Creek Campground.

Facilities: 17 tent and RV sites up to 32 feet long, drinking water, picnic tables, restroom, and several trails. The main trail is Wyeth Trail 411, which runs south 0.75 mile to a 120-foot tiered horsetail waterfall on Gorton Creek. Beyond the falls the trail climbs 3,900 feet through steep switchbacks for 7.3 miles into the Hatfield Wilderness Area.

Dates: Open Memorial Day to Labor Day.

Fees: There is a charge for camping and trail use.

Closest town: Cascade Locks, approximately 6 miles west.

For more information: Columbia River Gorge National Scenic Area, 907 Wasco, Hood River, OR 97031. Phone (541) 386-2333.

Trail 411 is open year-round and most of the lower segments are nearly always snow free. The upper elevation mountain areas are usually snow covered from Nov. to June.

Directions: I-84 Exit 51. The trailhead is in Wyeth Campground.

Trail: 7.3 miles one way.

Elevation: Trailhead is at 400 feet and the high point is 3,900.

Degree of difficulty: Strenuous.

Surface: Dirt and rock.

Fees: There is a charge for a trail park pass.

VIENTO STATE PARK CAMPGROUND

[Fig. 9(1)] This picturesque state park is the closest public campground to Hood River. Campsites are large and well spaced, and some enjoy a canopy of shade trees. Camping and day-use segments are on both sides of the rumbling interstate traffic. There is a rough boat access to the Columbia River for boats that can be hand carried. The launch is used mostly by wind surfers. *Viento* is Spanish for "wind" and the park is extremely popular with surfers during high-wind periods. If the wind is howling through here, rarely is an open campsite available.

Directions: Located along I-84 west of Hood River at Exit 56, the park grounds are divided by the interstate.

Activities: Wind-surfing, camping, and hiking.

Facilities: 58 full hook-up and 17 tent sites. Maximum site size is 30 feet long, picnic tables, restroom, hot showers, 1.1-mile hiking trail, Columbia River access (hand carry, no ramp), summer campfire programs. South of the interstate a path leads to an abandoned one-mile section on the Historical Columbia River Highway State Trail. The old roadbed is a level 1-hour round-trip walk west to Starvation Creek State Park picnic area.

Dates: Mar. 1 to Nov. 30

Fees: There is a charge for camping.

Closest town: Hood River, about 8 miles east.

For more information: The campground phone is (541) 374-8811. For campsite information, phone (800) 551-6949. Oregon State Parks Department, 1115 Commercial Street NE, Salem, OR 97301-1002.

TOWN OF HOOD RIVER

[Fig. 9] There are only two traffic lights and 5,110 people in Hood River, the largest town in the Columbia River Gorge. Hood River is the county seat of 536-square mile Hood River County, which is the second smallest county in Oregon. Yet this small town is an international mecca attracting thousands of summer recreationists.

Hood River has earned worldwide attention for the sport of wind-surfing on sailboards. The notoriously strong winds that steadily rake the Columbia River around Hood River attract thousands of wind-surfers, millions of dollars, and have established the region as a summer destination for international surfers.

Since the 1980s, the wind and waves at Hood River have consistently ranked in the top two surfing sites in the world.

On any breezy day, River Front Park, just west of the OR 35 Columbia River bridge, becomes an international community; an amazing collage of neon-colored sails, surfboard style sailboards, skin-tight wet suits, and cars outfitted with roof rack towers designed to hold multiple sailboards and mountain bikes.

Wind-surfing anchors a developing $30 million recreation industry that is being credited with reversing an economic downward spiral caused by the loss of timber and agricultural jobs. Dozens of small related businesses have sprung up, and the town's population has boomed.

Outdoor recreations of all types flourish here. The local chamber of commerce has a "Things To Do" list that includes 72 activities, and all but 18 take place outdoors. The unusually diverse recreation opportunities in this mountain, snow, and water community run from

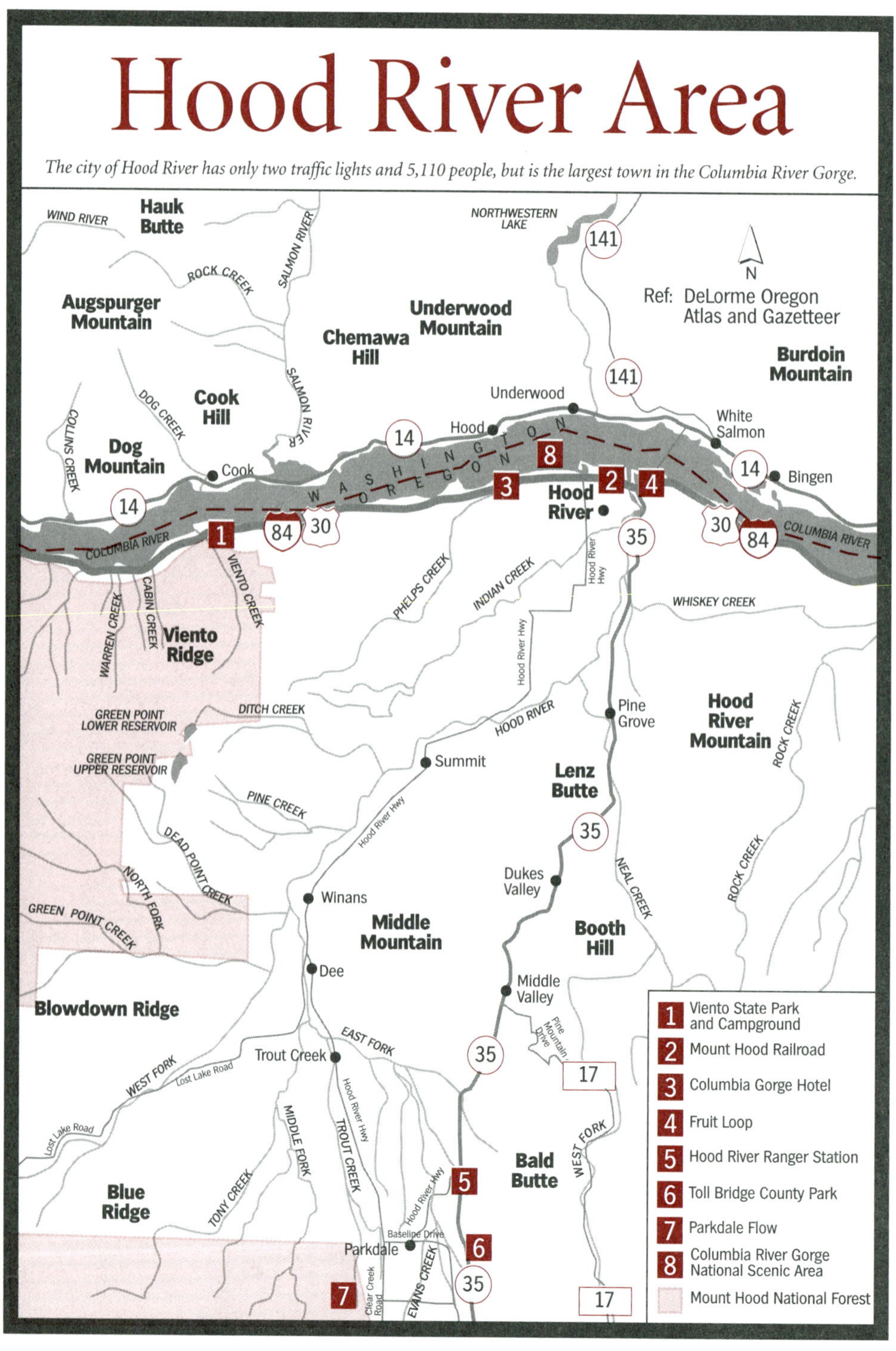
Hood River Area
The city of Hood River has only two traffic lights and 5,110 people, but is the largest town in the Columbia River Gorge.
Ref: DeLorme Oregon Atlas and Gazetteer
N
Wind River
Hauk Butte
Rock Creek
Salmon River
Northwestern Lake
Augspurger Mountain
Underwood Mountain
Chemawa Hill
Burdoin Mountain
Cook Hill
Dog Creek
Collins Creek
Dog Mountain
Cook
Underwood
Hood
White Salmon
Bingen
Washington
Oregon
Hood River
Columbia River
Viento Creek
Cabin Creek
Warren Creek
Viento Ridge
Phelps Creek
Indian Creek
Hood River Hwy
Whiskey Creek
Green Point Lower Reservoir
Ditch Creek
Green Point Upper Reservoir
Pine Creek
Summit
Hood River
Pine Grove
Hood River Mountain
Rock Creek
Lenz Butte
Dead Point Creek
North Fork
Green Point Creek
Dukes Valley
Neal Creek
Winans
Middle Mountain
Booth Hill
Dee
Middle Valley
Blowdown Ridge
East Fork
Pine Mountain Drive
Trout Creek
West Fork
Lost Lake Road
Middle Fork
Trout Creek
Bald Butte
Blue Ridge
Tony Creek
Baseline Drive
Parkdale
Evans Creek
Clear Creek Road
1 Viento State Park and Campground
2 Mount Hood Railroad
3 Columbia Gorge Hotel
4 Fruit Loop
5 Hood River Ranger Station
6 Toll Bridge County Park
7 Parkdale Flow
8 Columbia River Gorge National Scenic Area
Mount Hood National Forest

hiking trips with llamas that carry the supply packs, to whitewater rafting, golfing to skeet shooting, skiing to mountain biking, and fishing to fruit tasting.

Hood River is near the midpoint of the 80-mile long gorge, and is the headquarters of the Columbia River Gorge scenic area (*see*, Columbia River Gorge National Scenic Area, page 23). It is a crossroad for northern Oregon highways, and an important junction for gorge travelers.

Oregon Highway 35, the east leg of the Mount Hood Loop, intersects I-84 at Exit 64 and runs south through 14,775 acres of pear, apple, and cherry orchards to Mount Hood ski areas. This state highway merges with US 26 on the south shoulder of Mount Hood. US 26 is the east-west arterial between Portland and US 97 in the Deschutes River breaks at Madras. Northbound OR 35 crosses the Columbia River into Washington State on a narrow two-lane toll bridge.

By continuing east on I-84, travelers enter the open semiarid region of the Columbia Gorge. Mountains steeped in dense green forests give way to rounded, lightly wooded hills, rocky gorges, sagebrush plateaus, and the paved eastern leg of US 30.

Within 40 miles of Hood River there is a 65-inch difference in annual precipitation. Cascade Locks in western Oregon receives 76.24 inches of rain and snow. At midgorge, Hood River receives 30.65 inches, and the eastern region measured at The Dalles gets only 12 inches.

The impact of this rainfall variation is most visible in the forests. West of Hood River trees are often 200 feet tall, growing in dense mixed conifer and deciduous forests. The dominant trees are water-loving Douglas fir, western hemlock and bigleaf maples.

East of Hood River trees are well-spaced and interspersed with grasslands. The types of trees found east of Hood River require less water and run mostly to pines, especially red-barked ponderosa pine (*Pinus ponderosa*), and Oregon white oak (*Quercus garryana*), easily identified by deeply lobed dark green leathery leaves. One of the most common ground covers east of Hood River is the three-leaf cluster of poison oak (*Rhus diversiloba*).

Hood River's recreation activities don't stop when summer ends. First snow kicks off an intense 11-month winter ski and snow-board season on Mount Hood, which towers above this river town like a giant white pyramid.

Directions: I-84 Exit 64 goes into the center of town at the junction of OR 35.

Activities: Wind-surfing, boating, mountain biking, fishing, hiking, picnicking.

Facilities: River Front Park, which has a picnic area, swim beach, marina, and boat ramp. All traveler services, including private RV parks and motels.

For more information: Hood River County Chamber of Commerce and Information Center, 405 Portway Avenue, Hood River, OR 97031. Phone (541) 386-2000 or 1-800-366-3530. Web site: www.gorge.net/hrccc. Use I-84 Exit 63. Hood River County Parks, 918 18th Street, Hood River, OR 97031, phone (541) 387-6888.

MOUNT HOOD RAILROAD

[Fig. 9(2)] Folded into the mix of Hood River's extreme sports is the gentle scene of Mount Hood Railroad excursions through the orchards and foothills south of Hood River.

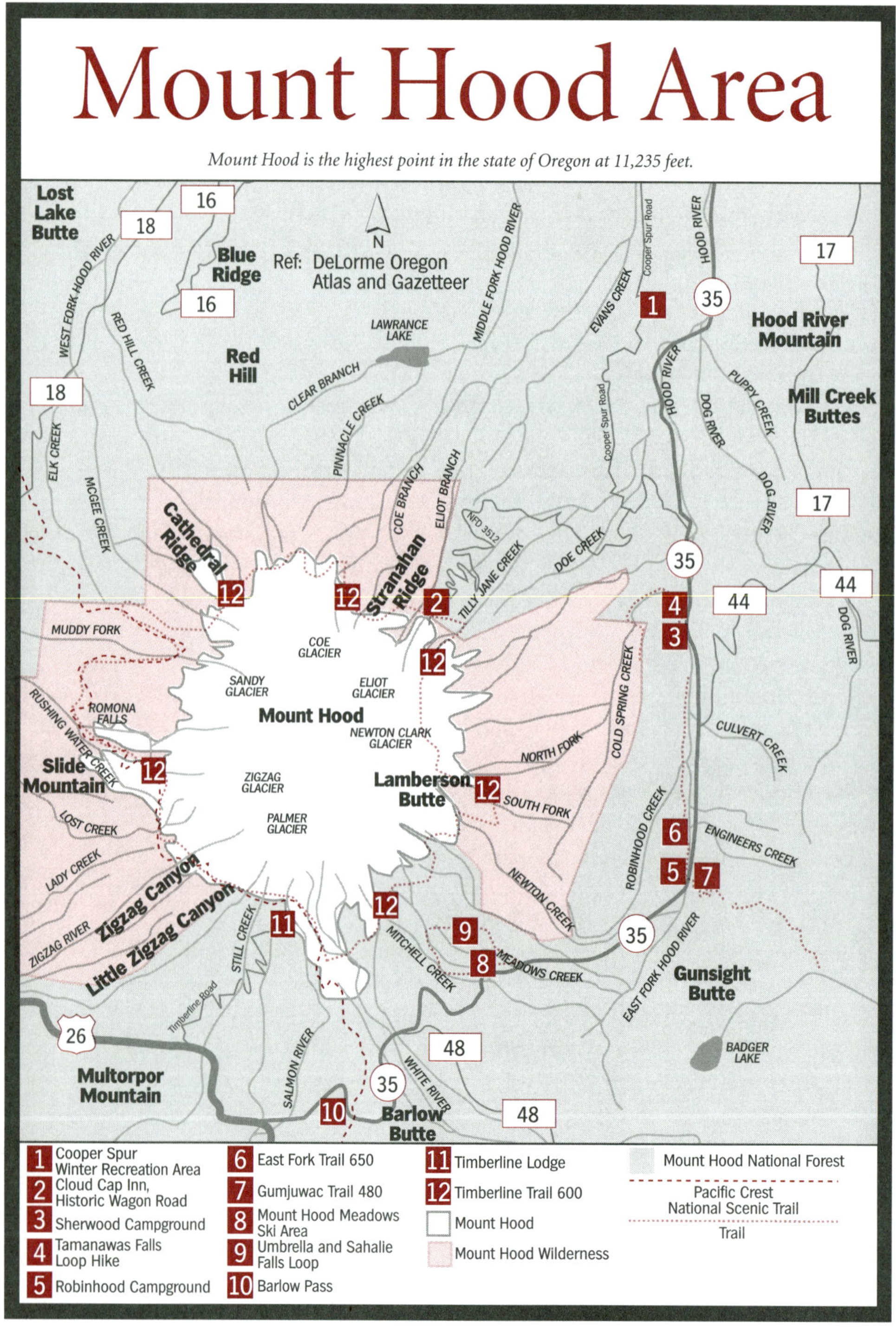
Mount Hood Area
Mount Hood is the highest point in the state of Oregon at 11,235 feet.
Ref: DeLorme Oregon Atlas and Gazetteer
N
Lost Lake Butte
Blue Ridge
Red Hill
Hood River Mountain
Mill Creek Buttes
Cathedral Ridge
Stranahan Ridge
Mount Hood
Lamberson Butte
Slide Mountain
Zigzag Canyon
Little Zigzag Canyon
Gunsight Butte
Multorpor Mountain
Barlow Butte
LAWRANCE LAKE
BADGER LAKE
COE GLACIER
SANDY GLACIER
ELIOT GLACIER
NEWTON CLARK GLACIER
ZIGZAG GLACIER
PALMER GLACIER
ROMONA FALLS
WEST FORK HOOD RIVER
RED HILL CREEK
CLEAR BRANCH
PINNACLE CREEK
MIDDLE FORK HOOD RIVER
EVANS CREEK
Cooper Spur Road
HOOD RIVER
PUPPY CREEK
DOG RIVER
ELK CREEK
MCGEE CREEK
COE BRANCH
ELIOT BRANCH
NFD 3512
TILLY JANE CREEK
DOE CREEK
MUDDY FORK
COLD SPRING CREEK
CULVERT CREEK
RUSHING WATER CREEK
NORTH FORK
SOUTH FORK
LOST CREEK
LADY CREEK
ROBINHOOD CREEK
ENGINEERS CREEK
NEWTON CREEK
ZIGZAG RIVER
STILL CREEK
MITCHELL CREEK
MEADOWS CREEK
EAST FORK HOOD RIVER
Timberline Road
SALMON RIVER
WHITE RIVER
16
18
17
35
44
26
48
1 Cooper Spur Winter Recreation Area
2 Cloud Cap Inn, Historic Wagon Road
3 Sherwood Campground
4 Tamanawas Falls Loop Hike
5 Robinhood Campground
6 East Fork Trail 650
7 Gumjuwac Trail 480
8 Mount Hood Meadows Ski Area
9 Umbrella and Sahalie Falls Loop
10 Barlow Pass
11 Timberline Lodge
12 Timberline Trail 600
Mount Hood
Mount Hood Wilderness
Mount Hood National Forest
Pacific Crest National Scenic Trail
Trail

The excursion railway winds south through 75-year-old orchards that are growing in volcanic soils and produce 30 percent of the world's winter pear crop. In April, the orchards glow with pink and white fruit blossoms.

The railroad is a National Historic Site. It was built in 1906 to bring logs cut in Mount Hood National Forest to mills and shipping barges in Hood River.

The rail system was restored in 1988, and the train was outfitted with ornate coach cars from the early 1900s. It is now used exclusively for passenger tours of the valley. The most popular tours are in April and May, when the miles of orchard trees are blooming.

Two trips are offered. A 49-mile, four-hour excursion leaves Hood River at midmorning and stops at shops in Parkdale. A 17-mile, two-hour trip leaves at midafternoon. The schedule of operation, however, varies with the season, and it's best to call in advance for current information and reservations.

Directions: The depot is located on the south side of I-84 Exit 63 to Railroad Avenue.

Facilities: Rail passenger tours from Hood River through orchards to the foothills of the Cascade Range. Meal trips available.

Dates: Apr. through Dec. Reservations are recommended.

Fees: There is a charge for passage, and food service.

Closest town: Hood River.

For more information: Mount Hood Railroad, 110 Railroad Avenue, Hood River, OR 97031. Phone (800) 872-4661 or (541) 386-3556.

COLUMBIA GORGE HOTEL

[Fig. 9(3)] This big-band era hotel is listed on the National Historic Register. It sits atop a 210-foot waterfall on a bluff above the Columbia River, surrounded by 11 acres of landscaped grounds and gardens. The hotel was built in 1921 and has been restored to original luxury.

For centuries the site of the hotel has been a meeting place for Indians, pioneers, prospectors and businessmen. In 1903, Hood River entrepreneur Robert Rand built the Waw-Gwin-Gwin Hotel on this site. The name is derived from a local Indian word for "running water," in recognition of the nearby 210-foot waterfall. Wah-Gwin-Gwin Falls is behind the hotel. There is a viewing area of the top of the falls.

When Columbia River steamer boats approached the Waw-Gwin-Gwin Hotel, the pilots would use the steam whistle to signal the number of passengers who would need rooms: one toot per boarder. When the boat landed, the hotel staff would have the appropriate number of rooms ready. Rand sold his hotel and surrounding 23 acres in 1920 to timber baron Simon Benson, who tore it down and constructed the Columbia Gorge Hotel. The three-story, Spanish-style hotel became a hideaway for early Hollywood celebrities. Singer Rudolph Valentino was a frequent guest, and a lounge is now named for him.

Directions: Take Exit 62 from I-84 west of Hood River to Westcliff Drive.

Activities: Waterfall and garden viewing, and dining.

Facilities: Restored historic hotel, 1920s-era dining room, landscaped grounds, walkways, and elevated viewpoints.

Dates: Open year-round.

Fees: There is a charge for dining and overnight accommodations.

Closest town: Hood River.

For more information: Columbia Gorge Hotel, 4000 Westcliff Dr., Hood River, OR 97031. Phone (800) 345-1921 or (541) 386-5566.

Historic Columbia River Highway (US 30 East)

[Fig. 7(1), Fig. 11(1)] By abandoning I-84 at Exit 76 to Mosier for the paved two lanes of US 30, east-bound travelers exchange expediency for a country-road drive to the explosive color of wildflowers at the Tom McCall Nature Area, the Columbia Gorge Discovery Center, and the pioneer city of The Dalles.

The town of Mosier provides access to the eastern leg of the Columbia River Gorge Scenic Highway US 30. The town is a Main Street community of small rural homes. Locate US 30 where it slips up the hill at the east end of town, rolling toward the Rowena Plateau through hills bent with wild grass, small orchards and rugged canyons.

Between Mosier and The Dalles on US 30 are 38 miles of winding two-lane, lightly traveled farm road. Drivers are more likely to meet a lumbering combine than a truck, or to crawl through a cattle herd walking down the road between pastures. The few ranches along this road are tucked behind hills of pale blue sage (*Artemisia tridentata*) and yellow rabbit brush (*Chrysothamnus nauseosus*), or in the protection of rocky creek bottoms.

The constant breeze blowing over the ridges washes US 30 with pleasant aromas and spinning dust devils. Along most of the drive, the interstate is far below and comfortably out of sight.

East of Mosier, the historic highway rides the curve of the canyon wall well above and out of sight of the interstate buzzing below. Keep a sharp eye around the orchards for mule deer, and valley quail (*Lephortyx californicus*) with their distinctive comma-shaped head plumes. Long-tailed black-billed magpies *(Pica pica)* loop across the open sky, and a careful look at rock piles often reveals the furry heads of yellow-bellied marmots *(Marmota flaviventris)*, a woodchuck-like animal that lives in rocky burrows and startles hikers with its shrill alarm whistle.

This is dry, arid country and the hillsides show the cracks and sears of high summer temperatures, penetrating winter cold and strong year-round winds. The gray-brown parasol seed heads of cow parsnip *(Heracleum lanatum)*, and crinkled leaves of arrowleaf balsamroot *(Balsamorrhiza sagitatta)* are scattered between bright, colorful patches of blue elderberry *(Sambucus cerulea)*, Cascade aster *(Aster ledophyllus)* and low, pink clumps of hardy little spreading phlox *(Phlox diffusa)*.

Less than two miles east of Mosier, population 290, on US 30, and seemingly 2,500 miles out of place, the tawny western landscape rolls into the front yard of a Southern antebellum-style mansion.

Mayer Mansion was built in 1914; a three-story, white house with porch columns that would easily fit behind a long rail fence in the pre-Civil War South.

It was constructed by Portland businessman Mark Mayer to serve as a gentleman's headquarters from which he could oversee his 250-acre ranch. This photogenic structure is privately owned and tours are not offered.

Directions: From the west on I-84, Exit 69 into Mosier. From the east, at The Dalles on I-84, take Exit 82 and go west on the scenic highway US 30.

Activities: Scenic drive.

Facilities: Overlooks and wildflower areas.

Dates: Open year-round.

Fees: None.

Closest town: Mosier.

For more information: Columbia River Gorge National Scenic Area, 902 Wasco Avenue, Suite 200, Hood River, OR 97031. Phone (541) 386-2333.

ROWENA CREST AND TOM MCCALL PRESERVE

[Fig. 11(2)] The high point on the nine-mile section of scenic US 30 between Mosier and Rowena is located on the crest of a windswept ridge 3 miles west of the tiny hard-scrabble community of Rowena.

The attraction is Rowena Crest, and the adjoining Tom McCall Preserve. The large parking lot provides spectacular views of the Rowena Loops, a winding section of the scenic highway wrapped around the hillside in a steady easterly descent toward the river.

West of the parking lot, a stile crosses a wire fence into Tom McCall Preserve, 231 acres of wild plants, flowers and desert wildlife conserved in the name of Oregon's 30th governor.

Maintained by The Nature Conservancy, the preserve is on a nearly treeless plateau, elevation 594 feet, that supports more than 300 native species of plants and wildflowers, including three species unique to the gorge: Thompson's broadleaf lupine (*Lupinus latifolius thompsonianus*), Columbia desert parsley (*Lomatium columbianum*), and Thompson's waterleaf (*Hydrophyllum capitatum thompsonii*).

Two trails explore the preserve. The lower path is an easy 1-mile walk, with a gradual 200-foot elevation change. It crosses the plateau, skirts a permanent pond, and ends at the edge of a 300-foot cliff overlooking the interstate. The second route gains 1,000 feet over two miles ending at the area's high spot, McCall Point, elevation 1,722 feet. The upper trail is closed from November 1 to April 30, but the lower trail is open year-round. Flower blooms are at their peak in April, May and June.

During the Missoula Floods, this wildflower plateau was covered by 400 feet of water, scouring it down to bedrock, which was later buried by four feet of volcanic ash spewed during the formative eruptions of Mount Saint Helens, 60 miles to the northwest in Washington. The mysterious mounds and swales prevalent on the preserve are remnants of that ash fall.

Showy wildflowers emerge as early as late February. Expect to see varieties of yellow bells, gold stars, balsamroot, fringecups, shooting stars and milkvetch.

The plateau is an oasis for wildlife, including Pacific rattlesnakes (*Crotalus viridis*), Pacific tree frogs (*Hyla regilla*), meadowlarks (*Sturnella neglecta*), great horned owls (*Bubo virginianus*), small saw-whet owls (*Aegolius acadicus*), and the striking cornflower-colored mountain bluebirds (*Sialia currucoides*). You may also see horned larks (*Eremophila alpestris*), and Oregon juncos (*Junco hyemalis*). The scrub white oak around the ponds frequently attracts Lewis woodpeckers (*Melanerpes lewis*), a common yet rarely seen jay-size bird with distinctive pink breast, red face mask and rounded green head.

The view from Rowena Crest is of Columbia River hillsides and gullies unfolding to the east in rounded waves of open plateaus separated by grasslands, talus slopes, and rock-walled gorges with trickling seep creeks. A few of the wider plateaus support green and burnished-gold fields of irrigated winter wheat, but most are a mix of tough, invasive cheatgrasses, rabbit brush, bluegrass, bunchgrass, and scattered sage.

It's a lonesome land inhabited by buff gray coyotes (*Canis latrans*), belly-dragging badgers (*Taxidea taxus*), spotted bobcats (*Felis rufus*) and mule deer. Songbirds, valley quail, and chukar partridge live in the brush, hiding from the raptors that seem to hang forever in the sky, held up by silent invisible updrafts. Golden eagles (*Aquila chrysaetos*) red-tailed hawks (*Buteo jamaicensis*), and prairie falcons (*Falco mexicanus*) are common. It's not unusual to see ospreys (*Pandion haliaetus*) and bald eagles (*Haliaeetus leucocephalus*) hunting for fish along the river.

US 30 drops off the Rowena Plateau to the interstate in a series of sweeping curves known as the Rowena Loops, descending 3.5 miles east to a geologic formation at Rowena Gap.

Directions: On I-84 East, exit Mosier, 5 miles east of Hood River. Head east on US 30, beyond milepost 6. The Preserve is on both sides of the highway.

Activities: Nature walks and photography. There is a path through the natural concentration of wildflowers, and occasional desert wildlife.

Facilities: There is a large parking lot on the east side of US 30 with elevated views of the Columbia River. The wildflower area is on the west side of the highway. There is a loop path through the preserve. Maps of the preserve are sometimes available in a covered box at the start of the path.

Dates: The lower trail is open year round. Apr. to June is the peak period for wildflower blooms. The high trail is open May 1 to Oct. 31.

Fees: None.

Closest town: Mosier.

For more information: Contact The Nature Conservancy of Oregon, 821 SE 14th Avenue, Portland, OR 97214. Phone (503) 230-1221.

MEMALOOSE OVERLOOK AND ISLAND

[Fig. 11(3)] Memaloose Overlook is a small gravel parking area on the lofty plateau edge above the Columbia River. Seen below are the twin asphalt strips of I-84, and to the east, wedged between the interstate and river, is the shading canopy of Memaloose State Park, a popular oasis for camping and picnicking and a rest stop for travelers on I-84.

The stark rock islet visible in the Columbia River at the edge of the park is Memaloose Island, once a burial ground for indigenous tribes. It now testifies to the collision of tribal and European cultures that is this river's history.

The irony of this one-time Indian burial ground is that the only person now buried here is a white man, Victor Trevitt, who died in the winter of 1883. Trevitt, once popular with both white settlers and native tribesmen, ended up offending both groups by demanding to be buried with the Indians on Memaloose Island.

Trevitt was a politician, gambler, tavern-keeper and strong supporter of local tribes when it wasn't popular to be so. When his instructions to be buried with the Indians on Memaloose Island were carried out, survivors of the interred tribal members were offended rather than pleased by his show of eternal support. They complained the burial site was despoiled, and many of the native dead were exhumed and reburied on the mainland. The rest of the Indian dead were removed and reburied when it became obvious that most of the 3-acre island would be inundated by water rising behind Bonneville Dam. Only New Hampshire-born Victor Trevitt is still buried on the half acre that remains.

Visible on the north side of the Columbia River is the tan stain of roiled sand at the shallow mouth of Washington's Klickitat River, deep canyons painted with white oaks, and treeless slopes etched with miniature terraces pounded flat by cattle traveling head-to-tail.

The junction of I-84 at Exit 76 is in the Ortley Anticline geological area. This area is generally regarded as the physiographic beginning of the Columbia River Gorge, and the historic end of wagon traffic on the Oregon Trail. The geologic formation identifying the

BOBCAT
(Felis rufus)
Similar in appearance to the lynx, the bobcat is found only in North America, where it is the most common wildcat.

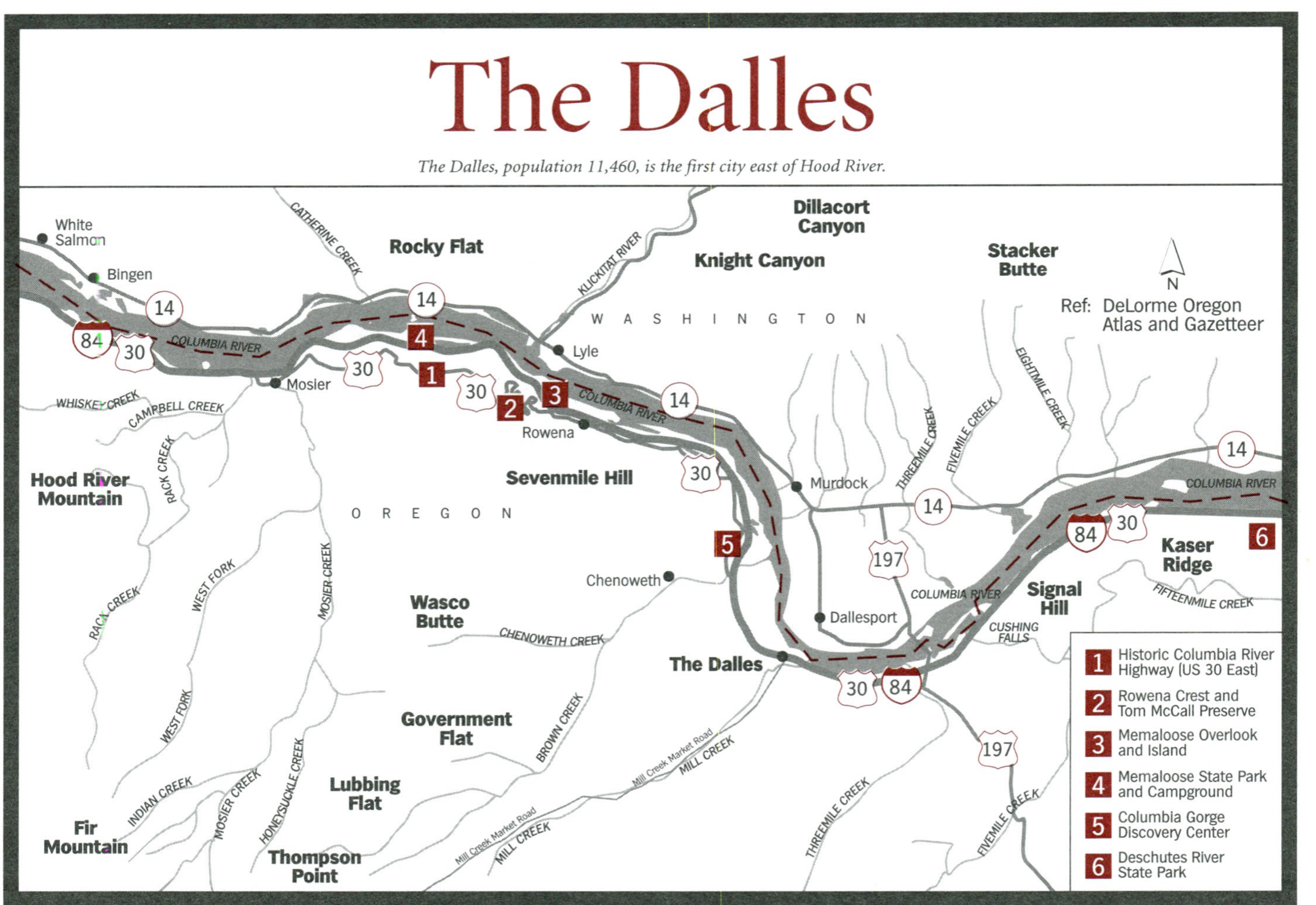
The Dalles
The Dalles, population 11,460, is the first city east of Hood River.
Ref: DeLorme Oregon Atlas and Gazetteer
N
1 Historic Columbia River Highway (US 30 East)
2 Rowena Crest and Tom McCall Preserve
3 Memaloose Overlook and Island
4 Memaloose State Park and Campground
5 Columbia Gorge Discovery Center
6 Deschutes River State Park
WASHINGTON
OREGON
COLUMBIA RIVER
White Salmon
Bingen
Mosier
Lyle
Rowena
Murdock
Dallesport
Chenoweth
The Dalles
Rocky Flat
Dillacort Canyon
Knight Canyon
Stacker Butte
Signal Hill
Kaser Ridge
Sevenmile Hill
Wasco Butte
Government Flat
Lubbing Flat
Thompson Point
Fir Mountain
Hood River Mountain
CATHERINE CREEK
KLICKITAT RIVER
EIGHTMILE CREEK
FIVEMILE CREEK
THREEMILE CREEK
FIFTEENMILE CREEK
CUSHING FALLS
MILL CREEK
Mill Creek Market Road
BROWN CREEK
CHENOWETH CREEK
MOSIER CREEK
HONEYSUCKLE CREEK
WEST FORK
INDIAN CREEK
RACK CREEK
CAMPBELL CREEK
WHISKEY CREEK
14
30
84
197

anticline is an arch of stratified rock angled downward.

Directions: I-84 to Exit 76, and follow US 30 east to the top of the hill.

Activities: Scenic viewing.

Facilities: None.

Dates: Open year-round.

Fees: None.

Closest town: The Dalles is about 8 miles east on US 30.

For more information: Oregon State Parks, 1115 Commercial Street NE , Salem, OR 97301-1002. Phone (800) 551-6949.

MEMALOOSE STATE PARK CAMPGROUND

[Fig. 11(4)] Memaloose State Park is the largest state campground in the gorge. Its 337 acres are accessible from the Columbia Gorge Scenic Highway or from the westbound lanes of I-84. There is no direct access to the park from the eastbound lanes of I-84. The picnic area and campground are located on a bluff above the river north of I-84.

Directions: Westbound on I-84 about 11 miles west of The Dalles, exit at the Memaloose State Park Exit. Eastbound, you must continue to Exit 76 and return in the westbound lane to the Memaloose State Park Exit.

Activities: Picnicking, camping, and fishing.

Facilities: 43 full hook up sites and 67 tent sites, RV dump station, picnic tables, some with wind breaks; restrooms, hot showers, summer campfire and interpretive programs.

Dates: Open Apr. 1 to Nov. 2.

Fees: There is a charge for camping.

Closest town: The Dalles.

For more information: Phone the resident manager at (541) 478-3008 or contact Oregon State Parks, 1115 Commercial Street NE , Salem, OR 97301-1002. Phone (800) 551-6949.

THE DALLES

[Fig. 11] If there is a gateway to western Oregon, The Dalles is it.

The Dalles, population 11,460, county seat of Wasco County, is the first city east of Hood River and anchors the eastern terminus of the Historic Columbia River Scenic Highway. It is also the junction of US 197, which connects with US 97 and runs south to California along the eastern front of the Oregon Cascades..

Until they were flooded by the turn-of-the-century construction of Bonneville Dam, a series of dangerous and often unnavigable rocky-tooth rapids roared below The Dalles.

Wagons westbound on the Oregon Trail were pinched off by a steep wall of solid lava that flowed directly into the river and the fearsome rapids. The cliff and whitewater formed a barricade and natural end to the overland Oregon Trail. Many Oregon settlers remained here. Others built rafts and charged westbound pioneers to descend the river rapids, a risk that many pioneer families declined.

In 1846, an alternative route was pioneered by Sam Barlow. After refusing to pay the steep fees required to float the river, Barlow forced his wagons on a rugged, roadless mountain crossing south of the gorge. In 1846, Barlow put gates on both east and west ends of his new route, which became known as Barlow Road, and charged a $5 toll for wagons and stock to detour around the treacherous gorge. His road ran south through a mountain pass, climbed the Cascades south of Mount Hood and descended to the Willamette River at Oregon City south-east of Portland. Sections of it are still driveable today (*see* Sam Barlow's Toll Road, page 74).

Lewis and Clark camped in The Dalles in October 1805, and doled out strips of blue ribbon to Indian women. Over the centuries, as many as 10 different indigenous tribes from as far away as western Montana would congregate here in the late summer to trade and fish for salmon.

The Dalles was a boom-town trade and transportation center during Oregon and Idaho gold rushes. Gold flowed so freely in the 1880s that the federal government built a mint here. Before a single coin could be minted, the boom collapsed.

The gold, the wagon trains, and the days as a central trading center are gone. Today, the major source of revenue is The Dalles Dam at I-84 Exit 87. The imposing concrete facility is the second hydro-electric dam and lock system on the Columbia above the ocean. The dam has an interpretive center in Seufert Park, three picnic areas, and a tour train. From April to September, the train takes travelers on an unusual tour through the mammoth facility. The rail tour is free.

Completion of the dam in the 1950s flooded Celilo Falls, a foaming canyonlike set of multiple falls and rapids near the mouth of the Deschutes River. The falls were the most important and productive traditional Indian fishing site on the lower Columbia River. The fishermen stood on rickety platforms extended over churning rapids, dipping long-handled nets into the turbulent water for salmon thrashing up through the falls.

Artists have transformed the walls of downtown buildings in The Dalles into multi-story murals "in the footsteps of Native Americans, sailors and soldiers, fur trappers and river rats, scalawags, bankers and hellfire preachers, hogheads and mutton-chopped leaders of commerce," according to the chamber of commerce, which offers a map of the self-guided mural tour.

Directions: Exits 82, 83, 84 and 85 lead from I-84 into The Dalles. Exit 84 goes into the business district.

Activities: Columbia Gorge Discovery Center, museums, tours of The Dalles Dam, boating, fishing, tour of downtown wall murals, picnic areas, and city parks. The annual Fort Dalles Rodeo is a 4-day professional event that dominates the 3rd week in July.

Facilities: The Dalles has full traveler services, and accommodations, including private RV parks.

For more information: The Dalles Area Chamber of Commerce, 404 W. Second Street, The Dalles, OR 97058. Phone (800) 255-3385 or (541) 296-2231. The Dalles Mural Society, 402 E. 2nd Street, The Dalles, OR 97058. Phone (541) 296-8500. The Dalles Dam, I-84 Exit 87, phone (541) 296-9778.

DESCHUTES RIVER STATE PARK

[Fig. 11(6)] About 15 miles east of The Dalles is a major campground in Deschutes River State Recreation Area at the confluence of the Columbia and Deschutes rivers. The campground is built on the site of an Oregon Trail immigrant camp. Wagon ruts from the original Oregon Trail are still visible in the recreation area. The park is heavily used by whitewater rafters, fishermen, boaters, hikers, horseback riders, and campers.

There's a free boat ramp on the west side of the river at Heritage Landing. In mid- to late-summer the park is a popular bank-fishing spot and launch area when fishing seasons open for upriver bound steelhead and salmon. The lower 2 miles of river are open to fishing from the banks only.

Directions: I-84 to Exit 97.

Activities: Camping, picnicking, fishing, boating, and trails including access to a 22-mile round-trip equestrian trail, an 8-mile hiking path and 17-mile bike trail.

Facilities: The campground has 34 RV sites with electrical hookups and 35 primitive sites with nearby boat ramp, drinking water and flush-toilet restrooms. A covered wagon that sleeps four can be rented for the night. There is an interpretive display about the region's history.

Dates: Year-round. The park office is open weekdays 8-5.

Fees: There is a charge for camping and Deschutes River boating passes. River passes are available weekdays at the park office or from nearby sporting goods outlets, including Braggables, 616 E. 3rd Street, The Dalles, OR 97058. Phone (541) 296-8434.

Closest town: The Dalles is 15 miles west on I-84.

For more information: Phone the park resident manager at (541) 739-2322. Oregon State Parks, 1115 Commercial Street NE , Salem, OR 97301-1002. Phone (800) 551-6949.

COLUMBIA GORGE DISCOVERY CENTER

[Fig. 11(5)] For an eye-opening understanding of the cultural and geological history of the complex Columbia River and Gorge, stop at the combined Columbia Gorge Discovery Center and Wasco County Historical Museum.

The center is located on a 50-acre plateau just west of The Dalles on old US 30. The open ridge top is in the Chenoweth Scablands, the only volcanic scablands in the gorge, and is nearly always sun-washed and wind-scoured.

The complex includes a state-of-the-art interpretive center where 40 million years of gorge evolution unfold in a mixed medium of films, robotics, dioramas, oral histories, turn-of-the-century photographs, life-size models, and written explanations of the unique geology and climates, original inhabitants, and explorers. The outside grounds include a paved path to scenic overlooks, pioneer-era orchards and gardens, artifacts, and a picnic area.

Directions: From I-84 westbound use Exit 84 to W. 2nd Street, turn west at the first stop light onto Webber Street, then north at the first stoplight onto W. 6th, which is also US 30. Continue 3 miles to Discovery Drive and the center.

The Dalles Boating And Fishing

Ramps are available for sport-fishermen to launch boats above and below The Dalles Dam. Many fishermen try for walleye (professional guides believe the next world record will be caught here), sturgeon, and smallmouth bass. There is fishing for salmon and steelhead in season. One of the hot spots for smallmouth and walleye is below the dam in the rock rubble of island reefs known as Three Mile Rapids. Boating enthusiasts use I-84 Exit 85 to reach the free boat ramp at The Port Of Dalles Marina.

To launch above the dam on Lake Celilo, continue east on I-84 to Exit 97 at Celilo Park. There's no launch fee and it's a favorite put-in point for walleye fishing at Miller Island, and steelhead and salmon fishing below the mouth of Deschutes River.

For the latest information on fishing, hunting and whitewater boating opportunities, seasons, and licenses, stop at Braggable's Sporting Goods, 616 E. 3rd Street, The Dalles, OR 97058. Phone (541) 296-8434.

Eastbound travelers use I-84 Exit 82, turn north onto Historic Columbia River Highway US 30 and continue east 1.5 miles to Discovery Drive.

Dates: Open daily 10-6, except Thanksgiving, Christmas, and New Year's Day.

Fees: There is a charge for admission to the center buildings. Features on the outside grounds are free.

For more information: Columbia Gorge Discovery Center, 5000 Discovery Drive, The Dalles, OR 97058, Phone (541) 296-8600.

OREGON 35 LEG OF THE MOUNT HOOD LOOP

[Fig. 9] OR 35 is one of the most important highways leading into the Hood River Recreation Area and the 1,061,381-acres of Mount Hood National Forest.

Looking southbound, the highway appears to run directly into the snow-covered apron of 11,240-foot Mount Hood. The views are sometimes larger-than-life panoramas filling the windshield with glistening snow fields, crevasse-streaked glaciers, and vertical ice walls.

OR 35 is the connecting route between I-84 and US 26, and the only highway leading south from the Columbia River into the heart of the Cascades of northern Oregon. South of Hood River Valley, Highway 35 angles steadily to the junction with US 26 on the shoulder of Mount Hood, east of the mountain community of Government Camp.

FRUIT LOOP

[Fig. 9(4)] Fruit trees stand in regimented rows on both sides of OR 35 between Hood River and the first steep slopes into the mountains. This is a celebrated fruit-growing region, and a great place to stock up with sweet July cherries, juicy August peaches, and crisp September pears and apples.

The orchards were started in 1854 and today the fertile volcanic soil produces more than 30 percent of the nation's winter pears. Locals proudly proclaim it as "Oregon's

Largest Fruit Growing District."

The Fruit Loop, a whimsical but perfectly descriptive name, ropes together a string of country roads and highways connecting 21 orchards, farms, and roadside vegetable and fruit markets in the valley. Many of the farms provide tours, pick-it-yourself crops, and stands stocked with fresh fruit, vegetables and farm crafts. There are no fewer than nine special farm-related events celebrated annually in this valley.

The Fruit Loop is easy to find. It's identified with colorful guide signs posted along OR 35, which forms the eastern leg of the loop. A Fruit Loop map, which includes a directory of farms, orchards, produce markets and pick-it-yourself site locations, is available at most Hood River businesses catering to travelers.

Directions: From the north, take I-84 to Exit 64. From the south, US 26 to OR 35 junction east of Government Camp.

Activities: Sight-seeing, fruit and vegetable picking.

Facilities: Access to recreation areas.

Dates: Open year-round.

Fees: None.

Closest town: Hood River.

For more information: Hood River County Chamber of Commerce and Information Center, 405 Portway Ave., Hood River, OR 97031. Phone, (541) 386-2000 or (800) 366-3530.

HOOD RIVER RANGER STATION

[Fig. 9(5)] About 14 miles south of Hood River on the west side of OR 35 is the headquarters of the Hood River Ranger District of Mount Hood National Forest. An information counter is staffed weekdays and on the weekends in summer.

This is a good stop for maps of Mount Hood National Forest, the Columbia Gorge National Scenic Area, Hatfield and Mount Hood wilderness areas, and most of the Hood River drainage. Also available are pamphlets on seasonal opportunities for hiking, mountain biking, mushrooming, fishing and hunting and other forest use opportunities. Trail park passes are sold weekdays at the ranger station.

Directions: The district headquarters and information station complex is located on the west side of OR 35, 14 miles south of Hood River.

Activities: Hiking, mountain biking, cross-country and downhill skiing, whitewater kayaking, trout fishing, deer, elk, bear and grouse hunting, mushrooming, rock climbing, camping, and berry picking.

Facilities: Ranger station with information center.

Dates: The ranger station is open weekdays 8 to 4:30. From May 30-Sept. 6 it remains open daily.

Fees: There are charges for some campgrounds and trail use. Trail passes can be bought at the ranger station or at local businesses catering to recreationists. Where there is a charge for camping, fees are collected on site. All trails entering the Mount Hood and

Hatfield Wildernesses require trail park passes.

Closest town: Hood River is 14 miles north on OR 35.

For more information: Hood River Ranger Station, 6780 Highway 35 Mt. Hood - Parkdale, OR 97041. Phone, (541) 352-6002.

TOLL BRIDGE COUNTY PARK

[Fig. 9(6)] Toll Bridge County Park, the largest campground on OR 35, is located at an elevation of 1,600 feet on the banks of the East Fork of Hood River, a fast-dropping riffle and rock trout stream that in summer is likely to be the color of chocolate chalk. The color is created by glacial flour, the icy silt that melts off glaciers on Mount Hood during warm summer days. The river runs strikingly clear during cool weather.

Directions: Adjacent to OR 35 about 17 miles south of Hood River.

Activities: Camping, stream fishing for trout, hiking, and equestrian trails.

Facilities: 82 campsites, including 20 full-service sites, 44 with water and electricity, 16 tent and 2 group sites. There is a picnic area with tables and grills, shelter house, and restrooms with potable water, and hot showers. Reservations are accepted.

Dates: Open Apr. 1-Oct. 31.

Fees: There is a charge for camping and picnic area use.

Closest town: Parkdale is about 2 miles west.

For more information: The resident manager's phone is (541) 352-5522. Hood River County Parks and Buildings, 918 18th Street, Hood River, OR 97031, phone (541) 387-6889.

PARKDALE FLOW

[Fig. 9(7)] The Parkdale Flow is the youngest formative lava breach on Mount Hood. It's located off Clear Creek Road about 1 mile south from Parkdale. The lava beds geological site attracts little public attention with the exception of geology students. There are no facilities other than an informational sign and dirt paths into the lava area.

The lava flow is 6,000-year-old, 3.5-mile long basalt lava. It is hemmed in by fruit orchards, farm lands, and second-growth timber, and can be difficult to see.

Directions: From OR 35, turn southwest on the Parkdale Road. At Parkdale the road joins Clear Creek Road. There are no national forest access points or parking lots. Access in via private land.

Activities: Trail walking in geological area.

Facilities: None.

Closest town: Parkdale.

For more information: Hood River Ranger Station, 6780 Highway 35 Mt. Hood - Parkdale, OR 97041. Phone (541) 352-6002.

COOPER SPUR WINTER RECREATION AREA

[Fig. 10(1)] Cooper Spur Winter Recreation Area is the smallest of Mount Hood's four ski areas, and the jumping off place to historic Cloud Cap Inn. Compared with the world-class ski slopes and black diamond ski runs offered by the three other Mount Hood ski areas, Cooper Spur is a laid-back family-oriented area. The ski area reflects its turn-of-the-century construction. The gentle beginner and intermediate slopes make this a favorite winter destination for families with small children.

Directions: Follow OR 35 about 23 miles south from Hood River to the 4,000-foot level on Mount Hood where Forest Service 3510 intersects from the west. Cooper Spur ski area is 2.5 miles west on Forest Service Road 3510 road.

The ski area is about 1.5 miles beyond the Inn At Cooper Spur, a contemporary log-walled restaurant-lodge complex with sweeping views of the valley and Mount Hood. Located at an elevation of 4,000 feet, the inn is a seasonal center for mountain bikers, downhill and cross-country skiers, and elk, deer and bear hunters.

Activities: Winter downhill and cross-country trail skiing Dec.-Mar., 500 vertical feet rated easy. Summer mountain biking, hiking. Hours and openings vary. Call for current hours.

Facilities: T bar, rope tow and warming hut with snack bar. The nearby Inn At Cooper Spur is one of only a handful of overnight accommodations on the south end of OR 35.

Dates: Ski area operates weekends from Dec. through Mar. Weekday hours vary.

Watch For Wild Turkeys

Wild turkeys are thriving in the open forests, oak groves and ranch lands of the Hood River Valley and Rowena Plateau near Mosier. State wildlife biologists estimate populations that range between six and 15 wild turkeys per square mile in this area, the highest density north of Albany in the Willamette Valley.

Turkeys are not native to the Beaver State, but transplant releases of imported Merriam's and Rio Grande subspecies beginning in 1961 have established flocks in most good habitat areas, especially in the Hood River area. April turkey hunting is the fastest growing hunting sport in Oregon.

It's not uncommon to catch a glimpse of wild turkeys feeding in orchards, coulees and open creek bottoms shaded by oak trees.

Oregon's wild turkeys are easy to mistake for domestic varieties, because they look almost alike. Toms weigh 14 to 25 pounds, and have a 3- to 10-inch clump of hairlike feathers, known as a beard, extending from their breast. The featherless head is reddish, with splotches of white and blue. The feathers, including the fanlike tail, are iridescent and black-tipped, which gives a tom a dark, polished look.

Hens are smaller, generally eight to 12 pounds, with dull gray-blue colored heads that often sport a few odd strands of feather. The buff-tipped body feathers lack the iridescent sheen of toms.

For hunting and license information contact Oregon Department of Fish and Wildlife, PO Box 59, Portland, OR 97207. Phone (503) 872-5268.

Fees: There are charges for ski area facilities.

Closest town: Hood River is 23 miles north on OR 35.

For more information: Cooper Spur Ski Area, Highway 35, Hood River, OR, 97031. Phone (541) 352-7803. Inn At Cooper Spur, phone (541) 352-6692.

CLOUD CAP INN AND HISTORIC WAGON ROAD

[Fig. 10(2)] Cloud Cap Inn is the most historic building on Mount Hood. The remnant buildings of this inn, the first destination lodge on Mount Hood, can be reached by driving up Ghost Ridge along a gravel road that follows a one-time wagon road. The switchbacks end at the doorstep to the inn and a breath-taking pass at the foot of Mount Hood's northern glaciers.

The road begins just west of Cooper Spur ski area, where the pavement of Forest Service Road 3512 narrows, becomes gravel and continues into the forest roughly following a route originally carved by the iron-rimmed wheels of horse-pulled wagons.

From the ski area, the single lane road climbs for 11 miles in a series of switchbacks up Ghost Ridge to the 6,000-foot edge of Mount Hood, Cloud Cap Inn, and nearby Tilly Jane Campground. The road is rutted and in June or early July may be difficult for low-slung passenger cars or campers. The route is not recommended for motor homes.

At the inn, the road passes a trailhead access to Timberline Trail No. 600, which follows a circuitous 40.7-mile long route around Mount Hood (*see* Timberline Trail 600, page 87).

Now a designated national historic site, the log-walled aerie was built in 1889 at the edge of Mount Hood's crevasse-trenched Eliot Glacier. The grounds are open, but the interior of the inn is not maintained for public access.

During snow-free months, the unpaved route along the one-time wagon road to Cloud Cap Inn is lined with pink blossoms of wild rhododendrons, orange splatters of Indian paintbrush (*Castillia hispida*) and soft purples of subalpine lupines (*Lupinus latifolius*). Wiry green stalks of blossoming white beargrass (*Xerophyllup tenax*) glow at the edge of the road. The forest and flowers are little changed from 1890 when travelers paid $12.50 to ride six hours in an open wagon to stay at Cloud Cap Inn.

Natural attractions and 11 designated viewpoints are along this twisting forest road, and the original wagon ruts are still plainly visible. If you stop nowhere else on this route, pull over at Inspiration Point, 3.3 miles into the drive at the only guardrail on the road. Follow the short path to an inspiring view of the 100-foot plunge of Wallalute Falls, the slide-scoured walls of Weygandt Canyon and far below the white ribbon of the Eliot Branch of Hood River.

Cloud Cap Inn is maintained by The Crag Rats, a Hood River-based climbing club and rescue group. Built of sturdy log walls, with a thick cedar-shake roof, and warmed by two huge native stone fireplaces, the inn was built to survive the Arctic-like winters on Mount Hood. To keep the inn from blowing off the ridge, heavy cables were passed over the roof and anchored into rock.

The view from the porch is spectacular, sweeping from Cooper Spur Ridge to Eliot Glacier, up the vertical icy North Face, which is the most treacherous climbing route to the summit. The northeast boundary of Mount Hood Wilderness Area begins almost at the edge of the road at the inn.

In the early 1900s Cloud Cap was the heart and soul of Mount Hood recreation, hosting various climbing and snowshoe clubs and an almost nonstop parade of Portlanders on holiday. The inn lost its dominance in 1938 when massive Timberline Lodge opened on the more accessible and less hazardous south face (*see* Timberline Lodge, page 86). Cloud Cap Inn continues to command the most spectacular view of Mount Hood's craggy north face.

Mount Hood National Forest

[Fig. 5, Fig. 9, Fig. 10] The west boundary of the 1,061,381-acre Mount Hood National Forest is 20 miles east of Portland and the heavily populated northern Willamette River Valley, making it one of the most popular outdoor destinations in Oregon.

Mount Hood National Forest extends south from the Columbia River Gorge across more than 60 miles of forested mountains, 160 lakes, 4,000 miles of streams, and 1,200 miles of trails to Olallie Scenic Area, a high lake plateau under the shielding slopes of Mount Jefferson.

Forest recreation includes fishing, camping, boating, rock climbing, mountain biking and hiking in the summer, hunting in the fall, and skiing and other snow sports in the winter. Because the snow pack is usually more than 20 feet deep, and lasts well into August, Mount Hood has the longest snow ski season in the U.S., closing for about one month in late summer and early fall.

Berry-picking, gold panning, and mushroom gathering are popular, and for many area residents a December trek to cut the family Christmas tree is a tradition.

The national forest's roots go back a century to 1893, when the Cascade Range Forest Reserve was established. In 1908 the reserve was divided into several national forests, and the northern portion was merged with the Bull Run Reserve. The pristine 95,382 acre Bull Run watershed is now Portland's primary source for drinking water, a source so pure that it does not require a treatment plant. The area was first named Oregon National Forest. In 1924, it was changed to Mount Hood National Forest.

The most popular destinations in the forest are Timberline Lodge, built in 1937 below the glaciers on Mount Hood, campgrounds at Lost Lake, Trillium Lake, Timothy Lake, Rock Creek Reservoir, and portions of the historic Oregon Trail and Barlow Toll Road.

Despite the next-door proximity to Oregon's population center, there are 189,200 acres of designated wilderness area in the forest. The largest section is Mount Hood Wilderness, which is 46,520 acres in size and includes the volcano's summit and upper slopes. Other wilderness areas are Badger Creek, 24,000 acres; Hatfield (formerly Columbia), 39,000; Salmon-Huckleberry, 44,550 and Bull-of-the-Woods, 34,884. In addition, 4,743 acres of the 106,958-acres Mount Jefferson Wilderness Area are in Mount

ENGELMANN SPRUCE
(*Picea engelmannii*)
This spruce grows up to 120 feet tall and is identified by four-sided blue-green needles and cones with wavy edges on the scales.

Hood National Forest.

Free permits are required to go into the wilderness areas, and some trailheads will require trail park passes. The wilderness permits are available at ranger district offices and from self-issuing stands at some trailheads.

On the south end of the forest is the Olallie Scenic Area, a basin sprinkled with mountain lakes largely dedicated to primitive recreation. A historic yet functional lodge and campground are located at Olallie Lake. (*see* Olallie Scenic Area, page 127).

The Mount Hood forest is a mix of conifer species, running heavily on the west slopes to Douglas fir, hemlock and western red cedar. The East Slope is mostly ponderosa and lodgepole pine tapering east into the high desert and clumps of short, stout juniper.

On the high slopes are the scraggly silhouettes of whitebark pines (*Pinus albicaulis*), conical-shaped mountain hemlock (*Tsuga mertensiana*) and the dense evergreen towers of alpine fir (*Abies lasiocarpa*). The steep slopes are open with clusters of dwarf juniper (*Juniperus communis*,) red heather (*Phylodoce empetriformus*) and thickets of spindly mountain ash (*Sorbus sitchensis*).

The mountain sides are hardened with octagonal streaks of columnar basalt, talus, jointed andesite and littered with pyroclastic rock fragments.

The most popular and heavily used trailheads and trail systems require a trail park pass. There is a charge. These passes are not required for trail use, but must be displayed inside the lower left corner of the windshield of vehicles parked within 0.25 mile of designated trailheads, campgrounds and fee sites. Daily and annual passes are available. Golden Age and Golden Access passport holders are entitled to a 50 percent discount.

Trail park passes are sold at ranger stations and many local businesses that cater to recreationists. The vehicle passes are not available at trailheads or parking areas.

Two popular forest service campgrounds are on the high slopes of Mount Hood along OR 35. Both are in shaded forest settings on the west side of the highway along the East Fork of Hood River. Tent and RV sites are spread out in both camping areas with lots of privacy. Either camp makes a convenient base for exploring Mount Hood's recreational opportunities.

Directions: Follow OR 35 abut 23 miles south of Hood River to the forest's north boundary 1.5 miles north of Forest Service Road 3512 cut-off to Cooper Spur Ski Area, and Cloud Cap Inn. The forest is also accessible on the west side from US 26 and OR 224 by driving less than 15 miles east of the Portland metro area.

Activities: Winter skiing, hiking, bicycling, horseback riding, fishing, hunting, gathering, photography, mountain climbing, whitewater boating, and camping.

Facilities: Campgrounds, commercial ski lodges, trails, boat launches, and regional information centers.

Dates: The forest is open year-round. The Mount Hood Information Center is open daily, except Christmas, 7:30 to 4:30.

Fees: Some trails and campgrounds require trail park passes, and camping fees.

Closest town: Portland, Troutdale, Estacada, and Hood River.

For more information: Contact Mount Hood Information Center, 65000 E. Highway 26, Welches, OR 97067. Phone (503) 622-7674. Internet web site is: www.fs.fed.us/r6/mthood.

SHERWOOD CAMPGROUND AND DAY USE AREA

[Fig. 10(3)] **Directions:** OR 35, 2 miles south of the Cooper Spur Road junction.

Facilities: This is a barrier-free campground, with 14 sites up to 16 feet long. No RV hookups. Vault-style toilets, tables, and fire pits are provided. The site is located at an elevation of 3,000 feet.

Activities: There is fair stream fishing in the East Fork Hood River for trout and trail hiking.

Dates: Generally snow free and open in May.

Fees: A fee is charged for camping.

Closest town: Parkdale is about 9 miles north.

For more information: Hood River Ranger Station. 6780 Highway 35
Mt. Hood - Parkdale, OR 97041. Phone: (541) 352-6002.

TAMANAWAS FALLS LOOP HIKE

[Fig. 10(4)] The trail from Sherwood Campground to Tamanawas Falls can be extended into a loop route that begins along OR 35 about 0.25 mile north of Sherwood Campground . The loop is easily hiked in two hours and allows plenty of time to picnic in the cool mist at the bottom of the 100-foot high falls.

Directions: Look for a sign marking the East Fork Trailhead about 0.25 mile north of Sherwood Campground on OR 35. Follow East Fork Trail 650 for 0.5 mile to where it connects to Tamanawas Falls Trail 650A. Follow 650A to 650B, turn left and continue 0.5 mile to the falls.

To complete the loop hike from the falls, follow 650B on an easy climb out of the canyon to Elk Meadows Trail 645. Turn right on 645 and loop back to the East Fork Trail. Follow the trail upstream to the highway trailhead.

Trail: 5.5 miles as a loop through a conifer forest.
Elevation: 3,000 feet.
Degree of difficulty: Moderate to strenuous with minor elevation changes.
Dates: Snow free Apr. to Nov.

ROBINHOOD CAMPGROUND AND DAY USE AREA

[Fig. 10(5)] Located at an elevation of 3,500-feet, this site is generally snow free by late May. There is stream fishing for rainbow trout, and trail hiking.

Directions: Adjacent to OR 35, 2.2 miles south of the junction of Dufur Valley Road Forest Service 44.

Facilities: A barrier-free campground with 24 campsites up to 18-feet long. No RV hookups. Well water, vault-style toilets, tables, and fire pits are provided.

Dates: Open Memorial Day to Labor Day.

Fees: A fee is charged for camping.

Closest town: Hood River is about 31 miles north on OR 35.

For more information: Hood River Ranger Station. 6780 Highway 35 Mt. Hood - Parkdale, OR 97041. Phone: (541) 352-6002.

EAST FORK TRAIL 650

[Fig. 10(6)] This easy trail on the northeast side of Mount Hood National Forest makes a pleasant day hike along the upper East Fork of Hood River, with gradual elevation gains, and multiple access points from the highway. It is restricted to walkers and bicyclists.

Directions: Drive south 25 miles from Hood River on OR 35 to Polallie Creek Picnic Area or continue 6 miles south to Robinhood Campground. There is a trailhead at both sites. One-way hikers often drop off a shuttle vehicle at the destination trailhead.

Dates: Open year-round, snow free May to Nov.

Trail: 12 miles round-trip, but most hikers divide the route into short segments between access points.

Elevation: There is an elevation change of 600-feet distributed across 12 miles of trail. North trailhead elevation is 2,900 feet and the south trailhead is 3,500 feet.

Degree of difficulty: Easy.

Surface: Natural duff.

GUMJUWAC TRAIL 480

[Fig. 10(7)] This switch-back trail

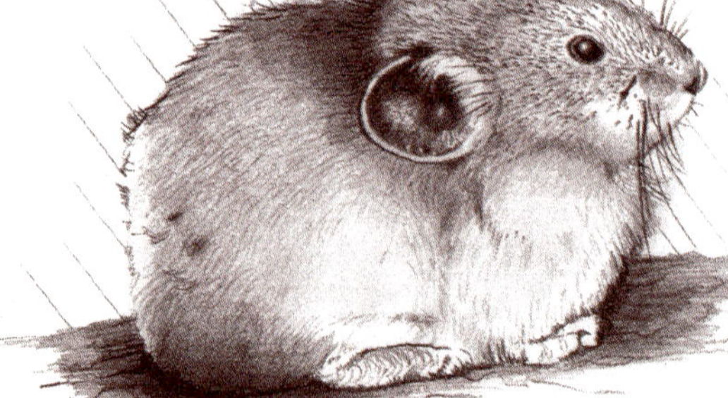

PIKA
(Ochotona princeps)
Although this small mammal looks like a rodent with ratlike head and body, it is actually related to the rabbit. The vocal pika communicates with nasal bleats and is known for its ventriloquist talents as well.

climbs 800 feet from Robinhood Campground to a saddle with sweeping views of the surrounding peaks, and meadows that are often ablaze with summer wildflowers, including lupine and penstemon, sedum, phlox and white sandwort.

The mountain view is dramatic. Hikers can see from Broken Top west of Bend to Mount Rainier 40 miles from Seattle. Trail use is restricted to walkers, horseback riders, and bicyclists.

Directions: Drive OR 35 to Robinhood Campground. Cross the river on the bridge east of the highway to the trailhead. The trail climbs steadily in a series of switch backs to Forest Service 3550. You can continue on Trail 480 to Gumjuwac Saddle or on Trail 458 to Lookout Mountain.

Dates: Snow free from June to Oct.

Trail: 4.4 miles round trip.

Elevation: Beginning elevation 3,307 feet, ending at 4,101 feet, a gain of 794 feet. Continuing to the 6,525-foot summit of Lookout Mountain involves an additional 2,424-foot elevation change.

Degree of difficulty: Strenuous.

DUFUR VALLEY ROAD

[Fig. 12] Dufur Valley Road, which is also Forest Service Road 44, angles almost unnoticed east from OR 35. The paved two-lane road rides east-west along the top of a ridge between Wolf Run and Ramsey Creek. It gradually descends from the Mount Hood highlands to the farm town of Dufur.

The road is a 27-mile long transitional route from the mountains and deep forests along OR 35 to the open sagebrush land along US 97. It passes stunted 20-foot high white pines, and crosses rock slides, old timber cuts, and grassy meadows shaded with stands of ponderosa pine. The road is often lined with a summer mast of yellow, white and purple wildflowers, and leads to out-of-the-way camping spots like Knebal Springs, Fifteen Mile Creek, and Camp Baldwin. Two forest service fire lookouts are available for rent. At Clinger Springs, about 2.5 miles east of OR 35, Forest Service 4410 leads south to Lookout Mountain Trail 450. The 6,525-foot summit of Lookout Mountain offers magnificent views of Mount Hood.

Dufur Valley Road is closed to wheeled vehicles between December 15 and March 15, when snowmobilers, snowshoers, and cross-country skiers take over.

Directions: Dufur Valley Road intersects OR 35 from the east about 12 miles north of the junction of OR 35 and US 26,

Activities: Scenic drives, fishing, snowmobiling, hiking, mountain biking, wildlife viewing.

Facilities: Campgrounds, fire lookouts, trails.

Dates: The road is closed to wheeled vehicles Dec. 15 to Mar. 15.

Fees: There are charges for trail park passes and lookout rental.

Closest town: Dufur on the east end of Forest Service 44.

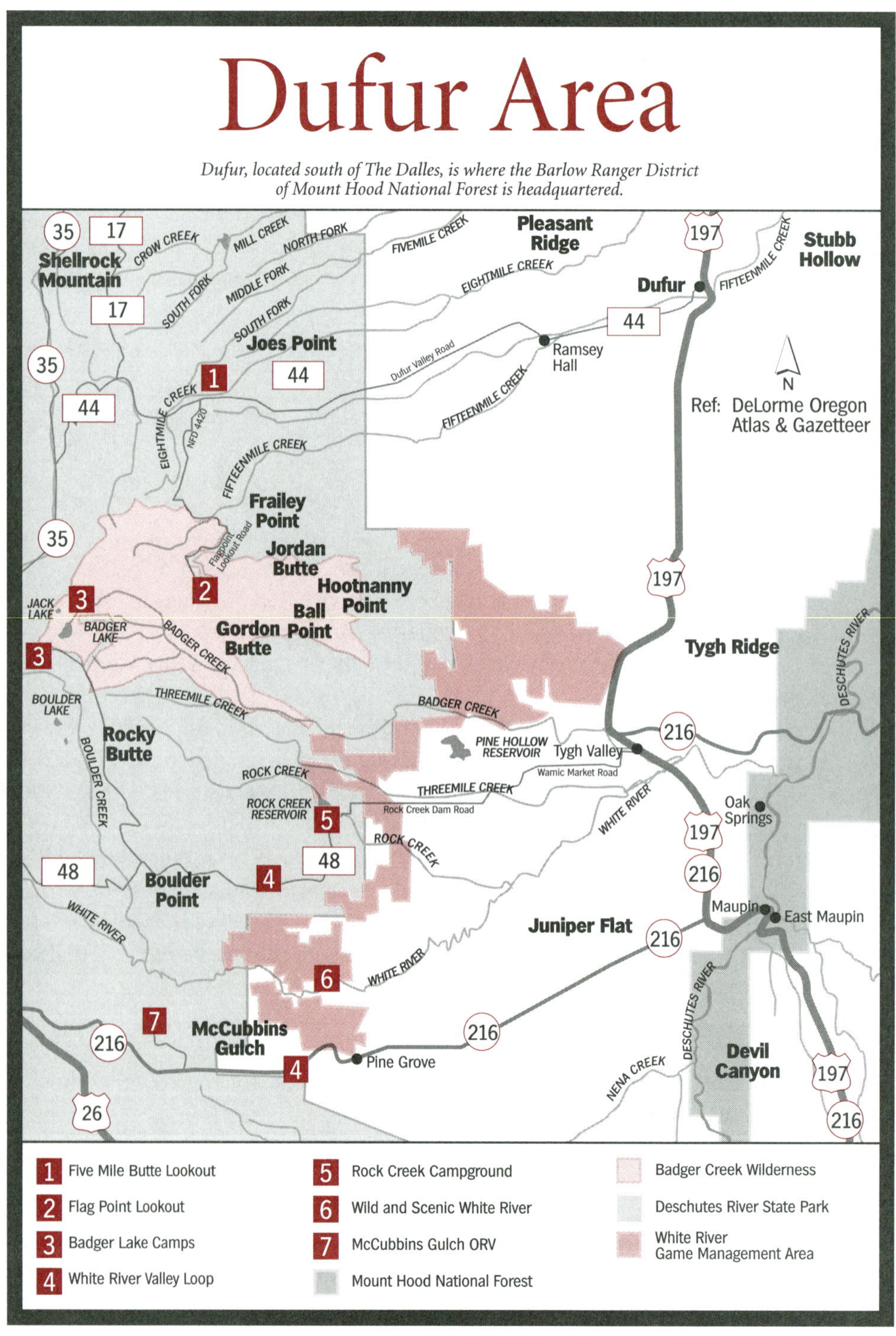
Dufur Area
Dufur, located south of The Dalles, is where the Barlow Ranger District of Mount Hood National Forest is headquartered.
Shellrock Mountain
Pleasant Ridge
Stubb Hollow
Dufur
Joes Point
Ramsey Hall
Ref: DeLorme Oregon Atlas & Gazetteer
Frailey Point
Jordan Butte
Hootnanny Point
Ball Point
Gordon Butte
Tygh Ridge
Rocky Butte
Pine Hollow Reservoir
Tygh Valley
Wamic Market Road
Rock Creek Reservoir
Rock Creek Dam Road
Oak Springs
Boulder Point
Juniper Flat
Maupin
East Maupin
McCubbins Gulch
Pine Grove
Devil Canyon
1 Five Mile Butte Lookout
2 Flag Point Lookout
3 Badger Lake Camps
4 White River Valley Loop
5 Rock Creek Campground
6 Wild and Scenic White River
7 McCubbins Gulch ORV
Mount Hood National Forest
Badger Creek Wilderness
Deschutes River State Park
White River Game Management Area

For more information: Barlow Ranger District Dufur Ranger Station, 780 NE Court St., Dufur, OR 97021. Phone (541) 467-2291. The station is closed weekends.

TOWN OF DUFUR

[Fig. 12] Dufur, population 605, is a ranch and farm town that could be the model for a Norman Rockwell illustration. It is tucked into a bucolic, irrigated valley along a creek somewhat protected from the arid and often harsh weather of the Deschutes River breaks. The streets are shaded by century-old locust and maple trees. Businesses have names like The Branding Iron, and the home crowd cheering the Dufur Rangers high school football team fits on a five-row bleacher.

Barlow Ranger District headquarters of Mount Hood National Forest, located here, is a weekday source of national forest travel and recreation information. Trail park passes, available at the ranger station are required to use these trails and campgrounds: Badger Trail, Boulder Lake Trail, Eightmile Loop, High Prairie Trail, Knebal Springs, Little Badger Trail, McCubbins Campground, McCubbins ORV Day Use, and McCubbins Overflow Campground.

Directions: US 197 south from The Dalles or east from OR 35 on Dufur Valley Road Forest Service 44.

Facilities: Gasoline, groceries, U.S.F.S. Barlow Ranger District headquarters.

For more information: The Dalles Area Chamber of Commerce, 404 W. Second Street, The Dalles, OR 97058. Phone (800) 255-3385 or (541) 296-2231.

FIVE MILE BUTTE LOOKOUT

[Fig. 12(1)] The lookout is a 14 by14-foot rental cabin atop a 30 foot tower at 4,627 feet. It offers sweeping views of the east side of Mount Hood National Forest, and the open ranch lands to the east. There is gravel road access during the summer. Getting there in the winter means a four hour cross-country ski trip.

Directions: Follow Dufur Valley Road Forest Service 44 roughly 6 miles east of OR 35 to Bottle Prairie. Turn north on graveled Forest Service Road 120 for about one mile to Five Mile Butte Lookout Tower.

Activities: Lodging.

Facilities: Lookout tower cabin.

Dates: Open year-round.

Fees: There is a charge for nightly rental.

RED-TAILED HAWK
(*Buteo jamaicensis*)

FLAG POINT LOOKOUT

[Fig. 12(2)] Available for winter rental only, this Forest Service lookout is a 14 by 14-foot cabin atop a 60 foot tower at an elevation of 5,650 feet. There is room for four people. Furnishings include a propane stove, single bed, table, chairs, and firewood.

Winter access requires an eight-hour cross-country ski trip not recommended for novices. The tower is two miles inside Badger Creek Wilderness, however a creative boundary line allows the lookout to be reached by road vehicles during snow-free months.

Directions: Turnoff from Forest Service 44 to Flag Point Lookout is 1 mile east of the Five Mile Butte Lookout turnoff. Go south on Forest Service 4420 and follow signs to Fifteen Mile Campground. Continue 1 mile east of Fifteen Mile Campground to a dirt road that turns south for 3 miles to the lookout.

Activities: Winter lodging.

Facilities: Forest Service lookout cabin.

Dates: Available for rent from Nov. 1 to May 30.

Fees: There is a rental charge.

MOUNT HOOD MEADOWS SKI AREA

[Fig. 10(8)] Covering 2,100 acres west of OR 35, Mount Hood Meadows is the largest downhill ski area on Mount Hood. It has 10 ski lifts, 4,000 vertical feet of runs, and is a major cross-country skiing and snowshoeing destination. It provides 82 groomed trails and rental equipment.

During summer, the ski area is a jumping-off spot for trail hiking and mountain biking. The chairlifts, lodge, and restaurant complex are at the 4,000-foot level on Mount Hood. Downhill skiing begins by Thanksgiving and runs into May. Skiers can sometimes use the highest runs near the 7,300-foot level until July.

In summer bring hiking boots. A trail system links the area with forest trails that climb onto the shoulder of Mount Hood and into the Mount Hood Wilderness Area. Short hikes lead from Meadows to Elk Meadows, Sahalie Falls and Forest Service Trail 667 to Umbrella Falls. These are easy walks, none longer than 0.2 mile.

Directions: From OR 35 about 5 miles northeast of US 26, turn west onto Forest Service 3555 for 1.3 miles.

Activities: Winter downhill and cross-country skiing. Summer trail hiking and mountain biking.

Facilities: Ski lifts and lodge accommodations, rental equipment, and restaurant. No overnight lodging.

Dates: Open mid-Nov.-end of Apr.

Fees: There is a charge for lift tickets.

Closest town: Hood River is 35 miles north, and Welches is 25 miles west on US 26.

For more information: Mount Hood Meadows Ski Resort, PO Box 470, Mount Hood, OR 97041. Phone (503) 337-2222. Web site: www.skihood.com.

UMBRELLA AND SAHALIE FALLS LOOP

[Fig. 10(9)] Just north of the ski area at Mount Hood Meadows is a loop trail that leads to two high waterfalls connected by a picturesque footpath along the East Fork Hood River. Summer trail use is restricted to walkers and bicyclists.

Directions: Drive 34 miles south from Hood River on OR 35 to Hood Meadows turnoff, 1 mile north of Mount Hood Meadows Ski area turnoff.

Follow the road to a graveled parking area. Take Elk Meadows Trail 645 about 0.5 mile to trail 667C to the 50-foot shower of Umbrella Falls. To finish the loop, backtrack to trail 667C which goes to Sahalie Falls, a 75-foot high horsetail falls. The trail continues from Sahalie Falls to the graveled parking lot.

For a little more exercise continue past Umbrella Falls on Forest Service 667 to Timberline Trail, turn northeast under a ski lift and walk 0.5 mile to Pencil Falls.

Dates: Snow free June to mid-Oct.

Trail: Loop Trail 645-667-667C, 4.1 miles.

Elevation: From 5,200 feet to 5,800 feet.

Degree of difficulty: Moderate.

BADGER CREEK WILDERNESS AREA

[Fig. 12] Small when compared with other Mount Hood National Forest wilderness areas, 24,000-acre Badger Creek Wilderness has few lakes to lure fishermen, and few developed trails to attract overnight hikers into the dry hills east of OR 35 where elevations vary from 2,000 to 6,500 feet.

The wilderness area is southeast of Mount Hood and east of OR 35 on Forest Service Road 4410. The east side of the wilderness borders the White River State Game Management Area, which is managed by Oregon Department of Fish and Wildlife as a black-tailed deer wintering area.

Elk also live in this wilderness along with mule deer, cougar, black bear, turkey, and blue and ruffed grouse.

The topography is steep with 30 to 70-degree slopes, talus slides and basalt outcrops. There are three drainages; Badger Creek, Little Badger Creek, and Tygh Creek. Glacial features dominate the wilderness.

Lookout Mountain (*see* Dufur Valley Road, page 65) and a high-elevation grassland known as High Prairie are the most popular destinations. Three-mile long High Prairie Trail 493 is clear of snow from July to October. Forest Service trail crews rate it as the most spectacular trail in the Barlow Ranger District, with commanding views of Mount Rainier in Washington, the high desert of eastern Oregon, and the Three Sisters volcanoes.

Directions: The western wilderness boundary comes within 2 miles of OR 35 near Robinhood Campground. From OR 35 turn east on Forest Service 44 and then south on 4410 to the wilderness boundary. On the south side, the best way to enter is by following Forest Service Road 48 to 4860 and turning north to Badger Butte.

Activities: Wildlife viewing, hiking, horseback riding, camping, fishing, hunting, and rock hounding.

Facilities: Primitive camping areas, and 55 miles of trails, including Badger Creek National Recreation Trail. Wheeled vehicles are not allowed.

Dates: Open year-round except for snow.

For more information: Dufur Ranger Station, 780 Court St., Dufur, OR 97021. Phone (541) 467-2291.

BADGER LAKE

[Fig. 10, Fig. 12] Forest Service 48 is a paved spine with gravel-road ribs leading into the outback. One of the longest ribs is Forest Service 4860, which winds through mile-high elevations to the south edge of the Badger Creek Wilderness Area. It passes three campgrounds, a rental forest cabin, and ends at a productive trout fishing lake. This highroad is generally snow-free from June to October.

Badger Lake, at an elevation of 4,400 feet, is the major attraction and although the lake is inside a wilderness area the road has been exempted to allow vehicles to reach the lake. The road into the lake, however, is narrow and trailers are prohibited.

Badger Lake is stocked with rainbow trout and supports wild brook trout up to 14 inches in size. Boats are allowed, but not outboard motors. On the north end of the lake there is a free and rarely crowded Forest Service campground with four primitive sites.

The Forest Service's Valley View mountain cabin is just a few hundred yards up Badger Lake Road from Forest Service 4860. Built in the early 1950s at an elevation of 5,600 feet, the cabin is available year-round for overnight rental. Winter access can be difficult and requires skis or snowmobiles. The cabin can accommodate four, and includes a single bed, wood stove, propane heater, firewood and a table. To inquire about overnight stays at the Dufur Ranger Station, phone (541) 467-2291.

Directions: From Forest Service 48 about 6 miles southeast of Barlow Crossing, turn north onto Forest Service 4860.

Activities: Sightseeing, camping, fishing, hunting.

Facilities: The first of the three primitive campgrounds on Forest Service 4860 is 2 miles north of Forest Service 48 at Post Camp, elevation 4,600, with four sites. At the end of the road, Camp Windy, at 5,200 feet has three sites.

Dates: Open year-round, but snow bound from Nov. to Apr.

Fees: There are charges for camping, trail park passes, and cabin rental.

Closest town: Tygh Valley is about 10 miles east of Rock Creek Reservoir near US 97.

For more information: Mount Hood Information Center, 65000 E. Highway 26, Welches, OR 97067. Phone (503) 622-7674 or (888) 622-4822.

BARLOW PASS

[Fig. 10(10)] Barlow Pass, elevation 4,155, is the low spot on the high ridge where OR 35 merges into US 26, and one of the most historic stops on the Mount Hood Loop.

The Mount Hood Loop turns west here onto US 26 and leads to the massive Works Progress Administration-era Timberline Lodge, a winter skiing and summer hiking complex 6,000 feet up Mount Hood at the base of Palmer Glacier.

US 26 is the southern leg of the Mount Hood Loop, an attraction-studded mountain drive between Mount Hood and Portland.

Southeast of Barlow Pass, US 26 leads into the open, semiarid region on the East Slope of the Cascades, passing through the Warm Springs Tribal Reservation, en route to the Deschutes River Recreation Area and US 97.

Directions: The pass is at the junction of OR 35 and US 26 on Mount Hood.

Activities: Historical appreciation, scenic drives, and hiking.

Facilities: None.

Dates: Open year-round.

Fees: None.

Closest town: Government Camp is 7 miles west on US 26.

For more information: Mount Hood Information Center, 65000 E. Highway 26, Welches, OR 97067. Phone (503) 622-7674 or (888) 622-4822.

US 26 To Mount Hood

US 26 is most important and heavily traveled east-west route crossing the Cascade Mountains in Oregon. It connects the Portland metropolitan area in the heavily populated Willamette Valley with US 97 at Madras, population 4,770, a center for Deschutes, Metolius and Crooked River trout fishing, river rafting, backpacking, rock climbing and mountain biking.

Through the mountains, US 26 rides the south shoulder of Mount Hood and connects to a web of high roads that lead to year-round recreation, and historic and geologic attractions. Most winter and much summer recreation is focused on three ski area complexes accessible from the highway. When downhill skiers call it quits in late June, they are replaced by backpackers, hikers, summit climbers, mountain bikers, berry pickers, bird watchers, and photography buffs.

US 26 is an entrance to hundreds of hiking and biking trails, including the Pacific Crest Trail 2000, and gravel roads through prime wildlife and wildflower zones. There are dozens of trout lakes and large campground complexes. The highway leads to three federally designated wild and scenic rivers, spans two nationally acclaimed trout rivers, two wilderness areas, and bisects the largest intact block of tribal reservation land in Oregon.

The confederation includes three separate tribes that traditionally occupied parts of eastern Oregon. The Wascos were Columbia River fishermen and traders. The Walla Wallas (later became Warm Springs) were hunters and fishermen. The Paiute were nomadic hunters and gatherers who lived mostly on the high plateaus.

The Confederated Tribes Of The Warm Springs Reservation includes 600,000 acres of high desert established in 1855. It occupies territory bordered by the Deschutes and Metolius rivers and the crest of the Cascade Mountains. The reservation has its own

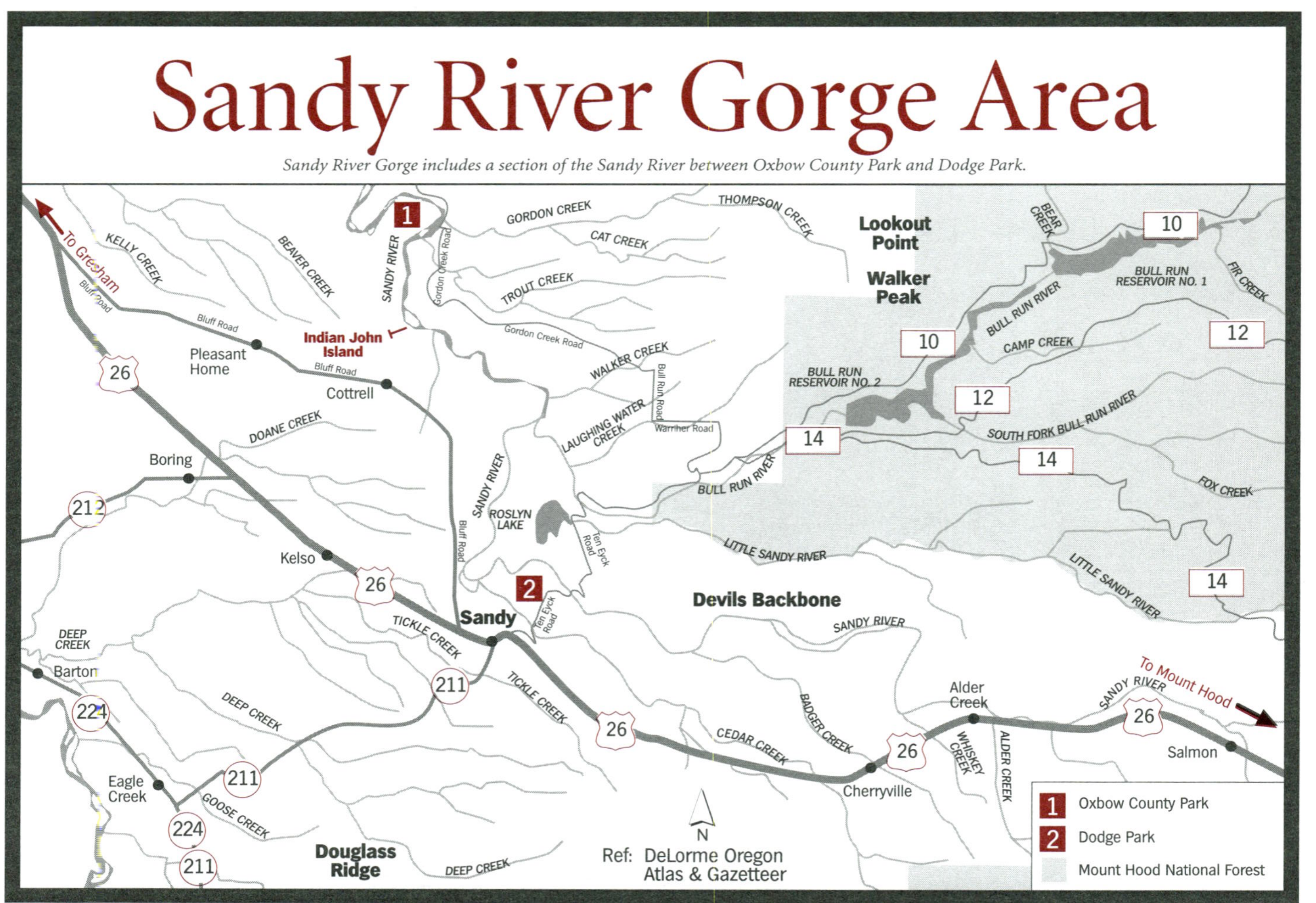
Sandy River Gorge Area
Sandy River Gorge includes a section of the Sandy River between Oxbow County Park and Dodge Park.
To Gresham
KELLY CREEK
BEAVER CREEK
SANDY RIVER
Gordon Creek Road
GORDON CREEK
CAT CREEK
THOMPSON CREEK
Lookout Point
Walker Peak
BEAR CREEK
BULL RUN RESERVOIR NO. 1
FIR CREEK
TROUT CREEK
Bluff Road
Indian John Island
Pleasant Home
Cottrell
WALKER CREEK
Bull Run Road
BULL RUN RIVER
CAMP CREEK
BULL RUN RESERVOIR NO. 2
LAUGHING WATER CREEK
Warriner Road
SOUTH FORK BULL RUN RIVER
DOANE CREEK
Boring
ROSLYN LAKE
Ten Eyck Road
FOX CREEK
LITTLE SANDY RIVER
Kelso
Sandy
Devils Backbone
DEEP CREEK
Barton
TICKLE CREEK
CEDAR CREEK
BADGER CREEK
WHISKEY CREEK
ALDER CREEK
Alder Creek
Cherryville
To Mount Hood
Salmon
Eagle Creek
GOOSE CREEK
Douglass Ridge
N
Ref: DeLorme Oregon Atlas & Gazetteer
1 Oxbow County Park
2 Dodge Park
Mount Hood National Forest
26
211
212
224
10
12
14

constitutional form of government and is considered a sovereign nation by the United States. Tourism is now a major reservation industry. Attractions include Kah-Nee-Ta Resort, hot springs, a lodge and convention center, a casino, and a museum. Recreation includes an 18-hole golf course, mountain biking, kayaking, horseback riding, fishing, and hiking (*see* Warm Springs Reservation, page 105).

The Mount Hood National Forest Service information center at Welches is well stocked with forest information and maps. It is a recommended stop.

Most travelers enter US 26 from the west, connecting at I-205 in the Portland suburb of Gresham.

WEST GATE TO MOUNT HOOD

The US 26 west gateway to Mount Hood is at Sandy, population 4,895, where the pastures of the Willamette Valley end and the foothills of the Cascades begin.

This route follows the Sandy River, which begins as a trickle of Reid Glacier ice melt on the west side of Mount Hood and ends in the Columbia River below Broughton's Bluff near Troutdale. The river supports great runs of summer and winter steelhead and salmon, and includes a magnificent 700-foot deep gorge. It has 24.9 miles of designated wild and scenic water. Rarely, however, is the river visible from US 26.

Directions: From Portland area, US 26 East joins I-205 south of Gresham.

SANDY RIVER GORGE

[Fig. 13] Sandy River Gorge includes a rough and tumble 12.5 mile section of the Sandy River between Dodge Park, a picnic area about 6 miles north of Sandy, and Oxbow County Park east of Gresham.

The 700-foot high cliffs that wall in the gorge protect a rich diversity of plants and animals, including one of Oregon's best remaining examples of low elevation old-growth Douglas fir just 20 miles east of Portland. The old growth escaped early logging because of the difficulty loggers had in getting to the bottom of the gorge. Later, the old growth was protected for conservation. Some of these ancient firs measure 7 feet across and were a century old when Christopher Columbus sailed from Spain.

Much of the gorge is inaccessible except from whitewater boats or by rugged hikes. Four hundred acres are preserved as an Area of Critical Environmental Concern by The Nature Conservancy and Salem District office of the Bureau of Land Management.

Winter and summer steelhead anglers fish the gorge upstream from Oxbow or downstream from Dodge following rough paths along the bank. Fishing from boats is not allowed above Oxbow, but the section is a favorite challenge for kayakers and whitewater enthusiasts. The campground at Oxbow is the only one along the lower river.

The wild and scenic segments of the Sandy are divided into a 12.5 mile section between Dodge and Oxbow parks, and 12.4 miles at the headwaters.

The topographic isolation and habitat diversity of the gorge has produced a haven for wildlife once common over much of western Oregon. There are good numbers of black

Barlow Toll Road

Barlow Toll Road was hacked into the wilderness in 1846 by Kentuckian Samuel K. Barlow, extending a bypass of the Oregon Trail around dangerous cliffs and rapids in the Columbia River Gorge.

Barlow built his wagon road from The Dalles south to Tygh (pronounced Tie) Valley, then west across the mountains at Barlow Pass, and downhill to Willamette Valley at Oregon City. He later placed a gate near Wamic, a few miles west of Tygh Valley, and collected tolls of $5 per wagon, and 10¢ a head for stock. Tracks of the wagons of intrepid pioneers are still visible near Barlow Pass.

Oregon Trail travelers claimed the steep, edge-of-the-world Barlow Road was the most dangerous place on the route. West of Barlow Pass, the perilous wagon road followed a sharp incline that now parallels and criss-crosses modern US 26. About 3 miles west of Government Camp the trail pitched down Laurel Hill. One fearful pioneer described the descent as wagons moving like "shot off a shovel." Another wrote, "The road on this hill is something terrible. It is worn down in the soil from 5 to 7 feet, leaving steep banks on both sides, and so narrow that is almost impossible to walk alongside of the cattle for any distance without leaning against the oxen." It was common for wagoneers to drag a tree as a brake, or to belay from ropes.

Eastern sections of this pioneer road, deeply rutted into the mountain sides, are used by hikers, deer hunters, mountain bikers, 4-wheel drive enthusiasts and snowmobilers. In fact, the asphalt for OR 35 near Barlow Pass was laid in the ruts of Barlow Road.

One of the unexpected finds in the pass area is along Forest Service 3531 about 1.5 miles east of the OR 35. A pullover where roadside brush has been cleared reveals a horizon-to-horizon view of Mount Hood's glacier-encrusted east side. On the uphill side, a natural spring bubbles into a manmade cistern bowl mortised from native rocks. The spring gushes from a hillside dark with old growth cedar trees and is overhung with huckleberries. The water is delicious.

Barlow Road can be traveled by foot, horseback, or, in places, by vehicle. The road east is primitive and narrow, with large water bars and even larger potholes. Road conditions will sometimes limit passenger vehicles to all-wheel drive, high-clearance models.

On the eastern Barlow Road between OR 35 and Wamic Toll Gate historic attractions include pioneer campsites at Devil's Half Acre, a meadow often filled with blooming wildflower; Klinger's Camp, and White River Station.

Westward along US 26, a replica of the original gate, which operated from 1879 to 1919, marks Barlow's West Tollgate. Original wagon ruts are preserved 4 miles south of the tollgate at the Bureau of Land Management's Wildwood Recreation Area.

The road ends at the End Of The Oregon Trail Interpretive Center in Oregon City, phone (503) 657-9336.

bear, elk, black-tailed deer, red fox, beaver, mountain beaver, river otter, short-tailed weasel, raccoon, and flying squirrels. The gorge is home to wood ducks, blue and ruffed grouse, pileated woodpeckers, osprey, bald eagles, water ouzels, great blue herons, harlequin ducks and mergansers.

Sandy River is an ancient flow that began before the Cascade Mountains were formed when most of Oregon was covered with tropical forests. The gorge walls expose a cross-section of seven major geologic formations. Volcanic rocks (Columbia River basalt, Rhododendron Formations and Boring Lava) are interspersed between water-deposited sediments of sand, silt, clay, pebble, and mud stone. The area frequently serves as a living laboratory for Portland college students.

The supply center for gorge recreationists is Sandy, population 4,895, which has full traveler services, and is the headquarters of Mount Hood National Forest. The National Forest offices provide interpretive displays, and forest maps, and sells trail park passes and Sno-Park permits.

Directions: Take I-84 East from Portland to Exit 17. Turn right on 257th St. and travel 1 mile. Turn left on SE Division St. and drive 5 miles to Oxbow Regional Park.

Activities: The gorge is primitive with no developed recreation areas beyond Dodge and Oxbow parks. Hiking through old growth trees, whitewater boating, and summer

Pioneer Woman's Grave

Just 0.1 mile north of US 26, Forest Service Road 3531 angles south from OR 35 for 0.4 mile to a parking area and the Pioneer Woman's Grave historic site. The grave was discovered by engineers building the Mount Hood Loop. The bed of a wagon had been used as a coffin for the nameless pioneer mother of two small children. The spot is marked with a rock cairn and many of today's travelers pay tribute by placing flowers and native plants on the cairn.

Across the road from the grave are tracks of the original wagon trail and a 1-mile trail to a state Sno-Park, winter fee area, at Barlow Pass.

OLIVE-SIDED FLYCATCHER
(*Contopus borealis*)
The flycatcher's call is *pip-whee-beer* or, when alarmed, *pip-pip-pip-pip*.

and winter steelhead fishing.

Facilities: None.

Dates: Open year-round.

Fees: None.

Closest town: Sandy

For more information: Metro Parks and Green Spaces, 600 NE Grand Ave., Portland, OR 97232-2736. Phone (503) 797-1850. Salem District office of the Bureau of Land Management, 1717 Fabry Rd. SE, Salem, OR 97306. Phone (503) 375-5646. The Nature Conservancy of Oregon, 821 SE 14th Street, Portland, OR 97214. Phone (503) 230-1221.

DODGE PARK

[Fig. 13(2)] Dodge Park, a day use area, is the eastern entry point into the Sandy River Gorge.

Directions: From US 26 in Sandy, go 5 miles northeast on Ten Eyck Road to the Sandy River bridge.

Facilities: Restrooms, drinking water, river access, picnic tables, and grills.

Dates: Open year-round.

Fees: None.

Closest town: Sandy, about 5 miles south on Ten Eyck Road.

For more information: Multnomah County, Parks Department, 1021 SW 4th Avenue, Portland, OR 97204. Phone (503) 248-3511.

OXBOW COUNTY PARK

[Fig. 13(1)] Oxbow County Park is the only developed campground in the gorge, and provides access from the west end.

Directions: From Dodge Park, continue across the Sandy River Bridge to Lusted Road. Follow Lusted Road for about 3.5 miles along the bluff above the gorge. Turn north at the junction of Oxbow Parkway Road. It's about 2 miles to the park.

Facilities: 45 tent and RV campsites with full hookups, restrooms, drinking water, boat ramp, and picnic area.

Dates: Open year-round.

Fees: There is a charge for day use and camp sites.

Closest town: Gresham is 8 miles west.

For more information: Metro Parks and Green Spaces, 600 NE Grand Ave., Portland, OR 97232-2736. Phone (503) 797-1850 or Multnomah County Parks Department, 1021 SW 4th Avenue, Portland, OR 97204. Phone (503) 248-3511.

MOUNT HOOD INFORMATION CENTER

[Fig. 15(7)] Mount Hood Information Center is a multiagency complex near Mount Hood that serves as the centralized information headquarters for all of Mount Hood National Forest. It is located on US 26 at Welches about 14 miles east of Sandy in Mount Hood Village.

This is possibly the most comprehensively stocked and staffed mountain information source in Oregon. It offers regional and topographical maps of the forest, individual ranger districts, trail systems, Mount Hood recreation and attractions, and listings of recommended seasonal activities and areas. It also has a bookstore, interpretive displays, pamphlets identifying forest flowers, mushrooms, wildlife, fishing, and other forest uses. Forest trail park passes, wilderness use permits, and Sno-Park permits may be obtained here.

The staff includes local and federal representatives who are exceptionally efficient and informed about not only Mount Hood and the nearby national forest, but adjoining national forests, Bureau of Land Management sites and other areas managed by county, state and federal agencies.

Directions: The Mount Hood Information Center is on US 26, 14 miles east of Sandy at Mount Hood Village.

Facilities: Staffed information center regarding Mount Hood National Forest and surrounding region. There are interpretive displays, restrooms, and picnic tables. Adjacent Mount Hood Village includes an RV park, dump station, camping area, gas stations, picnic area, gift shops, groceries, restaurants, Laundromat, and exercise and swimming facilities.

Dates: The information center is open daily except Thanksgiving and Christmas.

Fees: Trail park use and Sno-Park use permits can be purchased here.

Closest town: Sandy, 14 miles west on US 26.

For more information: Mount Hood National Forest, 65000 E. Highway 26, Welches, OR 97067. Phone (503) 622-7674 or (888) 622-4822.

WILDWOOD BUREAU OF LAND MANAGEMENT RECREATION SITE

[Fig. 15(8)] The nationally unique Salmon River is one of Oregon's most striking, but relatively obscure, wild and scenic rivers, and the centerpiece for the Bureau of Land Management's 560-acre Wildwood Recreation Site.

The 33-mile Salmon River is the only river in the lower 48 states protected as a national wild and scenic river for its entire length. It begins in the Palmer Snow Field on Mount Hood and joins the Sandy River, 3 miles east of Wildwood. At Wildwood, the river is spanned by a 190-foot wooden bridge, and in the fall and early winter chinook salmon and steelhead trout may sometimes be seen spawning.

Wildwood is open only during the day, and camping is not allowed. The maze of nature trails includes a wheelchair-accessible 2.5 mile path that incorporates a 0.75 mile wetland loop. The trails have interpretive signs, and range from 0.5 to 2.5 miles, winding across mostly level terrains with minimal obstacles. Wildwood is also the trailhead for popular Boulder Ridge Trail into adjacent Salmon-Huckleberry Wilderness Area.

Directions: Wildwood is 15 miles east of Sandy, on the south side of US 26, about .5 mile east of the Mount Hood Information Center.

Activities: Hiking, picnicking, and fishing.

Facilities: Picnic tables, shelter houses, trails, and interpretive signs.

Dates: Open May-Oct.

Fees: None.

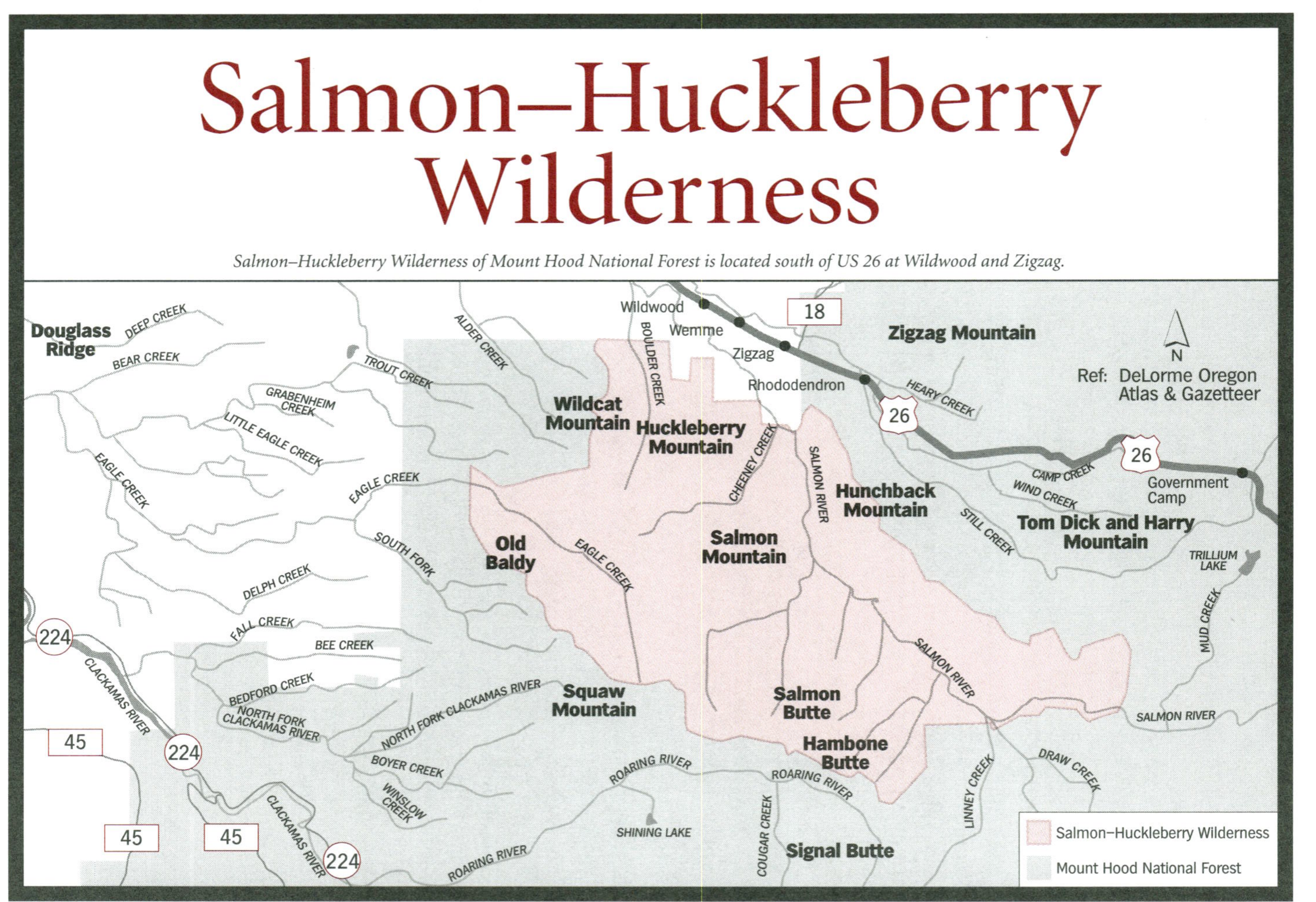

Salmon–Huckleberry Wilderness

Salmon–Huckleberry Wilderness of Mount Hood National Forest is located south of US 26 at Wildwood and Zigzag.

Closest town: Sandy.

For more information: Bureau of Land Management, Salem District, 1717 Fabry Road SE, Salem, OR 97306. Phone (503) 375-5646.

SALMON-HUCKLEBERRY WILDERNESS

[Fig. 14] Salmon-Huckleberry Wilderness of Mount Hood National Forest is south of US 26 at Wildwood and Zigzag. Its 44,600 acres are popular with hikers because it's easily entered from the highway and has multiple trails.

Two drainages divide the wilderness: Salmon River and Eagle Creek. Salmon River flows south from the upper slopes of Mount Hood into the wilderness, then turns north again to join the Sandy River near Mount Hood Village. Eagle Creek drains east, eventually winding into the Clackamas River southeast of Portland.

Major geologic features include volcanic plugs, pinnacles and dramatic cliffs. It is steep country with sharply dissected slopes that commonly run at angles of 60 to 90 degrees. Elevations vary from 1,400 to 4,800 feet.

The middle and lower slopes support western hemlock and the upper slopes, Pacific silver fir. Salmon Butte and Huckleberry Mountain have high-elevation ecosystems. The Salmon River National Recreation Trail wraps around the mountainside several hundred feet above the thundering falls of the Salmon River Gorge.

For more information about Salmon-Huckleberry Wilderness see page 97.

Directions: Popular access points are from the Wildwood BLM site on US 26 west of Government Camp; Salmon River Road south of US 26; Highway 224, and Forest Service 2613, which is also called the Sherar Burn Road.

Facilities: Primitive campsites, and 70 miles of maintained trails.

Dates: Open year-round.

Fees: There is a charge for trail park passes at trailheads.

Closest town: Sandy is about 15 miles west on US 26.

For more information: Mount Hood Information Center, 65000 E. Highway 26, Welches, OR 97067. Phone (503) 622-7674 or (888) 622-4822.

LOLO PASS TO LOST LAKE

[Fig. 15(1)] The Lolo Pass to Lost Lake route is a back-road driving adventure through the rounded low mountains north of US 26 at Zigzag. The windshield is often filled with Mount Hood glaciers, and rivers that drop from mountains in thin veils of mist. There are hiking paths passing rough-barked towers of sweet-smelling conifer trees in cathedrals of ancient old growth, and scenic forest campsites.

Lolo Pass Road, also identified as Forest Service 18, begins its 21-mile northerly route at Zigzag on US 26. It ends north of Lolo Pass, elevation 3,420 feet, at Lost Lake in the Hood River drainage. This is the only passenger car route around the west side of Mount Hood, and is closed from late November to late May by snow that accumulates to depths of 20 feet.

Lolo Pass Road Forest Service 18 is paved for 10 miles between US 26 and an intersection with the Pacific Crest Trail at Lolo Pass. Where the pavement ends, Forest Service 18 becomes Forest Service 1810. The remaining 11 miles are graded gravel, and is well maintained although there are twists, turns and hills. Forest Service 1810 follows the West Fork Hood River from the pass to Forest Service 13, a paved road that continues 7 miles south to Lost Lake. Four miles northeast of US 26, Forest Service 1825, a paved side road, forks east from Forest Service 18 into the Sandy River Valley at the edge of Mount Hood. Three major campgrounds are located here (*see* Camping At Lolo, bottom of page), as is the trailhead of a popular and easy hiking trail to a plunging waterfall. This is also the confluence for two dramatically different forks of the Sandy River.

The silt-stained fork of the Sandy River, sometimes identified as Muddy Fork because of the thick glacial sediment in it called "glacier flour," comes in from its headwaters under Reid and Sandy glaciers. Both glaciers are visible from Forest Service 18.

In transparent contrast, the Clear Fork begins in springs on the side of Hiyu Mountain just below Lolo Pass, and is so clear that individual stones can be counted at the bottom of deep pools. The Clear Fork offers decent trout fishing for wild cutthroat. Getting there can be a bushwhack, but that's what keeps the fishing good.

The summit at Lolo Pass is in a logged-over area thick with vine maple, squaw berries, salmonberries and wild rhododendrons that bloom pink in June. From the pass to Forest Service 13 is a mix of lofty valley views, conifers draped with strands of club moss, and huckleberry bushes. Spring creeks rocket off the steep mountainside along dark sluiceways through tunnels of thorny devils club into bogs that sometimes glow with the brilliant yellow hoods of skunk cabbage (*Lysichitum americanum*).

Directions: Turn north off US 26 onto Lolo Pass Road Forest Service 18 at the Zigzag Mountain Store in Zigzag.

Activities: Scenic drive, camping, fishing, hunting, hiking, horseback riding.

Facilities: Campgrounds, maintained trails, wheelchair fishing pier, picnic tables, and grills.

Dates: Open year-round, but often not completely free of snow until May.

Fees: There are charges for camping and trail park passes.

Closest town: Zigzag.

For more information: Mount Hood Information Center, 65000 E. Highway 26, Welches, OR 97067. Phone (503) 622-7674 or (888) 622-4822.

CAMPING AT LOLO

[Fig. 15(2)] Three campgrounds are clustered south of Lolo Pass along Forest Service 1825. All three are reached from Forest Service 18, which is paved. The elevations at the campgrounds vary from 2,000 to 2,600 feet.

MCNEIL CAMPGROUND

Directions: US 26 to Zigzag, turn north on Forest Service 18. At the junction of Forest Service 1825, turn east. All three campgrounds are within 2 miles of the junction.

Activities: Camping, hiking, and fishing.

Facilities: 34 tent and RV sites up to 22 feet, picnic tables, grills, but no hookup services or water.

Dates: Open Apr. through Oct.

Fees: There is a charge for camping.

RILEY HORSE CAMP

Activities: Horseback riding, camping, fishing, and hiking.

Facilities: 14 tent and RV sites to 16 feet, and well water, stock loading and staging areas, hitch rails, picnic tables, and grills. No hookups or water.

Dates: Open Apr. through Oct.

Fees: There are charges for camping and trail use passes.

LOST CREEK CAMPGROUND

Activities: Camping, hiking, fishing, and picnicking.

Facilities: 16 tent and RV sites to 22 feet long, barrier-free paths, fishing pier, paved trail, picnic tables, grills, and well water.

Dates: Open Apr. through Sept.

Fees: There are charges for camping and trail park passes.

RAMONA FALLS LOOP TRAIL 797

[Fig. 15(3)] This trail from the Lolo Pass camping area is well marked and so heavily used that Forest Service officials are considering restricting access. The trail goes through groves of centuries old Douglas fir and western hemlock, with Mount Hood looming overhead. The wide fan of the 45-foot namesake waterfalls are a kaleidoscope of water and light falling in hundreds of tiny shimmering pyramids down a black basalt rock wall.

Directions: From Forest Service 18, about 4 miles northeast of Zigzag, go north on Forest Service 1825, cross the Sandy River, continue 3.5 miles and park at the end of the road. Continue 1.5 miles—Sandy River trail connects to Ramona Falls trail. Follow Trail 797 across a bridge to connect with the loop trail to the falls.

Trail: 7.5 miles, loop.

Elevation: Trailhead is at 2,500 feet, and the trail gradually gains 900 feet in about 3.5 miles.

Degree of difficulty: Easy.

Surface: Forest duff.

Dates: Open year-round. Snow free from May to Nov. Seasonal bridge at Sandy River installed May through Oct.

Fees: There is a charge for trail park passes.

Closest town: Zigzag.

For more information: Mount Hood Information Center, 65000 E. Highway 26, Welches, OR 97067. Phone (503) 622-7674 or (888) 622-4822.

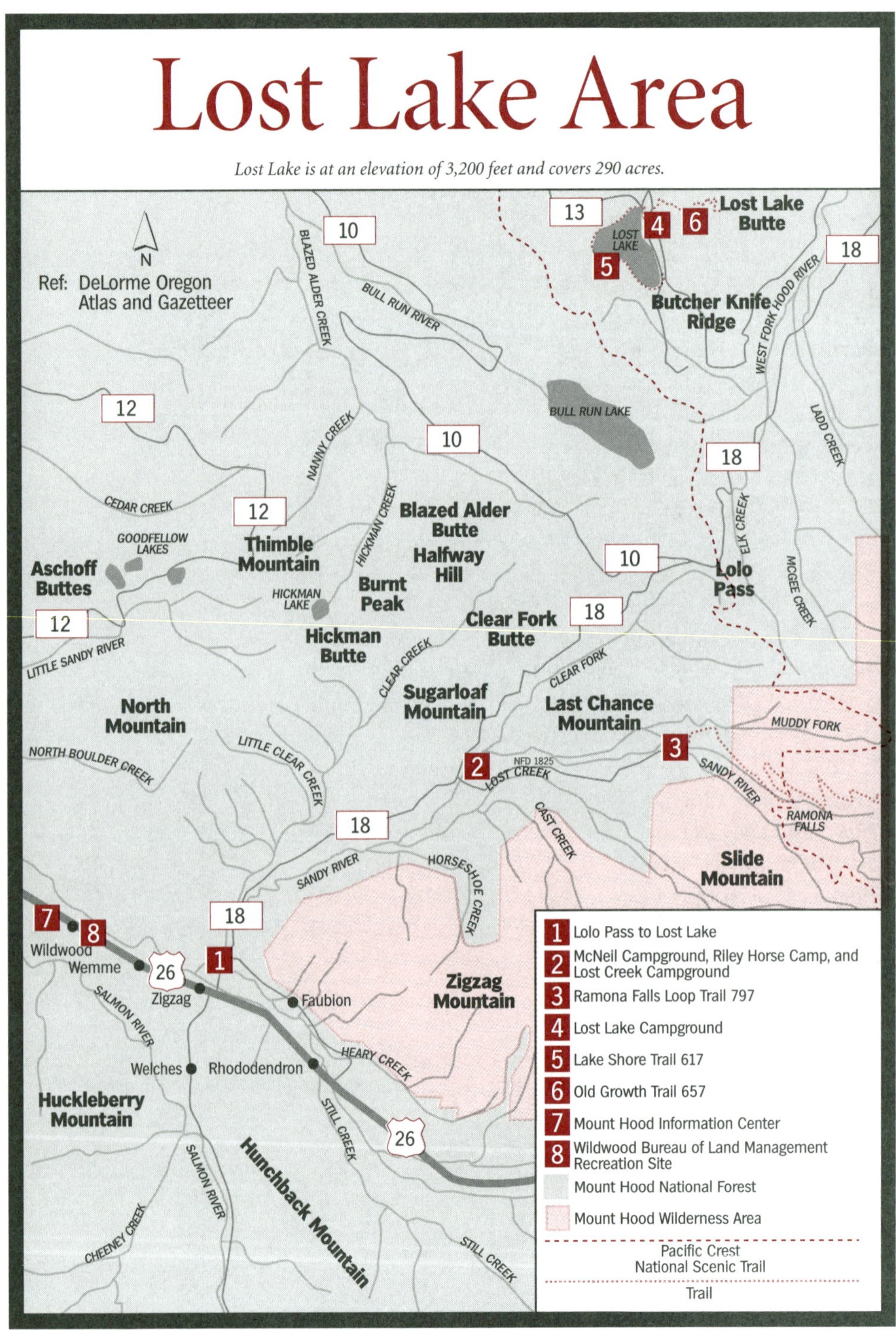
Lost Lake Area
Lost Lake is at an elevation of 3,200 feet and covers 290 acres.
N
Ref: DeLorme Oregon Atlas and Gazetteer
Lost Lake Butte
Lost Lake
Butcher Knife Ridge
West Fork Hood River
Blazed Alder Creek
Bull Run River
Bull Run Lake
Ladd Creek
Nanny Creek
Cedar Creek
Goodfellow Lakes
Aschoff Buttes
Thimble Mountain
Hickman Creek
Blazed Alder Butte
Halfway Hill
Burnt Peak
Hickman Lake
Elk Creek
Lolo Pass
McGee Creek
Clear Fork Butte
Hickman Butte
Little Sandy River
Clear Creek
Clear Fork
Sugarloaf Mountain
Last Chance Mountain
North Mountain
Muddy Fork
North Boulder Creek
Little Clear Creek
NFD 1825
Lost Creek
Sandy River
Cast Creek
Ramona Falls
Horseshoe Creek
Slide Mountain
Wildwood
Wemme
Zigzag
Faubion
Zigzag Mountain
Salmon River
Welches
Rhododendron
Heary Creek
Huckleberry Mountain
Still Creek
Hunchback Mountain
Cheeney Creek
1 Lolo Pass to Lost Lake
2 McNeil Campground, Riley Horse Camp, and Lost Creek Campground
3 Ramona Falls Loop Trail 797
4 Lost Lake Campground
5 Lake Shore Trail 617
6 Old Growth Trail 657
7 Mount Hood Information Center
8 Wildwood Bureau of Land Management Recreation Site
Mount Hood National Forest
Mount Hood Wilderness Area
Pacific Crest National Scenic Trail
Trail

Lost Lake

[Fig. 15] Shimmering in a natural mountain bowl 10 miles northwest of Mount Hood, Lost Lake is one of the most pristine and popular camping, hiking and fishing destinations in Mount Hood National Forest. The 290-acre lake is the centerpiece of a heavily used forest recreation region. On windless summer days, the lake surface becomes a mile-long mirror reflecting Mount Hood, a photo opportunity that has become one of Oregon's most popular postcard images.

Native Hood River tribes called the lake *E-e-kwahl-a-mat-yam-ishkt.* It translates poetically to Heart Of The Mountains. In 1880 the name was reduced to simply "Lost Lake" by explorers who failed to find the lake on their first sortie. Heart Of The Mountains is now one of 13 Lost Lakes in Oregon. The lake is at an elevation of 3,200 feet, protected by thick walls of Douglas fir, mountain hemlock, red cedar, and white pine. There is a Forest Service 125-site campground, trailhead complex, and private resort at the lake.

Seasonal access is regulated by winter snow depths, but the lake is usually open from mid May to late October. Summer cabins and rental boats are available at Lost Lake Resort. Fishermen try for brook, rainbow, and brown trout and landlocked kokanee salmon. Gasoline boat motors are prohibited. The surrounding hills are webbed with trail systems through conifers, alder, and huckleberry brush. Wildlife is plentiful. Watch for river otters (*Lutra canadensis*), beaver (*Castor canadensis*), occasional pine martens (*Martes americana*), and black-tailed deer. Black bear, cougar, and bobcat are seldom seen but are fairly common in the surrounding forest. Black and white ospreys (*Pandion haliaetus*) or fish hawks, are often seen plunging into the lake from great heights, sometimes emerging in a shower of water with an unlucky trout in their talons. The trout and salmon also attract common mergansers (*Mergus merganser*), common loons (*Gavia immer*), and deep-diving cormorants (*Phalacrocorax auritus*).

Directions: From Hood River drive OR 35 about 13 miles south and turn west onto Woodworth Road. Continue 3 miles to Dee Highway OR 281. Take OR 281 south for 5 miles to Dee Forest Products Mill where Lost Lake Road Forest Service 13 begins. Follow it to the lake.

From US 26 turn north at Zigzag onto Lolo Pass Forest Service Road 18 and continue north 21 miles to the junction of Forest Service 13. Turn left for 7 miles to Lost Lake.

Activities: Camping, row boating (electric motors are allowed), fishing, hiking, mountain biking, organized nature walks.

Facilities: Campground, boat ramp, resort, trails, picnic area, shelter houses, and showers. Cabin and boat rentals at Lost Lake Resort.

Dates: Open mid-May to Oct.

Fees: There are charges for camping and trail park passes.

Closest town: Hood River is about 28 miles north.

For more information: Mount Hood Information Center, 65000 E. Highway 26, Welches, OR 97067. Phone (503) 622-7674 or (888) 622-4822. Campsite reservations, phone (800) 280-2267. Lost Lake Resort, phone (541) 386-6366.

LOST LAKE CAMPGROUND

[Fig. 15(4)] This is one of the largest and most popular forest service campgrounds in northern Oregon. Most campsites are barrier free, and separated by native underbrush and trees. Some sites are always available on a first-come basis, but campsite reservations are recommended. During prime camping periods there are few days when this campground is not full.

Directions: See Lost Lake.

Activities: Camping, boating, fishing, hiking, interpretive walks.

Facilities: 125 tent and RV sites to 32 feet long, well water, showers, picnic areas, grills, shelter houses, boat launch, interpretive programs, and a private resort with 7 cabins, rental boats and a small store.

Dates: The campground is usually free of snow from mid May through Oct.

Fees: There are charges for campsites, trail park passes, cabin and boat rentals.

LOST LAKE HIKES

Several hiking trails provide a mix of casual forest walks, and overnight backpacks into the surrounding mountains. Trail park passes are required and are sold at the entrance to Lost Lake Campground.

LAKE SHORE TRAIL 617

[Fig. 15(5)] Lake Shore Trail 617 is the most popular hike. The trail follows the shoreline in a canopied forest with reflected views of Mount Hood. There is a stand of old-growth western hemlock. At the northeast end of the lake the trail connects with a strenuous 2-mile uphill route, through a large grove of old-growth Pacific silver fir (*Abies amabilis*) to the top of the ridge and Pacific Crest Trail 2000.

Directions: From Forest Service 13, follow access road into Lost Lake campground, bear west past the resort to a parking lot at the end of the road. The trailhead is on the far side of the parking lot.

Trail: 3.2 miles, one way.

Elevation: 3,200 feet.

Degree of difficulty: Easy. First mile is barrier-free.

Surface: Forest duff.

OLD GROWTH TRAIL 657

[Fig. 15(6)] A paved, wheelchair-accessible interpretive trail through old-growth Douglas fir, western hemlock and western red cedar—some measuring seven feet in diameter. Bicycles and vehicles, excluding wheelchairs, are prohibited.

Directions: From Forest Service 13, follow access road into campgrounds. Bear west and follow lakeside drive past resort to the end of the road in a day-use parking area where the trailhead is marked.

Trail: 2 miles, loop.

Elevation: Begins and ends at 3,200 feet, no appreciable elevation changes.

Degree of difficulty: Easy

Surface: Pavement.

Mount Hood

Zigzag Mountain Store

The Zigzag Store is a colorful country throwback with a massive rock fireplace, planed log columns, worn floors and sleeping dogs. The store is at the junction of US 26 and Lolo Pass Road and is a supply oasis for adventurers who need gas, groceries, fishing tackle, live bait, firewood, or a Zigzag T-shirt.

Behind the Zigzag Mountain Store is the Zigzag River, a short, 12-mile long sluiceway for whitewater spilling from pocket to pool along US 26 from headwaters on Mount Hood.

The glacier-caped centerpiece of the Oregon Cascades, Mount Hood is, at 11,235-feet, the highest point in the state, and a year-round playground for Portland's metro area just 45 miles west via US 26. Indigenous tribes called it *Wy'east,* the mountain god who spouts flame and hurls boulders. On Oct. 29, 1792, British Lt. William Broughton renamed the volcano Mount Hood, to honor Lord Samuel Hood, an English naval hero. Thirteen years later, Lewis and Clark coming overland through The Dalles called it Falls Mountain, but no one else ever did.

The steep pyramid silhouette of the fourth highest peak in the Cascade Range commands horizon views from eastern Oregon deserts to the Willamette Valley population center. Snow never leaves the upper slopes, frozen in 12 glaciers and snow fields that are wedged between five major ridges. Geologically, Mount Hood is a 780,000-year-old Quaterenary stratovolcano composed of lava flows, domes and volcaniclastic deposits. The bulk of the volcano is built of andesite. The remains of an older volcano, the Sandy Glacier Volcano, are exposed on the west side of Hood. The summit area comprises several andesite or dacite domes that appear to be weakening and, according to geologists, are susceptible to a potentially catastrophic slope failure.

Geologists estimate that 1,000 feet of the volcano has already either eroded or exploded. The last eruption was in 1907, and geologists emphatically note the volcano is dormant, not extinct. Climbers confirm smelling wafts of rotten egg-like sulfur fumes at fumaroles in the Devil's Kitchen area at 10,200 feet. Occasionally a sigh of steam escapes near the summit.

Volcanic mud flows from Hood have been uncovered 25 miles from the peak. The last major eruptive period ended in 1865. Seventy-two years later, Timberline Lodge was dedicated by President Roosevelt and the volcanic slopes swarmed with downhill skiers. They still do. Four ski resorts ring the mountain and one, Timberline, is the only year-round ski area in the country.

The north flank of the mountain is included in 47,100-acre Mount Hood Wilderness Area. Permits are required. Much of the south side is a broad, relatively smooth fan that slopes down to US 26 at Government Camp. The White River, a wild and scenic designate, flows south and east from the mountain to the Deschutes River. The Salmon River, also designated as wild and scenic, takes a long circuitous course down the south face. The Sandy River heads on the west side of the volcano.

The village of Government Camp, elevation 3,888 feet, is an oasis for travelers on US

26 below Timberline Lodge. Named for a disastrous 1849 bivouac by the First U.S. Mounted Rifles, Government Camp is a hub for summer and winter recreationists. US 26 and OR 35 provide easy highway access to the mountain's web of recreational trails including the 40.7-mile Timberline Trail 600, which circles around the peak. The highest and most popular mountain access point is at Timberline Lodge.

Directions: From Portland go east on US 26 45 miles. From Hood River go south 40 miles on OR 35.

Activities: Mountain climbing, hiking, mountain biking, sight-seeing, downhill and cross-country skiing, and fishing.

Facilities: Restaurants, chairlifts, ski resorts, museum, hiking trails, picnic areas, and lodging.

Dates: Open year-round.

Fees: There are charges for lodge, ski, and resort services, trail park passes at selected trailheads.

Closest town: Hood River.

For more information: Mount Hood Information Center, 65000 E. Highway 26, Welches, OR 97067. Phone (503) 622-7674 or (888) 622-4822.

TIMBERLINE LODGE

[Fig. 10(11)] Timberline Lodge sits at an elevation of 6,000 feet on the south side of Mount Hood where the blue-green wall of spire like sub-alpine fir ends and the rocky heather basins that slope up onto the glacial ice of the Palmer Snowfield begin. More than a year-round ski area, Timberline is a historic institution, and a must-stop for northern Oregon mountain travelers. Completed on September 28, 1937, the massive native beam and stone-built lodge was a Works Progress Administration (WPA) project that became a showcase for Northwest artisans and craftsmen. It has been a national historic landmark since 1972, and is a showcase of Depression-era stained glass windows and murals, hand-hooked rugs, hand-loomed upholstery, appliquéed curtains, fitted oak floors, sturdy hand-built furniture, and hand-crafted stone, wood and iron fixtures.

The 11,235-foot summit of Mount Hood creates a lofty backdrop. The lodge's peaked roof line deliberately resembles the mountain's silhouette. Chiseled lava-rock walkways and castlelike steps of the lodge offer sweeping views of lesser Cascade mountains that fade into the distance like great folds of purple and green fog.

A section of the lodge is set aside as the Rachel Griffin Historic Exhibition Center, with Indian carvings and a wildlife mosaic. Lining the rock-sculpted walls are displays of yellowing photographs, antique clothing, turn-of-the-century ski equipment and climbing gear. The lodge functions as a hotel, restaurant and a downhill and cross-country ski center. It is the only lodge in North America where skiers rocket downhill 11 months of the year. During the summer, the U.S. Olympic ski team trains on the fast ice of the Palmer snow field above the lodge.

Chairlifts take summer sightseers to the upper slopes. A thousand feet above the lodge is a Cascadian-style Silcox Hut. Originally built as a warming station for skiers and mountain climbers, the stone building has been renovated to accommodate up to 24 overnight guests in bunkhouse-style. Reservations can be made through the lodge.

Directions: US 26 east of Portland to Government Camp. North on Timberline Road to the lodge at 6,000 feet elevation on Mount Hood.

Activities: Hiking, downhill and cross-country skiing.

Facilities: Lodge restaurants, chairlifts, overnight accommodations, interpretive displays, historical exhibition center, forest service information area, mountain trails and wildflower areas.

Dates: Open year-round.

Fees: There is no access fee, but there are charges for services.

Closest town: Portland is 60 miles west on US 26 and Hood River is 40 miles north on OR 35.

For more information: Contact Timberline Lodge, phone (503) 272-3311 or (800) 547-1406.

TIMBERLINE TRAIL 600

[Fig. 10(12)] Timberline Trail 600 forms a 40.7 mile scalloped circle around Mount Hood. Dozens of spur trails drop away from this arterial route like spokes from a hub, leading to ridges, lakes and backpack destinations in Mount Hood Wilderness Area, and to forest access roads.

Carved into the steep mountainside in the 1930s by the Civilian Conservation Corps (CCC), the trail has been worn into a wide, flat pathway by thousands of thick-soled hiking boots that pound the crunching lava soils almost nonstop during the brief snow-free window from mid-July to mid-September. At several points hikers need to ford frigid glacial streams. The trail was designed to ride the undulating line separating blue-green conifer forests from the treeless open heather slopes, permanent snow fields and a dozen glaciers that skirt the summit. The trail is restricted to hikers, except on the south and west sides, where it shares the route with Pacific Crest Trail 2000 and horses are allowed.

The trail's lowest elevation is at 3,200 feet on the west side above Ramona Falls. The high spot at 7,320 feet is diametrically opposite on the east flank, where the trail climbs between Lamberson Butte and Cooper Spur (*see* OR 35, Cloud Cap Inn, page 60). To hike the entire trail means puffing up and scrambling down 9,000 feet of elevation changes. While the Timberline Trail is heavily used and brightened with the sunny blooms of alpine flowers, don't be lulled. This is a steep, rugged, unforgiving route where people have died in sudden weather extremes and falls, sometimes only a few hundred yards from the protection of the lodge.

Directions: The trail is accessible from many of the roads and trails around Mount Hood. The most heavily used trail access is 200 yards north of Timberline Lodge. The second major entry is on the northeast side of Mount Hood at Cloud Cap.

Dates: Often snow free mid-July until mid-Sept. Some exposed southern segments, including the area near Timberline Lodge, open in mid-June.

Fees: None. A free wilderness permit is required where the trail is inside Mount Hood Wilderness Area.

Trail: 40.7 miles encircling the upper slopes and snow fields of Mount Hood near tree line.

Elevation: Undulates from a low of 3,200 feet to a high of 7,320 feet.

Degree of difficulty: Moderate to strenuous. Short loop hikes can be planned that are rated easy to moderate. The area near Timberline Lodge is fairly flat and rated easy.

Surface: Dirt, rock, and ice.

MOUNT HOOD WILDERNESS AREA

[Fig. 10] The wilderness area covers 47,100 acres of Mount Hood National Forest, a 73-square mile area with the summit of Mount Hood as the focal point. Most of this wilderness is above the 6,500-foot tree line on open slopes, ridges and snow fields. Elevations vary from 3,500 to 11,235 feet.

The wilderness lies within a frame roughly formed by US 26 on the south, OR 35 on the east, and Lolo Pass Road Forest Service 18 on the west. The north boundary is about 4 miles north of the summit. Eleven trails, including Timberline Trail 600, are closed to pack and saddle stock, and all areas within the wilderness are closed to mountain bikes, hang-gliders and wheeled vehicles.

Snowfall may occur any month. In an average year, snow covers the upper slopes of Mount Hood down to 4,000 feet until at least June. The West Slope receives the heaviest rain and snowfall, which promotes thick brush and dense conifer forests. On the East Slope, a rain shadow behind the summit creates a semiarid area and a mix of meadows and open forests. Douglas fir is the dominant tree on the lower slopes. As the elevation increases, the dominant trees are western hemlock, Pacific silver fir, noble fir, mountain hemlock, subalpine fir, and white bark pine.

Under the West Slope canopy grow huckleberries (bring a picking bucket in September), vine maple, Oregon grape, salal, rhododendron, and devil's club. On the drier east side are chinkapin, boxwood, poison oak and prince's pine. More than 150 species of birds and 40 species of mammals live in the wilderness. State fishing and hunting regulations apply. Some of the streams offer limited success for small, wild trout. There are only five small lakes, Hidden Lake, Devils Lake, Dumbbell, Cast and Burnt, all in the Zigzag Mountain region.

All of the land within the wilderness originated in Mount Hood eruptions, and is composed of ash, pumice, and rock fragments interbedded with thin flows of lava and mud. Steam and gas fumaroles are visible at Crater Rock on the south side of the wilderness.

Directions: The three most popular entry points are from US 26 at Timberline Lodge; From OR 35 at Cloud Cap Saddle on Forest Service 3512; and from Lolo Pass Road Forest Service 18 on Ramona Falls Trail 797.

Activities: Mountain climbing, hiking, hunting, fishing, and camping.

Facilities: Trails and primitive camping areas.

Dates: Open year-round.

GRAY JAY
(*Perisoreus canadensis*)

Fees: None, but a free wilderness use permit is required. They are self-issued on each trail at entry points.

Closest town: Hood River is about 35 miles north.

For more information: Mount Hood Information Center, 65000 E. Highway 26, Welches, OR 97067. Phone (503) 622-7674 or (888) 622-4822.

White River Valley

One of the least-traveled loops in the Mount Hood region is on a paved forest service road that runs east into semiarid sagebrush and returns on a lightly traveled state highway. Forest Service Road 48 and OR 216 follow opposite walls of the White River Valley for almost 40 miles. Forest Service 48 follows the north side of the valley above the chalky, gray glacial waters of the White River, easily the least known federally designated wild and scenic river in Oregon. It follows a ridge above the canyon to Rock Creek Reservoir and campground. This 100-acre reservoir is a popular family fishing site for stocked rainbow trout, largemouth bass, and bullhead catfish.

OR 216 is the southern leg which roughly parallels the south side of the valley. Both legs are wide, paved and suitable for family sedans and motor homes. Traffic is nearly always light.

White River begins at Crater Rock near the icy summit of Mount Hood and drains to the Deschutes River just south of the Badger Creek Wilderness Area. Forest Road 48 joins the curving north bank of the river just east of OR 35, and about 3 miles north of US 26.

The south leg of the White River Valley loop is on OR 216, across 43 miles of lonesome high prairie between the tall green of Mount Hood and the dry Deschutes River breaks near Tygh Valley (pronounced *Tie* Valley). Lightly traveled OR 216 connects US 197 at Maupin, population 495, with US 26 about 12 miles southeast of Government Camp. This two-lane route is steeped in ruralism. About three miles west of US 197, a rusting windmill tower stands in a field tracked by mule deer. The words "Aermotor, Chicago" are faded yet still legible on the vane. In the early morning, the shadow of the windmill stretches into the collapsed ruin of a pioneer homestead. Mount Hood glows in the distance.

The few houses along the highway are mostly ranches tucked into protective draws between scatterings of blue-green sage and rocky fields etched with plow marks. At Walters Corner (gas and groceries) is the Wapinitia junction, which, if followed south, goes 28 miles to the heart of the Warm Springs reservation lands and a hot spring resort complex (*see,* Warm Springs Reservation, page 105.)

The only town on OR 216 is Pine Grove, 5.3 miles west of Walters Corner. There is a store, RV park with cabin rentals, showers and laundry, gas station, and mini-mart supplies. Old homes sit behind old fences beneath older shade trees. Huge ivory-tipped racks of elk antlers are nailed onto garage walls. On porches and sidewalk stoops, antique kitchen pots overflow with red geraniums and purple and white petunias. A few miles west of Pine Grove are two forest service campgrounds and a major off-road vehicle area.

Directions: To reach Forest Service 48 from the junction of US 26 and OR 35, drive north on OR 35 and east on Forest Service 48. OR 216 connects with US 197 at Maupin, and with US 26 about 12 miles southeast of Government Camp.

Activities: Scenic drives, camping, picnicking, mountain biking, hiking, berry picking, fishing, and hunting.

Facilities: Campgrounds, hiking trails, and off road vehicle area.

Dates: Open year-round, but usually snow covered Nov. through May.

Fees: There are charges for camping, and trail park passes.

Closest town: Maupin.

For more information: Mount Hood Information Center, 65000 E. Highway 26, Welches, OR 97067. Phone (503) 622-7674 or (888) 622-4822.

ROCK CREEK CAMPGROUND

[Fig. 12(5)] This is a large shaded forest service campground on the south shore of Rock Creek Reservoir.

Directions: From OR 35 near Barlow Pass, drive east for 19 miles on Forest Service 48. The campground is on the south end of Rock Creek Reservoir at an elevation of 2,200 feet.

Activities: Camping, fishing, and boating.

Facilities: 33 campsites for tents and RVs to 18 feet long, drinking water, tables, and grills. There is a launch ramp for nonmotorized boats. The area is wheelchair accessible and campsite reservations are accepted.

Dates: Open mid-Apr.-mid-Oct., depending on weather.

Fees: There is a charge for camping.

Closest town: Wamic.

For more information: Barlow Ranger District, Dufur Ranger Station, PO Box 67, Dufur, OR 97021. Phone (541) 467-2291. For campsite reservations phone (877) 444-6777.

WILD AND SCENIC WHITE RIVER

[Fig. 12(6)] The wild and scenic White River draws its name from its summer color when the normally clear waters are clouded with suspended glacial silt from snow melt at Crater Rock at the summit of Mount Hood. The river runs for 46.5 miles between Forest Service 48 and OR 216 before spilling into the Deschutes River north of Maupin. Just east of the national forest's eastern boundary, the river drops into a gorge at Smock Prairie. Dedicated anglers hike into the gorge early in the season, before snow melt discolors the water, to catch rainbow trout. The trout are small, few more than a foot long, but the scenery and experience is large.

The best trout fishing takes place where the river flows through the flat ground between the prairie and a trio of waterfalls about three miles above the Deschutes confluence. There is some expert kayaking on this river, but the hazards are extreme.

Wildlife viewing, however, is considered excellent. There are good numbers of mule deer, coyotes, golden-mantled ground squirrels, and birds. Especially numerous are ravens (*Corvus corax*), black-billed magpies (*Pica pica*), whiskey jacks (*Perisoreus canadensis*), also called gray jays; Canada jays, camp robbers, and a variety of small songbirds. Watch the sky for raptors riding updrafts. It's not unusual to see golden eagles (*Aquila chrysaetos*), red-tailed hawks (*Buteo jamaicensis*) and prairie falcons (*Falco mexicanus*).

Directions: From OR 35 at Barlow Pass, turn east on Forest Service 48, which parallels the north bank of the river to Rock Creek Reservoir.

Activities: Trout fishing, whitewater boating, and wildlife watching.

Facilities: None.

Dates: Open year-round.

Fees: None.

Closest town: Maupin is at the eastern end of the White River near its confluence with the Deschutes River.

For information: Bureau of Land Management, Prineville District Office, 185 E. Fourth Street, Prineville, OR 97754. Tel: (541) 416-6700.

MCCUBBINS GULCH OFF ROAD VEHICLE AREA AND CAMPGROUND

[Fig. 12(7)] On OR 216, McCubbins Gulch and Bear Springs Campground are camping hubs for four-wheeler, dirt-bike and snowmobile enthusiasts using McCubbins Gulch ORV Area, the largest off-road vehicle (ORV) playground in the region. The off-road vehicle area opened in 1997, and includes miles of loop trails north of OR 216.

Directions: ORV area is two miles north of OR 216 on Forest Service 2110.

Activities: Camping, ORV use.

Facilities: 5 campsites at McCubbin Gulch and 21 sites at Bear Springs Campground, which also has well water, picnic tables, and grills.

Dates: Open year-round, although riding in the winter is strongly discouraged.

Fees: There are charges for campsites and ORV area use. Oregon Department of Motor Vehicle registration stickers are required for off-road vehicles.

Closest town: Pine Grove, about 7 miles east on OR 216.

For more information: Bear Springs Work Station, 73558 Hwy 216, Maupin, OR 97037. Phone (541) 328-6211.

CHINOOK SALMON
(Oncorhynchus tshawytscha)
The chinook is the largest of the five species of salmon that spawn in Oregon, occasionally exceeding 70 pounds.

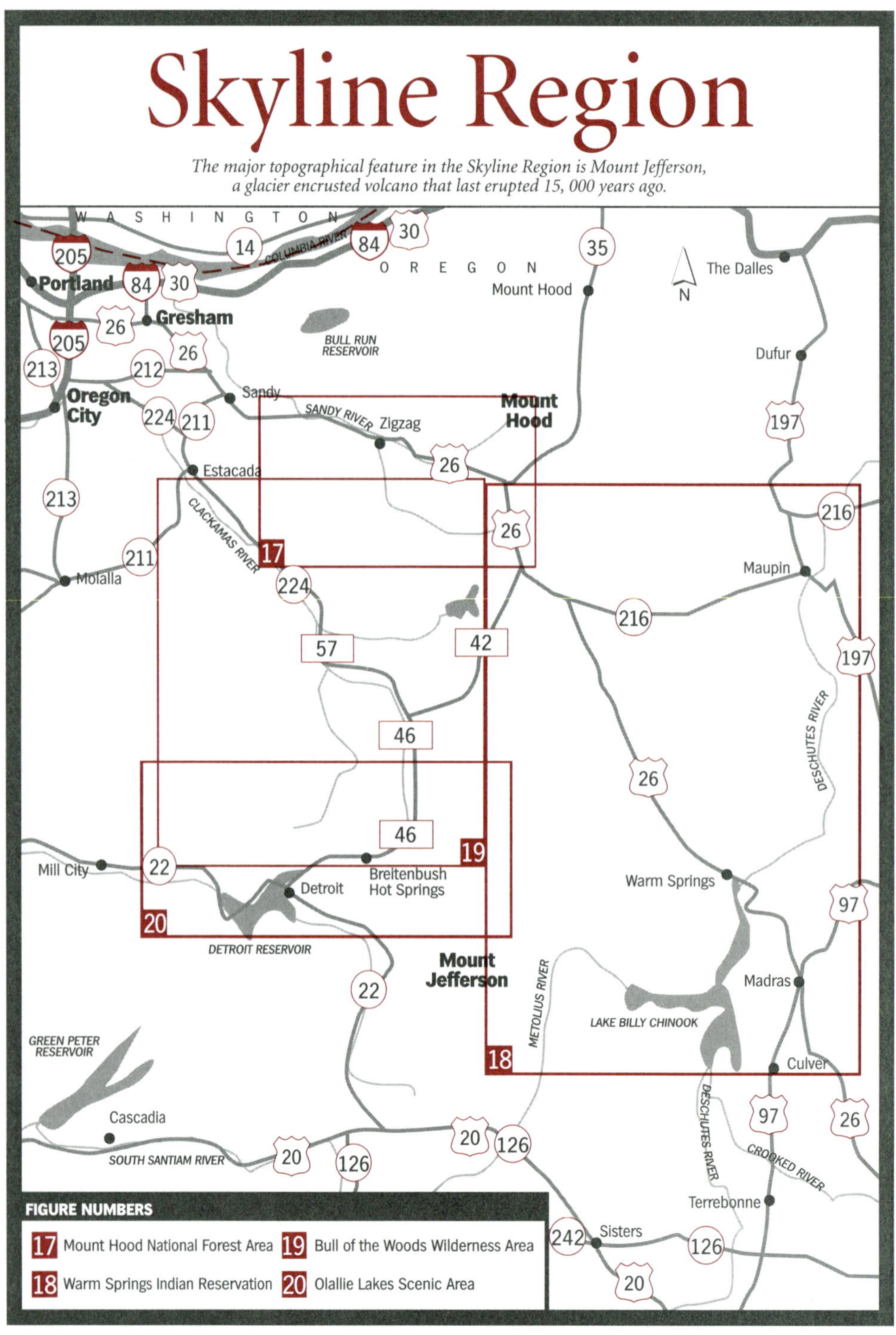

Skyline Region
The major topographical feature in the Skyline Region is Mount Jefferson, a glacier encrusted volcano that last erupted 15, 000 years ago.
WASHINGTON
OREGON
COLUMBIA RIVER
Portland
Gresham
Oregon City
Sandy
Estacada
Molalla
Mount Hood
The Dalles
Dufur
BULL RUN RESERVOIR
SANDY RIVER
Zigzag
Mount Hood
CLACKAMAS RIVER
Maupin
DESCHUTES RIVER
Mill City
Detroit
Breitenbush Hot Springs
DETROIT RESERVOIR
Mount Jefferson
METOLIUS RIVER
Warm Springs
Madras
LAKE BILLY CHINOOK
Culver
GREEN PETER RESERVOIR
Cascadia
SOUTH SANTIAM RIVER
DESCHUTES RIVER
CROOKED RIVER
Terrebonne
Sisters
FIGURE NUMBERS
17 Mount Hood National Forest Area
18 Warm Springs Indian Reservation
19 Bull of the Woods Wilderness Area
20 Olallie Lakes Scenic Area

Skyline Region

In many ways, the vast forests of the Cascade Mountains south of US 26 are more attractive to wilderness lovers than the tourist attractions and heavily used natural areas surrounding Mount Hood.

The first of these remote forest and lake regions, the Skyline Region, begins immediately south of US 26, where it wraps around Mount Hood. It is a 50-square-mile area of trout lakes, campgrounds, hiking trails, logging roads, wildlife, and scenic drives. Forest Service Road 42, which is appropriately named Skyline Road, runs north and south directly through the center of the region along the crest of the Cascade Range. The road provides paved arterial access to all of the recreational opportunities between US 26 on the north and OR 22 on the south.

This mountainous and heavily forested region includes Oregon's second-highest peak, Mount Jefferson, at an elevation of 10,497 feet. It also includes all or part of four

[*Above:* In the Skyline Region, beautiful waterfalls can be seen]

wilderness areas: Salmon-Huckleberry, Bull Of The Woods, Mount Jefferson, and Molalla River/Table Rock. Fishermen, campers, horseback riders, hikers, and wildlife enthusiasts enjoy Olallie Lakes Scenic Area, plus several federal and state designated scenic waterways and byways, long soaks in natural hot springs, stocked trout lakes, and hundreds of camping opportunities.

Compared with the recreation areas around Mount Hood, the Skyline Region has few commercial attractions. Skyline Road follows the backbone of the Cascade Range where elevations range between 4,000 and 5,000 feet. Snow from November though May makes it impassable to wheeled vehicles, but it remains a popular route for snowmobilers.

Almost limitless opportunities are found here to fish for trout and salmon, camp, hunt for grouse, bear, deer, and elk, hike, gather, photograph, boat, snowmobile, explore scenic back roads, bicycle, picnic, and gold pan. The region's volcanic legacy also means that energized days of mountain fun can be capped by long soaks in natural hot springs. The hot springs bubbling from prehistoric fissures in the earth's mantle are reminders of the area's violent origin in fire and ice. Most of the mountains here were either created by, or are, dormant or extinct volcanoes. Some of these peaks were spewing lava just a few thousand years ago, a blink of time by geological standards. More than two dozen volcanoes have been counted by geologists in the foothills south of US 26 above Portland.

The permanent snow fields that crown the highest peaks in glistening white ice year-round are actually the remnants of massive Ice-Age glaciers that scoured out the river valleys, shaved the foothills, and chiseled the stone faces of the most dominating peaks.

Oregon's largest city, Portland, is built mostly on gravels that washed downhill from these volcanic peaks and settled into a wide fault-block during the Pliocene Era that ended about 3 million years ago. Geologists have estimated, conservatively, that 75 extinct volcanoes are in the Portland area. The volcanoes that make up most of the West Slope of the Cascades through here are rounded because they were eroded into mounds, and buried beneath outpourings from the younger volcanoes that now sit along the crest of the Cascades.

The major topographical feature in the Skyline Region is Mount Jefferson, a glacier-encrusted volcano that last erupted 15,000 years ago. The peak bears a striking resemblance to the familiar pyramid shape of Mount Hood, about 55 miles north. The similarity ends with the shape, however. Mount Jefferson is the centerpiece of a roadless wilderness that may be visited only by hikers, and where summit climbs involve expedition-style treks. The peak does not support any of the commercial development that flanks Mount Hood.

Most of Skyline Region is within Mount Hood National Forest. Willamette National Forest encroaches into the south end of the region, and on the east side of this region is Warm Springs Indian Reservation.

Skyline Road follows the crest of the Cascades so closely that it parallels and sometimes crosses Pacific Crest National Scenic Trail 2000 (PCT 2000) on the trail's 2,638-mile long route along the backbone of the Sierra Nevadas and Cascades between Mexico and Canada. Designated as a national scenic trail in 1968, PCT 2000 enters the Cascade's of southern Oregon just east of I-5 at Pilot Rock, elevation 5,910 feet, and follows the top of the range north along the highest peaks. The trail crosses from Oregon into Washington just 104-feet above sea level on The Bridge Of The Gods which spans the Columbia River at Cascade Locks.

Most of Oregon's high Cascade trails incorporate parts of PCT 2000. The transcontinental path of PCT 2000 skirts the edge of the lake at Crater Lake National Park and winds through most designated wilderness areas in the Oregon Cascades. The segment that cuts through the mostly undulating terrain in the Skyline Region is one of the most moderate legs of the entire route.

For travelers heading into the Skyline Region, aptly named Skyline Road is the arterial route for passenger cars and RV traffic. It connects with US 26 east of Mount Hood, and immediately leads to a nearby cluster of camping and lake recreational areas. The scenic two-lane road resembles a black ribbon of asphalt trimmed with wildflowers and grasses that seems to be continually unrolling north-south between 60-foot-high walls of pole-straight conifers.

At the southern extreme, Skyline Road joins Forest Service Road 46, which is a national scenic byway. Forest Service 46 is an east-west route along the wild and scenic Clackamas River that connects the West Slope community of Estacada and the mountain town of Detroit.

This scenic byway also leads to the high lake wonderland of Olallie Lakes Scenic Area, one of the greatest concentrations of mountain lakes in the Oregon Cascades. South of Olallie lakes, Forest Service 46 crosses a spectacular low-elevation pass that forms the topographical divide between the Clackamas River drainage and the headwaters of the sprightly Breitenbush River.

The Breitenbush is a beautiful tumbling trout stream falling downhill for 15 miles in a series of riffles and pools. The river is nearly always within sight and earshot of the road. In its final mile the Breitenbush bulges into an arm of 3,000-acre Detroit Lake, one of the most popular and congested water-oriented recreation area in the high Cascades.

HORSEFLY
(Tābanidae)
Found near running water, these biting flies are the curse of human visitors to the mountains and forests.

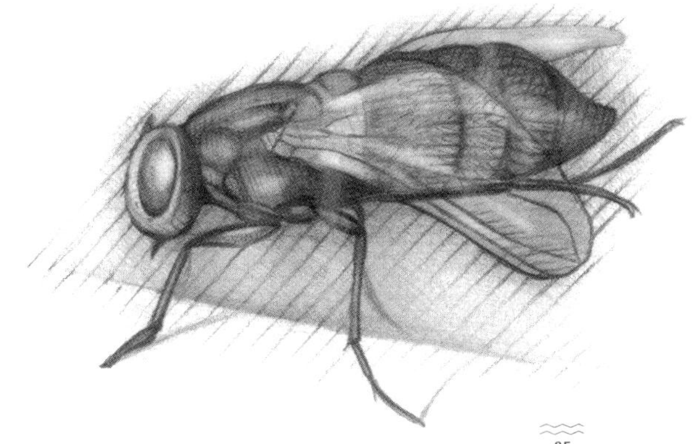

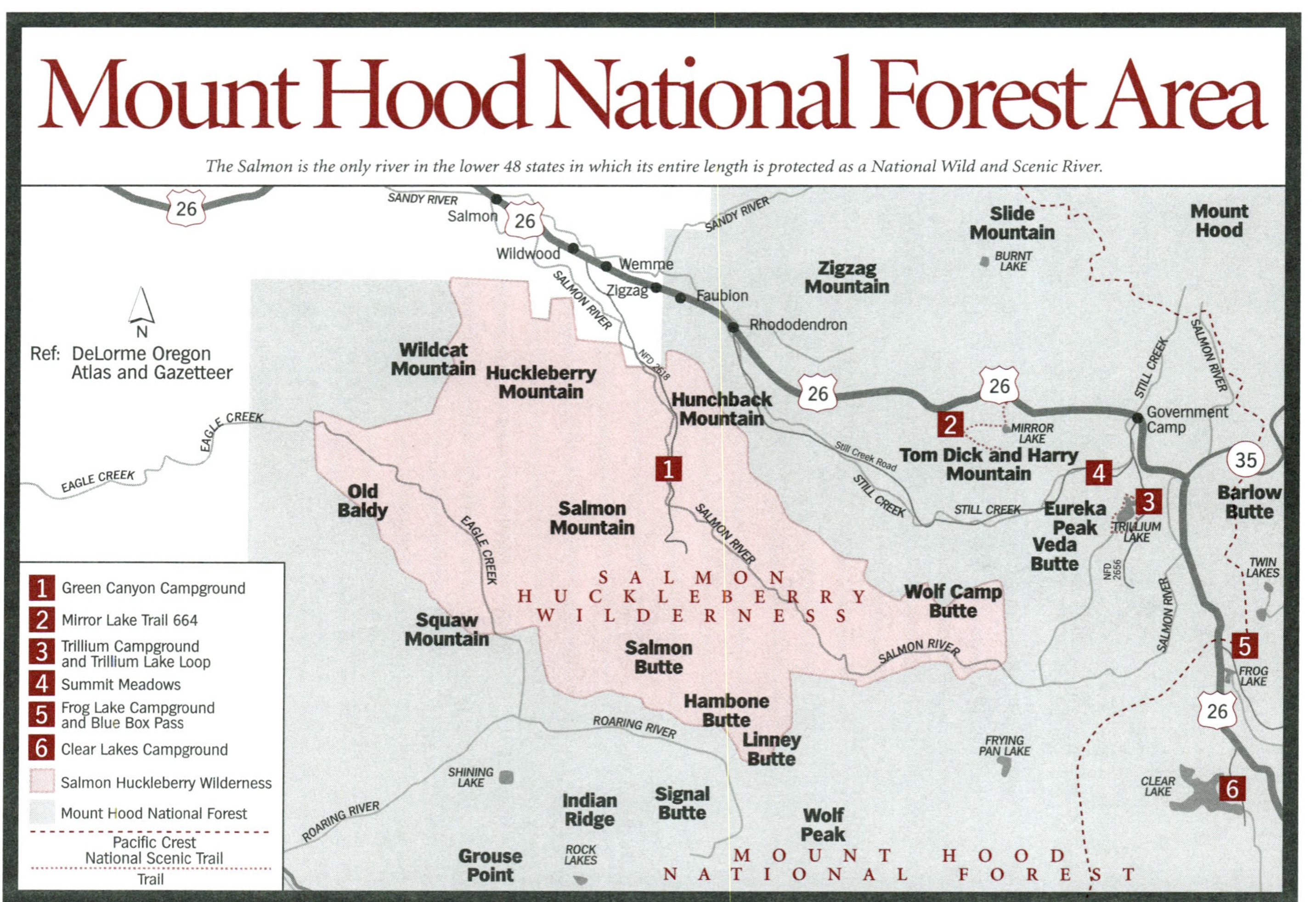

Mount Hood National Forest Area
The Salmon is the only river in the lower 48 states in which its entire length is protected as a National Wild and Scenic River.
N
Ref: DeLorme Oregon Atlas and Gazetteer
1 Green Canyon Campground
2 Mirror Lake Trail 664
3 Trillium Campground and Trillium Lake Loop
4 Summit Meadows
5 Frog Lake Campground and Blue Box Pass
6 Clear Lakes Campground
Salmon Huckleberry Wilderness
Mount Hood National Forest
Pacific Crest National Scenic Trail
Trail
26
Sandy River
Salmon
Wildwood
Wemme
Zigzag
Faubion
Rhododendron
Salmon River
NFD 2618
Zigzag Mountain
Slide Mountain
Burnt Lake
Mount Hood
Still Creek
Government Camp
35
Barlow Butte
Twin Lakes
Frog Lake
Clear Lake
Mirror Lake
Tom Dick and Harry Mountain
Still Creek Road
Eureka Peak
Veda Butte
Trillium Lake
NFD 2656
Wildcat Mountain
Huckleberry Mountain
Hunchback Mountain
Eagle Creek
Old Baldy
Salmon Mountain
Salmon Huckleberry Wilderness
Wolf Camp Butte
Squaw Mountain
Salmon Butte
Hambone Butte
Linney Butte
Roaring River
Shining Lake
Frying Pan Lake
Indian Ridge
Signal Butte
Wolf Peak
Grouse Point
Rock Lakes
Mount Hood National Forest

Mount Hood Area

SALMON-HUCKLEBERRY WILDERNESS

[Fig. 14, Fig. 17] Salmon-Huckleberry Wilderness of Mount Hood National Forest comes within 1 mile of US 26 at the Bureau of Land Management-operated Wildwood Recreation Area, 15 miles east of Sandy. The 44,600-acre wilderness area is formed around the 33.5-mile wild and scenic Salmon River. Its other main feature is a national recreation trail cut into the steep mountain side above the river that leads to a series of dramatic waterfalls in a gorge.

Geologic features include massive lava rocks that once formed plugs as they cooled inside erupting volcanoes, chimney-like pinnacles, and basalt cliffs. The mountains are steep, averaging angles between 60 and 90 degrees, and are thick with evergreens and spindly underbrush such as Oregon grape and huckleberry bushes. Steep side slopes are dominated by western hemlock and the high ridges support hardy stands of Pacific silver firs. Elevation and climate zones in the wilderness vary from lush temperate zones at 1,400 feet elevation to alpine regions at 4,800 feet.

The Salmon River National Recreation Trail (NRT) follows the Salmon River upstream from US 26 and penetrates into the wilderness. The trail follows the river course, but usually rides the hillsides several hundred feet above the water. The river and trail are on the same level only for the lower 2.5 miles. Green Canyon Campground is located 1.5 miles before the road end. It is a convenient base for enjoying the river and exploring trails. Inside the wilderness, Salmon River NRT links with trails to Eagle Creek, Wildcat, and Huckleberry mountains.

Because of the steepness of the terrain and dearth of natural lakes there are few opportunities for fishing, except for two lightly fished rivers. Fishermen sometimes find cutthroat and summer-run steelhead in the scenic salmon river (*see* Salmon River, page 98). The other possible fishing spot is Eagle Creek, which flows through the remote west side into the Clackamas River near Estacada. Forest Service Trail 501 follows the north bank of Eagle Creek for fly-fishermen hiking in for wild cutthroat. It's a two-mile hike, however, from the trail head just to reach Eagle Creek and few fishermen tackle the walk.

A national fish hatchery on lower Eagle Creek outside of the wilderness, stocks the creek with sea-run salmon and steelhead. Fishing for salmon and steelhead, however, is not allowed in the wilderness area. The seasons and requirements for trout fishing vary annually and fishermen need to check current Oregon fishing regulations before wetting a line.

Oregon has one of the largest state and federal fish hatchery programs in the United States. Steelhead and salmon are anadromous fish that are hatched in freshwater, migrate to the ocean to mature, then return to spawn in freshwater. Millions of salmon and steelhead are stocked in streams and rivers that drain to saltwater in order to supplement native fish for Indian and nontribal commercial fishing, as well as sport-fishing. Because most runs of steelhead and salmon have been severely overharvested for decades, many native runs are now extinct or endangered and fishermen rely exclusively on hatcheries to provide fish to catch. In 1999 dozens of Oregon's wild salmon and steelhead runs were declared endangered or threatened, and are now completely protected from harvest.

The state also raises and stocks many freshwater lakes and rivers with trout and landlocked salmon for sport fishermen.

Directions: The easiest access to the north side of the Salmon-Huckleberry Wilderness is from US 26 at Wildwood near Welches. Turn south onto Forest Service 2618 Salmon River Road and follow it through a narrow corridor that penetrates 5 miles inside the wilderness area.

From the west, the entry route begins two miles southeast of Estacada on OR 224. From OR 224, follow Abbot Road past Hesperin Camp to Forest Service Road 4614 which climbs to the wilderness boundary near Githens Mountain. Forest Service Trail 504 leads into the wilderness from a trailhead on Forest Service Road 4614.

Activities: Camping, hiking, trout and steelhead fishing, and hunting.

Facilities: Maintained trails.

Dates: Open year-round.

Fees: None.

Closest town: Sandy is about 15 miles west on US 26.

For more information: Mount Hood Information Center, 65000 E. Highway 26, Welches, OR 97067. Phone (503) 622-4822, toll free outside Portland area (888) 622-4822.

GREEN CANYON CAMPGROUND

[Fig. 17(1)] This popular campground is on the wild and scenic Salmon River, and is surrounded on three sides by the Salmon-Huckleberry Wilderness. It can be reached by paved road, and is a good base for exploring the wilderness, fishing the river, or hiking on the Salmon River National Recreation Trail.

Directions: From US 26 at Wildwood turn south on Forest Service 2618 Salmon River Road and follow it 4.5 miles through the river corridor, which penetrates into the Salmon-Huckleberry Wilderness Area.

Activities: Camping, hiking, and river fishing.

Facilities: 15 sites for tents and RVs to 22 feet long, well water, toilets, barrier-free access, picnic tables.

Dates: Open May through Oct. The campground is heavily used, and often filled to capacity on summer weekends.

Fees: There are charges for campsites.

WILD & SCENIC SALMON RIVER

[Fig. 17] Designated a wild and scenic river, the Salmon River is paralleled by a national scenic trail that leads into the Salmon-Huckleberry Wilderness to a cool misty gorge stair-stepped with thundering waterfalls.

The Salmon is the only river in the lower 48 states in which its entire length, 33.5

miles, is protected as a national wild and scenic river.

The river begins on Mount Hood in the Palmer Snow Field above Timberline Lodge. It drains into the Sandy River near US 26 three miles west of Wildwood at Brightwood. Between Wildwood and Green Canyon Campground it is paralleled by Forest Service Road 2618.

From the end of the road, hikers can continue into the wilderness on Salmon River National Recreation Trail 742, which follows the river for another 11 miles upstream.

This narrow, rocky and shallow river is not considered suitable for boating, but that doesn't stop a few hard-core kayakers from banging through the rocks between Green Canyon Campground and US 26.

The river flows evenly through deep woods, sliding from pool to pool. Summer-run steelhead move into the river in June, and remain well into the cold months. On hot afternoons silt from the glacial headwaters may discolor the typically gin-clear water.

In late summer and fall, coho and chinook salmon are in the river to spawn, and are protected from fishing. From the falls upstream die-hard fishermen who are willing to work for their fun may tangle with beautifully colored wild cutthroat trout. From Forest Service 2618 bridge upstream, though, fishermen are restricted to using fly-fishing tackle.

Hikers are likely to spot large red-crowned pileated woodpeckers and the tiny, curved-beak brown creepers (*Certhia familiaris*) where the trails pass through sections of old-growth trees. Birds commonly seen along the river are American dippers (*Cinclus mexicanus*) which are also called water ouzels for their unique habit of walking underwater; belted kingfishers (*Ceryle alcyon*); and nesting hooded mergansers (*Lophodytes cucullatus*).

Directions: US 26 about 3 miles east of Wildwood to a south turn onto Forest Service Road 2618, which is also called Salmon River Road.

Activities: Camping, fishing, hiking.

Facilities: None.

Dates: Open year-round, usually snow-free from May through Nov.

Fees: None.

MIRROR LAKE TRAIL 664

[Fig. 17(2)] Because of the spectacular reflection of Mount Hood on the 8-acre surface of Mirror Lake, this is one of the most popular hiking routes on Mount Hood. A round trip to the lake takes about three hours. In late August, hikers stain fingers purple picking the wild huckleberries that grow in dense patches along the trail. Mirror Lake can be fished for small rainbow and brook trout.

From Mirror Lake the trail continues to the top of Tom, Dick and Harry Mountain.

Directions: Take US 26 to 1 mile west of Government Camp, where there is a large parking area on a sweeping curve at Yocum Falls. The trailhead is on the far side of the Camp Creek bridge.

Dates: Usually snow-free June through Oct.

Fees: None.

Trail: 4 miles round trip.
Elevation: The trailhead is at 3,500 feet gaining 650 feet at the lake.
Degree of difficulty: Easy to moderate.
Surface: Natural forest duff.

TRILLIUM LAKE

[Fig. 17] Trillium Lake is one of the most popular picnic, camping, fishing, hiking, and photography stops in an area that overflows with such opportunities. Forest Service Road 2656, the entry road, intersects US 26 just east of Government Camp.

The lake is a 57-acre impoundment of Mud Creek with a dazzling view of Mount Hood, a major forest service campground on the east bank, stocked trout, a wheelchair accessible fishing pier, and a loop trail that's as popular with cross-country winter skiers as summer hikers.

The lake is shallow, rippled with shoals and is a late summer favorite with fly-fishermen attracted by stocked rainbow and brook trout 9- to 12- inches long. Boats with motors of any kind are not allowed. There's a ramp for rowboats and canoes, and a fishing pier at the campground. This is a good place for kids to fish; plenty of access and willing trout.

If huckleberry picking is on the menu, take Forest Service Road 2613 from the west side of the lake and drive southwest to Sherar Burn. The road is rough, and not recommended for passenger cars or trailers, but the picking is great from mid-August to mid-September. Look for concentrations of mountain huckleberries (*Vaccinium ovatum* and *Vaccinium parvifolium*) along the road between Eureka and Devils peaks. Huckleberries are also plentiful along Veda Lake Trail 637; Dry Lake Trail 672; Fir Creek Trail 674, and Hunchback Trail 793.

Directions: From US 26 about 1 mile east of Government Camp turn south onto paved Forest Service 2656 for 1 mile to the lake.

Activities: Fishing for stocked trout, paddling or rowboating, camping, huckleberry picking in season, hiking, picnicking, winter cross-country skiing.

Facilities: Campground, boat ramp, fishing pier, picnic areas, and hiking trails.

Dates: Open Memorial Day through Labor Day.

Fees: There is a charge for day-use picnics, parking at the dam, and overnight camping.

Closest town: Sandy is about 30 miles west on US 26.

For more information: Mount Hood Information Center, 65000 E. Highway 26, Welches, OR 97067. Phone (503) 622-4822, toll free outside Portland area (888) 622-4822.

TRILLIUM CAMPGROUND

[Fig. 17(3)] This is a large, popular barrier-free campground on Trillium Lake near Mount Hood at an elevation of 3,600 feet that also provides day use and picnic facilities. The lake is stocked with rainbow and brook trout.

Directions: Follow US 26 east of Government Camp to the junction of Forest Service

Road 2656, then south on Forest Service 2656 1 mile. The campground is on the east side of Trillium Lake.

Activities: Camping, hiking, fishing, picnicking, and berry picking.

Facilities: 57 tent and RV sites to 40 feet long, plus an overflow camping area. Well water, toilets, tables, fire pits, fishing pier, and boat ramp.

Dates: The campground is open Memorial Day through Labor Day.

Fees: There are charges for camping and parking passes, required for day-use parking. Reservations are recommended for campsites, especially on weekends.

For more information: For campsite reservations phone (800) 280-2267.

TRILLIUM LAKE LOOP

[Fig. 17(3)] Trillium Lake Loop Trail 761 encircles the lake on a maintained route that includes elevated boardwalks across alpine wetlands. Wildlife is commonly spotted and in late summer there is often clusters of wildflowers including the shade-loving namesake western trillium (*Trillium ovatum*).

The trail is open for hiking from mid-May through October. The road system loop is heavily used by cross-country skiers on winter weekends.

Directions: Drive 2 miles east of Government Camp on US 26, then south for 2 miles on Forest Service 2656 past Trillium Lake Campground to the day-use area. During the winter Forest Service 2650 is snow-closed and becomes part of a 41-mile network of cross-country ski trails.

Fees: There is a charge for day-use parking (summer) and Sno Park parking (winter).

Trail: 2 miles, loop.

Elevation: 3,600 feet with minor variances.

Degree of difficulty: Easy.

Surface: Dirt.

SUMMIT MEADOWS

[Fig. 17(4)] Bogs in Summit Meadows on the approach to Trillium Lake are ablaze with wildflowers from June through August. Varieties include gentians (*Gentiana simplex* and *Gentiana calycosa*), lupines, and wild orchids. An especially colorful bloom takes place in the wet area of the meadows where slender bog orchids (*Habenaria saccata*) thrive. These delicate green flowers sometimes appear to carpet the bogs with blooms.

Still Creek Road continues west from the meadows as a primitive road looping away from US 26 through a narrow mountain canyon before merging with US 26 between Zigzag and Rhododendron. Forest Service 2612 closely follows the transparent waters of Still Creek, which offer fair fishing for wild cutthroat trout from late June until snow closes the road in late October.

Directions: From US 26 take the Trillium Lake Road Forest Service 2656 cut-off south. Just before reaching Trillium Lake turn west onto Still Creek Road Forest Service 2612 for a short distance to the meadow and wildflower area.

Activities: Wildflower and bog scenery, photography.

Facilities: None.

Dates: Open year-round, but the road is closed by snow during the winter.

Fees: None.

Closest town: Government Camp is 2 miles west of Trillium Lake Road.

For more information: Mount Hood Information Center, 65000 E. Highway 26, Welches, OR 97067. Phone (503) 622-4822, toll free outside Portland area (888) 622-4822.

FROG LAKE AND CAMPGROUND, BLUE BOX PASS

[Fig. 17(5)] Several remarkable mountain attractions are concentrated near a slight divide on US 26 about 5.75 miles southeast of the Trillium Lake cut-off. Within 1 mile the highway crosses the Pacific Crest Trail 2000, goes through two mountain passes, then slides around a small shallow lake with a big campground and an even bigger morning reflection of Mount Hood.

Hikers on Pacific Crest National Scenic Trail (PCT) 2000 cross the highway at Wapinitia Pass, elevation 3,949 feet. The crossing also marks an east turn onto Forest Service 2610 to Frog Lake, where PCT 2000 hikers may head south to a campground and recreation complex at Timothy Lake, or north to Twin Lakes where there is good brook trout fishing.

Blue Box Pass, elevation 4,024 feet, is just south of Frog Lake on US 26. The unusual name originated with a 10-foot high wooden box, painted blue, that in the early 1900s contained a telephone that was a lifeline connected to the nearby Clackamas Lake Ranger Station.

Forest workers and other mountain travelers on the then-primitive road used the phone to signal the ranger station to send a horse-drawn sleigh to the pass. Passengers were shuttled on a 9-mile-long sleigh ride through deep snow and evergreens to the ranger station, which still stands near Timothy Lake.

The old trail is still followed by Forest Service 2660, a rough two-track, for three miles to Clear Lake. The former sleigh route is an easy hike, or can be driven by high-clearance vehicles. It is not advised for passenger cars.

From US 26, Forest Service 2610 goes to Frog Lake in a corridor cut through a thick wall of conifers that screens the Frog Lake Campground from the traffic buzz on the highway. The lake is small at 11 acres, but is famous for amazingly crisp sunrise reflections of Mount Hood, and as a great place to camp and fish with children. The lake is shallow, heavily stocked by the state with pan-size rainbow trout, and just as heavily fished. Rowboats are allowed but outboard motors are prohibited.

From the 3,800 foot elevation campground, unimproved Forest Service Road 220 continues 1.5 miles to Frog Lake Butte. Beginning in mid-August the shoulders of this rough road are overhung with delicious purple huckleberries. The dirt road is not recommended for low-slung passenger vehicles. The road makes a good hiking path, and it's an easy 0.5 mile walk to the huckleberry area.

Directions: 9 miles east of Government Camp on US 26 to Forest Service 2610. Turn east and follow signs to Frog Lake, less than 1 mile from the highway.

Activities: Camping, rowboating, trout fishing, berry picking, and hiking.

Facilities: Frog Lake Campground, barrier-free, 33 tent and RV sites to 22 feet long, well water, tables, fire pits, and vault toilets.

Dates: Open when snow-free, usually from Memorial Day to Labor Day.

Fees: There are charges for campsites, and trail park passes.

Closest town: Government Camp is about 9 miles west on US 26.

For more information: Contact Hood River Ranger District, 6780 Highway 35 S., Mount Hood-Parkdale, OR 97041. Phone (541) 352-6002. For camping reservations phone (800) 280-2267.

CLEAR LAKE AND CAMPGROUND

[Fig. 17(6)] Forest Service Road 2630 plunges south from US 26 into thick fir and hemlock forests to emerge in less than 1 mile at 475-acre Clear Lake, one of the largest lakes in the region.

This impounded horseshoe-shaped lake is a favorite summer destination for trout fishermen trolling or baitfishing for stocked rainbow and brook trout. There are no resort facilities or rental boats. Trailered boats may be launched at a ramp at the east shore campground.

A lake speed limit of 10 mph keeps jet skiers and speed boats at bay.

It's a shallow lake, averaging 15.6 feet. By midsummer, the lake level can be drawn down to meet irrigation demands, revealing long stretches of stump-studded mud bottom. The aesthetics suffer.

This is an excellent crayfish (*Pacifastacus trowbridgii*) lake. Bring a crayfish trap, butter to melt, and in one night's set you can have the makings for a freshwater shellfish

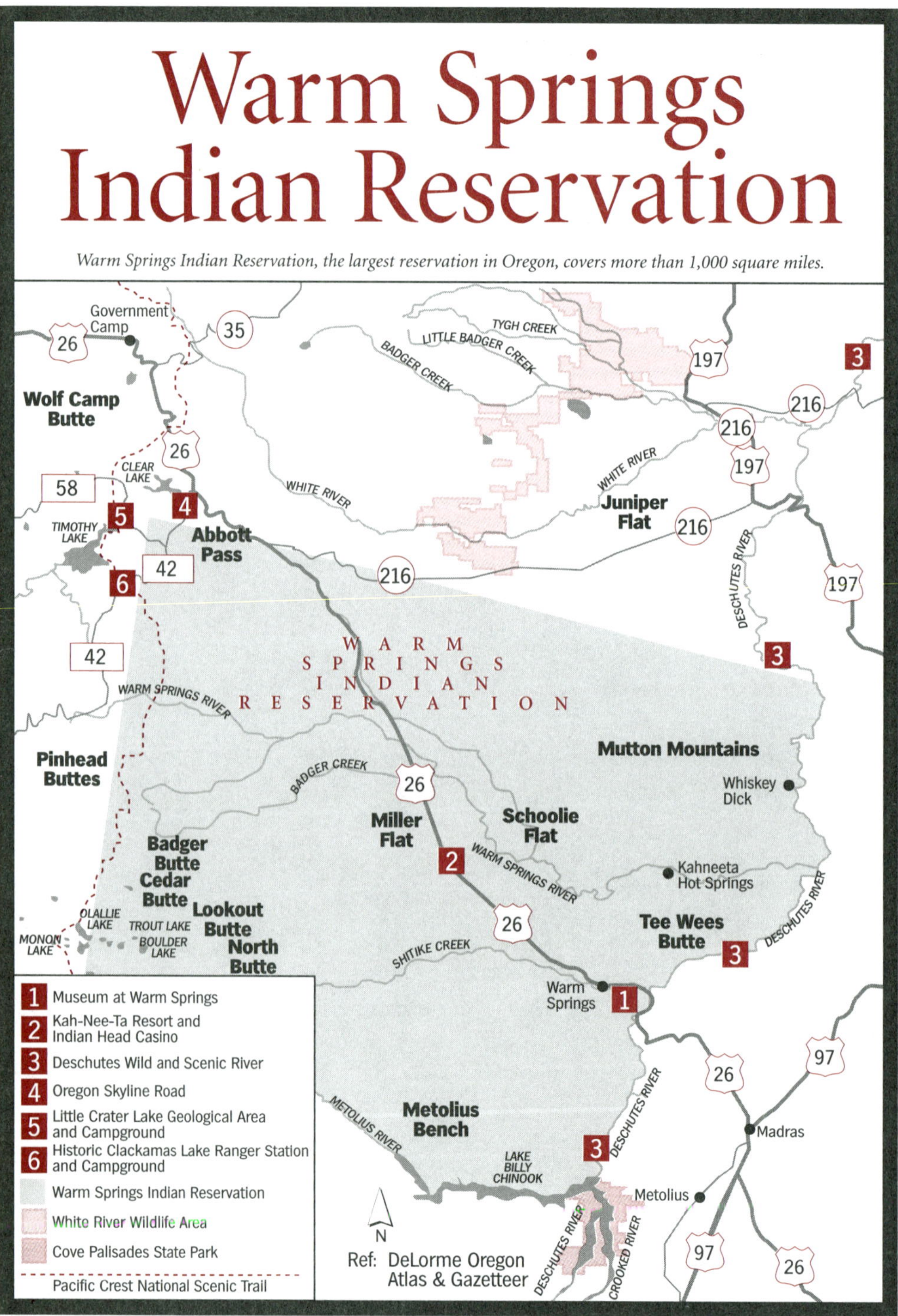
Warm Springs Indian Reservation
Warm Springs Indian Reservation, the largest reservation in Oregon, covers more than 1,000 square miles.
Government Camp
26
35
TYGH CREEK
LITTLE BADGER CREEK
BADGER CREEK
197
3
Wolf Camp Butte
216
26
CLEAR LAKE
58
WHITE RIVER
197
WHITE RIVER
Juniper Flat
TIMOTHY LAKE
5
4
Abbott Pass
216
42
216
DESCHUTES RIVER
6
197
42
WARM SPRINGS INDIAN RESERVATION
3
WARM SPRINGS RIVER
Mutton Mountains
Pinhead Buttes
BADGER CREEK
26
Whiskey Dick
Miller Flat
Schoolie Flat
Badger Butte
2
WARM SPRINGS RIVER
Kahneeta Hot Springs
Cedar Butte
OLALLIE LAKE
TROUT LAKE
Lookout Butte
26
Tee Wees Butte
DESCHUTES RIVER
MONON LAKE
BOULDER LAKE
North Butte
3
SHITIKE CREEK
Warm Springs
1
26
97
METOLIUS RIVER
Metolius Bench
DESCHUTES RIVER
Madras
3
LAKE BILLY CHINOOK
Metolius
N
DESCHUTES RIVER
CROOKED RIVER
97
26
Ref: DeLorme Oregon Atlas & Gazetteer
1 Museum at Warm Springs
2 Kah-Nee-Ta Resort and Indian Head Casino
3 Deschutes Wild and Scenic River
4 Oregon Skyline Road
5 Little Crater Lake Geological Area and Campground
6 Historic Clackamas Lake Ranger Station and Campground
Warm Springs Indian Reservation
White River Wildlife Area
Cove Palisades State Park
Pacific Crest National Scenic Trail

feast. The meat of crayfish that inhabit the clear, cool waters of lakes above 2,000 feet elevation is generally free of the "muddy" taste common to crayfish in muddy low-lying lakes.

Directions: Follow US 26 to Forest Service Road 2630, 11 miles east of Government Camp. The paved turnoff from the highway is well-marked, and continues about 1 mile to the lake and campground. The campground can also be reached from Skyline Road Forest Service 42, but requires an 8 mile drive on gravel road around the lake.

Activities: Camping, swimming, trout fishing, crayfish trapping, rowboating, and hiking.

Facilities: A barrier-free campground with 28 tent and RV sites to 32 feet long, well water, boat ramp, toilets, tables, and fire pits.

Dates: The campground opens when the snow melts, usually by the first week in June, through Sept.

Fees: A camping fee is charged. Free access to the boat ramp.

Closest town: Government Camp.

For more information: Mount Hood Information Center, 65000 E. Highway 26, Welches, OR 97067. Phone (503) 622-4822, toll free outside Portland area (888) 622-4822. For campsite reservations phone (800) 280-2267.

East Slope Region

WARM SPRINGS INDIAN RESERVATION

[Fig. 18] The largest Indian reservation in Oregon makes up much of the Skyline Region east of Mount Hood.

US 26/Mount Hood Highway runs through the heart of the vast Confederated Tribes of the Warm Springs Reservation west of Madras. Covering more than 1,000 square miles, the reservation includes most of the upper slope from the summit of the Cascade Mountains and snowcapped Mount Jefferson at 10,497 feet, east to the Deschutes River's 1,000-foot elevation marker. The Metolius River and Lake Billy Chinook form the southern boundary. The reservation was created in 1855, four years before Oregon statehood.

The tribal lands are a microcosm of the effect the Cascade Mountains rain shadow has on the East Slope Region climate extremes. The west side of the reservation receives about 120 inches of rain and 200 inches of snow annually, compared with the east side, which gets about 10 inches of rain and 15 inches of snow.

Indigenous tribes, which are united under the Warm Springs Confederation, include Wasco, northern Paiutes, and Walla Wallas, which later became the Warm Springs Tribe. Most of the 3,400 members live in the community of Warm Springs, the only town on the reservation.

The reservation economy is based on natural resources and tourism, including hydropower, forest products, ranching, casino gambling, and resort recreation. About half of the reservation is forested with Ponderosa pine and Douglas fir. The balance is open range land. Nontribal members are excluded from reservation lands, except for the resort facilities and permit-access recreation sites.

Kah-Nee-Ta Resort leads the confederation's efforts to attract tourism, and includes a cultural museum, hot springs spa, lodge, and recreation facilities. A program is being developed to offer nontribal members guided trout and steelhead fishing, and recreational trips on the reservation.

The three tribes of the confederation descended from different bands, which historically lived and hunted on the Columbia Plateau and fished the Columbia River at places like Celilo Falls and other salmon spawning streams. (Celilo Falls was inundated behind The Dalles Dam in 1957.)

Each tribe's history and heritage is unique. The Wasco bands on the Columbia River were the easternmost group of Chinookan-speaking Indians. The Warm Springs bands lived along the Columbia's tributaries, spoke Sahaptin, and were their closest upriver neighbors. The Paiutes were nomadic hunters and gatherers, and traditional rivals of the Columbia tribes. They lived in southeastern Oregon and spoke a Shoshonean dialect.

Wasco were principally fishermen and traders who remained at permanent village sites along the Columbia River throughout the year. The Warm Springs bands moved between winter and summer villages, and depended more on game, roots, and berries. Salmon was also an important staple for the Warm Springs bands. Both tribes built scaffolding over falls in the river and used long-handled dip nets to harvest salmon and other migrating fish.

The Paiutes migrated frequently and widely for the plants and game. Their language was foreign to other tribes, and trade with other Indians was infrequent. In fact, before 1879, when 38 Paiutes were moved onto the Warm Springs Reservation, most contact between the Paiutes and the Wasco or Warm Springs Indians occurred during skirmishes.

The three-tribe confederacy was formed in 1937.

Directions: The reservation is on US 26 between US 97 and Government Camp on Mount Hood about 119 miles east of Portland.

Activities: Gaming, golf, tennis, horseback riding, guided fishing, spa recreation, swimming, mountain biking, RV camping, salmon bakes.

Facilities: Kah-Nee-Ta Resort, Indian Head Casino, The Museum at Warm Springs, restaurant, campground, hot springs. Gasoline is not available on the reservation.

Dates: Open year-round.

Fees: There are charges for all services.

Closest town: Madras is 12 miles east on US 26 at US 97.

For more information: Confederated Tribes of the Warm Springs, PO Box C, 1233 Veterans Street, Warm Springs, OR 97761. Phone (541) 553-1161.

MUSEUM AT WARM SPRINGS

[Fig. 18(1)] The 27,000-square-foot, $7.6 million museum houses the single largest collection of artifacts from one tribe under one roof, according to the Smithsonian Institute in Washington D.C. The museum is along Highway 26, 1 mile south of Warm Springs. The contemporary structure resembles a traditional encampment along Shitike Creek in Deschutes River Canyon.

Visitors experience storytelling, craft making, and dancing. There are art displays and interactive exhibits. The museum's permanent collections include artifacts, historic photographs, narratives, graphics, murals, and rare documents. Traditional dwellings, a tule mat lodge, wickiup, and plankhouse have been meticulously constructed to show life as it was long ago.

Dates: Open daily.

Fees: There is an admission charge.

For more information: The Museum at Warm Springs, 2189 Highway 26, Warm Springs OR 97761. Phone (541) 553-3331.

KAH-NEE-TA RESORT AND INDIAN HEAD CASINO

[Fig. 18(2)] Kah-Nee-Ta Resort is designed as an upscale retreat to the past. Accommodations range from the village RV park, cottages, hot springs swimming pool, camping, and teepees to the modernistic lodge. Visitors may experience a traditional-style Indian salmon bake and dancing and singing. The tribe's newest commercial venture is Indian Head Casino, which features 340 slot machines, blackjack, and poker.

Directions: The resort is 11 miles north of Warm Springs on US 26.

Facilities: Tennis courts, swimming pools, golf course, 2 restaurants, mineral springs, exercise rooms, riding stables, whitewater rafting service, bike paths, fishing area, 129-room lodge, 25 cottages, 60 RV sites with hookups, 21 teepees, and 30 tent sites.

Dates: Open year-round.

Fees: There are charges for most services.

For more information: Kah-Nee-Ta Resort, PO Box K, Warm Springs OR 97761. Phone (541) 553-1112 or 1-800-554-4786.

WHITE RIVER WILDLIFE AREA

[Fig. 18] Northwest of Maupin in the rolling brown hills of the East Slope (for more on the East Slope of the Cascades, *see* the Natural History of the Oregon Cascades, page 1) along Jordan Creek is the Oregon Department of Fish and Wildlife's White River Wildlife Area, and one of the best places in the state to see wild turkeys, deer, and elk.

In December and February, the wildlife area is a wintering area for mule deer that migrate to lower elevations from the high Cascades.

A mix of fir, pine, and Oregon oak forests offer diverse habitats for a variety of wildlife. The wild turkey population is the highest in northern Oregon, according to ODFW. Western gray squirrels (*Sciurus griseus*) are abundant.

Spring and summer are the best times to see uncommon Lewis' woodpeckers (*Melanerpes lewis*). These birds are about 11 inches long and have distinctive pink breasts and red faces.

The wildlife area is a popular hunting spot during fall big game seasons. After hunting seasons, ODFW maintains feeding stations to supplement available natural foods. The stations are good places to see and photograph deer and elk during the winter.

Directions: From The Dalles: Go 31 miles south on Hwy. 197. Turn west onto Wamic Market Road at the blinking light at Tygh Valley and follow the signs to Wamic. As you enter Wamic, continue straight on Dodson Road through three 90-degree turns. Turn left on the gravel road (0.25 mile past last curve) and continue approximately 1.5 miles to cattleguard and area signs. The headquarters is located just beyond the cattleguard.

Activities: Wildlife viewing, spring turkey and fall big game hunting.

Facilities: Winter feeding stations for deer and elk, staffed ODFW office.

Dates: Open year-round, best big game viewing is from Dec. to Feb. Vehicle travel is restricted in winter.

Fees: None.

Closest town: The Dalles.

For more information: ODFW White River Wildlife Area Manager, 78430 Dodson Road, Tygh Valley, OR 97063. Phone (541) 544-2126.

LAKE BILLY CHINOOK

[Fig. 18] Located in a sun-splashed high desert canyon 8 miles southwest of Madras, population 5,000, sprawling Lake Billy Chinook is a watery magnet for summer campers, water skiers, house boaters, fishermen, and rockhounds prospecting for thundereggs (*see* Thundereggs, page 244). The reservoir covers 6 square miles behind Round Butte Dam, which was built at the confluence of Deschutes, Crooked, and Metolius rivers to produce hydroelectricity for Portland General Electric. Those impounded rivers are three of the largest drainages in the East Slope Region, and now form the arms of the reservoir.

The Metolius River arm makes up the largest part of the reservoir. It borders the Confederated Tribes of Warm Springs Reservation. The tribe manages recreation in that arm, and require permits for boating access.

The arms of the Deschutes and Crooked rivers are controlled by various state and federal agencies. Cove Palisades State Park, Oregon's second largest state park, has extensive facilities here.

The biggest attractions are 300 days of sunshine, deluxe facilities at the state park, house boat rentals, water skiing, and fishing for a thriving kokanee salmon population. Anglers also try for rainbow and brown trout, and smallmouth bass may be caught in the Metolius River arm.

Between Madras and Lake Billy Chinook are 155,000 acres of public land and wildlife habitat set aside as Crooked River National Grassland. It's one of six federally designated grasslands in the country. The undeveloped semiarid region is believed to support 375 species of wildlife, including Oregon's big game animals: mule deer, elk, pronghorn antelope, and mountain lions. Raptors and songbirds are plentiful.

Directions: From Madras on US 97, go south to the Culver turnoff, then west to Culver State Park. The road is paved and the route well-marked. From the southwest, travelers follow Forest Service 63 from Sisters and Forest Service 11 from Camp Sherman (*see* Sisters, page 189) to smaller campgrounds on the south shore.

Activities: Camping, boating, swimming, fishing, and rockhounding.

Facilities: Cove Palisades State Park, Three River Recreation Area and houseboat rentals, Round Butte Observatory and picnic area at the dam, boat ramps at Perry South Campground, and at 4 locations in Crooked and Deschutes arms.

Dates: Open year-round, but fishing seasons and access may vary. The observatory grounds are open during daylight hours from May 25 to Sept. 30.

Fees: There are fees for tribal permits, and state park services.

Closest town: Madras is about 15 miles east.

For more information: Madras-Jefferson County Chamber of Commerce, 274 SW 4th Street, Madras, OR 97741 Phone (541) 475-2350. Confederated Tribes Of Warm Springs, PO Box C, Warm Springs, OR 97761. Phone (541) 553-1161. Oregon Parks and Recreation Department, 525 Trade Street SE, Salem, OR 97310. Phone (800) 452-5687. Palisades Cove State Park (541) 546-3412.

COVE PALISADES STATE PARK

[Fig. 18] This is the second-largest state park in Oregon and an exceptionally popular summer oasis area on the east shore of Billy Chinook Reservoir. The park includes two state campgrounds, at Deschutes and Crooked rivers. Reservations are recommended for campsites.

Directions: See Lake Billy Chinook, page 108.

Activities: Camping, fishing, swimming, hiking, and boating.

Facilities: Deschutes Campground has 87 sites with RV hookups and 94 tent sites. Crooked River has 91 sites with electricity. At Cove Palisades State Park there are 3 log cabins, marina, general store, wheelchair-accessible pier, picnic and swimming areas, trails for biking and hiking, 2 boat ramps, showers, flush toilets, picnic tables, grills, and dump station.

Dates: Open May through Sept.

Fees: There are charges for campsites and day use of swimming and picnic areas.

For more information: Oregon Parks and Recreation Department, Reservations NW, PO Box 500, Portland, OR 97207-0500. Phone (800) 452-5687. Palisades Cove State Park (541) 546-3412. Campsite reservations: (800) 452-5687.

Skyline Road

[Fig. 18] Hemmed into a woodland corridor, Skyline Road Forest Service 42 is a delight to drive. It flows south off Mount Hood beneath a canopy of towering conifers along the crest of the Cascades from US 26 to the mossy quiet in the trout-rich headwaters of Clackamas River, a wild and scenic designate. This high road route is encased in a forest that often presses to the roadsides. In summer, the shoulder is sprinkled with the pink blossoms of wild rhododendron, red paintbrush, blue lupines, and the woolly white heads of white pearly everlastings *(Anaphalis margaritacea)*.

Road berms are pocked with the tracks of black-tailed deer and, occasionally, elk, but catching a glimpse of their reddish-brown forms in the dense timber is difficult. Cougars, black bears, coyotes (*Canis latrans*), and bobcats (*Felis rufus*) also live here but are man-shy and hardly ever seen.

Travelers are likely, though, to spot golden-mantled ground squirrels (*Spermophilus laterealis*) and the electric quick little Townsend's chipmunk (*Eutamias townsendi*) darting across the roadway.

Several species of birds that are common on the Skyline Road are rarely seen outside of mountain areas. The most noticeable is the raucous and iridescent black raven (*Corvus corax*). Ravens are remarkable birds, with 27-inch-long bodies, and wings that can span a yardstick. Their extensive vocabulary ranges from a series of quick pops, to harsh croaks, and musical tinklings. Ravens are famous for spinning, diving, and looping aerobatics, and figure prominently in local Indian lore.

Even more common than ravens are gray jays (*Perisoreus canadensis*), gregarious, black-masked beggars that campers commonly identify as whiskey jacks. Nearly every campground in the Oregon Cascades has a resident flock of gray jays, which are both delight and pest. These fearless, robin-size birds will swipe food from a sizzling skillet, snatch raisins from a stranger's open palms, and hunt through clothes for hidden nuts. They also make it impossible to leave food unattended, and can be maddening during picnics.

Gray jays are sometimes confused with the larger, and far less gregarious Clark's nutcracker (*Nucifraga columbiana*). These birds are about pigeon-size, and like gray jays are white, gray, and black. They are especially plentiful around stands of whitebark pine where they can be seen prying seeds from cones, a favorite food. Clark's nutcrackers are rarely seen elevations below 2,000 feet. You can quickly distinguish nutcrackers from gray jays, by their notably larger size, and lack of a black headband. The size difference is the most obvious distinction. In fact, William Clark, on his 1804-06 exploration with Meriweather Lewis identified the nutcracker as a new species of woodpecker and ornithologists later referred to the sizeable bird as "Clark's Crow."

A more commonly seen bird, yet very striking is the Steller's jay (*Cyanocitta stelleri*). Larger than white and blue Eastern bluejays (*Cyanocitta cristata*), Stellers have dark blue feathers and charcoal-colored crested hoods. Steller jays are common at all elevations.

Skyline Road is a good two-lane paved arterial with generous pullovers and a capillary network of forest roads that lead to campgrounds, fishing waters, trails, and hot springs. Most of these roads were built for logging operations, and while they offer adventurous routes into remote areas, they can be rough and difficult for passenger cars.

Common sense, caution, and a full gas tank become requirements any time you turn off the maintained pavement of Skyline Road.

Skyline Shelter is about 0.5 mile southwest of US 26 on Skyline Road. It's a log cabin warmed with a double-barreled wood stove, furnished with long plank-wood tables, and includes a restroom. The cabin is maintained by a snowmobile club as a staging area for winter snowmobile adventures. In summer the park-like setting is a pleasant spot to check the map or have a picnic.

Elevations along the Skyline route vary from 3,200 to 4,000 feet. Winter snow drifts may linger until late May or early June. Expect the first snow to blanket the road in mid-October.

Most recreation-seekers turn off at Timothy Lake. Those who continue south will find few developed forest attractions. Skyline Road is paved to the junction of OR 224, but 17 miles south of US 26 it narrows into one lane with pullovers. There are some steep grades that will challenge drivers pulling RV trailers, and the Oregon forest squeezes hard against the side of the road. Deer tracks occasionally stitch the iron-orange soil on the berms, and wild rhododendrons are thick.

At the junction of Skyline Road Forest Service 42 and Clackamas River Road Forest Service 46, travelers have two options. Turning northwest on Forest Service 46 follows a paved route downstream on the Clackamas River to the foothill town of Estacada, population 2,065.

By turning south on Forest Service 46, travelers can go into the Olallie Lakes Scenic Area and the headwaters of the Breitenbush National Scenic Byway.

Directions: On the north, Skyline Road Forest Service 42 intersects US 26 about 3 miles south of Blue Box Pass. On the south it joins the Clackamas-Breitenbush National Scenic Byway Forest Service Road 46 and intersects OR 22 at Detroit Lake.

Activities: Camping, hiking, fishing, boating, wildlife watching, hunting, and mountain biking.

Facilities: Campgrounds, boat launches, picnic areas.

Dates: Open year-round and usually snow-free from Memorial Day through Labor Day. The road is closed to cars in winter but open to snowmobiles.

Fees: There are charges for camping at improved campgrounds, trail park passes, hunting and fishing licenses.

For more information: Mount Hood Information Center, 65000 E. Highway 26, Welches, OR 97067. Phone (503) 622-7674.

LITTLE CRATER LAKE GEOLOGICAL AREA

[Fig. 18(5)] Little Crater Lake Geological Area is scenic treasure just far enough off the beaten path to be missed by most travelers beelining toward a nearby major recreation area. The tiny, nearly transparent lake is the centerpiece of a natural area at 3,200-foot elevation that includes a lightly used campground, wildflower meadow, and a level, paved trail.

The pool is small and surprisingly deep. The water is so remarkably transparent that the skeletal remains of waterlogged trees are clearly visible on the bottom, 45 feet down. The pool is fed by 34-degree water from an artesian well and never freezes. Little Crater Lake is an ancient lake created when an underground fault shifted, allowing an artesian spring to work to the surface in a boggy meadow. Over the centuries, the percolating spring has gradually eroded the soft meadow muck into a craterlike lake filled with cold, transparent spring water, and the surrounding meadow has become a wildflower wonderland.

A barrier-free, paved 250-yard pathway leads from a campground to the 0.25-acre lake. The nearly flat pathway crosses the meadow through seasonal colors of blooming lilies, bog orchids, blue asters, orange paintbrush, and long yellow grasses that sway in the breeze. Blooms are at their peak from June through August.

Directions: From Forest Service 42 about 3 miles south of the Clear Lake turnoff, turn west at Abbot Pass onto Forest Service 58 and follow it 2.3 miles to Little Crater Lake Campground.

Activities: Geological attraction and wildflower marsh meadow, camping, and hiking.

Facilities: Campgrounds, paved interpretive path.

Dates: Open Memorial Day through Labor Day.

Fees: None.

Closest town: Nearest traveler's services are at Government Camp on US 26, about 17 miles northwest.

For more information: Mount Hood Information Center, 65000 E. Highway 26, Welches, OR 97067. Phone (503) 622-7674. Campsite reservations are accepted, phone (800) 280-2267.

LITTLE CRATER LAKE CAMPGROUND

[Fig. 18(5)] **Directions:** Adjacent to Little Crater Lake Geological Area.

Activities: Camping, hiking. A natural meadow, crossed by an 800-foot long, paved, barrier-free path and seeming to explode with wildflowers blooms in early summer. PCT 2000 passes the west edge of Little Crater Lake and can be hiked to nearby Timothy Lake.

Facilities: 16 tent and RV sites up to 22 feet long are well-spaced in an oasis of large conifer trees. There is well water, tables, fire pits, and an on-site camp host.

Dates: Open May through Oct.

Fees: There is a charge for campsites.

FOREST SERVICE ROAD 58

[Fig. 18] From Little Crater Lake, Forest Service Road 58 continues southwest into a remote backcountry area south of wild and scenic Roaring River, a major trout-fishing tributary to the Clackamas River. This is a region for self-sufficient adventurers who enjoy primitive campsites, exploring logging roads, uncrowded trout fishing, and wildlife.

The road leads to uncrowded natural areas with names like Black Wolf Meadow, Lynx Creek, High Rock Springs, Lightning Creek, and Hideaway Lake, where there can be good cutthroat trout fishing.

Bring a Clackamas River Ranger District Map of Mount Hood National Forest, and fill the gas tank; there are no services out here. The paved road may be rough in places, but it is maintained and regularly traveled.

Southwest of Little Crater Lake at Shellrock Creek, Forest Service 58 merges with Forest Service 57. A paved section of Forest Service 57 travels westward along Oak Grove Fork of the Clackamas River to intersect with OR 224 and Forest Service 46 east of Estacada.

There is good fishing for native rainbow and cutthroat trout for 15 miles along the Oak Grove Fork. At OR 224 turn northwest and continue to the town of Estacada or turn south on Forest Service 46 and loop back to Skyline Road (*see* OR 224, page 92).

Directions: Forest Service Road 58 intersects with Skyline Road Forest Service 42 about 3 miles south of the Clear Lake turn-off. It is the marked route to Little Crater Lake.

Activities: Camping, backroad explorations, wildlife viewing, fishing, hunting, and mountain biking.

Facilities: Improved and primitive campgrounds, maintained trails.

Dates: Open year-round, but snow bound from Dec. through May.

Fees: There are charges for camping at improved sites, and trail park passes are needed at some trailhead parking areas.

Closest town: On the north, the nearest travelers service are at Government Camp on US 26, about 17 miles northwest. On the west, traveler services are available at Estacada on OR 224.

For more information: Clackamas River Ranger District, Mount Hood National Forest, 595 NW Industrial Way, Estacada, OR 97023, phone (503) 630-6861.

TIMOTHY LAKE

[Fig. 18] Timothy Lake is the largest lake on Skyline Road and is very popular with boaters, fishermen, and campers. The lake's 1,282-acres were impounded in 1956 by a 110-foot-high, 740-foot-long hydroelectric dam on Oak Grove Fork of Clackamas River. The dam flooded Timothy Meadows, which was named by herders who grazed sheep on timothy grass in the meadow. Campers are attracted by the lake's seven Forest Service campgrounds, including an unusual primitive site on Meditation Point, which is accessible only by boat or trail.

The popularity of this pretty mountain retreat, unfortunately, has also led to crowding, vandalism, and natural resource abuse. Campsite reservations are recommended. First-come, first-served sites are often full during July and August.

A 10 mph maximum speed limit eliminates speed boats, and promotes fishing for the lake's stocked rainbow, cutthroat, brook trout, and kokanee, a trout-size land-locked salmon. Brook trout grow to trophy proportions in Timothy Lake. Five pounders are taken each year. The lake's abundant crayfish population gets credit for the trophy-size fish. The crustaceans are a nutritionally rich food source, and are so thick on the lake bottom that they are commercially trapped.

Crayfish tails are both a favorite bait for big trout and an excellent shellfish treat when boiled, doused with lemon juice, and dredged through melted butter.

Early season fishing is always slow, improving as the weather warms. The best catches occur in late summer and early fall when the brook trout are preparing to spawn. When winter's first snowflakes drop, they land on fly fishermen who are casting fly patterns at big brook trout that are gathering near the mouths of tributaries preparing to head upstream to spawn.

Directions: From Skyline Road Forest Service 42, turn west at Joe Graham Campground onto Forest Service 57, and continue 2 miles to the lake. From Estacada, follow OR 224 to Forest Service 57 and follow it northeast to Timothy Lake.

Activities: Camping, trout fishing, boating (10 mph speed limit), and hiking.

Facilities: Seven campgrounds, 2 picnic areas, multiple boat launches, and hiking trails. All of the campgrounds have vault toilets, well water, tables, and fire pits. Campground hosts are on site during the summer. Forest Service Trail 528, an easy route, circles the lake on an 8-mile long loop with minor grade changes. Campgrounds and the number of sites include Gone Creek 50; Oak Fork 47; Hoodview 43 plus picnic area; Pine Point 25 plus picnic area; Cove 10; North Arm 8, and Meditation Point 5. Reservations are accepted and recommended at the 3 largest campgrounds.

Dates: The lake is at an elevation of 3,200 feet and the campsites are usually snow-free and open by Memorial Day, and close shortly after Labor Day.

Fees: There are charges for camping at Gone Creek, Oak Fork, Hoodview, and Pine Point.

For more information: Mount Hood Information Center, 65000 E. Highway 26, Welches, OR 97067. Phone (503) 622-7674. For campsite reservations phone (800) 280-2267.

HISTORIC CLACKAMAS LAKE RANGER STATION

[Fig. 18(6)] The historic complex of the Clackamas Lake Ranger Station is almost unchanged since it was completed in 1935. The station is located on Skyline Road Forest Service 42 at the junction of Forest Service 57.

Volunteers are available to guide history buffs on a walking tour of the log-walled complex that includes a district ranger office, mess hall, bunkhouse, blacksmith shop, a restored 1935 fire truck, warehouses, a residence, and a mule barn.

The Clackamas Lake buildings were built by the Civilian Conservation Corps as a forest service headquarters. The outpost was originally designed as a basic, no frills complex, but the advent of larger CCC budgets encouraged designers to upgrade the plans with labor-intensive features. This served to keep workers employed longer.

The detailed masonry, fitted rock pathways, and hand-finished wood and metal work attest to the CCC's budget and the skills of its workers.

The ranger station was placed on the National Historic Register in 1979, and is still used by the Forest Service as a visitor information center, as an equipment warehouse. There is a campground at nearby Clackamas Lake.

Directions: From US 26 about 11 miles east of Government Camp, turn south on

Skyline Road Forest Service 42 and continue 9 miles. The ranger station is just east of Timothy Lake.

Activities: A walking tour of 1933-era forest service ranger complex.

Facilities: Volunteer-staffed information and interpretive center, and well water.

Dates: The staffed information center and building tour is open weekends 9 to 5 from Memorial Day to July 4, and Wednesday through Saturday from July 4 to Labor Day. The grounds are open at all hours.

Fees: None.

Closest town: Government Camp.

For more information: Mount Hood Information Center, 65000 E. Highway 26, Welches, OR 97067. Phone (503) 622-7674.

CLACKAMAS LAKE CAMPGROUND

[Fig. 18(6)] **Directions:** From US 26, drive 9 miles south on Skyline Road Forest Service 42 then east at the junction of Forest Service 4270 to Clackamas Lake. The 11-acre mosquito bog is in a large marshy meadow at 3,400 feet elevation. Campers in this area frequently report damage from black bears. Warning signs are posted, and food should be stored in vehicles.

Activities: Camping, hiking, horse-trail riding.

Facilities: 46 tent and RV campsites to 32 feet long, drinking water, tables, fire pits, pit toilets, and stock ramp. Corrals and other stock facilities are located on the north side of Clackamas Lake at the Joe Graham pioneer camp adjacent to the Clackamas Lake historic ranger station.

Dates: Open Memorial Day through Labor Day.

Fees: There is a charge for overnight camping.

Clackamas/Breitenbush National Scenic Byway

[Fig. 19(1)] Forest Service Road 46 is part of a national scenic byway that loops into the Oregon Cascades between Estacada and the recreation-oriented mountain community of Detroit. The paved two-lane forest road runs east and west along Clackamas River, which is a national wild and scenic waterway. On the southeast end is Olallie Lakes Scenic Area and a 3,500-foot elevation mountain divide into the Breitenbush River drainage to Detroit Lake. On the northwest end, the scenic byway goes to Estacada in the Willamette Valley southeast of Portland. This national byway is actually two very different mountain roads in two national forests that join atop the Breitenbush divide at a sweeping overlook.

The Clackamas segment is the northern part of the byway and is within Mount Hood National Forest. It is the most heavily used of the two legs, and follows the wild and scenic Clackamas near its headwaters at Olallie Lakes to Estacada. The paved route follows the river and provides easy entry to excellent steelhead and trout fishing. The Clackamas leg, which includes OR 224, passes the Forest Service Ripplebrook Guard Station, four major

Water Ouzel

Some birds walk on water. The strange little water ouzel walks under it.

If you see a starling-size slate-gray bird step off a rock and disappear under the quick, clear waters of a mountain stream or river, don't run for the rescue net—it's probably a water ouzel (*Cinclus mexicanus*).

Dipper is the common name for this uncommon bird. Without obvious physical adaptations, such as webbed feet, the dipper seems to be as much at home submerged and walking on the stones at the bottom of a stream as in the air.

It's not unusual to spot dippers on river rocks, bobbing in knee bends, then stepping into the river. Look into the water and you might see the bird walking along the bottom, probing among stones for insects, larvae, and nymphs. Ouzels sometimes walk up to 10 feet along the bottom before popping to the surface and swimming to shore.

Ouzels are gray, about 8-inches long, with short tails, stocky frames and yellow legs. You can't mistake them, they're the only birds you'll see walking along the bottom of mountain streams.

tributaries, a major fishing and boating site at North Fork Reservoir, more than a dozen campgrounds and picnic sites, hiking trails through giant old-growth conifers, and a regionally famous hot springs. The much shorter Breitenbush segment is the southern leg and parallels the tumbling Breitenbush River between the divide near Olallie Lakes and Detroit Reservoir. Most of this section is within the Willamette National Forest.

The Breitenbush leg is lightly traveled, and doesn't support nearly as many developed forest attractions. It is, however, an exceptionally scenic drive that passes a popular natural mineral hot spring, four campgrounds, many side-of-the-road picnic areas, and miles of picturesque trout fishing opportunities.

Directions: The Clackamas-Breitenbush National Scenic Byway can be reached from the north by taking US 26 to Skyline Road Forest Service 42, and south to Forest Service 46, which intersects the byway about 14 miles southeast of Ripplebrook Guard Station. The east gateway is Forest Service 46 at Detroit on OR 22. West entrance is OR 224 from Estacada.

Activities: Camping, fishing, hiking, boating, whitewater boating, hunting.

Facilities: Campgrounds, resorts, picnic areas, boat launches, trails for walking and mountain biking, and a natural hot spring.

Dates: The byway is open year-round in low-elevation areas, but higher elevation areas are not maintained during heavy snow months from Nov. through Apr.

Fees: There are charges for some campsites and trail park passes.

Closest town: Estacada is at the west entrance and Detroit is at the south entrance.

For more information: For fishing information contact Oregon Department of Fish and Wildlife, Columbia Region, 17330 SE Evelyn Street, Clackamas, OR 97015. Phone (503) 657-2000. For forest information, Mount Hood National Forest Clackamas River Ranger District, 595 NW Industrial Way, Estacada, OR 97023. Phone (503) 630-6861.

Wild and Scenic Clackamas River

The Clackamas River is a designated wild and scenic waterway, an important trout, salmon and steelhead fishery, and a favorite rock and rapid challenge for whitewater boaters. Summer and winter steelhead trout run the Clackamas, from the Willamette Valley to the Big Bottom Area inside Mount Hood National Forest, north of Olallie Lakes. Most of the river is paralleled by the OR 224 and Forest Service 46 leg of the Clackamas-Breitenbush National Scenic Byway.

Clackamas River is the major West Slope drainage in a checkerboard of logging areas and forest lands west of Skyline Road. Its headwaters flow through a vast remote region that is favored by fishermen, big game hunters, and mushroom gatherers.

The mild winters and nutritionally rich duff floor of the forests, a compost sometimes a 0.5 foot of decaying leaves, conifer needles, and sticks, provides a rich environment for hundreds of mushroom species. Among the most plentiful edibles are sponge-shaped edible morels (*Morchella esculenta*), yellow chanterelles (*Cantharellus cibarius*), shaggy manes (*Coprinus comatus*), varieties of boletus (*Suillus*), and coral (*Hericum*). Beware, however, this is also prime growing ground for numerous inedible varieties, plus potentially deadly varieties, such as death cup (*Amanita phalloides*), panther amanita (*Amanita pantherina*), destroying angel (*Amanita ocreata*), and fly amanita (*Amanita muscaria).*

Most of this beautiful, fish-rich river, however, is followed closely by paved road. The lower river is less than one hour's drive from Portland, and the competition for recreation from campers, whitewater enthusiasts, and fishermen can be heavy, especially on weekends. The Clack, as locals call it, is the rumbling product of innumerable clear-water creeks and five large tributaries. Four of those major tributaries begin in the westward draining mountains of Mount Hood National Forest. The drainages are south of US 26 and north of OR 224. All of these tributaries have developed and primitive campsites, and promising trout fishing.

The Clackamas is a freestone river, characterized by transparent but nutritionally poor water, multicolored boulders tumbled by the powerful current until they are smooth and round, deep pools and noisy rapids. It flows through forests, steep canyons, and basalt crags. The scenic combination plus its storied recreation potential has earned the upper 47 miles status as a federal wild and scenic river. Fourteen Forest Service campgrounds are along the highway and river between North Fork Reservoir and the mouth of the Collawash River.

The Clackamas is not a wide river. A spin fisher can cast across most of it. State fishery managers, however, recognize it as one of the most important salmon and steelhead producing rivers in the state. The river is a challenge for boaters. There are five launches below Estacada where rafting is popular, especially the 8-mile float from Milo McIver State Park downstream to Barton County Park. A couple of Class II and III rapids add zest to this otherwise quiet float. Above the North Fork Dam, however, the river is a real whitewater challenge. The rocks, powerful currents, and rapids limit floaters to speciality craft: kayaks, double-ended McKenzie drift boats, or sturdy rafts. Boaters should be skilled enough to handle the dangerous class III and IV rapids in the upstream section. Primitive launches for river boats are scattered along OR 224.

North Fork Reservoir is impounded behind a power-generating dam 7 miles upstream from Estacada. The reservoir is 4 miles long with 350 surface acres of water stocked with rainbow, brown, and cutthroat trout. The lake is popular for fishing, swimming and boating. One region of the lake is open for speed boats and the rest is set aside for fishing. The managing power company, Portland General Electric, provides boat ramps, picnic areas, and a campground at Promontory Park. At the east end of the lake is a marina, boat rental, swimming beach, and small grocery.

The Clackamas has a long tradition of outstanding fishing. In the 1980s chinook salmon weighing up to 50 pounds were caught in this scenic river. Few of these lunkers survive today's intense commercial net fishery, but 10- to 25-pound chinook are caught every year. The salmon fishing takes place downstream of Estacada closer to the confluence with the Willamette River. The state has imposed a mixed-bag of conservation restrictions on tackle and fish limits, so check the Oregon Department of Fish and Wildlife regulations before wetting a line.

Directions: From Estacada, follow OR 224 up the main stem of Clackamas River. Mount Hood National Forest begins just above North Fork Reservoir. About 0.5 mile east of Ripplebrook Guard Station, OR 224 becomes Forest Service 46. Forest Service 46 continues along the Clackamas River to a point near the headwaters at Olallie Lake Scenic Area. To reach the river from the north, follow Skyline Road Forest Service 42 south from US 26. (*see* Skyline Road, Page 109).

Activities: Fishing for salmon, steelhead, and trout; camping, whitewater boating.

Facilities: 14 developed campgrounds and several roadside picnic areas, primitive boat launches.

Dates: Open year-round, but the road above Ripplebrook Guard Station is often closed by snow during winter months.

Closest town: Estacada is on OR 224, about 8 miles west of the national forest boundary.

For more information: For fishing information contact Oregon Department of Fish and Wildlife, Columbia Region, 17330 SE Evelyn Street, Clackamas, OR 97015. Phone (503) 657-2000. For forest information, Mount Hood National Forest Clackamas River Ranger District, 595 NW Industrial Way, Estacada, OR 97023. Phone (503) 630-6861.

CAMPING ON THE CLACKAMAS

Fourteen developed forest service campgrounds and three picnic sites are sprinkled along the Clackamas River between North Fork Reservoir and the forks at the Collawash River confluence. Yet, because the heart of this scenic corridor is only two hours from Portland, campgrounds can be overwhelmed on summer weekends.

Some of the tent and RV sites at 12 of the campgrounds are set aside for advance reservations. The balance of sites are on a first-come basis. Campgrounds accepting reservations, and the total number of sites in each, are: Indian Henry, 86; Lazy Bend, 21;

Armstrong, 12; Carter Bridge, 17; Riverside, 16; Lockaby, 30; Fish Creek, 24; Roaring River, 19; Sunstrip, 9; Rainbow, 17; Ripplebrook, 13, and Raab, 27.

Four of these campgrounds, with a combined 87 tent and RV sites up to 22 feet in length, are included in a cluster of camps between the Big Cliff area and the confluence of Fish Creek about 8 miles east of the forest's west boundary. They are Lazy Bend, Armstrong, Lockaby, Fish Creek. Carter Bridge Camp is also here.

Indian Henry with 86 tent and RV sites up to 22 feet long, is the largest campground in the corridor, and the only one with a RV dump station. Indian Henry is about 7 miles east of the Fish Creek campground. A second cluster of campgrounds is about 8 miles southeast of Indian Henry near the mouth of the Collawash River; River Ford has 10 sites, Riverside, 16, and Raab, 27. Day-use picnic areas with tables and fire pits beneath canopies of riverside trees are at Big Eddy, Carter Bridge, and Two Rivers.

Directions: Clackamas River corridor campgrounds are scattered along the river at intervals on OR 224, which continues into the Mount Hood National Forest as Forest Service 46.

Activities: Camping, hiking and river fishing for steelhead and trout.

Facilities: All of the campsites, except for River Ford, Raab, Carter Bridge, Ripplebrook, Alder Flat, and Rainbow, have potable water. They all offer picnic tables, and restrooms.

Dates: Open Memorial Day through Labor Day.

Fees: There are charges for camping, and trail park passes.

Closest town: Estacada, west on OR 224.

For more information: Mount Hood National Forest Clackamas River Ranger District, 595 NW Industrial Way, Estacada, OR 97023. Phone (503) 630-6861.

ALDER FLAT TRAIL 574

[Fig. 19(2)] This nearly-level trail goes through a grove of huge old growth fir, western hemlock, and cedar past a complex of beaver dam-ponds to Alder Flat Campground. The campground has 6 free tent sites with tables and fire pits, but no potable water. Walk-in and bicycle access only. The campground is along the Clackamas River in an area known for good steelhead and trout fishing.

Directions: Follow OR 224, about 26 miles southeast of Estacada to Ripplebrook Guard Station. The trailhead and one campsite are across the road from the guard station.

Dates: Open year-round.

Trail: 0.9 mile, one way.

Elevation: 1,300 to 1,400 feet.

Degree of difficulty: Easy.

Surface: Forest duff.

CLACKAMAS RIVER TRAIL 715

[Fig. 19(3)] Forest Service Trail 715 follows the Clackamas River between Fish Creek and Indian Henry campgrounds. It's an easy hike with lots to see, including 100-foot high Pup Creek Falls, rocky outcropping, old growth western hemlock, and wildflowers. In April and May, the area is bright with snow queen (*Synthyris reniformis*). The forest floor is often carpeted with a large variety of moist forest herbs including vanilla leaf, wood sorrel, violets, trillium, and Solomon's seal.

Directions: Travel southeast from Estacada on OR 224 for 16 miles, turn south onto Forest Service 54 and cross over the bridge. The trail begins across the road from the parking area, which is just beyond the end of the bridge.

Trail: 15.6 miles round trip along the Clackamas River.

Elevation: Begins on the east at 900 feet, gradually rising on the west to 1,250 feet.

Degree of difficulty: Easy.

Surface: Forest duff.

RIVERSIDE NR TRAIL 723

[Fig. 19(4)] Riverside has been designated as a national recreation trail because of its outstanding scenic qualities. The trail weaves along the Clackamas River among old-growth groves between Rainbow and Riverside campgrounds. The trail is open to bicyclists and hikers.

Directions: Follow OR 224 from Estacada 27 miles east to Rainbow Campground near the Ripplebrook Guard Station. Or, follow Skyline Road Forest Service 42 south from US 26 to Forest Service 57 for 15 miles, to Rainbow Campground, at the junction of Forest Service 46.

Dates: Open year-round, but snow-free Apr. to Nov.

Fees: There is a charge for trail park passes.

Trail: 4 miles, one way, along Clackamas River.

Elevation: 1,400 feet, follows river level.

Degree of difficulty: Easy.

Surface: Forest duff.

FISHING THE FOUR FORKS OF THE CLACKAMAS

The four largest tributaries feeding into the Clackamas River are promising trout fisheries, especially productive for anglers willing to walk into areas away from major access points. Summer steelhead may also be caught in the lower reaches. All four forks may be reached from OR 224 and Forest Service 46 along the main Clackamas River.

The North Fork collects on the steep slopes of Squaw Mountain at the south edge of the Salmon-Huckleberry Wilderness Area and flows into the Clackamas River, at North Fork Reservoir about 5 miles southeast of Estacada. Reach the river from Forest Service Road 4610, which runs north from OR 224. The forest road roughly parallels the river, but mostly at a distance. The road is often snow-free by the end of April. Fishing is mostly for wild cutthroat in the 8-to 12-inch range. Waterfalls and steep canyon sections make this river a challenge to fish.

The Roaring River is about 15 miles long. Because it is difficult to get to, it is one of the least fished trout and summer steelhead rivers in the region. Roaring is a federally designated wild and scenic river that is located west of Skyline Road near High Rock Springs, and runs west through a roadless canyon area. If you enjoy hike-in fishing to unfished, secluded trout pools, this is your river. The lower river flows through a steep gorge, and much of the upper river is in a deep canyon. The remote upriver canyon areas are rarely fished. Summer steelhead migrate from the Clackamas River for 3 miles upstream to the base of an impassable falls. Above the lowest falls there are wild rainbow and cutthroat trout. A popular access point is at the mouth, where a bushwhack path picks a primitive route upstream from OR 224. The Roaring River joins the Clackamas River near Roaring River Campground.

The Oak Grove Fork, in contrast, is conveniently paralleled on both banks by forest roads with easy access in limited locations. Trout fishing is productive and yields a mix of rainbows, cutthroats, brookies, and browns. The best water is below Timothy Lake on Forest Service 57. The Oak Grove Fork is about 25 miles long, flowing from small headwater creeks in the northwest corner of the Warm Springs Indian Reservation. The river crosses beneath Skyline Road and flows southwest to empty into the Clackamas River above Ripplebrook Guard Station. It's followed for most of its length by Forest Service 57, both a paved and gravelled road. State regulations require that fishing lures and flies be barbless and restricted to single hooks. If you keep trout, they must be at least 8 inches long but no longer than 12 inches.

The Collawash River is a beautiful small freestone flow that joins the upper Clackamas River about 30 miles southeast of Estacada. Fishermen hook summer steelhead, resident rainbow trout, and an occasional brook trout. Forest Service Road 63 follows the river for 9 miles from the junction with Forest Service 46, often within sight of the Collawash's deep pools and rumbling rapids. Undeveloped pull-over campsites are limited along the river. Three Forest Service campgrounds with tables, grills, and restrooms are near the Clackamas confluence (Riverside has water). River Ford has 10 sites, Riverside, 16, and Raab, 27. Two Rivers Picnic Area, a day-use area, is also at the confluence. This tributary's major tributary, Hot Springs Fork, offers good fishing for pan-size and larger trout. Hot Springs Fork anglers often top off a day's fishing with a hot mineral water soak at nearby Bagby Hot Springs.

For more information: For fishing regulations and seasons, contact Oregon Department of Fish and Wildlife, Columbia Region, 17330 SE Evelyn Street, Clackamas, OR 97015. Phone (503) 657-2000. For forest information, Mount Hood National Forest Clackamas River Ranger District, 595 NW Industrial Way, Estacada, OR 97023. Phone (503) 630-6861.

BAGBY HOT SPRINGS

[Fig. 19(5)] One of the most popular natural hot springs in northern Oregon, Bagby Hot Springs is in the headwaters of the Hot Springs Fork of the Collawash River. There are three soaking areas, including two open-sky tub houses with log benches, and tubs formed from hollowed-out cedar logs or 6-foot cedar rounds. A 150-foot-long log flume diverts the naturally hot water into the tubs. The grounds include a cabin from a 1913 ranger station. The spring is located at an elevation of 2,270 feet and winter snows are common.

Directions: The springs are a short hike and 40 miles southeast of Estacada. Follow OR 224 southeast. About 0.5 mile east of Ripplebrook Guard Station OR 224 becomes Forest Service 46. Continue 3.5 miles to the junction with Forest Service 63. Go south along the Collowash River on Forest Service 63 for 3.5 miles. Turn west at the junction of Forest Service 70 and go 6 miles upstream along Hot Springs Fork to Bagby Trail 544. The trail is

Bull of the Woods Wilderness Area

Bull of the Woods Wilderness Area is due east of Salem and 68 miles southeast of Portland.

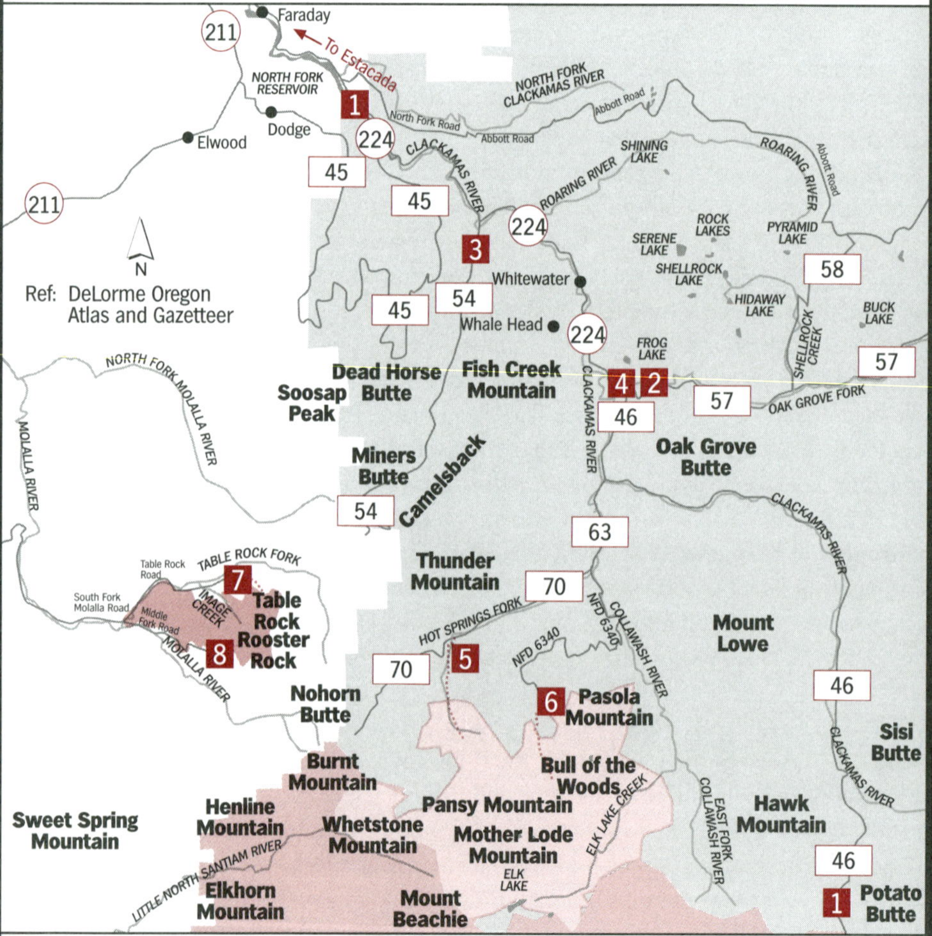

Ref: DeLorme Oregon Atlas and Gazetteer

1 Clackamas–Breitenbush Nat. Scen. Byway
2 Alder Flat Trail 574
3 Clackamas River Trail 715
4 Riverside Trail 723
5 Bagby Hot Springs
6 Bull of the Woods Trail 550
7 Table Rock Trail
8 Old Bridge Trail

Table Rock Wilderness
Bull of the Woods Wilderness
Mount Hood National Forest
Willamette National Forest
Trail

an easy 1.5 mile hike through old-growth Douglas firs and cedars.

Activities: Soaks in natural mineral hot springs.

Facilities: Two springs with water temperatures of 136 degrees Fahrenheit, shelter houses, and log tubs.

Dates: Open year-round, but snow can be an access problem during winter.

Fees: There is no charge, but donations are accepted by the Friends of Bagby.

Closest town: Estacada, 40 miles northwest.

For more information: Contact the Friends of Bagby, PO Box 15116, Portland, OR 97215 or the Mount Hood National Forest Clackamas River Ranger District, 595 NW Industrial Way, Estacada, OR 97023, phone (503) 630-6861.

BULL OF THE WOODS WILDERNESS AREA

[Fig. 19] Small by Western standards at 34,885 acres, Bull of the Woods Wilderness Area is due east of Salem, on the west side of the Pacific crest between the Clackamas and North Santiam rivers. The wilderness is 68 miles southeast of Portland in Mount Hood National Forest. Springs and small creeks originating in the wilderness form the headwaters of three major western Oregon rivers, including the north-flowing Collawash River, a major tributary of the upper Clackamas River (*see* Wild and Scenic Clackamas River, page 117).

Bull Of The Woods Wilderness is characterized by very steep, mountainous terrain that is scored by streams running through deep, steep canyons. Elevations of the mountains inside the wilderness vary from 2,000 to 5,523 feet. A dozen lakes larger than one acre are scattered in the forest well separated by ridges and canyons. The lakes are connected by 75 miles of maintained trails. Trout anglers fish the lakes for rainbow, cutthroat, and brookies.

The mountains are thickly covered with dense stands of timber, including groves of massive old-growth Douglas fir, mountain hemlock and Pacific silver fir. In places, hikers find evidence of past mining activity, including shafts and pieces of equipment. The most popular feature is the Bull of the Woods Lookout which, at 5,523-feet, is the highest point in the wilderness and commands sweeping views of the surrounding mountains. The trail into the lookout starts from the end of Forest Service Road 6340.

Directions: From the east, follow OR 224 to Forest Service 46, then Forest Service 63 to the wilderness. From the north, follow Forest Service 7020 south beyond Bagby Hot Springs. The road touches the edge of the wilderness at several points.

Activities: Backpacking, day hikes, fishing, and hunting.

Facilities: 75 miles of hiking trails, Bull of the Woods Lookout.

Dates: Open year-round, higher trails may not be snow-free until June.

Fees: None

Closest town: Salem is 65 miles west.

For more information: Mount Hood National Forest, Estacada Ranger Station, 595 NW Industrial Way, Estacada, OR 97023. Phone (503) 630-6861.

BULL OF THE WOODS TRAIL 550

[Fig. 19(6)] This is the most popular hike in the wilderness. The main attraction is

Bull of the Woods fire lookout, and a sweeping view from 5,523 feet, the highest point in the wilderness. The trail follows a gradual incline through Douglas fir, western hemlock, wild rhododendrons, beargrass, and lupine to the lookout. The hike can be extended by continuing 2.5 miles east from the lookout on Trail 554 to the Welcome Lakes. Going on to Welcome Lakes involves an elevation change of 1,243 feet. The two largest lakes, Lower and West Welcome, have brook trout that average about 9 inches.

Directions: From Estacada, drive southeast on OR 224 to Forest Service 46, continuing to Forest Service 63 at the confluence of the Collowash River. Follow Forest Service 63 for 5.7 miles, then turn onto Forest Service 6340 and continue for 7.8 miles to a fork. Stay left on Forest Service 6340 and continue for another 1.5 miles. The trailhead parking is at the end of the road.

Dates: Open year-round, but usually snow-free from June to Nov.

Trail: 6.4 miles round trip on the west side of a ridge below North and South Dickey peaks.

Elevation: From the trailhead, the trail gains 500 feet over 3.2 miles, ending at the summit at 5,523 feet.

Degree of difficulty: Moderate to lookout, strenuous if you continue to Welcome Lakes.

Surface: Forest duff.

Table Rock Wilderness

[Fig. 19] Table Rock Wilderness is the only wilderness area in Oregon managed by the Bureau of Land Management. It is located between Salem and Bull Of The Woods Wilderness, about 3 miles west of the Mount Hood National Forest Boundary. The wilderness incorporates 5,500 acres and 20 miles of steep hiking trails. The rugged hills are made up of cliffs, closely spaced conifers and meadow areas well-known for colorful midsummer wildflower blooms. Sixteen miles of trail go through ancient forests carpeted with the green clover-shaped leaves of wild sorrel, delicate lady slippers, and many varieties of ferns. There are wild rhododendrons, clumps of beargrass, acres of dense mountain ash and jungles of thimbleberry (*Rubus parviflorus*). The raspberry-shaped red fruit is bland and rather dry. It ripens in late summer, and what it lacks in quality in makes up for in quantity.

The centerpieces of this small wilderness area are two prominent rock spires; Table Rock at 4,827 feet elevation and Rooster Rock at 4,663 feet. Both pinnacles may be reached by hiking trails. The summits are believed to have formed more than 10 million years ago as part of a stratovolcano, which are built in layers by a series of small eruptions, instead of the singular massive explosions that build shield volcanoes. From these high points, hikers get panoramic views of glaciered Cascade volcanoes stretching from Mount Rainier in Washington to Three Sisters near Bend. Table Rock Wilderness is located in a wedge between the upper Molalla River and Table Rock Fork both well-known for wild cutthroat and rainbow trout fishing. The streams are paralleled by maintained roads south from the community of Molalla. The wilderness has a surprisingly amount of wildlife, especially black-tailed deer and black bear.

The south-facing slope is a mix of grassy meadows and timber that provides food and cover for a resident herd of Roosevelt elk (*Cervus canadenis roosevelti*), Oregon's native species.

Directions: From OR 211 in Molalla go south on South Mathias Road to South Feyrer Park Road. Continue 1.7 miles on South Feyrer, cross the Molalla River and turn onto South Dickey Prairie Road for 5.3 miles. Cross the river and turn onto South Molalla Road. Continue 13 miles to Middle Fork Road and follow this gravel road for 2.6 miles to Table Rock Road. Continue 5.8 miles to the trailhead leading to the top of Table Rock.

Activities: Hiking, hunting, wildflower viewing. Trout fishing in streams. Dogs must be leashed.

Facilities: Hiking trails and marked trailheads. There is no potable water. A map and information pamphlet is available from the district BLM office.

Dates: Open year-round

Fees: None

Closest town: Molalla is 17 miles northwest.

For more information: Bureau of Land Management Salem District Office, 1717 Fabry Road SE, Salem, OR 97306. Phone (503)375-5646.

TABLE ROCK TRAIL

[Fig. 19(7)] This trail is the shortest and most popular route to the summit of Table Rock in the Bureau of Land Management wilderness area.

Directions: From South Molalla Road at the west boundary, follow Table Rock Road 5.8 miles and cross Image Creek. The trailhead is in the parking area near the terminus of the road.

Trail: 5.2 miles round trip.

Elevation: 3,625 feet at trailhead to 4,827 feet on the summit.

Degree of difficulty: Moderate, with cliffs and rock areas.

Surface: Forest duff and rock.

OLD BRIDGE TRAIL

[Fig. 19(8)] This is the most popular route to Rooster Rock summit in Table Rock Wilderness.

Directions: From South Molalla Road, turn north onto Middle Fork Road and continue 0.1 mile. The trailhead is on the east side of the road.

Trail: 17.5 miles round trip to Rooster Rock summit at 4.663 feet elevation.

Elevation: The trail gains about 3,000 feet to the top of the ridge.

Degree of difficulty: Strenuous with steep switchbacks.

Surface: Dirt and rock.

STRIPED SKUNK
(*Mephitis mephitis*)

Olallie Lakes Scenic Area

Olallie Lakes Scenic Area has approximately 60 lakes connected by a network of hiking trails.

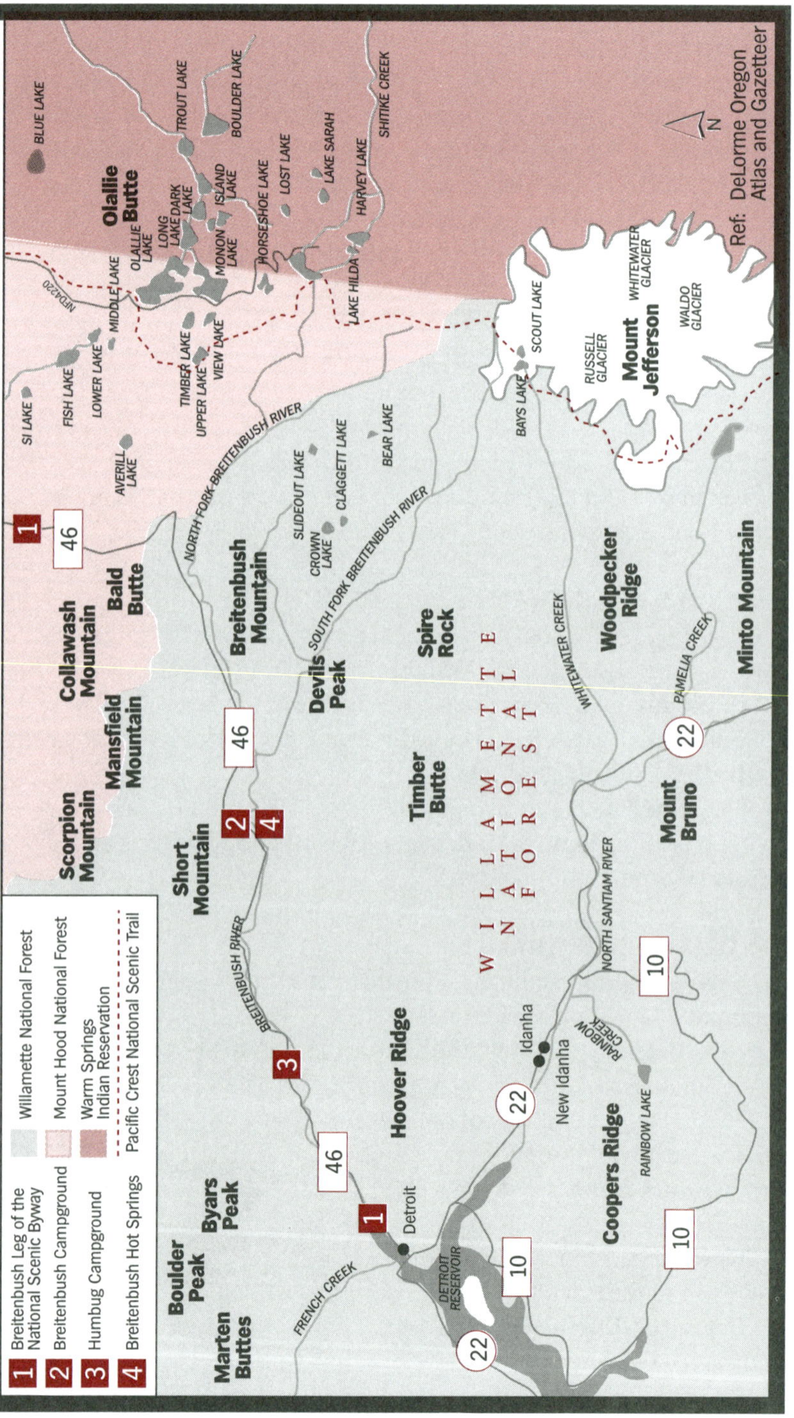

1 Breitenbush Leg of the National Scenic Byway
2 Breitenbush Campground
3 Humbug Campground
4 Breitenbush Hot Springs

Willamette National Forest
Mount Hood National Forest
Warm Springs Indian Reservation
Pacific Crest National Scenic Trail

Scorpion Mountain
Collawash Mountain
Mansfield Mountain
Bald Butte
46
Si Lake
Fish Lake
Lower Lake
Averill Lake
NFD4220
Middle Lake
Olallie Lake
Olallie Butte
Blue Lake
Long Lake
Dark Lake
Trout Lake
Timber Lake
Upper Lake
View Lake
Monon Lake
Island Lake
Boulder Lake
Horseshoe Lake
Lost Lake
Lake Sarah
Lake Hilda
Harvey Lake
Shitike Creek
Boulder Peak
Marten Buttes
Byars Peak
Short Mountain
Breitenbush River
Breitenbush Mountain
North Fork Breitenbush River
Slideout Lake
Crown Lake
Claggett Lake
Devils Peak
South Fork Breitenbush River
Bear Lake
French Creek
Detroit
Hoover Ridge
Timber Butte
Spire Rock
Detroit Reservoir
22
10
Willamette National Forest
Idanha
New Idanha
Whitewater Creek
Bays Lake
Scout Lake
Russell Glacier
Mount Jefferson
Whitewater Glacier
Waldo Glacier
Coopers Ridge
Rainbow Creek
Rainbow Lake
North Santiam River
Woodpecker Ridge
Mount Bruno
Pamelia Creek
Minto Mountain
N

Ref: DeLorme Oregon Atlas and Gazetteer

Olallie Lakes Scenic Area

[Fig. 20] Olallie Lakes Scenic Area has approximately 60 lakes connected by a network of hiking trails, sprinkled across a remote high-mountain plateau where the shockingly clear water reflects glaciated volcanoes, and rounded cinder cones (which are small basalt volcanoes that erupt a conical pile of rock fragments), and one or two lava flows. Dense stands of conifers lie like dark green carpets across the ridges between lakes and wildflower meadows.

The owners of the only resort in this 400-square-mile area promote it as "40 miles from any civilization, and a place of extraordinary beauty." Few visitors argue. Located at 4,900 feet elevation, the area's number of lakes, remoteness, lack of major recreation developments, variety of wildlife, and a topography given to rolling meadows, bogs, and dense stands of pine trees give it a unique niche in Oregon's mountains. The area is generally snow-free from June to October. Mount Jefferson and the rugged Mount Jefferson Wilderness (*see* Mount Jefferson Wilderness, page 151) is just south of Olallie Lakes Scenic Area. The reflection of that snow-encrusted 10,498-foot volcano fills many of the lakes. Cinder cone towers of andesite, reminders of the area's volcanic legacy, jut into the horizon in all directions. The largest cone is Olallie Butte at 7,215 feet, which is also the largest cinder cone in the Cascade Range. Nearby cones are Badger Butte at 5,485 feet and Sisi Butte at 5,617 feet elevations.

The eastern edge of the area abuts the Warm Springs Indian Reservation. The main entry point for vehicles is on the west side. Follow Forest Service 46 along the upper Clackamas River to a well-marked east turn onto Forest Service 4690. Forest Service 4690 connects with Forest Service 4220,which continues 5 miles to Olallie Lake. At 238 acres, and more than a mile long, Olallie Lake is the largest in the area. The road in is partially paved. Drive slowly and watch for deer, elk, black bear, beaver, or squirrels. The woods and marsh are home to an almost endless variety of forest birds that can range from diminutive Rufous hummingbirds (*Selasphorus rufus*) to largc bald eagles. Jays, nutcrackers, ravens, ospreys, nuthatches, finches, and woodpeckers are especially plentiful. Deer and elk are often spotted at the edges of meadows and bog areas where tall grasses and white tufts of beargrass provide both food and cover. This is a popular big game hunting region in October and November. In the lakes, trout fishermen challenge rainbows and brookies from June through October, always looking for one of the 10-pounders that are caught every year. Most trout, though, average about a foot long, although there is a fair number of 20-inchers. Few people fish in this remote area compared with more accessible waters.

Photographers and gatherers are attracted by the area's lake and forest scenery, and proliferation of wildflowers, mushrooms, and huckleberries. The area is famous for succulent wild berries that ripen in late August and September. In fact, the name Olallie is derived from the Chinook Indian word *klalelli,* meaning berries.

The dozens of lakes and remote camping areas are linked by more than 47 miles of maintained trails that are shared by hikers, horseback riders and bicyclists. The West's most famous trail, Pacific Crest National Scenic Trail 2000, crosses north-south through the heart of the area and passes down the shoreline of Olallie Lake.

Directions: The scenic area is 35 miles south of US 26. Follow Skyline Road Forest Service 42 to Warm Springs Meadow, then continue on Forest Service 4220 south 12 miles to Olallie Lake. From Estacada follow OR 224 to Forest Service Road 46. Continue on Forest Service 46 and cross the Clackamas River bridge, then turn east on Forest Service 4690. The first 8 miles of Forest Service 4690 are paved. A few miles before the lake, turn south onto Forest Service 4220. From the south, follow OR 22 to the east side of Detroit Lake, turn northeast at Breitenbush River onto Forest Service 46 and continue to Forest Service 4220, which turns east for 3 miles to Breitenbush Lake. The 75-acre lake is one of the few fishing lakes on the Warm Springs Indian Reservation where non tribal anglers are allowed to fish without a tribal permit. It's a good place to bring the family for pan-size rainbow and brook trout, especially in August and September. Go north from Breitenbush Lake on Forest Service 4220 to Olallie Lake. This route is recommended for high clearance vehicles only. Passenger cars should stay on Forest Service 46 to 4640.

Activities: Trout fishing, rowboating, camping, deer and elk hunting in season, hiking, horseback riding, mountain biking, berry, and mushroom gathering.

Facilities: The 1920s-era Olallie Lake Resort rents rowboats, 11 rustic cabins, 4 yurts, and has a boat launch, camping area, groceries, tackle, and showers. There are 7 Forest Service campgrounds in the Olallie Lakes Scenic Area. Only one—Paul Dennis Campground, adjacent to the resort—has drinking water. The others are Peninsula, Camp Ten, Horseshoe Lake, Lower Lake, Triangle Lake Horse Camp, and Olallie Meadow. They have a total of 91 tent and RV sites. Reservations are accepted at Paul Dennis only. Forty-seven miles of hiking, horseback riding, and bike trails wind through the forested area.

Dates: Open year-round, and generally snow-free from June through Oct. The resort is open June to Oct.

Fees: There are charges for camping, trail park passes, and resort services.

Closest town: Detroit is 30 miles southwest on Forest Service 46.

For more information: Clackamas River Ranger District, 595 NW Industrial Way, Estacada, OR 97023. Phone (503) 630-6861. Olallie Lake Resort, 13445 Golden Mantle Road, Crooked River Ranch, OR 97760. Phone (541) 504-1010 or (503) 557-1010.

OLALLIE LAKE

[Fig. 20] The centerpiece of the Olallie Lake Scenic Area, Olallie Lake is a mile long, and covers 238 acres with water so pure it's used as a source for drinking. Because of that, outboard motors and swimming are prohibited.

Located at an elevation of 4,900 feet, the lake is a favorite stop for summer fishermen searching for rainbow trout, which can weigh 10 pounds. The lake is generally snow- and ice-free by mid-July, and fishing is good through October. Rowboats may be rented, and there is a launch area for personal boats.

The Pacific Crest Trail 2000 follows the northern edge of the lake and leads to a number of smaller trout lakes. The scenic area's only resort is on the north end of Olallie Lake, adjacent to Paul Dennis Campground, which is the only source for potable water.

Facilities: Olallie Lake Resort has cabins, campsites, yurts, rowboats, groceries, ice, tackle, bait, fishing licenses, public showers, and fast foods. Gasoline is not sold. Three Forest Service campgrounds are on the lake and provide a total of 62 sites.

Dates: Open from mid-June through Oct.

Fees: There are charges for camping, trail pass parking, and resort services.

For more information: For fishing information contact Oregon Fish and Wildlife Columbia Region office, 17330 SE Evelyn Street, Clackamas, OR 97015. Phone (503) 657-2000. For resort information, Olallie Lake Resort, 13445 Golden Mantle Road, Crooked River Ranch, OR 97760. Phone (541) 504-1010 or (503) 557-1010.

Breitenbush Leg of the State Scenic Byway

[Fig. 20(1)] Forest Service Road 46 is the southern leg of the West Cascades Scenic Byway, a lightly traveled connection between the wild and scenic Clackamas River recreation areas, Olallie Lake Scenic Area, and popular Detroit Lake. Southeast of Olallie Lakes Scenic Area, the Breitenbush route crosses a divide, elevation 3,500 feet, at an overlook near Bald Butte. The sweeping view takes in both river valleys, rock escarpments, and the ragged cliffs, crevasses, and glaciers on the north face of Mount Jefferson. Viewed from the overlook, the Clackamas Valley is a patchwork of mountain meadows and bowls divided by dark green fingers of dense conifers, and active avalanche chutes.

Northbound from the divide the paved, two-lane Breitenbush Road heads into the Clackamas River drainage of Mount Hood National Forest. Southbound, it enters the Willamette National Forest, and follows along the banks of rollicking Breitenbush River.

The byway is terraced into the granite mountainside near the North Fork Breitenbush River, which is a dandy trout stream. Four campgrounds are spread along the 12 miles of byway between Detroit Lake and a resort at Breitenbush Hot Springs.

Directions: From OR 22 at Detroit, turn northeast on Forest Service 46 and follow the Breitenbush River upstream to the Clackamas divide.

Activities: Camping, stream fishing for trout, mountain biking, and hiking.

Facilities: 4 campgrounds, most with tables, fire grills, vault toilets, and potable water.

Dates: Open year-round, but upper elevations are closed in winter, except for snowmobile traffic. Campgrounds are operated with services from Memorial Day to September.

Fees: There is a charge for campsites.

Closest town: Detroit, 9.8 miles southwest on OR 22.

For more information: Willamette National Forest, Detroit Ranger District, Box 320, Mill City, OR 97360. Phone (503) 854-3366.

BREITENBUSH CAMPGROUND

[Fig. 20(2)] This is the most northern and largest campground on Forest Service 46 in the Breitenbush segment of the Clackamas-Breitenbush National Scenic Byway. It's a

Pacific Crest Trail

The Pacific Crest Trail spans 2,650 miles from Mexico to Canada through three states.

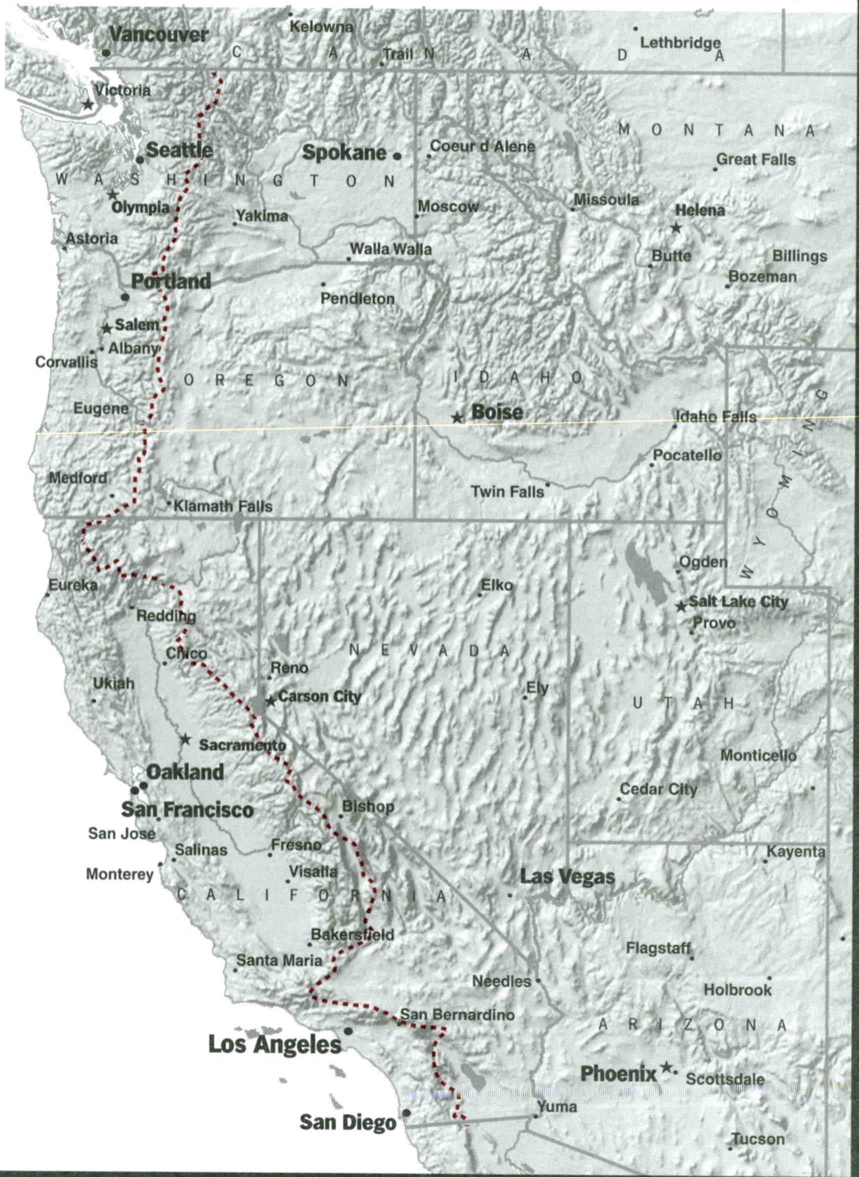

favorite headquarters for trout anglers fishing the Breitenbush River.

Directions: The campground is on Forest Service Road 46, 9.8 miles northeast of OR 22 at Detroit.

Activities: Camping, stream fishing for trout, and hiking.

Facilities: 30 campsites with tables and fire grills, 8 vault toilets, potable water, and firewood provided during the summer. Long RV trailers may have difficulty negotiating some of the tight corners.

Dates: Open year-round, but snowed out mid-Nov. through Apr.

Fees: There is a charge for camping during summer.

HUMBUG CAMPGROUND

[Fig. 20(3)] This shaded Forest Service campground is along the Breitenbush River and makes a convenient base for campers enjoying the nearby Detroit Reservoir recreation opportunities. Use is heavy during the summer.

Directions: The campground is on FS 46 about 5 miles northeast of Detroit.

Activities: Camping, stream fishing for trout, and hiking.

Facilities: 21 tent and RV sites with tables and fire grills, vault toilets, potable water during the summer.

Dates: Open year-round, but snowed out mid-Nov. through Apr.

Fees: There is a summer charge for campsites.

BREITENBUSH HOT SPRINGS

[Fig. 20(4)] Privately owned by a holistic community, Breitenbush Hot Springs is open to the public for a fee. It's a rustic facility 11 miles northeast of Detroit on Forest Service 46 at an elevation of 2,300 feet. The hot springs is on the banks of the Breitenbush River. There are four outdoor soaking pools, three mineral foot baths in a meadow near the river, a sauna and steam room, and cabins that can be rented for overnight. The natural mineral water flows from springs at 180 degrees, and is cooled before flowing into the soaking areas. Bathing suits are required from 9 a.m. to noon, and optional after that.

Directions: Follow OR 22 to Detroit, turn northeast on Forest Service 46 and continue 11 miles to the marked driveway.

Facilities: Rock pools for soaking in natural mineral hot spring water, a sauna and steam room, and rental cabins.

Dates: Open year-round.

Fees: There are charges for resort facilities.

For more information: Breitenbush Hot Springs, PO Box 578, Detroit, OR 97342. Phone (503) 854-3314.

AMERICAN GOLDFINCH
(*Carduelis tristis*)

Willamette–Santiam Region

The youngest eruptions are the highest peaks in the Cascades and form what geologists call the High Cascades Province.

N

46
42
20
221
Silverton
Salem
23
Clackamas River
46
Stayton
5
North Santiam River
22
Mill City
Detroit
Breitenbush Hot Springs
24
226
Detroit Reservoir
Albany
25
Mount Jefferson
22
Metolius River
Lebanon
Green Peter Reservoir
20
Brownsville
Cascadia
Sweet Home
South Santiam River
20
20
126
228
Calapoola River
5
Mohawk River
126
242
Sisters
McKenzie Bridge
Vida
26
Three Sisters
McKenzie River
126
Springfield
Creswell
Lowell
58
19
Cottage Grove
Westfir

FIGURE NUMBERS

23 Willamette National Forest Area
24 Mount Jefferson Wilderness Area
25 Green Peter Reservoir Area
26 Middle Santiam Wilderness Area

Willamette-Santiam Region

The Willamette-Santiam Region is a picturesque puzzle, where the major pieces are three secluded wilderness areas, and two large resort lakes. The pieces are outlined by green walls of conifer forests that divide along the crooked lines of mountain valleys, wild rivers, and scenic highway corridors.

Most of this region lies along the West Slope of the Cascade Range within the Willamette National Forest. The Cascade crest is the dividing line between west and east drainages, and is a north-south imaginary line passing near the center of 111,177-acre Mount Jefferson Wilderness Area. On the far east side the region includes part of Deschutes National Forest.

Nearly all of Oregon's central mountain range was first crossed by eastern pioneers coming west. The Santiam region, however, was settled by Willamette Valley entrepreneurs pushing east. The tracks of their wagons are still visible in the blue clay of the

[*Above:* Detroit Lake State Park with Mount Jefferson in the background]

Santiam Wagon Road, a trade route between Willamette Valley settlements, and the cattle ranches and mines in eastern Oregon. The valley corridor of Quartzville Creek, now a wild and scenic river, was settled by gold prospectors sluicing, panning and digging their way east into the central Cascades. Amateur prospectors may still find color in their gold pans here.

The myriad streams, creeks, and springs that seem to fill every dip and glen in the heavily wooded West Slope, empty into one of three forks of the Santiam River, which flows into the Willamette River in the Interstate 5 corridor north of Albany.

The landscape these waterways continue to erode was shaped by 55 million years of volcanic eruptions. The west-flowing forks of the Santiam River are part of the oldest formative events in the Cascades. Mountains in the Willamette-Santiam Region are worn and heavily forested. They form a somewhat gentle apron where the Cascades taper into the Willamette Valley. These rounded summits and ridges are typical of the Western Cascade Geologic Province, which was created by two volcanic episodes over the past 55 million years.

The youngest eruptions are the highest peaks in the Cascades and form what geologists call the High Cascades Province. The province was formed over the last 3.5 million years during a period of reoccurring fire and ice cataclysms that produced the chain of 2-mile-high, treeless glaciers and peaks that now form the crest of the Cascades. The chain of volcanoes includes hundreds of dormant and extinct volcanoes, including Mount Hood, Mount Jefferson, Three Sisters, Broken Top, Mount Thielsen, Diamond Peak, the imploded remains of Mount Mazama at Crater Lake National Park, and Mount McLoughlin near the California border. Lava flows, cinder accumulations, and silt from these young mountains buried or eroded the older, lower peaks on the West Slope, including these in the Willamette-Santiam Region.

About 60 million years ago this was sea bed. The fossilized remains of ancient fish species and tropical plants are believed to be entombed beneath the mountains and foothills by layers of accumulated lava and ash and deposits from the Lake Missoula floods (*see* Columbia River Corridor, page 19).

Evidence of the unimaginably cataclysmic collisions of pyroclastic eruptions and grinding ice caps can be seen along the highways: walls of columnar basalt, granitic intrusions, ash beds, and building-size chunks of andesitic magma that cooled into granite rock. The greenish gray rocks that often jut from mountainsides above the roads were bleached by steam venting from the earth's core millions of years ago.

Paved OR 22 delineates the north boundary of the Willamette-Santiam Region. The southern boundary is formed by US 20, which is an east-west connector route between two major north-south highways: I-5 at Albany and US 97 at Bend.

On the west side of the Cascade crest, US 20 follows the South Fork Santiam River along the floor of a steeply walled canyon. At the top of the mountain range, the highway crosses through Santiam Pass, elevation 4,817 feet, and continues eastward through an open patchwork of hardened lava flows from Belknap Crater and the numerous vents and cones of the Sand Mountain complex. Along the side of the road is nearly white volcanic ash from those eruptions that is estimated to be about 25 million years old. The highway continues through high plains, grassy meadows, and pine groves to the Western-theme town of Sisters, population 765. From Sisters, US 20 continues to US 97 at Bend, population 29,425.

The most popular attraction in this vast, heavily forested region is 9-mile-long Detroit Reservoir, a 3,580-acre lake impounded at an elevation of 1,600 feet behind a power dam on the North Fork Santiam River. The reservoir is popular with swimmers, water skiers, and boaters. It is also heavily stocked with trout, supports five major campgrounds, picnic areas, several trailheads, and the relocated mountain community of Detroit. The town is a collection of private resorts, restaurants and recreation-oriented businesses. The original townsite was flooded in 1952 when the river water rose behind the dam.

The Bureau of Land Management's Quartzville Recreation Corridor runs through the heart of the region, linking the mountain community of Marion Forks on OR 22 and the Willamette Valley at Foster Reservoir on the outskirts of Sweet Home.

A paved but narrow mountain road follows Quartzville Creek, through most of the east-west corridor. The creek is a federally designated wild and scenic water, and the route is a picturesque and lightly traveled back-road alternative to the heavily used cross-mountain state and federal highways. The corridor route will take you through an early mining region, and is one of the few areas with recreational gold panning. Even first-time panners frequently "find color" in the sand and gravel of Quartzville Creek.

The Willamette-Santiam region supports a rich variety of wildlife, which includes river otter (*Lutra canadensis)*, beaver (*Castor canadensis*), pine marten (*Martes americana*), mink (*Mustela vision*), porcupine, (*Erethizon dorsatum*) snowshoe hare (*Lepus americanus*), bobcat, cougar, black bear, black-tailed deer, and elk. Bald eagles, ospreys, and ravens are common sights at the large reservoirs, and mergansers, water ouzels, and diving ducks are numerous in the creeks and rivers. Ruffed and blue grouse are often spotted in the gravel at the edges of mountain roads. Pileated and hairy woodpeckers are common, and northern flickers are abundant. Such rarities as three-toed woodpecker (*Picoides tridactylus*), Williamson's sapsucker (*Sphyrapicus thyroideus*), western tanager (*Piranga ludoviciana*), and green-tailed towhee (*Pipilo chlorurus)* are sometimes seen.

On the west, at the edge of Willamette Valley, the Cascade Mountains evolve into rounded green foothills, and a checkerboard mix of private, state, and Bureau of Land Management ownerships. The mountains rise about 15 miles east of Interstate 5, which provides easy connections to both OR 22 and US 20. After leaving the Willamette Valley, the only full-service community in this mountainous region is Detroit, 50 miles east of Salem and 78 miles west of Bend.

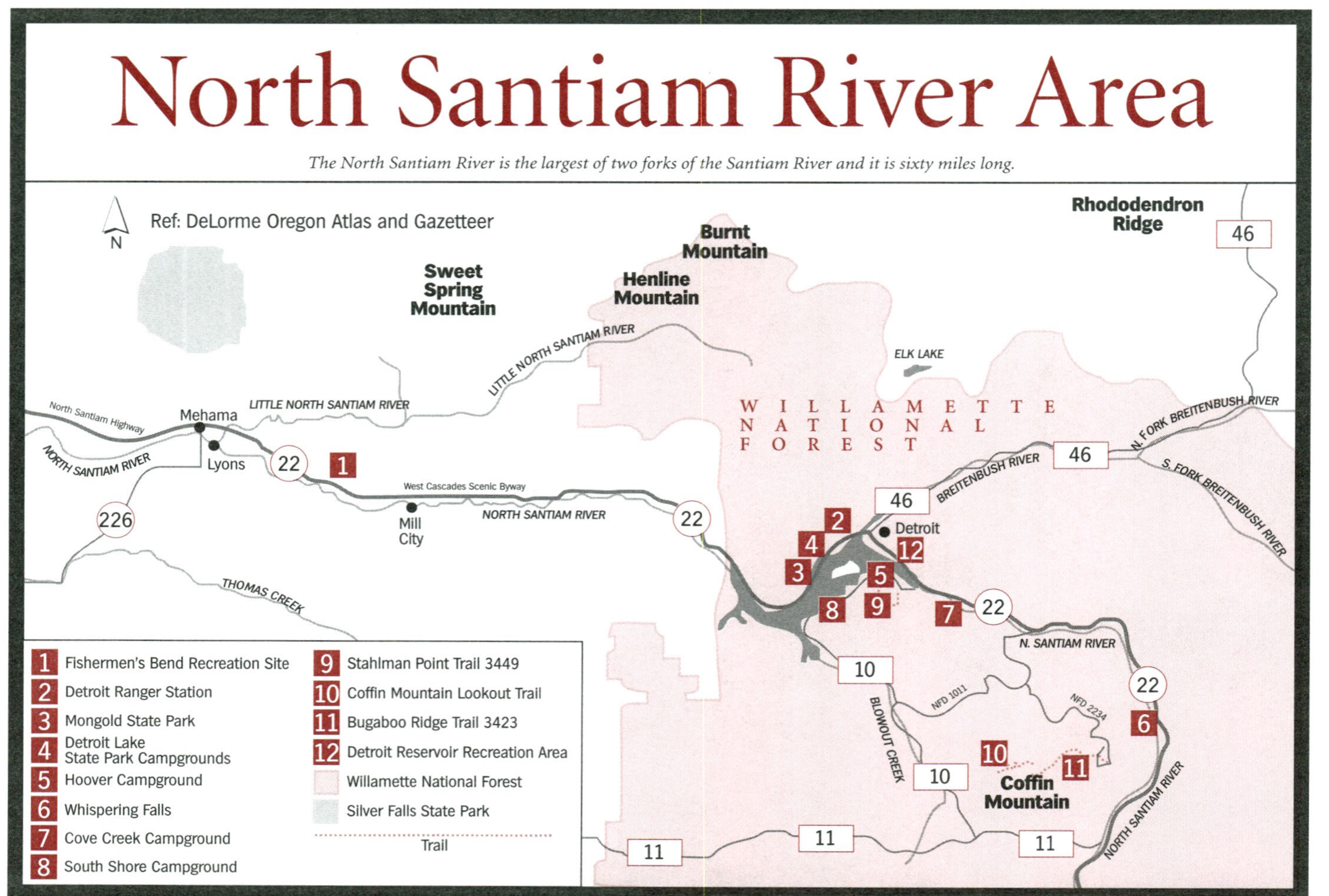
North Santiam River Area
The North Santiam River is the largest of two forks of the Santiam River and it is sixty miles long.
N
Ref: DeLorme Oregon Atlas and Gazetteer
Sweet Spring Mountain
Burnt Mountain
Henline Mountain
Rhododendron Ridge
46
LITTLE NORTH SANTIAM RIVER
ELK LAKE
WILLAMETTE NATIONAL FOREST
N. FORK BREITENBUSH RIVER
S. FORK BREITENBUSH RIVER
BREITENBUSH RIVER
North Santiam Highway
Mehama
Lyons
NORTH SANTIAM RIVER
22
1
West Cascades Scenic Byway
Mill City
226
THOMAS CREEK
Detroit
N. SANTIAM RIVER
10
NFD 1011
NFD 2234
BLOWOUT CREEK
Coffin Mountain
11
1 Fishermen's Bend Recreation Site
2 Detroit Ranger Station
3 Mongold State Park
4 Detroit Lake State Park Campgrounds
5 Hoover Campground
6 Whispering Falls
7 Cove Creek Campground
8 South Shore Campground
9 Stahlman Point Trail 3449
10 Coffin Mountain Lookout Trail
11 Bugaboo Ridge Trail 3423
12 Detroit Reservoir Recreation Area
Willamette National Forest
Silver Falls State Park
Trail

Willamette National Forest

[Fig. 25, Fig. 23] Willamette National Forest stretches for 110 miles, mostly along the western slopes of the Cascades. It extends from the Mount Jefferson Wilderness Area to the Calapooya Mountains northeast of Roseburg, and includes the Willamette-Santiam Region.

The forest covers about 1.6 million acres, a region that is about the size of the state of New Jersey. Cross-mountain highways connect to a web of recreation, forest, and logging roads and trails. The area is crammed with recreational opportunities, including camping, hiking, boating, swimming, hunting, fishing, mountain climbing, skiing, and snowmobiling. It's also a popular source of wild mushrooms and berries.

Mushroom gathers have hundreds of varieties from which to chose. Some of the most prized for their table qualities are yellow chanterelles (*Cantharellus cibarius*), coral hydnum (*Hericium abietis*), shaggy manes (*Coprinus comatus*), prince (*Agaricus augustus*), king boletus (*Boletus edulis*), and several varieties of morels (*Morchella esculenta* and *Morchella elata*).

In late summer, berry gatherers fill their buckets with edible wild red and blue varieties of elderberries (*Sambucus racemosa* and *Sambucus cerulea*), red and purple types of huckleberries (*Vaccinium parvifolium* and *Vaccinium ovatum*), blueberries (*Vaccinium deliciosum*), salmonberries (*Rubus spectabilis*), and Pacific blackberries (*Rubus ursinus*).

The Willamette National Forest is a glaciated landscape of mountain peaks and volcanoes, rock pinnacles, lava fields, craters, and cinder cones. Four of Oregon's highest peaks, and Collier Glacier, the state's largest glacier, are on the forest's rugged east side in Three Sisters Wilderness.

More than 80 campgrounds and picnic sites are maintained, and most have water and vault or flush toilets. Some campgrounds have a user fee. All campsites are filled on a first-come, first-served basis, although a limited number of sites can be reserved in advance in the most popular campgrounds.

Hikers, bikers, horseback riders, and cross-country skiers select from 1,400 miles of maintained trails. Three exceptionally scenic low-elevation trails—the McKenzie River, Fall Creek, and South Breitenbush Gorge Trails—have been designated as national recreation trails. All three can be reached year-round by highway, and are close to population centers. Fall Creek and McKenzie River trails are within 50 miles of Eugene (public buses run from Eugene to McKenzie Bridge). South Breitenbush Gorge Trail is 60 miles east of Salem.

The eight wilderness areas all or partially within the forest encompass 380,805 acres, a land mass equal to about half of the size of Rhode Island. These are remote, rugged, roadless areas that are popular with hikers, backpackers, fishermen, and mountain climbers. A free wilderness permit is required to enter all designated wilderness areas from Memorial Day through October 31. Self-issuing permit dispensers are at most trailheads, and permits are also available at ranger district offices.

Wilderness areas in the Willamette-Santiam Region include Mount Jefferson, Menagerie, and Middle Santiam wildernesses. The Bull of the Woods Wilderness is east of Salem. Three Sisters, Mount Washington, Waldo Lake, and Diamond Peak wildernesses are in the high mountain region in the southeast part of the forest.

Over 350 lakes are contained in the forest. Most of these are high lakes above 4,000 feet, and anglers willing to hike are rewarded with solitude and excellent fishing. Many of the high lakes are not ice-free until late June. The large number of high country lakes is the result of the region's heavy annual precipitation, which fills in rocky bowls left over from the last round of volcanic eruptions and grinding ice ages.

Heavily fished lakes are restocked annually. More isolated ones are planted every two or three years. Fish found in the Willamette's lakes and rivers include rainbow, cutthroat, brook, and steelhead trout. Some of the most consistent producers are Daly, Parish, Riggs, and Gordon lakes. Rivers and streams recommended for fishing are South Santiam, Quartzville, Calapoonia, North Fork Middle Fork Willamette River, Salmon Creek, Salt Creek, and the Middle Fork of the Santiam.

Winter sports are popular. There are two developed ski areas on the Willamette National Forest, Hoodoo and Willamette Pass, and many forest roads and trails lend themselves to cross-country skiing. Snowmobiling is popular on Waldo Lake Road and in the Big Lake area near Santiam Pass.

The forest is open to hunting and fishing in state-regulated seasons. Regulations and licensing are established by the Oregon Department of Fish and Wildlife.

Rainfall on the Willamette National Forest varies from 40 to more than 150 inches a year, much of it as snow that blankets the higher Cascades. The rains and melting snow furnish water for over 500,000 Willamette Valley residents.

Willamette National Forest is nearly always the top timber producer among the 156 national forests in the United States.

Directions: From the west between Eugene and Salem follow state and federal highways east from I-5. Preferred routes are US 20, OR 22, 126, and 58. From the east follow state and federal routes west from US 97. Preferred routes are US 20, and OR 126, 242, 372, and 58.

Activities: Camping, hiking, boating, swimming, hunting, fishing, mushrooming, gold panning, mountain climbing, skiing, and snowmobiling.

Facilities: Campgrounds, maintained hiking trails, boat ramps, toilets, water, picnic areas, and interpretive centers.

Dates: Open year-round, although many of the higher roads are closed in winter by snow, or restricted to cross-country skiers, snowshoers and snowmobilers. Nearly all roads in the Willamette are snow-free by early June, and major highways are maintained year-round.

Fees: There are charges for trail park passes required at many popular trailheads and picnic grounds, and for improved campsites.

For more information: Willamette National Forest headquarters, Federal Building, 211 East 7th Avenue, PO Box 10607, Eugene, OR 97440. Phone (541) 465-6521

Landlocked Salmon

Most large reservoirs and many deep lakes in the Oregon Cascades are stocked by the state fish and wildlife department with landlocked salmon, to supplement recreational trout fishing opportunities.

Three species of salmon are stocked, kokanee (*Oncorhynchus nerka*), coho (*Oncorhynchus kisutch*), and chinook (*Oncorhynchus tshawytscha*). These salmon are called landlocked because dams or lack of outlet streams prevent them from migrating out of their freshwater habitats. They are spawned and raised to fingerling-size in state fish hatcheries, stocked directly into lakes, and, unlike their famous ocean-roaming cousins, never get a whiff of salt water. Migratory salmon are anadromous fish that have been spawned in freshwater rivers, migrate to the ocean to mature, and in three to five years return to their natal rivers to spawn.

Landlocked salmon never grow as large as their ocean-roaming cousins. Most lake salmon average a trout-like 10 to 20 inches long. The kokanee variety, which is the landlocked version of sockeye salmon, is the most heavily stocked. Kokanee are prized for their bright pink, oily meat (great smoked) and hard fighting qualities. In fall, the blue-backed kokanee will become bright red with green heads, and where they can get up an inlet stream, they will stage spawning runs. In some places, such as Lake Billy Chinook, huge schools of spawning salmon seem to paint the river bottoms red and attract concentrations of bald eagles.

Some of the best landlocked salmon fishing lakes include Detroit and Green Peter reservoirs, Crescent, Odell, Suttle, Billy Chinook, Paulina, and Lemolo lakes. These are deep-water fish, and you'll need a boat to reach them. Most fishermen troll small spoons, spinners sweetened with a kernel of corn or worm, or stillfish using worms, corn, or single salmon eggs for bait. It's best to check locally for the lake's latest hot rig.

There are special bag limits and regulations for salmon in trout water so be sure to consult the Oregon Department of Fish and Wildlife sport-fishing regulations booklet.

NORTH SANTIAM HIGHWAY AND WEST CASCADES SCENIC BYWAY

[Fig. 23] OR 22, locally called the North Santiam Highway, is one of the most important cross-Cascade routes in this region, and the primary road to winter and summer recreation in the Detroit Lake area. It is also one leg of the West Cascades Scenic Byway, Oregon's newest scenic byway.

The state highway is a wide, heavily traveled, year-round route between the densely populated Willamette Valley south of Portland and recreationally important east-side towns of Sisters and Bend.

From the Willamette Valley, North Santiam Highway connects with I-5 just south of Salem, and follows the north bank of the North Santiam River east through Fox Valley, past Detroit Lake, the junction of Clackamas-Breitenbush Scenic Byway, to within 8 miles

OSPREY
(Pandion haliaetus)
Also known as the fish hawk, the osprey hovers over water before plunging in feetfirst to grasp the fish with its talons.

of the river's trickling headwaters west of Santiam Junction.

From eastern Oregon, the most direct entry into the forest is to drive west on US 20 from US 97 at Bend, through Sisters, to Santiam Junction.

The North Santiam River Highway is a favorite route for campers, pleasure boaters, fishermen, trail users, and hunters heading for recreation spots either along the river or at Detroit Reservoir. There is a little commercial truck traffic, but most big rig drivers prefer to cross the Cascades on US 20 to the south.

The largest concentration of public and commercial recreation facilities is in the Detroit-Breitenbush area. (*see* Breitenbush Leg Of The National Scenic Byway, page 129). Recreationists are attracted by the concentration of mountain, lake, and river options at Detroit, including 9-mile-long Detroit Reservoir, Clackamas-Breitenbush Scenic Byway, Breitenbush Hot Springs, multiple federal and state campgrounds, a large state park, resorts, picnic areas, hiking and mountain biking trails, and the Detroit Ranger District headquarters of Willamette National Forest.

There is also challenging whitewater kayaking, good trout, landlocked salmon, and steelhead fishing in the lakes and rivers, and marinas for pleasure boating on the 3,580-acre reservoir.

You can expect this popular area to be congested on most summer weekends. Solitude seekers find quiet campgrounds a few miles from Detroit either by turning north along Breitenbush River, or east along North Santiam River.

OR 22 is a leg of West Cascades Scenic Byway that connects three other national forest scenic byways and links the small mountain communities of Detroit, Oakridge, Westfir, McKenzie Bridge, Idanha, and Estacada.

The entire 220-mile route is paved, and snow-free for wheeled-vehicle traffic from late spring through fall. In winter Forest Service roads 19 and 46 on the byway are closed because of snow, but the routes are often used by snowmobilers.

This is an exceptionally scenic route accompanied by several of Oregon's most beautiful trout and steelhead rivers. In several places the byway parallels stretches of river that have federal wild and scenic classification.

Directions: The West Cascades Scenic Byway is accessible at many different points.

Starting on the south, it begins in Oakridge, follows OR 58 to Forest Service 19, then to OR 126 East up the wild and scenic McKenzie River. At Santiam Junction, turn west on OR 22 to Detroit, then bear north on Forest Service 46, which is the Clackamas-Breitenbush Scenic Byway. Forest Service 46 joins OR 224 at Ripplebrook and the byway ends in Estacada.

Activities: Camping, hiking, mountain biking, lake and river fishing, hunting, pleasure and whitewater boating, scenic drives, picnicking, and swimming.

Facilities: Campgrounds, picnic areas, and boat launches, Oregon State Park, ranger district headquarters.

Dates: Open year-round. Forest Service roads 19 and 46 are closed in winter.

Fees: There are charges for most campsites, state park services, and trail park passes.

Closest town: Detroit on OR 22, about 50 miles east of Salem.

For more information: Willamette National Forest Headquarters, 211 E. 7th Avenue, Eugene, OR 97401. Phone (541) 465-6521. Also, Detroit Ranger Station, Willamette National Forest, HC 73, Box 320, Mill City, OR 97360. Phone (503) 854-3366. For updated road conditions phone (541) 889-3999.

NORTH SANTIAM RIVER

[Fig. 23] Sixty miles long, the North Santiam River is the larger of two forks of the Santiam River and a famous trout, steelhead, and salmon flow.

The North Santiam parallels OR 22 from the Willamette Valley to within 8 miles of the headwaters in the high mountain country near Santiam Junction. The river course includes two reservoirs impounded behind Big Cliff Dam and Detroit Reservoir Dam.

Above and below the dams, the North Santiam is a lively and productive fishery for skilled whitewater boaters and bank fishermen. Below the dams, the river is one of Oregon's top winter and summer steelhead producers. The upstream migration of these ocean-going game fish stops at the dams.

The river flow above the dams is fast, and filled with whitewater chutes, rapids, and boulder fields that provide good habitat for foot-long rainbow and cutthroat trout and productive fly and light tackle action for wading anglers. The hottest trout fishing is said to be between Idanah and Marion Forks. Don't be surprised to see mink, deer, elk, or even black bears foraging along the river.

North Santiam fly fishermen are fond of the steelhead area downstream from the dams, and the trout water above. The peak of winter steelhead fishing is from March through May. Summer-run steelhead are in the river from May through December. Trout are in the river year-round, and fishing is best after snow runoff in mid-to-late summer.

Boat launches are located downstream of Big Cliff Dam at Packsaddle County Park, Kimmel Park, Fishermen's Bend Bureau of Land Management Park, North Santiam State Park, John Neal County Park, Mehama Bridge, Stayton Island, and Bridge and Buell Miller Boat Ramp.

Much of the North Santiam River is challenging whitewater for boaters, and not recommended for novices. The river is littered with boulder gardens, rapids, tight chutes, and logjams created by high water runoff during spring snowmelt. Caution is advised.

Above the reservoir the river is shallow and rocky and there is little opportunity for boating. Most anglers wade or bank fish this area.

Directions: Follow OR 22 east from Salem or west from Santiam Junction. The highway follows the north bank of the river.

Activities: Trout and steelhead fishing, whitewater boating, camping.

Facilities: Boat launches, and adjacent campgrounds, picnic sites with toilets, grills and tables.

Fees: None.

Closest town: Detroit and Stayton on OR 22.

For more information: Detroit Ranger Station, Willamette National Forest, HC 73, Box 320, Highway 22, Mill City, OR 97360. Phone (503) 854-3366. For fishing information, Oregon Department of Fish and Wildlife, 2501 SW First Avenue, PO Box 59, Portland, OR 97207-0059. Phone (503) 872-5268.

FISHERMEN'S BEND RECREATION SITE

[Fig. 23(1)] Nestled along a forested bend of the North Santiam River, 32 miles west of Salem on OR 22, Fishermen's Bend Recreation Area includes a campground, picnic area, boat launch, nature center, trails, and playgrounds. The top of one remarkable picnic table is a single 80-foot long slab cut from an old-growth Douglas fir.

The complex, the largest between the Willamette Valley and Detroit Reservoir, is managed by the Salem district office of the Bureau of Land Management. There are resident campground hosts.

Directions: East of Salem on OR 22 about 1.5 miles west of Mill City.

Activities: Camping, fishing, river boating, hiking, picnicking, bicycling.

Facilities: 21 RV campsites with water hookups and 18 tent or camper units with a shared water supply. Restrooms, showers, RV dump station, picnic units, boat ramp, group picnic areas, nature center and trail, amphitheater, playground, and athletic courts.

Dates: Open mid-May through Oct.

Fees: There is a charge for day use and camping facilities.

Closest town: Mill City, 1.5 miles east on OR 22.

For more information: Fishermen's Bend Bureau of Land Management Recreation Site, PO Box 785, Mill City, OR 97360. Phone (503) 897-2406.

Town of Detroit

[Fig. 23] Detroit is a small mountain community on OR 22 at an elevation of 1,569 feet. The year-round population of 370 triples during the summer when thousands of recreationists flock to adjacent Detroit Lake.

The original town, founded in 1891, was flooded in 1952 when Detroit Dam on

North Santiam River was completed. The town was rebuilt on the northeast shore and today is a crossroads center for the local recreation seekers.

Many of the original settlers were natives of Michigan, explaining the name.

Directions: On OR 22 about 45 miles east of Salem.

Facilities: Motels, bed and breakfast rooms, restaurants, gasoline, grocery, and marinas.

For more information: Detroit Lake Recreation Area Business Association, PO Box 574, Detroit, OR 97342.

DETROIT RANGER STATION

[Fig. 23(2)] Located on OR 22 at Mill City, the Detroit Ranger Station is a comprehensive source for maps, Forest Service recreational permits, and general information about the upper North Santiam River, Detroit Reservoir and Willamette National Forest.

Directions: Drive OR 22 East to milepost 48, 1.5 miles west of Detroit.

Activities: An information kiosk, permit and map sales.

Facilities: A source for information about the Detroit Lake area and adjacent forest, recreational roads and trails maps, trail park passes, wilderness permits, and current flora and fauna information. Restrooms.

Dates: Open year-round 7 days a week in the summer, 5 days a week in the winter.

Closest town: Detroit

For more information: Detroit Ranger Station, Willamette National Forest, HC 73, Box 320, Mill City, OR 97360. Phone (503) 854-3366.

DETROIT RESERVOIR RECREATION AREA

[Fig. 23(12)] Detroit Reservoir is a marine-blue crown at the head of a popular recreation area in North Santiam Canyon, just 45 miles east of I-5 and Oregon's capital city Salem.

If there is a downside to this beautiful recreation area it's that the number of lake and mountain recreationists who enjoy it often surpasses the year-round populations of many rural towns.

The lake, however, can absorb a lot of use with five tree-canopied campgrounds, multiple clear-water swimming beaches, two marinas, 35.5 miles of mostly public shoreline, massive stockings of trout and landlocked salmon, myriad hiking opportunities, and plenty of off-lake mountain attractions.

The water in Detroit Reservoir is so transparent that a white rock can be spotted on the bottom at 18 feet.

The reservoir backs up for 9 miles behind 463-foot high Detroit Dam across a canyon section of the North Santiam River. This is an extraordinarily deep lake, averaging 121 feet, with one area surveyed at 440 feet. In most areas the steep hillsides around the lake continue their plunge underwater, leaving little beach area. Swimming beaches have been developed at campgrounds. The lake's only shallow area, a stump-studded flat just off

Detroit, sometimes goes dry late in the summer.

Piety Island is just west of the Detroit shallows and is one of the most coveted camping spots on the lake. Twelve free tent sites with tables and fire grills are available on a first-come basis year-round. The island also has a picnic area. It can be reached only by private boats and is a popular base for swimming, water skiing, and picnicking. There are four vault restrooms on the island.

Four road-accessible federal and state park campgrounds also ring the lake.

Two marinas supply gas, moorage, boat rentals, and full services for recreational boating. For information on marina services at Detroit Lake Marina, phone (503) 854-3423. Public boat launches are at Mongold Day Use Area, Detroit Lake State Park, Detroit, and South Shore Campground. Boat ramps are also upstream from the main lake on Breitenbush and North Santiam River tributaries.

Detroit Reservoir is the most heavily stocked freshwater lake in Oregon and fishing is a major attraction. Annually the state stocks more than 100,000 rainbow trout and landlocked chinook and kokanee salmon. The trout average about a foot long, and landlocked salmon vary from 9 to 15 inches. The pink salmon meat is considered by many Oregon fish fanciers as among the state's tastiest.

A wheelchair-accessible public fishing dock extends into the lake at Detroit Lake State Park Campground. Similar fishing platforms are available at south shore Forest Service campgrounds.

Directions: Follow OR 22 east from Salem for 45 miles, or west from Bend for 78 miles. Detroit Reservoir can be reached from Mount Hood to the north by way of Skyline Road Forest Service 42, or east from Estacada on Clackamas-Breitenbush Scenic Byway Forest Service 46. The lake is on the densely forested West Slope of the Cascade Range at an elevation of 1,569 feet.

Activities: Camping, boating, fishing, picnicking swimming, hiking, biking, and nearby hot springs.

Facilities: 5 state and federal campgrounds with a total of 418 tent and RV sites, 3 picnic areas, 4 boat ramps, 2 marinas, rental boats and Jet Skis, motels, resorts, commercial RV camps, swimming beaches, gasoline, fishing tackle and full travel services.

Dates: Fishing year-round; campground closed in winter.

Fees: There are charges for most state and federal camping areas, trail park passes, and all private services.

Closest town: Detroit.

For more information: Detroit Lake Recreation Area Business Association, PO Box 574, Detroit, OR 97342. An information kiosk is located in the center of town. Detroit Ranger Station, Willamette National Forest, HC 73, Box 320, Highway 22, Mill City, OR 97360. Phone (503) 854-3366.

MONGOLD STATE PARK

[Fig. 23(3)] A heavily used state day-use and boat launch area on the north shore of

Detroit Reservoir. No camping.

Directions: The park is on the south side of OR 22 about 2 miles southwest of Detroit Ranger Station.

Activities: Swimming, picnicking, boating, and fishing.

Facilities: 75 picnic tables and fire grills, boat ramp with parking, swim beach, flush toilets, and drinking water.

Dates: Open year-round.

Fees: A user fee is charged.

Closest town: Detroit is 4 miles east.

For more information: Oregon State Parks, 1115 Commercial Street NE, Salem, OR 97310. Phone (800) 551-6949.

DETROIT LAKE STATE PARK AND CAMPGROUNDS

[Fig. 23(4)] There are several drive-in campgrounds and one state park around Detroit Lake

By far the largest campground on the reservoir, Detroit Lake State Park Campground is the heart of lake recreation. The park includes a large but congested tent and RV campground, and extensive day-use area.

Most tent and RV sites are small and close together, giving the appearance of a tent city during peak summer weekends. Campsite reservations are strongly recommended. Some sites are available first-come, first-serve.

Directions: On OR 22 on the north shore of Detroit Lake, 2 miles west of Detroit.

Activities: Camping, swimming, fishing, boating, picnicking, and interpretive walks, and nature programs.

Facilities: 134 tent sites, 70 electrical sites, 107 RV sites with full hookups, tables and fire pits, hot showers, well water, utility buildings, telephones, boat ramp, moorage, fishing docks, swimming beach, amphitheater, interpretive area, picnic area, and playground. Facilities are wheelchair accessible.

Dates: Open Mar.-Nov., with campsite reservations accepted year-round.

Fees: There is a charge for campsites, and day use facilities. All permits are available at the park office.

Closest town: Detroit is 2 miles east.

For more information: Detroit Lake State Recreation Area, OR 22, PO Box 549, Detroit, OR 97342. Phone (503) 854-3346. Campsite reservations (800) 452-5687. Reservations are accepted up to 11 months in advance, but no less than 2 days before arriving.

OTHER DETROIT LAKE CAMPGROUNDS

Hoover Campground: [Fig. 23(5)] Follow OR 22 southeast of Detroit about 3 miles to an east turn onto Blowout Road Forest Service 10. Cross North Santiam River and continue northeast about 1.1 miles from the highway. 37 tent and RV sites, tables, fire rings, some grills, wheelchair access, drinking water, flush toilets, boat ramp, and fishing pier.

Cove Creek Campground: [Fig. 23(7)] 0.2 mile beyond Hoover Campground. 63 tent and RV sites to 70 feet, coin-operated showers, a central water faucet, flush restrooms, and boat ramp. There are charges for camping, and boat ramp parking.

South Shore Campground: [Fig. 23(8)] About 2 miles beyond Cove Creek on Blowout Road. 32 tent and RV sites to 70 feet long, central water, vault toilets, tables, fire grills, boat ramp, and a picnic area. There are charges for camping and boat ramp parking.

STAHLMAN POINT TRAIL 3449

[Fig. 23(9)] The trail climbs steeply through old and second growth forests, with occasional views of Detroit Reservoir. It ends at a former lookout tower site. There are good summit views of the lake and Mount Jefferson.

Directions: The trailhead is 8.5 miles from Detroit and just east of South Shore Campground.

Dates: Open early spring into early winter.

Fees: None.

Trail: 2.5 miles one way.

Elevation: The trail begins at 1,800 feet and climbs to 3,045 feet at the summit.

Degree of difficulty: Strenuous, steep.

Surface: Natural duff, very few rocks.

COFFIN MOUNTAIN LOOKOUT TRAIL

[Fig. 23(10)] Southeast of Detroit a small logging road, Forest Service 2234, turns west and connects with a series of logging roads that end at a trail into old-growth forest that leads to a fire tower 5,771 feet high on Coffin Mountain. Carry water. The tower may be staffed during fire season. The lower trail is through old-growth Douglas fir, changing at higher elevations to sub-alpine mountain hemlock, and creeping juniper.

Directions: Drive east from Detroit Ranger Station on OR 22 for 7.7 miles. Turn onto Forest Service 2234 (Coopers Ridge Road). At 4 miles turn southwest onto Forest Service 1003. After 0.75 mile turn left (south) onto Forest Service 2236 and go 2 miles to Forest Service 130. Between Aug. 15 and Nov. 30 Forest Service 130 is gated to protect wildlife. The trailhead is 1.75 mile up Forest Service 130 from the gate.

Dates: Open year-round, snow-free May through mid-Oct.

Trail: 2.5 miles one way from the end of Forest Service 130 to the summit of Coffin Mountain.

Degree of difficulty: Strenuous, steep, occasionally narrow.

Elevation: The trailhead is at 4,100 feet, climbing to 5,771 feet.

Surface: Natural duff and rock.

BUGABOO RIDGE TRAIL 3423

[Fig. 23(11)] This is a popular hike from Forest Service Road 2234 into the high ridges south of OR 22. Impressive flower displays bloom along upper portions of trail in early summer. The trail offers views of Mount Jefferson and Three Fingered Jack. The top of Bachelor Mountain has a panoramic view that includes Coffin Mountain, Mount Hood, Three Sisters, and Diamond Peak. Carry water. There are impressive stands of old-growth Douglas and noble firs at lower elevations and mountain hemlock at higher elevations.

Directions: Follow OR 22 18.8 miles east from Detroit Ranger Station; turn south onto Forest Service 2234 (Bugaboo Road) for 3.2 miles; left on Forest Service 260 for about 400 feet. Trail begins on the right.

Trail: 2.5 miles one way to junction with trail 3420.

Elevation: 4,400 feet at trailhead and 5,400 feet at the high point.

Degree of difficulty: Easy, with some moderate stretches

Surface: Forest duff.

Dates: Open year-round, snow-free from late May through mid-Oct.

Fees: There is a charge for trail park passes.

WHISPERING FALLS AND CAMPGROUND

[Fig. 23(6)] This is a small Forest Service campground 9 miles southeast of Detroit Lake, located across the river from a plunging waterfall. Whispering Falls is also a convenient camp for trout fishermen trying for the rainbows and cutthroats in one of the best fly-fishing sections of the North Santiam River.

Directions: Located on OR 22 along North Santiam River about 9 miles southeast of Detroit.

Activities: Camping, trout fishing, waterfall scenery.

Facilities: 16 campsites with tables and fire grills, flush toilets, and drinking water. No hookups. Whispering Falls is a 60-foot cascade of Misery Creek into North Santiam River.

Dates: Open mid-Apr. though mid-Sept.

Fees: There is a charge for camping.

Detroit Ranger District

PAMELIA LAKE CORRIDOR

[Fig. 24(1)] The Pamelia Lake Corridor and trailhead are the heaviest used entry points into the west side of 111,177-acre Mount Jefferson Wilderness Area. Pamelia Lake Trail is the only hike in the Willamette National Forest where the Forest Service restricts the number of hikers. Free permits are required to hike.

All hikers must carry limited entry permits. A wilderness access permit is also required for overnight stays and hiking destinations beyond Pamelia Lake. The limited entry permits are available up to 30 days in advance at the Detroit Ranger District office. A self-issuing wilderness access permit dispenser is at the trailhead.

Corridor road Forest Service 2246 ends at a washed out bridge at 3,100-foot elevation, where Pamelia Lake Trail 3439 begins. The shallow lake is at an elevation of 4,000 feet, covers 45 acres, and is intensely fished for wild cutthroat trout.

Directions: About 3 miles south of Whispering Falls Campground on OR 22, paved Forest Service Road 2246 cuts east just before the highway crosses Pamelia Creek. Head uphill for 3.2 miles to Pamelia Lake Trailhead at the edge of spectacular Mount Jefferson Wilderness Area.

Activities: Hiking, backpacking, camping, and fishing.

Facilities: Trail, parking area, and permit dispenser.

Dates: Open year-round, snow-free from late May through mid-Oct.

Fees: None.

Closest town: Detroit is 12 miles northwest on OR 22.

For more information: Detroit Ranger Station, Willamette National Forest, HC 73, Box 320, Mill City, OR 97360. Phone (503) 854-3366.

PAMELIA LAKE TRAIL 3439

[Fig. 24(2)] This is a heavily used trail and only 20 parties (maximum of 12 hikers per party) a day are allowed on the trail. Overnight stays and hikes into the Mount Jefferson Wilderness beyond Pamelia Lake also require wilderness permits, which are dispensed at the trailhead. Limited entry permits must be obtained in advance at the Detroit Ranger Station.

Directions: From OR 22 about 3 miles south of Whispering Falls Campground, turn east onto Forest Service Road 2246 and continue 3 miles along the creek to the trailhead.

Trail: 2.3 miles one way to Pamelia Lake along Pamelia Creek.

Elevation: Trailhead is at 3,100 feet and the lake is at 3,884 feet.

Degree of difficulty: Easy.

Surface: Forest duff and rock.

MARION FORKS AND CAMPGROUND

[Fig. 24(3)] Twenty miles south of Detroit Ranger Station on OR 22, Marion Creek joins the North Fork Santiam River at the small community of Marion Forks, a junction with several attractions, including a state fish hatchery, campground, restaurant, and access to the Mount Jefferson Wilderness Area.

Fishermen try their luck at the nearby North Santiam River and Marion Creek, which supports wild trout, but is brushy and difficult to fish.

At Marion Forks Fish Hatchery, Oregon Fish and Wildlife Department (ODFW) raises fingerling salmon. The hatchery is open to the public on weekdays. For information, contact ODFW, Columbia Region Office, 17330 SE Evelyn Street, Clackamas, OR 97015. Phone (503) 657-2000.

Marion Forks Campground is a small Forest Service campground at an elevation of

2,500 feet, located near the salmon hatchery.

Directions: Follow OR 22 for 18 miles southeast of Detroit to Forest Service 052 at Marion Forks.

Activities: Camping, river fishing, salmon hatchery tours, and hiking.

Facilities: 15 tent and RV sites to 50 feet long, tables and fire grills, potable water, 2 vault toilets.

Dates: Open year-round, except when there is too much snow.

Fees: There is a charge for campsites.

Closest town: Marion Forks.

For more information: Detroit Ranger Station, Willamette National Forest, HC 73, Box 320, Mill City, OR 97360. Phone (503) 854-3366.

MARION FORK ROAD 2255

[Fig. 24] Forest Service Road 2255 follows Marion Creek 4.5 miles upstream past two well-used hiking trails and a cascading 100-foot high waterfall, before ending on the edge of Mount Jefferson Wilderness Area at a trail that leads to trout fishing in Marion Lakes.

The road is well maintained and heavily used. Travelers enjoy sweeping territorial views from the road, and access to Independence Rock Trail, Gatch Falls, and Marion Lake Trail. Wilderness permits are dispensed at the Marion Lake trailhead.

Directions: On OR 22 at Marion Forks, turn southeast onto Forest Service Road 2255.

Activities: Scenery appreciation and hiking.

Facilities: Trailhead parking and wilderness permit dispenser.

Dates: Open year-round, but snow-free from May through mid-Oct.

Fees: None.

Closest town: Marion Forks.

For more information: Detroit Ranger Station, Willamette National Forest, HC 73, Box 320, Mill City, OR 97360. Phone (503) 854-3366.

INDEPENDENCE ROCK TRAIL 3431

[Fig. 24(4)] The trail winds through old-growth Douglas fir to an overlook at an elevation of 2,800 feet. Watch for exceptionally large anthills along the trail.

Directions: Turn east from OR 22 onto Forest Service 2255 and continue 0.12 mile to the trailhead on the north side on the road.

Dates: Snow-free from May to early Nov.

Trail: 2.2 miles loop route

Elevation: The trailhead is 2,454 feet and the summit 2,800 feet.

Degree of difficulty: Easy to moderate with some steep pitches.

Surface: Forest duff some rock.

GATCH FALLS TRAIL

[Fig. 24(5)] Gatch Falls is a picturesque 100-foot cascade in Marion Creek. Fishing is not allowed above the falls. A short path leads from the parking area to the falls. Be aware this trail is on private land and access may be limited.

Mt. Jefferson Wilderness Area

This entire area is dominated by Mount Jefferson, which is Oregon's second highest peak at 10,497 feet.

1 Pamelia Lake Corridor
2 Pamelia Lake Trail 3439
3 Marion Forks and Campground
4 Independence Rock Trail 3431
5 Gatch Falls Trail
6 Marion Lake Trail 3436
7 Santiam Junction and Sand Mt. Lava Flow
Mount Jefferson Wilderness
Willamette National Forest
Trail
Pacific Crest National Scenic Trail

Ref: DeLorme Oregon Atlas and Gazetteer

Directions: At Marion Forks, about 18 miles south of Detroit, turn east from OR 22 onto Forest Service 2255 and continue 3.5 miles. Turn south on Forest Service 850 and continue 0.2 mile to a parking area.

Activities: Hiking, waterfall viewing.

Dates: Open year-round and generally snow-free from May to early Nov.

Elevation: 2,500 feet.

Fees: None.

Closest town: Marion Forks.

For more information: Detroit Ranger Station, Willamette National Forest, HC 73, Box 320, Highway 22, Mill City, OR 97360. Phone (503) 854-3366.

MARION LAKE TRAIL 3436

[Fig. 24(6)] The 350-acre lake is a popular destination for day hikers looking for incredible scenery, and trout fishermen seeking rainbows, brookies and cutthroat. A small raft or float tube is handy for anglers fishing for trout that average about 11 inches long but there are trophies that can weigh as much as 5 pounds.

Directions: The trailhead is at the end of Forest Service 2255.

Dates: Open year-round, and generally snow-free from Memorial Day through Oct.

Trail: 2 miles one way to Marion Lake.

Elevation: Parking lot elevation is 3,360 feet and the lake elevation is 4,130 feet.

Degree of difficulty: Easy.

Surface: Dirt and rock.

MOUNT JEFFERSON WILDERNESS AREA

[Fig. 24] The rugged volcano, ice, rock, and conifer topography of Mount Jefferson Wilderness forms the second largest and possibly the most spectacular of eight designated wilderness areas in Willamette National Forest.

The 111,177 acres in this wilderness are mostly high mountain, alpine regions. In the alpine regions, the thick forests of the lower slopes give way to open basins that are carpeted with bristly 6-inch-high plants of red heather (*Phylodoce empertriformus*), dwarf junipers (*Juniperus communis*), and swatches of mountain ash, beargrass, Indian paintbrush, and the daisylike blue petals of alpine asters (*Aster alpigenus*).

The trails are narrow brown ribbons that often cut through green meadows and wrap around the gray faces of rock outcroppings. Woodchuck-size yellow-bellied marmots (*Marmota flaviventris*), and round-eared pikas (*Ochotona princeps*) whistle shrill alarms as hikers pass by.

This entire area is dominated by the craggy, ice-encrusted tower of Mount Jefferson, which at 10,497 feet, is Oregon's second highest peak (*see* Mount Jefferson, page 153). Only Mount Hood, Mount Jefferson's sister peak to the north, is higher. An almost equally prominent peak dominates the south end of the wilderness. Three-Fingered Jack Mountain is a triad of needle-steep eroded cones that top out at 7,841 feet.

The wilderness is part of a large volcanic plateau between Olallie Lakes Scenic Area on the north, OR 22 on the west, Warm Springs Indian Reservation on the east and US 20 on the south.

This is a vast and rugged mountainous region where the lowest elevations are marked at 3,000 feet rising to 10,497 feet. Winter arrives early, generally in September, and remains until July. Snow depth is often higher than two-story buildings.

Named by Lewis and Clark in honor of President Thomas Jefferson, the pyramid-shaped volcano has a mantle of five glaciers: Jefferson Park, Milk Creek, Waldo, Russell, and Whitewater. Geologists believe that Mount Jefferson's last eruption was about 15,000 years ago, but the magma chamber far below the peak still glows with activity. Some scientists suspect the magma chambers and lava tubes below Mount Jefferson Wilderness provide the heat that warms the water in area hot springs, including the popular soaking pools at Breitenbush, Bagby, and Kah-Nee-Ta on the Warm Springs Reservation.

The wilderness contains many small volcanic cones, but none have been active for at least 6,000 years. Some of the youngest cones, Fork Butte, South Cinder Peak, and Red Butte last erupted about 6,500 years ago and retain their original mounded shapes. Older cones that formed during the Mount Jefferson eruptions are severely eroded and have steep walls.

The lower mountain slopes were formed by ancient talus and pumice deposits that now support dense conifer forests. The higher mountains are steep talus rock, rimmed with sheer cliffs and outcroppings. Wedged into basins between 5,000 and 6,000 feet in elevation are alpine meadows and u-shaped valleys with more than 150 lakes. About half of the lakes have trout.

There are numerous lava flows to explore. The most prominent formations are the long, narrow flows at Jefferson and Cabot creeks.

The wilderness is divided north-south by the crest of the Cascades and 36 miles of the Pacific Crest Trail 2000. All totaled, 190 miles of maintained hiking trails weave through the wilderness.

The wilderness receives 75 inches of precipitation annually, most of it snow that begins to stick on the ground in September. Snow falls every month of the year at the higher elevations.

About 62 percent of the wilderness is canopied by conifer forests, mostly Douglas, silver, and subalpine firs; mountain hemlock, lodgepole and ponderosa pines; and several varieties of cedar. The underbrush is a colorful mix of ferns, vine maple, rhododendrons, and huckleberry bushes.

Summer and fall recreation is heavy and at the most popular lake destinations camping is restricted to marked sites. Lakes with designated sites include Scout, Bays, Park, Russell, Rock, Pamelia, Duffy, Wasco, and Square.

Climbers have found nearly a dozen routes to the icy summit of Mount Jefferson. Most climbers establish base camps at Russell or Scout lakes and ascend the summit from Whitewater Glacier. The routes are technical climbs, requiring several days, specialized climbing equipment, and training. It is considered a hazardous climb to be attempted only by experienced climbers.

The wilderness is a popular destination for summer fishermen and fall deer hunters, horse pack trips, and backpacking.

Directions: The most popular entry points are from US 20 at the south end on Pacific Crest National Scenic Trail 2000 and Summit Trail 65. Best west side access is from Marion Lake Trail 3436 and Pamelia Lake Trail 3439 off Forest Service 2246 (*see* Pamelia Lake Trail 3439, page 148). From the north most hikers enter on the PCT 2000 from Breitenbush Lake. From the east, most hikers enter either on Cabot Lake Trail 3437, Road 1234 at Jack Lake, or Jefferson Lake Trail 4001 from Forest Service Road 1292.

Activities: Backpacking, hikes, camping, summit climbs, fishing and hunting, and huckleberry picking

Facilities: 190 miles of hiking trails, 150 lakes.

Dates: Open year-round, but generally snow covered from mid-Oct. through early June.

Fees: Some access trails require a trail use pass for which there is a daily charge. Wilderness permits required to go inside the wilderness are dispensed from self-issuing stations at most trailheads. Trail use passes can be bought at the Detroit Ranger District office.

Closest town: Sisters is 19 miles southeast on US 20 and Marion Forks is 5 miles west on OR 22.

For more information: Willamette National Forest Supervisors Office, 211 East 7th Avenue, Eugene, OR 97401. Phone (503) 465-6521. Detroit Ranger District, HC 73, Box 320, Mill City, OR 97360. Phone (503) 854-3366.

MOUNT JEFFERSON

[Fig. 24] Once believed to have been more than 12,000 feet high, glacier-shrouded Mount Jefferson, at 10,497 feet, is still the second highest peak in Oregon and a dominating silhouette straddling the crest of the Cascade Mountains.

The sharply pointed peak is visible for hundreds of miles, a white pyramid that marks the northern panhandle of Mount Jefferson Wilderness Area. Mount Jefferson is sometimes mistaken for its taller sister volcano Mount Hood.

Geologists have described Mount Jefferson as an enormous pile of andesites built on a foundation of basalt. The first eruptions were almost

QUAKING ASPEN
(*Populus tremuloides*)
Like other poplar trees, this is a pioneer tree that can be found in logged or burned-over areas.

entirely basalt lava, followed by peak-building eruptions of andesites. The oldest rocks found at the mountain are 6.5 million years old, and the eruptions that formed the present face of Mount Jefferson are believed to have begun 680,000 years ago, and ended about 15,000 years ago.

The upper slopes of the volcano have become encased in five permanent glaciers. Melt from these ice fields form the headwaters of some of Oregon's finest rivers.

Some scientists believe Mount Jefferson is permanently dormant, but others, less certain, note recent nearby basalt flows and hot springs indicate that magma chambers still glow deep inside the mountain. Located in a roadless wilderness area where vehicles are prohibited, the peak is accessible only by walking trails. The most well known is Pacific Crest Trail 2000, which crosses the west shoulder.

Another popular route enters from OR 22. Follow Forest Service Road 2243 about 7 miles up Whitewater Creek to the edge of the wilderness boundary and the beginning of Whitewater Creek Trail. This route leads 5 miles to spectacular Jefferson Park at the 5,800-foot north base of the mountain. This alpine park was once called Hanging Valley. It is 1 mile wide, about 3 miles long, and is framed between the glaciers on Mount Jefferson and a perpendicular rock wall to the north.

Amateur hikers are warned away from the steep areas of scree and ice above Jefferson Park. Summit climbers rate the north face of Mount Jefferson as one of the most technical and dangerous climbs in the Cascades. Near the top the rock is too rotten to anchor ropes or climbing protection and climbers are forced to free climb, unprotected, to the summit. The climbing season runs from mid-July to mid-September. Allow up to 10 hours to summit from Jefferson Park.

The lower slopes are much more gentle, and in late summer sometimes seem to glow purple and red with wild huckleberries and strawberries.

Politically, the mountain is divided by an invisible north-south line that passes directly through the summit. The area east of the line is within the Warm Springs Indian Reservation. West is the Willamette National Forest.

Directions: The mountain is not accessible by vehicle, including mountain bike, but there are a number of good hiking trails. The most direct access is from OR 22. About 12 miles southeast of Detroit, turn east onto Forest Service Road 2243 and continue 7 miles up Whitewater Creek to the edge of the wilderness area. Whitewater Creek Trail 3429 leads 5 miles to Jefferson Park on the 5,800-foot level on the northern base of the mountain.

Activities: Hiking, mountain climbing, and berry picking.

Facilities: Hiking trails, including Pacific Crest Trail 2000, self-issuing wilderness permit dispensers are positioned at most popular trailheads. Primitive campsite

Dates: Open year-round, but higher trails are generally snow bound from mid-Oct. through June.

Fees: None. Free wilderness permits are required, and are available at trailheads.

Closest town: Detroit on OR 22.

For more information: Willamette National Forest Supervisor Office, 211 East 7th

Avenue, Eugene, OR 97401. Phone (503) 465-6521. Detroit Ranger District, HC 73, Box 320, Mill City, OR 97360. Phone (503) 854-3366.

Santiam Junction Area

SANTIAM JUNCTION/SAND MOUNTAIN LAVA FLOW

[Fig. 24(7)] Acres of exposed nearly barren lava encase the approaches to Santiam Junction in folds of hardened rock. The desolate miles of dark, seemingly lifeless lava create a stark and somewhat sudden contrast to the conifer green corridors lined with bright wildflowers leading into the junction from the north and west.

The junction is where OR 22 merges with US 20/OR 126. Travel northbound on OR 22 to reach Detroit Lake and the Clackamas-Breitenbush Scenic Byway. East on US 20 is the Old West theme town of Sisters, headwaters of the trout-rich Metolius River; and Bend, the largest city along the East Slope. West on US 20 is Albany, the I-5 corridor, the west leg of McKenzie Pass-Santiam Pass Scenic Byway, and the cut-off to Eugene.

The junction is located in the collapsed bed of an ancient lava lake. Hardened wrinkles of once-molten lava flow are visible from the highway at several places near the junction. For travelers coming from the north or west this is the first contact with the huge lava areas unique to the crest of the central Cascades. A clump of lava along OR 22 just north of the junction originated in Nash Crater, visible just south of the junction. The Nash flows are estimated to be 3,800 years old.

South, east, and west of the junction is a hardened flow known as the Sand Mountain lava field. This pyroclastic event oozed from a row of at least 22 closely spaced minor volcanoes that are lined up north to south on a line that crosses US 20 just east of Santiam Junction.

Ridges of basalt can be seen south of the junction. These are the eroded edges of the lava lake. Geologists believe about 3,000 years ago, the surface of the lake solidified on top of molten lava. When the molten materials drained away, the thin lava lid caved in, forming a slight depression where the highways now run.

During the last Ice Age this entire area was covered by glaciers and ice.

Directions: The junction is just west of the crest of the Cascades at the interchange of US 20 and OR 22.

Activities: Sight-seeing.

Facilities: The only facilities at the junction are a state highway work area, and the runway of Santiam Junction State Airport.

Dates: Open year-round, but expect snow from Nov. through May.

Fees: None.

Closest town: Sisters, about 19 miles east on US 20/OR 126.

For more information: Central Oregon Visitors Association, 63085 N. Hwy. 97,

No.104, Bend, OR 97701. Phone (541) 382-8334 or (800) 800-8334. Sisters Area Chamber of Commerce, 222 W. Hood Avenue, Sisters, OR, phone (541) 549-0251.

QUARTZVILLE RECREATION CORRIDOR AND BACK COUNTRY BYWAY

[Fig. 26(3)] Gold fever!

You can almost feel it sizzling seductively in the mountain air, and see it in the washed gravel rolling in the stiff current of Quartzville Creek. This is one of the few mountain areas where hopeful prospectors can still pan for "color" in unclaimed public waters, much as they did in 1863 when Jeremiah Diggs filed the first gold claim.

Quartzville Creek Corridor is a 50-mile-long Bureau of Land Management scenic byway through Oregon gold mining history. The scenic and historic corridor follows an east-west route between OR 22 south of Detroit and US 20 near Sweet Home, and much of the route has been set aside for public gold panning.

The corridor is threaded by a paved, one-lane road, which is one of the least traveled scenic byways in the state. The road parallels Quartzville Creek, a federally designated wild and scenic river that tumbles between rapids and clear pools. The byway passes the one-time boomtown of Quartzville. The townsite is now on private land, and the remains, swallowed in second-growth forest, are difficult to find.

The Quartzville gold boom was actually more of a pop. In 30 years of intense mining, the area produced only about $200,000 worth of gold and silver. The meager legacy, however, doesn't stop modern-day 49ers from trying their luck. Only two private mining claims are in the corridor. The rest of the creek is open to the public for panning. The panning area is between Rocky Top Bridge and the Willamette National Forest boundary.

Amateur prospectors won't need permits to search for gold unless they are using suction dredges or highbank mining equipment, which require free permits from the Oregon Department of Environmental Quality. Most amateur prospectors use gold pans, rockers, or sluice boxes. The Quartzville byway is a true backcountry experience. There are no travel services, residences, or buildings along the route. Ten miles west of OR 22, the road climbs to the top of a ridge dividing drainages to Detroit Lake and Quartzville Creek. There are primitive campsites and a viewpoint with sweeping views that include Mounts Jefferson and Hood.

On the east end the byway connects with OR 22. An outdoor kiosk and map of the route is posted along Road 11 west of the North Santiam River Bridge.

On the west you can reach the byway from US 20, about 1 mile east of Sweet Home. The byway heads east along the north shore of Green Peter Reservoir. Two Bureau of Land Management recreation sites, including a campground and trail, are located along lower Quartzville Creek, which is now used more by swimmers and trout fishermen than gold prospectors.

The entire 50-mile-long corridor is easily driven in less than two hours. The route passes through a mix of old-growth and second-growth conifers, mostly Douglas fir. The drive is accented by gray rock outcroppings, huckleberry patches, wildflowers and leggy vine maple plants.

Directions: From the east on OR 22, turn right onto Straight Creek Road BLM 11 about 2 miles south of Marion Forks. From Sweet Home, follow US 20; turn left on Quartzville Rd., heading towards Green Peter Reservoir. The Quartzville Creek Corridor begins along the north side of the reservoir.

Activities: Sight-seeing, gold panning, fishing, camping, swimming, and boating.

Facilities: Primitive camping along the creek, and two Bureau of Land Management recreation sites with developed campgrounds. Recreational mining corridor can be found on the BLM section of the Byway. There is a map and information kiosk on Straight Creek Road near OR 22.

Dates: Closed from Nov. through Apr. by snow.

Fees: None.

Closest town: Sweet Home and Detroit.

For more information: An informational brochure, gold mining guidelines, and map of the corridor are available from Bureau of Land Management Salem District Office, 1717 Fabry Rd., SE, Salem, OR 97306. Phone (503) 375-5646. The east segment is within the Willamette National Forest. Contact, Sweet Home Ranger District, 3225 Hwy. 20, Sweet Home, OR 97386. Phone (503) 367-5168.

WILD AND SCENIC QUARTZVILLE CREEK

[Fig. 26(1)] Quartzville Creek is a romping pool and riffle stream that by any definition is picturesque. It's a small stream, shallow enough to be crossed in hip waders, and rarely more than a few yards wide. The lower 9.6 miles between Green Peter Reservoir and the Willamette National Forest boundary are designated as wild and scenic.

Quartzville Creek is the major drainage dividing the mountains between the larger North and South Santiam rivers. It was included among the nation's wild and scenic waters by Congress because of the corridor's outstanding scenic drive, opportunities for recreational gold prospecting, and whitewater boating.

Congress didn't mention trout fishing, but local fishermen do.

Oregon outdoor writer Maddy Sheehan describes the tumbling clear water as "an excellent trout stream." It's a small, quick stream that invites light spinning and fly tackle for challenging rainbow and cutthroat trout. Plenty of roadside parking areas are available for fishermen and stream-side picnickers.

Directions: Follow the Quartzville Byway west from OR 22 south of Marion Forks, or east from Green Peter Reservoir on US 20 east about 22 miles east of Sweet Home.

Activities: Trout fishing, gold panning, kayaking, swimming, camping.

Facilities: 1 developed campground and many primitive riverside tent sites.

Dates: Open year-round, snow-free from Apr. through Oct.

Fees: None.

YELLOWBOTTOM RECREATION SITE

[Fig. 26(2)] Yellowbottom Recreation Site is a Bureau of Land Management-operated picnic and campground complex that is nestled in old-growth forest along the wild and

Green Peter Reservoir Area

This U. S. Army Corps of Engineers-managed lake covers 3,720 acres and has 48 miles of shoreline.

226
Rogers Mountain
N
Crabtree Creek
226
Ref: DeLorme Oregon Atlas and Gazetteer
Snow Peak
Crabtree Creek
Brewster Road
Crabtree Creek
Yellowbottom Creek
Green Mountain
Green Mtn. Creek
Yellowstone Mountain
Quartzville Creek
20
Round Mountain
Lebanon
Keel Mountain
Middle Santiam River
South Santiam River
Bald Peter
Green Peter
Green Peter Reservoir
20
Green Peter Dam
Lower Soda Falls Creek
South Santiam River
Foster Reservoir
Sweet Home
20
South Santiam River
20
228
228
Calapooia River
Brush Creek
Green Mountain
Swamp Mountain
Calapooia River
Calapooia River
Oshkosh Mountain

1 U. S. 20 South Santiam Corridor
2 Cascadia State Park
3 Lower Soda Falls
Willamette National Forest

scenic section of Quartzville Creek. Located just west of the Willamette National Forest boundary, the recreation site is a popular base for fishermen, fall hunters, gold panners, and sightseers.

Directions: Follow Straight Creek Road 11 west from OR 22 for about 40 miles or Quartzville Creek Corridor Road east for about 10 miles from Green Peter Reservoir. The campground is near the boundary dividing Bureau of Land Management and Forest Service lands at an elevation of 1,500 feet.

Activities: Picnicking, camping, trout fishing, hiking, hunting, and gold panning.

Facilities: 21 campsites for tents and trailers to 28 feet long, 6 picnic tables, wheelchair accessible vault toilets, and potable water.

Dates: Open May 15 through Sept. 21.

Fees: There is a charge for overnight camping.

RHODODENDRON TRAIL

[Fig. 26(4)] The trail winds uphill behind Yellowbottom Recreation Site through old-growth Douglas fir, western red cedar, and an understory of rhododendrons.

Trail: 1.2 miles one-way

Dates: Open May 15 through Sept. 21.

Elevation: 1,500 feet.

Degree of difficulty: Easy

Surface: Natural forest duff.

GREEN PETER RESERVOIR

[Fig. 25] Green Peter Reservoir is a 10-mile-long flood control impoundment on lower Quartzville Creek and Middle Santiam River, about 8 miles northwest of Sweet Home. It also produces irrigation water and electrical power for the Willamette Valley. This leggy U.S. Army Corps of Engineers-managed lake covers 3,720 acres yet recreation use is light compared with other Cascade impoundments.

It's in a beautiful area at the west end of Quartzville Creek Scenic Corridor. The reservoir's 48 miles of scalloped shoreline rises almost unbroken into the steep canyon walls. The upper lake collects below two inlet arms fed by Quartzville Creek and Middle Santiam River. Above the Middle Santiam Arm, a private logging road follows the river upstream to the edge of the Middle Santiam Wilderness Area. It may be reached from US 20, about 1.5 miles west of Cascadia. The road is rough, but provides access for diehard anglers who want to challenge the Middle Santiam's wild cutthroat and rainbow.

The mountains surrounding Green Peter Reservoir are forested but logging clear-cuts or treeless avalanche chutes sometimes reveal walls of columnar basalt that are common in this area.

At about midlake on the north shore is Whitcomb Creek Park, operated by Linn County as a picnic area sheltered in a large grove of old-growth trees scattered on top of a peninsula high above the water. Secluded tables and grills are set in a shaded glade of drooping deer and sword ferns, beneath towering spars of dark green old-growth hemlocks. The sites are well separated and divided by rangy limbs of vine maple. Swags of club moss hang from tree branches, and where the sun pokes through the canopy grow patches of red huckleberries and Oregon grape. The ground is a soft mat of conifer needles and decomposing fern leaves. Sites are linked by fern-lined trails. A few paths lead daringly down the steep hillside to the lakeshore, but there is no ready access to the water from the picnic area.

The park includes a wide concrete boat launch and campground below the picnic area in a glade of old-growth. Crowds are rarely a problem. A second public boat ramp is available downlake at Thistle Creek Park.

Summer fishermen troll for rainbow trout and kokanee salmon, which get up to 12 inches long. Some largemouth bass fishing takes place, but bass fishing in the deep (the lake's depth averages 114 feet) water is difficult. Primitive, free campsites are wedged into flat spots along the lake's north shore, especially in the Quartzville Creek Arm.

Tours of the dams at Green Peter Reservoir and Foster Lake can be arranged by phoning (541) 367-5127. Like many dams, fish ladders have been built to allow steelhead to migrate upstream beyond the impoundments. What sets these ladders apart is that the rungs at the top of the ladders are actually part of elevator systems that shuttle the fish from the ladder into the lakes where they're released to continue migrating to spawning areas.

Directions: From the I-5 corridor, go east on Hwy 20 through Sweet Home. Continue east from Sweet Home. Turn left on Quartzville Rd., past Foster Reservoir to a north turn up the Quartzville Recreation Corridor. Reservoir recreation facilities are on the north shore of Green Peter Reservoir.

Activities: Boating, camping, fishing, and picnicking.

Facilities: Two boat ramps with restrooms are on the north shore at Thistle Creek and Whitcomb Creek county parks. There is camping and picnicking at Whitcomb Creek County Park.

Dates: Lake open year-round; park open Apr.-mid-Sept.

Fees: There is a charge for camping.

Closest town: Sweet Home is 8 miles west on US 20.

For more information: A map and recreation guide is available from the Army Corps of Engineers, Portland District, PO Box 2946, Portland, OR 97208-2946. Phone (503) 808-5150. For recreation information contact Linn County Parks and Recreation, phone (541) 967-3917.

FOSTER LAKE

[Fig. 25] Foster Lake is the lowest reservoir on Middle Santiam and South Santiam rivers. It is a regulating dam for Green Peter Reservoir, which is about 2.5 miles west. Its 1,200 acres offer fishing, water skiing, boating, camping, and picnicking. The south bank is followed by US 20. The north shore is paralleled by the North River Road extension of Quartzville Scenic Byway.

Directions: 3 miles east of Sweet Home on US 20.

Activities: Camping, fishing, picnicking, swimming, and boating. Weekday tours of the dam can be arranged by phoning (541) 367-5127.

Facilities: Foster Lake has 4 parks and access areas. Only Sunnyside Park offers campsites for tents and RVs with electricity. Sunnyside also has restrooms, drinking water, a picnic area, and a boat launch. Other lakeside parks with boat launches are Gedney Creek Access and Andrew S. Wiley Park. South Santiam State Fish Hatchery and Sweet Home Ranger Station are just west of the reservoir on North River Road and US 20, respectively.

Dates: Reservoir open year-round; Sunnyside Park open Apr.-early Nov.

Fees: A fee is charged for camping at Sunnyside Park.

Closest town: Sweet Home, 3 miles west on US 20.

For more information: A map and recreation guide is available from the Army Corps of Engineers, Portland District, PO Box 2946, Portland, OR 97208-2946. Phone (503) 808-5150. For recreation information contact Linn County Parks and Recreation, (541) 967-3917.

US 20 SOUTH SANTIAM CORRIDOR

[Fig. 25(1)] Like parallel ribbons, US 20 and South Santiam River weave a scenic route linking the crest of the Cascades near Santiam Junction and the lowland community of Sweet Home on the edge of Willamette Valley. US 20 connects with I-5 at the south edge of Albany. East of Sweet Home, travelers in the South Santiam Corridor will find groves of old-growth conifers, waterfalls, a pioneer wagon road, spur routes leading to wilderness areas, campgrounds, riverside picnic sites, covered bridges, nature paths, fire lookouts, hundreds of logging roads and hiking trails, and mile after mile of challenging trout and steelhead fishing.

About 15 miles east of Sweet Home, the two-lane federal highway enters the Sweet Home Ranger District of Willamette National Forest and remains in the forest until it crosses Santiam Pass into Deschutes National Forest and eastern Oregon.

Driving between Sweet Home and the community of Cascadia travelers may occasionally see country grocery stores, some with gas pumps, and front yard stands offering home-grown vegetables and flowers. A covered bridge spans the river two miles west of Cascadia at Maples Store. Turn north from US 20 onto High Deck Road. The road immediately crosses Short Bridge. The towering white-painted covered span was built in 1945. A picnic area is near the bridge.

In a meadow just west of the Cascade crest US 20 merges into OR 126 and continues east to Sisters as part of the McKenzie Pass-Santiam Pass Scenic Byway. The Ranger Station in Sweet Home is an excellent source of maps and information for this route.

Directions: From I-5 turn east on US 20. From Santiam Junction go west on US 20.

Dates: Open year-round.

Fees: There are charges for camping and trail park passes within the corridor.

For more information: Sweet Home Chamber of Commerce, 1575 Main Street, Sweet Home, OR 97386. Phone (541) 367-6186. Willamette National Forest Sweet Home Ranger District, 3225 Highway 20, Sweet Home, OR 97386. Phone (541) 367-5168.

SOUTH SANTIAM RIVER

[Fig. 25] This is an 80-mile-long trout and steelhead river followed for most of its length by US 20 from Albany to its headwaters below the Cascade Crest. Below Foster Dam, South Santiam is a very productive and heavily fished summer-steelhead river. Above the reservoir it's a trout fishery. The upper river is wedged into a narrow, shallow run at the bottom of a steep mountain canyon, and spills westward in a series of classic trout pools, riffles and rapids.

While the lower South Santiam gets a small run of winter steelhead from January through May, it's the large run of summer steelhead, averaging about 8 pounds, that most fishermen come for. Summer steelheading begins in May lasts into October, and peaks in June and July. Summer-runs are available into December, but few anglers try for them after cold weather settles in. One of the best winter and summer steelhead fishing spots is at Wiley Creek Park below Foster Dam. Thousands of steelhead, blocked by the dam from continuing upstream, stack in this area, attracting hopeful steelheaders.

Above Foster Dam, South Santiam is a beautiful trout stream too small to boat yet perfect for wading fishermen. There is roadside access to the water from US 20, plus a series of campgrounds and parks. At Yukwah Campground a wheelchair-accessible fishing platform extends over the water.

Rainbow and wild cutthroat trout up to 14 inches are fun on light spinning rods or fly tackle. A lot of people fish near the campgrounds, but there is also lots of less-crowded water to explore. The upper South Santiam is rarely more than a few yards wide and there are many shallow areas for wade fishing. Fishing is the most popular recreation attraction on the South Santiam River, but wildlife watchers may also enjoy an occasional glimpse of beavers, river otters, mink, black-tailed deer, great blue herons, belted kingfishers, and families of common and red-breasted mergansers.

Directions: The river is followed by US 20 from the crest of the Cascade Mountains to below Sweet Home in the Willamette Valley.

Activities: Fishing for steelhead, salmon, and trout.

Dates: Open year-round, but fishing seasons can vary annually.

Fees: None. There is a charge for fishing licenses.

Closest town: Sweet Home.

For more information: Oregon Department of Fish and Wildlife, Columbia Region, 17330 SE Evelyn Street, Clackamas, OR 97015. Phone (503) 657-2000. Fishing licenses, regulations, and current fishing conditions can be picked up at tackle shops in Sweet Home and along US 20.

CASCADIA STATE PARK

[Fig. 25(2), Fig. 26(5)] Once a thriving 312-acre resort on South Santiam River famous for "medicinal" spring water, much of Cascadia is now a state park with campgrounds, nature trails, picnic area, and river frontage. A nearby waterfall plunges across a triple tier drop. The natural spring pumps out water that is unusually high in calcium, potassium, and iron. In the late 1800s local entrepreneurs built a resort that catered to believers who came to soak away illnesses and injuries in the so-called medicinal spring. The water is still rich in minerals and other natural elements but most people today are looking for a picnic table, quiet campsite, or scenic walk to nearby Lower Soda waterfall.

The campground and park are in a grove of huge bigleaf maples, hemlocks, and firs. Cascadia Cave, a few hundred yards east on OR 20, is one of the oldest known Indian sites in Oregon. Archeologists believe the cave was used 8,000 years ago as a temporary shelter during hunting and berry-gathering treks. Faded petroglyphs can be seen at the cave, but there are no facilities, and the cave can be difficult to locate.

Directions: Follow US 20, 14 miles east of Sweet Home along the South Santiam River.

Activities: Camping, picnicking, fishing, swimming, and hiking.

Facilities: 25 primitive tent and RV sites to 35 feet long, picnic area with tables and grills, potable water, a 1.5 mile round trip nature walk.

Dates: Open year-round for day use. Campground open mid-Apr. through Oct.

Fees: There is a charge for camping.

For more information: District park office at Detroit Lake State Park (503) 854-3406, or contact Oregon Parks and Recreation, 1115 Commercial Street NE, Salem, OR 97301-1002. Phone (800) 551-6949.

LOWER SODA FALLS

[Fig. 25(3)] Lower Soda Creek Falls is a thin stream that drops 180 feet in three tiers into a sylvan setting of moss-covered rocks and tree canopy. There's a 0.5 mile path from Cascadia State Park.

Directions: The trail to the falls begins at the north side of Cascadia State Park on US 20.

Facilities: None.

Dates: Open year-round.

Fees: None.

GREAT BLUE HERON
(Ardea herodias)
Often spotted standing or stalking in water, this heron catches fish by using its bill, like pincers. It grows to 4 feet tall and has a wingspan of 6 feet.

Sweet Home Area

SANTIAM WAGON ROAD

[Fig. 26(6)] Santiam Wagon Road parallels US 20 for 19 miles through South Santiam Valley between Cascadia State Park and the Cascade Crest at OR 126. Hikers may reach the road and walk in the tracks of Oregon pioneers from the highway at dozens of picnic areas, rest stops, and parks.

Unlike other early wagon roads that were built to bring settlers west into the Willamette Valley, Santiam Wagon Road was hacked eastward through the wilderness. The purpose of the road was to get Willamette Valley cattle to pasture lands and beef markets in the gold mining regions east of the Cascades.

The route is maintained by the Forest Service as a trail for hikers, horseback riders, and mountain bikers. A short segment near Tombstone Pass is sometimes open to vintage pre-1940 vehicles and horse-drawn wagons. Permits are required from the Sweet Home or McKenzie ranger district offices.

The vintage auto traffic is allowed to commemorate automotive history that was made on this road June 20, 1905. Dwight Huss drove west on the Santiam Wagon Road in a 1904 Oldsmobile during the first-ever continental crossing by automobile. The trip also marked the first car on the Oregon Trail, and the first automobile crossing of the Oregon Cascades. It took Huss 44 days to drive from New York to Portland. A commemorative plaque is posted at Tombstone Pass.

Directions: US 20 follows the Santiam Wagon Road and provides many entry points between Cascadia State Park and Tombstone Pass.

Activities: Hiking, mountain biking, and horseback riding.

Facilities: None, although there are campgrounds and Forest Service picnic areas on US 20.

Dates: Open year-round, but upper elevations are snow-covered from Nov. through Apr.

Fees: There is a charge for trail use parking permits.

Closest town: Sweet Home is about 15 miles west of the western terminus.

For more information: Linn County Tourism Coalition, Albany Visitors Association, 300 2nd Avenue SW, Albany, OR 97321. Phone (541) 928-0911. Sweet Home Ranger District, 3225 Highway 20, Sweet Home, OR 97386. Phone (541) 367-5168.

TROUT CREEK

[Fig. 26] Jammed into an otherwise woodsy two-mile section of US 20 19 miles east of Sweet Home are a pair of large Forest Service campgrounds, a jump-off to two wilderness areas, a popular hiking trail, rock climbing pinnacles, an elk-viewing interpretive area, and a pretty stretch of good trout fishing.

The valley is a migration corridor for herds of elk that spend summers grazing in the meadows at the top of surrounding ridges, and winters in the often snow-free forests near the lower river. This site is often used by elk moving between summer and winter ranges.

Directions: On US 20 between Trout Creek and Fernview campgrounds at an elevation of 1,200 feet.

Activities: Camping, fishing, wildlife viewing, rock climbing, hiking.

Facilities: Campgrounds, trails, interpretive center.

Dates: Open year-round.

Fees: There are charges for camping and trail park passes.

Closest town: Sweet Home.

For more information: Sweet Home Ranger District, 3225 Highway 20, Sweet Home, OR 97386. Phone (541) 367-5168.

TROUT CREEK CAMPGROUND

[Fig. 26(7)] **Directions:** Alongside US 20 about 19 miles east of Sweet Home.

Activities: Camping, hiking, picnicking, swimming, fishing and interpretive trail.

Facilities: 24 tent and RV sites, potable water, tables, grills, and wheelchair-accessible restroom.

Dates: Open year-round.

Fees: There is a charge for camping.

WALTON RANCH INTERPRETATIVE TRAIL 3418

[Fig. 26(8)] The trail begins at Trout Creek Campground, crosses Trout Creek and ends at two viewing platforms. The first viewpoint overlooks Walton Ranch interpretive site and wildlife habitat area. The second platform offers a better view of the west end of the ranch meadow where elk often spend the winter feeding below the snow line that encases the upper elevation feeding areas in many feet of snow.

Directions: Adjacent to Trout Creek Campground area.

Fees: None.

Trail: 0.25 mile, wheelchair accessible.

Elevation: 1,300 to 1,400 feet.

Degree of difficulty: Easy.

Surface: Gravel.

BEAVER (*Castor canadensis*)

YUKWAH CAMPGROUND

[Fig. 26(9)] Just east of Trout Creek Campground, at an elevation of 1,300 feet, is Yukwah Campground. The unusual feature of this camp is the fishing platforms, accessible to wheelchairs, which are built at the edge of South Santiam River. River pools below the platforms are heavily stocked with trout throughout the summer.

Activities: Camping, hiking, swimming, and fishing.

Facilities: 20 tent and RV campsites, potable water, tables, grills, restroom, fishing platforms, and barrier-free access.

Dates: Open mid Apr. through Oct.

Fees: There is a charge for camping.

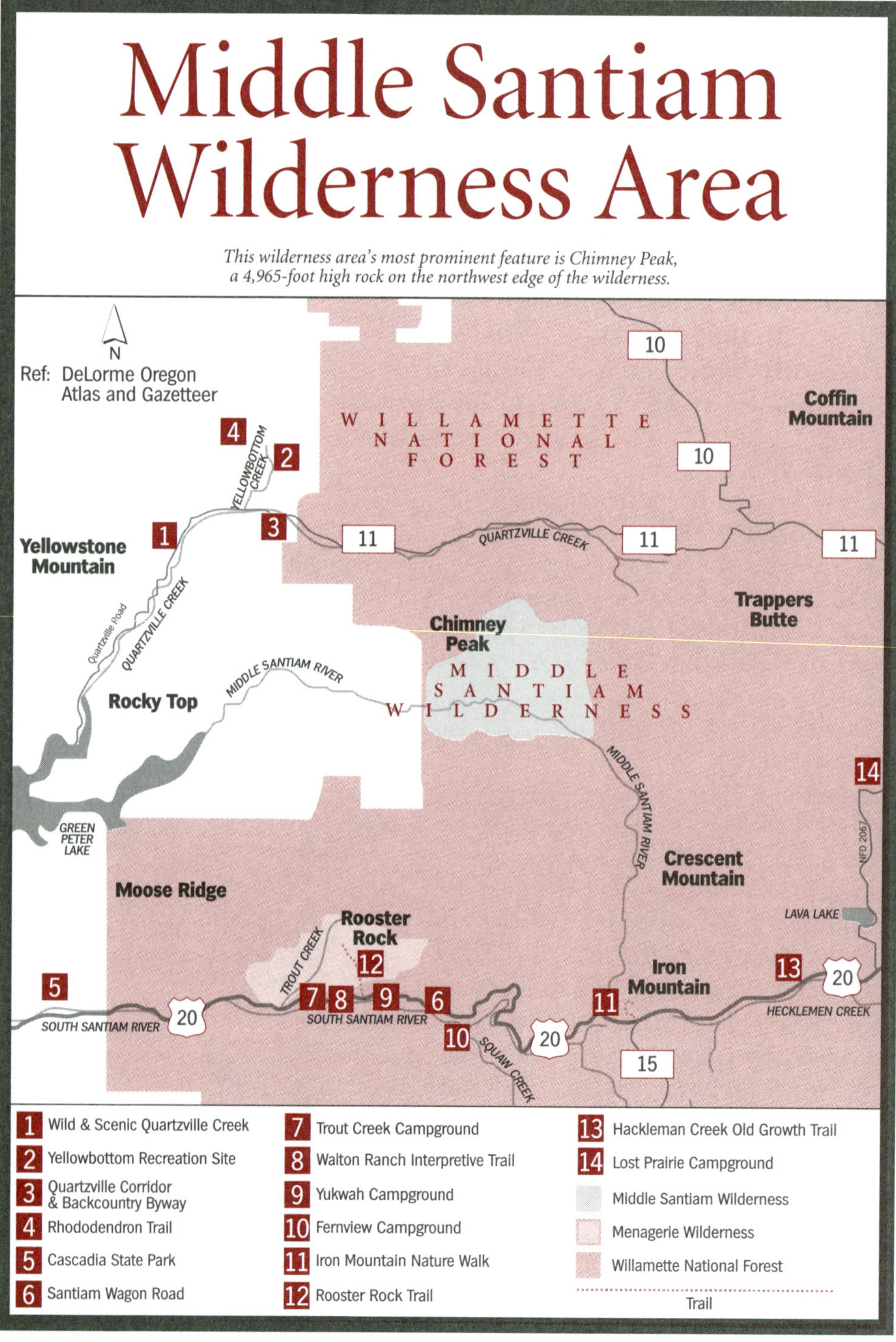
Middle Santiam
Wilderness Area
This wilderness area's most prominent feature is Chimney Peak, a 4,965-foot high rock on the northwest edge of the wilderness.
N
Ref: DeLorme Oregon Atlas and Gazetteer
WILLAMETTE NATIONAL FOREST
Coffin Mountain
Yellowstone Mountain
YELLOWBOTTOM CREEK
QUARTZVILLE CREEK
Quartzville Road
Trappers Butte
Chimney Peak
MIDDLE SANTIAM WILDERNESS
MIDDLE SANTIAM RIVER
Rocky Top
GREEN PETER LAKE
Moose Ridge
Rooster Rock
TROUT CREEK
Crescent Mountain
NFD 2067
LAVA LAKE
Iron Mountain
SOUTH SANTIAM RIVER
SQUAW CREEK
HECKLEMEN CREEK
1 Wild & Scenic Quartzville Creek
2 Yellowbottom Recreation Site
3 Quartzville Corridor & Backcountry Byway
4 Rhododendron Trail
5 Cascadia State Park
6 Santiam Wagon Road
7 Trout Creek Campground
8 Walton Ranch Interpretive Trail
9 Yukwah Campground
10 Fernview Campground
11 Iron Mountain Nature Walk
12 Rooster Rock Trail
13 Hackleman Creek Old Growth Trail
14 Lost Prairie Campground
Middle Santiam Wilderness
Menagerie Wilderness
Willamette National Forest
Trail

MIDDLE SANTIAM WILDERNESS

[Fig. 26] If you are searching for an outdoor adventure far from the beaten path, the Middle Santiam Wilderness is waiting. This is one of the smallest, most isolated, and rarely visited wilderness areas in Oregon. Its 8,542 acres form the headwaters of the Middle Santiam River. The region is a remote wedge of unlogged mountains north of busy US 20, south of popular Quartzville Scenic Byway Forest Service 11, and east of Green Peter Reservoir. From some vantage points it seems to be an island of ancient old-growth conifers in a sea of clear-cut logging tracts. The heavily eroded topography ranges from steep slopes, to sharp peaks and ridges in the higher areas, to gentle slopes and benches at lower elevations. The most prominent feature is Chimney Peak, a 4,965-foot high rock on the northwest edge of the wilderness at the head of McQuade Creek. Elevations in the wilderness range from 1,600 to 5,022 feet. Donaca Lake and Middle Santiam River both have wild trout and are rarely fished. Donaca Lake is located at 2,700 feet. Although it is only 3 acres in size, it is 41 feet deep, and has cutthroat trout. Middle Santiam River flows from the west side of the wilderness, and is so rarely fished that few of Oregon's fishing guidebooks even mention it. It's a pretty stream, small and easily fished for native cutthroat and rainbow trout. A mix of federal and private dirt and gravel logging roads approach the wilderness on all sides. Three trail systems web through dense stands of old-growth Douglas fir, western red cedar, and western hemlock. Silver fir grows at the highest elevations. Nearly all of Oregon's large mammals can be found here, including black-tailed deer, elk, black bear, and cougar (*Felis concolor*). Sometimes called mountain lion, Oregon's cougar population has been climbing in recent years because of hunting restrictions. Sightings of these wary predators are increasing in frequency, but are still rare. The big cats are attracted by the deer and elk herds that live in Middle Santiam Wilderness, are most active at night, and generally give hikers and backpackers a wide berth.

Directions: From the north, follow OR 20 to Quartzville Scenic Byway Forest Service 11. Abut 3 miles east of Yellowbottom Campground, turn south onto Forest Service 1142 and continue to the marked McQuade Creek Trail 3397, which goes into the wilderness area to Chimney Park. From the south, one mile east of Fernview Campground on US 20, turn north onto Forest Service 2041 and continue about 12 miles to the south boundary. This is a long, dusty, sometimes rough road and may not be suitable for cars with low ground clearance. Turn right onto 646 Spur and drive 1.5 miles to the trailhead.

Activities: Backpacking, camping, trout fishing, fall hunting, and rock climbing.

Facilities: 3 trail systems for walkers or horseback riders.

Dates: Open year-round, but most of the access roads are snow covered from late Oct. through May.

Fees: There is a charge for trail park passes to use trails at Chimney Peaks 1 and 2, Gordan Peak, Swamp Peak, and McQuade Creek. A free wilderness permit is required from Memorial Day through Oct. 31.

Closest town: Sweet Home.

For more information: Sweet Home Ranger District, 3225 Highway 20, Sweet Home, OR 97386. Phone (541) 367-5168.

IRON MOUNTAIN NATURE WALK

[Fig. 26(11)] This is one of the most compressed and interesting hikes in the South Santiam River Corridor. More than 300 species of wildflowers have been documented on this hillside, and many botanists describe it the most spectacular wildflower display in western Oregon. A short, steep switchback trail leads through 11 habitat zones to a manned fire lookout. The lookout is on the 5,455 foot summit of Iron Mountain, a 30 million-year-old remnant of an ash and lava spewing volcano. There are 20 interpretive stops along the mile-long trail, explaining rock formations, meadow habitats, and boreal forests. The most unusual feature is a xeric meadow, which is an arid habitat so dry and harsh that naturalists call it a mountainside desert. The rocky meadow is exposed to full summer sun, and the imposing bulk of Iron Mountain screens away most rain clouds. The results are a near-desert habitat surrounded by lush forests. Because of the variety and variable blooming periods, wildflowers are in bloom along the trail spring, summer, and fall. Bright pink swags of Davidson's penstemon (*Penstemon davidsonii*) thrive along with 299 other species. The best time to view blooming wildflowers is mid-June through Labor Day. Pick up a guide pamphlet keyed to designated stops on the nature walk at the trailhead or through the Sweet Home Ranger District office.

Directions: From Sweet Home drive 34 miles east on US 20 to Forest Service Road 15. Turn right and travel .5 miles. The trailhead will be on the right. Another option is to drive 1.25 miles west on Forest Service 15 to a north turn onto Civil road 035 and follow 035 to its end. A vault restroom is available at this trailhead, and the summit is a 0.9 mile hike.

Dates: Snow-free from June through Oct.

Fees: There is a charge for trail park passes at both trailheads.

Closest town: Sweet Home.

For more information: Sweet Home Ranger District, 3225 Highway 20, Sweet Home, OR 97386. Phone (541) 367-5168.

Trail: Iron Mountain 3389, 1.6 miles one way.

Elevation: Trailhead, about 2,600 feet; summit 5,455 feet.

Degree of difficulty: Strenuous. The trail is steep, narrow, and sometimes runs along the edge of nearly vertical slopes. Pets are permitted but it is advised they be leashed. Carry water.

LOST PRAIRIE

[Fig. 26] While searching this area for a lost herd, a cattleman is reported to have found the west side of what later became the Santiam Pass route from the Willamette Valley to central Oregon. The route is now part of the historic Santiam Wagon Road (*see* Santiam Wagon Road, page 164), which passes through the prairie. Nearby attractions include trails to Echo Basin Old Growth, Road 2067 to vanishing Lava Lake, and the junction of OR 126, which is the west leg of McKenzie Pass-Santiam Pass Scenic Byway.

US 20 crosses Tombstone Pass at an elevation of 4,236 feet. The pass is named for an 1871 tragedy. Eighteen-year-old James McKnight was accidentally killed by his own gun while the pioneer family camped. His grieving mother erected a monument, which became a landmark for pioneers who followed.

Pre-1940 vehicles and horse-drawn wagons are allowed on the Santiam Wagon Road between Tombstone Pass and Fish Lake (*see* Santiam Wagon Road, page 164). Special vehicle permits are required, and can be obtained at the Sweet Home Ranger District office. Lava Lake, which is just north of US 20, is a large snow melt lake with the annoying habit of disappearing into a lava fault during the summer when there is little precipitation in this area. Follow paved Forest Service Road 2067 north to the lake. Forest Service 2067 continues on a loop route that joins OR 22 north of Santiam Junction. The cut-off makes a nice side trip through this picturesque forest, meadow, and lava rock country. Spur roads lead west into the Three Pyramid Mountains. Just east of Lost Prairie, US 20 spills out of the forest and into a meadow studded with lava boulders, and a commanding view of Three-Fingered Jack Mountain jutting 7,841 feet into the sky above the Mount Jefferson Wilderness Area.

This is the junction of OR 126. Turn south and you'll follow the scenic byway along the McKenzie River to Eugene. Turn north and about 1.1 mile northeast of the merge is a short trail to Sawyer's Cave, which is a lava tube encrusted with permanent ice. Lava tubes were formed by fingers of molten lava that burned tapered passageways underground. When the lava flows drained away, what remained were lengthy carrot-shaped caverns with walls coated with a veneer of basalt lava. Lava tube caves are found around most of the Northwest's most recently active volcanoes. Enough moisture sometimes dripped into some lava tubes, including Sawyer's Cave, to form ice during the winter. The cold cavern temperatures preserved the frozen water for much of the summer, and provided a source of ice for pioneers.

Sawyer's Cave is marked at the highway. Continue northeast on US 20/OR 126 to Santiam Junction where OR 22 cuts off north to Detroit Lake. The recreationally important East Slope cities of Sisters and Bend are east of Santiam Junction along US 20/OR 126. In winter Lost Prairie is a favorite destination for snowmobiling and cross-country skiing. In the summer campers use Lost Prairie Campground as a base for exploring the intriguing local high country.

LOST PRAIRIE CAMPGROUND

[Fig. 26(14)] **Directions:** Follow US 20 east of Sweet Home for 37 miles to Lost Prairie near the summit of the Cascades.

Activities: Camping, fishing, picnicking, mountain biking, and hiking.

Facilities: 4 barrier-free tent and RV sites, and a day use picnic area with 6 tables, and well water.

Dates: Open year-round.

Fees: There are charges for campsites, and trail park passes.

SPOTTED OWL

The spotted owl is identified by its large, dark eyes and white spots on the head, back, and underparts.

Fig. 27: McKenzie-Santiam Pass Loop

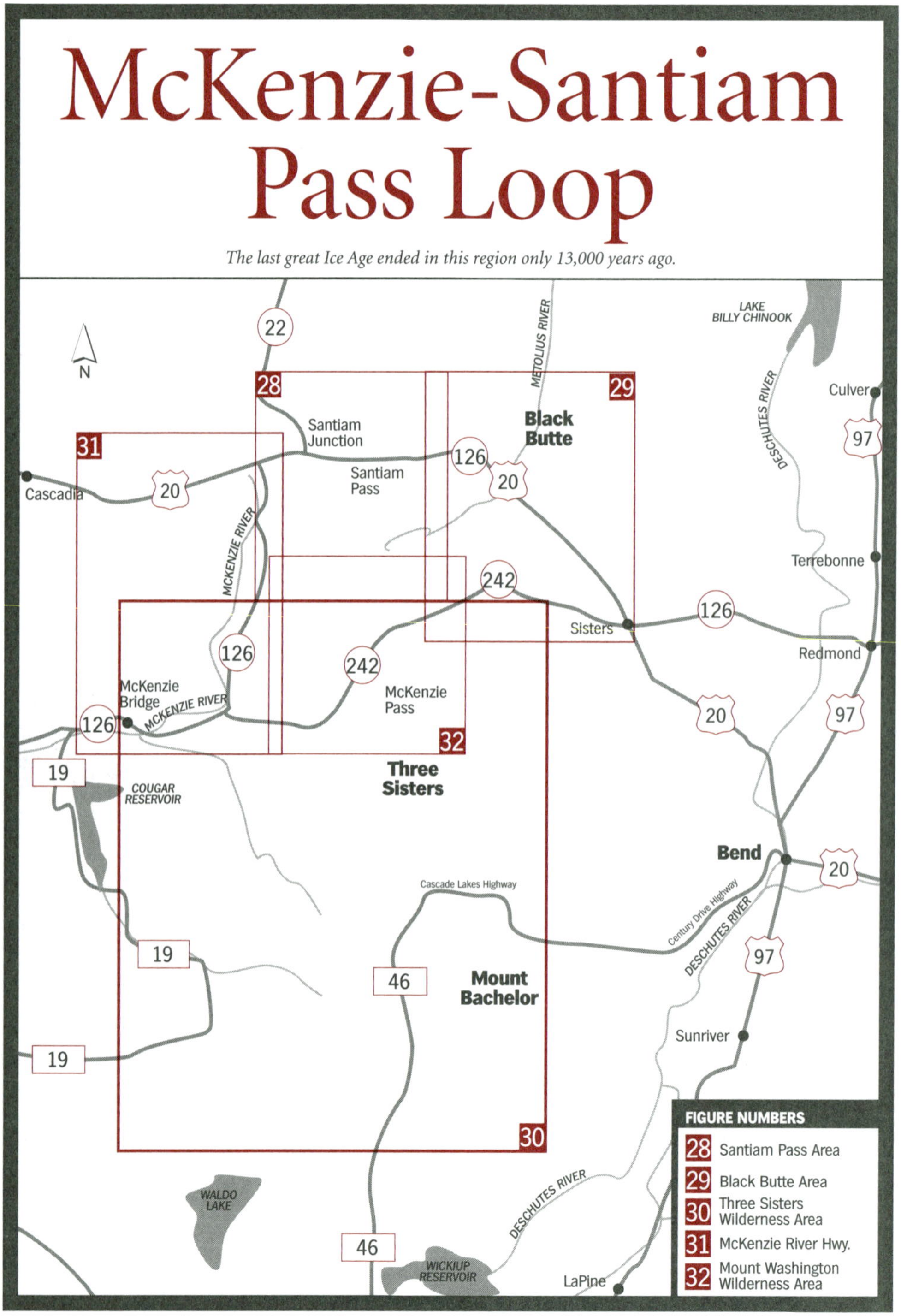

McKenzie-Santiam Pass Loop
The last great Ice Age ended in this region only 13,000 years ago.
N
22
28
29
31
32
30
METOLIUS RIVER
LAKE BILLY CHINOOK
DESCHUTES RIVER
Culver
97
Santiam Junction
Black Butte
Santiam Pass
126
20
Cascadia
MCKENZIE RIVER
242
Terrebonne
Sisters
Redmond
McKenzie Bridge
McKenzie Pass
Three Sisters
19
COUGAR RESERVOIR
Bend
Cascade Lakes Highway
Century Drive Highway
46
Mount Bachelor
Sunriver
WALDO LAKE
WICKIUP RESERVOIR
LaPine
FIGURE NUMBERS
28 Santiam Pass Area
29 Black Butte Area
30 Three Sisters Wilderness Area
31 McKenzie River Hwy.
32 Mount Washington Wilderness Area

McKenzie–Santiam Pass Loop

Four of Oregon's most scenic highways converge at Santiam Junction, a mountain hub situated roughly between the west and East Slope cities of Salem and Sisters.

The Hudson's Bay Company, the powerful British fur dealing organization that built Fort Vancouver near Portland, first sent European explorers through this gap. Peter Skene Ogden led the first party. He came through in 1825, headed for Santiam Pass with 32 mountain men instructed to trap into extinction any beaver they found in order to discourage American trappers who might follow.

The brigade managed to obtain only 460 pelts. After learning that Modoc Indians near the California border were hostile, Ogden returned to Fort Vancouver and recommended against the British establishing a fort on the East Slope. That recommendation left the interior of Oregon open to American exploration, which came 20 years later. By

[*Above:* Anglers fish from a McKenzie boat, a dory-shaped riverboat that was named for the McKenzie River.]

1850, Oregon Trail pioneers had begun to settle along the East Slope.

This pastoral saddle in the central Cascades is probably little changed from the time when Ogden crossed, except for the four modern highways that converge at the hub, presenting travelers with a choice of scenic direction.

This is a region of massive lava flows, volcanic peaks, craters, mountainous wilderness areas, and spring-fed rivers and lakes. The McKenzie-Santiam Pass Loop, an 82-mile paved scenic route, encircles the region.

Attractions along the loop include a downhill ski and winter recreation area, the recreationally oriented Western theme town of Sisters, a massive lava flow with a paved interpretive trail and rock-house observatory (*see* McKenzie Pass, page 203), wild and scenic rivers, rock spires, several geologic oddities, dozens of trout lakes, campgrounds, three wilderness areas, and miles of hiking trails.

The east and south borders of the McKenzie-Santiam Region are formed by McKenzie Pass Highway/OR 242, which angles between McKenzie River Highway/OR 126 East at Sisters and OR 126 West at Belknap Hot Springs. This mountain pass route is closed during winter. Some years, it's mid-July before enough snow melts for the pass to open.

McKenzie Pass is a lava wonderland on a natural divide between Three Sisters and Mount Washington wilderness areas. The road is built on top of hardened lava flows that extend for miles on either side of the highway. One flow covers 65 square miles with black lava and is believed to be about 2,700 years old — almost new in geological time.

Except for ranches and a few private timber holdings along the highways, nearly all of this land is public and managed by the Forest Service. On the lower McKenzie River, Forest Service land gives way to a mix of ownerships as it slides into the Willamette Valley. Land management in the lowlands is divided among the Bureau of Land Management, several state departments, and private timber producers.

Some of the most productive timber harvests in the nation come from this area. The Willamette National Forest usually ranks in the nation's top five timber-producing national forests. That fact pleases foothills communities with timber-based economies, and rankles conservationists and preservationists who are calling for harvest reductions, protection of old-growth conifers, road closures, and an end to clear-cut logging practices.

Elevations in this region vary from 1,000 feet in the western foothills to 10,495 feet atop Mount Jefferson. Above 3,000 feet elevation, snow blankets the peaks and ridges from October through May, supplying water for more than 1,500 miles of rivers and streams and almost 400 lakes.

Most of the West Slope is covered with Douglas fir, western red cedar, and hemlock, including many stands of old-growth.

The East Slope is in the rain shadow and is a much more arid land where forests are dominated by less water-dependent pines, especially ponderosa and lodgepole. Drought-tolerant sagebrush (*Artemisia tridentata*); bitterbrush (*Purshia tridentata*), an important winter food for deer; and the sunflower-like arrowleaf balsamroot (*Balsamorhiza sagitta-*

ta), grow on the lower skirts of the East Slope.

This is one of the best places in the state to get a close-up look at the Cascade Range's volcanic creation. According to an official at the Deschutes National Forest, "more good examples of different kinds of volcanic features can be found here than anywhere else in the United States." Some of the most distinctive features may be found at McKenzie Pass southwest of Sisters (*see* page 208), and south of Bend at Lava Lands Visitor Center and Newberry National Monument (*see* page 251).

The last great Ice Age ended in this region only about 13,000 years ago, a microsecond in geologic time. Slabs of glaciers from that period are still wedged into crevasses near the summits of Mount Jefferson, Three Sisters, Diamond Peak, and Mount Thielsen.

The topography shows the scars of glacial scouring, lava flows, and erosion. Volcanic cones and lava fields ranging in size from a few acres to massive shields that cover many square miles are scattered across the landscape.

More than 300 species of fish and wildlife are found here, including the uncommon northern spotted owl (*Strix occidentalis*), which stirred up a controversy in the late 1970s. When it was discovered that spotted owls required old-growth conifers for habitat, federal officials shut down many logging areas, infuriating timber-oriented industries and workers. Harlequin ducks (*Histrionicus histrionicus*), a sea species, are sometimes seen in fast-moving mountain streams during the summer in this region. They come to breed and nest, and return to the ocean in the fall and winter.

Golden eagles and other birds of prey soar on the updrafts along the East Slope, while most water areas on the West Slope are visited by hunting bald eagles and ospreys.

More common are the big game animals such as black-tailed and mule deer, elk, black bear, and cougars. Bears and cougars are rarely a problem, but they do inhabit almost the entire region. Bears have been known to attack unattended picnic baskets. Oregon's only poisonous reptile, northern Pacific rattlesnakes (*Crotalus viridis oreganus*) live in the river breaks and sagebrush areas along the lower East Slope. The non-venomous ringneck snake (*Diadophis punctatus*) is also found in western Oregon and has been spotted in this area.

Most day-use areas and hiking and biking trails along the byway require that a trail park pass be purchased. Venturing into the Jefferson, Washington and Three Sisters wilderness areas requires permits, which are free. Permits and trail park passes can be picked up at the Sisters Ranger District office, located on US 20 on the west outskirts of Sisters. Don't count on finding a source for forest use passes beyond the Sisters' business area.

Santiam Junction

[Fig. 28(1)] Santiam Junction is a lava-littered meadow where the west side's wet green forests and the east side's dry brown sagebrush prairies collide in a high mountain saddle. The mountain region north of Santiam Junction is lush and full of water drained by Oregon's twin cloud catchers, Mounts Hood and Jefferson. Drenched by nine months and more than 25 feet of annual rain and snow, northern mountain forests are thick with giant conifers (some more than 200 feet tall) and dense underbrush. Walls of Oregon greenery press into roadways, overhang river banks, and plug treeless clear-cuts with tangles of leggy vine maples, scrub alders, and wads of thimbleberry and salmonberry stalks.

South, away from the wet influence of the mountain giants, the air is drier, the landscape more open, and there are miles of Oregon's volcanic history. Lava flows, sometimes miles wide, lie across the mountains like wrinkled gray sheets. The massive flows are starkly barren except for scattered islands of juniper and pine that grow incongruously from small plots of spare soil encircled by hardened lava.

East brings travelers to sagebrush, clear skies, and llama, horse, and cattle pastures studded with room-size chunks of black basalt from eruptions during the volcanic formation of the High Cascades. River banks are eroded into bald folds, one laid on top of the next like rows of fallen dominoes. Between the folds are silken flows famous for trout, steelhead, and whitewater thrills.

The north-south path of Pacific Crest Trail 2000 forms a climatic and political demarcation line roughly through the center of the region. The moist West Slope is in Willamette National Forest. The drier East Slope is mostly in Deschutes National Forest. Traveler services and private tourism services are few and far between in this mountainous region. The other highways that meet at Santiam Junction include OR 22 north, US 20 west, and OR 126 west.

OR 22 goes north from Santiam Junction to Detroit Lake, and North Santiam Canyon. The highway closely follows North Santiam River and connects with paved scenic byways along the Breitenbush and Clackamas wild and scenic rivers. This highway also intersects Skyline Road Forest Service 42, which can be driven north through the Skyline Region to Mount Hood.

US 20 crosses west and east, and is a two-lane link between the Willamette Valley and the sun-splashed town of Sisters. West from Santiam Junction, US 20 follows South Santiam River to Sweet Home on the edge of the I-5 corridor. East of the junction, US 20 merges with OR 126, and the combined state and federal highways form the northern loop of McKenzie-Santiam Scenic Byway. En route to Sisters, this route passes near the Hoodoo Ski Area, Black Butte, several campgrounds, and the headwater spring of the trout-rich Metolius River. The combined federal and state highways follow an open 5,000-foot elevation ridge where the landscape seems harsh, almost Arctic at times, and is filled with volcanic cinder cones, stunted pine trees, trout lakes, and red lava rocks.

McKenzie River Highway/OR 126 turns south and west from the junction. Southbound it follows the densely timbered West Slope for about 20 miles along the headwaters of McKenzie River, then bends west to continue along the river to Eugene. Shortly after the west turn, OR 126 is intersected by Aufderheide Memorial Drive. The Aufderheide route goes south from OR 126 over a divide and descends along the North Fork Middle Fork Willamette River, past several remote campgrounds to OR 58 at Oakridge.

Directions: Follow US 20/OR 126 west from Sisters or US 20 east from Sweet Home. From Eugene follow OR 126 east and north. From Detroit, follow OR 22 east and south.

Activities: Sight-seeing.

Facilities: None.

Dates: Open year-round.

Fees: None.

Closest town: Sisters, about 21 miles east on US 20/OR 126.

For more information: McKenzie Ranger District, Willamette National Forest, Hwy. 126, McKenzie, OR 97413. Phone (541) 822-3381.

LOST LAKE

[Fig. 28] Lost Lake is about 2 miles east of Santiam Junction, on the north side of US 20/OR 126. Its cold 50 acres of shallow snow melt are a favorite destination for mountain fishermen after trout and Atlantic salmon. There's a campground on the west shore.

The red and black cinder cones around the lake were active just 2,000 years ago. Snow-capped Three-Fingered Jack Mountain, elevation 7,841, towers against the northern sky.

Directions: US 20/OR 126 about 2 miles east of Santiam Junction or 19 miles west of Sisters.

Activities: Camping, fishing.

Facilities: Primitive, undesignated tent sites, no services.

Dates: Open Memorial Day through Labor Day.

Fees: None.

Closest town: Sisters.

For more information: McKenzie Ranger District, Willamette National Forest, Hwy. 126, McKenzie, OR 97413. Phone (541) 822-3381.

HOODOO SKI BOWL

[Fig. 28(2)] This is a small, family-oriented winter ski area offering both downhill and cross-country runs.

Directions: US 20 west from Sisters across Santiam Pass then south on Forest Service Road 2690 to the ski area.

Activities: Downhill and cross-country ski runs.

Facilities: Day lodge with cafe, ski rentals, 5 lifts, 17 runs, 1,035 foot vertical drop.

Elevation: 4,668 at base to 5,703.

Dates: Open mid-Dec. through mid-Apr.

For more information: Hoodoo Ski Bowl, Sisters, OR 97759. Phone (541) 822-3799.

BIG LAKE

[Fig. 28] South of Hoodoo Ski Bowl, on Forest Service 2690, is tree-encircled Big Lake, 250 acres of water recreation at an elevation of 4,639 feet near the summit of the Cascade

Range. This is a popular destination for camping, trout fishing, and boating. The nearby forest of conifer snags is the result of a devastating 7,700-acre forest fire in 1967.

Directions: US 20/OR 126 west from Sisters across Santiam Pass then south on Forest Service Road 2690 for 4 miles.

Activities: Fishing for rainbow, brook, and cutthroat trout and kokanee salmon; camping, water skiing, and hiking.

Facilities: There are 2 campgrounds with restrooms. Big Lake Campground is on the north shore and offers 11 day-use picnic sites, 49 tent and RV sites, and water. On the west bank, Big Lake West, is a walk-in access with 11 tent sites, but no water. Sites include tables and fire grills.

Dates: The lake is open to fishing year-round, but the campgrounds close in winter.

Fees: There is a fee for camping at both campgrounds.

For more information: McKenzie Ranger District, Willamette National Forest, Hwy. 126, McKenzie, OR 97413. Phone (541) 822-3381.

SAND MOUNTAIN LOOKOUT

[Fig. 28(3)] A gable-roofed Forest Service lookout sits atop 5,459-foot Sand Mountain west of Big Lake. It's maintained as an interpretive site and is not available for rent.

Directions: US 20 west from Sisters across Santiam Pass, then south on Forest Service Road 2690 for 4 miles, turning west on Forest Service Road 810 at the north end of Big Lake. This dirt road can be rough and portions are unsuitable for passenger cars. The lookout site is about 5 miles west on Forest Service 810.

Activities: Regional vistas.

Facilities: Interpretive site in a lookout built to resemble a 1930s facility. The lookout is not a tower, sitting just 12 feet off the ground.

Dates: The road is snow-free generally from July 1 through Oct. 15.

Fees: None.

PATJENS LAKES LOOP TRAIL 3395

[Fig. 28(4)] This trail offers a rare opportunity for a short loop hike to lakes in the Mount Washington Wilderness. The trail is in a mixed forest of lodgepole pine, western hemlock and alpine fir. Three small lakes, two with trout, are near the trail. Middle Patjens, 6 acres, is stocked with rainbow trout. Upper Patjens, 3 acres, has brook trout.

Directions: The trail is on the east and west sides of Big Lake. The main trailhead is in West Campground.

Dates: Open year-round, snow-free in late May through Oct.

Fees: There is a fee for passes to park at the trailhead. Free wilderness permits are required and are dispensed at the trailhead.

Trail: 5.5-mile loop route into Mount Washington Wilderness.

Elevation: 4,650 feet at trailhead, with a 500 foot change.

Degree of difficulty: Easy.

Surface: Dirt and rock.

Deschutes National Forest

[Fig. 5] The word "diverse" best describes the Deschutes National Forest's 1,852,497 acres of central Oregon, which extend for about 100 miles along the east side of the Cascade Mountains crest. The forest includes alpine areas, geologic formations, dense evergreen forests, mountain lakes, caves, desert areas, and high-mountain meadows.

Elevations range from 1,950 feet at Lake Billy Chinook north of Sisters to 10,358 feet at the top of South Sister Mountain, the third highest peak in Oregon.

Deschutes National Forest is one of the most popular forests in the Pacific Northwest, annually attracting more than 8 million people to camp, fish, hike, bike, hunt, ski, kayak, boat, snowmobile, cave dive, rock climb, and gather dozens of different mushroom species. The diversity of recreation opportunities makes it a year-round vacation land.

Twenty peaks of volcanic origin stretch higher than 7,000 feet, including three of Oregon's five highest peaks. There are more than 150 lakes and 500 miles of streams, including 135 miles of wild and scenic rivers. Most of the lakes are in the mountains, many in the forest's five wilderness areas. Other attractions are six wild and scenic rivers, the Newberry National Volcanic Monument, and the Oregon Cascades Recreation Area.

Deschutes National Forest is also home to two specialized operation centers: a regional seed extractory and the Redmond Air Center. The Redmond Air Center dispatches smokejumpers, fire crews, aircraft, and fire equipment to wildfires throughout the nation. Both facilities offer tours.

Wild and scenic rivers in the forest include sections of Upper Deschutes, Little Deschutes, and Metolius rivers, Big Marsh, Crescent and Squaw creeks.

More than 300 species of fish and wildlife live within the Forest. Special elk and deer habitat management areas have been preserved to secure summer and winter browsing and grazing ranges, with the goal to increase the numbers of these large animals. An effort is being made to significantly reduce the 9,000 miles of roads in Deschutes National Forests to lessen the impact on wildlife. Still, more than 1,300 miles of trail now weave through the forest for hikers, bicyclists, and horse riders.

The region's volcanic legacy makes it ripe for development of geothermal energy sites. Geologists believe there is a potential to tap up to several hundred megawatts of geothermal energy from trapped steam and heat. Molten rock has been detected less than a mile below the forest's floor.

Summer camping season starts at the forest's 101 campgrounds as early as mid-April and lasts until late September at developed sites. Some camps remain open into November to accommodate hunters. Camping also occurs near the lakes within the Newberry National Volcanic Monument. This monument, southeast of Bend, combines the Lava Lands Visitor Center, the Lava Butte Observatory, Lava River Cave, and Newberry Crater.

Downhill and cross-country skiing are popular. Mount Bachelor Ski and Summer Resort attracts nearly three-quarters of a million people annually. For those who enjoy vacationing away from the crowds, the Deschutes National Forest offers vast tracts of undeveloped empty land linked by 1,300 miles of trails for hikers, horseback riders, snowmobilers, skiers, and mountain bikers.

Five congressional designated wilderness areas cover 183,000 acres within the forest. Wilderness areas that are partially within Deschutes National Forest include Diamond Peak, Mount Jefferson, Mount Thielsen, Mount Washington, and Three Sisters.

Pacific Crest National Scenic Trail 2000 winds through and connects many of these wilderness areas. Portions of the forest are open to off-highway vehicles (OHV) and snowmobiles. Wildernesses, roadless areas, research, and experimental forests, and some wildlife winter ranges, are closed to OHVs. During the summer, OHV operators often use logging roads. Snowmobiling is very popular on the forest's 346 miles of snowmobile trails.

Directions: From the west follow state and federal highways east from I-5 between Eugene and Salem. Preferred routes are US 20, and OR 126, and 58. From the east US 97 south of Bend passes through the heart of the national forest. Other main routes from US 97 are US 20, and OR 126, 242, 46, and 58.

Activities: Camping, hiking, boating, swimming, hunting, fishing, mushroom gathering, caving, gold panning, mountain and rock climbing, skiing, snowmobiling, and whitewater boating.

Facilities: 1,300 miles of hiking trails and 346 miles of snowmobile trails, and 4 ranger district offices. The Redmond Air Center, 1740 SE Ochoco Way, Redmond, OR 97756. Phone (503) 548-5071.

Dates: Open year-round, although many of the higher roads are closed in winter by snow, or restricted to cross-country skiers, snowshoers, and snowmobilers. Nearly all roads and campgrounds are snow-free by early June, and major highways are maintained year-round.

Fees: Trail park pass and Sno-Park fees are charged at most popular trailheads and picnic grounds. Fees are charged for campsites with services. Wilderness use permits are required in designated wilderness areas, but there is no charge.

For more information: Deschutes National Forest, Forest Supervisor Headquarters, 1645 East Highway 20, Bend, OR 97701. Phone (541) 388-2715. Web site: www.fs.fed.us/r6/deschutes/desnf/recreate/recreate.html.

Ranger District Offices are located at 1230 NE 3rd Street, Bend, OR 97701. Phone (541) 388-5664. PO Box 208, Crescent, OR 97733. Phone (541) 433-2234. PO Box 249, US 20, Sisters, OR 97759. Phone (541) 549-2111.

SANTIAM PASS

[Fig. 28(5)] Santiam Pass marks the boundary between the Willamette and Deschutes National Forests. Waters west of Santiam Pass flow into the Willamette River Valley. On the east side of the pass, waters drain into the Deschutes River Basin.

This US 20 divide is the high point of the Oregon Cascades through this area. The Canada-to-Mexico Pacific Crest Trail 2000 crosses north to south through the pass. There is a trailhead with parking.

Santiam is a high spot on a wide, open ridge, not one of the Northwest's spectacular, top-of-the-world mountain passes. Still, it is a panoramic vantage point for photographing the imposing crags of Three Fingered Jack Mountain and Mount Washington. A large vehicle turnout 4.8 miles east of the pass, which is 4,817 feet high, offers a spectacular view of Mount Washington. Southeast of the pass is Black Butte, a striking cinder cone with an elevation of 6,436 feet that marks the springs at the headwaters of the Metolius River, one of the most productive trout rivers in Oregon. Black Butte was an active volcano during the last Ice Age. Long inactive, it is covered with dense forests of pine and supports native mule deer.

Directions: US 20/OR 126 about 15 miles west of Sisters.

Dates: Pass is maintained year-round.

Closest town: Sisters.

For more information: Sisters Ranger District, Deschutes National Forest, PO Box 249, Sisters, OR 97759. Phone (541) 549-2111 or McKenzie Ranger District, Willamette National Forest, Hwy. 126, McKenzie, OR 97413. Phone (541) 822-3381.

CACHE MOUNTAIN LAKES

[Fig. 28] Small trout lakes are scattered along both sides of Forest Service Road 2076 beneath 5,579-foot Cache Mountain. The largest lake is 18 acres. The main road to Cache Mountain Lakes is Forest Service 2076, which is improved gravel. Short spur roads lead to smaller lakes but most are rutted and not suited for passenger cars. There are no developed facilities.

The first lake, Island Lake, is about 1 mile south of US 20/OR 126. The short roads leading from Forest Service 2076 to nearby tarns are mostly fire breaks and two-tracks. Some of the roads are dry enough to be driven by mid-June. Many anglers park on Forest Service 2076 and make the short walk to the lakes.

Bring the fly rods and light spinning tackle for a variety of cutthroats, brookies, and rainbows. There are primitive camping sites at Link and Meadow lakes. At 18 and 16 acres respectively, they are the largest lakes in the Cache Mountain chain.

Directions: Follow US 20/OR 126 to Forest Service 2076 about 3 miles east of Santiam Pass. Go

MARTEN

(*Martes americana*)

Male martens are quarrelsome and associate with females only in the summer mating season.

Santiam Pass Area

Santiam Pass marks the boundary between Willamette and Deschutes National Forests.

DUFFY LAKE
NORTH SANTIAM RIVER
N
Ref: DeLorme Oregon Atlas & Gazetteer
SANTIAM LAKE
Three Fingered Jack
Maxwell Butte
BERTLEY LAKES
FIRST CREEK
FIRST CREEK
To Detroit
22
1
Santiam Junction
LOST LAKE
LOST LAKE CREEK
LOST LAKE CREEK
ROUND LAKE
SQUARE LAKE
LONG LAKE
20
126
To Sisters
5
NFD 2690
NFD 2076
BLUE LAKE
DARK LAKE
ISLAND LAKE
Hoodoo Butte
2
Hayrick Butte
LINK LAKE
HAND LAKE
CACHE LAKE
Sand Mountain Road
NFD 810
NFD 2690
NFD 2076
3
Sand Mountain
MEADOW LAKE
CUB LAKE
NFD 810
Cache Mountain
Little Cache Mountain
BIG LAKE
PATJENS LAKES
4

1	Santiam Junction		Deschutes National Forest
2	Hoodoo Ski Bowl		Willamette National Forest
3	Sand Mountain Lookout		Mt. Jefferson Wilderness
4	Patjens Lake Loop Trail		Pacific Crest National Scenic Trail
5	Santiam Pass		Trail

south on Forest Service 2076. Lakes are not identified by signs, so a map might be useful.

Activities: Primitive camping and trout fishing.

Facilities: The major trout lakes along Forest Service 2076 are, Island, 8 acres, cutthroat and brookies; Link, 18 acres, cutthroat, brookies and rainbow, primitive campsites; Meadow, 16 acres, cutthroats and brookies, primitive campsites; Hand, 4 acres, cutthroats and brookies; Cache, 8 acres, a meadow lake that can be weed choked by July, cutthroat and brookies.

Dates: Lakes are generally ice-free and accessible from mid-June through mid-Oct.

Fees: None.

Closest town: Sisters, east on US 20.

For more information: Sisters Ranger District, Deschutes National Forest, PO Box 249, Sisters, OR 97759. Phone (541) 549-2111.

BLUE LAKE

[Fig. 28] Blue Lake occupies a spectacular water-filled 54-acre, 300-feet deep crater that geologists believe was blasted out of solid rock by tremendous underground steam explosions 3,500 years ago. The extreme depth was created by multiple explosions. The nearly pure water bubbling from springs 240 feet deep makes the lake an unusual aquamarine color. On clear, windless days the surface reflects the sharp peaks of Mount Washington. Many travelers compare the crater of Blue Lake with the much larger and internationally famous Crater Lake at Crater Lake National Park to the south (*see* Crater Lake National Park, page 315).

Directions: South of US 20/OR 126, about 14 miles west of Sisters at an elevation of 3,453 feet. Follow Forest Service Road 2070 south to the lake.

Activities: Camping, fishing for stocked rainbow trout, picnicking, and hiking.

Facilities: There is private resort with lodging and camping, rental boats, fee boat ramp, and store supplies. Picnic tables at Elliott Corbett Memorial State Recreation Site. A 2.5 mile trail loops around the crater rim.

Dates: Usually snowbound from Nov. through late May.

Closest town: Sisters, 14 miles east on US 20/OR 126.

For more information: Sisters Ranger District, Deschutes National Forest, PO Box 249, Sisters, OR 97759. Phone (541) 549-2111.

SUTTLE LAKE

[Fig. 29] This is a 253-acre water skiing, fishing, camping, and resort destination on the crest of the Cascades just east of Blue Lake. Suttle Lake averages 70 feet in depth and lies in a forested trough scoured into the landscape by glaciers 10,000 years ago. It is visible from US 20/OR 126.

Suttle Lake is a favorite late summer destination for families who enjoy its three Forest Service campgrounds, swimming beaches, resort, picnic area, and recreation that includes hiking, trout fishing, water skiing, wind-surfing, sailing, and swimming. An almost level hiking trail loops around the lake.

The camps are 3,438 feet in elevation, and may be snowed in until mid-April. As a rule, the sites are open from April through September. South Shore Campground is the largest with 38 tent and RV sites. Link Creek Campground has 33 sites, and Blue Bay Campground has 24 sites. Campsites are available for reservation by calling (877) 444-6777.

Just east of Suttle Lake, Forest Service Road 12 intersects US 20/OR 126 from the north and provides access to the neighboring Mount Jefferson Wilderness. Forest Service 12 is paved and is an arterial route connecting with secondary forest roads, trailheads and camping areas along the east side of Mount Jefferson Wilderness.

Some of the most popular wilderness entry points from Forest Service 12 are Forest Service 1210 to Round Lake; Forest Service 1234 to Jack Lake; Forest Service 1235 to Bear Valley Trail; and Forest Service 1230 to Cabot Lakes Trail. These are popular jumping-off points for hikers backpacking into the east side of Mount Jefferson Wilderness.

Suttle Lake is a very popular destination for water and Jet Skiers in late July and August, but because of the elevation, the water is slow to warm and quick to cool. It's fished heavily in May for kokanee salmon and in summer for whitefish and brown trout. The banks of the lake are steep, rapidly dropping to 60 feet in most areas. Yet, the deepest spot is only 75 feet.

The lake was created by glacier scouring during the Pleistocene Epoch, when all of Oregon's high mountains were buried by the last Ice Age. The valley is broad, and easily recognizable as a glacial trough. Suttle Lake is a misspelled honorarium to John Settle, one of the construction supervisors of the Cascade Mountain Military Wagon Road, built in the 1860s. Settle found the lake while hunting.

Directions: From the east or west follow US 20/OR 126 to the Suttle Lake turnoff 7 miles east of Santiam Pass.

Activities: Full range of water sports, including fishing and pleasure boating, swimming, hiking, hiking, and camping.

Facilities: Three Forest Service campgrounds, a picnic area, a year-round private resort with campsites, cabin rentals, and boats, restaurant, and store. All three campgrounds offer vault restrooms, drinking water, tables, grills, and boat ramps.

Dates: Open year-round. Campgrounds open mid-Apr. through mid-Oct.

Fees: Fees are charged for camping, and resort services.

Closest town: Sisters is 14 miles west on US 20/OR 126.

For more information: Sisters Ranger District, Deschutes National Forest, PO Box 249, Sisters, OR 97759. Phone (541) 549-2111. Suttle Lake Resort and Marina, US 20/OR 126, Sisters. Phone (541) 595-6662.

SUTTLE LAKE LOOP TRAIL

[Fig. 29(1)] The trail encircles 253-acre Suttle Lake in a canopy of mixed conifer trees. It's accessible from all of the campgrounds and roadways.

Trail: Forest Service 4030 is 3.2 miles between lake and forest. Horses are prohibited, but mountain bikes are allowed.

Elevation: 3,450 feet, with a 50-feet in elevation change.

Degree of difficulty: Easy.

Surface: Dirt.

Fees: None.

SUTTLE/BLACK BUTTE TRAIL

[Fig. 29(2)] This is a popular and easy hiking and mountain biking forest trail that roughly parallels US 20/OR 126 between Suttle Lake and Black Butte. It is very popular with mountain bikers.

Directions: Trial heads are on US 20/OR 126 at Suttle Lake, 14 miles west of Sisters and Black Butte at Sherman Jct., 10 miles west of Sisters.

Trail: Suttle Tie Trail No. 4094, 5 miles one-way.

Dates: Generally snow-free from mid-April through mid-Oct.

Fees: There is a charge for trail park pass.

Elevation: Varies from 3,400 feet at Suttle Lake to 3,200 at Black Butte.

Degree of difficulty: Easy.

Surface: Dirt and rock.

BLACK BUTTE

[Fig. 29] The imposing conical-shaped tower of Black Butte, elevation 6,436 feet, is a prominent local landmark. The extinct cinder cone volcano rises dramatically above the pine forest at the north edge of US 20/OR 126, about 10.2 miles west of Sisters.

The cinder cone sits between two major forest roads, Forest Service Road 14 and Forest Service 11, that lead north into the beautiful Metolius River Valley. On the south side of US 20/OR 126 is Black Butte Ranch, one of central Oregon's best known guest ranches.

Black Butte volcano is 1.4 million years old, five times older than towering Mount Washington, visible 6.9 miles to the south. Unlike the other mile-high mountains nearby, Black Butte is glacierless. That's because Mount Washington so effectively shields Black Butte from incoming weather fronts that not enough water falls on it to develop permanent snow packs. The marshes along the US 20/OR 126 just south of the volcano were believed to have been created when lava rock under the cone obstructed spring flows.

A hiking trail leads to the summit.

Directions: Adjacent to US 20/OR 126 about 10 miles west of Sisters.

Activities: Hiking, resort recreations.

Facilities: Hiking trail and nearby resort ranch with two 18-hole golf courses, tennis courts, riding stable, trout fishing, restaurant, and full resort accommodations.

Dates: Open year-round.

Fees: There are charges for trail park passes and resort services.

Closest town: Sisters is 10 mile east on US 20/OR 126.

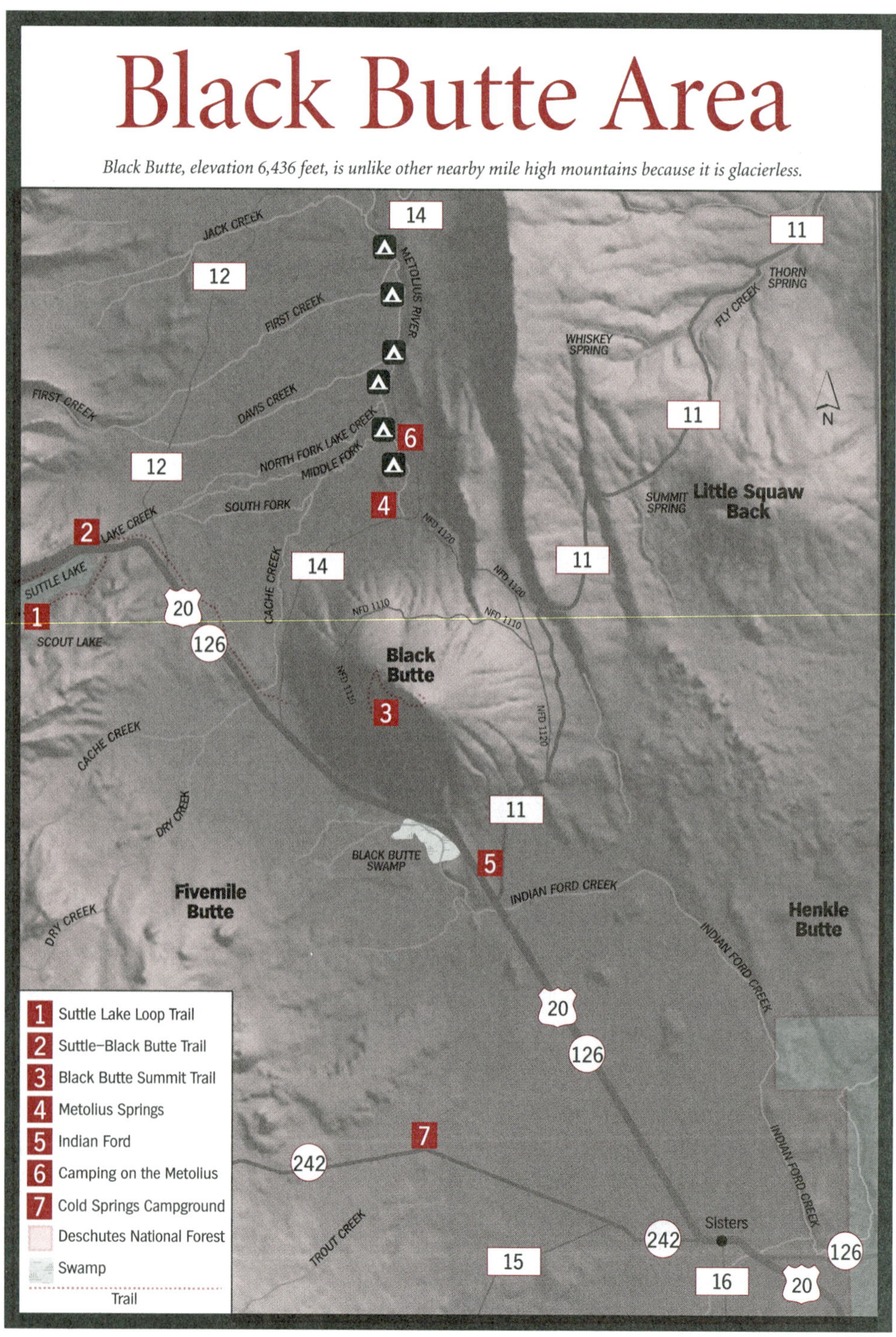
Black Butte Area
Black Butte, elevation 6,436 feet, is unlike other nearby mile high mountains because it is glacierless.
14
11
JACK CREEK
12
METOLIUS RIVER
FIRST CREEK
THORN SPRING
FLY CREEK
WHISKEY SPRING
FIRST CREEK
DAVIS CREEK
11
N
NORTH FORK LAKE CREEK
MIDDLE FORK
6
12
SUMMIT SPRING
Little Squaw Back
SOUTH FORK
4
NFD 1120
2
LAKE CREEK
CACHE CREEK
14
11
SUTTLE LAKE
NFD 1120
20
NFD 1110
NFD 1110
1
SCOUT LAKE
126
Black Butte
NFD 1110
3
NFD 1120
CACHE CREEK
DRY CREEK
11
BLACK BUTTE SWAMP
5
INDIAN FORD CREEK
Fivemile Butte
Henkle Butte
DRY CREEK
INDIAN FORD CREEK
20
126
INDIAN FORD CREEK
7
242
TROUT CREEK
Sisters
242
126
15
16
20
1 Suttle Lake Loop Trail
2 Suttle–Black Butte Trail
3 Black Butte Summit Trail
4 Metolius Springs
5 Indian Ford
6 Camping on the Metolius
7 Cold Springs Campground
Deschutes National Forest
Swamp
Trail

For more information: Sisters Ranger District, Deschutes National Forest, PO Box 249, Sisters, OR 97759. Phone (541) 549-2111. For resort information contact Black Butte Ranch, PO Box 8000, Black Butte Ranch, OR 97759. Phone (800) 452-7455.

BLACK BUTTE SUMMIT TRAIL 4026

[Fig. 29(3)] The trail climbs steeply up this symmetrical volcano through a forest of large ponderosa pines. In the second mile of the hike, the forest gives way to open slopes. While the view is commanding, summer temperatures on the open mountainside can be extreme. There is a fire tower lookout at the summit. Horses are allowed by permit, but mountain bikes are prohibited on the trail.

Directions: US 20/OR 126 to the junction of Forest Service Road 11 about 10 miles west of Sisters. Drive north on Forest Service Road to Forest Service 1110, turn west and follow Forest Service 1110 to the trailhead.

Dates: Open June through mid-Nov.

Fees: There is a charge for a trail park pass.

Trail: 2 miles one-way to the summit.

Elevation: Trailhead is 4,800 feet, summit at 6,436 feet.

Degree of difficulty: Moderate. Upper reaches are unshaded and summer temperatures can be extreme. Carry water.

Surface: Dirt and rock.

METOLIUS RECREATION AREA

[Fig. 29] One of the prettiest spring-fed rivers in central Oregon, the Metolius gushes clear and nearly pure from a spring beneath Black Butte and flows for 28.6 miles along the west slope of Green Ridge before feeding into Lake Billy Chinook on the Warm Springs Indian Reservation. It's one of Oregon's 20 wild and scenic rivers, and the heart of the Metolius Recreation Area.

Much of the transparent, spring-fed Metolius River is restricted to fly-fishing and it is well known for its native population of challenging rainbows. A portion of the river is open year-round (check the Oregon Regulation Synopsis for fishing information), but the most productive fishing takes place between April and July.

The wild and scenic segment of the river begins at Metolius Springs on the north side of Black Butte flowing downstream through pines, Engelmann spruce, Douglas firs, larch, lush meadows and cattail marshes. It is followed by paved Forest Service Road 14. The pavement and the wild and scenic designation end at Lower Bridge camp near the south border of the reservation.

A rough dirt road closed to motorized vehicles, Forest Service 1499 continues north along the river, which now forms the south boundary of the reservation. River access is more difficult in this area and often requires strenuous hikes along steep paths between the road and water levels. At about 5 miles, the Metolius veers east into a remote gorge, 1,500 feet deep in places, and widens into the west arm of Lake Billy Chinook. The lake is a popular destination for house-boaters, water skiers, and fishermen. Lake recreation areas are reached from US 97 south of Madras.

Wizard Falls State Fish Hatchery is on the west side of the river near Allen Springs campground. There are 12 Forest Service campgrounds along the river, plus picnic areas, a trout viewing bridge, hiking trails, and several private resorts and RV camps are scattered in the yellow ponderosa pines and grassy meadows along the river.

Camp Sherman is the supply center for the valley with a circa-1917 store, groceries, camping supplies, fishing information, restaurant, and a post office. Three private resorts provide campsites, rental cabins, fishing tackle, groceries, gas, and ice. Fishing guides can also be arranged here. A bridge at Camp Sherman spans a deep green pool in a no-fishing zone, where tourists toss food to big trout. There is little commercial development beyond Camp Sherman except for Forest Service river-side campgrounds. The trout are what attract fishermen to this beautiful valley. Rainbows five pounds and up are not uncommon, but are notoriously difficult to catch.

Fishermen easily wade the upper sections of the wild and scenic section, although rafts and river drift boats are also used. Kayaking is also popular.

The Metolius Recreation Area's unusual gushing headwater, open forest setting, wildflowers, wildlife, and scenery invite bicyclists, picnickers, photographers, and hikers. The upper river resembles a park. Open forests are carpeted with long yellow wild grasses, divided by bogs and meadows, and always a sprinkling of wildflowers. Botanists believe that this river bottom produces the thickest concentrations of wild penstemon (*Penstemon peckii*) in Oregon.

Several varieties of penstemon thrive here, ranging in color from the purplish-blue of the foot-high small-flowered variety (*Penstemon procerus*), to the pink of the 2- to 6-inch-high Davidson's penstemon (*Penstemon davidsonii*), which grows in brightly colored mats that resemble throw rugs on the forest carpet. Look for the Davidson's variety in rocky areas, and the small-flowered type in moist places. The best time for wildflowers is May through June, but something is always in bloom through the end of September.

The elusive native rainbow trout, averaging 8 to 16 inches and reaching 5 pounds, is the main fishery. A few browns stray in from Lake Billy Chinook and brookies drift down tributaries from higher lakes. The "lunker" fish in this river is the bull trout, a char that can weigh 15 pounds. These big predators, however, are protected by endangered species status, and fishing is not allowed.

In September the lower river runs scarlet red and olive green with the spawning colors of thousands of kokanee salmon moving upstream from Lake Billy Chinook to propagate in the flowing water. Like all salmon, these kokanee die after spawning. Dozens of bald eagles often descend on the lower river to take advantage of the seasonal feast.

There are strict state restrictions governing tackle, fishing areas, and lures on the Metolius. An 11 mile section near Camp Sherman is restricted to fly-fishing only. It's a good idea to check current regulations before wetting a line. In October this is a popular deer hunting area.

The elevation of the upper valley is about 3,000 feet and snow will be on the ground from November through March. US 20/OR 126 and Forest Service 14 is maintained year-round.

Several conservation, research, primitive, scenic, and heritage areas are designated in the Metolius Valley. Special areas include:

Metolius Conservation Area is composed of portions of Mount Jefferson Wilderness and Green Ridge. Its 86,000 acres encompass the bend in the Metolius, where the river hooks sharply to the east and forms the boundary between the Deschutes National Forest and the Warm Springs Indian Reservation.

Metolius Heritage Area, 24,300 acres, was created to protect ancient yellow-belly ponderosa pine and spring-fed streams.

Metolius Wildlife-Primitive Area, 13,100 acres, provides undisturbed habitat for bald eagle, cougar, and deer.

Metolius Black Butte Scenic Area, 10,600 acres, protects Black Butte forests of mature trees and snags, which are valued as nesting sites and produce insect foods for a variety of woodpeckers, sapsuckers, and birds of prey.

Metolius Special Interest Area, 1,700 acres, is a geological, biological, and cultural area that includes the summits of Black Butte and Castle/Cathedral Rocks.

Metolius Scenic Views Area, 4,800 acres, overlooks mountain peaks, rock formations and geological features.

Metolius Old Growth Area, 1,800 acres, protects ancient trees in the Black Butte Old Growth Unit and the Glaze Meadow Unit. Western junipers in this area are 800 to 1,000 years old. Some of the area has been preserved by The Nature Conservancy.

Most of these special use areas are identified with interpretive signs on Forest Service 14.

The Metolius supports a lot of wildlife. Watch for black-tailed deer, elk, black bear, otter, mink, and beaver. Overhead may be bald and golden eagles, osprey, many varieties of hawks, and herons. Great blue herons (*Ardea herodias*), with their 6-foot wingspans and 47-inch height are sometimes seen stalking frogs, salamanders and small fish in marsh and bog areas.

Directions: From US 20/OR 126, about 10 miles west of Sisters, Forest Service Road 14 turns north at Black Butte and follows the river down the valley.

Activities: Camping, fishing, hunting, hiking, mountain biking, picnicking, whitewater boating, wildlife viewing, and cross-country skiing.

Facilities: 12 campgrounds, resorts, grocery store, hiking, mountain biking, and picnic areas.

Dates: Open year-round.

Fees: There are charges for trail park passes, campsites, and resort services.

Closest town: Sisters is 9.6 miles east on US 20/OR 126.

For more information: Sisters Ranger District, Deschutes National Forest, PO Box 249, Sisters, OR 97759. Phone (541) 549-2111. Oregon Department of Fish and Wildlife, High Desert Regional Office, 61374 Parrell Road, Bend, OR 97702. Phone (541) 388-6363.

METOLIUS SPRINGS

[Fig. 29(4)] Unlike most Oregon rivers that collect from tiny trickles and rain-fed mountain tributaries the wild and scenic Metolius River bursts out of the ground beneath Black Butte full-grown, cold, and populated with trout.

The 48-degree water gushes from the spring at the rate of 50,000 gallons per minute. More springs supplement the flow, and actually lower the water temperature within a half mile of the headwaters.

The source of Metolius Springs is an ongoing debate. One school claims it wells from underground flows impounded by geological shuffling beneath Black Butte. Others argue that it flows from an underground river on the fault line that created Green Ridge.

Deschutes National Forest maintains day-use facilities at the springs, including a paved wheelchair-accessible 200-yard path from the parking lot to the springs overlook. It's a peaceful, noncommercialized setting framed by a rail fence, tall pines, wildflowers and a reflection of Mount Jefferson. Riverside and Camp Sherman campgrounds are just downstream from the springs. The elevation here is 3,000 feet.

Directions: The springs are 9.6 miles northwest of Sisters on US 20/OR 126. Immediately west of Black Butte turn north onto Forest Service 14 and continue 4.4 miles to the day use area. It's well marked.

Activities: Scenic view, picnicking.

Facilities: Fenced overlook, paved path, 3 picnic tables, and 1 vault-style restroom. There is no drinking water or camping.

Dates: Open year-round, but snowbound from Nov. through Mar.

Fees: None.

CAMPING ON THE METOLIUS

[Fig. 29(6)] Twelve small Forest Service campgrounds are liberally sprinkled in the open pine and fir forests along the 28.6 miles of Metolius River between the headwater springs and Lake Billy Chinook. Fee campgrounds have well water. All of the sites have picnic tables, fire pits, and vault restrooms.

Additional campsites, including some with RV hookups, are available at private parks in the Camp Sherman area, where there is also a small grocery store, gas station, and restaurant.

Directions: The turnoff to the Metolius River camp area is 9.6 miles west of Sisters at Forest Service Road 14. Turn north on Forest Service 14, which is paved to Lower Bridge Campground.

Activities: River trout fishing, camping, hiking, wildflower viewing, mountain biking, and in the winter, cross-country skiing and snowmobiling.

Facilities: Riverside Forest Service campgrounds and their number of sites are as follows: Allen Springs, 17; Allingham, 10; Camp Sherman, 15; Candle Creek, 4; Canyon Creek, 4; Gorge 18; Lower Bridge, 12; Monty, 20; Pine Rest, 8; Pioneer Ford, 20; Riverside, 16; and Smiling River, 38. The campgrounds near Lake Billy Chinook are more easily reached from the east on US 97 and Forest Service 63.

Dates: Most of the campgrounds are open from Apr. through Sept. and 6 remain open through Oct.

Fees: Campsite fees are charged at all sites except Candle Creek and Canyon Creek.

INDIAN FORD

[Fig. 29(5)] A small Forest Service campground at the site of a historic Indian crossing of what is now called Indian Ford Creek. According to historians, Indian trails from all points on the compass, including some followed inland by the Columbia River bands of Wallowas, converged at this spot in the woods. The trails connected summer and winter campsites of several bands, and lead to mountain areas for berry gathering, hunting, and inter tribal trading. Several hiking trails now wind through the vicinity.

Directions: Turn north from US 20/OR 126 at milepost 95.

Activities: Camping, hiking, bird-watching, deer hunting in the fall.

Facilities: 25 campsites, vault restroom, and drinking water (hand pump).

Dates: Open May through Sept.

Fees: There is a charge for camping.

SISTERS

[Fig. 29] Sisters, with a population of 820, and at 3,182 feet elevation, is more than a Western theme town. It's a recreation and supply center, and the junction of several important cross-Cascade highways. It has full travelers' services, including a city park that welcomes campers.

A Forest Service office and information center is located here. Deschutes National Forest Sisters Ranger District headquarters has a selection of maps, books, and informational pamphlets about the area. You can also secure wilderness use and trail pass parking permits at the office, which is located on the west edge of town at the junction of US 20/OR 126 and OR 242.

Oregon 242 runs southwest from Sisters and is the McKenzie Pass leg of the McKenzie-Santiam Scenic Byway. It reconnects with OR 126 on the McKenzie River. McKenzie Pass, elevation 5,325 feet, is closed during winter. The rest of the year it's an amazing route that passes through vast lava fields within sight of volcanic craters, between wilderness areas, along crystalline trout lakes, and includes dozens of hiking and biking trails. During peak summer travel periods, Sisters seems to bulge with recreational vehicles, four-wheel drive trucks, mountain bikes, backpacks, whitewater boats, and vacationers.

The Fly Fisher's Place, 151 W. Main Street, sells fishing licenses and can provide current angling information.

By early afternoon, the "Sorry Full" sign is often posted at the four motels and four bed and breakfast inns. Campers, however, can usually be squeezed into the two private RV parks and spacious Sisters City Park, which have water and RV hookups. Nearly every day during the height of summer vacation season, the 16 eateries and five gas stations have waiting lines, and traffic is hood-to-trunk past the storefronts on Cascade Avenue.

Incredibly, there are 11 art galleries in this small town. The second week of July launches five days of the nation's largest outdoor quilt show. (For information, phone 541-549-6061).

On OR 242, about 0.5 mile west of Sisters, is Patterson Arabian Ranch. In addition to breeding Polish Arabian horses, this ranch supports a llama herd of from 250 to 500 animals, plus Rocky Mountain elk. Local boosters believe this is the West's largest herd of domestic llamas. Tours aren't scheduled but visits can be arranged. There are roadside photo opportunities. Phone (541) 549-1215. Close-up visits with 250 llamas are offered Monday through Saturday at Hinterland Ranch 3.5 miles east of Sisters on US 20/OR 126. Phone (541) 549-1215. The ranch also sells llama fleece and yarn.

Sisters is located at the imaginary crease where the green forests of the Oregon Cascades unfold into the semiarid sage and steppe regions that identify the Deschutes River Breaks. It's a city surrounded by federal wilderness areas. Looking northwest from Sisters, you see the snowy peaks in Mount Jefferson Wilderness Area. West is Mount Washington Wilderness Area, and southwest are the glaciated summits in Three Sisters Wilderness Area.

Recreation continues year-round in this snow and lake country. By late fall, cross-country skiers replace summer hikers, snowmobilers replace mountain bikers, snowshoers replace golfers, and hunters replace fishermen.

Founded in 1888, Sisters is named for the glaciated, pinnacle peaks of the Three Sisters Mountains that dominate their namesake wilderness.

At midsummer, daytime high temperatures usually poke into the 80s and low 90s, dropping into the 40s at night. Summer days are almost predictably bright and clear, night skies are thick with stars, and the air is dry with very low humidity.

The town's calendar of annual events is crowded. Most weekends, year-round, there is a carnival, festival, show, or event celebrating everything from fossils (from fossil beds in eastern Oregon) to custom cars, motorcycles, and farm produce which is trucked in from valley agricultural areas. The elevation of Sisters means a short growing season. The summer highlight is the Sisters Rodeo and Parade, the second weekend in June. Contact Sisters Rodeo Association, phone (541) 549-0121.

Camp Polk Road leads north into a rugged, lightly populated area of back roads to Squaw Back Ridge, and creeks flowing at the bottoms of steep, eroded coulees. This is a popular area for mountain biking.

Camp Polk was a military outpost built in 1865, under the command of Captain Charles LaFollette, who was from Polk County, Oregon. It was manned by 40 members of the Oregon Volunteer Infantry, but was never involved in any of the Indian skirmishes of that time. In 1870, the first white settlers staked claims. Ten years later, the post office at Camp Polk was moved to the present location of Sisters, and the outpost was ended.

Directions: At the junctions of US 20/OR 126, and OR 242 about 20 miles northwest of Bend.

Activities: Rodeo, weekend expositions and jamborees, camping.

Facilities: All traveler services are available here, including a tree-shaded city park

Rare Birds

Sisters can be a bird watcher's paradise.

The many habitats that form in the forest-to-desert transition zone near Sisters attract an unusual mix of birds, including several uncommon and rare species.

Habitat zones of old lava flows, wild meadows, semiarid steppe prairies, and forests of mixed fir, juniper, and ponderosa and lodgepole pine overlap each other in this region.

Cold Springs Campground, five miles west of Sisters on McKenzie Pass Highway (OR 242), attracts a concentration of white-headed woodpeckers (*Picoides albolarvatus*). Considered uncommon to rare, this bird is about 9 inches long and has a distinctive white head and a brilliant red nape. When it flies, you can see a large patch of white on its wing. The birds prefer ponderosa pine and Douglas fir, probing the thick bark for insects. Cold Springs is also favored by rare red-naped sapsuckers (*Sphyrapicus varius*), which are sometimes called yellow-bellied sapsuckers.

Western tanagers (*Piranga ludoviciana*), with their distinctive yellow bodies and red heads, are fairly common in the Sisters region. The colorful plumage of the male looks tropical. It can be tough to spot because it's a rather sedentary bird, but if it is moving, it will most likely be seen high in the tall conifers. Females are drab olive green, and nest in braids of twigs and conifer needles, usually in the highest trees. Black-and-orange-colored Rufous-sided towhees (*Pipilo erythrophthalmus*), and varied thrushes (*Ixoreus naevius*), which look like robins with black breast bands, are often seen kicking and scratching for insects and worms in the ground duff.

Two of the West's rarest birds can be found in the lodgepole forests: black-backed woodpeckers (*Picoides arcticus*) and flammulated owls (*Otus flammeolus*). Flammulated owls, at 6 to 7 inches tall, are one of the smallest owls in North America. This area is also home to the largest owl in North America, the great gray owl (*Strix nebulosa*), which grows to a height of 33 inches.

Turquoise-colored mountain bluebirds (*Sialia currucoides*) are often seen in juniper groves, and the open lava outcroppings are home to gray-crowned rosy finches, (*Leucosticte tephrocotis*) one of the rarest birds in the country.

The Sisters area is also well-known for soaring turkey vultures (*Cathartes aura*), red-tailed hawks (*Buteo jamaicensis*), and bald (*Haliaeetus leucocephalus*) and golden (*Aquila chrysaetos*) eagles.

with tent and RV campsites, and the Sisters Ranger District headquarters information center.

For more information: Sisters Chamber of Commerce, 222 W. Hood Avenue, Sisters, OR 97759. Phone (541) 549-0251. Sisters Ranger District, Deschutes National Forest, PO Box 249, Sisters, OR 97759. Phone (541) 549-2111.

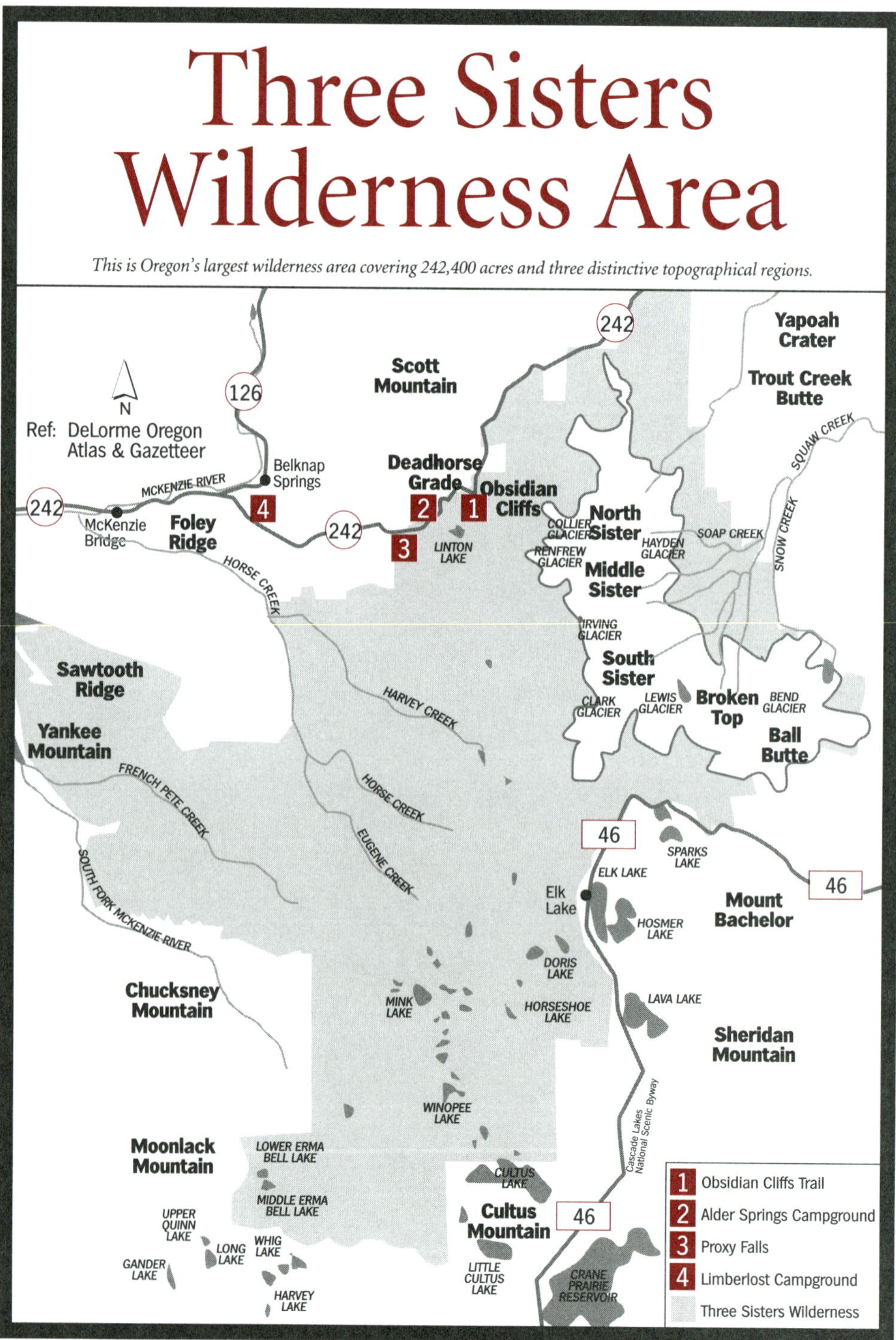
Three Sisters Wilderness Area
This is Oregon's largest wilderness area covering 242,400 acres and three distinctive topographical regions.
N
Ref: DeLorme Oregon Atlas & Gazetteer
242
126
Scott Mountain
Yapoah Crater
Trout Creek Butte
SQUAW CREEK
Belknap Springs
MCKENZIE RIVER
McKenzie Bridge
Foley Ridge
Deadhorse Grade
Obsidian Cliffs
LINTON LAKE
COLLIER GLACIER
North Sister
RENFREW GLACIER
HAYDEN GLACIER
SOAP CREEK
SNOW CREEK
Middle Sister
HORSE CREEK
IRVING GLACIER
South Sister
Sawtooth Ridge
Yankee Mountain
HARVEY CREEK
CLARK GLACIER
LEWIS GLACIER
Broken Top
BEND GLACIER
Ball Butte
FRENCH PETE CREEK
EUGENE CREEK
46
SPARKS LAKE
ELK LAKE
Elk Lake
Mount Bachelor
SOUTH FORK MCKENZIE RIVER
HOSMER LAKE
DORIS LAKE
Chucksney Mountain
MINK LAKE
HORSESHOE LAKE
LAVA LAKE
Sheridan Mountain
Cascade Lakes National Scenic Byway
WINOPEE LAKE
Moonlack Mountain
LOWER ERMA BELL LAKE
MIDDLE ERMA BELL LAKE
CULTUS LAKE
Cultus Mountain
UPPER QUINN LAKE
LONG LAKE
WHIG LAKE
GANDER LAKE
HARVEY LAKE
LITTLE CULTUS LAKE
CRANE PRAIRIE RESERVOIR
1 Obsidian Cliffs Trail
2 Alder Springs Campground
3 Proxy Falls
4 Limberlost Campground
Three Sisters Wilderness

COLD SPRINGS CAMPGROUND

[Fig. 29(7)] Located beside McKenzie Pass National Scenic Highway/OR 242, about 5 miles west of Sisters and 10 miles east of McKenzie Pass, Cold Springs Campground is a convenient base for enjoying the shops in Sisters while exploring the hiking and biking trails and volcanic scenery on the boundary between Mount Washington and Three Sisters wilderness areas. The campground is a favorite sighting area for bird watchers. You could see rare white-headed woodpeckers and red-naped sapsuckers in the trees here.

Directions: Drive west from Sisters on McKenzie Pass National Scenic Highway/OR 242 to Cold Springs Road at milepost 88. The campground is adjacent to the north side of the highway in a shaded grove of ponderosa pine, at an elevation of 3,400 feet.

Activities: Camping, bird-watching, and hiking. The hills and forests north and south of Cold Springs camp are heavily roaded, some paved and some not, providing almost unlimited opportunities for mountain biking, hiking, fall deer and grouse hunting, wildlife watching, and scenic drives. A map of the Forest Service road system is available from the Sisters ranger station.

Facilities: 23 tent and RV sites, vault restroom, drinking water (hand pump), tables and fire pits.

Dates: Open Apr. through Sept.

Fees: There is a charge for camping.

Three Sisters Wilderness

[Fig. 30] The largest and arguably most spectacular wilderness area in Oregon is Three Sisters Wilderness, which covers 242,400 acres and three distinctive topographical regions including its heavily glaciated namesake peaks. The snow-encrusted summits of North, Middle and South Sister mountains are skyline landmarks that can be seen for almost 100 miles in all directions. The wilderness includes the Cascades south of McKenzie Pass National Scenic Highway, west of Bend, and east of Aufderheide National Scenic Byway. It's crossed north-south by 40 miles of Pacific Crest National Scenic Trail 2000.

The wilderness area's dominating peaks are Oregon's third, fourth and fifth highest. There are 17 permanent glaciers, more than 300 lakes, miles of forest—mostly hemlocks, pines, and firs—rolling heather basins, moraines, and waterfalls. Lake and streams support rainbow and brook trout, and wildlife include black-tailed deer, elk, black bear, and cougar. Hikers explore 260 miles of high-elevation hiking trails.

Three Sisters Wilderness is the largest glacial area in the United States south of the 45th Parallel. The wilderness' northern region is heavily volcanic. Lava fields intermix with meadows and pockets of timber, mainly silver fir, sub-alpine fir, true fir, and lodgepole pine. The west-central region is channeled by deep canyons and sharp-walled ridges, fast-dropping streams, and dense tracts of Douglas fir. The south is a giant plateau sprinkled with trout lakes, and walled in by deep Douglas fir forests.

The highest and youngest peak is South Sister, elevation 10,354, followed by its adjoining sibling summits, North Sister, elevation 10,094, and Middle Sister, elevation 10,053. Just south of the Sisters is Broken Top Mountain, elevation 9,175 feet, a distinctive jagged peak.

Glaciers embedded in this string of hacksaw summits are icy white landmarks visible from as far away as the high desert of central Oregon. Seen from a distant roadway the Three Sisters are awesome. Up close they're inspirational. One of the glaciers is the largest in Oregon. Collier Glacier is 1.5 miles long and 0.75 mile wide and appears as a vast snow field between North Sister and Middle Sister.

All of the snow-capped peaks, and most of the smaller mountains in this wilderness, are cinder cones or volcanoes honed into peaks by erosion (*see* Know Your Volcanoes, page 238). North Sister, a shield volcano, and Middle Sister, a stratovolcano, last erupted 100,000 and 50,000 years ago and are believed to be extinct. South Sister, also a stratovolcano, last spewed basaltic andesite and rhyolite 1,500 years ago. It is alive, but dormant. About 90 feet of snow and ice plugs the crater of South Sister.

Other major geologic features in the wilderness include Rock Mesa and Yapoah Crater. Alpine meadows, waterfalls, lava fields, glaciers and glacial lakes are abundant.

Hikers and horsemen enjoy 260 miles of maintained trail. Vehicles, including mountain bikes and hang gliders, are not allowed.

Most of the trailheads entering the wilderness begin at roads near the boundary. They start either in the dense forest of Douglas fir on the West Slope of the Cascades, or towering ponderosa pines on the east. Nearly all of the trails eventually lead from beneath the tree canopy into open, alpine basins and ridge backs carpeted with wild heathers and landscaped with the slim, twisted trunks of alpine and silver firs.

There are many permanent lakes in Three Sisters Wilderness and most support trout, usually rainbows, cutthroats or brookies. As a rule, the fish are rarely larger than a foot, a result of the long winters and short growing seasons at these elevations. Hikers often share trails with golden-mantled ground squirrels, family flocks of seemingly fearless blue grouse (*Dendraqapus obscurus*), and high mountain black-tailed and mule deer. Black bears and cougars are fairly common, but rarely seen. The shrill whistles of yellow-bellied marmots (*Marmota flaviventris*) and pikas (*Ochotona princeps*) often ring out from the rock piles above tree line.

The forests in this wilderness consist mainly of Douglas, silver, sub-alpine, and true firs, mountain and western hemlocks, lodgepole and ponderosa pines. Popular areas are Green Lakes, Obsidian, Sunshine, Erma Bell Lakes, the South Sister climbing trail.

Directions: The most convenient access points are from McKenzie Pass on OR 242, Cascade Lakes Highway OR 46, and McKenzie River Highway OR 126.

Dates: Upper elevations are snowbound from Dec. through June. McKenzie Pass is open only during summer.

Fees: There is no charge for wilderness use permits, required from Memorial Day through Oct. 31. Wilderness permits are self-issued from dispensers at some trailheads, or available at Sisters and McKenzie ranger stations. Fee trail park pass permits are required at most trailheads.

Closest town: Sisters, Bend, and McKenzie Bridge.

For more information: Sisters Ranger Station, PO Box 249, US 20, Sisters, OR 97759. Phone (541) 549-2111. McKenzie Ranger Station, Willamette National Forest, 57600 McKenzie Hwy., McKenzie Bridge, OR 97413. Phone (541) 822-3381. Willamette National Forest Supervisors Office, 211 East 7th Avenue, Eugene, OR 97440. Phone (541) 465-6521. Deschutes National Forest Supervisors Headquarters, 1645 East Highway 20, Bend, OR 97701. Phone (541) 388-2715.

OBSIDIAN CLIFFS TRAIL 3518

[Fig. 30(1)] Obsidian Cliffs is a popular hiking destination, and the trail is a favorite connecting route for backpackers continuing to Yapoah and Collier Craters, Oppie Dilldock Pass and Pacific Crest Trail 2000. The trail runs south along the cliffs to meadows on the flanks of the Three Sisters.

The cliffs were formed about 3,000 years ago by an upheaval of rhyolite magmas that were too dense to retain steam moistures, and hardened into brittle obsidian.

Hikers enjoy dramatic views of Collier Glacier and Three Sisters mountains.

Directions: The trailhead begins on the south side of McKenzie Pass Highway/OR 242 at the top of Deadhorse Grade.

Dates: Snow free and open July through Oct.

Fees: A limit-entry permit is required for those entering the Obsidian/Sunshine area. Permits are available only from McKenzie Ranger District in person or via mail or fax.

Closest town: Sisters.

Trail: 14.8 miles one way. The cliffs are about 5 miles from the trailhead.

Elevation: Varies from 5,200 to 7,334 feet.

Degree of difficulty: Moderate.

Surface: Dirt, rock and crushed lava cinders.

For more information: McKenzie Ranger Station, Willamette National Forest, 57600 McKenzie Hwy., McKenzie Bridge, OR 97413. Phone (541) 822-3381.

ALDER SPRINGS CAMPGROUND

[Fig. 30(2)] Sitting at the foot of Deadhorse Grade, this small campground is at the winter-closure gate of McKenzie Pass National Scenic Byway. Deadhorse Grade is a steep, hairpin, switchback section of McKenzie Pass Highway/OR 242 with an elevation change of more than 1,000 feet in about 4 miles. Combination vehicles that exceed 35 feet are prohibited east of the gate.

The top of the grade is at about 5,000 feet elevation, where the topography is alpinelike with heather undergrowth, alpine and silver fir, and clumps of juniper. The bottom of the grade is at an elevation of 3,600 feet and is lush with sword ferns that lean into the roadway, contorted clumps of vine maples, and wild huckleberries.

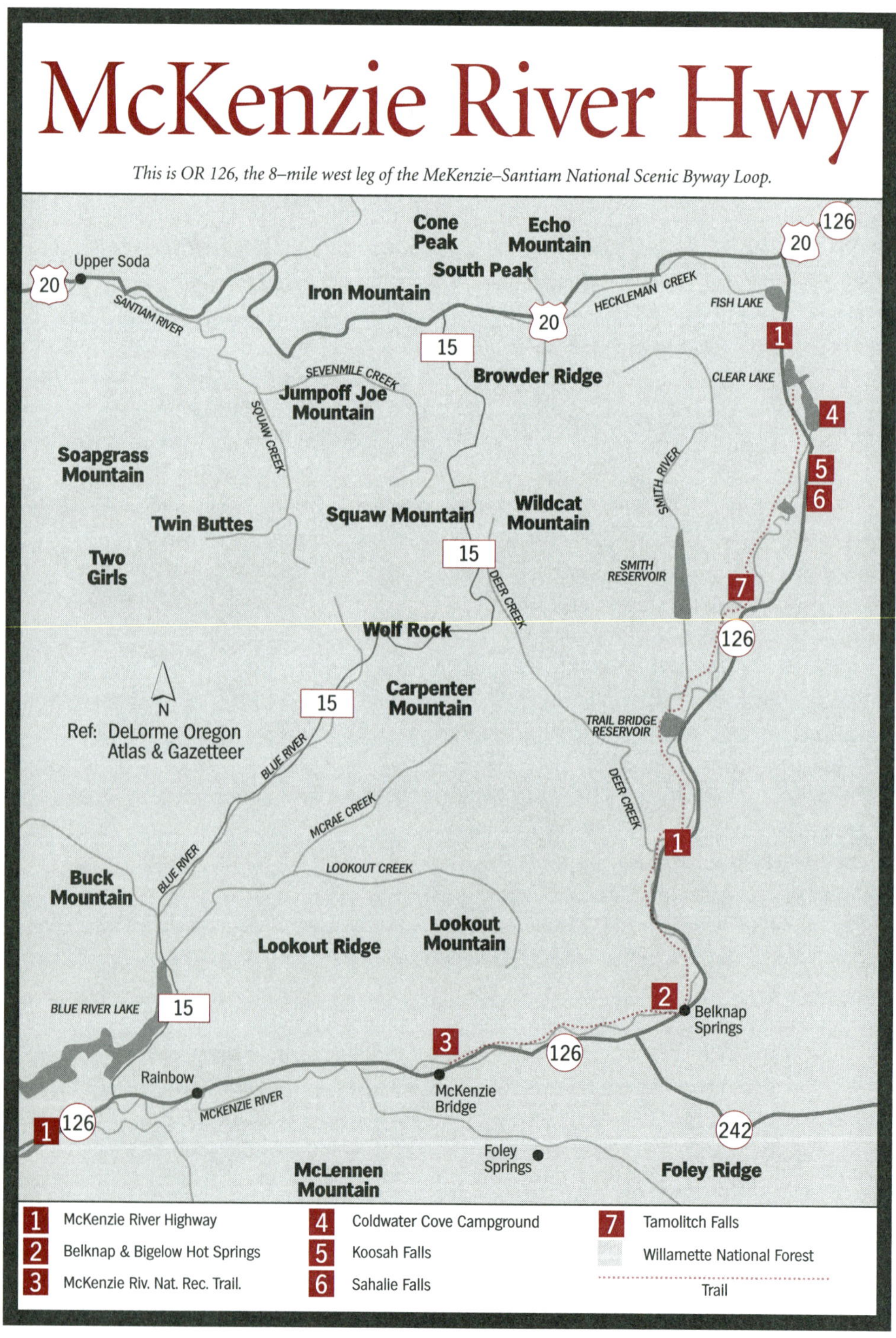
McKenzie River Hwy
This is OR 126, the 8–mile west leg of the MeKenzie–Santiam National Scenic Byway Loop.
Cone Peak
Echo Mountain
South Peak
Upper Soda
Iron Mountain
Santiam River
Heckleman Creek
Fish Lake
Sevenmile Creek
Browder Ridge
Jumpoff Joe Mountain
Clear Lake
Squaw Creek
Soapgrass Mountain
Smith River
Twin Buttes
Squaw Mountain
Wildcat Mountain
Two Girls
Smith Reservoir
Deer Creek
Wolf Rock
Carpenter Mountain
N
Ref: DeLorme Oregon Atlas & Gazetteer
Blue River
Trail Bridge Reservoir
McRae Creek
Lookout Creek
Buck Mountain
Lookout Ridge
Lookout Mountain
Blue River Lake
Belknap Springs
Rainbow
McKenzie River
McKenzie Bridge
Foley Springs
McLennen Mountain
Foley Ridge
20
126
15
242
1 McKenzie River Highway
2 Belknap & Bigelow Hot Springs
3 McKenzie Riv. Nat. Rec. Trail.
4 Coldwater Cove Campground
5 Koosah Falls
6 Sahalie Falls
7 Tamolitch Falls
Willamette National Forest
Trail

Directions: Follow McKenzie Pass Highway/Or 242, 11.5 miles east from McKenzie Bridge.

Activities: Camping, picnicking, and hiking.

Facilities: 7 tent sites, no water.

Dates: Open year-round, generally snow-free by Memorial Day.

Fees: None.

For more information: McKenzie Ranger Station, Willamette National Forest, 57600 McKenzie Hwy., McKenzie Bridge, OR 97413. Phone (541) 822-3381.

PROXY FALLS

[Fig. 30(3)] Two waterfalls cascade down basalt lava into sylvan glens of moss-carpeted logs, ferns, wild rhododendrons, and huckleberries. Just after snow melt, the access trail is brightened by a carpet of wild trilliums (*Trillium ovatum*). The falls are at an elevation of 3,200 feet and are an extremely popular destination for day hikers. The one-way loop route, in fact, was built to help minimize congestion. This is a popular spot for picnicking. Lower Proxy Falls is considered the most impressive of the two, dropping 200 feet in a misty fan shape. A short spur trail leads from Trail 3532 to an overlook. Upper Falls is a segmented 125-foot gush from a steep wall.

Directions: Follow McKenzie Pass Highway/OR 242 for 6.3 miles east of OR 126 to a marked pullover at Proxy Falls Trail 3532, an easy 1.25 mile loop walk through towering Douglas firs to the falls on Proxy Creek.

Activities: Waterfall viewing, hiking.

Dates: Open year-round, snow-free from about Memorial Day through Oct.

Fees: There is a charge for trail park pass.

For more information: McKenzie Ranger Station, Willamette National Forest, 57600 McKenzie Hwy., McKenzie Bridge, OR 97413. Phone (541) 822-3381.

McKenzie River Highway

[Fig. 31] On bright summer days the pavement of this north-south highway is painted with the long shadows of old-growth Douglas firs that tower above the highway shoulder. The effect is like driving in an extended glen alongside a swirling trout river, through a carpet of wildflowers, flickering leaves, and lacy ferns. This is OR 126, the 8-mile west leg of McKenzie-Santiam National Scenic Byway loop, and the connecting route between Eugene and OR 242 on the south and US 20 near Santiam Junction.

The road follows an easy, winding grade at the bottom of a steep lava-walled canyon that is pinched between the West Slope of the Cascades and the rushing McKenzie River. The river corridor is sprinkled with natural and scenic attractions, including two thundering waterfalls, a dry falls, two hot springs, a marsh popular with bird watchers, a national recreation trail, three campgrounds, and an ancient forest standing upright on the bottom of spring-fed Clear Lake. Standout attractions on the upper McKenzie River

Blue Grouse

Blue grouse (*Dendragapus obscurus*), the largest of Oregon's three species of forest grouse, are up to 21 inches long, can weigh more than 2 pounds, and flush with a thunderous roar of wings that's guaranteed to startle the unwary.

Blues are found in the high mountains on both sides of the Cascade Crest, nearly always in areas with a mix of wild berries, meadows, and conifer trees. The males are slate-colored with a yellow eye comb and black-tipped tail. The female is brown and heavily barred.

Blues are often seen along the edges of gravel roads in the mornings and evenings. In the early summer, you're likely to find entire family clutches of birds. They come to eat gravel that packs into their gizzards and helps break down tough foods for easier digestion.

Unlike most wildlife, blue grouse migrate in the winter to the high mountains, where there are few predators to contend with. Blues feed on evergreen buds, and for protection during extremely harsh weather conditions, will huddle under drooping branches bowed down by the weight of snow.

In the spring, it's common to hear males hooting their courtship calls. It seems the males are able to throw their voices, for although their calls carry far, they are almost impossible to track.

Blue grouse spend about as much time walking as perching or flying, and are an important source of food for most mountain predators and raptors, including grouse hunters, who savor the delicate white meat. The birds feed on seeds, berries, insects, and buds.

Highway include Belknap and Bigelow hot springs, Sahalie, Koosah, and Tamolitch falls, the McKenzie River National Recreation Trail and Clear Lake. The dominating attraction is the rumbling headwaters flow of 89-mile long McKenzie River. Its upper 12.7 miles, including the section paralleled by OR 126, are part of the national wild and scenic rivers program. The river's clear, cold, rushing water and plunging falls are a scenic wonder for travelers, and a challenge for white-water enthusiasts and trout fishermen. The McKenzie is one of Oregon's most productive and popular trout rivers. It begins in a natural spring at Clear Lake and ends at a confluence with the Willamette River west of I-5 in Eugene. The wild and scenic headwater section below Clear Lake is spectacular, a delight to fish, and there are enough rainbow trout to make each cast suspenseful. Below Leaburg Dam, the river also supports anadromous runs of summer steelhead and spring chinook salmon. The cold, clear upper river draws whitewater enthusiasts. The dory-style McKenzie drift boat, popular with whitewater fishermen, was named for this river.

BELKNAP AND BIGELOW HOT SPRINGS

[Fig. 31(2)] Belknap is a small commercial mineral spring located at Belknap Lodge on OR 126 about 6 miles east of McKenzie Bridge, near the junction of McKenzie Pass Highway/

OR 242. The natural hot spring water is channeled into two swimming pools and six Jacuzzis. Clothing is required. Bigelow Hot Springs is a small, undeveloped fern-rimmed pool somewhat hidden adjacent to the McKenzie River at Deer Creek Road Forest Service 2654. The turn from OR 126 is halfway between mileposts 15 and 14. Cross the McKenzie River, park at the Deer Creek Road bridge, and follow the footpath downstream to the unseen pool. Water temperature averages 103 degrees Fahrenheit, and there's room for four soakers. The hot spring is closed at night. Clothing is optional, but swimwear is the accepted standard.

Dates: Both hot springs are open year-round, but Bigelow is restricted to daytime use.

Fees: No charge at Bigelow, but commercial fees are charged at the Belknap Hot Springs.

Closest town: Eugene is about 60 miles southwest on OR 126.

For more information: Belknap Hot Springs Lodge, Rt. 1, McKenzie Bridge, OR 97413. Phone (541) 822-3512. McKenzie Ranger Station, Willamette National Forest, 57600 McKenzie Hwy., McKenzie Bridge, OR 97413. Phone (541) 822-3381.

FALLS OF THE MCKENZIE

Three waterfalls in the McKenzie River off OR 126 are worth stops en route through the upper canyon. Two of the falls are roaring torrents and the third is dry, the result of an unnatural phenomenon. Koosha and Sahalie falls are about 6 miles north of OR 242, at a large, paved pull-out and interpretive sign area on the west side of the highway. Sahalie Falls [Fig. 31(6)] is a gushing 140-foot plunge through a cleft in basalt rock into a plunge pool. It's a glen with towering cedar and fir trees, walls of vine maple entanglements, where ferns grow out of black rocks and the river banks are carpeted with mosses. There is a developed viewpoint, paved path, and access to the McKenzie River National Recreation Trail.

Koosah Falls [Fig. 31(5)] is less than 0.5 mile south of Sahalie Falls at Ice Cap Campground. Koosah drops 80 to 120 feet in segments. It can be reached by footpath from Sahalie Falls parking area, or follow OR 126 south to a marked parking area. Tamolitch Falls [Fig. 31(7)] is about 1 mile south of the Sahalie interpretive area.

To reach the dry falls, park at Trail Bridge campground and follow the McKenzie River NR Trail north for 1 mile. The McKenzie River dropped 60 feet down a rock wall into a plunge pool, before the river was diverted into power reservoirs 3 miles upstream. The undiverted

LODGEPOLE PINE

(*Pinus contorta*)
Growing up to 80 feet tall, this pine has needles growing in twisted pairs and cones that are closed and prickly, pointing away from the branch.

water of the McKenzie River resurface below the dry falls wall in a strikingly blue pool fed by a capillary system of natural springs. The trail is easy walking and this is an intriguing stop.

Directions: The falls are in a 1-mile section of the McKenzie River about 5.2 miles south of US 20 or 6 miles north of US 242. Watch for signs.

Facilities: Interpretive signs, restrooms, paved pathway and developed viewpoints.

Dates: Open year-round.

Fees: None.

Closest town: Eugene.

For more information: McKenzie Ranger Station, Willamette National Forest, 57600 McKenzie Hwy., McKenzie Bridge, OR 97413. Phone (541) 822-3381.

MCKENZIE RIVER NATIONAL RECREATION TRAIL 3507

[Fig. 31(3)] McKenzie River National Recreation Trail follows 26.5 miles of upper McKenzie River above McKenzie Bridge, and is accessible in many areas from OR 126 which parallels both the river and the trail at the bottom of the McKenzie Canyon.

Most hikers and mountain bikers divide this trail into short treks or loop routes between highway access points. The entire trail can be hiked easily in two days. Three days leaves a lot of time for enjoying the postcard quality river scenery and unusual volcanic features. The trail crosses several splashing tributaries on log bridges, and works around Clear Lake and its adjacent lava flows. The lower section of river trail goes through fern and moss-carpeted stands of 600-year-old Douglas firs. The upper trail passes waterfalls and ancient lava flows. Nearly the entire route is through cool, green glens of conifer forests. Developed campsites, toilets, and potable water are available at Paradise, Trailbridge and Coldwater Cove campgrounds, and Clear Lake Picnic Area.

Dates: Lower sections are usually snow-free year-round, and the upper elevations are clear by May.

Fees: None.

Closest town: McKenzie Bridge is at the southern terminus.

For more information: McKenzie Ranger Station, Willamette National Forest, 57600 McKenzie Hwy., McKenzie Bridge, OR 97413. Phone (541) 822-3381.

Trail: 26.5 miles one-way.

Elevation: The low point is 1,450 feet rising to 3,200 feet at Clear Lake..

Degree of difficulty: Easy to moderate.

Surface: Natural forest duff.

CLEAR LAKE

[Fig. 31] Three thousand years ago, a 3-mile-long river of lava flowed downhill from Little Nash Crater and blocked several spring creeks. When the lava hardened, it impounded the springs and created the coldest, possibly clearest, lake in Oregon, formed the headwaters of the McKenzie River, and entombed a standing forest preserved in near-freezing water.

The jumble of lava from this flow still encases the hillside on the southeast side of Clear Lake. About 200 feet deep, Clear Lake is fed by springs, which are the headwater source of the wild and scenic McKenzie River. The river gushes full-grown from a corner of the lake. One of the most amazing characteristics of this exceptionally scenic lake is the ancient forest that still stands beneath it. On the bottom of the lake, at the north end, a ghost forest of trees nearly 3,000 years old stands upright, preserved in 100 feet of frigid, unpolluted water. The water is so clear that boaters can see the tops of the standing forest poking up from the lake bottom.

Anglers fish from nonmotorized boats for wild cutthroat and brook trout, and stocked rainbow trout. Fishing licenses and timely fishing information is available at Clear Lake Resort and Crockett Lodge. The small fish camp is operated by Santiam Fish and Game Association that rents cabins, RV sites, and boats. The resort and lodge are on the north end of the lake. The Forest Service's Coldwater Cove Campground is on the south end of the lake adjacent to the McKenzie River National Recreation Trail (NRT). The NRT is part of a 5 mile long, mostly level and partially paved loop trail that encircles the lake. Watch for bald eagle nests on the west side of the lake.

McKenzie Glacier Age

During the last Oregon Ice Age, about 12,000 years ago, most of the high Cascades in the McKenzie region were covered by a solid sheet of moving ice.

Glaciers filled the McKenzie Valley as far west as Blue River, and evidence that the glaciers once covered McKenzie Pass is found in striations on the old andesite rocks at Craig Lake. These scratches were caused by rocks locked in the ice rubbing against bedrock, and reveal the direction the glacier was moving.

Between the peaks of Three Sisters and Mount Washington, the retreating ice sheet gouged out great depressions in the landscape, and carved tons of material from the newly formed mountains. The retreat began about 10,000 years ago. Today's snow fields and glaciers high on the mountains are actually the last remnants of that Ice Age.

The glaciers continue to move and grind rock from the mountains. The rock residue can be seen deposited in moraines at the foot and sides of the glaciers.

Directions: Along the east side of OR 126 about 4 miles south of US 20 or 18 miles north of McKenzie Bridge.

Activities: Camping, picnicking, fishing, hiking, wildlife watching, and big game hunting.

Facilities: Resort with rustic rental cabins, RV sites, some groceries and tackle, restaurant, boat rentals, Forest Service campground, 2 boat ramps, lake shore hiking trail.

Dates: Generally snow-free from Memorial Day through Oct. The resort is sometimes open during winter.

Fees: There is a charge for camping and resort services.

Closest town: McKenzie Bridge, 18 miles south on OR 126.

For more information: McKenzie Ranger Station, Willamette National Forest, 57600

Mount Washington Wilderness Area

According to geologists, this area erupts lava about every 1,500 years and last erupted 1,500 years ago.

Sand Mountain
BIG LAKE
Pacific Crest National Scenic Trail
CUB LAKE
Cache Mountain
Little Cache Mountain
PATIENS LAKES
Pacific Crest National Scenic Trail
DRY CREEK
Mount Washington
MOUNT WASHINGTON WILDERNESS
GEORGE LAKE
Dugout Butte
ROBINSON LAKE
Belknap Crater
Little Belknap
Pacific Crest National Scenic Tr
KUITAN LAKE
Black Crater
242
McKenzie Pass
Twin Craters
Millican Crater
Scott Mountain
HAND LAKE
CAMPERS LAKE
Condon Butte
BENSON LAKE
YAPOAH LAKE
SCOTT LAKE
FROG CAMP CREEK
MELAKINA LAKE
Sims Butte
MINNIE SCOTT SPRING

1 McKenzie Pass Nat. Scen. Byway
2 Lava Sea Overlook
3 Milican Crater Trail
4 Black Crater Trail 93
5 Lava Camp Lake
6 McKenzie Pass
7 Lava River Trail
Mount Washington Wilderness
Three Sisters Wilderness
Pacific Crest National Scenic Trail
Trail

McKenzie Hwy., McKenzie Bridge, OR 97413. Phone (541) 822-3381. For Forest Service campsite reservations phone (800) 280-2267. Crockett Lodge cabin reservations are made by mail only. Contact Santiam Fish & Game Association, PO Box 500, Lebanon, OR 97355.

COLDWATER COVE CAMPGROUND

[Fig. 31(4)] **Directions:** On the south end of Clear Lake at an elevation of 3,100 feet.

Activities: Camping, fishing, hiking, rowboating.

Facilities: 35 well spaced and shaded tent and RV sites, tables, grills, potable water, vault toilets, barrier-free access, boat ramp, and paved lakeside trail. There is a resident manager, and reservations are accepted.

Dates: Open Memorial Day through Sept.

Fees: There is a charge for campsites.

McKenzie Pass National Scenic Byway/OR 242

[Fig. 32(1)] "No one who would claim to be in search of the soul of Oregon should pass this road by," writes Ralph Friedman about the McKenzie Pass Highway in his 1990 book, *In Search of Western Oregon.* Less adventurous travelers, however, might argue that if Friedman is right, then Oregon's soul is twisted, steep, narrow, and trapped in a volcanic wonderland.

But most travelers will probably agree with the descriptions of another Oregon writer, William Mainwaring, in his book, *Exploring Oregon's Central and Southern Cascades*: "The drive over McKenzie Pass has few peers for scenic diversity—you'll see deep canyons, waterfalls, sparkling mountain lakes, snowcapped peaks, vast forests, and the most extensive relatively recent volcanic activity in the continental United States."

McKenzie Pass National Scenic Highway/OR 242 is a spectacular two-lane, 40-mile long east-west summer route between Sisters and the McKenzie River Highway 126. It is a national scenic byway that forms the southern leg of the McKenzie-Santiam Pass Loop.

The route is closed by mountainous accumulations of snow from December through June. Combination vehicles longer than 35 feet are prohibited at all times. The long vehicle and winter snow closure areas are in the high elevations west of milepost 85 and east of Alder Springs. The restrictions are a maintenance and safety concession to the byway's steep grades and tight curves. Steering large motor homes over this route can be challenging. Wide berms and pullovers help. There are no commercial businesses that service motorists inside the national forest segment of the route.

The two-lane highway passes through astonishing vistas of past volcanic activity. Near McKenzie Pass, elevation 5,342-feet, the highway crosses 75 square miles of moonscape-like broken lava rocks, and the ominous remains of Belknap Crater, elevation 6,872 feet. The land is spotted with dark cinder cones, craters, ragged blankets of jumbled lava, land islands crowded with groves of dwarf pine and fir trees, obsidian beds, crystalline trout lakes, and distant glaciers.

The road slides between two federal wilderness areas, Mount Washington to the north

Dwarf Trees

The McKenzie Pass lava area is dotted with natural bonsai trees that have been stunted by the harsh environment.

The short growing seasons, scarcity of summer water, and lack of topsoil has produced conifer trees that are short, stunted, dense and very old. Most are mountain hemlock (*Tsuga mertensiana*), lodgepole pine (*Pinus contorta*) and Western juniper (*Juniperis occidentalis*).

It's not unusual for a root system to be several times larger than the trunk in order to supply enough food to support the tree. These small, often wind-twisted trees, can be several centuries old, and the wood is so dense that it's difficult to cut with a hatchet.

and Three Sisters on the south. It is the only highway to actually adjoin the border of the popular Three Sisters Wilderness Area. Wilderness permits are not required to drive through the area, but are needed to hike into the wilderness areas. All of the improved trails require trail park passes. Like a black crown, a lava-walled observatory built in 1930 sits at the summit of McKenzie Pass. The observatory resembles a rock turret pierced by 11-slotted windows, each directed at a different mountain.

A 0.5-mile-long, paved, wheelchair accessible, interpretive trail leads from the observatory parking area into the surrounding desolation of the Yapoah lava field. East of McKenzie Pass travelers enjoy an elevation change that gradually shifts 2,150 feet in 15 miles of ranch lands, meadows sprinkled with wild grasses and flowers, dense conifer stands, and open ridges. West of the pass, the route is more dramatic, changing 4,000 feet in 21 miles. Along the summit ridge, piles of broken lava press against the road, twisted white skeletons of weather-killed conifer trees poke at the sky, and dirt side roads cut north and south to campgrounds, lakes, and trails. About 4 miles west of the summit at Deadhorse Grade the mountain sides steepen, and the tree-lined highway folds into a series of accordion switchbacks. The western snow closure begins at the bottom of the grade near Alder Springs.

This national scenic byway began as a cross-mountain summer trail for tribes coming from the Columbia River area to trade with Indians in the McKenzie River Valley. In 1862, Felix Scott Jr. widened the trail into a wagon road to supply Idaho mining camps with food and equipment from the Willamette Valley. The Indian trail varied routes as it crossed the jumbled lava fields. In the late 1860s, the present route was pushed up Lost Creek Canyon and was literally carved out of the rocks. It became a toll road in 1872, a free road in 1898, and a state highway in 1917.

Today, it's one of the most unusual national scenic byways in America.

Directions: From the east, OR 242 intersects with US 20 on the west edge of Sisters. On the west it intersects with OR 126 just west of Belknap Springs.

Dates: Open July through Nov. depending on snow accumulations.

Fees: Free wilderness and fee trail park passes are available at both Sisters and McKenzie ranger stations. Campsite fees for campgrounds along the highway are collected on site.

Closest town: McKenzie Bridge on the west, and Sisters on the east.

For more information: East, Sisters Ranger Station, Deschutes National Forest, PO Box 249, Sisters, OR 97759. Phone (541) 549-2111. On the west at McKenzie Ranger Station, Willamette National Forest, 57600 McKenzie Hwy., McKenzie Bridge, OR 97413. Phone (541) 822-3381.

MOUNT WASHINGTON WILDERNESS

[Fig. 32] The steeple-peak summit of an extinct shield volcano, Mount Washington, elevation 7,794 feet, is the dominant feature of 52,516-acre Mount Washington Wilderness. The peak overlooks the rounded cinder cone of Belknap Crater, elevation 6,872 feet. Less than 1,000 years ago, at the end of the last Ice Age, Belknap volcano delivered one of the most powerful and explosive pyroclastic events in the war between fire and ice that shaped the Cascades. It gushed miles of molten basaltic lava that formed the now-hardened basalt that blankets this wilderness. Viewed from roadside overlooks, the dark, dormant Belknap Crater now appears to be imprisoned in desolate isolation at the center of miles of hardened "aa" basalt.

Geologists also speculate that, given this area's molten underpinnings and braids of fault lines, there is a real possibility that new eruptions could occur. The topography of Mount Washington Wilderness is not composed of the thick forests, alpine basins, and lake meadows that are typical of Oregon wilderness areas. The stony landscape is nearly waterless. Trees grow in wedges of composted earth walled in by vast wrinkled flows of broken basalt, andesite, rhyolite, and ash.

The wilderness area is shared by Willamette and Deschutes national forests. It lies on a high plain south of US 20/OR 126, west of Sisters, and north of McKenzie Pass National Scenic Byway OR 242. The lowest point in this high-mountain wilderness area is 3,000 feet, and the highest is the summit of Mount Washington. Most of this rugged lava land is between 4,000 and 5,000 feet in elevation. Immense tracts are treeless. The few hardy trees that survive here are mostly lodgepole pine and mountain hemlock.

Mount Washington rises above 75 square miles of lava-strewn plains. This is a rugged region, primarily used by hunters, hikers and mountain climbers. Most of the water is near the outside boundary of the wilderness area. Twenty-eight small lakes, some little more than large puddles, offer limited trout fishing.

Pacific Crest National Scenic Trail 2000 runs through 16.6 miles of the wilderness and is the primary access trail. Several short trail systems are used, though. The most popular trails are Patjens Lake Trail 3395, Benson Lake 3502, and Hand Lake Trail 3513.

The Mount Washington Wilderness includes examples of some of the youngest volcanic activity in the Oregon Cascades, lava shields, cinder cones, and lava flows. The youngest cones, Yopoah and Collier, may be 1,500 years old. According to geologists, this area erupts lava about every 1,500 years. The last lava flow was about 1,500 years ago.

Directions: From the north, take US 20 to Forest Service 2690 (Big Lake Road) and go south to Big Lake West Campgrounds, where Patjens Lake Trail 3395 loops into the wilderness. From the east, there is summer trailhead to the Pacific Crest Trail 2000 at

DOUGLAS FIR
(Pseudotsuga menziesii)

McKenzie Pass on OR 242. West side entry is from OR 126 north of Trail Bridge Reservoir. Turn east onto Forest Service Road 2664 to Robinson Lake trailhead on the edge of the wilderness.

Dates: Upper elevations are snowbound from Dec. through June. McKenzie Pass OR 242 is open only during summer.

Fees: There is no charge for wilderness use permits required from Memorial Day through Oct. 31. Permits are self issued at some trail heads, and available at Sisters and McKenzie ranger stations. There is a charge for trail park passes which can be purchased at the ranger stations.

Closest town: Sisters.

For more information: Sisters Ranger Station, PO Box 249, US 20, Sisters, OR 97759. Phone (541) 549-2111. McKenzie Ranger Station, Willamette National Forest, 57600 McKenzie Hwy., McKenzie Bridge, OR 97413. Phone (541) 822-3381.

LAVA SEA OVERLOOK

[Fig. 32(2)] A wide pullover with interpretive signs at Windy Point, 11.5 miles west of Sisters on McKenzie Pass/OR 242, provides a sweeping view of the choppy sea of lava that less than 1,500 years ago gushed from several craters. Belknap Crater, the largest, rises to 6,872 feet on the horizon 3.9 miles west. Scientists believe Belknap last erupted about 1,000 years ago, and the lava sea was formed by three flows that occurred 3,000 to 1,000 years ago. The steeple peak of Mount Washington stands above the desolate lava plain.

The black sea of broken basalt lava covers 20 square miles, and looks very much as it did immediately after the eruption. Little plant life has taken hold in this forbidding region. The lava at this overlook is part of an 8-mile-long, 0.5-mile-wide flow from an eruption at Yapoah Crater about 1,500 years ago. Yapoah is out of sight to the southeast, near North Sister Mountain, and is believed to have last erupted less than 400 years ago. It's believed to be dormant and may erupt again.

From this elevated overlook you can also see Little Belknap Peak, elevation 6,305 feet, which is 3.2 miles west; Mount Washington, elevation 7,794 feet, 4.8 miles west. North are Three Finger Jack, elevation 7,841 feet, at 14 miles; Mount Jefferson, elevation 10,497 feet 27 miles, and Mount Hood, elevation 11,235 feet, 75 miles. The Belknap craters can be reached by hiking across the lava field on nearby Pacific Crest Trail 2000. The trailhead is near the overlook. The Lost Creek Valley to the west is a glacial moraine at the end of a tongue of ice that flowed from Middle Sister about 10,000 years ago. The banks of Lost Creek are a favorite area with rock hounds looking for bits of obsidian that originated on Middle Sister Mountain. In places, Lost Creek disappears beneath the porous lava rock, and continues downstream as underground braids following old stream gravelways.

Directions: Follow McKenzie Pass National Scenic Byway/OR 242 west from Sisters for 11.5 miles. The viewpoint, at an elevation of 4,850 feet, is on the north shoulder.

Facilities: Interpretive signs explaining the volcanic sequences that created the vast lava fields, trailhead to Pacific Crest Trail 2000.

Dates: This section of the scenic byway is open only from late June through Nov.

Fees: None.

BLACK CRATER TRAIL 93

[Fig. 32(4)] Beginning less than a quarter of a mile west of Windy Point overlook, Black Crater Trail heads south from OR 242 on a strenuous route into Three Sisters Wilderness. The trail is open to hikers and horses, but not bicycles. From the trailhead, Black Crater Trail climbs steeply, moderating slightly as it enters a thick stand of mountain hemlock (*Tsuga mertensiana*) on the north side of the crater. The upper section of the trail gradually emerges onto open cinder slopes. The summit is a rocky outcrop with dramatic views of North Sister Mountain, Mount Washington and McKenzie Pass lava flows. On a clear day Mount Adams is visible 100 miles north in Washington State. A fire lookout once stood on the site.

Directions: Follow OR 242 west from Sisters for 11.75 miles to a trailhead parking area just west of Windy Point overlook.

Dates: Usually snow-free June through Nov.

Fees: Trail park passes are required to park at the trailhead, and free wilderness area passes are self-issued at trailhead dispensers.

Closest town: Sisters.

For more information: Sisters Ranger Station, Deschutes National Forest, PO Box 249, Sisters, OR 97759. Phone (541) 549-2111.

Trail: Black Crater Trail 93, 3.8 miles to the open summit of Black Crater in Three Sisters Wilderness.

Elevation: Trailhead is at 4,900 feet and the summit is at 7,251 feet.

Degree of difficulty: Strenuous.

Surface: Dirt and rock.

LAVA CAMP LAKE

[Fig. 32(5)] A small, sparkling blue surprise, Lava Camp Lake is an oasis of shade trees and picnic tables surrounded by a McKenzie Pass landscape so lunar-like that in 1964 astronauts practiced walking and working here in preparation for the first moon landing. Within a mile of the paved highway are Lava Camp Lake, Millican Crater Trail and the Pacific Crest Trail 2000. The elevation is 5,300 feet and night-time temperatures below freezing are common even in summer. This is an ideal base for day-hike explorations of the surrounding lava fields and nearby wilderness areas.

Directions: The campground is 14.6 miles west of Sisters, just east of McKenzie Pass on OR 242. At milepost 78 turn onto Forest Service 900, a red cinder road with ruts, holes, and dust that could be problematic for low-slung vehicles.

Activities: Camping and hiking.

Facilities: 10 campsites, vault toilets, picnic tables, and fire pits. No water.

Dates: Open May through Oct.

Fees: None.

MILLICAN CRATER TRAIL

[Fig. 32(3)] The trail to Millican Crater is through open conifer stands and lava rock to the crater in Three Sisters Wilderness Area. It's possible to continue on intersecting trails for a loop route back to Lava Camp Lake Campground. To make the circle, continue about a mile south of the crater, to Trail 4066, and turn southwest to Yopoah Lake. Continue through Scotts Pass, elevation 6,100 feet, to the PCT. Take the PCT north to Lava Camp Lake Campground.

Directions: The trailhead is at the far end of Lava Camp Lake campground on McKenzie Pass Highway/OR 242. At milepost 78 turn onto Forest Service 900, a red cinder road and continue through the campground to the trailhead.

Dates: Open late June through Nov.

Fees: There is a charge for trail park passes. Free wilderness passes are dispensed at the trailhead.

Trail: Millican Crater Trail 4066, 4.6 miles one way.

Elevation: The trailhead is 4,870 feet and the crater is at 5,120 feet.

Degree of difficulty: Moderate.

Surface: Dirt and rock.

MCKENZIE PASS

[Fig. 32(6)] The crown of McKenzie Pass National Scenic Byway/OR 242 is McKenzie Pass, elevation 5,342 feet, a rustic centerpiece surrounded by natural exclamation points and man-made wonders. The summit is accessible only from July through November, and sits on a pyroclastic hump centered in miles of broken, black "aa" lava that 1,500 years ago gushed white hot and molten from Yopoah Crater to the south.

On a clear day you can see the Oregon Cascades' five highest peaks from the pass. The glacier-streaked crags of Three Sisters and Broken Top Mountain dominate the southern horizon, Mount Washington stands to the north and in the distance are the pyramidal peaks of Mounts Jefferson and Hood. It's difficult to imagine, but from 1866-72 the McKenzie Salt Springs and Deschutes Wagon Road crossed this vast lava plain, wooden wheels and hooves picking across razor sharp clinkers and jagged boulders. Another testimonial to pioneer hardships lies a mile west of the summit at a memorial to postman John Templeton Craig. In 1877 while carrying Christmas mail between McKenzie Bridge and Camp Polk (now Sisters), 56-year-old Craig was caught in a blizzard and took refuge in a small cabin. He was found frozen to death, curled up inside the fireplace, where he apparently tried to soak up the last of the residual heat from the hearth stones.

Perched atop a pile of lava rock at the high point on the pass is Dee Wright Observatory, a two-story, fortress-looking aerie with a commanding view of Oregon. The landmark is open to the public. It is named for a Forest Service horse packer and foreman of the CCC construction crew that built the observatory in 1935. Wooden supports for the rock-walled facility were heavily damaged by a lightning strike, and extensive renovations were completed in 1998. At the base of Dee Wright Observatory is the start of Lava River National Recreation Trail 3540. At 0.5 mile, this paved path is probably one of the shortest nationally recognized trails in America.

Directions: Follow McKenzie Pass National Scenic Highway 15 miles west of Sisters.

Facilities: Observatory, national hiking trail, restroom, and paved parking lot.

Dates: Open July through Nov.

Fees: None.

Closest town: Sisters.

For more information: Sisters Ranger Station, Deschutes National Forest, PO Box 249, Sisters, OR 97759. Phone (541) 549-2111. McKenzie Ranger Station, Willamette National Forest, 57600 McKenzie Hwy., McKenzie Bridge, OR 97413. Phone (541) 822-3381.

LAVA RIVER NATIONAL RECREATION TRAIL 3540

[Fig. 32(7)] This short, paved interpretive trail winds through the Yapoah Crater lava flow from the 5,342-foot summit of McKenzie Pass on OR 242. It begins and ends below Dee Wright Observatory. Lake River Trail offers remarkable see-and-touch opportunities in the lava field, with interpretive signs explaining geologic formations along the trail.

Dates: Open July through Nov.

Fees: None.

Trail: 0.5 mile through a lava flow.

Elevation: 5,342 to 5,350.

Degree of difficulty: Easy.

Surface: Paved, wheelchair accessible.

SCOTT LAKE

[Fig. 32] A picture-perfect photo stop, Scott Lake, 4,680 feet in elevation, is a heavily used campground and picnic area west of McKenzie Pass in the Willamette National Forest. On windless days the lake mirrors a dramatic reflection of The Three Sisters. This is a good stop for picnicking, and short forest walks on an 1866 wagon trail. Nearby Sims Butte is a small volcano that poured several thin basalt lava flows into the Lost Creek Valley since the last Ice Age.

Directions: Follow McKenzie Pass Highway/Oregon 242 about 4 miles west of McKenzie Pass, or 14 miles east of OR 126. Turn north on Scott Lake Road.

Activities: Camping, boating (no motors), trout fishing, hiking, and picnicking.

Facilities: 20 walk-in tent sites, potable water, picnic tables, fire pits.

Dates: Open July through Sept.

Fees: A trail park pass is required for the trails leaving the campground area.

For more information: McKenzie Ranger Station, Willamette National Forest, 57600 McKenzie Hwy., McKenzie Bridge, OR 97413. Phone (541) 822-3381.

Cascades Lakes Region

This region falls within the management of Willamette National Forest and Deschutes National Forest.

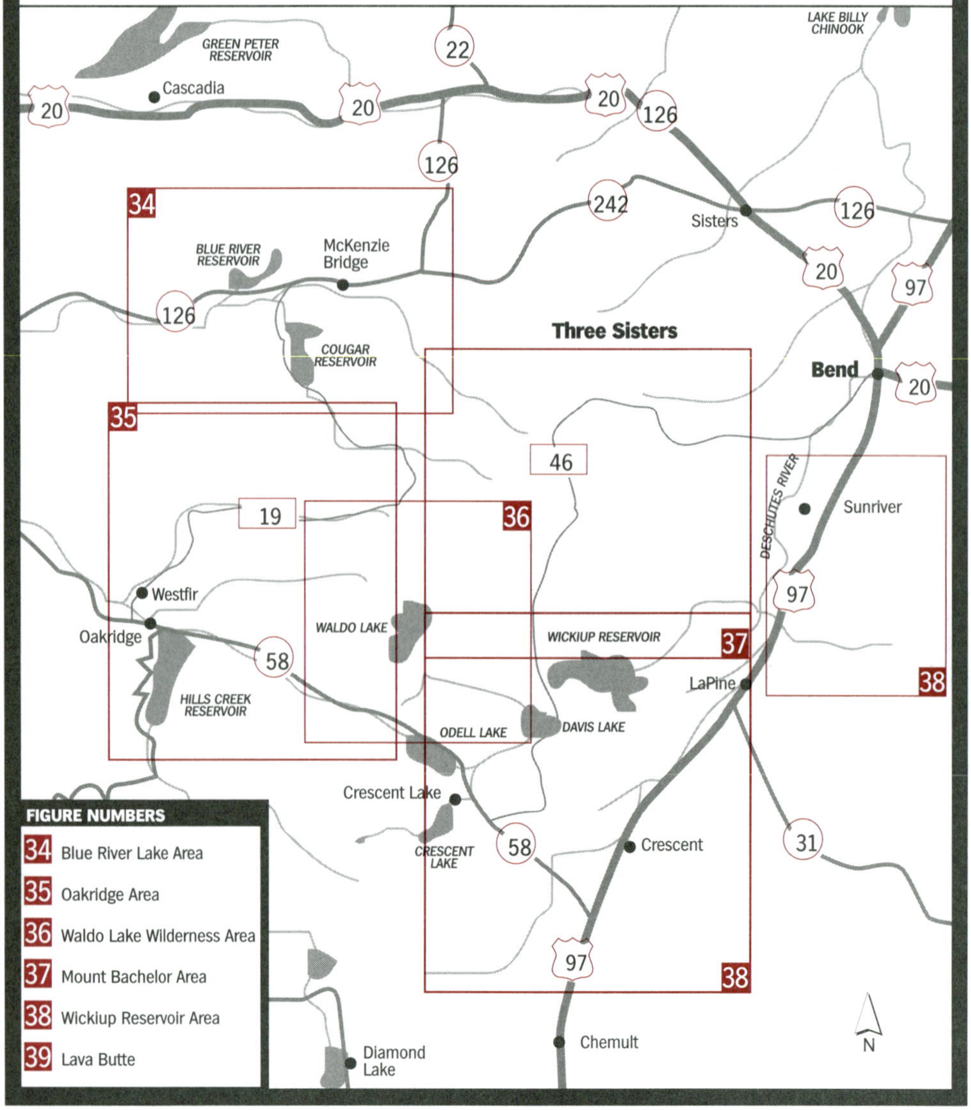

LAKE BILLY CHINOOK
GREEN PETER RESERVOIR
Cascadia
22
20
20
20
126
126
242
Sisters
126
20
97
BLUE RIVER RESERVOIR
McKenzie Bridge
126
COUGAR RESERVOIR
Three Sisters
Bend
20
46
19
DESCHUTES RIVER
Sunriver
Westfir
Oakridge
58
WALDO LAKE
WICKIUP RESERVOIR
97
LaPine
HILLS CREEK RESERVOIR
ODELL LAKE
DAVIS LAKE
Crescent Lake
CRESCENT LAKE
58
Crescent
31
97
Chemult
Diamond Lake
N

FIGURE NUMBERS

34 Blue River Lake Area
35 Oakridge Area
36 Waldo Lake Wilderness Area
37 Mount Bachelor Area
38 Wickiup Reservoir Area
39 Lava Butte

Cascade Lakes Region

The Ice-Age glacial scouring, volcanic scars, ice-encased peaks, shattered sheets of hardened lava flows, and other souvenirs from Oregon's fire and ice beginning have evolved into areas with peculiar and spectacular natural features. There are few regions, however, where the results are as evident, and recreationally beneficial as in the Cascade Lakes Region.

The region is named for a necklace of natural and manmade high lakes strung together by a nationally recognized scenic route along the east shoulder of the Cascades. The lakes range in size from a few grassy acres of leftover snowmelt to the 10,000-acres of Deschutes River water impounded by the federal Bureau of Reclamation (BOR) in Wickiup Reservoir for lowland irrigation. Most of the natural lakes were gouged out by Ice Age glaciers thousands of feet thick. The lakes are favorite destinations for camping, boating, and fishing.

[*Above:* Every ounce of Waldo Lake is pure enough to drink, making it one of the most pristine lakes in the world.]

Lakeside campgrounds are also used as base camps for hikers, mushroom and berry gatherers, and hunters exploring the surrounding forests. The volcanic soil is fertile growing ground for many varieties of mushrooms, especially the coveted Japanese pine mushrooms known as Matsutake (*Tricholoma ponderosum*), and at least a dozen varieties of edible boletes (*Boletus*). There is also a profusion of purple huckleberries that ripen in early September, and in the low-elevation valleys are jungle-like patches of non-native Himalaya and Evergreen trailing blackberries (*Rosaceae*). The range is shared by mule and black-tailed deer, and elk. The mixed habitats offered by high elevation lakes, rivers, forests, and open mountains supports and interesting mix of wildlife. This is one of the few places in Oregon where biologists suspect that wolverines (*Gulo gulo*) still range. Beavers, mink, otters, and pine martens are fairly common, as are the major predators such as black bear (*Ursus americanus*), mountain lion (*Felis Concolor*) and bobcat (*Felis rufus*). Occasionally lynx (*Felis lynx*) sightings are reported. Porcupines (*Erethizon dorsatum*) are plentiful, but are rarely seen because they are largely nocturnal and rarely come down from the towering conifers where they feed on bark, cambium, and buds. In rock slides along open mountain peaks live yellow-bellied marmots (*Marmota flaviventris*), a groundhog-size rodent that's usually seen perched atop rock piles, and makes its presence known by shrill whistles and loud chirps. Nervous 6-inch-long Douglas squirrels (*Tamiasciurus douglasii*) are very common tree dwellers. It's almost impossible to escape their incessant chattering and scolding trills.

Geographically, this region includes the remote mountains, rivers, valleys, and forests between the cities of Eugene in the rain-drenched lush Willamette Valley and Bend in the semiarid sage and juniper flats in the rain shadow at the east edge of the Cascades. It also includes the Newberry National Volcanic Monument on the East Slope of the Cascades. The north border runs east-west, roughly following McKenzie Pass Scenic Byway/OR242. The south boundary is an east-west line formed by Middle Fork Willamette River and OR 58, a heavily used cross-mountain highway that parallels the river.

Two paved national scenic byways follow paralleling, but well-separated, north-south routes through the region. Cascade Lakes National Scenic Byway runs along the open top of the Cascades and Aufderheide National Scenic Byway tracks the tree-canopied bottom of river valleys below mile-high mountains.

The Cascade Lakes National Scenic Byway runs along the eastern side of the region on a 93-mile-long north-south route that combines OR 372 and Forest Service 46. Until it was designated as a national scenic byway, this nearly-100-mile-long route was known as Century Drive. That name still appears on many maps.

The route follows a high, undulating ridge composed of 7,000-year-old andesite deposits left from the series of devastating volcanic explosions, implosions, and eruptions of Mount Mazama. It offers top-of-the-world views and connects many important central Cascade recreation areas, including internationally known ski areas at Mount Bachelor. From May through November (the route is closed in winter) the byway is the scenic string that connects a chain of Cascade lakes and 25 Forest Service campgrounds.

Cascade Lakes National Scenic Byway roughly follows the spine of the Cascade Range and is a geological, topographical, and climatological division line.

Oregon's Cascades are actually two parallel mountain ranges separated by millions of years of volcanic upheaval and Ice Age glacial erosion. The Cascade Lakes National Scenic Byway roughly traces the division line between these two ranges.

West are the rounded mountains of the Western Cascades. These are the oldest mountains in the Cascade Range and were formed between 8 and 45 million years ago. East is the High Cascades, a belt of young volcanos that erupted during the last five million years, and includes Oregon's most spectacular peaks.

It was the eruption of these younger mountains that buried much of the older Western Cascades. Summits that were once as high as the glacier-encrusted High Cascade peaks are now rounded, buried under lava that formed the foundation of the High Cascades. Much of the geologic history of the Western Cascade Range is inaccessible. The answers to geological questions are buried beneath hundreds of feet of lava, sedimentary rock, and other volcanic debris that flowed in molten blankets of lava during the explosive development of the younger, higher High Cascade Range.

The youngest volcanos were active in the last 10,000 years, and the eruptions that buried the older mountains also created Oregon's most impressive peaks: Mount Thielson, Diamond Peak, Mount Washington, Mount Jefferson, Three Sisters, and Mount Hood. Many of these volcanoes are now considered extinct, but Mount Hood and Three Sisters are likely to erupt again, according to geologists.

The highway corridor is also a dividing line for weather and flora. Most of the low, moisture-heavy clouds coming in from the Pacific Ocean are blocked by the mile-high wall of the Western Cascades. Banked against the mountains, the clouds drop more than 100 inches of rain, and 30 feet of snow on these steep slopes every year.

The result is humid air, jungle-like underbrush, dense forests of towering, thickly packed deciduous and conifer trees, especially red alder, bigleaf and vine maples, cottonwood, Douglas fir, hemlock and western cedar.

Where sunlight sprays through the canopy are lush meadows often filled with wildflowers such as pink fireweed, purple lupines, magenta foxgloves, white oxeye daisies,

NORTH AMERICAN PORCUPINE

(*Erethizon dorsatum*)
When threatened, the porcupine strikes with its tail, leaving some of its 30,000 barbed quills embedded in its enemy; the quills are actually modified hairs loosely attached to the porcupine's skin.

blue penstemons, yellow skunk cabbage, goldenrod and yarrow, and the white swab-like heads of pearly everlastings.

In the shade grow lush, tropical-like clusters of kinnickinnick (*Arctostaphylos uva-ursi*), rose purple Pacific rhododendron (*Rhododendron macrophyllum*), the broad leaves of wild ginger, white blooms of Solomon's plume, American vetch, trillium, and mats of shamrock-like sorrel.

Ferns are everywhere on the west side. More than 30 species grow in the damp, shaded Douglas fir duff. They range from the sturdy head-high stalks of bracken (*Pteridium aquilinum*), to bouquets of sword fern (*Polystichum munitum*) to the delicate leaves of lace fern (*Cheilanthes gracillima*).

Berries are abundant. In prime spots it's possible to pick five varieties without moving. The most abundant are snowberries (*Symphoricarpos albus*), red elderberry (*Sambucus racemosa*), Oregon grape (*Berberis nervosa*), wax currant, (*Ribes cereum*) red (*Vaccinium parvifolium*), and purple huckleberries, pinemat manzanita (*Arctostaphylos nevadensis*), salmonberries (*Rubus spectabilis*), thimbleberries (*Rubus parviflorus*), blueberries, salal (*Gaultheria shallon*), Mountain ash (*Sorbus scopulina*), blackberries (*Rubus ursinus*), blackcap raspberries (*Rubus leucodermis*), and many other varieties, some edible and some not—such as the bright red fruit on spiny devil's club (*Oplopanax horridum*).

East of the byway, deprived of heavy rain, the weather is semiarid, summer and winter temperature swings are more extreme, and the land more open.

Trees grow in scattered lots separated by thin carpets of rangy wild grasses, clumps of poison oak, and tangles of brush. Pines are the dominant trees, including ponderosa, lodgepole, Jeffrey, and western white varieties. Also look for large stands of western larch, incense cedar (*Caolocedrun decurrens*) and hardy deciduous trees such as quaking aspen (*Populus tremuloides*), black cottonwood (*Populus trichocarpa*), Oregon oak (*Quercus garryana*), black hawthorn (*Crataegus douglasisii*), and chokecherry (*Prunus virginiana*).

Underbrush seems to grow in clumps determined by water availability. Where there's year-round water, the brush can be impenetrable tangles of wild rose (*Rosa nootkana*), chokecherry, antelope (bitter) brush (*Purshia tridentata*), spiraeas (*Spiraea densiflora*), greenleaf manzanita (*Arctostaphylos patula*) and sagebrush (*Artemisia tridentata*).

Flowers are generally tough, stalky species that do well on little water. The broad leaves and yellow blooms of arrowleaf balsamroot (*Balsamorrhiza sagitatta*), often erroneously called sunflowers, are possibly the most widespread large flower east of the Cascades. Six-foot high stalks of woolly mullein (*Verbascum thapus*) poke through broken soils, especially along roadways. You might also see yarrow, spreading dogbane (*Apocynum androsaemifolium*), phlox (*Phlox diffusa*), and woolly sunflowers (*Eriophyllum lanatum*).

In alpine areas you are likely to see bright magenta splashes of paintbrush (*Castilleja miniata*), fuzzy clusters of pussypaws (*Spraguea umbellata*), the broad green leaves of rosy twisted-stalk (*Streptopus roseus*), and the thick fleshy branches of spreading and creamy stonecrop (*Sedum divergens* and *S. oregonense*), along with the white cottony heads of beargrass.

East Slope wildlife includes most species found west of the crest, but the lower elevations also include sagebrush lizards (*Sceloporus graciosus*), racer snakes (*Coluber constrictor*), gopher snakes (*Pituophis melanoleucus)* and Pacific rattlesnakes (*Crotalus viridis*).

Rattlesnakes are Oregon's only poisonous snake. Few are found in western Oregon and those are mostly in the south near the California border. Mid and lower elevations on the entire east side, including the skirts of the Cascade Range, however. Pacific rattlers are 12-to 62-inches-long, olive, gray or brown with large dark brown or black blotches and the telltale rattles on the tail. Gopher snakes are often mistaken for rattlesnakes. Both have large dark blotches and live in similar habitats. Gopher snakes, however, can reach more than 8 feet long. Few Pacific rattlesnakes exceed half that size.

On the west side of this vast region of the central Cascades is Aufderheide National Scenic Byway, a 65-mile long route between McKenzie Pass Highway/OR 126 near the community of Blue River and OR 58 at Oakridge. Also known as Aufderheide Memorial Drive and Forest Service 19, most of the paved byway is in the corridors of two adjoining river valleys. It links the South Fork McKenzie River and North Fork Middle Fork Willamette River drainages at a low saddle at Box Canyon Campground. North of Box Canyon the byway follows the McKenzie into Blue River. South of the saddle it follows the wild and scenic tributary of the Willamette River into Oakridge. Ten campgrounds are scattered along the Aufderheide route, many in groves of massive, 200-foot high bigleaf maple trees, cedars, and Douglas fir.

Inside this geographically huge and topographically diverse area travelers explore the southern part of Three Sisters Wilderness (*see* page 193), the crystalline pure water of Waldo Lake and the adjoining wilderness area, natural hot springs, an exceptional chain of sparkling trout lakes, several wild and scenic rivers, and mountains of wrinkled lava that form the west edge of central Oregon lava lands.

The Cascade Lakes Region falls within the management reach of two national forests. The entire central Cascade region west of the crest and the west edge of Three Sisters and Waldo Lake wilderness areas is in Willamette National Forest. The eastern area, which includes Cascade Lakes National Scenic Byway and adjoining lakes, is in Deschutes National Forest.

Town of Blue River

[Fig. 34] Gold prospectors built this little riverside community while chasing an 1863 strike in the McKenzie River. Today the McKenzie River and its impounded tributary Blue River Lake continue to support the town, not with gold, but with travel and recreation businesses.

Located 41 miles east of Eugene on OR 126, Blue River is at the confluence of the Blue and McKenzie rivers, and is the regional headquarters for a thriving whitewater boating industry and McKenzie River trout fishing trips. The Willamette National Forest's Blue

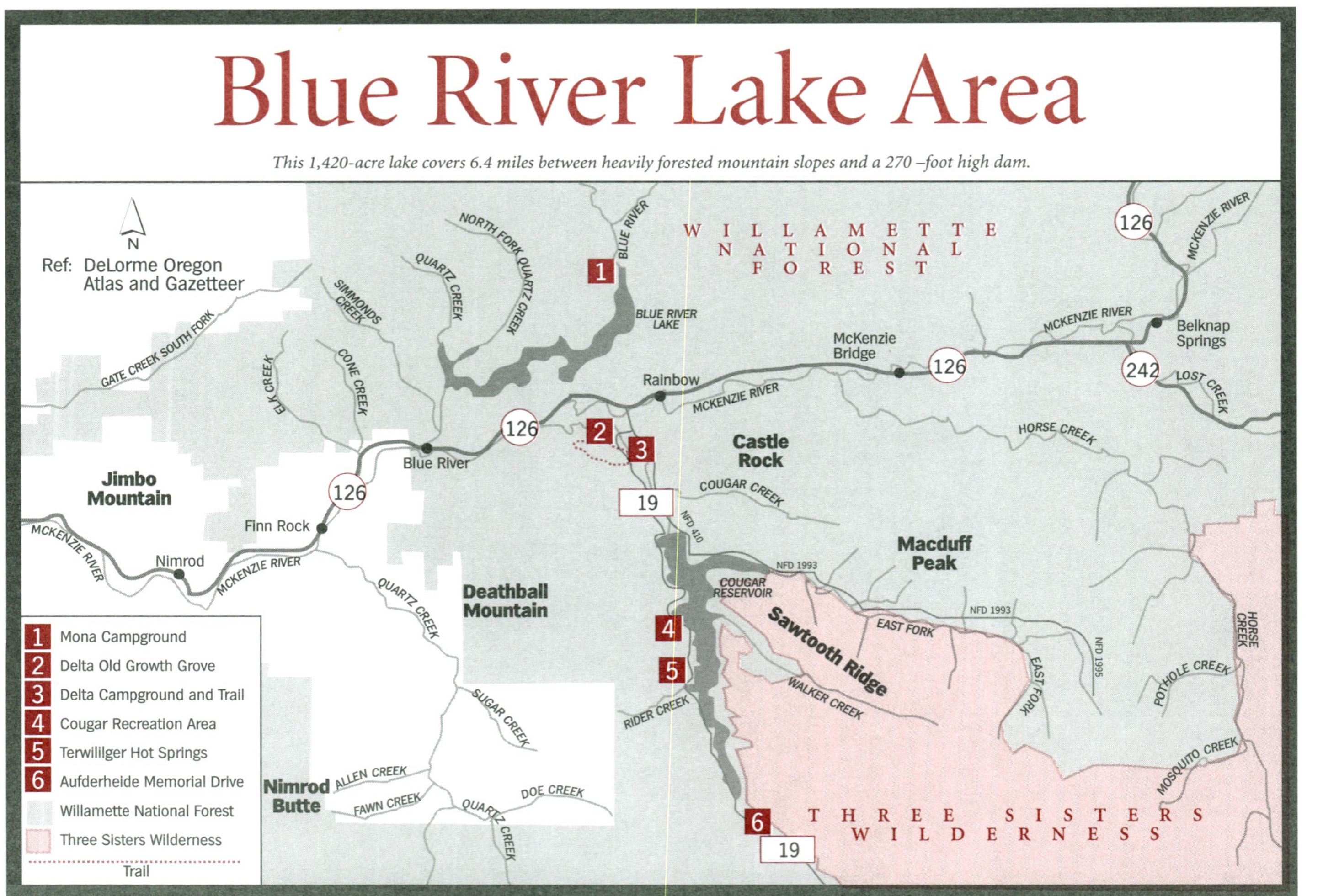

Blue River Lake Area
This 1,420-acre lake covers 6.4 miles between heavily forested mountain slopes and a 270 –foot high dam.
N
Ref: DeLorme Oregon Atlas and Gazetteer
WILLAMETTE NATIONAL FOREST
THREE SISTERS WILDERNESS
Jimbo Mountain
Deathball Mountain
Nimrod Butte
Castle Rock
Macduff Peak
Sawtooth Ridge
Blue River
Rainbow
McKenzie Bridge
Belknap Springs
Finn Rock
Nimrod
MCKENZIE RIVER
BLUE RIVER
BLUE RIVER LAKE
COUGAR RESERVOIR
NORTH FORK QUARTZ CREEK
QUARTZ CREEK
SIMMONDS CREEK
CONE CREEK
ELK CREEK
GATE CREEK SOUTH FORK
LOST CREEK
HORSE CREEK
COUGAR CREEK
EAST FORK
POTHOLE CREEK
MOSQUITO CREEK
WALKER CREEK
RIDER CREEK
SUGAR CREEK
ALLEN CREEK
FAWN CREEK
DOE CREEK
NFD 410
NFD 1993
NFD 1995
126
242
19
1 Mona Campground
2 Delta Old Growth Grove
3 Delta Campground and Trail
4 Cougar Recreation Area
5 Terwillilger Hot Springs
6 Aufderheide Memorial Drive
Willamette National Forest
Three Sisters Wilderness
Trail

River Ranger District office and information post is also here. Blue River is a supply center for campers, boaters, hikers, and fishermen staying at nearby Blue River Lake, and the jumping-off point to the upper McKenzie River recreation area (*see* Aufderheide Memorial Drive/Forest Service 19, page 221). The Blue River, a shallow, easily waded, trout fishery, is only 11 miles long. Ten miles of river are above Blue River Lake and 1 mile is between the dam and the McKenzie River confluence. The river above the lake is paralleled by Forest Service Road 15 and there are many scenic spots where primitive camps can be set.

Just north of the compact business center on the way to Blue River Lake is Blue River Ranger Station, a weekday source of local and regional recreation opportunities, attraction, and travel information and permits. Turn north from OR 126 in Blue River and continue through the business district 0.5 mile to the ranger office. The station is open weekdays 7:45 a.m. to 4:30 p.m.

Directions: Blue River is on OR 126, about 41 miles east of Eugene and I-5.

Activities: River and lake camping, fishing, and boating.

Facilities: Grocery stores, gas stations, restaurant, motel, RV camps, whitewater rafting companies, and forest service information station.

For more information: Blue River Ranger Station, Willamette National Forest, PO Box 199, Blue River, OR 97413. Phone (541) 822-3317. Lane County Convention and Visitors Association, 115 W. 8th, Suite, 190, Eugene, OR 97440. Phone (541) 484-5307 or (800) 547-5445. Email: travel@cvalco.org.

BLUE RIVER LAKE

[Fig. 34] The 1,420 acres of Blue River Lake cover 6.4 miles between steep, heavily forested mountain slopes behind a 270-foot high dam built in 1969 by the U.S. Army Corps of Engineers impounding Blue River.

The lake is regulated for downstream flood control and water levels fluctuate widely. By late summer the water level may be drawn down significantly, exposing muddy banks, but boating facilities are usually usable. This is a popular destination for rainbow trout fishermen from April through mid-June, and for water skiers and boaters from mid-July into September.

The river above Blue Lake is followed closely by Forest Service Road 15. Fishermen enjoy wade-fishing for rainbow and cutthroat trout, 8- to 12- inches-long, and wildlife enthusiasts watch the road edge for black-tailed deer and elk. Sharp-eyed bird watchers may see red-breasted mergansers, belted kingfishers, and water ouzels. There are black bears, beavers, coyotes, and porcupines here, but they're rarely seen.

Directions: There are two entry points. The dam and a viewpoint are reached by leaving OR 126 at Blue River and following Road 125 for less than 1 mile north. To reach boat launches, campgrounds, picnic and swim area, continue east of Blue River on OR 126 for 3.5 miles, turn north on Forest Service 15 and follow the signs about 4.5 miles around the end of the lake to Mona Campground.

Activities: Camping, fishing, boating, and water skiing.

Facilities: Forest Service campground, 2 boat ramps, picnic area, swimming beach, viewpoint at dam.

Dates: Open year-round.

Fees: None.

For more information: Portland District U.S. Army Corps of Engineers, PO Box 2946, Portland, OR 97208. Phone (503) 808-5150.

MONA CAMPGROUND

[Fig. 34(1)] Mona Campground is the only overnight facility on Blue River Lake. Operated by the Forest Service, the camp is located on the northwest side of the upper lake, directly across the lake from Look Creek boat ramp and swimming area.

Directions: Drive 3.5 miles east of Blue River on OR 126, turn north on Forest Service 15 and follow the signs north about 4.5 miles around the upper end of the lake. The campground is on the west shore.

Activities: Camping, picnicking, fishing, boating, swimming, and water skiing.

Facilities: 23 tent and RV sites, swimming area, and potable water.

Dates: Open year-round.

Fees: There is a charge for campsites.

DELTA OLD-GROWTH GROVE

[Fig. 34(2)] Trees that were centuries old before Christopher Columbus landed on the East Coast of North America in 1492 now form a 200-foot-high canopy over campers. Walls of native red huckleberry (*Vaccinium parvifolium*), sword fern (*Polysticum munitum*), and vine maple grow at Delta Old-Growth Grove.

Carved into this dense, heavily shaded underbrush are a woodsy campground, amphitheater, picnic area, and a 0.5 mile interpretive trail along the braided waters of Delta Creek. Keep an eye out for beavers that live in the slow-moving creek.

Foresters estimate that some of these trees are more than 650 years old. The dominant old-growth species are Douglas fir, western red cedar, hemlock, and Pacific yew (*Taxus brevifolia*).

The grove is a microcosm of the importance of old-growth trees.

Pacific yew wood was once used by native hunters for bows and weapon handles. Today, the bark is valued by some as an agent in cancer treatment. Stringy cedar and thick fir bark have been used as lodge coverings, sleeping mats, baskets, and clothing. Fir pitch was used for fire starting, glue, and waterproofing.

Northwest Indians used hemlock bark for house material and used the sap for a variety of medicines. Hemlocks are one of the few trees able to sprout and grow in the shade of old-growth firs. Where forests are uncut, hemlocks will eventually replace the sun-loving fir trees that protected them as saplings.

Directions: Follow OR 126 about 6 miles east of Blue River, turn south onto Forest Service 19 (Aufderheide Memorial Drive), then west onto Forest Service 400 into the grove.

Activities: Camping, picnicking, fishing, and hiking.

Dates: Open from the end of Apr. through Oct.

Fees: There are charges for campsites and trail park passes.

Closest town: Blue River is 6 miles west on OR 126.

For more information: Blue River Ranger Station, Willamette National Forest, PO Box 199, Blue River, OR 97413. Phone (541) 822-3317.

DELTA CAMPGROUND AND TRAIL

[Fig. 34(3)] The highlight of this cool, heavily shaded campground is a 0.5 mile loop trail with 10 interpretive stations. The trail is fairly flat and an easy walk. It begins and ends in the campground.

Directions: On the east side of Delta Old-Growth Grove, 6 miles east of Blue River, and south of OR 126. The elevation at the campground is 1,200 feet.

Activities: Camping, picnicking, fishing, and hiking.

Facilities: 38 tent and RV sites, 3 picnic sites, potable water, barrier free access, restrooms, hiking trail.

Dates: Open from late Apr. through Oct.

Fees: There are charges for campsites.

COUGAR RECREATION AREA

[Fig. 34(4)] The heart of Cougar Recreation Area is about 46 miles east of Eugene at Cougar Lake, a narrow 6-mile-long impoundment in the South Fork McKenzie River. The east shore of the lake squeezes against the west boundary of Three Sisters Wilderness.

The lake is a U.S. Army Corps of Engineers project, impounded behind 452-foot-high Cougar Dam, which is the tallest rock dam in Oregon. Unusual terraces that are carved into the basalt cliffs near the dam are the source of much of the rock used in building the dam. Guided tours of the dam can be arranged Monday through Friday by telephoning (503) 367-5124.

The steep, green hills above 1,280-acre Cougar Lake shelter six Forest Service campgrounds, including three with boat ramps and picnic areas. One of Oregon's most popular natural hot springs and soaking pools is a short walk from a large parking area on the northwest side of the lake.

The recreation area is located just south of McKenzie River Highway/OR 126 on Aufderheide Memorial Drive. Most of the area lies within a river valley beneath the conifer walls of Sawtooth Ridge, and the French Pete area of Three Sisters Wilderness. The lake is popular with trout fishermen, campers, and picnickers. French Pete Campground is just south of the impoundment and is heavily used by river fishermen trying their luck on the South Fork McKenzie rainbow trout. The quiet coves and protective peninsulas make this big lake a good spot to water ski.

The lake is also a promising place to catch a glimpse of ospreys, bald eagles, and red-tailed hawks. Black-tailed deer are frequently spotted browsing along the shoreline.

The campgrounds are managed by the Forest Service. Most sites are either at the south end of the lake or tucked along the remote east shore. The road along the east side

What Is Old Growth?

"Old growth" is a phrase you're likely to hear often and with confusing definitions in Oregon's Cascade Mountains.

The title usually, but not always, refers to conifer trees. Some argue that century-old deciduous trees such as Oregon ash, bigleaf maples, and white oaks should be included.

If nothing else the term is controversial, and subject to far-flung interpretations.

Old growth logs have always been desirable for forest products because these large diameter trees produce high quality lumber and plywood. At the same time, many biologists and ecologists believe that old growth ecosystems provide a complex and biologically rich pool of benefits other than timber products.

Preservationists use the term as a political label to define ancient groves. Foresters and loggers use it as a general identification for exceptionally large conifers, usually fir, cedar and hemlock giants growing at mid and low elevations. At high elevations, however, where growing seasons are brief, old growth conifers may be short, thin, with dense twisted trunks and several hundreds years old. Environmentalists see it as a specific habitat complex that combines ancient conifers and deciduous trees with brush, duff and deep shade. The multilayered canopy is required for some wildlife, including endangered species such as marbled murrelets (*Brachyramphus marmoratus*) and northern spotted owls (*Strix occidentalis*). Murrelets are sea birds that fly inland to nest under the protective canopy of ancient forests.

The most common definition of old growth is a tree at least 32 inches in diameter or 200 years old. Courts have accepted this definition during the frequent legal skirmishes waged between timber companies and preservationists arguing tree cutting issues. Many of the trees in preserved areas are 500 to 1,000 years old, according to the Oregon Department of Forestry.

Most old growth trees on private lands have been logged. Nearly all of what remains is on public Forest Service or park lands, and will not be harvested either because it is in wilderness areas or critical habitat zones for endangered species.

No one knows for sure how much old growth remains. A Wilderness Society study reports there are 1.1 million acres of old growth in Oregon and Washington. The Forest Service estimates almost 4.5 million acres of old growth remain.

is gravel. None of the Cougar Lake sites has utilities, but all have restrooms, and with the exceptions of Sunnyside and Cougar Crossing campgrounds, all have potable water. Boat ramps are available at Echo Park, Slide Creek and Sunnyside.

Aufderheide Memorial Drive/Forest Service 19 follows the curves of the west shore and offers elevated views overlooking the water. The largest overlook is on the northwest side of the lake at Rider Creek and is also the trailhead to Terwilliger Hot Springs, a day-use area.

Directions: Take OR 126 for 46 miles east of Eugene and turn south on Aufderheide

Memorial Drive/Forest Service 19. Continue south 6 miles to the dam, and the west side of the lake.

Activities: Camping, fishing, boating, water skiing, picnicking, hiking, wildlife observation, hot spring soaking.

Facilities: 6 campgrounds, 3 boat ramps, picnic areas, and a swimming beach at Slide Creek Campground.

Dates: Open year-round, but campgrounds are maintained during snow-free months only.

Fees: There is a charge for campsites, trail park passes to use picnic and other developed areas. Permits are dispensed at each site.

Closest town: Blue River is 12 miles northwest of the dam on OR 126.

For more information: Blue River Ranger Station, Willamette National Forest, PO Box 199, Blue River, OR 97413. Phone (541) 822-3317. Free maps of the recreation area are available from the U.S. Army Corps of Engineers, Portland District, PO Box 2946, Portland, OR 97208-2946. Phone (503) 808-5150.

TERWILLIGER HOT SPRINGS

[Fig. 34(5)] On a hillside just above the west bank of Cougar Lake is Terwilliger Hot Springs, a very popular primitive area that features five natural soaking pools positioned in stair-step fashion down a ravine on Rider Creek.

The natural springs are sheltered by a high forest canopy, in a primal, woodland setting of moss-covered rocks and massive cedar logs. The spring emerges from the hillside at 116 degrees Fahrenheit, and the water temperature drops at each succeeding pool. By the time it reaches the lowest pool the water has cooled to about 95 degrees. Clothing is optional.

Directions: Follow Aufderheide Memorial Drive/Forest Service 19 south from OR 126 for 7.5 miles along the west shore of Cougar Lake to a large pullover parking area at Rider Creek. The trail leaves from the parking lot and goes 0.3 mile past a lagoon to the hot spring.

Activities: Hot spring soaks.

Facilities: A primitive outhouse is located near the springs.

Dates: Open year-round, daylight hours only.

Fees: There is a per-person-use charge. Permits available at the Blue River ranger district office, Cougar Recreation Area information site on the lake, and local stores.

AUFDERHEIDE MEMORIAL DRIVE/FOREST SERVICE 19

[Fig. 34(6), Fig. 35(1)] Aufderheide National Scenic Byway/Forest Service 19 is a paved connection that links McKenzie River Highway/OR 126 in the north with OR 58 at Oakridge in the south. Identified on some maps as Aufderheide Memorial Drive, this scenic byway crosses a forested saddle between two low-elevation mountain valleys and is nearly always within earshot of one of three rivers that rumble alongside the byway.

The route, named for former Willamette National Forest supervisor Robert Aufderheide, follows the pioneer-era route of a horse and wagon trail. The divide between the two drainages is located near Box Canyon Horse Camp, which is marked by restored 1933 Civilian Conservation Corps log cabin.

Elk often show up in the meadow near the cabin. The meadow was once heavily grazed by sheep, but the area is now closed to livestock. With the sheep gone, the ridge has been reclaimed by wild elk as a spring calving and summer grazing range.

The divide is at an elevation of 3,728 feet and is closed by snow during winter. From late April through November, however, the entire 70-mile-long byway is maintained for passenger vehicle traffic. Be sure to top off the gas tank and get necessary supplies before you head up the byway. There are no commercial traveler services on the route. The Forest Service operates seven riverside campgrounds between Cougar Lake and Oakridge.

There are so many unusual features along this lightly traveled scenic route that the Forest Service offers an auto audio tape with a mile-by-mile guide to special interest areas. Free loaner cassettes may be borrowed for the drive at either the Blue River Ranger Station on OR 126, or Oakridge Ranger Station in Oakridge on Salmon Creek Road north of OR 58.

North of the Box Canyon saddle, the byway follows the plunging 37-degree water of Roaring River to its confluence with the South Fork McKenzie River and eventually into Cougar Lake. South of the saddle, the road closely winds along the North Fork Middle Fork Willamette River, a designated wild and scenic waterway. The river is not stocked and fishermen are required to use fly tackle for the native trout.

Some of the highlights along the Aufderheide National Scenic Byway include:

Office Covered Bridge. At 180 feet, Oregon's longest covered bridge crosses the North Fork Middle Fork Willamette River at Westfir about 2 miles northeast of Oakridge. The bridge was built in 1945 as part of once thriving company mill town owned by Western Lumber Company.

The Gorge. This is a spectacular canyon cut into 3-million-year-old lava on the North Fork Middle Fork Willamette above Westfir. The falls-and-rapids water in the gorge makes it popular with kayakers.

Constitution Grove. This stand of 200-year-old Douglas firs was dedicated in 1987 to commemorate the 200th anniversary of the signing of the U.S. Constitution. Plaques with the names of the signatories are placed on the two-century-old firs. There is a short, flat trail through the grove.

The Incline. This historic site is 8 miles north of Oakridge at the base of a 72-degree grade below Huckleberry Creek. In the 1920s and 1930s, amazingly, rail tracks went up this nearly vertical mountainside to a logging area. A powerful belt-driven steam engine called a donkey winched the trains 0.66 mile up and down the wall, shuttling raw logs from the cutting area to the mill at Westfir. Empty trains hauled to the top of the grade continued 7,000 feet to the logging site at Huckleberry Flat where flatbed cars were packed with cut logs, then lowered down the incline tracks to river level. The last locomotive was lowered in 1937 and the incline tracks were demolished.

Directions: The south end of Aufderheide National Scenic Byway/Forest Service 19 is entered from OR 58 at Oakridge. The north end intersects with OR 126 between Blue River and McKenzie Bridge.

Activities: Scenic and historical sight-seeing, camping, hiking, boating, lake and river trout fishing, deer and elk hunting in the fall. Audio cassette travel guides may be borrowed from Willamette National Forest ranger district offices in Blue River and Oakridge.

Facilities: 7 Forest Service campgrounds on Cougar Lake, South Fork McKenzie River and North Fork Middle Fork Willamette River, Cougar Lake boat ramps and picnic areas.

Dates: Open Apr. through Nov.

Fees: There is a charge for campsites with water, and trail park passes.

Closest town: Oakridge and Blue River.

For more information: Blue River Ranger Station, Willamette National Forest, PO Box 199, Blue River, OR 97413. Phone (541) 822-3317. Middle Fork Ranger Station, 49098 Salmon Creek Road, PO Box 1410, Oakridge, OR 97464. Phone (541) 782-2283. In Summer/Fall 2000, Middle Fork Ranger District office will be located at 46375 Hwy 58, Westfir, OR 97492. Call to confirm new mailing address.

KIAHANIE CAMPGROUND

[Fig. 35(2)] Kiahanie Campground is a centrally located base for campers exploring the adjacent Aufderheide National Scenic Byway, and fly fishermen challenging native trout in the North Fork Middle Fork Willamette River.

The 2,200-foot elevation campground is located in a grove of massive old-growth Douglas firs. The sites are scattered along the wild and scenic river, and are so isolated by vine maples, wild dogwoods, rhododendrons, drapes of club moss, and walls of hemlock and fir branches that it's rare to see a neighbor's evening fire. This is a lightly used campground where campers enjoy near-wilderness solitude and scenery, and are often surprised by wildlife such as black-tailed deer, raccoons, Douglas squirrels, and bushy-tailed wood rats (*Neotoma cinerea*), a nocturnal 9-inch long squirrel-like rodent with a bushy tail and white underbelly.

Directions: From Westfir follow Aufderheide byway 20 miles north.

Activities: Camping, picnicking, fly fishing, whitewater boating, and hiking.

Facilities: 19 tent and RV sites, well water, vault toilets, fire rings, picnic tables, and a recycle center. There is a resident camp manager.

Dates: Open Apr. 20 to Oct. 30.

Fees: There is a charge for campsites.

SHALE RIDGE TRAIL 3567

[Fig. 35(3)] Sometimes called the Waldo Lake Wilderness Trail, Shale Ridge Trail 3567 connects Aufderheide scenic byway with the northern part of the wilderness area. The trail passes a bog in a grove of ancient western red cedar, crosses the North Fork Middle Fork River, gains elevation at a series of switchbacks, then follows above the river to a ridge on the lake-littered north edge of Waldo Lake Wilderness. Shale Ridge Trail is considered a

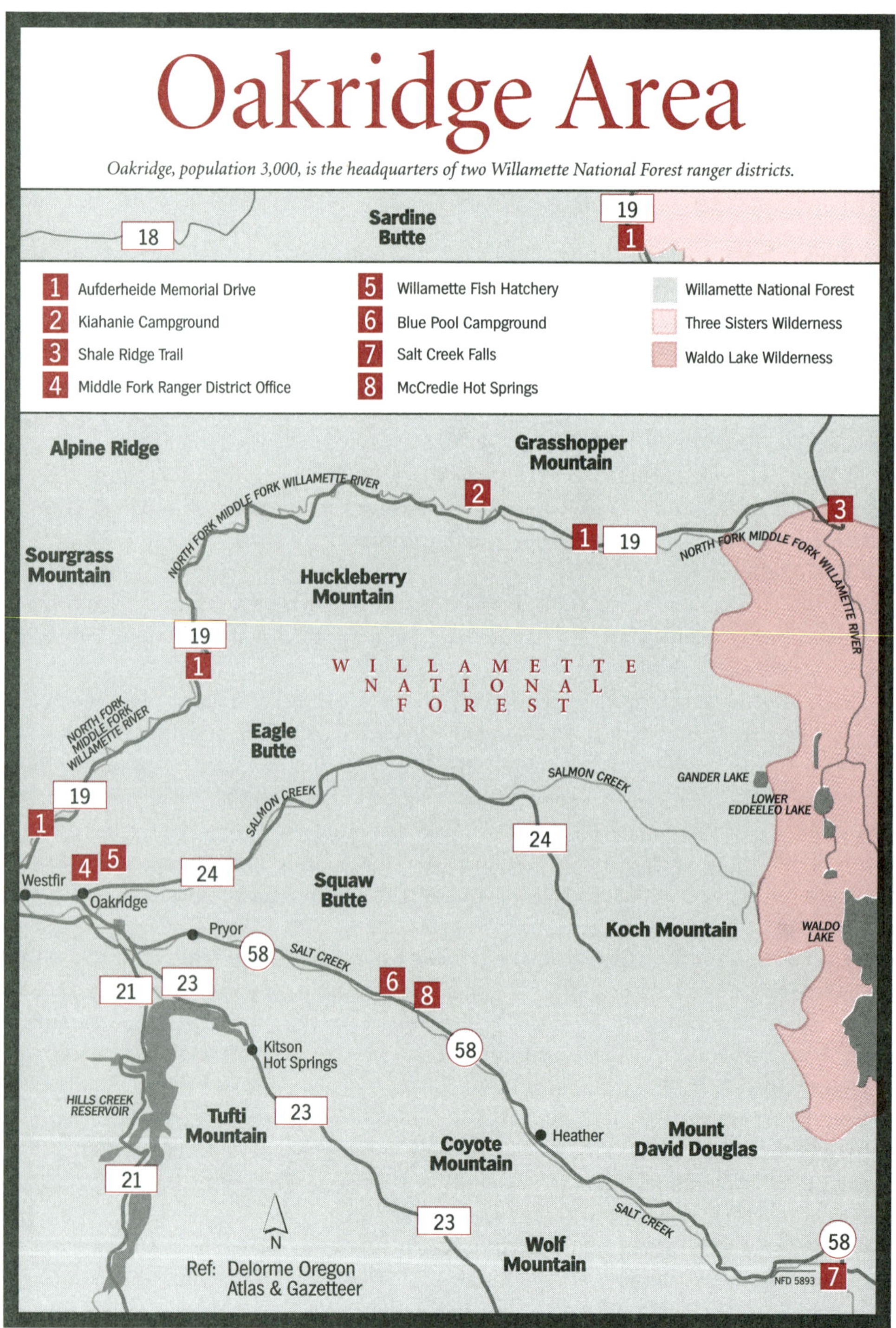
Oakridge Area
Oakridge, population 3,000, is the headquarters of two Willamette National Forest ranger districts.
Sardine Butte
1 Aufderheide Memorial Drive
2 Kiahanie Campground
3 Shale Ridge Trail
4 Middle Fork Ranger District Office
5 Willamette Fish Hatchery
6 Blue Pool Campground
7 Salt Creek Falls
8 McCredie Hot Springs
Willamette National Forest
Three Sisters Wilderness
Waldo Lake Wilderness
Alpine Ridge
Grasshopper Mountain
North Fork Middle Fork Willamette River
Sourgrass Mountain
Huckleberry Mountain
Willamette National Forest
Eagle Butte
Salmon Creek
Gander Lake
Lower Eddeeleo Lake
Westfir
Oakridge
Squaw Butte
Pryor
Salt Creek
Koch Mountain
Waldo Lake
Kitson Hot Springs
Hills Creek Reservoir
Tufti Mountain
Coyote Mountain
Heather
Mount David Douglas
Wolf Mountain
NFD 5893
N
Ref: Delorme Oregon Atlas & Gazetteer

poor route for horse travel and is closed to bicycles and motorcycles.

Directions: Follow Aufderheide byway 30 miles north of Westfir. The trailhead is on the east side of the road at a sharp curve. It is well marked.

Trail: 5.5 miles one-way.

Elevation: Beginning at 3,000 and ending at 4,500 feet.

Degree of difficulty: Strenuous.

Surface: Dirt and rock.

Town of Oakridge

Oakridge, population 3,000, is 42 miles east of Eugene in the heart of Cascade Mountain recreation, scenery, and history. Oakridge is the headquarters of two Willamette National Forest ranger districts, Rigdon and Oakridge, and is the site of an intriguing and little-known state fish hatchery/museum/wildlife complex. Popular McCredie Hot Springs, a natural riverside soaking pool, is a 10 minute drive east of town on OR 58.

Oakridge is a jumping-off point to Aufderheide National Scenic Byway and the historic Oregon Central Military Wagon Road; Willamette Pass ski area; 500 miles of public hiking, biking and snowmobile trails; and a 7.6-mile-long turquoise-colored lake that trout fishermen, campers, boaters, water skiers, picnickers, and swimmers find hard to resist. The food sources and cover in the overgrown clear-cuts, and thick underbrush of surrounding mountains, support some of the most productive black-tailed deer, elk, and black bear hunting regions on the West Slope.

This region's vast spider web-like network of trails is the site of one of the community's largest annual festivals. The Oakridge Fat Tire Festival is held on the fourth weekend in July. The festival features mountain bike races for all age levels, guided scenic mountain bike tours, and exhibition riding. Thousands of mountain bike enthusiasts turn out, transforming this small mountain town into a carnival crowded with brilliantly colored, Lycra-encased adrenaline junkies. For festival information phone (541) 782-4228.

The Middle Fork Willamette River and North Fork Middle Fork Willamette River flow through Oakridge and adjoining Westfir, population 2,000. Both towns are surrounded by Willamette National Forests lands, yet are within sight of Umpqua National Forest to the south.

Directions: Oakridge is on Willamette Pass Highway/OR 58 about 42 miles east of Eugene and 96 miles west of Bend.

Facilities: 5 motels, 7 trailer parks, 1 RV park, a 9-hole golf course, several gas stations, grocery supplies; Rigdon and Oakridge Ranger Districts Headquarters, Oregon Department of Fish and Wildlife museum, wildlife exhibit, and fish hatchery. Green Waters Park, 0.5 mile east of town, has an information kiosk, boat ramp into the Middle Fork Willamette River, picnic area, restrooms, and nature trails.

For more information: Oakridge/Westfir Chamber of Commerce, PO Box 217,

Moss And Lichens

The wet west side of Oregon's Cascade Range is a living laboratory for mosses and lichens. According to studies at the University of Oregon more than 900 species of moss and 1,200 lichens are common in the Northwest.

It usually requires a microscope to tell one from another. Two of the most common and interesting are tree dwellers and are abundant in lowlands, especially steep-walled, heavily shaded river valleys.

One of the most important is Old Man's Beard (*Alectoria sarmentosa*), which hangs in gauzelike drapes from tree branches at all elevations below tree line. The yellow green sheets are commonly called club moss, but are actually a wispy lichen that grows up to 30 feet long and is a critical food source for deer and elk. The lichen helps the animals absorb nutrients from the other plants that compose the majority of their diet. In areas with high populations of deer and elk, the drapes will be trimmed off at the maximum height of the browse line. If you find an area where drapes of Old Man's Beard reach the ground, you can bet there are few, if any, deer or elk nearby.

In the dampest areas, tree trunks and branches are often encased in green sheaths of *Isothecium myosuroides* . This moss grows mostly along rivers, creeks, and springs in cool, damp, heavily shaded areas. Where growing conditions are ideal it encases almost everything: boulders, trees, logs, and branches, giving them a green fuzzy appearance. The mats of moss can be several inches thick and are used as nesting material by many animals and birds.

Oakridge, OR 97463. Phone (541) 782-4146.

MIDDLE FORK RANGER DISTRICT OFFICE

[Fig. 35(4)] The offices of the Middle Fork Ranger District of Willamette National Forest are housed in the Rigdon headquarters on Salmon Creek Road, east of Oakridge. In the Summer/Fall of 2000, the district office will be located at 46375 Hwy 58, Westfir, OR 97492. This is the best source for forest information in this area, and a good place to pick up trail park passes required to park at most of the popular trailheads and picnic areas in the national forest.

Books, maps, and permits are sold here. Audio cassette taped tours of Aufderheide National Scenic Highway can be picked up or returned.

Directions: Follow OR 58 to the only stoplight in Oakridge and turn north, cross an overpass and turn east (right) onto East 1st Avenue. Continue 2 miles east to Salmon Creek Road and the ranger station.

Facilities: Public restrooms.

Dates: Open year-round during business hours.

Fees: There are charges for some maps, books, and permits. The tour cassettes are loaned at no charge.

For more information: Middle Fork Ranger Station, 49098 Salmon Creek Road, PO Box 1410, Oakridge, OR 97464. Phone (541) 782-2283. In Summer/Fall 2000, Middle Fork Ranger District office will be located at 46375 Hwy 58, Westfir, OR 97492. Call to confirm new mailing address.

WILLAMETTE FISH HATCHERY

[Fig. 35(5)] What may be one of the most interesting wildlife exhibits you've never heard of is two miles east of Oakridge at a wide spot on Salmon Creek, where the Oregon Department of Fish and Wildlife operates Willamette Fish Hatchery.

In addition to the usual hatchery self-guided tours of juvenile and spawning fish, the complex includes a wildlife viewing area with live Rio Grande turkeys, chukar (*Alectoris graeca*) and red-legged partridge (*Alectoris rufa rufa*), several species of pheasant, valley quail (*Lophortyx californicus*) and other game birds.

An observation pond holds five white sturgeon between 5-and 8-feet-long, lunker-size rainbow trout, and chinook salmon. There is a coin-operated dispenser of fish food. This hatchery rears 3.4 million spring chinook salmon, 100,000 rainbow trout, 200,000 winter and summer steelhead.

The Oregon State Police Museum, next to the sturgeon pool, includes excellent dioramas of central Oregon native wildlife in natural habitats. The diorama is built around taxidermy mounted models of wildlife in strikingly lifelike poses. Included are life-size mule deer, black bear, red (*Vulpes vulpes*), gray (*Urocyon cinereoargenteus*) phases of fox, fisher (*Martes pennanti*), wolverine (*Gulo gulo*), coyotes (*Canis latrans*), northern Pacific rattlesnake (*Crotalus virdis oreganus*), bobcats (*Felis rufus*), cougars (*Felis concolor*), lynx (*Felis lynx*), ruffed grouse (*Bonasa umbellus*) beavers (*Castor canadensis*), pine martens (*Martes americana*), and birds of prey.

Band-tailed Pigeons

If you're deep in the high mountain forests of the central Cascades, miles from civilization, and are suddenly buzzed by a flock of birds that look strangely like barnyard pigeons, you've just been introduced to Oregon's wild band-tailed pigeon (*Columba fasciata*).

Band-tails are larger than most domestic or rock doves, often growing longer than 15.5 inches, and spend their lives in treed foothills or mountains. They are hardly ever seen in suburban areas, and are more common on the West Slope than on the East Slope.

The birds have grayish feathers with a pale broad band across the end of the fanlike tail, and a white crescent ring on the back of the neck. They have distinctive yellow legs, while domestic rock doves have red feet.

They always perch in trees, generally on the highest branches, and feed on berries. Band-tails are especially fond of cascara, elder, and mountain ash berries, and sometimes flocks of a dozen birds will swarm good berry trees.

Band-tails are migratory, wintering in California and summer nesting in the Cascades. They arrive in the mountains as the snow pulls back, generally arriving in the lower foothills in March and April.

Band-tailed pigeons were once a popular game bird, but seasons have been discontinued in Oregon and Washington to help the birds recover from an overall population decline believed to be linked to habitat problems.

Adjacent to the wildlife interpretive display is a floor-to-ceiling glass tank that holds live rainbow, brown, cutthroat, and brook trout, crappie, largemouth and smallmouth bass, whitefish, pea-mouth chubs, and squawfish.

Directions: Follow OR 58 to milepost 37 on the east side of Oakridge, and turn north onto Fish Hatchery Road.

Activities: Viewing of live wildlife and fish displays, wildlife dioramas, museum, fish feeding station, and hatchery tours.

Facilities: Museum, wildlife area, and fish ponds.

Dates: Hatchery and wildlife area open daily. Museum is open weekdays and summer weekends.

Fees: None.

Closest town: Oakridge.

For more information: Willamette Fish Hatchery, 76389 Fish Hatchery Road, Oakridge, OR 97463. Phone (541) 782-2933.

BLUE POOL CAMPGROUND

[Fig. 35(6)] In a grove of old-growth fir trees east of Oakridge on OR 58, Blue Pool Campground provides a riverside camping base for exploring the many recreational opportunities and historic attractions in the Oakridge region. Three of these attractions are very near the camp: Salt Creek, a splashy trout stream flowing around massive log jams; Salt Creek Falls, second highest waterfall in Oregon; and McCredie Hot Springs, a 105-degree soaking pool just 40 yards south of OR 58. The campground is at an elevation of 2,000 feet, and is snow-free much of the year.

Directions: Follow OR 58 about 9.5 miles east of Oakridge. The campground is 0.25 mile west of milepost 45.

Activities: Camping, picnicking, swimming, and fishing.

Facilities: 25 tent and RV sites, including 5 tent walk-in sites; 5 picnic sites with grills, potable water, flush toilets, vault toilets, and fire rings.

Dates: Open May 25 to Sept. 15.

Fees: There are charges for camping and trail park passes.

Closest town: Oakridge is about 9.5 miles west on OR 58.

For more information: Middle Fork Ranger Station, 49098 Salmon Creek Road, PO Box 1410, Oakridge, OR 97464. Phone (541) 782-2283. In Summer/Fall 2000, Middle Fork Ranger District office will be located at 46375 Hwy 58, Westfir, OR 97492. Call to confirm new mailing address. Oakridge/Westfir Chamber of Commerce, PO Box 217, Oakridge, OR 97463. Phone (541) 782-4146.

SALT CREEK

[Fig. 35] Flowing 28 miles from a mountain lake on Willamette Pass along OR 58 to Oakridge, Salt Creek is a rough and tumble stream heavily scoured from powerful floods during snow runoff. The quick flow swirls around log jams, car-size boulders, and natural debris deposited by annual spring floods. It's an attractive trout stream, with easy access, and is heavily fished. Unfortunately, the cold rushing waters offer little habitat, are nutritionally poor, and support only a small number of wild trout.

Directions: The creek parallels OR 58 east of Oakridge and can be reached from numerous roadside pullovers.

Activities: Trout fishing, picnicking, and swimming.

Facilities: Picnic areas and restrooms at Blue Pool and Salt Creek Falls.

Dates: Open for fishing from the fourth Saturday in Apr. through Oct. 31.

Fees: There is a charge for a state fishing license, and trail park passes are required at some riverside picnic areas.

SALT CREEK FALLS

[Fig. 35(7)] Salt Creek water plunging over the lip of Oregon's second highest waterfall free-falls for four seconds before smashing into the plunge pool 286 feet below. The continuous spray and mist feed a smooth carpet of undisturbed brilliant green moss that paints the rocks and stream banks below the falls. From the plunge pool, Salt Creek flows clear and quiet through the dripping green like a blue ribbon winding around black rocks and towering conifers.

The observation area is connected to the parking lot by a paved, wheelchair-accessible pathway that is framed between wild rhododendrons, wind-twisted hemlocks, and shiny clumps of Oregon grape. The overlook provides an excellent vantage point to see the falls from the top and front. The observation area is at an elevation of 4,000 feet. Another path, not wheelchair accessible, goes to within 100 feet of the base of the falls. A shaded area near the lookout offers one of the most pleasant summer picnic or rest stops on OR 58. In winter this is a popular destination for cross-country skiers heading out on the nearby network of trails and logging roads.

Directions: Follow OR 58 about 15.5 miles east from Blue Pool Campground and turn south on Forest Service Road 5893 to the observation area.

Activities: Waterfall sightseeing, hiking, and picnicking.

Facilities: Observation overlook, paved pathways, flush toilets, picnic tables.

Dates: Open year-round.

Fees: None.

MCCREDIE HOT SPRINGS

[Fig. 35(8)] At a wide pullover on the shoulder of OR 58 about 0.5 mile east of Blue Pool Campground, a well-pounded path leads 40 yards upstream along Salt Creek to a chain of shallow pools fed by natural hot springs. The pools are little more than rock-rimmed depressions with water temperatures that vary from 95 to 105-degrees Fahrenheit.

Although McCredie Hot Springs is within a rock toss of a major cross-Cascades highway, clothing is optional. The springs are very popular, especially on weekends. A few small soaking pools on the far side of the creek offer a bit more solitude. This is, however, a heavily used hot springs, as indicated by the largest pool's nickname, "Party Pool." The best opportunities for a quiet soak are on weekday mornings.

Directions: Follow OR 58 for 0.5 mile east of Blue Pool Campground to a large

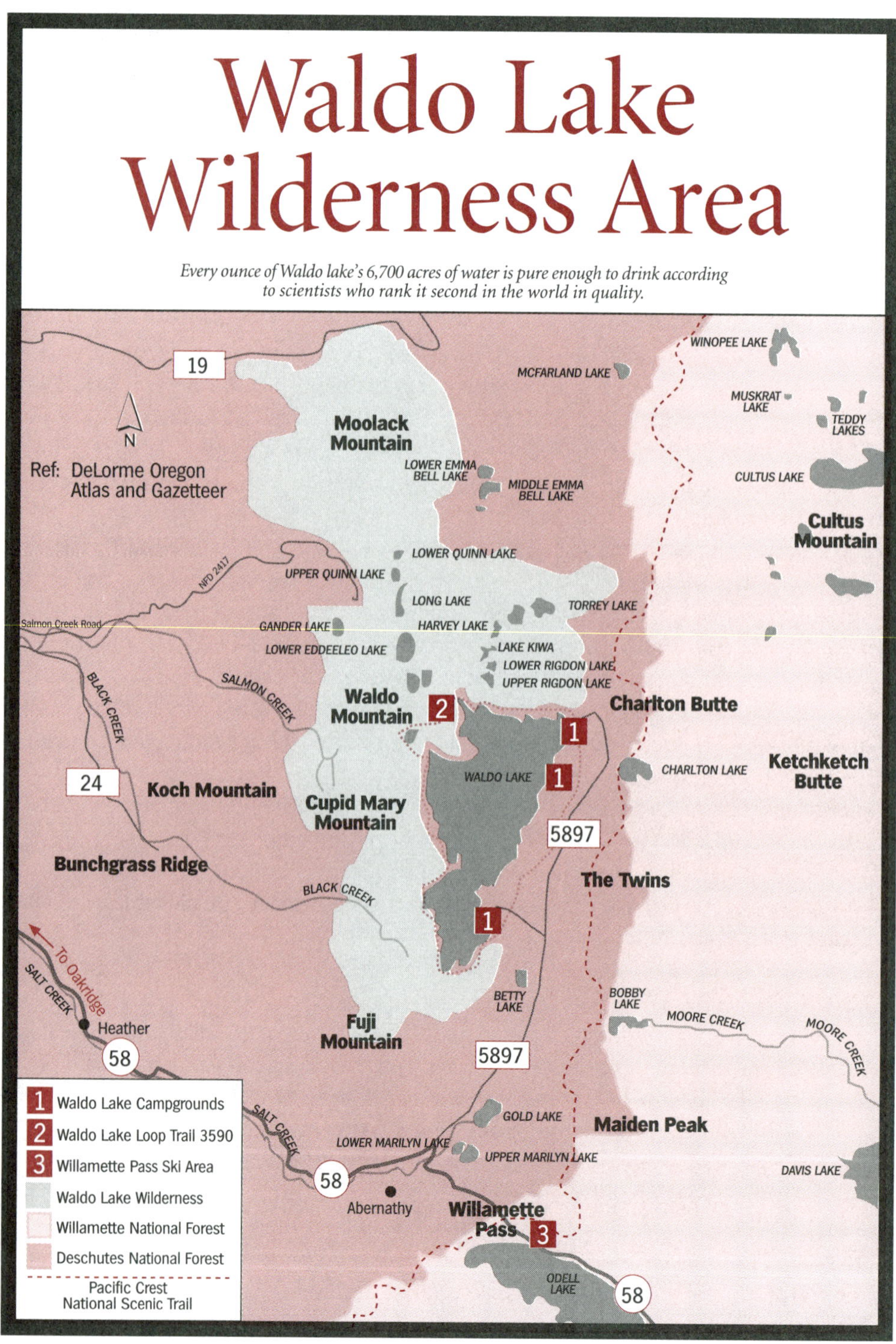
Waldo Lake
Wilderness Area
Every ounce of Waldo lake's 6,700 acres of water is pure enough to drink according to scientists who rank it second in the world in quality.
19
N
Ref: DeLorme Oregon Atlas and Gazetteer
Moolack Mountain
MCFARLAND LAKE
WINOPEE LAKE
MUSKRAT LAKE
TEDDY LAKES
LOWER EMMA BELL LAKE
MIDDLE EMMA BELL LAKE
CULTUS LAKE
Cultus Mountain
LOWER QUINN LAKE
UPPER QUINN LAKE
NFD 2417
LONG LAKE
TORREY LAKE
Salmon Creek Road
GANDER LAKE
HARVEY LAKE
LOWER EDDEELEO LAKE
LAKE KIWA
LOWER RIGDON LAKE
UPPER RIGDON LAKE
BLACK CREEK
SALMON CREEK
Waldo Mountain
2
Charlton Butte
1
WALDO LAKE
1
CHARLTON LAKE
Ketchketch Butte
24
Koch Mountain
Cupid Mary Mountain
5897
Bunchgrass Ridge
The Twins
BLACK CREEK
1
To Oakridge
SALT CREEK
BETTY LAKE
BOBBY LAKE
MOORE CREEK
MOORE CREEK
Heather
Fuji Mountain
58
5897
GOLD LAKE
Maiden Peak
SALT CREEK
LOWER MARILYN LAKE
UPPER MARILYN LAKE
DAVIS LAKE
58
Abernathy
Willamette Pass
3
ODELL LAKE
58
1 Waldo Lake Campgrounds
2 Waldo Lake Loop Trail 3590
3 Willamette Pass Ski Area
Waldo Lake Wilderness
Willamette National Forest
Deschutes National Forest
Pacific Crest National Scenic Trail

pullover on the south shoulder. Follow the 40-yard-long path from the parking area upstream along Salt Creek.

Activities: Natural hot spring soaks.

Facilities: None.

Dates: Open year-round during daylight hours.

Fees: There is a charge for the trail park pass that is required for parking at the highway pullover.

WALDO LAKE

[Fig. 36] Not only is Waldo Lake one of the most unusual natural lakes in the Cascade Range, but it is also one of the most pristine in the world. Located more than a mile high at an elevation of 5,414 feet, the lake covers 10 square miles with incredibly clear, pure water. The white volcanic sand shoreline laps at the irregular edge of a dark conifer forest that rings the lake creating colorful calendar-quality views from all directions.

Every ounce of the lake's 6,700 acres of water is pure enough to drink, according to state health officials, and scientists rank the quality of water as the second best in the world. Only the water in Siberia's Lake Baikal is more pure. Waldo Lake's crystal water fills a 420-foot deep depression that was scoured by glaciers in a high-plateau area that is now sandwiched between the vast Waldo Lake Wilderness and the crest of the Cascade Range.

The lake was formed during the creation of two distinct geologic provinces that were created by a series of volcanic eruptions occurring over millions of years. The west part of the lake was formed within the 25-million-year-old Western Cascade province, and the east section was created within the High Cascade province, which geologists believe is less than 10,000 years old. Except for three large Forest Service campgrounds, the lake has been spared commercial development, a restraint that is at least partially credited for Waldo Lake remaining one of the world's two purest lakes.

Most of the credit for the unusual purity goes to the lake's lack of a permanent inlet that would bring in nutrients, fertilize plant growth, and compromise purity. The water in Waldo Lake comes entirely from precipitation, and on calm days it's difficult to visually separate air and water. A secchi dish, a visual tool used to measure clarity, is visible from the surface when it's lowered 125 feet into the water. Submerged drop-offs and reefs often appear to boaters to be deceivingly close to the surface.

While the lake is pure, it's not sterile and does support fish. In June and October rainbow and brook trout and kokanee salmon move into the near-shore waters and provide a limited sport fishery. Better trout fishing, though, is usually found in smaller nearby lakes such as Bobby, Hidden, Johnny, and Charlton.

When sunlight penetrates Waldo's transparent water all of the colors of the spectrum are absorbed except for blue, which gives the huge lake a spectacular indigo color. The sandy beaches that ring much of the lake are silicates deposited 6,000 years ago from an eruption at Mount Mazama, which is the centerpiece of Crater Lake National Park (*see* Crater Lake, page 316).

Archaeological digs around the lake have unearthed ancient stone tools and artifacts dating back several thousand years. European settlers arrived in the late 1800s, and established fur buying stations and sheep pastures.

Today, Waldo Lake is the heart of a year-round recreation area. Deep accumulations of snow attract snowmobilers and cross-country skiers. In warm weather months, campers come for the 200 developed camping sites at three Forest Service campgrounds, or head for dozens of primitive sites dispersed around the lake. Some of the dispersed sites are reached by boat and others by trail. Bring lots of mosquito repellent; the region is infamous for swarms of these biting pests. The lake is encircled by Waldo Lake Loop Trail 3590, a 21-mile foot and bike path that connects with the region's 170-mile network of trails into the backcountry. The loop trail is open to hikers, horseback riders, and bicyclists. Bicycles are not allowed on spur trails that lead into Waldo Lake Wilderness, which borders the west side of the trail on the west side of the lake.

Motor boats are limited to 10 mph while on the lake, making the water unusually attractive to sailors who enjoy a predictable southwest wind that blows constantly between 11 a.m. and sunset. Diehard sailors trailer sailboats as long as 30 feet into this remote lake to enjoy the winds, wilderness, scenery, and water.

Directions: Drive OR 58 about 23 miles east of Oakridge to a north turn onto Forest Service Road 5897. Continue north for about 6.5 miles to a west turn onto Forest Service Road 5896, which leads to Shadow Bay Campground on the south end of the lake. The lake shore can also be reached at Islet and North Shore campgrounds by continuing north on Forest Service 5897. Campground turnoffs are well marked.

Activities: Camping, swimming, picnicking, boating, fishing, hiking, hunting (fall only), bicycling, snowmobiling, and cross-country skiing.

Facilities: 3 Forest Service campgrounds with amphitheaters, boat ramps, flush toilets, drinking water, fire rings, tables, swimming beaches, picnic areas.

Dates: The lake is open year-round, and the campgrounds are open from July 1 to Sept. 30, depending on snow conditions.

Fees: There are charges for campsites, and trial park passes.

Closest town: Oakridge is about 33 miles west on OR 58.

For more information: Middle Fork Ranger Station, 49098 Salmon Creek Road, PO Box 1410, Oakridge, OR 97464. Phone (541) 782-2283. In Summer/Fall 2000, Middle Fork Ranger District office will be located at 46375 Hwy 58, Westfir, OR 97492. Call to confirm new mailing address. Oakridge/Westfir Chamber of Commerce, PO Box 217, Oakridge, OR 97463. Phone (541) 782-4146.

WALDO LAKE CAMPGROUNDS

[Fig. 36(1)] Three large, developed Forest Service campgrounds are aligned on the east shore of Waldo Lake. Primitive campsites are dispersed around the lake and may be reached by boat or trail. One of the most popular of these remote sites is Rhododendron Island, a wild rhododendron-covered islet just off the west shore across the lake across from Shadow Bay Campground.

Directions: See Waldo Lake.

Activities: Camping, fishing, hiking, boating, bicycling, and swimming.

Facilities: North Waldo Campground has 58 tent and RV sites, Islet Campground has 55 tent and RV sites, and Shadow Bay Campground has 92 tent and RV sites. All three camps have flush toilets, drinking water, garbage containers, fire pits, tables, boat ramps, swimming areas, amphitheaters, and picnic areas.

Dates: Open July 1 to Sept. 30, depending on snow conditions.

Fees: There are charges for campsites and trail park passes.

WALDO LAKE LOOP TRAIL 3590

[Fig. 36(2)] The trail roughly follows the shoreline of Waldo Lake, and consists mostly of easy grades through forested rolling country. Much of the trail is in the forest and out of view of the lake. Numerous primitive campsites are along the lake and trail. The best way to reach the water sites is by boat.

In some areas, trail users can enjoy good views of Mount Bachelor, Broken Top and the Three Sisters mountains. The trail is open for hikers, horseback riders, and bicyclists, and closed to motorized vehicles.

Directions: The main trailhead is on the north side of the boat launch at North Waldo Campground (*see* Waldo Lake, page 231), or can be entered at Islet and Shadow Bay campgrounds.

Dates: Open July through Oct.

Facilities: A shelter is on the south end of the lake.

Trail: 21.8 miles on a one-way loop.

Elevation: 5,400 feet with minor grades.

Degree of difficulty: Easy but long.

Surface: Dirt and rock.

CHARLTON LAKE

[Fig. 36] Campers at crystalline Waldo Lake usually enjoy better fishing 2 miles east in the fertile 100 acres of Charlton Lake, which is well known for producing 10-to 16-inch-long brook trout. Gasoline powered motors are not allowed, and there is a 0.25 mile walk from the parking lot to the water. A gravel road continues 8 miles east from Charlton Lake to intersect with the paved Cascade Lakes Scenic Byway Forest Service 46 between Crane Prairie Reservoir and Davis Lake. The route is rough and lightly traveled, but it's the shortest route between Waldo Lake and the Cascade Lakes Byway, and there's a good chance of seeing deer. In September, this is a great place to fill a bucket with wild huckleberries.

Directions: From the Waldo Lake Road Forest Service 5897, bear east at milepost 9 onto graveled Forest Service 4290 and continue less than 1 mile to the well-marked parking lot at an elevation of 5,700 feet.

Facilities: Primitive campsites at the lake.

Dates: Generally snow-bound from Oct. through June.

Fees: There is a charge for trail park passes.

WALDO LAKE WILDERNESS

[Fig. 36] Most of the small lakes and bogs in 37,162-acre Waldo Lake Wilderness are west and north of Waldo Lake in a mosquito-infested corner of Willamette National Forest.

The northern boundary of Waldo Lake Wilderness meets the southern border of volcano-peppered Three Sisters Wilderness. The northwest corner edges close to the shoulder of Aufderheide National Scenic Byway at Constitution Grove (*see* Aufderheide National Scenic Byway, page 221). Countless small lakes, bogs, and potholes are scattered through the wilderness area. Many are filled with water from snow melt left from the many feet of snow that falls here. Many of the lakes are stocked with rainbow, brook and cutthroat trout. The largest lakes and chains are popular hiking destinations, especially Six Lakes Basin, Eddeeleo Lakes, Wahanna Lakes, and Quinn Lakes.

The topography varies from steep mountain pitches to nearly flat meadows. Hikers will see many basin areas, with grassy, sometimes boggy meadows and heather-streaked rock outcrops. Nearly the entire wilderness is forested, mostly with lodgepole pine, Douglas fir, western hemlock, western fir, and true fir.

Elevations vary from 2,800 feet to 7,144 feet. The high point is at the top of Fuji Mountain, which is on the southern borderline of the wilderness. Another landmark is a Forest Service lookout tower jutting from the summit of 6,357-foot high Waldo Mountain.

Hikers and horseback riders have about 84 miles of maintained trails to explore. Vehicles, including bicycles, are not allowed anywhere in the wilderness. Compared with many of Oregon's wilderness areas, this is lightly used and campsites located in solitude and sylvan settings are common. Don't, however, forget insect repellent. The lakes and bogs that keep this woodland so beautifully green also grow dense clouds of aggressive mosquitoes.

Directions: The most heavily used entry points are at Waldo Lake, Salmon Creek Road Forest Service 24 which runs northeast from Oakridge, Aufderheide Road at Constitution Grove, and Box Canyon Summit.

Activities: Hiking, camping, fishing, hunting, and huckleberry picking.

Facilities: 84 miles of maintained hiking trails.

Dates: Open year-round.

Fees: There are charges for trail park passes. Free wilderness use passes are available at the Oakridge ranger station.

Closest town: Oakridge is just southwest of the wilderness on OR 58.

For more information: Middle Fork Ranger Station, 49098 Salmon Creek Road, PO Box 1410, Oakridge, OR 97464. Phone (541) 782-2283. In Summer/Fall 2000, Middle Fork Ranger District office will be located at 46375 Hwy 58, Westfir, OR 97492. Call to confirm new mailing address.

WILLAMETTE PASS

[Fig. 36] Almost a mile high, Willamette Pass, elevation 5,128 feet, is a popular destination on OR 58 for summer trout fishermen at nearby Gold Lake, and winter skiers and snowmobilers.

The forested pass is the dividing point for Willamette and Deschutes national forests. Rivers south of the pass drain into the Middle Fork Willamette and North Fork Umpqua drainages. North of the pass is the Cascade Lakes region, which is one of the most popular camping and trout fishing areas in Oregon.

The most visible feature here is Willamette Pass Ski Area, a small downhill ski complex north of the highway.

Directions: The pass is on OR 58 about 70 miles east of Eugene and 85 miles west of Bend near Odell Lake (*see* Odell Lake, page 270).

Activities: Downhill and cross-country winter skiing, and trout fishing.

Facilities: Ski resort, roadside snow shelters, and Sno-Parks.

Dates: The pass is maintained and open year-round.

Fees: A trail park pass is required to park at the pass, and to use nearby Sno-Parks and cross-country ski shelters.

Closest town: Oakridge is about 28 miles west on OR 58.

For more information: Middle Fork Ranger Station, 49098 Salmon Creek Road, PO Box 1410, Oakridge, OR 97464. Phone (541) 782-2283. In Summer/Fall 2000, Middle Fork Ranger District office will be located at 46375 Hwy 58, Westfir, OR 97492. Call to confirm new mailing address. Willamette Pass Ski Area, Cascade Summit, OR 978401. Phone (541) 484-5030.

WILLAMETTE PASS SKI AREA

[Fig. 36(3)] This is a commercial ski area featuring downhill and cross-country skiing. The summit is 6,666 feet high with a 1,525 foot drop to the base at 5,141 feet.

Directions: See Willamette Pass.

Activities: Winter downhill skiing.

Facilities: 5 chairlifts, snow play tow, day lodge with restaurant, Nordic skiing, day care center, and restrooms.

Dates: Open mid-Nov. through mid-Apr.

Fees: There is a charge for lift tickets.

GOLD LAKE

[Fig. 36] A short side trip on Forest Service Road 500 north of OR 58 at Willamette Pass will bring you to Gold Lake, a 0.5-mile long, 100-acre fly-fishing honey hole for big rainbow and brook trout. Fishing is restricted to fly tackle, and boats with gasoline-

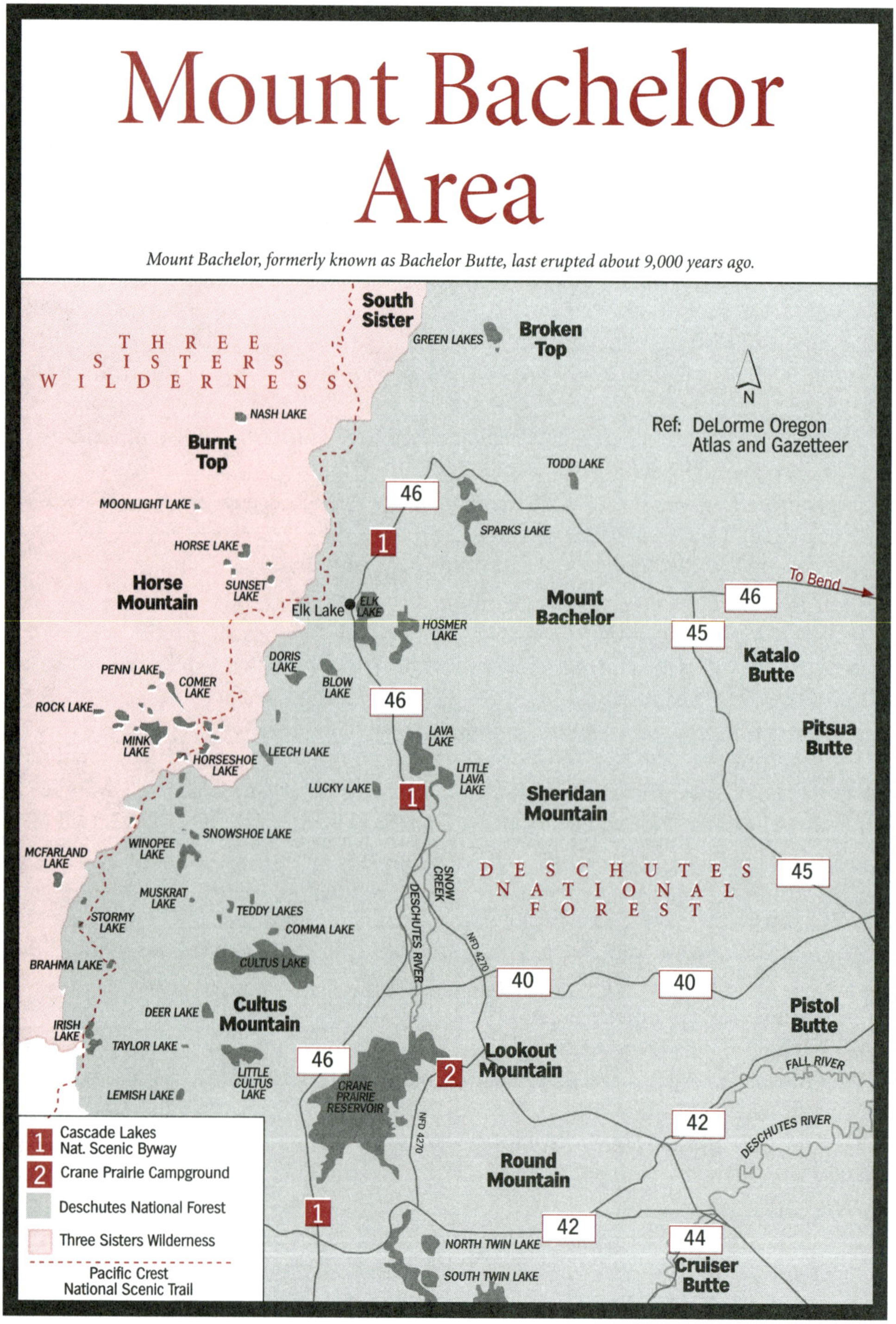

Mount Bachelor Area

Mount Bachelor, formerly known as Bachelor Butte, last erupted about 9,000 years ago.

South Sister
Broken Top
GREEN LAKES
THREE SISTERS WILDERNESS
N
Ref: DeLorme Oregon Atlas and Gazetteer
NASH LAKE
Burnt Top
TODD LAKE
46
MOONLIGHT LAKE
SPARKS LAKE
1
HORSE LAKE
To Bend
Horse Mountain
SUNSET LAKE
Elk Lake
ELK LAKE
Mount Bachelor
46
HOSMER LAKE
45
Katalo Butte
DORIS LAKE
PENN LAKE
COMER LAKE
BLOW LAKE
46
ROCK LAKE
Pitsua Butte
MINK LAKE
LAVA LAKE
HORSESHOE LAKE
LEECH LAKE
LITTLE LAVA LAKE
LUCKY LAKE
1
Sheridan Mountain
SNOWSHOE LAKE
MCFARLAND LAKE
WINOPEE LAKE
SNOW CREEK
DESCHUTES NATIONAL FOREST
45
MUSKRAT LAKE
DESCHUTES RIVER
STORMY LAKE
TEDDY LAKES
COMMA LAKE
NFD 4270
CULTUS LAKE
BRAHMA LAKE
40
40
DEER LAKE
Cultus Mountain
Pistol Butte
IRISH LAKE
TAYLOR LAKE
46
Lookout Mountain
2
FALL RIVER
LITTLE CULTUS LAKE
LEMISH LAKE
CRANE PRAIRIE RESERVOIR
NFD 4270
42
DESCHUTES RIVER
Round Mountain
1
42
44
NORTH TWIN LAKE
Cruiser Butte
SOUTH TWIN LAKE

1 Cascade Lakes Nat. Scenic Byway
2 Crane Prairie Campground
Deschutes National Forest
Three Sisters Wilderness
Pacific Crest National Scenic Trail

powered motors are prohibited. The road is usually snow-free by June. Gold Lake is the headwater of Salt Creek, the picturesque stream that parallels OR 58 into Oakridge.

Directions: About 28 miles east of Oakridge turn north from OR 58 onto Forest Service 500 to the lake.

Activities: Trout fishing, camping, picnicking, swimming, and rowboating.

Facilities: Boat ramp and Forest Service campground with 25 tent and RV sites, a picnic area.

Dates: Open June to Oct.

Fees: There is a charge for campsites.

Mount Bachelor

[Fig. 37] An extinct stratovolcano 9,065 feet high, Mount Bachelor is an imposing snow-crowned cinder cone that dominates both the skyline of the eastern Cascade Range and winter and summer mountain recreation in the Bend area.

The mountain is the acknowledged capital of Oregon winter sports. Sno-Parks, snowmobile, and cross-country ski trails lead from just about every wide spot along the highway between Bend and the Dutchman Flat parking area for the mountain's winter and summer resort recreation area.

The snow-capped peaks visible from Dutchman Flat have made it a popular setting for movies, including *Homeward Bound, How The West Was Won,* and *Rooster Cogburn.*

The resort area is about 21 miles southwest of Bend on Cascade Lakes Scenic Byway/ Forest Service Road 46, where the road wraps around the 6,200-foot level of the mountain. A spur road leads into the parking lot.

Until a few years ago, Forest Service 46 west and south of Mount Bachelor was called Century Drive, a name that still appears on some maps. The spectacular scenery along the route has earned it a federal designation and a new name, The Cascade Lakes National Scenic Byway (*see* page 239), a spectacular top-of-the-world highway along the spine of the Cascades connecting dozens of clear trout lakes, forest campgrounds, and trails. This scenic byway is closed during winter at a gate just west of the Mount Bachelor ski resort, at which time it becomes a winter-trail corridor for snowmobilers and skiers.

Mount Bachelor has earned international recognition as a world-class downhill ski area with 3,365 feet of vertical drop and 3,686 acres of dry, knee-deep powder snow. Downhill and cross-country skiers and snow boarders zip across the slopes from mid-November through the Fourth of July. In recent years, recreational activities have been expanded to 365 days a year, and include dog sledding, cross-country skiing, snowmobiling, snowshoeing and snow camping. During the snow-free months there is mountain biking, hiking, and chairlift sight-seeing rides to the 9,065-foot-high summit. The wide dome top of Mount Bachelor is actually a cluster of small pyroclastic cones and shallow craters. The summit of Mount Bachelor is the highest, most northerly spot on the West

Know Your Volcanoes

Two different types of volcanoes built the Oregon Cascades: stratovolcanoes and shield volcanoes.

The difference between them is in the composition and amount of water in the materials that erupted from them.

Stratovolcanoes, which include most of the highest peaks; Mount Hood, Mount Jefferson, and Three Sisters; are formed by alternating eruptions of lava and ash. The alternating eruptions create a volcano composed of stratified layers and various lavas from eruptions often centuries apart. Some of the stratovolcanoes first produce basalt, then rhyolite and andesite. Each of these dome-building eruptions adds small portions of different materials to the cone.

Stratovolcanoes are usually craggy and pinnacle-crowned, with steep, heavily eroded flanks. This is due to intense erosion by vanished ice age glaciers.

Shield volcanoes are built of a single dominating material, usually basalt lava.

Formative eruptions of shield volcanoes are more of an ooze of molten basalt than an explosion of hot magma. The low-powered eruptions form squat, low-profile mountains. One geologist wrote that shield volcanoes more closely resemble "a puddle of cold molasses than a volcano." Belknap Crater is one of Oregon's best-known shield volcanoes.

Coast accessible to foot passengers.

At tree line, which is about 7,700 feet in elevation, short old-growth hemlock forests give way to open meadows that are streaked with old snow and lava rock in summer. In the winter these alpine meadows are often buried under 25 feet of snow, while the city of Bend, just 21 miles east, averages less than 10 inches of snow a year. The contrast is typical of the weather extremes in these mountains.

Mount Bachelor, formerly known as Bachelor Butte, last erupted about 9,000 years ago. Mount Bachelor rises more than 2,000 feet above neighboring buttes and creates its own localized weather. July and August snowfalls are not uncommon. During most late summer evenings, thunderstorms develop around the peak when the hot air in the desert basin east of Bend is carried up the front range of the Cascades by thermal winds. Thunderheads develop when the hot thermals collide with the cool air that nearly always collects around Mount Bachelor. Most storms are short-lived and mornings dawn clear beneath blue skies.

Botanists are attracted to Mount Bachelor by one of the rarest plants in the Northwest, the pumice grape fern (*Botrychium pumicola*). Approximately 100 of the plants live on the mountain, and they occur in only four other alpine locales, plus sites in Central Oregon lower-elevation pumice openings within lodgepole pine forests. To root, the plant needs loose pumice, which is found only in areas that were blanketed by fallout from the eruption of Mount Mazama. Those areas are in what is now Crater Lake National Park, or in areas within the fallout zone from an eruption from Newberry Crater, located 10 miles south of Bend.

Directions: From U.S. 97 in Bend, drive about 21 miles west on Hwy 46 to the resort and ski area parking lot. The route is well signed.

Activities: Winter downhill, cross-country skiing, snow boarding, snowshoeing, snowmobiling, dog sledding, and snow camping. Summer, mountain biking, hiking, and chairlift rides to the summit.

Facilities: 4 day-use lodges, restaurant/cafes, 11 chairlifts, 70 ski runs, 12 cross-country ski trails, 7.5 miles of mountain bike trails. Bicycles, hiking boots, and ski equipment may be rented. The nearest overnight accommodations are about 15 miles east on Hwy 46.

Dates: Open year-round, the resort's winter snow season is from mid-Nov. through July 4.

Fees: There are charges for commercial services, and Forest Service parking passes are required at nearby trailheads.

Closest town: Bend.

For more information: Bend Ranger District, Deschutes National Forest, 1230 NE 3rd., Bend, OR 97701. Phone 541-388-5664, or Deschutes National Forest (541) 388-2715. Mount Bachelor Ski Area, Bend, OR 97709, phone (800) 829-2442, or (541) 382-2442. Dog sled rides may be arranged by phoning the numbers listed for Mount Bachelor Ski Area.

Cascade Lakes National Scenic Byway

[Fig. 37(1)] An 87-mile-long paved route that follows the spine of the Cascade Range, the Cascade Lakes National Scenic Byway connects dozens of mirrorlike alpine trout lakes, forest service campgrounds, rustic resorts, hiking trails, and wildlife areas.

Open only from June through October (winter snows often are more than 20 feet deep) the byway runs west from Bend to the north side of Mount Bachelor where it turns south on Forest Service 46. The route is a mountain connection that links OR 46 on the north to OR 58 on the south. At the junction of OR 58, drivers have the option of turning west toward Eugene and I-5, or east to US 97 south of Bend.

The route was dedicated as a national scenic byway in 1989, and before that was called Century Drive, a name that refers to the route's 100 miles and which still appears on many maps.

Cascade Lakes National Scenic Byway is known for two attractions: high-mountain scenery, and a necklace of lakes that press against the road like turquoise gemstones dangling from an asphalt chain.

With the exception of a few small, shallow ponds, all of the lakes have improved Forest Service campgrounds with tent and RV sites, and drinking water. There are 25 Forest Service campgrounds scattered along the route. The largest lakes have rustic resorts.

The byway crosses paths made by some of the first explorers of the Northwest, including trappers Peter Skene Ogden, Nathaniel J. Wyeth, Captain John C. Fremont, and Kit Carson.

Like much of the West, it was rival trappers who first explored this region while searching for undiscovered caches of beavers to trap. In the early 1800s both British and American forces were struggling for control of this region. In 1825-26, the British-owned Hudson's Bay Company, based at Fort Vancouver near Vancouver, Washington, sent a party of trappers led by Ogden across Santiam Pass and south along the East Slope of the Cascades. It was the first intrusion by European descendants south of Lewis and Clark's Columbia River route. Ogden was under orders to destroy any beaver colonies he found, in order to discourage American trappers from moving into the region. He found few beavers, however, and discouraged Hudson's Bay Company officials from establishing an outpost on the East Slope.

Seventeen years later, Ogden's route was followed by Captain Fremont, an American. The exploration included government cartographers and produced the first maps of this area. For two years the Fremont group explored the east side of the Cascade Range guided by legendary American scout Kit Carson and free trapper Old Bill Williams. Carson and Williams were involved in the first skirmishes between European descendants and the local Klamath and Modoc Indian bands. Fremont became known as the Great American Pathfinder, a title he carried into his unsuccessful 1856 campaign as the first Republican Party candidate for the U.S. presidency. He lost to James Buchanan.

The landscape visible from the byway is volcanic in origin, formed by centuries-old eruptions and lava flows that built the surrounding peaks, and created the series of natural lakes. Summers along the byway are usually warm, dry, and sunny, with cool nights. The road flows along the base of the mountains.

A highlight along this national byway is the winter and summer recreation at Mount Bachelor Resort, which is a popular backdrop for Western films. Dutchman Flat is also unique—the protected area has a blanket of pumice gravel so thick at the site that plants can't find soil enough to root, giving the appearance of a high-elevation desert.

At Devils Garden, ancient cultural clashes intersect with space travel. The site is just north of Sparks Lake, and is a lush spring-fed meadow where wild elk sometimes graze. The colorful grasses and wildflowers in the meadow dramatically border a barren black lava flow so moonlike that in the 1960s astronauts trained here for Apollo lunar missions. Astronaut James Irwin took a chunk of Devils Garden rock to the moon, where it remains today. In the same area where the astronaut picked up that lunar-bound lava is a boulder with an ancient pictograph that marks an Indian trail, and an ambush site where Klamath warriors attacked a group of Warm Springs warriors.

Elk Lake and Hosmer Lakes are well-known respectively for sailing and fly-fishing for large brook trout and Atlantic salmon (*Salmo salar*). Cultus Lake is one of the few lakes along the byway with shallow, sandy beaches that invite swimming. Vast Crane Prairie Reservoir is famous for a standing forest of flooded lodgepole pine snags, big rainbow trout, and the largest concentration of nesting ospreys (*Pandion haliaetus*) in the conterminous United States. A short path leads to a viewpoint at Osprey Observation Point (*see* Crane Prairie Reservoir, page 243).

North and South Twin Lakes are geological rarities. The lakes occupy almost perfectly round, deep volcanic craters called "maars," which have no inlet or outlet. They're fed entirely by rainfall and snowmelt. Nearly this entire top-of-the-world byway is within Deschutes National Forest.

Directions: From the north, drive west from Bend on OR 46. From the south, follow OR 58 to Crescent Creek and turn north onto Forest Service 46. A third option is to drive from US 97. At the junction community of Crescent, turn west on Deschutes County Road 61 and continue west to intersect with Cascade Lakes National Scenic Byway/Forest Service 46 south of Davis Lake.

Activities: Sight-seeing, hiking, trout and bass fishing, fall hunting for deer, elk, bear, and grouse; swimming, camping, mountain biking, boating, and picnicking.

Facilities: 25 Forest Service campgrounds, most on lakes. Private resorts and campgrounds, boat launches, picnic areas, many hiking and bicycling trails. A historic and rustic Forest Service guard and information station, staffed by volunteers from Memorial Day through Oct., is on the west side of Elk Lake near Elk Lake Resort.

Dates: Open to wheeled vehicles June through Oct. Snowmobilers use the snow-buried highway from Nov. to late May.

Fees: There are charges for campgrounds, trail park passes, and resort services.

Closest town: Bend.

For more information: Deschutes National Forest, 1645 Highway 20 E., Bend, OR 97701. Phone (541) 388-2715. Central Oregon Visitors Association, 63085 N. Hwy. 97, Suite 104, Bend, OR 97701. Phone (800) 800-8334 or (541) 389-8799. Web site www.fs.fed.us/r6/deschutes.

ELK LAKE

[Fig. 37] Stiff summer winds attract wind-surfers and sailors, and mirrored morning reflections of South Sister, Broken Top and Mount Bachelor mountains bring sightseers and photographers to this lake. Fishermen come for brook trout and kokanee salmon, and the exotic Atlantic salmon in nearby Hosmer Lake. Campers stake out 127 nearby tent and RV sites. A log-style resort on the west shore is open year-round. When Forest Service 46 is closed for the winter, guests arrive at the remote lodge on cross-country skis, snowmobiles, or by arranging through the resort to ride a Snow Cat shuttle. In summer the resort is used mostly by mountain bikers, boaters, and fishermen.

Elk Lake, at an elevation of about 4,893 feet, covers 390 acres in a dense forest of lodgepole pine, low-bush blueberries, and huckleberries. The lake averages 25 to 35 feet deep and the unroiled water is so transparent that nearly the entire bottom is visible from the surface. One mile south of Elk Lake is 160-acre Hosmer Lake, which is famous among fly-fishermen for its wary Atlantic salmon and large brook trout. Hosmer is ringed by tule reeds and the depth never exceeds 8.5 feet. The lake is used almost exclusively by fishermen. State regulations limit anglers to using fly tackle and all catches must be released.

Directions: Elk Lake is on the east side of Cascade Lakes National Scenic Byway/

Forest Service 46 about 10 miles south of Mount Bachelor. A gravel road encircles the lake, and connects several campgrounds and the resort.

Activities: Camping, boating (10 mph limit), fishing, hiking, swimming, windsurfing, cross-country skiing, snowmobiling,

Facilities: 4 Forest Service campgrounds: Little Fawn, 31 sites; Sunset Cove, 27 sites; Elk Lake, 22 sites; and Point, 9 sites. Nearby Hosmer Lake offers an additional 38 campsites. Elk Lake Resort can provide rustic cabins, boats, restaurant, store, fishing tackle, and winter Sno-Cat shuttle service from Mount Bachelor. Boat ramps are at Elk Lake Resort, Little Fawn and Point campgrounds. Most of the campgrounds have well water, restrooms, tables, and fire pits.

Dates: Campgrounds are open Memorial Day through Sept. The resort is open year-round.

Fees: There are fees for most campsites, and all resort services.

For more information: Elk Lake Resort, PO Box 789, Bend, OR 97709. Phone (541) 317-2994.

Deschutes Wild And Scenic River

[Fig. 37] The Deschutes is one of Oregon's premier rivers, and a nationally acclaimed wild and scenic river. It flows north for 252.2 miles, paralleling the east front range of the Oregon Cascades through ruggedly beautiful scenery that varies from pristine forests at its Lava Lake headwater to semiarid scablands where it meets the Columbia River east of The Dalles. Along the way are 173.4 miles of wild and scenic designated water, dozens of Class III to Class V rapids, unnavigable falls, stark rock canyons, isolated encampments and downtown parks.

The Deschutes is famous for outstanding whitewater boating, and a renowned sport fishery for steelhead, brown trout, and native rainbow trout. Most of the upper flow of the Deschutes River is through public land, although portions flow past private holdings.

Geographically, the Deschutes is divided into three segments—the Upper, Middle, and Lower. The upper river rambles along the top of the Cascade Crest and features primarily flatwater boating with limited whitewater and excellent trout fishing opportunities. The middle Deschutes near Bend has excellent hiking with spectacular geologic formations and waterfalls, and limited boating opportunities. Maupin is near the center of the lower Deschutes, which offers the greatest opportunities for whitewater rafting, and steelhead and trout fisheries.

French fur traders first named it *Riviere des Chutes*, which translates to "River of Falls."

Its headwaters are at Little Lava Lake, about 87 miles southwest of Bend. The 53 miles from Wickiup Dam to Bend are favorites with whitewater enthusiasts, offering a mix of thrills and scenery from Class V rapids to bucolic flats. Professional rafting guides run from Aspen Camp to Lava Island.

Humans have lived along the Deschutes River for 9,000 years, according to artifacts at

Island Rockshelter in Bend. Nomadic hunters and gathers were following the river while nearby volcanoes of Mount Mazama, Newberry Volcano, and Mount Jefferson were cracking, popping and dumping an 8- to 10-foot-deep blanket of ash and pumice on the land. Traditional Indian fishing platforms may be seen pinned to the columnar basalt walls at Shearer's Falls, a popular salmon fishing site northeast of Maupin.

The river is often an oasis in near-desert environments, and attracts a variety of wildlife, including bald and golden eagles, ospreys, and great blue herons stalking frogs, crayfish, and slow fish.

You may also see beavers, river otters, mule deer, elk, black bear, garter and Pacific rattlesnakes, and assorted lizards.

Deschutes River recreation opportunities also include developed and primitive spots for camping and picnicking. Trails are used for hiking, biking and horseback riding.

For more information: Bureau of Land Management, Prineville District, 3050 NE 3rd Street, Prineville, Oregon 97754, phone (541) 416-6700. Deschutes National Forest, 1645 Highway 20 East, Bend, OR 97701. Phone (541) 388-2715. Web site: www.empnet.com/dnf. Central Oregon Visitors Association, 63085 N. Highway 97, Suite 104, Bend, OR 97701, phone (541) 389-8799 or (800) 800-8334.

CRANE PRAIRIE RESERVOIR

[Fig. 37] Crane Prairie Reservoir is 5 square miles of shallow, tree-snag studded trout, bass, and osprey water on the south segment of Cascade Lakes National Scenic Byway. The big lake is ringed by good roads, large well-developed Forest Service campgrounds, a resort-marina complex, and miles of hiking and bicycling trails.

The reservoir was impounded to store irrigation water in 1928 by a dam on the upper Deschutes River that flooded the namesake prairie and a standing forest of lodgepole pine trees. The skeletonized snags of those drowned trees mark the flooded channels of the Deschutes, Cultus, and Quinn rivers. But a benefit more important to wildlife enthusiasts is that the sun-bleached, barkless towers have become nesting sites for the greatest concentration of ospreys in the United States. Bird fanciers bring their spotting scopes to an osprey observation area on the west side of the lake. The gravel road to the observation point is well-marked from the scenic byway, and suitable for RVs. Look for the turnoff about a mile south of the resort. Turn west onto Forest Service Road 200 and continue 0.6 mile to the observation area, where there is also a swimming beach and primitive campsites.

Ospreys, often called fish hawks, are black-and-white raptors that dive from as high as 100 feet into the water, often disappearing beneath the water in a streamlined plunge targeting swimming fish. Back in the air, the big birds will rotate the luckless catch in their talons until the fish is aerodynamically positioned headfirst into the wind for the flight back to the nest.

The sprawling lake averages about 11 feet deep. The standing trees and fertile, often weedy shallows provide excellent habitat for fish. Rainbow trout grow two inches a

Thundereggs

Central Oregon is thunderegg country. If you've never seen one it's almost guaranteed that you will the first time you stop for gas or snacks along US 97. It's hard to find a gas station or store along US 97 that doesn't have a display of sliced thundereggs on the counter.

Oregon's state rock is actually a composite of brilliantly colored agates that have formed inside a nondescript rhyolite geode. The rough gray outer rock of the shell gives no hint of the beautiful colored crystal formations inside.

Thunderegg agates are found only in light colored volcanic ash. Some digging sites are in forest areas, but the best known digs are in the stark, desertlike steppes where the east front of the Cascades meets the Columbia Plateau of central Oregon. Madras and Prineville are especially productive areas. Richardson's Recreation Ranch, also called Pridy Ranch, is believed to be the world's richest known deposit of thundereggs. In late June, there's a rock hound convention at the Jefferson County Fairgrounds in Madras, population 5,000.

Most thundereggs range from baseball to basketball size, and are formed either as nodes or geodes. One of the most unusual finds is 3 feet long and 3 inches across; some say it resembles a fat gray worm.

Thundereggs are formed as circulating water slowly fills the cavity of a rhyolite rock with silica, forming quartz crystals that blend brilliant colors into distinctive patterns. Crystal colors inside the geodes range from pastel blue to translucent red, yellow, and white.

Some eggs have well-developed calcite crystals and others contain pseudomorphs of chalcedony. Sawing a thunderegg in half to reveal the inside color usually reveals internal layers of coloring in formations similar to what you see by halving a head of cauliflower. Collectors often slice thundereggs into thin translucent plates called cabochons, or work the rock into colorful jewelry.

Value varies with color and gemstone qualities. Some eggs are filled with pastel jaspers, others have a variety of opal that can range from opaque blue and red to translucent yellow, blues, and whites. Jewelers are sometimes able to facet these opals, and a very tiny percentage are true opals. You can buy a slice of thunderegg for a dollar or two although exceptional quartz formations have brought more than $100 per slice.

There are public agate digs for rock hounds, many in the Madras area, where thundereggs can be dug free on public ground. The odds of a big find, however, generally favor those who dig at private fee sites. Prineville Chamber of Commerce, (541) 447-6304, can provide a list of public and private sites, and information on the state stone.

month during the summer, and there are lots of trout in the 4- to 10-pound range. The food-rich lake also supports a population of wild brook trout, kokanee salmon, and largemouth bass. Anglers travel hundreds of miles to challenge this big lake's lunker fish.

Boat speed is limited to 10 mph, which eliminates water skiing and speed boats.

The lake also attracts a variety of wildlife, including sandhill cranes, cormorants, migrating waterfowl, deer, elk, black bear, mink, beaver, and otter. Wildlife watching is a favorite pastime for boaters and campers.

The devastation that can be caused by wildfires in this remote area is visible at the north end of Crane Prairie Reservoir, which is surrounded by a standing forest of charred pine trees; casualties of a fire that ravaged the region several years ago. Wildfires are not uncommon in this area, especially in late summer and early fall when forests are the driest.

Directions: Follow Cascade Lakes National Scenic Byway/Forest Service 46 about 38 miles south from Bend. A shorter route is to go 15 miles south of Bend on US 97, turn west at Sunriver onto Forest Service 40 and continue 22 miles to the junction of Forest Service 4270. The resort is 4 miles south of the junction.

Activities: Camping, fishing, boating, hiking, mountain biking, wildlife watching, and swimming.

Facilities: 4 large Forest Service campgrounds, 5 boat launches, and Crane Prairie Resort, which provide a full-service RV park, marina, moorage, gas and oil, tackle shop, groceries, laundry, showers, and restaurant. Trips with fishing guides can also be arranged at the resort.

Dates: Fishing is allowed from the fourth Saturday in Apr. to Oct. 31, and that's when the resort and most of the campgrounds are open.

Fees: There is a charge for camping and resort services.

Closest town: Bend is about 38 miles north on Cascade Lakes National Scenic Byway/ Forest Service 46.

For more information: Deschutes National Forest, 1645 Highway 20 E., Bend, OR 97701. Phone (541) 388-2715. Central Oregon Visitors Association, 63085 N. Hwy. 97, Suite 104, Bend, OR 97701. Phone (800) 800-8334 or (541) 389-8799. Web site: www.fs.fed.us/r6/deschutes. Crane Prairie Resort, PO Box 1171, Bend, OR 97709. Phone (541) 383-3939.

CRANE PRAIRIE CAMPGROUND

[Fig. 37(2)] Crane Prairie Campground is the largest Forest Service campground on the Cascade Lakes National Scenic Byway. It is located on the east side of Crane Prairie Reservoir in a sandy flat divided by groves of lodgepole pine, patches of wild huckleberries, and lumps of lava boulders. This spacious campground adjoins a resort that has a small store, restaurant, tackle, boats, and camping supplies. Smaller campgrounds on the east side of the lake can be entered directly from the byway. The elevation here is 4,445 feet and remnants of the winter snow pack frequently linger well into May. Snow may fall during any month at this elevation.

Directions: From the scenic byway north of Crane Prairie Reservoir turn east onto Forest Service 40, then south on Forest Service 4270. The campground is about 4.5 miles south of the junction on the lake's northeast shore.

Activities: Camping, swimming, fishing, boating, and bird watching. Bicyclists enjoy

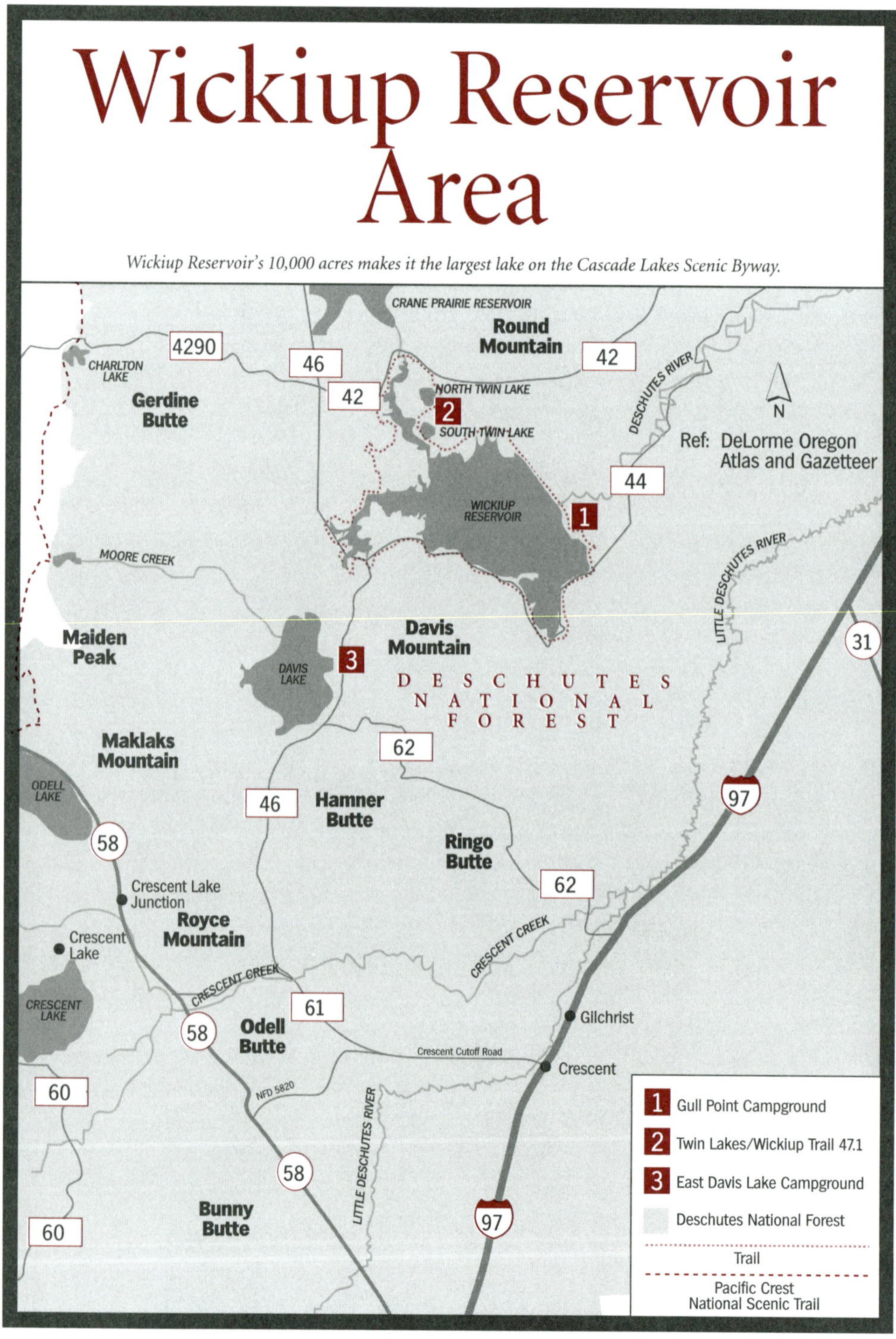
Wickiup Reservoir Area
Wickiup Reservoir's 10,000 acres makes it the largest lake on the Cascade Lakes Scenic Byway.
CRANE PRAIRIE RESERVOIR
Round Mountain
4290
46
42
CHARLTON LAKE
Gerdine Butte
NORTH TWIN LAKE
SOUTH TWIN LAKE
DESCHUTES RIVER
N
Ref: DeLorme Oregon Atlas and Gazetteer
44
WICKIUP RESERVOIR
MOORE CREEK
LITTLE DESCHUTES RIVER
Maiden Peak
Davis Mountain
DAVIS LAKE
31
DESCHUTES NATIONAL FOREST
Maklaks Mountain
62
ODELL LAKE
Hamner Butte
97
58
Ringo Butte
Crescent Lake Junction
Royce Mountain
Crescent Lake
CRESCENT CREEK
CRESCENT LAKE
61
Odell Butte
Gilchrist
Crescent Cutoff Road
Crescent
60
NFD 5820
Bunny Butte
1 Gull Point Campground
2 Twin Lakes/Wickiup Trail 47.1
3 East Davis Lake Campground
Deschutes National Forest
Trail
Pacific Crest National Scenic Trail

the network of roads that loop through the campground.

Facilities: 146 tent and RV sites, full hookups, tables, grills, water, showers, amphitheater, picnic area, boat ramp, dock. There is an on-site campground host/manager.

Dates: Open Apr. to Oct.

Fees: There is a charge for campsites.

WICKIUP RESERVOIR

[Fig. 38] Covering 10,000 acres behind a dam on the upper Deschutes River, Wickiup Reservoir is the largest lake on the Cascade Lakes National Scenic Byway, and an extremely popular summer stop for fishermen, water skiers, sail boarders, and campers.

On the north side of Wickiup Reservoir, Forest Service Road 42, which intersects with Forest Service 46, goes east to US 97 at the town of La Pine, south of Bend. Forest Service 42 is paved and is the primary connection between the Cascade Lakes National Scenic Byway/Forest Service 46 and US 97. To continue south through the mountains, travelers continue on Forest Service 46 to Davis Lake and OR 58.

The reservoir was impounded in 1949 to store irrigation water. It was named for the wickiup poles that supported temporary shelters, and were permanently left here by Indians who camped in the meadow during seasonal fishing and hunting trips. The framework poles were positioned in a circle and covered with brush to form temporary wickiups, or shelters. Wickiup Reservoir is encircled by a combination of Forest Service roads that provide access to seven campgrounds and four boat ramps. There is no resort on the lake but nearby Twin Lakes Resorts maintains a fleet of rental boats on the Deschutes River arm. The deepest spot in this wind-swept reservoir is 60 feet, but most of the lake is less than 20 feet deep and summer drawdowns to irrigate crops in the Central Oregon area expose much of the bottom.

Wickiup is considered one of the best fishing lakes for big trout in central Oregon. It has a large population of wild brown trout and kokanee, and is stocked with rainbow trout, and coho salmon. The lake has given up brown trout that weigh 24 pounds. Boat ramps are at Gull Point, North Wickiup, South Twin and Reservoir campgrounds.

Wickiup is also popular with water skiers and Jet Skiers and the predictable afternoon winds that chase fishermen and water skiers off the water attract wind surfers to the east end of the lake. Most campgrounds have swimming beaches.

The largest campground is Gull Point, on Forest Service Road 4260 on the north shore.

The lake's developed campgrounds, and the many others at nearby lakes and streams, are popular even during late summer when water is siphoned off for irrigation. This is because of the lake's central location to regional recreational opportunities. Canoe and raft paddlers can float and fish the Deschutes River for 40 miles from Wickiup Dam to Benham Falls south of Bend. The upper Deschutes River flows through meadows and gravel bars and is a fly-fisherman's dream. Forest roads wind through a woodland setting where wildlife, especially deer, are often seen. The roads lead to a variety of attractions such as Round Mountain Lookout, which is 2 miles north of the lake on a 5,900 feet elevation perch.

Dozens of hiking and mountain biking trails cut through the meadows and rolling lodgepole pine forests. One of the most popular trails is Twin Lakes/Wickiup Route 47.1, which begins near North Twin Lakes Campground.

Directions: Wickiup Reservoir is about 13 miles north of OR 58 on the east side of Cascade Lakes National Scenic Byway. Campgrounds on the north side of the lake can be reached by turning east on Forest Service 42 then south on Forest Service 4260. The south shore is followed by Forest Service 44, a good gravel road.

Activities: Trout fishing, camping, hiking, mountain biking, picnicking, sailing, wind surfing, and water skiing.

Facilities: There are 7 campgrounds; 4 are on the lake and 3 on connecting channels. Gull Point is the largest camp on the lake. Boat ramps are at Gull Point and North Wickiup campgrounds, West South Twin Campground, Reservoir Campground, and Wickiup Butte Campground. Developed campgrounds have drinking water, tables, fire pits, and vault toilets.

Dates: Fishing season opens the fourth Saturday in Apr. and closes Oct. 31. Most of the campgrounds operate during the fishing season.

Fees: There is a charge for camping and trail park passes, are required to park at most trailheads.

Closest town: Bend is about 45 miles north on US 97.

For more information: Deschutes National Forest, 1645 Highway 20 E., Bend, OR 97701. Phone (541) 388-2715. Central Oregon Visitors Association, 63085 N. Hwy. 97, Suite 104, Bend, OR 97701. Phone (800) 800-8334 or (541) 389-8799.

GULL POINT CAMPGROUND

[Fig. 38(1)] The largest of seven Forest Service campgrounds on Wickiup Reservoir, Gull Point is on the north bank at the mouth of the Deschutes River Channel. Sites are well-spaced in an open setting. The campground is at an elevation of 4,350 feet.

Directions: Follow Cascade Lakes National Scenic Highway about 15 miles north of

Oregon Grape

If your tent site is overrun by a bush with octopus-like branches, stiff, raspy leaves and grapelike berry clusters: congratulations. You've just met Oregon's state flower, the Oregon grape (*Mahonia aquifolium*).

Oregon grape is prolific and so abundant that in many areas it's regarded as a problem plant. The plants often appear as dense, tangled patches of underbrush in open areas beneath a canopy of Douglas pine. Their shallow, weblike root system is well suited to the thin, rocky soil of the Oregon Cascades, and in many areas it's difficult to find a place where this hardy plant won't grow.

In late summer, ruffed and blue grouse and other wildlife feed on the plant's grapelike clusters of blue berries, which are edible but seedy and dry, and may make your mouth pucker. Indigenous tribesmen used roots and wood from Oregon grape plants to make medicines and yellow dyes.

OR 58 and turn east on paved Forest Service Road 42. Continue east across the Deschutes River. Turn south onto Forest Service 4260. Drive southeast on Forest Service 4260 past North and South Twin lakes to the campground.

Activities: Camping, swimming, fishing, boating, hiking, and mountain biking.

Facilities: 80 campsites for tents and RVs up to 30 feet long, picnic tables, fire grills, water, RV dump station, and both vault and flush toilets, boat ramp, swimming area.

Dates: Open late Apr. through Oct.

Fees: There are charges for camping and trail park passes.

TWIN LAKES/WICKIUP TRAIL 47.1

[Fig. 38(2)] Mountain biking and hiking are very popular in the rolling forests around Wickiup Reservoir, and this woodland route encircling the reservoir is a favorite. Most hikers allow two days for the entire loop, or break the loop into shorter segments.

Directions: The trailhead is at North Twin Lakes Campground. Follow Cascade Lakes National Scenic Highway to the north side of Wickiup Reservoir and turn east on Forest Service 42, then south on Forest Service 4260 to the campground.

Dates: Snow-free from late Apr. through mid-Oct.

Fees: There is a charge for trail park passes.

Trail: 30 miles, loop.

Elevation: Trailhead elevation is 4,340 feet and the high point is 4,449 feet.

Degree of difficulty: Easy but long.

Surface: 5 miles are paved and 25 miles are dirt and rock.

DAVIS LAKE

[Fig. 38] Flanked on the north by the rock-hard wrinkles of the largest lava flow on Cascade Lakes National Scenic Highway south of Mount Bachelor, and on the south by a sea of marsh reeds, Davis Lake seems to be a must stop for every fly-fisherman traveling through the Cascades. Float tubes and neoprene boot waders greatly outnumber beach blankets and swimsuits.

Fly-fishermen are attracted by Davis Lake's fly fishing only regulations, and the promise of a chance to hook big rainbow trout and largemouth bass. There are three campgrounds on the lake. One is closed during the summer to protect nesting eagles, and the other two serve primarily as base camps for anglers.

Davis Lake, elevation 4,400 feet, is an attractive natural mountain lake framed between ponderosa and lodgepole pine forests. Nowhere is the lake more than 25 feet deep, and the very shallow south end is wrapped in acres of marsh divided by boat channels. The glacier-white peaks of distant volcanoes are reflected in the mirror of the lake's surface.

Evidence of the lake's volcanic origins can be seen at nearby Davis and Black Rock vents, which are Holocene cinder cones and andesite lava flows. Davis vent, the most northerly of these flows, created the lake about 5,500 years ago when a wall of molten lava believed to be more than 100 feet high poured from the vent across Odell Creek and hardened into a natural dam. The lava is at the edge of Lava Flow Campground, the only campground on the north end of the lake. Lava Flow is only open September 1 to December 31 to protect nesting bald eagles. Two other campgrounds are open during the summer. West and East Davis campgrounds are on the south end of the lake separated by a wide channel of water.

While there are opportunities to find prized Matsutake (*Tricholoma ponderosum*) and morel (*Morchella esculenta*) mushrooms in nearby pine forests, to watch birds, (especially waterfowl and grebes), and to hike; most people come to Davis Lake for the fly-fishing. Rainbow trout weighing 2 to 5 pounds are plentiful and often can be seen resting in the shade of floating logs, lined up like pickets, or feeding on insects at the grassy edges of the vast marsh. The most productive fishing is in May and June and September and October, but every open-water month can be good.

Directions: From OR 58 about 3 miles east of Crescent Lake Junction turn north onto Deschutes County Road 61 and continue 3 miles to Forest Service 46 and another 12 miles to Davis Lake's south shore. Cascade Lakes National Scenic Byway/Forest Service 46 runs along the east shore of the lake, but is screened by thick pines. The lake is at an elevation of 4,400 feet and snow is present from Nov. through Apr.

Activities: Fly-fishing, boating, waterfowl watching, camping, mushroom gathering.

Facilities: 3 campgrounds with boat ramps, vault toilets, drinking water, picnic tables and fire grills.

Dates: The lake is open for fishing year-round. Campgrounds are closed during heavy snow months.

Fees: There is a charge for camping.

Closest town: Bend is about 50 miles northeast on U. S. 97.

For more information: Deschutes National Forest, 1645 Highway 20 E., Bend, OR 97701. Phone (541) 388-2715. Central Oregon Visitors Association, 63085 N. Hwy. 97, Suite 104, Bend, OR 97701. Phone (800) 800-8334 or (541) 389-8799.

EAST DAVIS LAKE CAMPGROUND

[Fig. 38(3)] The largest of three campgrounds on Davis Lake, East Davis Campground is in a shady grove of pine trees along the southeast shore and can be reached on a spur road from Cascade Lakes National Scenic Byway/Forest Service 46. Neighboring West Davis Campground, with 25 tent and RV sites, can be seen from East Davis Campground on the lake's opposite shore, but to reach it requires a 10 mile drive around the south end of the lake. Short trails lead from East Davis Lake campground into the marsh, and along the lake shoreline. Because of the soggy, reed-filled shoreline, most of the fishing takes place from boats or float tubes.

Directions: Drive 7.7 miles north on Forest Service 46, about 17 miles north of OR 58. Turn west onto Forest Service Road 4600 and drive 2.6 miles to the campground.

Activities: Camping, fly fishing, boating, mushroom gathering, wildlife watching.

Facilities: 33 sites for tents and RVs to 22 feet long, picnic tables, grills, well water, vault toilets, and a rough boat launch.

Dates: Open from May through late Oct.
Fees: There is a charge for campsites.

Newberry National Volcanic Monument

[Fig. 39(1)] If you're even remotely interested in geology, volcanoes, eruptions, earthquakes, and the other cataclysmic events that formed Oregon's Cascade Range, plan to visit sprawling Newberry National Volcanic Monument.

The volcanic monument, located in the caldera of one of North America's largest volcanoes, is about 10 miles south of Bend. One of North America's truly unique geological areas, it covers 65,800 acres of exploded and imploded volcanic craters, basalt and obsidian flows, fossils, caves, lava, and special management areas.

Teachers, geologists, and students, as well as amateur naturalists, use the area as a living laboratory of easily accessible volcanic features, shaped by eruptions spanning the past million years. Visitors walk through cinder cones, pumice cones, lava flows, obsidian flows, Lava Cast Forest, caves, lakes, streams, waterfalls, and hot springs.

Some of the highlights include Big Obsidian Flow, which took place 1,300 years ago and covered 700 acres in a black, shiny obsidian field. A path traverses the flow. Major lava flows in the monument record the geologic history of the area. One flow changed the course of the Deschutes River. Another sudden lava flow created Lava Cast Forest, where visitors may see molds of downed trees and stumps frozen in time when the lava cooled.

Carrying lanterns, visitors may explore 1-mile-long Lava River Cave, which once ran white hot with molten rock. The cave temperature is now a constant 42 degrees, and it's one of the longest lava tubes in Oregon at 5,200 feet long, and 50 feet wide. The ceiling is as much as 60 feet high in places. The cave, with an elevation of 4,500 feet, is located off US. 97 about 12.5 miles south of Bend and 1 mile south of Lava Lands Visitor Center.

Strangely, some of the best recreational opportunities in Central Oregon occur within the often lunarlike surroundings of the 20- by 30-mile-wide Newberry caldera. East and Paulina lakes are home to trophy-size brown and rainbow trout, as well as kokanee and Atlantic salmon. The third largest brown trout in the world, 35-pounds, 8-ounces, came from 1,320-acre Paulina Lake. Seven campgrounds in the crater offer shoreline camping, boat ramps, vault toilets, group camping, and a horse camp with equestrian trails. In winter, the crater is a popular destination for snowmobilers and cross-country skiers. Miles of summer and winter trails run through the Monument to major lava flows and around portions of the crater rim. The northwest border of the Monument is the wild and scenic Deschutes River, where river rafters and kayakers bounce through whitewater rapids formed by narrow channels carved through the lava.

Before the last Ice Age, Mount Newberry formed as a shield-type volcano set apart from the Cascade Range to the west. This peak may have reached a height of 10,000 feet before it collapsed. Now the highest point in the crater is 7,897-foot Paulina Peak.

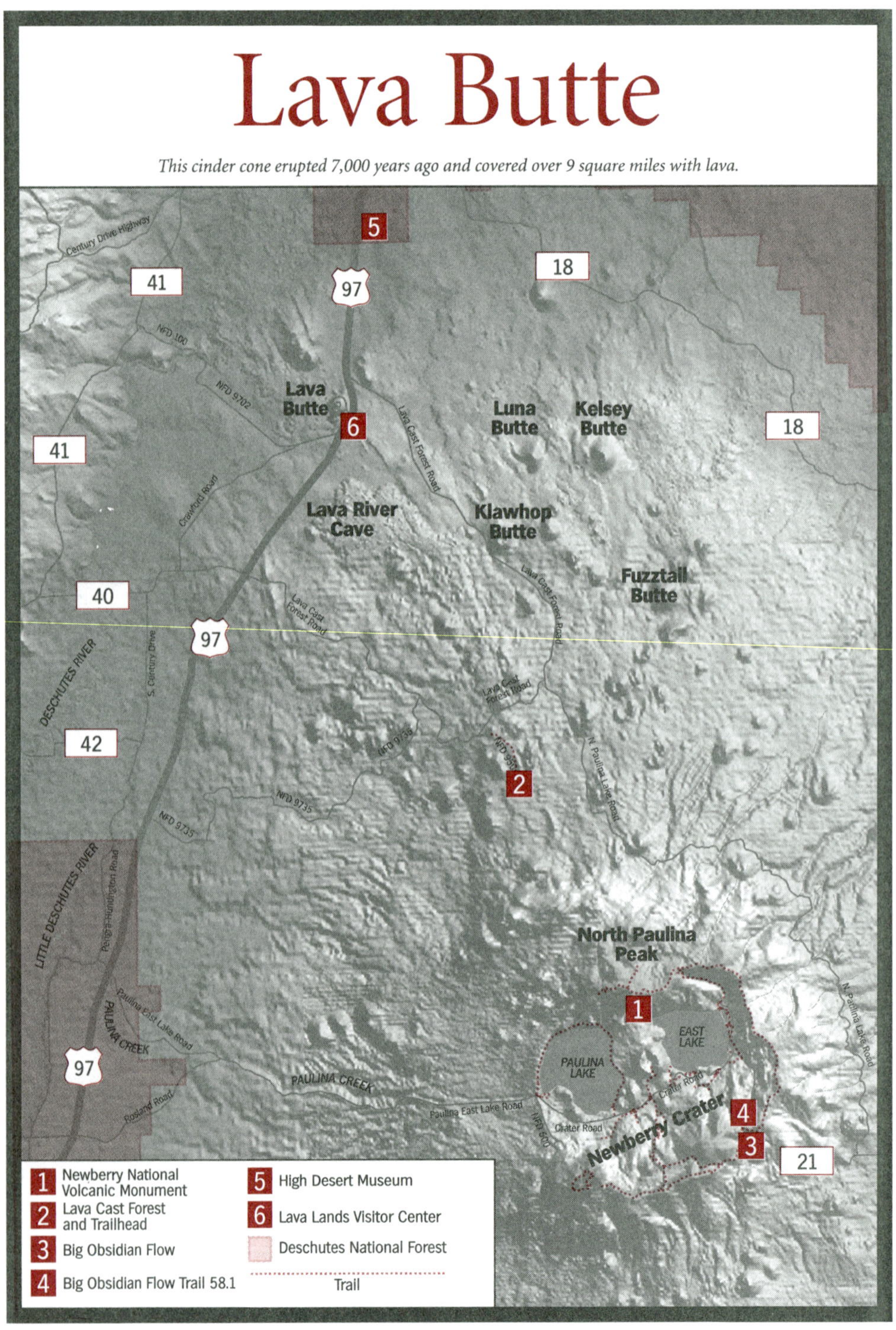
Lava Butte
This cinder cone erupted 7,000 years ago and covered over 9 square miles with lava.
Century Drive Highway
41
97
5
18
NFD 100
NFD 9702
Lava Butte
6
Lava Cast Forest Road
Luna Butte
Kelsey Butte
18
41
Crawford Road
Lava River Cave
Klawhop Butte
Lava Cast Forest Road
Fuzztail Butte
40
Lava Cast Forest Road
97
DESCHUTES RIVER
S. Century Drive
Lava Cast Forest Road
42
NFD 9735
2
N. Paulina Lake Road
NFD 9735
NFD 9735
LITTLE DESCHUTES RIVER
Pengra-Huntington Road
North Paulina Peak
1
EAST LAKE
N. Paulina Lake Road
PAULINA LAKE
Paulina East Lake Road
PAULINA CREEK
97
PAULINA CREEK
Paulina East Lake Road
Crater Road
4
Rosland Road
NFD 500
Crater Road
Newberry Crater
3
21
1 Newberry National Volcanic Monument
2 Lava Cast Forest and Trailhead
3 Big Obsidian Flow
4 Big Obsidian Flow Trail 58.1
5 High Desert Museum
6 Lava Lands Visitor Center
Deschutes National Forest
Trail

The caldera crater is at the top of 500-square-mile Newberry Volcano, a large shield-shaped volcano. The base of the volcano is at an elevation of about 4,400 feet. The mountain is so large and heavy that geologists believe it is has sunk hundreds, perhaps thousands, of feet into the ground. The gentle flanks of Newberry are studded with 400 cinder cones and at least that number of lava flows. Lava Butte (a cinder cone) and its lava flow are part of Newberry. The west and east flanks of Newberry are largely thick deposits of ash with channels, draws, and canyons eroded into them.

The crater is rimmed with steep 700- to 1,700-foot-high walls, except on the west side where Paulina Creek drains Paulina Lake. The floor holds barren obsidian flows, pumice, tuff, and ash covered plains and low cones. The southeast part of the caldera consists of steep slopes and flat, benchlike areas.

Cataclysmic eruptions, beginning 500,000 years ago, exhausted large magma chambers underlying Newberry Volcano. A series of collapses along concentric fractures created Newberry Crater. Small eruptions continued under the lake's surface. By 7,000 years ago, the central pumice cone and several lava flows had broken the surface of the lake and divided the caldera into the two lake basins. Magma is believed to lie about 2 miles under East Lake.

The last major caldera-forming eruption probably occurred about 200,000 years ago, and volcanologists believe that the next volcanic eruption in central Oregon will most likely occur either in Newberry Crater or at Three Sisters.

Deschutes National Forest Service staffs several public information centers for the monument on a seasonal basis. Visitors learn the geology, volcanology and the cultural history of the area at Lava Lands Visitor Center. On top of Lava Butte, a working forest fire lookout is partially open to the public with exhibits on the first floor. The Newberry Crater Information Center provides information about the crater and is operated under a special-use permit.

Directions: From Bend go south on US 97 for 11 miles to Lava Lands Visitor Center.

Facilities: Trails, interpretive centers, campgrounds, marinas, resorts, trails, restrooms, restaurants, boat ramps, and shuttle buses.

Dates: Open year-round. Lava Lands Visitor Center is open Apr.-Oct. Newberry Crater Information Center is open Memorial Day weekend to Labor Day weekend.

Fees: There are charges for admission, trail park passes, camping, and services.

Closest town: Bend.

For more information: Lava Lands Visitor Center, Deschutes National Forest, 58201 Hwy. 97 S., Bend, OR 97707. Phone (541) 593-2421.

LAVA BUTTE

[Fig. 39] Lava Butte rises 500 feet above its namesake, the Lava Lands Visitor Center. This cinder cone erupted 7,000 years ago and covered over 9 square miles with lava. The butte offers a panoramic view of central Oregon including a spectacular view of the Cascade Range and the northwest flank of Newberry. An interpretive trail circles the crater rim. A shuttle bus takes visitors to the top from Memorial Day to Labor Day.

Directions: See directions to Lava Lands Visitor Center under Newberry National Volcanic Monument.

Facilities: Trail, shuttle bus.

Fees: There are charges for entrance and shuttle trips.

LAVA CAST FOREST AND TRAILHEAD

[Fig. 39(2)] The geological area at Lava Cast Forest was established to protect the dozens of lava trees and tree molds that occur in the area. There is a 1 mile paved, self-guided interpretive trail for barrier-free access.

The trail loops through an area where hot molten lava erupted from the northwest flank of Newberry Volcano and engulfed a forest here 7,000 years ago. The landscape now includes the casts, or molds, of these ancient trees. Colonizing plants, such as delicate penstemon flowers and Indian paintbrush, have taken root in the rocky soil. Ponderosa pine trees have re-established so well that the landscape now includes a blend of the past and the present.

Directions: The forest is on Lava Cast Forest Flow in Newberry National Volcanic Monument, 14.8 miles south of Bend on Hwy. 97, then 8.6 miles east on Forest Service 9720, and then 0.7 mile south on Forest Service 9720-950.

Activities: Walking through a forest of lava-encased tree molds.

Facilities: Vault toilet, paved interpretive trail.

Dates: Open year-round.

Fees: There are charges for trail park passes.

Trail: 1 mile, one-way

Elevation: 5,750 feet at trailhead.

BIG OBSIDIAN FLOW

[Fig. 39(3)] The youngest dated volcanic feature in central Oregon and on Newberry Volcano is the Big Obsidian Flow, which is only 1,300 years old.

The volume of rock that was erupted at the Big Obsidian Lava Flow is 170 million cubic yards, enough to pave 70,000 miles of road 24 feet wide and 6 inches thick, circling the world three times. It would take a 10-cubic-yard dump truck, arriving every minute, 80 years to haul away the 416 million cubic yards of airfall pumice that was erupted from the Big Obsidian vent in only a few days.

Astronaut R. Walter Cunningham tested the mobility of a moon suit here in 1964.

Even stranger, every August the Obsidian Flow crawls with thousands of frogs. At times, it's hard to walk without stepping on one. Naturalists believe the frogs migrate up the flow from Lost Lake, like lemmings, but the reason the frogs do this is not clear.

Directions: From US 97 24 miles south of Bend, go east on Road 21 toward Paulina Lake Resort. Continue on Road 21 around the south side of Newberry Crater. The trail starts at Obsidian Flow Parking Lot.

Activities: Hiking.

Facilities: Interpretive trail with information signs.

Dates: Open year-round, but the road is not plowed during winter.

Fees: There are charges for trail park passes.

Closest town: Bend.

For more information: Lava Lands Visitor Center, 58201 Highway 97 South, Bend, OR 97707. Phone (541) 592-2421.

BIG OBSIDIAN FLOW TRAIL 58.1

[Fig. 39(4)] Seven interpretive signs are stationed along the trail explaining the geologic features of the unusual black glass of obsidian. The path is closed to bicycles and horses. The trailhead is east of Paulina Lake Resort on Road 21 at the south side of Newberry Crater.

Trail: 0.8 mile loop

Elevation: Trailhead is at 6,420 feet rising to 6,560 feet.

Degree of difficulty: Easy.

Surface: Crushed lava.

High Desert Museum

[Fig. 39(5)] Possibly the most informative two hours that travelers can spend in the East Slope Region is at the High Desert Museum outside of Bend. This nationally acclaimed nonprofit museum blends dioramas, live attractions, photography, cultural exhibits, and Indian artifacts into one of the most unusual and informative attractions in Oregon.

Located on the south outskirts of Bend, High Desert Museum includes daily presentations involving live otters, porcupines and birds of prey. There are 20 acres of nature trail and exhibits that include pioneer history and homesteads, a working sawmill, and extensive collections of western and wildlife art.

The indoor "Desertarium" showcases bats, kangaroo rats, and burrowing owls.

Directions: Go 3.5 miles south from Bend on US 97.

Activities: Museum tours and participatory presentations of nature, art, science, and history.

Facilities: The museum, 20 acres of trails and exhibits, cafe.

Dates: Open daily 9-5, year-round

Fees: There is a charge for admission.

Closest town: Bend.

For more information: High Desert Museum, 59800 S. Highway 97, Bend, OR 97702. Phone (541) 382-4754. Web site: www.highdesert.org.

BLACK-BILLED MAGPIE (*Pika pika*)

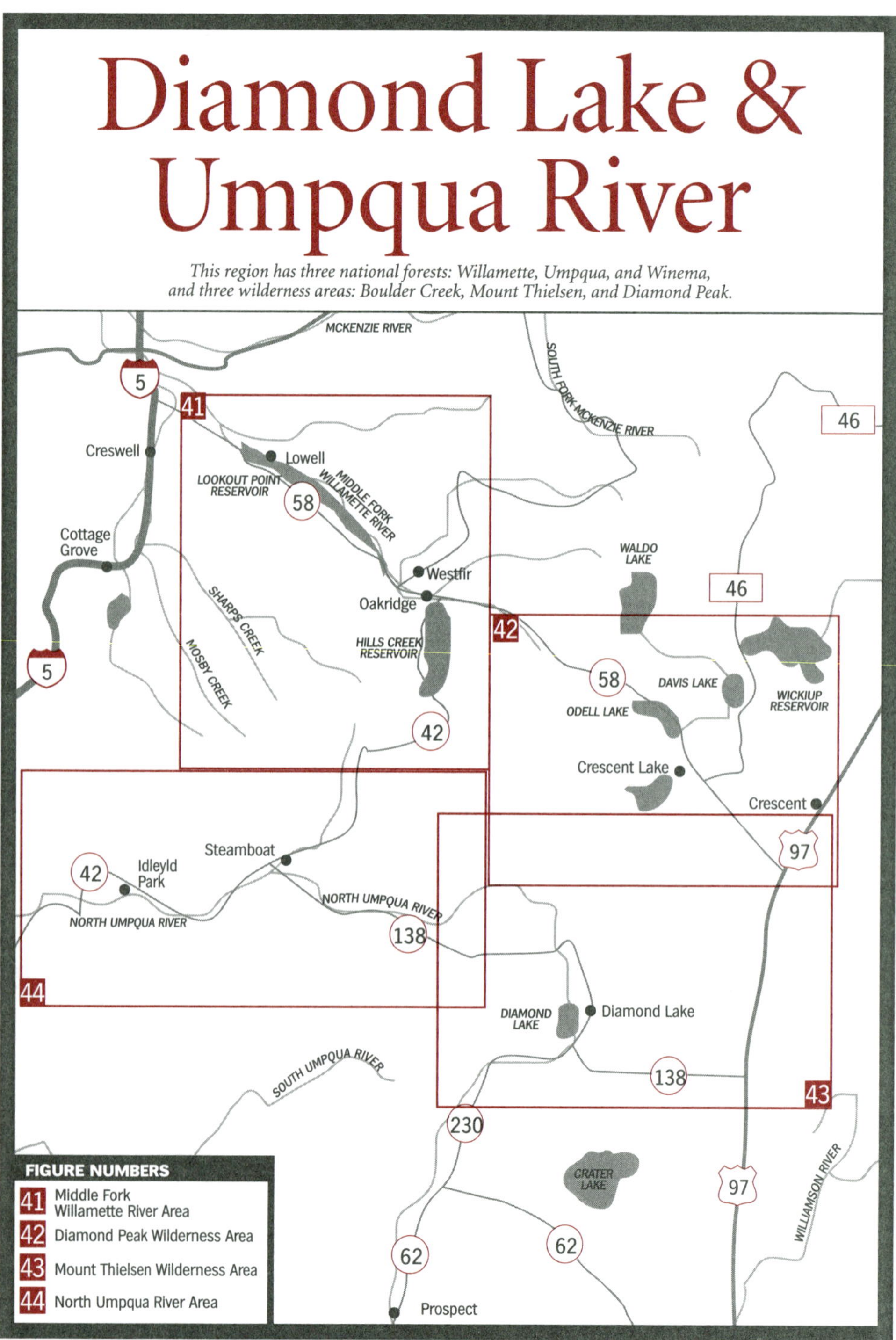
Diamond Lake &
Umpqua River
This region has three national forests: Willamette, Umpqua, and Winema, and three wilderness areas: Boulder Creek, Mount Thielsen, and Diamond Peak.
MCKENZIE RIVER
SOUTH FORK MCKENZIE RIVER
5
41
46
Creswell
Lowell
LOOKOUT POINT RESERVOIR
MIDDLE FORK WILLAMETTE RIVER
58
Cottage Grove
WALDO LAKE
Westfir
46
Oakridge
SHARPS CREEK
MOSBY CREEK
HILLS CREEK RESERVOIR
42
58
DAVIS LAKE
WICKIUP RESERVOIR
ODELL LAKE
42
Crescent Lake
Crescent
97
Steamboat
42
Idleyld Park
NORTH UMPQUA RIVER
NORTH UMPQUA RIVER
138
44
DIAMOND LAKE
Diamond Lake
SOUTH UMPQUA RIVER
138
43
230
CRATER LAKE
97
WILLIAMSON RIVER
62
62
Prospect
FIGURE NUMBERS
41 Middle Fork Willamette River Area
42 Diamond Peak Wilderness Area
43 Mount Thielsen Wilderness Area
44 North Umpqua River Area

Diamond Peak/ Umpqua River Region

The bloodlines of fire and ice that flow through the geological history of central Oregon's Cascade Range are very evident in the primitive, sometimes harsh, landscape formed from rock and water within the Diamond Peak/Umpqua River region.

Most of this mountainous region is rugged, lightly treaded forest, in a mix of extinct volcanoes and deep river valleys, lying mostly west of the Cascade Crest.

The north boundary is formed by OR 58. The south edge starts at a jagged 9,182-foot elevation summit of Mount Thielsen. The southern borderline is formed by the seemingly never-ending curves of OR 138 and the North Umpqua River.

This region has many distinctive natural features. Few attractions, however, are as well-known or revered as the North Umpqua River, a federally designated wild and scenic waterway. The water, clear and cold in the upper section, plunges along the highway like a glitter-spackled ribbon that connects a stairway of steps formed of deep, green pools and

[*Above:* Visitors may spot osprey nests along the North Umpqua River]

powerful, churning rapids. The river is lined by water-smoothed walls of black basalt and towers of Douglas fir and western red cedar. The river so stirs the imaginations of regional writers that its description as "holy water" has become cliché. Western novelist Zane Grey, an unabashed fishing enthusiast, first fished the North Umpqua in 1932 and was so enchanted that he immediately closed his famous fishing and writing camp at Winkler Bar on the Rogue River and relocated on the North Umpqua near Steamboat Creek.

It was the last place the globe-trotting author would ever fish.

On a summer day in 1937, Grey fished the North Umpqua during the cool of the morning. When the sun reached the water, he retired to a lounge chair overlooking the river, and suffered an apparent stroke. Grey was transported to his California home and died two years later.

Today, the North Umpqua continues to be revered as the holy water of Northwest summer-run steelhead fly-fishing. Yet fishing is only one of the attractions. In the summer, more than a dozen guides and outfitters run whitewater raft and kayak trips on the North Umpqua; campers select sites from a dozen riverside campgrounds; and mountain bikers and hikers explore the 79 miles of trail that follow every twist and turn of the river. In the fall, river camps accommodate elk and deer hunters, and mushroom gatherers.

Between the North Umpqua River and Oakridge are the Calapooya Mountains; four major lakes with large campground complexes; Diamond Drive, a mostly paved, lightly traveled scenic road along the Middle Fork Willamette River; and dozens of waterfalls, resorts, volcanic pinnacles, and remote places with names like Scared Man Creek.

In the mountains south of Oakridge is Indigo Springs, where five natural springs break out of the mountainside at an easy-to-miss three-site campground. The springs immediately blend into a stream that flows though the flickering shadow light of a woodsy cathedral canopied by giant cedars. The 38-degree water gushes through clusters of deer (*Blechnum spicant*) and northern maidenhair (*Adiantum pedatum*) ferns, and pours across red cedar logs in tiny waterfalls so pure, clear, and cold that they chill the summer air. Longtime local camper Roger Perkins unabashedly proclaims that Indigo Springs "has the best tasting water in the world," and few who fill water jugs here will argue.

This region occupies a geographic elbow where forest management is shared by Willamette, Umpqua, and Winema national forests and includes three wilderness areas: Boulder Creek, Mount Thielsen and Diamond Peak.

Hundreds of miles of hiking and mountain biking trails are etched into the mountains and river valleys affording trail lovers a variety of topographies, climates, seasons, and degrees of difficulty.

The arterial high route is Pacific Crest National Scenic Trail 2000, which weaves through the volcanic peaks in the west side of the region. A summer route, PCT 2000 connects the mountainous high points of the region. South of Crescent Lake it crosses the remote and little-known Oregon Cascades Recreation Area.

In topographical contrast, Fall Creek National Recreation Trail provides a low elevation year-round hiking route through old-growth Douglas fir, oxalis, and northern maidenhair ferns. Fall Creek NRT is about 30 miles east of Eugene east of Fall Creek Reservoir.

In contrast to the two extremes is the North Umpqua Trail, which tracks the North Umpqua River for 79 miles from the near-sea level lowlands at the community of Glide to an elevation of 6,000 feet at Maidu Lake.

The region grows a mix of conifer and deciduous trees. The moist, west slopes are heavily forested mostly with Douglas fir, western red cedar, and huckleberries. The lower river valleys grow bigleaf maples, cottonwoods, alders, dogwoods, rhododendrons, Oregon ash, white oaks, vine maples, and ponderosa pine. From the crest of the Cascade east, the forest is primarily a mix of mountain hemlock, lodgepole pine, Douglas fir, and mountain junipers. This is also mushroom country.

The Odell Lake area is well-known for its Matsutake mushrooms (*Armillarria ponderosa*), as well as black morels (*Morchella elata*), yellow chanterelles (*Cantharellus cibarius*), and shaggy manes (*Coprinus camatus*). Because of this, the area attracts armies of mycologists and commercial pickers in the fall. Competition for mushrooms is uncommonly fierce here and pickers—both commercial and amateur—are secretive and protective. Periods of abundance vary according to the type of mushroom, amount of rain, and elevation of the growing areas.

Poisonous mushrooms can be found in this area, especially the gilled species that are usually umbrella shaped. Although dozens of edible mushrooms grow in the Northwest, and varieties of most of them are found in this region, the region also includes the deadly poisonous members of the amanita family. Death cup (*Amanita phalloides*), panther (*Amanita pantherina*) destroying angel (*Amanita ocreata*), and fly (*Amanita muscaria*) are common. For current mushroom information check at a ranger district office.

Willamette National Forest

FALL CREEK NATIONAL RECREATION TRAIL

[Fig. 5, Fig. 41(1)] This nationally recognized 14-mile long hiker-only trail follows Fall Creek through the kind of low-elevation topography 30 miles east of Eugene that typifies many river valleys in western Oregon. The trail is framed by an understory of dogwood, alder, vine maple and bigleaf maples, and a canopy of western hemlock, red cedar and 500-year-old Douglas fir. It's a fairly level, streamside route with an elevation change of only 425 feet and can be hiked in segments accessible from Forest Service Road 18.

Most of the trail is snow-free year-round, and there are attractions for every season. Fall brings mycologists on the hunt for edible mushrooms, in the winter muddy hikers enjoy cold, wet, but deep solitude, spring produces waves of wildflowers including shade-loving bleeding hearts (*Dicentra formosa*). The trail is best known for cool escape during the summer months. There are carpets of shamrock-like oxalis (*Oxalis oregana*) and a

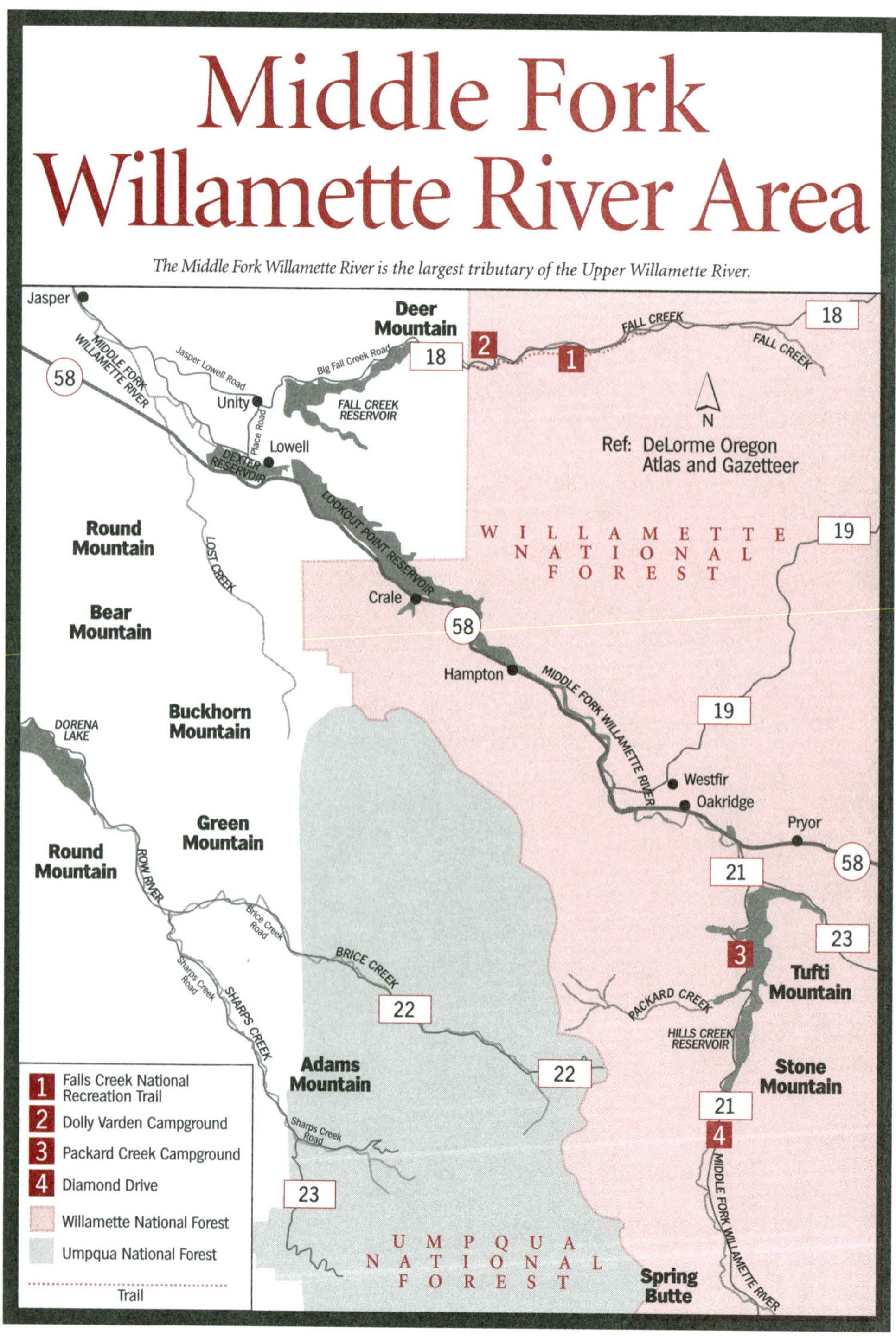
Middle Fork
Willamette River Area
The Middle Fork Willamette River is the largest tributary of the Upper Willamette River.
Jasper
Deer Mountain
MIDDLE FORK WILLAMETTE RIVER
Jasper Lowell Road
Big Fall Creek Road
FALL CREEK
58
18
Unity
FALL CREEK RESERVOIR
Place Road
Lowell
DEXTER RESERVOIR
LOOKOUT POINT RESERVOIR
N
Ref: DeLorme Oregon Atlas and Gazetteer
W I L L A M E T T E
N A T I O N A L
F O R E S T
19
Round Mountain
LOST CREEK
Bear Mountain
Crale
Hampton
Buckhorn Mountain
DORENA LAKE
Westfir
Oakridge
Pryor
Green Mountain
Round Mountain
ROW RIVER
21
23
Brice Creek Road
BRICE CREEK
Tufti Mountain
Sharps Creek Road
SHARPS CREEK
PACKARD CREEK
22
HILLS CREEK RESERVOIR
Adams Mountain
Stone Mountain
1 Falls Creek National Recreation Trail
2 Dolly Varden Campground
3 Packard Creek Campground
4 Diamond Drive
Willamette National Forest
Umpqua National Forest
Trail
U M P Q U A
N A T I O N A L
F O R E S T
Spring Butte

parade of backpackers and swimmers.

Nearby nature trails with interpretive stations are at Clark and Johnny Creeks. The 0.5 mile Johnny Creek Nature Trail is paved and wheelchair accessible and is reached by driving east on Forest Service 18, paralleling Fall Creek to Forest Service Road 1821, where there is a large parking area with picnic tables and restrooms.

A 51-acre old-growth grove of Douglas fir, hemlock and cedar is on the upper end of the trail near Marine Creek.

Directions: Take the Lowell exit from OR 58. Drive about 12 miles and turn right on Jasper Lowell Road to Unity Bridge. Turn right on Place Rd. (Forest Service 18) and head towards the dam. Stay to the left and drive about 8 miles to Dolly Varden campground, where the trail begins.

Activities: Hiking, camping, fishing, mushroom gathering, wildflower and wildlife watching.

Facilities: Developed Forest Service campgrounds are at Dolly Varden, Big Pool, Broken Bowl, Clark Creek, and Bedrock.

Dates: Open mid-June through fall months, depending on weather and trail conditions. Call Middle Fork Ranger District for update.

Fees: There is a charge for trail park passes.

Closest town: Lowell.

For more information: Middle Fork Ranger District, Willamette National Forest, 60 South Pioneer Street, Lowell, OR 97452. Phone (541) 937-2129.

Trail: 14 miles one-way.

Elevation: Trailhead is 960 feet elevation; high point is 1,385 feet.

Degree of difficulty: Easy.

Surface: Dirt.

DOLLY VARDEN CAMPGROUND

[Fig. 41(2)] This small streamside campground is a base camp for hikers and mountain bikers heading east on Fall Creek National Recreation Trail. The trailhead is at the south edge of the campground. This is also a point for anglers looking to fish Fall Creek's rainbow and cutthroat trout.

Directions: See Fall Creek National Recreation Trail directions.

Activities: Camping, hiking, fishing, seasonal mushroom gathering, and wildlife observation.

Facilities: Tent sites, restroom, fire pits; no water or hookups.

Dates: Open May-Sept.

Fees: There is a charge for campsites.

HILLS CREEK RESERVOIR

[Fig. 41] Hills Creek Reservoir is a popular summer and winter recreation site about 3 miles southeast of Oakridge. This big lake's west shore is followed by the north segment of Diamond Drive/Forest Service Road 21, a scenic route into a vast area along the wild and scenic Middle Fork Willamette River (*see* Diamond Drive, page 263). It's a favorite route for mountain biking, hiking, fishing, and fall deer and elk hunting.

The reservoir is formed by a 304-foot high dam across the Middle Fork just south of OR 58. The 7.6 mile long, 2,735-acre lake fills a narrow canyon with aqua-colored water impounded for flood control by the U.S. Army Corps of Engineers. The corps manages the lake and Willamette National Forest operates the lakeside campgrounds and picnic areas.

Hills Creek Reservoir is only 45 miles southeast of Eugene, and is very popular with summer boaters, water skiers, fishermen, and campers. The lake is at an elevation of about 1,500 feet in a valley that is protected from severe winter weather. Because of the moderate weather, Hills Creek Reservoir has earned a statewide reputation for good winter rainbow trout fishing.

Summer, however, also produces good fishing and boating opportunities.

Three boat ramps, two Forest Service campgrounds, and two picnic areas are scattered at intervals along the southwest side of the lake. The largest campground is Packard Creek Campground at mid-lake.

Directions: Drive 3 miles east of Oakridge on OR 58 to a right (east) turn onto County Road 6178/Kitson Springs Road and cross Salt Creek. Continue north on County Road 6178 to C. T. Beach Picnic Area and a spillway viewpoint, or turn south onto Diamond Drive/Forest Service 21 and continue to the campgrounds and picnic areas on the west shore.

Activities: Camping, fishing, water skiing, boating, swimming, and picnicking.

Facilities: Forest Service Campgrounds at Packard Creek and Sand Prairie; picnic areas at C. T. Beach and Cline-Clark near Larison Creek; boat launches at C. T. Beach, Packard CG, and Bingham Boat Ramp at the upper end of the lake; 2 dam viewpoints.

Dates: Open year-round.

Fees: There are fees for campsites and trail park passes.

Closest town: Oakridge is 3 miles west on OR 58.

For more information: Middle Fork Ranger Station, Willamette National Forest, 49098 Salmon Creek Road, PO 1410, Oakridge, OR 97463. Phone (541) 782-2283. In Summer/Fall 2000, Middle Fork Ranger District office will be located at 46375 Hwy 58, Westfir, OR 97492. Call to confirm new mailing address. U.S. Army Corps of Engineers, PO Box 2946, Portland, OR 97208-2946. Phone (503) 808-5150.

PACKARD CREEK CAMPGROUND

[Fig. 41(3)] Packard Creek Campground is the main overnight facility on Hills Creek Lake, and a center for boating activity. It is located at about mid-lake on the west shore.

Directions: The campground is entered from Diamond Drive/Forest Service 21 on the west side of Hills Creek Lake about 4 miles south of the dam.

Activities: Camping, boating, picnicking, swimming, fishing, hiking, and water skiing.

Facilities: 33 tent and RV sites, potable water, tables and fire rings, wheelchair-accessible restrooms, boat ramp, 5 picnic sites, group picnic area with shelter.

Dates: Open Apr. through Oct.

Fees: There are charges for campsites and trail park passes.

OREGON CENTRAL MILITARY WAGON ROAD

[Fig. 42(1)] At the south end of Hills Creek Lake, the remnants of the 1865 Oregon Central Military Wagon Road disappear under the impounded reservoir after following the Middle Fork Willamette River north for about 33 miles.

The road is a protected archaeological site, preserving the tracks of this cross-Cascade route built by a group of Eugene investors who hoped to link the upper Willamette Valley with the east part of the state.

The wagon road was maintained until the 1930s, and roughly follows the route of Diamond Drive/Forest Service 21 from Sand Prairie campground on Hills Creek Lake upstream on the Middle Fork Willamette River to Emigrant Pass at Summit Lake. Sections of the original road are visible along Diamond Drive at Rigdon Meadows, Indigo Springs, Beaver Creek and Alpine Lake.

Directions: Follow Diamond Drive/Forest Service 21 south along Hills Creek Lake to Sand Prairie Campground.

Activities: Historical sight-seeing.

Dates: Open year-round.

Fees: None.

DIAMOND DRIVE/FOREST SERVICE ROAD 21

[Fig. 41(4)] Diamond Drive/Forest Service 21 cuts a lightly traveled route through history, wildlife, and campgrounds in the backcountry of the Oregon Cascades between OR 58 at Oakridge and OR 138 near Diamond Lake.

Most travelers use busy US 97 between OR 58 and OR 138. Few, it seems, are even aware of the 60-mile scenic shortcut offered by Diamond Drive during the summer. The route is closed by snow from about November to June.

The drive is far enough from the beaten path to permit leisurely stops, lonesome camping, decent fishing, and an occasional glimpse of wildlife. This is definitely the road less traveled. Wildlife common to this area are Roosevelt elk, black-tailed deer, black bear, coyotes, several varieties of grouse, and many songbirds. The river attracts waterfowl, including the nesting harlequin duck (*Histrionicus histrionicus*), an uncommon seabird that ranges inland to breed and nest on fast, rocky rivers.

The route follows the Middle Fork Willamette River, a wild and scenic waterway, through the Calapooya Mountains, a range named for the Kalapuya Indians, who are believed to be the earliest human inhabitants of this region.

Elevations along the route vary from 1,200 to 5,400 feet. The entire route is paved, except for 18 graveled miles in Paddy's Valley and the Summit Lake area. There are no traveler services, including gas, on the route.

Overnight visitors have six Forest Service campgrounds, and a fire lookout tower on

Warner Mountain to select from.

Directions: From I-5 to the north entry, head east from Eugene on OR 58 for 37 miles, through Oakridge to Hills Creek Lake turnoff at Forest Service Road 21. To reach the south entry, go 73 miles east from I-5 at Roseburg on OR 138 and turn north onto Diamond Drive at Forest Service 2610 south of Lemolo Lake.

Activities: Sight-seeing, camping, river fishing, hiking, mountain biking, and hunting for grouse, deer, elk and bear.

Facilities: 6 Forest Service campgrounds are between Hills Creek Lake and Lemolo Lake, and a Forest Service fire lookout tower on Warner Mountain is available for nightly rentals during winter. Inquire at the Middle Fork Ranger Station. Well water is available at Sand Prairie, Campers Flat and Timpangos campgrounds, and potable spring water at Indigo Springs. Sacandaga Campground, with 17 forested sites, is the largest camping area south of Hills Creek Lake, but had no water in Fall of 1999. A new well is being built.

Dates: The road is closed by snow from Nov. to June.

Fees: There is a charge for camping and for trail park passes.

Closest town: Oakridge on OR 58, and Chemult on US 97. Groceries, gasoline and other traveler services are available at Diamond Lake.

For more information: Middle Fork Ranger Station, Willamette National Forest, 49098 Salmon Creek Road, Oakridge, OR 97463. Phone (541) 782-2283. In Summer/Fall 2000, Middle Fork Ranger District office will be located at 46375 Hwy 58, Westfir, OR 97492. Call to confirm new mailing address. Diamond Lake Information Center, Rural Station, Chemult, OR 97731. Phone (541) 793-3310.

MIDDLE FORK WILLAMETTE RIVER

[Fig. 41] The largest tributary of the Upper Willamette River, the wild and scenic Middle Fork is paralleled, usually at a short distance, by Diamond Drive, which provides excellent access for fishermen trying for the mountain river's plentiful rainbow and cutthroat trout.

The river begins on the spine of the Cascades near Timpanogas Lake and flows north into Hills Creek Lake at Oakridge before turning west toward the Willamette Valley.

This is a sprightly river averaging about 75 feet wide that flows easily between stretches of deep pools, long tailouts and rapids. Middle Fork Trail 3609 follows the river between Sand Prairie and Timpanogas Lake.

Directions: Accessible at many points south of Oakridge from Diamond Drive/Forest Service Road 21.

Activities: Hiking, mountain biking, horseback riding, fishing, camping, and hunting.

Facilities: None.

Dates: Open year-round. Fishing is allowed from the fourth Saturday in Apr. through Oct. 31.

Fees: There is a charge for trail park passes.

MIDDLE FORK TRAIL 3609

[Fig. 42(2)] This year-round trail seems to have something for everybody. It parallels the bank of the Middle Fork Willamette River for 27 miles from a trailhead at Sand Prairie Campground above Hills Creek Lake at Oakridge, then going south to Timpanogas Lake. The trail closely follows the gradient of the river on a gentle rolling course with gradual elevation changes. Many access points are marked on the shoulder of Diamond Drive. Expect to share the trail with backpackers, day hikers, fishermen, mountain bikers and horseback riders. The upper segments of the trail are downright lonesome.

Elk and deer are often seen in the forests of mixed conifers, cottonwoods, and bigleaf maples. This is a spring calving and summer grazing area for elk, which usually migrate down river valleys to the western foothills when snow forces them out of this high country.

Elk (*Cervus elaphus*) are the largest wild animal in Oregon. They commonly stand 5 feet high at the shoulder, and can be almost 10 feet from nose to tail. A large bull will weigh more than 1,000 pounds, but most weigh from 500 to 700 pounds.

In September and October, the breeding season, these hills ring with the melodious bugle call of bulls trying to attract cows to their harems and discourage rival bulls. Most of the bugling takes place at night or shortly after daylight.

Directions: Trailheads are at Sand Prairie Campground south of Hills Creek Lake and Timpanogas Lake north of Lemolo Lake. The trail can be divided into comfortable day-hike segments.

Activities: Hiking.

Facilities: 6 campgrounds on Diamond Drive are accessible from the trail.

Dates: Open year-round, higher elevations are snow covered from Nov. to June.

Fees: There is a charge for trail park passes.

Trail: 27 miles one-way, with a gradual elevation change.

Elevation: The north trailhead is at 2,000 feet and the south is at 5,300 feet. Changes are gradual.

Degree of difficulty: Easy hiking in segments, but to hike the entire trail would be strenuous.

Surface: Dirt and rock.

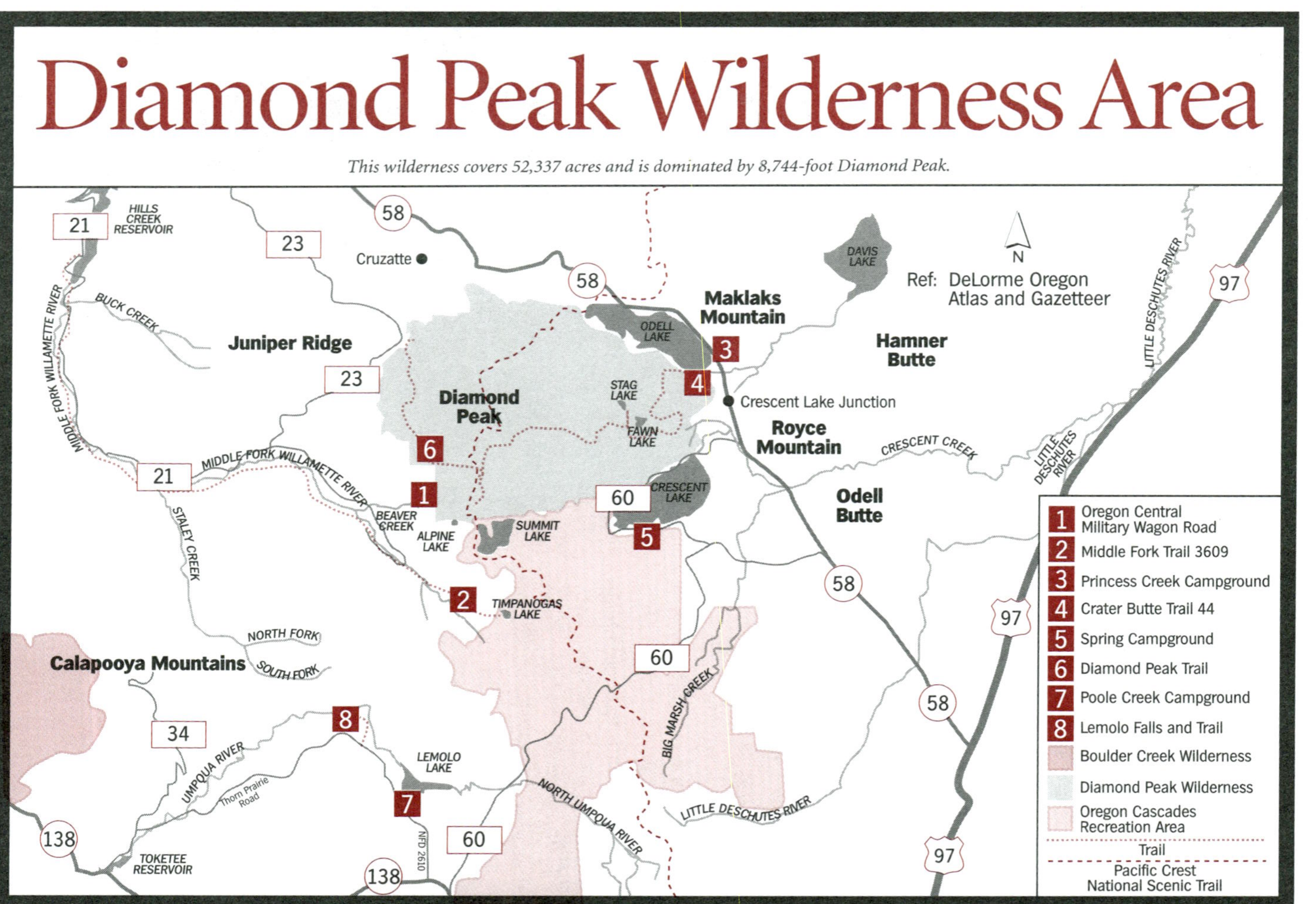
Diamond Peak Wilderness Area
This wilderness covers 52,337 acres and is dominated by 8,744-foot Diamond Peak.
HILLS CREEK RESERVOIR
21
23
58
Cruzatte
N
Ref: DeLorme Oregon Atlas and Gazetteer
DAVIS LAKE
97
LITTLE DESCHUTES RIVER
BUCK CREEK
Juniper Ridge
MIDDLE FORK WILLAMETTE RIVER
Maklaks Mountain
ODELL LAKE
Hamner Butte
Diamond Peak
STAG LAKE
FAWN LAKE
Crescent Lake Junction
Royce Mountain
CRESCENT CREEK
CRESCENT LAKE
Odell Butte
60
BEAVER CREEK
ALPINE LAKE
SUMMIT LAKE
STALEY CREEK
TIMPANOGAS LAKE
NORTH FORK
SOUTH FORK
Calapooya Mountains
BIG MARSH CREEK
34
UMPQUA RIVER
Thorn Prairie Road
LEMOLO LAKE
NORTH UMPQUA RIVER
LITTLE DESCHUTES RIVER
138
TOKETEE RESERVOIR
NFD 2610
1 Oregon Central Military Wagon Road
2 Middle Fork Trail 3609
3 Princess Creek Campground
4 Crater Butte Trail 44
5 Spring Campground
6 Diamond Peak Trail
7 Poole Creek Campground
8 Lemolo Falls and Trail
Boulder Creek Wilderness
Diamond Peak Wilderness
Oregon Cascades Recreation Area
Trail
Pacific Crest National Scenic Trail

DIAMOND PEAK WILDERNESS

[Fig. 42] Covering 52,337 acres of the southern Willamette and Deschutes national forests, Diamond Peak Wilderness straddles the crest of the Oregon Cascades in a heavily forested region dominated by the ragged, snow-encrusted summit of 8,744-foot elevation Diamond Peak.

OR 58 passes the north side of the wilderness and is the most convenient jumping-off point for backpackers, hikers, fishermen, and hunters. Most of the popular entrances are east of Willamette Pass from roads and trails in the Odell and Crescent lakes region. The southern boundary of the wilderness is formed by a rough, heavily rutted dirt road about 8 miles long that divides the wilderness area from the even more remote Oregon Cascades Recreation Area (*see* page 274). The dividing road is identified as Forest Service 6010, which connects the west end of Crescent Lake with Summit Lake and Diamond Drive (*see* Diamond Drive, page 263). Forest Service 6010 is recommended for all-wheel drive, high-clearance vehicles only.

A network of maintained hiking and horse trails leads to most of the wilderness area's outstanding attractions. All vehicles, including mountain bikes, are not allowed on wilderness trails. The remote area's major trail is a 14-mile segment of Pacific Crest Trail 2000, which follows a north-south route along the east side of Diamond Peak between Summit Lake and Willamette Pass.

Lost Wagon Train

The Odell-Crescent lakes area was almost the tragic final resting place for the legendary "lost wagon train" that left Allegheny City, Pennsylvania, for the Oregon Territory in 1853.

It's also a testimonial to pioneer fortitude and determination.

In October, the wandering wagon train rumbled westward from the hot desert south of Bend hoping to cross the Cascades into the Willamette Valley before winter. The road the pioneers expected to find going west from Crescent Lake, however, didn't exist.

Keeping Diamond Peak on their left, the determined pioneers plotted, chopped, and filled a rough road for the wagons to the summit at Willamette Pass. Again, they expected a road, and instead found a sea of densely packed conifers that seemed to extend to the ocean. At the end of October, with the first ghostly snows of winter falling into the evening campfires, they stopped. A scout was sent ahead, and days later returned with rescuers from the Willamette Valley. Some wagons were abandoned, household goods jettisoned, and the remaining wagons were practically willed through the forest in the natural lanes opened by Salt Creek and Middle Fork Willamette River.

According to historians, the remainders of the wagon train were forced to ford the swift, rocky streams 27 times on the descent before reaching what is now the community of Lowell.

The west side of the wilderness is crossed by Diamond Peak Trail 3699, a 10.3 mile dirt route around the west shoulder of Diamond Peak. Spur trails lead from Trail 3699 to the summit.

Most of this wilderness area is covered by mixed stands of mountain hemlock, lodgepole and western pine, and silver, noble and Douglas firs. Elevations vary from 4,790 to 8,744 feet, and wildflowers run strongly to alpine varieties such as lupine (*Lupinus species*), mountain monkeyflower (*Mimulus tilingii*), penstemon (*Penstemon davidsonii*), red heather (*Phylodoce empetriformus*) and Indian paintbrush (*Castillia hispida*) Wiry 30-inch high stalks of beargrass (*Xerophyllum tenax*) jut above the low heather and are easily identified by their single cottonlike creamy white bloom.

Wildlife is plentiful. The high-mountain forests and meadows are popular summer ranges for black-tailed and mule deer and elk. In winter this area is locked in 15 to 25 feet of snow, and the mule deer herds migrate east into the sage desert. Blacktails and elk prefer forested areas with grassy meadows and thick brush habitats and head for the West Slope to winter ranges below the snowline, generally under 2,000 feet elevation. Deer and elk are favorite prey for large predators such as cougars, bobcats, and coyotes, which follow the herds into the lower elevations. Black bears hibernate and most small mammals, such as marmots, snowshoe hares, squirrels, pine martens, and conies, stay year-round.

The most popular area in the wilderness is a collection of lakes near Diamond Peak. Campsites at Marie, Divide and Rockpile lakes are used as bases by summit climbers, and destination sites for backpackers. Compared with most other wilderness areas, however, Diamond Peak Wilderness is lightly visited, and is a favorite destination for solitude lovers.

Diamond Peak, 8,744 elevation, is the dominant geological feature. It's a massive extinct volcano on the southwest side of the wilderness. The white streaks of permanent snowpacks and dozens of small lakes that surround the peak were formed by glaciers that gouged out the rugged, rocky face of this landmark peak.

Directions: Several trailheads lead into Diamond Peak Wilderness from OR 58 in the Willamette Pass, Odell-Crescent lakes areas, and from Diamond Drive/Forest Service 21. A rough dirt road, Forest Service 6010, crosses the southern edge of the wilderness between OR 58 and Diamond Drive at Crescent and Summit lakes. Summit Lake, elevation 5,553 feet, is a favorite access point to Pacific Crest Trail 2000.

Activities: Camping, hiking, horseback riding, fishing, hunting, mountain and rock climbing, wildlife sight-seeing.

Facilities: None.

Dates: Open year-round, but trails are snow-free only June through Oct.

Fees: None, but from June 15 through Nov. 15, wilderness access permits are required, and are self-issued at trailhead dispensers.

Closest town: Oakridge is about 30 miles west on OR 57.

For more information: Middle Fork Ranger Station, Willamette National Forest, 49098 Salmon Creek Road, PO Box 1410, Oakridge, OR 97464. Phone (541) 782-2283. In Summer/ Fall 2000, Middle Fork Ranger District office will be located at 46375 Hwy 58, Westfir, OR

97492. Call to confirm new mailing address. Crescent Ranger District, Deschutes National Forest, PO Box 208 Crescent, OR 97733. Phone (541) 433-2234.

DIAMOND PEAK TRAIL 3699

[Fig. 42(6)] Trail 3699 is the main north-south trail on the west side of Diamond Peak Wilderness, and the best route to Happy, Blue, and Corrigan lakes, Diamond Rockpile, Pioneer Gulch, Bear Mountain and several popular climbing routes to the top of Diamond Peak.

Directions: From Oakridge, go south past Hills Creek Reservoir on Diamond Drive for 32 miles. Turn east on Forest Service 2154, go 5 miles and turn left onto 2160. Continue about 1.5 miles. Turn right on Road 380 and proceed 0.5 mile to the trailhead.

Activities: Hiking.

Dates: Open year-round; recommended use, July through Oct.

Fees: None. Wilderness use permit dispenser at trailhead.

Trail: 10.3 miles one-way.

Elevation: From 4,700 feet to 6,000 feet.

Degree of difficulty: Strenuous.

Surface: Forest duff, dirt, and rock.

DIAMOND PEAK

[Fig. 4(2)] While travelers on OR 58 sometimes claim to see the faint resemblance to a rough-cut diamond in the elongated summit of Diamond Peak, the mountain is actually named for pioneer explorer John Diamond, who scaled the peak in 1852.

Diamond was a settler in the Coburg area of the Willamette Valley, and was working with a party of road builders building a wagon route from the Willamette Valley to Idaho. He climbed the peak to look for the easiest route through the mountains, and from the summit saw Diamond Lake about 30 miles south. Diamond gave his name to both peak and lake.

The basaltic andesite shield volcano is believed to have last erupted 100,000 years ago and to now be extinct. Diamond Peak is 8,744 feet elevation, and is the major geologic feature visible from OR 58 south of Willamette Pass. It's also the dominant feature of Diamond Peak Wilderness.

Diamond Peak has a central pyroclastic cone surrounded by hardened lava flows. Permanent snow fields, remnants of a glacial period that ended 11,000 years ago, streak the summit year-round. Dozens of alpine lakes, some less than an acre and the largest 28 acres in size, surround the peak and were gouged into the rocks by the retreating glaciers.

The summit is usually reached from the south ridge by climbers who hike into the wilderness on Diamond Peak Trail 3699 or Pacific Crest Trail 2000. It is not considered a difficult climb, but there are steep areas and climbing equipment is advised. Summit climbers are rewarded with distant views of Three Sisters and Mount Washington, Odell, Crescent and Summit lakes, and Mounts Thielsen and Bailey.

Directions: Hike-in access from trailheads off OR 58 and Diamond Drive/Forest Service 21. Diamond Peak Trail 3699 is one of the most popular routes.

Activities: Hiking and climbing

Facilities: None.

Dates: Open year-round, but trails are snow-free only June through Oct.

Fees: None, but a free wilderness access permit is required June 15-Nov. 15. Trail park permits are required at trailheads.

Deschutes National Forest

ODELL AND CRESCENT LAKES

[Fig. 42] Two of the largest natural mountain lakes in Oregon lie in forested glacial troughs within a couple of miles of each other along OR 58 at the Cascade crest east of Willamette Pass. Odell and Crescent lakes are separated by less than 4 cross-country miles, and both lie at the edge of rugged Diamond Peak Wilderness. Both lakes are framed by mountain peaks that are dominated by the ragged, snow-streaked 8,744-foot elevation summit of Diamond Peak.

Multiple Forest Service campgrounds and private resorts provide accommodations that are popular with lake fishermen, sail boaters, sail boarders, and water skiers, and serve as base camps for hikers and mountain bikers exploring the myriad of nearby dirt roads and trails.

Anglers are attracted by trout, kokanee salmon, and especially the giant Mackinaw char (*Salvenlinus namaycushi)* that hug the bottoms of both Odell and Crescent lakes. The Oregon state record Mackinaw weighed 40 pounds and was caught at Odell Lake, which regularly gives up Macks from 20 to 30 pounds. Mackinaw is a Western term for lake trout that inhabit most of the extreme northern states and Canadian provinces. They are not native to Oregon. The first were stocked in Odell Lake in 1902 and stocking continued until 1965. They are now self-propagating. These are long-lived fish, often exceeding 30 years.

Many sailboaters come for the powerful afternoon winds that sweep both lakes. Winds are especially strong at Crescent Lake, which sits on an open ridge, marginally protected by a surrounding forest of short conifers from thermals that sweep up from the valleys. Odell Lake is somewhat more protected by high ridges and tall old-growth conifers. Still, its 6-mile length is raked by afternoon winds stiff enough to attract a colorful fleet of sail boarding enthusiasts.

Odell Lake is the larger of the pair, with 3,600 acres of dark blue water, and a depth of 305 feet. The elevation of the lake is 4,788 feet, high enough for sunny summer days with cool nights, and deep winter snows that arrive in late October and stay until May. It's a weather mix that recreationists appreciate. One of the interesting legends of Odell Lake is that a train, complete with locomotive, is entombed in the murk at the bottom. Some say it jumped from the Southern Pacific Railroad mainline, which follows the south shore.

Four campgrounds and two year-round resorts are scattered through the huckleberries, firs, pines and spruces that press against the oblong shoreline of Odell Lake.

Odell Lake Lodge is on the east end of the lake. The reddish-brown cedar-sided resort, reminiscent of the 1930s and smelling pleasantly of wood smoke, includes a lodge with large ax-hewn beams, a wooden floor and wall shelves that sag with the weight of an eclectic library and local artifacts. The resort also includes a restaurant that turns out near-gourmet dinners, a general store, rustic cabins, gasoline, and rental boats, cross-country skis, and mountain bikes. A trail system is established along the lake and adjoining hills for summer hiking, mountain biking, and cross-country skiing. The lodge also privately maintains and grooms a 5.5 mile cross-country ski trail. Popular Crater Butte Trail leaves from the lodge parking area for a 13.7 mile hike into Diamond Peak Wilderness.

Shelter Cove Resort is at the opposite end of Odell Lake on the southwest shoreline, 2.2 miles south of OR 58. It features a RV park, tent sites, cabins, boat rentals, groceries, gasoline, fishing tackle, boat docks, and 2.6 miles of groomed cross-country ski trails. Both resorts can arrange fishing guides.

Crescent Lake is shaped like a fluted bowl that is 5 miles long, 4 miles wide, 280-feet deep, and holds 3,600 acres of water at an elevation of 4,839 feet. The lake is ringed by roads, Forest Service campgrounds, a full-service resort, picnic areas, and miles of open sandy beach.

It's a summer and winter recreation destination similar to Odell Lake. While the deep cold water at Odell makes it a favorite with fishermen, the wide beaches, warmer water temperatures, and open setting of Crescent Lake make it popular with pleasure boaters, water skiers, wind surfers, and swimmers.

Crescent Lake can offer respectable fishing, however, especially in May and June, for Mackinaw char, kokanee salmon, and rainbow and brown trout. In the winter, Crescent Lake is popular with cross-country skiers and snowmobilers.

Crescent Lake Lodge, open year-round, rents cabins with kitchens, boats, skis, snowmobiles, and mountain bikes. The complex offers a restaurant, store, gas, groceries, moorage, boat ramp, and fishing tackle. The lodge is on the north end of the lake.

Crescent Ranger District headquarters of Deschutes National Forest is located in Crescent on Hwy 97, about 12 miles east of Crescent Lake on County Road 61. It's a good weekday source for forest and recreation maps, trailpark and snowpark passes, and information year-round and is open on Saturdays from Memorial Day to Labor Day.

ODELL LAKE

[Fig. 42] **Directions:** About 30 miles southeast of Oakridge, just east of Willamette Pass, Odell Lake can be seen along side OR 58. Marked turnoffs lead from the highway to the west and east ends of the lake.

Activities: Camping, boating, fishing, swimming, hiking, mountain biking, hunting, cross-country skiing. It's also a good area for seasonal berry and mushrooming picking.

Facilities: 2 resorts with full traveler services including gasoline, 4 Forest Service campgrounds, 5 boat ramps, hiking and mountain biking trails. Crater Butte and Whitefish/Yoran trailheads into Diamond Peak Wilderness. RV park with hookups at Shelter Cove Resort.

Dates: Open year-round.

Fees: There is a charge for campsites, trail park passes, and resort services.

Closest town: Oakridge is about 30 miles west on OR 58.

For more information: Crescent Ranger District, Deschutes National Forest, PO Box 208 Crescent, OR 97733. Phone (541) 433-2234. Odell Lake Resort, PO Box 72, Crescent Lake, OR 97425. Phone (541) 433-2540. Shelter Cove Resort, phone (541) 433-2548.

PRINCESS CREEK CAMPGROUND

[Fig. 42(3)] Princess Creek Campground is the largest of four Forest Service campgrounds on Odell Lake. Other lake shore campgrounds and the number of sites offered are Odell Creek, 22; Sunset Cove, 21; and Trapper Creek, 32. All but Odell Creek have boat ramps and Sunset Cove offers fully accessible boating, day use, and fish cleaning facilities.

Directions: Princess Creek Campground is located on the northeast side of the lake adjacent to OR 58.

Activities: Camping, fishing, boating, and picnicking.

Facilities: 46 tent and trailer sites, vault toilet, piped drinking water, boat launch with limited parking for day-use boating. Sunset Cove has ample parking and is a better choice for day-use boaters. It also has a wind-surfing deployment.

Dates: Open late May through late Sept.

Fees: There is a charge for campsites and trail park passes.

CRATER BUTTE TRAIL 44

[Fig. 42(4)] This popular hiking trail into Diamond Peak Wilderness begins near the east end of Odell Lake and ends at the junction of the Pacific Crest Trail near Marie Lake. The trail begins in a forest of Douglas and white fir, and hemlock, and ends in a forest of lodgepole pine and noble fir.

Directions: Trailhead is at Odell Lake Resort at the east end of Odell Lake.

Activities: Hiking, horseback riding. Mountain bikes are not allowed.

Facilities: None.

Dates: Open June through Nov.

Fees: There is a charge for trail park passes.

Trail: 13.7 miles one-way.

Elevation: Trailhead is at 4,850 feet, high point at 6,200 feet.

Degree of difficulty: Moderate.

Surface: Dirt and rock.

PONDEROSA PINE
(Pinus ponderosa)
Also called the western yellow pine, this tree grows to 180 feet tall with needles up to 7 inches long.

CRESCENT LAKE

[Fig. 42] **Directions:** From OR 58 about 2 miles southeast of Odell Lake at Crescent Lake Junction turn southwest on paved Forest Service 60 and continue about 2.2 miles to the lake.

Activities: Camping, boating, fishing, picnicking, swimming, hiking, mountain biking, cross-country skiing, and snowmobiling.

Facilities: 3 Forest Service tent and RV campgrounds, 1 horse camp with stalls, 1 universally accessible group campground, 1 primitive group campground, 3 picnic areas, 3 boat ramps, and Crescent Lake Lodge and Resort with rental boats, bikes, skis.

Dates: Open year-round.

Fees: There are charges for camping, trail park passes at trailheads, and resort services.

Closest town: Oakridge is about 35 miles west on OR 58.

For more information: Crescent Ranger District, Deschutes National Forest, PO Box 208 Crescent, OR 97733. Phone (541) 433-2234. Crescent Lake Lodge and Resort, PO Box 73, Crescent Lake, OR 97425. Phone (541) 433-2505.

SPRING CAMPGROUND

[Fig. 42(5)] The largest of four Forest Service campgrounds on Crescent Lake, this campground is located in a mostly open area on the southwest end of the lake. Other campgrounds on the lake and the number of camping sites are: Crescent Lake, 47; Contorta Point, 15; Whitefish Horse Camp, 17; Simax Group Camp, 3; and Windy Group Camp.

Directions: OR 58 to a southwest turn onto Forest Service 60 then southwest 8.1 miles. The campground is on the south side of Crescent Lake.

Activities: Camping, picnicking, swimming, fishing, boating, water skiing, wind surfing, hiking, mountain biking, and horseback riding.

Facilities: 68 tent and RV sites, swim beach, boat ramp, drinking water, vault toilets, tables, and grills. Many trails and gravel roads are available for hiking, mountain biking, and sight-seeing.

Dates: Open Apr. through Oct.

Fees: There is a charge for camping. Whitefish Horse Camp and Group sites are by reservation only (877) 444-6777.

OREGON CASCADES RECREATION AREA

[Fig. 42] Oregon Cascades Recreation Area (OCRA) may be the most remote and least visited designated recreation area in the Oregon mountains, and one of the few areas Congress has set aside specifically for recreational qualities.

The OCRA is a special designation created by Congress in 1984 to protect and enhance the recreational values of the area while allowing motor vehicles. Vehicles would have been prohibited if the area had been designated a wilderness area. By setting the OCRA aside for recreational use, Congress gave it some of the natural resource protections of a wilderness area without all of the prohibitions.

OCRA is 157,000 acres of primitive mountains along the crest of the Cascades. It's wedged between Diamond Peak and Mount Thielsen wilderness areas, mostly west of the Cascade crest.

Portions of the OCRA are within three national forests, Deschutes, Willamette, and Umpqua. The Winema National Forests borders it on the south. While vehicles are allowed, roads in the OCRA are few. The major road into the area is Forest Service 60, a gravel route that bisects the OCRA east-west between Crescent Lake and OR 138 south of Lemolo Lake. The route crosses Pacific Crest Trail 2000 at Windigo Pass, elevation 5,817 feet. The nearby Windigo Lakes are stocked with brook trout.

Other entry points into the OCRA are from Diamond Drive at Summit Lake, and Cinnamon Butte Lookout Road 4793 that runs east from OR 138 between Lemolo and Diamond lakes. The favorite route for hikers is Windy Pass Trail 3643, a strenuous 8.6 mile route to the Windy Lakes region southwest of Crescent Lake.

The OCRA's primary appeal is to winter snowmobile enthusiasts, big game hunters, back road sightseers, and hikers who enjoy bushwhacking. Very few maintained trails are in OCRA.

Directions: From OR 58 turn south on Forest Service 60 at Crescent Lake. Continue past the lake on Forest Service 60, which will cross the OCRA through Windigo Pass to OR 138.

Activities: Sight-seeing, hiking, hunting, winter snowmobiling.

Facilities: None.

Dates: Open year-round, but expect snow-covered roads Nov. through May.

Fees: None.

Closest town: Oakridge.

For more information: Deschutes National Forest, 1645 E. Highway 20, Bend, OR 97701. Phone (541) 388-2715.

Umpqua National Forest

[Fig. 5, Fig. 43] The second smallest national forest in the Oregon Cascades, Umpqua National Forest is still 554 square miles larger than Rhode Island. The forest also sits in a converging triangle of three unique provinces that make the range of flora, fauna, and geology unique. While small in size, it is large in diversity.

The heart of this West Slope forest is the North Umpqua, a frothing wild and scenic river flowing between black basalt cliffs, and towers of old-growth conifers. At first sight of this river, globe-trotting Western author Zane Grey was seduced, and set up a permanent fishing/writing camp at Steamboat Creek. More than half of the forest is still classified as old-growth habitat. At the top of the forest on the crest of the Cascades is Diamond Lake, 2 miles wide, 3 miles long, and a magnet for summer and winter recreationists. The 984,880 acres of national forest now used by sightseers and recreationists was used by five bands of Indians 150 years ago for hunting and fishing.

In the early nineteenth century, the mountains now included in Umpqua National Forest were used by tribal Indian bands of the Southern Molalla, Cow Creeks, Umpqua, Yoncalla, and Lower Umpqua. The resources of this area were rich enough that in 1830, Klickitat Indians from north of the Columbia invaded and settled in the Umpqua drainage lands.

Elk, black-tailed deer, black bear, cougar, otter, marten, coyote, bobcats, and snowshoe hares are common in these dense woods and river bottoms. Huckleberries, blueberries, and elderberries are prolific, and the North Umpqua and its tributaries still support thousands of ocean-going salmon and steelhead.

Today, these natural resources form the backbone of a booming recreational industry.

OR 138 follows the sweeping bends and drifting campfire smoke along the North Umpqua corridor from Roseburg east into the mountains until the river veers steeply north and east to its headwater at Maidu Lake in Mount Thielsen Wilderness. OR 138 turns south to Diamond Lake and connects with OR 230 near Crater Lake National Park and the headwaters of the nationally famous Rogue River drainage.

Umpqua National Forest is divided into four ranger districts: Cottage Grove, 78405 Cedar Park Road, Cottage Grove, OR 97424, phone (541) 942-5591; Diamond Lake, 2020 Tokette Ranger Station Road, Idleyld Park, OR 97447, phone (541) 498-2531; North Umpqua 18782 North Umpqua Highway, Glide, OR 97443, phone (541) 496-3532; and Tiller, 27812 Tiller Trail Highway, Tiller, OR 97484, phone (541) 825-3201.

Parts of two wilderness areas and all of a third are found here: Mount Thielsen, 55,100 acres is east of Diamond Lake; Boulder Creek, 19,100 acres is north of OR 138 at Umpqua Rocks; and Rogue-Umpqua Divide, 33,000 acres is southwest of Diamond Lake. Only Boulder Creek is completely within Umpqua National Forest.

Hikers and mountain bikers explore more than 500 miles of summer trails and 200 miles of winter trail—mostly in the Diamond and Lemolo lakes area—that are groomed for cross-country skiing and snowmobiling. One of the most popular trails is the 79-mile long North Umpqua Trail, which shadows the river until it's crossed by Pacific Crest Trail 2000. Sixty-three miles of trail are National Recreation Trails and another 30 miles are National Scenic Trails.

The North Umpqua River is also a favorite destination for whitewater rafters and kayakers (more than a dozen outfitters work the river), and for fly-fishermen attracted by the 31 miles set aside for fly-fishing and the challenge of summer-run steelhead.

Campers have 46 campgrounds to select from, and 10 forest service picnic areas. Most charge fees for camping. Campers at Tokette Lake Campground relax in the 106-degree Fahrenheit water at nearby Umpqua Hot Springs on a bluff overlooking the river.

Waterfall lovers love the Umpqua. With the number of waterfalls nearby, OR 138 is sometimes called "the Highway of Waterfalls." More than 25 major waterfalls, including the 272-foot plunge of Watson Falls, Oregon's third highest, are on the forest's waterfall circuit. Most of the best are described in detail in a free booklet, *Thundering Waters,* jointly published by Umpqua National Forest and Bureau of Land Management. The booklet is available at most information outlets along OR 138, or can be requested by phoning Roseburg District Bureau of Land Management, (541) 440-4930, Roseburg Visitors and Convention Bureau, (541) 672-9731, or Umpqua National Forest, (541) 672-6601.

Major geological areas are scattered throughout the forest. At Soda Springs Dam on the North Umpqua is a lichen-stained wall of perpendicular columnar basalt. At OR 138, milepost 32.2, turn north to Jobs Garden at the base of columnar basalt outcroppings. Between OR 138 and the south side of Boulder Creek Wilderness is a series of basalt pillars and odd geological formations. Examples are visible from the highway at Umpqua Rocks, Eagle Creek, and Slide Creek fossil beds.

For more information: Umpqua National Forest Supervisors Office, 2900 NW Stewart Parkway, Roseburg, OR 97470. Phone (541) 672-6601. Web site: www.fs.fed.us/r6/umpqua/.

LEMOLO LAKE

[Fig. 42] Lemolo Lake is 420 acres of jade green water with a robust brown trout and kokanee salmon population, four campgrounds, a resort, and two thundering waterfalls. It's best known, however, for great winter snowmobiling and cross-country skiing.

The lake is at an elevation of 4,230 feet and is the southern-most attraction on Diamond Drive. It is located 12 miles north of Diamond Lake, which is one of Oregon's most popular destinations, and for many provides a less harried base for enjoying the many recreational opportunities in this region.

Lemolo Lake was created by a power-generating dam that impounded the North Umpqua River, and is famous in angling circles for producing large brown trout. It's open year-round for fishing.

Sandy beaches, clear water and 8.3 miles of shoreline also invite summer boaters, and water skiers. Winter recreationists use nearly 400 miles of snowmobile trails that connect Lemolo to Crescent and Diamond lakes, and the surrounding Umpqua National Forest. In summer, the trails are used for off-road vehicle riding, hiking and mountain biking.

Two waterfalls are nearby. Both require short hikes to reach. Lemolo Falls is the most dramatic, but involves a steep 1.7 mile round-trip hike. Warm Springs Falls is at the end of an easy 0.3 mile path and features a 70-foot drop over columns of basalt. The route to the falls is signed on Forest Service Road 2610.

Directions: OR 138 about 73 miles east of Roseburg, turn north onto Forest Service 2610 for 6 miles to the lake.

Activities: Camping, fishing, hunting, water and snow skiing, snowmobiling, swimming, hiking, mountain biking, and ATV riding.

Facilities: 4 Forest Service campgrounds with a combination of 91 tent and RV sites, 2 boat ramps, Lemolo Lake Resort, store with camping and fishing supplies, restaurant, gasoline, marina, RV park with hookups, showers, and laundry.

Dates: Open year-round.

Fees: There is a charge for Forest Service campsites and resort services (charges for trail park passes may be initiated in 2000).

Closest town: Idleyld Park is about 58 miles west on OR 138. Most traveler supplies are available 12 miles southeast on OR 138 at Diamond Lake.

For more information: Diamond Lake Ranger District office, Umpqua National Forest, 2020 Toketee Road, PO Box 101, Idleyld Park, OR 97447. Phone (541) 498-2531. Lemolo Lake Resort, 2610 Birds Point Road, Idleyld Park, OR 97447. Phone (541) 643-0750.

POOLE CREEK CAMPGROUND

[Fig. 42(7)] Located next to the private resort, Poole Creek Campground is the largest of four Forest Service camps on Lemolo Lake, and the only campground with potable water and a boat launch. The campground lies just south of the mouth of Poole Creek in a lakeside grove of lodgepole pine, mountain hemlock and Shasta fir (*Abies shastensis*). This is about the northernmost growing area for Shasta firs. Plentiful in southern Oregon and northern California, Shastas reach 120-feet high, and may be as much as four-feet through at the base. They can be distinguished from other firs by the deeply-furrowed, cinnamon red bark. Some campsites are in open areas, and others are shaded. Other campgrounds on Lemolo Lake and the number of campsites at each are Bunker Hill, 5; East Lemolo, 15; and Inlet, 14.

Directions: To reach Poole Creek Campground, follow Forest Service Road 2610 north from OR 138 to the campground on the northwest side of Lemolo Lake.

Activities: Camping, swimming, boating, and fishing.

Facilities: 59 tent and RV sites to 35 feet long, 2 group sites (available through reservation), well water, tables, grills, boat ramp, vault toilets, swimming beach, wheelchair accessibility.

Dates: May 15 through Oct. 31.

Fees: There is a charge for campsites.

LEMOLO FALLS AND TRAIL 1468

[Fig. 42(8)] Forest Service Trail 1468 follows a steep route into the North Umpqua Canyon where North Umpqua River roars over Lemolo Falls in a thunderous 150-foot drop to the canyon floor. The now widely used name Lemolo is a Chinook Indian word for wild or untamed and originally applied to these falls.

Directions: Turn north from OR 138 onto Forest Service Road 2610 and continue north 4 miles to a west turn onto Forest Service Road 3401/Thorn Prairie Road. Continue to a north turn onto Forest Service 3401-800 and continue 1 mile to an east turn onto Forest Service 3401-840. The trailhead is at a picnic area at the end of the road.

Activities: Hiking, waterfall sight-seeing, picnicking.

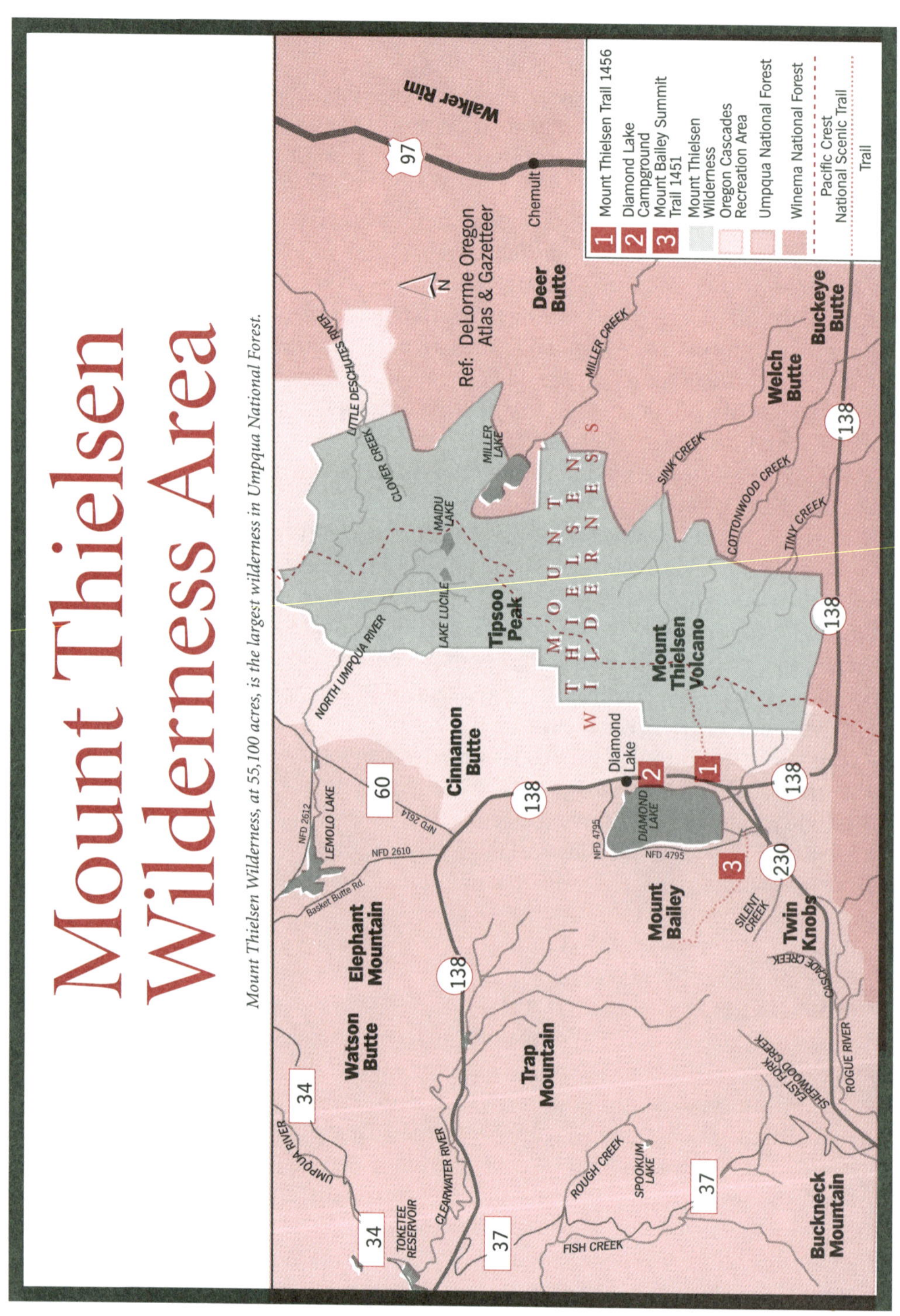
Mount Thielsen
Wilderness Area
Mount Thielsen Wilderness, at 55,100 acres, is the largest wilderness in Umpqua National Forest.
Ref: DeLorme Oregon Atlas & Gazetteer
N
1 Mount Thielsen Trail 1456
2 Diamond Lake Campground
3 Mount Bailey Summit Trail 1451
Mount Thielsen Wilderness
Oregon Cascades Recreation Area
Umpqua National Forest
Winema National Forest
Pacific Crest National Scenic Trail
Trail
Walker Rim
97
Chemult
Deer Butte
Buckeye Butte
Welch Butte
MILLER CREEK
SINK CREEK
COTTONWOOD CREEK
TINY CREEK
138
LITTLE DESCHUTES RIVER
CLOVER CREEK
MILLER LAKE
MAIDU LAKE
LAKE LUCILE
Tipsoo Peak
MOUNT THIELSEN WILDERNESS
Mount Thielsen Volcano
NORTH UMPQUA RIVER
Cinnamon Butte
Diamond Lake
DIAMOND LAKE
NFD 4795
230
60
NFD 2612
LEMOLO LAKE
NFD 2614
NFD 2610
Basket Butte Rd.
Elephant Mountain
Mount Bailey
SILENT CREEK
Twin Knobs
CASCADE CREEK
Watson Butte
Trap Mountain
EAST FORK SHERWOOD CREEK
ROGUE RIVER
34
UMPQUA RIVER
CLEARWATER RIVER
TOKETEE RESERVOIR
ROUGH CREEK
SPOOKUM LAKE
37
FISH CREEK
Buckneck Mountain

Facilities: Picnic table at trailhead.

Dates: Open year-round, snow-free from May through Oct.

Fees: None (charges for trail park passes may be initiated in 2000).

Trail: 1.7 mile round-trip, steep grade.

Elevation: Trailhead is at 4,100 feet.

Degree of difficulty: Strenuous.

Surface: Dirt.

MOUNT THIELSEN WILDERNESS

[Fig. 43] The dagger-like pinnacle of 9,182-foot Mount Thielsen juts into the clear mountain air in the heart of Mount Thielsen Wilderness, a landmark for climbers, hikers, hunters, and overnight backpackers. Mount Thielsen Wilderness, at 55,100 acres, is the largest wilderness in Umpqua National Forest. It is located east of Diamond Lake, about 80 miles east of I-5 at Roseburg. The major attractions include Forest Service Trail 1456 to the namesake peak, the headwaters of North Umpqua at Maidu Lake, and a 26-mile segment of Pacific Crest National Scenic Trail 2000. Elevations within the wilderness vary from 4,300 feet to 9,182 feet at the summit of Mount Thielsen, which is a popular destination for climbers. The wilderness contains 78 miles of hiking trails, and is divided between three national forests: Umpqua, Deschutes and Winema.

Directions: From OR 138 about 80 miles east of Roseburg, the wilderness area is located east of Diamond Lake along the crest of the Cascades. Popular entry points are at Miller Lake Forest Service Road 9772 from Chemult; Cinnamon Butte Lookout Road 4793 from OR 138 continuing past the lookout on Forest Service 100 to the west edge of the wilderness, or by trailheads from the east side of OR 138 at Diamond Lake.

Activities: Hiking, camping, summit climbing, and fishing.

Facilities: About 78 miles of hiking trails.

Dates: Open year-round, but expect snow to cover trails Nov. to Apr.

Fees: Free wilderness access permits are dispensed at most trailheads (charges for trail park passes may be initiated in 2000).

Closest town: Diamond Lake, an unincorporated community on OR 138 that provides most basic traveler services.

For more information: Diamond Lake Ranger District, 2020 Toketee Ranger Station Road, Idleyld Park, OR 97447. Phone (541) 498-2531. Diamond Lake Information Center is located on Forest Service Road 4798 at Diamond Lake Campground. It is open Memorial Day to Labor Day. Phone (541) 793-3310.

MOUNT THIELSEN VOLCANO

[Fig. 43] Nicknamed the "lightning rod" of the Cascades because of frequent strikes on its pinnacle-like summit, Mount Thielsen, elevation 9,182 feet, is an extinct shield volcano that last erupted about 290,000 years ago. Decades of repeated lightning strikes have fused rock particles near the summit into fulgurites, which are tapered tubes of brownish-green glass usually just a few inches long.

It is estimated that 1,000 feet has been eroded or erupted from the top of Mount Thielsen. It's made up of basaltic andesite, like most of the volcanoes in this region. The distinctive summit spire is a thick plug of andesite that filled the eruption crater. Glacial scouring and erosions have worn away most of the crater wall, leaving the plug exposed.

The toothy pinnacle is the centerpiece of Mount Thielsen Wilderness and a favorite destination for hikers from trailheads at Diamond Lake.

Directions: Located on the Cascade crest east of Diamond Lake and north of Crater Lake National Park.

Activities: Trail hiking and summit climbs.

Facilities: None.

Dates: Open year-round.

Fees: Free wilderness access permits are dispensed at trailheads (charges for trail park passes may be initiated in 2000).

DIAMOND LAKE

[Fig. 43] Wedged into a mile-high forest of lodgepole pines between the imposing silhouettes of two extinct volcanoes, Diamond Lake is atop the backbone of the Oregon Cascades, 5 miles from the north entrance to Crater Lake National Park. The lake is the centerpiece of the most popular summer and winter recreation destination on OR 138. The lake's ever-blue 3,030 acres of water fill a 52-feet deep oval more than 1.5 miles wide and 3.5 miles long. It's encircled by a paved forest road, and a nearly-level 11.5-mile paved loop pathway for hikers and bicyclists. Recreationists base their fun at three major Forest Service campgrounds, a resort, RV park and 102 summer homes.

On the west side of Diamond Lake, massive Mount Bailey, elevation 8,363 feet high, catches the first pink rays of daybreak. On the east side, the pinnacle lightning rod of Mount Thielsen, 9,182 feet high, reflects the glow of lingering sunsets. When seen from a boat adrift on the mirror of Diamond Lake, neither event will be forgotten.

Summer recreation includes mountain biking, hiking, water sports (10 mph boat speed limit), trout fishing, camping, horseback riding, and sight-seeing. Winter recreationists enjoy 300 miles of snowmobile trails, 200 miles of cross-country ski trails, snowshoeing, and inner tube sledding. One of the most unique winter attractions is Snowcat skiing on remote Mount Bailey. Advanced skiers and snowboarders are shuttled by Snowcat to the summit of Mount Bailey and 3,000 feet of vertical drop through waist-deep powder snow, open bowls, steep chutes and tree rows.

Small business areas with gasoline, groceries, restaurants, and information are stationed at the north and south ends on the east side of the lake off OR 138. Umpqua National Forest operates three campgrounds with 450 sites, 5 boat launches, picnic areas, and swimming beaches. The two largest campgrounds, Diamond Lake and Broken Arrow, both on the east shore. If there is a drawback to this superlative land, it's the cloud of mosquitoes that can engulf the lake from spring through mid-July.

Directions: Follow OR 138 east from Roseburg or west from US 97 north of Klamath

Falls. The lake is 5 miles north of Crater Lake National Park on the Rogue-Umpqua National Scenic Byway.

Activities: Winter and summer trail and water activities.

Facilities: 3 Forest Service campgrounds, Diamond Lake Resort, year-round trail system, horse corrals, marina, RV parking with hookups, 5 boat ramps, showers, laundry, groceries, gasoline, restaurants, visitor information center.

Dates: The lake, traveler services, and resort are open year-round. Forest Service campgrounds operate May 15-Oct. 31.

Closest town: Roseburg is 80 miles west on OR 138.

For more information: Diamond Lake Ranger District, 2020 Toketee Ranger Station Road, Idleyld Park, OR 97447. Phone (541) 498-2531. Diamond Lake Information Center is located on Forest Service Road 4798 at Diamond Lake Campground. It is open Memorial Day to Labor Day. Phone (541) 793-3310. Diamond Lake Resort, Diamond Lake, OR 97731. Phone (800) 733-7593.

DIAMOND LAKE CAMPGROUND

[Fig. 43(2)] On the northeast shore of Diamond Lake, next to the resort, Diamond Lake Campground is the largest of three Forest Service Campgrounds. The other campgrounds are Broken Arrow Campground with 147 sites and Thielsen View with 60 sites.

Directions: Follow directions to Diamond Lake.

Activities: Camping, fishing, picnicking, hiking, mountain biking, swimming, and boating.

Facilities: 238 tent and RV sites for trailers up to 35 feet, tables, fireplaces, barbecues, potable water, flush toilets, showers, RV dump stations, amphitheater, 2 boat ramps, and a fish cleaning station. There are also horseshoe pits, volleyball court, and a playground.

Dates: Open May 15 through Oct. 31.

Fees: There is a charge for campsites. Campsite reservations can be made in advance by phoning (877) 444-6777. Charges for trail park passes may be initiated in 2000.

MOUNT BAILEY SUMMIT TRAIL 1451

[Fig. 43(3)] The trail to the top of Mount Bailey begins on a lodgepole pine flat. Within about a mile, it climbs above timberline into a steep, rocky geological area that reflects the volcanic trauma that created the 8,363-foot mountain.

The first 2 miles are used by cross-country skiers in winter and mountain bikers in summer, as well as hikers. The entire trail is closed to motorized vehicles.

Directions: At the north entrance to Diamond Lake Recreation Area, turn west off OR 138 onto Forest Service Road 4795, and drive 3.5 miles along the east shore. Turn right on Forest Service 4795 and go 1.5 miles to a left turn onto Forest Service Road 4795-300 and drive 1.3 miles to the trailhead.

Activities: Hiking, mountain biking, and cross-country skiing.

Facilities: None.

Dates: Open year-round.

Fees: None (charges for trail park passes may be initiated in 2000).

Trail: 5 miles one-way.

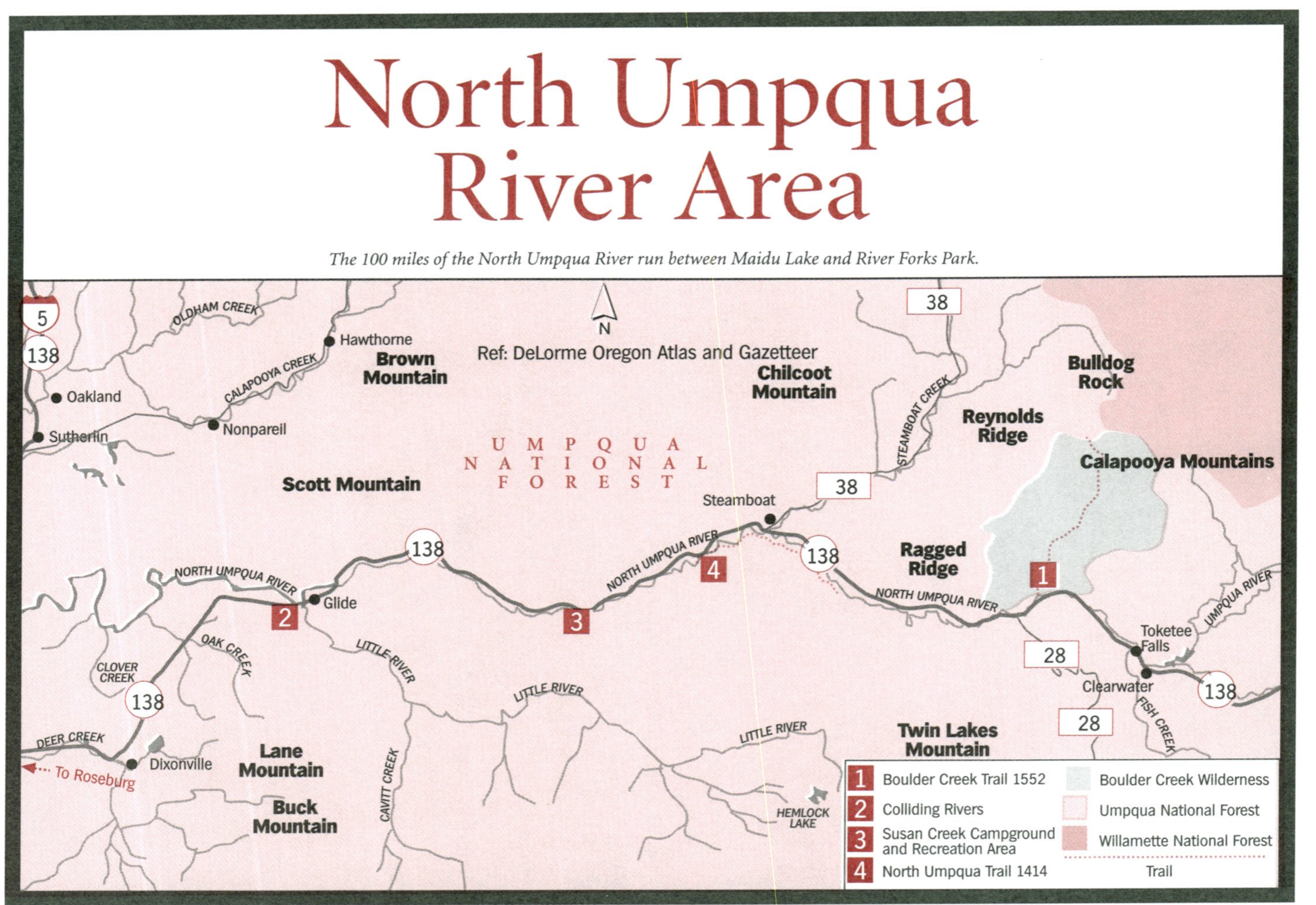

The 100 miles of the North Umpqua River run between Maidu Lake and River Forks Park.

Elevation: Trailhead is at 5,250 feet and the summit is at 8,363 feet.

Degree of difficulty: Lower 1 mile is moderate, the upper 4 miles are strenuous.

Surface: Dirt and rock.

MOUNT THIELSEN TRAIL 1456

[Fig. 43(1)] Beginning in lodgepole pine near Diamond Lake, Mount Thielsen Trail 1456 winds steeply to the rocky escarpments above timberline, and is the most popular route to the summit of Mount Thielsen. There's a breathtaking view of the peak 1.6 miles from the trailhead at Spruce Ridge Trail junction. The trail is steep, especially beyond timberline at 7,200 feet. The final 200 feet to the summit is vertical, and climbing protection is recommended. The top-of-the-world view goes south to California's Mount Shasta and north to the Three Sisters.

Directions: Trailhead is located on the east side of OR 138 about 1.5 miles north of OR 230 junction.

Activities: Summer hiking, winter cross-country skiing.

Facilities: Restroom at trailhead.

Dates: Open year-round.

Fees: None (charges for trail park passes may be initiated in 2000).

Trail: 4.9 miles one-way.

Elevation: Trailhead, 5,400 feet; summit, 9,182.

Degree of difficulty: Strenuous.

Surface: Dirt below timberline, and loose rock above.

BOULDER CREEK WILDERNESS

[Fig. 44] A mosaic of old forest fires, basalt rock spires, and towers of old-growth conifer, Boulder Creek Wilderness, at 19,100 acres, is the smallest wilderness area in Umpqua National Forest. Included in the wilderness is the 1,420-acre Umpqua Rocks geologic area, featuring massive volcanic basalt and andesite monolithic spires called Eagle Rock, Rattlesnake Rock, Old Man and Old Woman Rocks.

Hikers follow 30 miles of trails through old-growth ponderosa pine, oak groves, wildflower meadows, and small rumbling streams.

It is the only wilderness area located entirely within the Umpqua. While rock climbers find the area's 30-million-year-old spires appealing, since 1996 the most notable feature has been a very visible monument to the effects of wildfire. Named the Spring Fire, the 1996 burn involved 16,500 acres including much of the Boulder Creek area. Scientists have adopted the wilderness as a study area to determine long-term ecological effects of fire.

Directions: 50 miles east of Roseburg and north of OR 138.

Activities: Hiking, hunting, mushroom gathering, and rock climbing.

Facilities: 30 miles of maintained hiking trail.

Dates: Open year-round.

Fees: Free wilderness use permits required during the summer are dispensed at trailheads (charges for trail park passes may be initiated in 2000).

Closest town: Idleyld Park is about 29 miles west on OR 138.

For more information: Diamond Lake Ranger District, 2020 Toketee Ranger Station Road, Idleyld Park, OR 97447. Phone (541) 498-2531. Diamond Lake Information Center is located on Forest Service Road 4798 at Diamond Lake Campground. It is open Memorial Day to Labor Day. Phone (541) 793-3310.

BOULDER CREEK TRAIL 1552

[Fig. 44(1)] On and off, the trail follows Boulder Creek for the lower 6 miles, then leaves the creek and proceeds along the ridge top to Calapooya Divide. This is a fairly steep trail with many stretches exceeding 15 percent gradient. The trail winds mostly through a closed canopy of Douglas fir and hemlock, with very few open vistas.

About 2 miles from the trailhead is a large open stand of old growth ponderosa pine known as Pine Bench. This is the most popular spot in the wilderness. A small spring is located on the north side of the bench about 150 feet off the trail. This trail can be walked in one day, but an overnight camp out makes a more pleasant hike.

Directions: Turn north from Highway 138 onto Road 4775, the Medicine Creek Road. Go about 50 feet and turn left onto Road 4775-011 for 2.6 miles to a gate and small parking area. About 100 yards past the gate Boulder Creek Trail takes off to the right.

Dates: Open year-round.

Fees: None (charges for trail park passes may be initiated in 2000).

Trail: 10.6 miles one-way.

Elevation: From 1,600 to 5,400 feet.

Degree of difficulty: Begins easy; becomes strenuous with elevation gains.

Surface: Dirt and rock.

NORTH UMPQUA RIVER

[Fig. 44] The 100 miles of North Umpqua River between the headwater trickle at Maidu Lake on the Cascade crest and the sweeping eddies at the confluence of the River Forks Park near Roseburg are some of the most treasured river miles in a state that overflows with wild and scenic rivers. Fishermen love the North Umpqua for its cold water and internationally renowned runs of summer-run steelhead. Geologists and rock climbers are attracted by unique chimney spires of basalt lava. Whitewater enthusiasts come for the adrenaline rush of Class III and IV rapids, campers for the twenty-plus campgrounds, and sightseers enjoy it all. The wild and scenic section is from the community of Idleyld Park east to Soda Springs at the south edge of Boulder Creek Wilderness.

The lower river is framed by foothills carpeted with rolling grass pastures and groves of hardwoods; white oak, madrone (*Arbutus menziesii*), and manzanitas. East of Idleyld Park the river romps through shady corridors of dark green pine and fir trees, many more than 200 feet high, and tumbles between black walls of columnar basalt and volcanic rock sculptures. It's followed by OR 138, the north segment of Umpqua-Rogue National Scenic Byway. The two-lane highway tracks all but 20 miles of the winding river where it turns north and east to its headwater in Mount Thielsen Wilderness. Even when the green flow of the river is out of sight from the highway, it's not out of touch. Coolness hangs in the air.

Every campground, picnic area, waterfall, osprey nest, and other attraction along the North Umpqua may be reached from this highway, including 79 miles of North Umpqua Trail 1414. This hiking and mountain biking path follows along the river and parallels OR 138. The list of riverside attractions is long, and includes the osprey nest near Milepost 43, chimney spires at Eagle Rock Campground and the Umpqua Geologic Area, Watson Falls, Steamboat Inn, and more. Colliding River Visitor Center is a multiagency source of maps and information on North Umpqua recreation, accommodations, and attractions. It is located adjacent to the North Umpqua Ranger Station, 18782 North Umpqua Highway at Glide, and is a highly recommended stop for North Umpqua travelers. The visitor center has interpretive displays and an NWIA bookstore. In spring and summer, more than a dozen outfitters provide whitewater rafting and kayaking plunges through the whitewater sections, while summer-run steelhead fishermen cast flies in the dark green pools and troughs swirling past black ledges. North Umpqua is world famous in fly-fishing circles for its run of 7 to 20 pound summer-run steelhead trout.

The picturesque rapids and tailouts near the confluence of Steamboat Creek is the heart of the celebrated fly-fishing area. Steelheaders call it "the holy water," as much for its cathedral-like setting as for the quality of fishing found there. For years, Zane Grey, the Western author, maintained a writing and fishing camp at Steamboat Creek. Rooms at the nearby Steamboat Inn are as coveted as the meals served on its slab-wood tables, and both figure prominently in North Umpqua history.

The Bureau of Land Management has several recreational sites on the lower river west of the national forest boundary. One of the largest complexes is Susan Creek Campground and day-use area near the national forest boundary east of Glide.

Directions: From I-5 use Exit 124 at Roseburg and go east on OR 138. From US 97 north of Klamath Falls, go west on OR 138 toward Crater Lake National Park and Diamond Lake.

Activities: Fishing, whitewater boating, swimming, camping, hiking, rock climbing, picnicking, and sight-seeing.

Facilities: 20-plus Bureau of Land Management and U.S.. Forest Service campgrounds and picnic areas, hiking trails, and boat launches. Ranger district offices at Glide and Idlelyd Park, and information center at Colliding Rivers.

Dates: Call for seasonal updates.

Fees: There is a charge for trail park passes and campground sites.

Closest town: Roseburg.

For more information: North Umpqua Ranger District, Umpqua National Forest, 18782 North Umpqua Highway, Glide, OR 97443. Phone (541) 496-3532. Colliding Rivers Visitor Center, 18782 N. Umpqua Highway, Glide, OR 97443. Phone (541) 496-0157.

COLLIDING RIVERS

[Fig. 44(2)] Seventeen miles east of I-5, the powerful south-bound flow of the North

Umpqua runs head-on into the north-flowing Little River at one of the few places in North America where two rivers actually collide. The collision of currents at the Colliding Rivers site produces a swirl of eddies, small whirlpools, and turbulence in a narrow rock-walled trench. In the summer the collision pool is a favorite swimming and cliff diving area. Picnic tables overlook the narrows. Next to the attraction is Colliding Rivers Visitor Center and museum—the best source of recreation, history, and travel information on OR 138, and North Umpqua Ranger Station.

Directions: Colliding Rivers is on OR 138 at Milepost 17 near Glide.

Activities: Sight-seeing, picnicking, river swimming.

Facilities: Picnic tables, nearby information center for North Umpqua corridor, and North Umpqua Ranger Station.

Dates: Open year-round. Collision best seen in fall, winter, and spring.

Fees: None.

SUSAN CREEK CAMPGROUND AND RECREATION AREA

[Fig. 44(3)] Susan Creek Recreation Area is a major Bureau of Land Management site 12.5 miles east of Glide under a canopy of mature forest along the banks of the North Umpqua Wild and Scenic River. The site, at OR 138 milepost 29, is actually a complex that includes tent and RV campsites, picnic area, barrier-free hiking trail, historic Indian mounds, and a 40-foot waterfall on Susan Creek. The Indian mounds are moss-covered rock remnants of a spiritual site once visited by American Indian boys approaching manhood.

Directions: The site is on the south side of OR 138 about 12.5 miles east of Glide at an elevation of 930 feet.

Activities: Camping, picnicking, hiking, interpretive theaters, river and stream fly-fishing, swimming, and sight-seeing.

Facilities: 31 tent and RV sites, flush toilets, hot water, showers, picnic tables and grills, potable water, and nature trails. There is a resident campground host.

Dates: Open early May to late Oct., depending on weather.

Fees: There is a charge for campsites.

Closest town: Glide is 12.5 miles west on OR 138.

For more information: Bureau of Land Management, Roseburg District Office, 777 NW Garden Valley Boulevard, Roseburg, OR 97470. Phone (541) 440-4948.

NORTH UMPQUA TRAIL 1414

[Fig. 44(4)] One of the longest east-west trails in Oregon, the 79 miles of North Umpqua Trail 1414 begin east of Roseburg at Swiftwater Park near the community of Idleyld Park. The trail ends in an alpine junction with Pacific Crest Trail 2000 in Mount Thielsen Wilderness Area.

For nearly all its length, the gradual incline of the trail runs within a stone's throw of the North Umpqua River, usually in the woodland quiet on the opposite side of the river from the bank that parallels OR 138. Except for where it runs inside Boulder Creek and Mount Thielsen wildernesses, the trail is open to foot hikers, horseback riders, and mountain bikers. The trail is divided into 11 segments from 3 to 16 miles in length, each with separate entry points, and generally follows an up-and-down route (there are steep sections) carved into the forested hillsides above the winding river. Most segments, especially downstream from Boulder Flat Campground, are rated easy to most difficult. Above Boulder Flats, the trail steepens as it heads for the Cascade Crest and the route becomes strenuous in places.

One of the most colorfully named sections is the 13 miles in the Dread and Terror segment. Here the trail follows a strenuous route that is not recommended for mountain bikes or horses because of the steep narrow pathway. At the other end of the extreme sections of Tioga Segment are graveled, level trails designed for senior citizens and wheelchairs.

Sixteen campgrounds are scattered along the route. Several spur trails lead to waterfalls, fishing holes, primitive campsites, and natural areas unusually rich in plant and wildlife. The trail goes through several plant communities that change with the elevations. In the lowlands are thousands of old-growth Douglas firs, some of which are 6 feet at the base. The quivering canopies of bigleaf maples, twisted red-leafed vine maples, red alder (*Alnus rubra*) trees, devil's club (*Oplopanax horridum*), and red huckleberry bushes occur in the riparian zone. In higher elevations, the trail is shaded by lodgepole pines, mountain hemlock and noble firs. Delicate maidenhair and lady ferns are common along the trail. Many varieties of wildflowers spill onto the trail in the summer, including calypso orchids, called fairy slippers (*Calypson bulbosa*); tiger lilies (*Lilium columbianum*); trillium (*Trillium ovatum*); and wood violets (*Viola glabella*).

Hikers often spot ospreys, water ouzels, great blue herons, common mergansers, and blue Steller's jay. It's not unusual to share the trail with black-tailed deer or elk, and the riverbank is a highway for otters, beaver, pine martens, and mink.

Directions: The western trailhead is at Stillwater Park east of Glide, and the eastern entrance is from Pacific Crest Trail near Maidu Lake. There are numerous entry points from OR 138.

Activities: Hiking, mountain biking, horseback riding, camping, wildlife watching.

Facilities: Full service campgrounds are along the route, as well as primitive sites. Many of the midtrail entry points have restrooms.

Dates: Open year-round, but there can be blowdowns present. Call for more information.

Fees: There is a charge for trail park passes.

Trail: 79 miles, one-way, divided into 11 named segments.

Elevation: Gradient gradually varies from 1,000 to 6,000 feet.

Degree of difficulty: Most segments are easy to most difficult.

Surface: Gravel in high-use low elevation areas, natural duff and rock for most of the route.

For more information: Umpqua National Forest, 2900 NW Stewart Parkway, Roseburg, OR 97470. Phone (541) 672-6601.

Rogue River/Western Klamath Region

Some of the last major battles in Oregon between Indians and whites were fought in this region.

46 Mount McLoughlin Area

47 Rogue–Umpqua Divide Wilderness

48 Mountain Lakes Wilderness Area

49 Upper Klamath Lake

Rogue River–Western Klamath Region

The past and present of the upper Rogue River and western Klamath Region is a mixed bag of Indian wars, fur trappers, timber barons, whitewater rafting, volcanoes, a river that disappears into the ground only to reappear as one of America's first wild and scenic rivers, fire lookouts to rent, nearly a thousand miles of mountain trails, three wilderness areas, dozens of campgrounds, Jet Skis, scenic byways, and mile-after-mile of unbroken pine, hemlock, fir and spruce forests.

The lightly populated Rogue River-Klamath Region is bordered on the north by Diamond Lake and on the south by the Siskiyou Mountains (pronounced Sis-Q) and California border. The west side is formed by the narrow two lanes of OR 230/62, and on the east is Upper Klamath Lake, Winema National Forest, and Crater Lake National Park (*see* Crater Lake National Park, page 315), and America's only Volcanic Legacy Scenic Byway.

At the center are the corners of three National Forests; (Umpqua, Winema, and Rogue

[*Above:* Recreation along the Rogue River includes fishing and boating]

River) and three wilderness areas (Rogue-Umpqua Divide, Sky Lakes, and Mountain Lakes). Umpqua National Forest touches the northwest side of the region. Most of the region west of the crest is within Rogue River National Forest, and on the east is Winema National Forest.

Few highways cross this region east-west. The most heavily used, and arguably the most scenic, is the southern leg of the Rogue-Umpqua National Scenic Byway, OR 230/62, following the Rogue River about 90 miles between the Diamond Lake area and Medford on the I-5 corridor. Less traveled east-west crossings, and some will argue just as scenic, may be made on OR 140 and OR 66.

OR 66 rolls through an unpopulated, semi-open forest area as it crosses the Cascades between Klamath Falls and Ashland, rarely more than 10 miles from the California border. It is the southernmost paved road across the Oregon Cascades, and one of the least traveled. Traveling OR 66 is, however, the only way to get a sip of cold natural water at Tub Springs, a must-stop for travelers since 1846 when Applegate Trail immigrants camped here. There is an Oregon State Park interpretive display. The spring is in a cool green glen that in midsummer is surrounded by parched trees, heat-withered bushes, and long whips of seared brown grass. The wayside is 19 miles east of Ashland.

Mountains in the south part of the range enjoy a fairly uniform blend of West Slope and East Slope weather and temperature. This area's homogenized weather is an anomaly to the Cascades' trademark climatic differences that divide at the crests, into a lush, wet-cool West Slope, and semiarid, hot-cold East Slope.

South of Diamond Lake the mountains are lower and less of a dividing barrier. The canyons and valleys cut through the Cascades by the powerful Rogue and Klamath rivers allow hot desert winds generated in eastern Oregon to leak into western Oregon below the east-west range of Siskiyou Mountains. The Klamath is the only river south of the Columbia River that crosses the Cascade Range, and like the Columbia is a corridor for weather phenomena.

Summer weather in the southern Cascades is dry with temperatures often soaring to 100-degrees Fahrenheit, which is more like east-side temperatures than west. In fact,

BALD EAGLE

(*Haliaeetus leucocephalus*)

It is believed that bald eagles mate for life. The 40-inch-long bird, which can have a 7½-foot wingspan, builds a large nest in trees, cliffs, or on the ground that can weigh up to 1,000 pounds. Eagles eat carrion, fish, and waterfowl.

summer temperatures in the west-side cities of Medford and Ashland are often closer to readings in Klamath Falls on the east-side than to the more moderate west-side temperatures up the I-5 corridor at Roseburg and Eugene.

Natural attractions and geological oddities abound in the southern Cascades, but two features dominate. Mount McLoughlin, at 9,494 feet, is the highest peak in the southern Cascades and is believed to be a dormant volcano. Uneroded lava rocks piled along the shoulder of OR 140 at Fish Lake near an unnamed 5,105-foot elevation pass are believed to have been erupted from Mount McLoughlin to the north and Brown Mountain, elevation 7, 311 feet, in the south. Brown Mountain is an extinct volcano. Mount McLoughlin's snow-encased summit is visible from most vantage points.

The storied Rogue River flows from its headwaters near Crater Lake along a turbulent channel worn into 50-million-year-old lava rocks to Medford. The river continues west from Medford through the Siskiyous and flows into the Pacific Ocean at Gold Beach, Oregon.

The Rogue River flows more than 215 miles from its headwaters' gushing origin at Boundary Springs in the northwest corner of Crater Lake National Park. It flows through canyonlike corridors of black lava rocks for much of its downstream plunge to the ocean. Nearly 100 miles of the upper river are within the Rogue River-Klamath Region. Most of it is followed closely by OR 62, and Upper Rogue River National Recreation Trail between the Boundary Springs, source of the Rogue, and the Forest Service's Prospect Ranger Station, in the small town of Prospect 45 miles northeast of Medford.

The north, middle, and south forks come together 30 miles above Medford near Lost Creek Lake, a reservoir built to control the river's infamous monstrous floods. Downstream of the Lost Creek Lake Dam, the powerful main Rogue features rapids that churn white through black rock teeth, deep green pools, and towering canyon walls. This section attracts whitewater raft and kayak adventurers and provides spawning areas for thousands of wild and hatchery-reared steelhead, chinook, and coho salmon. In the early 1900s, the lower Rogue provided an intense commercial salmon fishery supporting dozens of canneries, which were rivaled in number and competitive ferocity only by those on the much larger Columbia River.

The river's commercial history was written in the 1800s by gold miners, salmon canners, fur trappers, and boatmen. Indians have lived along the Rogue for 9,000 years, according to carbon dated artifacts. The oldest sites were inhabited by Takelma bands, a fierce people for whom the river was named. It was called *La Riviere Aux Coquins* (The River of the Rogues) by French-Canadian trappers working for the Hudson's Bay Company after repeated skirmishes with the Takelmas. In 1854, the Oregon Territorial legislature, more concerned with economic development than respectful recognition of the river's warlike defenders, changed the name to Gold River. The new name lasted less than a year.

Some of the last major battles in Oregon between Indians and whites, including the 1855-56 Rogue River Indian War, were fought in the canyons along the Rogue. On the east side of the region, Modocs, who were as fierce as Takelmas, waged the Modoc War from 1872-78 in the lunarlike terrain at what is now Lava Beds National Monument.

Indian leaders were hanged at the site of Fort Klamath. The Klamath Indian people lived north of the Modocs and Klamath Falls. In 1961, the Klamath Indian Reservation, 1,350 square miles, was terminated by Congress and absorbed into the new Winema National Forest. Congress eventually paid the tribe $2.98 million.

Above Lost Creek Lake the forks, especially the 62 miles of the North Fork, are excellent trout streams, with strong populations of rainbow, cutthroat, brown, and brook trout. The forks are narrow streams, with plunging waterfalls, sweeping gravel bars, deep pools, and excellent access for the hundreds of anglers who fish and camp here from early June through October, the narrow window when this mile-high region is snow-free.

There is still far more wildlife in these mountains than people, even during the peak of summer travel season. The West Slopes have black-tailed deer, the East Slopes support mule deer, and elk graze on both sides of the Cascade crest. Black bears are fairly common, and cougar numbers seem to be growing. Blue and ruffed grouse are often seen pecking gravel at the edge of unpaved forest roads. In September the forest area along the backbone of the Cascades, especially in the Fish Lake and Lake of the Woods region on OR 140, is good pickin' for huckleberries.

Almost 1,000 miles of trails attract summer hikers, backpackers and winter cross-country ski and snowmobile enthusiasts. There's a 10-mile round trip trail to the top of Mount McLoughlin that's more of a steep walk than a technical climb, and the trail to National Creek Falls is an easy 0.5-mile family walk through shaded, mixed conifers to a cool, moist oasis fed by springs seeping through the flanks of Mount Mazama.

At Union Creek on OR 62, the Rogue is squeezed into a narrow 500-foot-long, 45-foot-deep slot, and roars between million-year-old rock formations at Rogue River Gorge. There's a paved, wheelchair-accessible 0.25-mile interpretive trail along the edge of the gorge. A second geological oddity is about 1.5 miles downstream, at Natural Bridge. South of the gorge the churning whitewater of the Rogue is again squeezed into a tight channel between lava walls, only this time it abruptly disappears underground. Fifty feet downstream, the river gushes back to the surface on the far side of the Natural Bridge and continues its romp to the ocean. The explanation, according to geologists, is that the river drops into a maze of hollow lava tubes, which worm beneath a massive block of basalt rock, which obstructs the riverbed.

Among other historic features in the Rogue River-Klamath Region is Hershberger Lookout. At an elevation of 6,285 feet atop the Rogue-Umpqua Divide, the cupola offers great views of Mount McLoughlin, Mount Shasta in California, and the rim of Crater Lake. En route to the summit, Forest Service Road 6515 wraps around a geological feature known as Rabbit Ears. The ears are two closely spaced, steep lava spires that are remnant lava plugs that once filled the neck of an ancient volcano. The volcano has eroded away leaving the pair of leaning plugs to challenge rock climbers who are sometimes spotted against the vertical face of the "ears." To get there from OR 230, turn west on Forest Service 6510, about 1 mile north of the junction with OR 62. Forest Service 6510 connects with Forest Service 6515 to the lookout. The road is good gravel and the route is marked.

Backpackers, hikers, and horse riders can find miles of hiking trails and hours of solitude in the region's three wilderness areas: Rogue-Umpqua Divide is west of Crater Lake National Park, Sky Lakes adjoins the south border of the park, and Mountain Lakes Wilderness is west of Upper Klamath Lake. During the narrow window between eight months of snow, this high country has much to offer boaters, campers, and fishermen. Lost Creek Lake's 3,500 acres are a very popular destination for campers, pleasure boaters, water skiers, and fishermen. The 11-pound, 4-ounce state record largemouth bass was caught here in 1988. Within 5 miles of each other on the 5,150-foot summit of OR 140, Fish Lake and Lake of the Woods provide some of the most scenic campgrounds in the region. In the southwest corner of this region, big Howard Prairie Lake and nearby Hyatt Reservoir are heavily stocked with rainbow trout for fishermen, and swept by predictable afternoon winds for sailors and Jet Skiers. Great camping facilities, too.

More than just a picturesque mountain top gateway to adrenaline-driven whitewater float trips on the Rogue, elk hunting at Butte Falls, and Oregon's only national park, the Rogue River-Klamath Region is large, scenic, and littered with historical and geological intrigue.

Rogue River National Forest

[Fig. 5, Fig. 46] Surrounding much of the Rogue Valley east and west of I-5 in southwestern Oregon, the 630,000-acre Rogue River National Forest includes about 53,800 acres in California. The forest can be entered on the west side by leaving I-5 at community exits and driving east, or from the north by continuing south from Diamond Lake on OR 230.

The forest is actually composed of two units each with its own mosaic of terrain and vegetation. On the west, the National Forest includes the headwaters of the Applegate River, within the complex geology of the Siskiyou Mountains. This is a country of narrow canyons and high, steep ridges. Elevations range from 1,600 feet on the Applegate River to 7,533 at the summit of Mount Ashland (the highest point in Oregon west of the Cascades). The variety of environments includes open oak woodlands, dense conifer forests, and barren, rocky ridge tops.

The climate from July through September is mostly mild with clear skies. Temperatures normally range between 30 and 80 degrees. However, frosty mornings can be expected. Rain, or even snow, may occur during any month of the year. Thunderstorms are common during late afternoon or evening hours.

To the east, the forest follows the upper reaches of the Rogue River, and the slopes of the younger, volcanic Cascade Range. Although the southern Cascades tend to have fairly gentle relief, several deep canyons, such as the Middle Fork of the Rogue and the South Fork of Little Butte Creek, are located in this part of the forest.

The highest point (9,495 feet) is the top of Mount McLoughlin, one of the major volcanic cones in the Oregon Cascades. The area's extensive forest of Douglas fir, ponderosa pine, and other conifers is opened by occasional meadows, lakes and streams. This part of the forest contains Huckleberry Mountain, the ancestral berry-gathering place of the Klamath Indians. Other historic sites include the route of the old military wagon road across the Cascades to Fort Klamath and the rustic buildings of the Union Creek Historic District.

The forest offers more than 40 developed campgrounds and picnic grounds, and about 400 miles of trails for hiking, mountain biking and horseback riding. The Pacific Crest National Scenic Trail runs the entire length of the forest, through the remote backcountry of the Sky Lakes Wilderness along the spine of the High Cascades, and extends westward along the crest of the Siskiyou Mountains. Most developed areas, including trailhead parking areas, require trail park passes, which can be purchased at the area ranger district offices. Fees are also charged for developed campsites with water, and most of the larger campgrounds have a resident manager.

Northeast of Medford, the scenic route along OR 62 and 230 provides access to the Wild and Scenic Upper Rogue River, Crater Lake National Park and popular recreation developments at Diamond Lake (Umpqua National Forest). Rogue River National Forest is divided into four ranger districts: the Applegate, Ashland, Butte Falls, and Prospect.

For more information: Rogue River National Forest Headquarters, 333 W. 8th Street, Medford, OR 97501. Phone (541) 858-2200. Butte Falls Ranger District PO Box 227, Butte Falls, Oregon 97522. Phone (541) 865-2700. Prospect Ranger District, 47201 Highway 62, Prospect, OR 97536. Phone (541) 560-3400. Ashland Ranger District, 645 Washington Street, Ashland, OR 97520. Phone (541) 482-3333. Applegate Ranger District, 6941 Upper Applegate Road, Jacksonville, OR 97530. Phone (541) 899-1812.

SKY LAKES WILDERNESS

[Fig. 47] Designated by Congress in 1984, Sky Lakes Wilderness is 116,300 acres of mountains, lakes, rocky ridges, and timbered slopes along the backbone of the southern Oregon's Cascade Range from Crater Lake National Park south to Highway 140.

The wilderness is about 6 miles wide and 27 miles long, with elevations ranging from 3,800 feet in the Middle Fork of the Rogue River canyon, to 9,495 feet at the top of Mount McLoughlin.

The twin hearts of the wilderness area are two lake basins, Seven Lakes Basin and Blue Canyon Basin, which feature a string of more than 200 lakes, ranging in size from ponds to lakes of 40 acres. Fourmile Lake, near the southern end of the area, contains 700 acres. The lake basins can sometimes be crowded with backpacking campers, but the wilderness has thousands of acres of alternative forest and scenic ridges for solitude lovers.

Many lakes are shallow and do not support fish, but the deeper lakes may have some brook trout. A few lakes may have rainbow trout. The South and Middle forks of the Rogue River and Red Blanket Creek also provide fishing. An Oregon State fishing license is required.

To protect this heavily used area, there are special rules, including a prohibition on motorized vehicles and equipment including hang-gliders, carts, wagons, bicycles, and all forms of mechanized transport. Disabled persons in wheelchairs are permitted.

Group size is limited to 8 persons; maximum number of stock per group is 12 pack/ saddle animals. Campsites must be at least 100 feet from lakeshores and 50 feet from streams. Keep pack and saddle animals at least 200 feet from lakeshores and 50 feet from streams. Grazing is not allowed before August 1.

In geologic terms, the Sky Lakes Wilderness is quite young. Geologic studies indicate that the earliest rocks in this part of the High Cascades began forming when a chain of volcanoes erupted between five and three million years ago. Less than one million years ago, during the Ice Age, the composite volcanoes of Mount Mazama and Mount McLoughlin began their initial build-ups. Just south of Sky Lakes, jumbled lava rocks still litter the forests, little changed in the 15,000 years since the lava erupted from Brown Mountain (elevation 7,311 feet). The mountain can be seen south of OR 140 between Fish Lake and Lake of the Woods.

The north and east slopes of Mount McLoughlin and other peaks bear the scars of glacial ice. Seven Lakes Basin and the deep canyon of the Rogue River's Middle Fork were carved by the massive ice fields, which once covered the highest elevations of the Cascades. As late as 12,000 years ago, minor lava eruptions and mudflows occurred at places like Big Bunchgrass Butte and Imagination Peak. A chain of cinder cones, extending from Goosenest Mountain north to Crater Lake National Park, formed during the post-glacial period. The biggest geologic event in this region was 6,700 years ago, when Mount Mazama imploded and collapsed, forming the caldera of Crater Lake. Some of the vast amount of rock and ash that was thrown into the air landed in the northern portion of Sky Lakes Wilderness, creating a pumice-covered desert.

On the timbered slopes are found many species of trees and smaller plants. Nearly two dozen tree species exist, including Pacific yew (*Taxus brevifolia*) in the lowlands to the mountain hemlock and subalpine fir in the high mountains. Lodgepole pine is common, and whitebark pine may be found high on the slopes of Mount McLoughlin. Shasta red fir dominates much of the wilderness. Prostrate juniper and heather may be seen in the rocks above Margurette Lake, and brilliant shoots of columbine in the talus rock at Lucifer. Kinnickinnick (*Arctostaphylos uva-ursi*) and huckleberries are common throughout the wilderness.

Wildlife is plentiful in most areas. You may see chipmunks, deer, or a herd of elk. Black bears and coyote are also here. Uncommon animals include yellow-bellied marmots, fishers, and pine marten. Often heard (but rarely seen) among the rocks of talus slopes is the tiny pika. Goshawks hunt under the tree canopy. Rattlesnakes (*Crotalus viridis oreganus*) are not known to live in Sky Lakes, but are sometimes seen near Upper Klamath Lake.

Summers tend to be warm and dry, and winters are bitterly cold with heavy snow. The snows often block full access to the wilderness before mid-July. Except for an occasional summer thunderstorm, there is normally little moisture from June to October.

Despite its remote, high-mountain location, people have been roaming Sky Lakes for several thousand years, beginning with the ancestors of the Klamath and the Takelma Indians who hunted game and gathered berries. Early white settlers hunted, trapped

Fig. 46: Mount McLoughlin Area

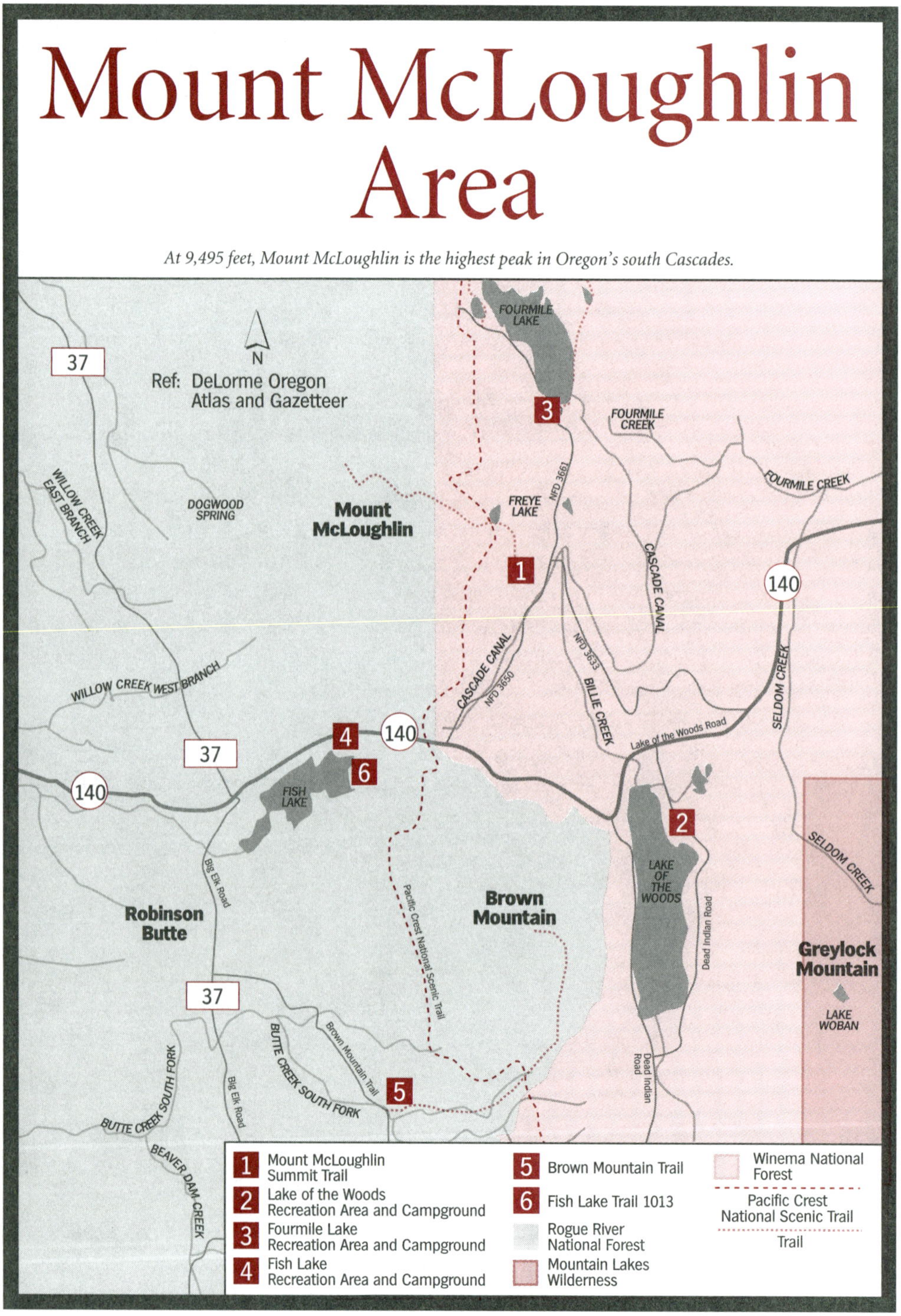

Mount McLoughlin Area
At 9,495 feet, Mount McLoughlin is the highest peak in Oregon's south Cascades.
N
Ref: DeLorme Oregon Atlas and Gazetteer
37
FOURMILE LAKE
3
FOURMILE CREEK
FOURMILE CREEK
WILLOW CREEK EAST BRANCH
DOGWOOD SPRING
Mount McLoughlin
FREYE LAKE
NFD 3661
1
CASCADE CANAL
140
NFD 3633
BILLIE CREEK
SELDOM CREEK
WILLOW CREEK WEST BRANCH
CASCADE CANAL
NFD 3650
4
140
Lake of the Woods Road
37
6
140
FISH LAKE
2
SELDOM CREEK
LAKE OF THE WOODS
Big Elk Road
Robinson Butte
Pacific Crest National Scenic Trail
Brown Mountain
Dead Indian Road
Greylock Mountain
LAKE WOBAN
37
BUTTE CREEK SOUTH FORK
Brown Mountain Trail
BUTTE CREEK SOUTH FORK
Big Elk Road
5
Dead Indian Road
BEAVER DAM CREEK
1 Mount McLoughlin Summit Trail
2 Lake of the Woods Recreation Area and Campground
3 Fourmile Lake Recreation Area and Campground
4 Fish Lake Recreation Area and Campground
5 Brown Mountain Trail
6 Fish Lake Trail 1013
Rogue River National Forest
Mountain Lakes Wilderness
Winema National Forest
Pacific Crest National Scenic Trail
Trail

beaver and marten in the winter, and grazed stock in the high meadows during the warm months. In August settlers from lower-elevation communities picked huckleberries at Stuart Falls and Twin Ponds. Thirty-five miles of Pacific Crest Trail 2000 go through Sky Lakes Wilderness. A trailhead on Highway 140, a mile east of Fish Lake, is the southern entrance. The trail passes through lake basins and crosses into Crater Lake National Park.

Directions: PCT trailhead at Fish Lake on OR 140 goes north into the wilderness. One of the most popular entry points is at Fourmile Lake Campground. Turn north on Forest Service 3661 at Lake of the Woods to the campground.

Activities: Hiking, fishing, hunting, berry picking, and camping.

Facilities: None.

Dates: Open year-round and snow-free mid-July through Oct. Access to trailheads prevented by deep snow in mid-winter.

Fees: Trail park permits are required at some trailheads.

Closest town: Klamath Falls.

For more information: Rogue River National Forest Headquarters, 333 W. 8th Street, Medford, OR 97501, phone (541) 858-2200 or Klamath Ranger District, 1936 California Avenue, Klamath Falls, OR 97601, phone (541) 885-3400.

MOUNT MCLOUGHLIN

[Fig. 46] Towering 9,495 feet above the southwest corner of Sky Lakes Wilderness, Mount McLoughlin is the highest peak in Oregon's south Cascades, and a regional landmark for modern travelers, just as it was centuries earlier for Takelma, Klamath, and Modoc tribes. It's the highest point between Three Sisters and Mount Shasta. The eastern base of the peak is in Winema National Forest but most of the mountain, including the summit, is in Rogue River National Forest. The mountain covers 20 square miles, and is tracked by a trail that leads hikers on a tough but nontechnical route to the summit.

Before 1905, when Oregon's legislature named the peak in honor of the head of the Hudson's Bay Company in Oregon, Dr. John McLoughlin, the mountain has had more than half-a-dozen names, including *Kesh yainatat*, a Klamath Indian name meaning, "dwarf old woman who controlled the west wind."

Mount McLoughlin is a relatively young composite volcano that began building less than a million years ago, and last erupted 12,000 years ago. Ice Age glaciers scoured away most of the mountain's northeast slope, leaving behind long, winding moraines of loose rock.

Below tree line the mountain is encased in a forest of Shasta red fir and mountain hemlock, with scattered lodgepole pines. Manzanita, huckleberry, and mountain ash bushes make up much of the understory. Hikers frequently see deer and elk in

BAND-TAILED PIGEON
(*Columba fasciata*)

the timber. The mostly open upper slopes are home to golden-mantled ground squirrels, pine martens, and Clark's nutcrackers. In 1917 the Forest Service anchored a fire lookout to the summit, but eventually abandoned and burned it.

MOUNT MCLOUGHLIN SUMMIT TRAIL

[Fig. 46(1)] It's possible to step onto the summit of southern Oregon's highest mountain without the technical protection required to climb most of Oregon's young volcanoes.

The trail to the summit begins on Forest Service Road 3650 between Fish and Fourmile lakes north of OR 140, and winds through rocky terrain, including a boulder field about 1 mile from the trailhead near the junction of Pacific Crest Trail 2000. Tree blazes mark the route through rock and boulder areas. Above tree line, head for the main ridge and follow it to the summit. The ascent is steep, but can be walked. Take water, it's a dry hike.

Directions: From OR 140 about 1 mile east of Fish Lake, turn north onto paved Forest Service 3650/Fourmile Lake Road and continue about 2 miles to the trailhead parking area on the west side of the road. Most of the trail is inside Sky Lakes Wilderness and vehicles, including mountain bikes, are not allowed.

Activities: Hiking, summit climbs.

Facilities: None.

Dates: Open year-round, and mostly snow-free from late May to mid-Oct.

Fees: There is a charge for trail park passes.

For more information: Butte Falls Ranger District, Rogue River National Forest, PO Box 227, Butte Falls, Oregon 97522, phone (541) 865-2700

Trail: 11 miles round-trip.

Elevation: Trailhead is about 5,600 feet and the summit is 9,495 feet.

Degree of difficulty: Strenuous.

Surface and Blaze: Dirt and rock, with tree blazes in places.

LAKE OF THE WOODS RECREATION AREA AND CAMPGROUNDS

[Fig. 46(2)] Located at an elevation of 4,961 feet in dense forest near the top of the Cascade Range on OR 140, Lake of the Woods and nearby Fish Lake are clear, cool refuges from the often 100-degree plus summer temperatures at lower elevations in Medford to the west and Klamath Falls on the east. Southern Oregon's largest lava flow, Brown Mountain, lies in slabs and boulders in pockets and massive rock gardens through this area. Two large Forest Service campgrounds with 127 sites are tucked into the conifer trees around 1,113-acre Lake of the Woods. Another 25 campsites are 6 miles north at 740-acre Fourmile Lake. An additional 44 Forest Service campsites, and a 50-site resort are at Fish Lake 7 miles west.

There are numerous trails in the forest around Lake of the Woods and Fish Lake that have easy grades and are open to hikers, mountain bikers, and horseback riders. All three lakes are popular with boaters, trout fishermen, and water skiers at Lake of the Woods. Lake Of The Woods and Fourmile are also excellent kokanee salmon producers.

The recreation area is engulfed in dense stands of old-growth white and Douglas firs and lodgepole pines. The conifer canopy opens across the water for great views of Mount McLoughlin. Lake of the Woods, the largest camping and recreation complex in the area, was formed when lava flows from Brown Mountain dammed the drainages of three small creeks. Both Lake of the Woods and Fish Lake also have private resorts that rent boats, sell groceries and camping supplies, and offer cafes, private RV sites with hook-ups, and cabins. Fishing licenses can also be bought there.

This recreation area is just south of the hiking and backpacking opportunities at Sky Lakes Wilderness Area and west of Mountain Lakes Wilderness.

This area shows the scars of two volcanic periods separated by millions of years. Vast flows of broken lava boulders lay in barren disarray along OR 140 near Fish Lake. The area was a geological division line between volcanic periods.

West of Fish Lake to Eagle Point, Oregon, the lava littering the roadside and lying in great barren swaths between conifer groves is believed to be about 75 million years old, which would place the region's development in the Cretaceous Era, when seawater still lapped at the west edge of these mountains. Some of the rocks have been discolored to hues of purple and green by thermal steam releases.

East along OR 140, from Fish Lake to Klamath Falls, the islands and fields of hardened lava are believed to be only about 7,000 years old, remnants of the eruptions that formed the highest peaks of the present-day Cascades. The black rocks are basalt, the grayish ones andesite, and those that appear bright red are stained by iron oxides.

The remote lava and forest lands south of OR 140 along Dead Indian Memorial Road to Howard Prairie Lake are popular with deer and elk hunters. The first seasons are archery hunts that begin in early September.

All three lakes in the recreation area, Fish, Lake of the Woods, and Fourmile, provide swimming, picnicking, hiking, fishing, and camping. Speed limits eliminate water skiing at Fourmile and Fish Lakes.

Directions: Lake of the Woods Recreation Area is alongside OR 140 at the crest of the Cascades, about 35 miles west of Klamath Falls and east of Medford.

Activities: Camping, swimming, boating, picnicking, hiking, mountain biking, seasonal hunting, trout and kokanee salmon fishing.

Facilities: At Lake of the Woods: 2 Forest Service campgrounds with 127 total sites, piped water, flush toilets, boat launches, picnic tables, fireplaces, waste water disposal, and trailer dump. A private year-round resort has tent and RV sites with hookups, a restaurant, store, gas, marina, boat rentals, and showers. A visitor center is located between the lake and highway and is open from Memorial to Labor Day. It stocks maps and recreational information.

At Fish Lake: 2 Forest Service campgrounds with 44 tent and RV sites; a private resort with another 50 sites, some with RV hookups. The resort also has cabins, bottled gas, showers, store, cafe, laundry room, and boat rentals.

At Fourmile Lake: 6.0 miles north of OR 140 on Forest Service 3661, there is 1 campground with 25 sites, vault toilets, picnic tables, fireplaces and drinking water.

Dates: Memorial Day to mid-Sept. The 5,744-foot elevation at Fourmile Lake is about 1,000 feet higher than OR 140, snow depths are greater and the campground sometimes doesn't open until early July.

Fees: There are charges for camping and trail park passes are required at the Mt. McLoughlin Trailhead.

Closest town: Klamath Falls is about 35 miles east, and Medford 35 miles west on OR 140.

For more information: Klamath Ranger District, Winema National Forest, 1936 California Avenue, Klamath Falls, OR 97601. Phone (541) 885-3400. Ashland Ranger District, Rogue River National Forest, 645 Washington Street, Ashland, OR 97520. Phone (541) 482-3333. Lake of the Woods Resort, phone (541) 949-8300, Fish Lake Resort, phone (541) 949-8500.

BROWN MOUNTAIN TRAIL 1005

[Fig. 46(5)] Brown Mountain Trail runs 7.8 miles, from Lake of the Woods in Winema National Forest west through the vast Brown Mountain lava flow to Rogue River National Forest Road 3705 at South Fork Little Butte Creek south of Fish Lake. The trail is open for hiking, mountain biking, and horseback riding. There are few places along the trail where 7,311-foot elevation Brown Mountain can be seen.

Much of the route is in shaded, old-growth forest and offers opportunities for morel mushroom hunting in the late spring; shade-loving wildflowers such as orchids and trilliums blanket the forest floor in early summer. Huckleberry picking is good in late summer, and there are brilliant fall colors. The trail intersects Pacific Crest National Scenic Trail 2000 west of Brown Mountain. Mountain bikes are not allowed on the Pacific Crest Trail.

Directions: Eastern trailhead is on the west shore of Lake of the Woods at Camp McLoughlin Boy Scout Camp. The western entry is reached by going south from OR 140 west of Fish Lake on Forest Service 37 for 6 miles to Forest Service 3705. Turn east onto 3705 and continue 3.5 miles to the trailhead. Parking is available for 4-5 vehicles

Activities: Hiking, mountain biking, mushroom and berry picking, hunting in fall.

Facilities: None.

Dates: Mid-May to Oct.

Fees: There is a charge for trail park passes in summer.

Trail: 7.8 miles one-way.

Elevation: 4850 feet at Road 3705 and 4,961 feet at Lake of the Woods.

Degree of difficulty: Moderate.

Surface: Dirt and rock.

FISH LAKE TRAIL 1013

[Fig. 46(6)] Fish Lake Trail offers easy hiking and mountain biking opportunities that range from a short stroll along the shore of Fish Lake or the North Fork of Little Butte Creek, to daylong excursions to the Brown Mountain Lava flows along the connecting Pacific Crest National Scenic Trail 2000. Mountain biking is not allowed on PCT.

At about mile point 4.8 on Trail 1013, an interesting geologic phenomenon can be viewed. In the early 1900s, the 11-mile Cascade Canal was built to carry water from Fourmile Lake to Fish Lake and subsequently to Medford. Near the trail, the water from the canal disappears into a lava tube and enters Fish Lake 1 mile away at a small pond.

Directions: To begin at Fish Lake's Doe Point or Fish Lake Campground, follow OR 140 to the Fish Lake turnoff, turn south and follow signs. Park at either of the day-use picnic areas.

Activities: Hiking, mountain biking, horseback riding.

Facilities: None.

Dates: Open May to Oct.

Fees: There is a charge of trail park passes.

Trail: 5.0 miles, one way.

Elevation: 4,560 feet at Forest Service Road 37, and 4,950 feet at the PCT.

Degree of difficulty: Easy

Surface: Dirt.

Rogue-Umpqua Divide Wilderness

[Fig. 47] Mountains range in elevation from 3,200 to 6,878 feet inside the 33,000-acre Rogue-Umpqua Divide Wilderness, which separates the drainages for the famed Rogue and Umpqua rivers. The wilderness is in Umpqua National Forest on the west border of Rogue River National Forest, about 80 miles southeast of Roseburg. The east boundary of the wilderness is about 5 miles directly west of Crater Lake National Park on the ridgeline above the west side of OR 230. This is a beautiful summer area of high mountain meadows and hill-hugging mists. The wilderness is a land of deep forests and subalpine meadows characterized by timbered valleys of Douglas fir, which rise to alpine meadows and mixed stands of pines and firs.

Large old-growth forests are along Acker Divide and Cripple Camp trails. Nearly all of the trails in Rogue-Umpqua Divide pass through subalpine meadows. In the spring, the openings are a palette of lush green grass, wildflowers, and trees in bud.

The forest inside this small wilderness area is a diverse mix of sugar pine, grand fir, mountain hemlock, western white pine, incense-cedar (*Calocedrus decurrens*), subalpine fir, western red cedar, white fir, ponderosa pine, Douglas fir, Alaska yellow cedar (*Chamaecyparis nootkaensis*), Shasta red fir, lodgepole pine, Pacific silver fir, western hemlock, and whitebark pine. Trails lead to many small lakes, meadows, and top-of-the-world vistas. The most popular trail is the 31.4 mile Rogue-Umpqua Divide National Recreation Trail.

Directions: Several roads approach the edge of the wilderness on all sides. South Umpqua River Road is a popular entry route on the west side. Follow the river northeast from Tiller. On the east side, Forest Service 6510/6515 leads from OR 230 west to Hershberger Lookout at the edge of the wilderness.

Activities: Hiking, backpacking, fishing, and hunting for deer and elk.

Facilities: None.

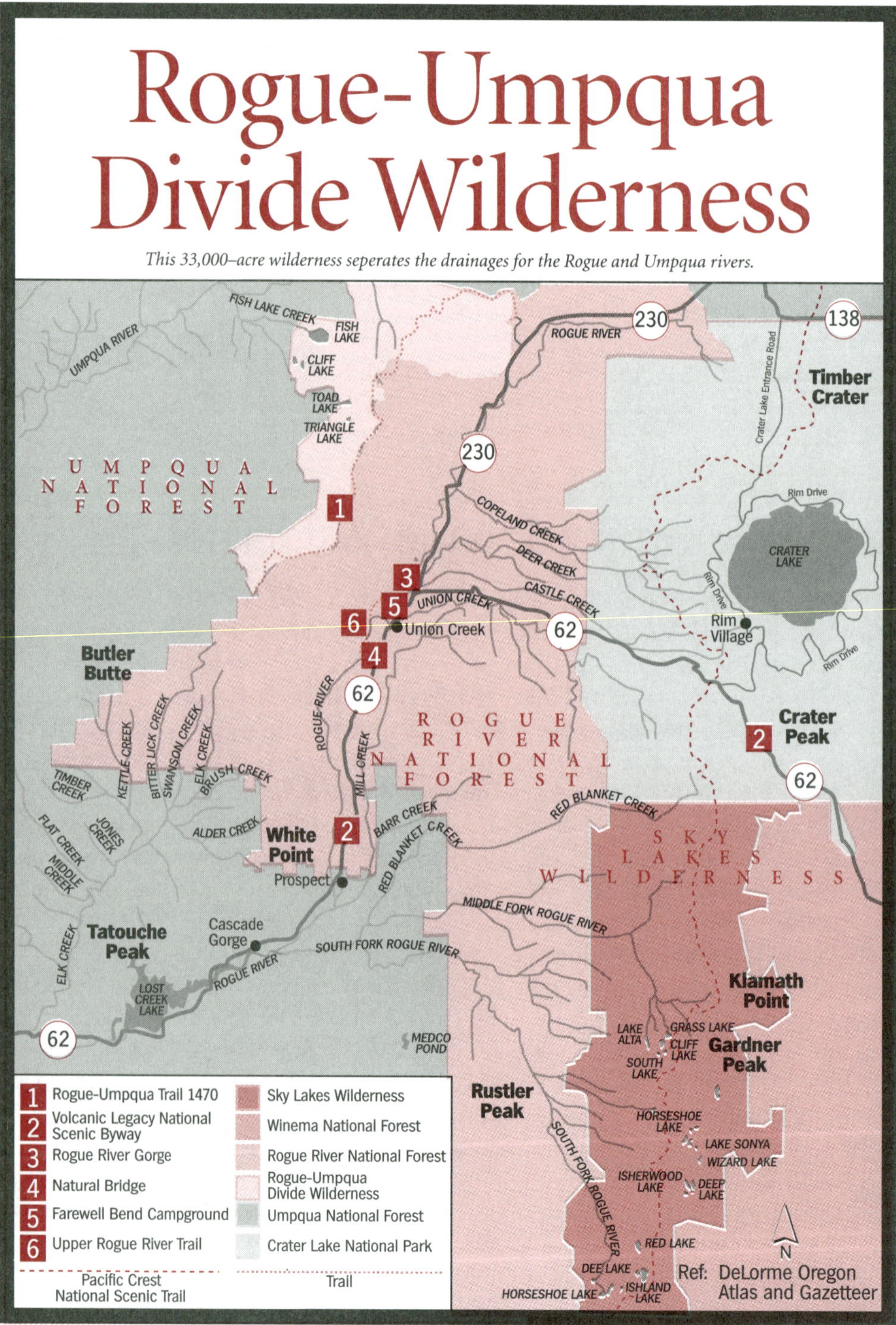
Rogue-Umpqua Divide Wilderness
This 33,000–acre wilderness seperates the drainages for the Rogue and Umpqua rivers.
UMPQUA NATIONAL FOREST
ROGUE RIVER NATIONAL FOREST
SKY LAKES WILDERNESS
Timber Crater
Crater Lake
Rim Village
Rim Drive
Crater Lake Entrance Road
Crater Peak
Butler Butte
White Point
Prospect
Union Creek
Cascade Gorge
Tatouche Peak
Lost Creek Lake
Medco Pond
Rustler Peak
Klamath Point
Gardner Peak
Fish Lake
Cliff Lake
Toad Lake
Triangle Lake
Lake Alta
Grass Lake
South Lake
Horseshoe Lake
Lake Sonya
Wizard Lake
Isherwood Lake
Deep Lake
Red Lake
Dee Lake
Ishland Lake
Umpqua River
Fish Lake Creek
Rogue River
Copeland Creek
Deer Creek
Castle Creek
Union Creek
Mill Creek
Kettle Creek
Bitter Lick Creek
Swanson Creek
Elk Creek
Brush Creek
Timber Creek
Jones Creek
Flat Creek
Middle Creek
Alder Creek
Barr Creek
Red Blanket Creek
Middle Fork Rogue River
South Fork Rogue River
230
138
62
1 Rogue-Umpqua Trail 1470
2 Volcanic Legacy National Scenic Byway
3 Rogue River Gorge
4 Natural Bridge
5 Farewell Bend Campground
6 Upper Rogue River Trail
Pacific Crest National Scenic Trail
Sky Lakes Wilderness
Winema National Forest
Rogue River National Forest
Rogue-Umpqua Divide Wilderness
Umpqua National Forest
Crater Lake National Park
Trail
N
Ref: DeLorme Oregon Atlas and Gazetteer

Dates: Open year-round, usually snow-free from mid-July through Oct.

Fees: None.

Closest town: Roseburg is 80 miles west on OR 138.

For more information: Umpqua National Forest, 2900 N. W. Stewart Parkway, Roseburg, OR 97470. Phone (541) 672-6601. Diamond Lake Ranger District, Box 101, Idleyld Park, OR 97447. Phone (541) 498-2531.

ROGUE-UMPQUA DIVIDE NATIONAL RECREATION TRAIL 1470

[Fig. 47(1)] The most popular trail in the wilderness is the 31.4 mile Rogue-Umpqua Divide National Recreation Trail. Views are exceptional from the trail, both east and west, as it weaves its way across the crest of the divide. To the west lies the irregular and deeply dissected terrain of the Umpqua drainage. To the east is the broad, open Rogue Basin, with the peaks of the high Cascades rising above. In addition to the sweeping vistas, the divide trail features a spectacular display of meadow wildflowers from mid-June until August.

Directions: About 2.5 miles west of the junction of OR 230 and 138 near Diamond Lake, turn north off OR 230 onto Forest Service 3703/Three Lakes Road. Continue for 6 miles. The trailhead is just west of Three Lakes Camp.

Activities: Hiking.

Facilities: None.

Dates: Open year-round, and usually snow-free from mid-June through mid-Oct.

Fees: None.

Trail: 31.4 miles, one-way.

Elevation: 5,250 feet to 6,020 feet.

Degree of difficulty: Easy to moderate.

Surface: Dirt and rock.

VOLCANIC LEGACY NATIONAL SCENIC BYWAY

[Fig. 47(2)] Volcanic Legacy National Scenic Byway threads through 140 miles of volcanic landscapes, which vary from the wonders of Crater Lake (*see* Crater Lake National Park, page 315), south to the high desert and wetlands of the Klamath Basin.

The north-south byway, designated by Congress in 1998, takes 5 to 7 hours to drive, begins and ends on US 97, and incorporates segments of OR 138, 62, and 140.

The byway was selected for national scenic status because it exemplifies outstanding scenic, historic, recreational and natural qualities.

The north entrance to Volcanic Legacy National Scenic Byway starts from the junction of OR 138, and continues into the national park. It leads to the young—7,000-years-old—caldera, now filled with Crater Lake. At 1,932 feet deep, it is the deepest lake in the United States and seventh deepest in the world. It passes the east side of Sky Lakes Wilderness, continues south along the west side of Agency and Upper Klamath lakes, and runs along the northeast side of Mountain Lakes Wilderness, before returning to US 97 at Klamath Falls. The route follows the incline of the East Slope of the Oregon Cascades, and is a good opportunity to see the rapid changes in climate, topography, and botany between the crest of the Cascades and the desert floor. Most of the byway is within Winema National Forest.

Klamath Basin is at the south end of the route, and contains the largest freshwater ecosystem west of the Great Lakes. Upper Klamath Lake (*see* Upper Klamath Lake and Refuge, page 311) has 90,000 surface acres, a self-guided canoe trail, renowned rainbow trout fishing, and Upper Klamath Wildlife Refuge. During peak fall migrations the refuge attracts more than one million birds. Biologists estimate that 80 percent of all waterfowl in the Pacific Flyway use the refuge during spring and fall migrations. More than 430 species of wildlife live here year-round.

The southern portal to the Volcanic Legacy National Scenic Byway is where US 97 crosses the California border at Francis S. Landrum Historic Wayside.

Most of the route is two lanes, paved, and designed for maximum scenery. Traveler services are available on US 97 and OR 140.

For more information: Winema National Forest Supervisor's Office, 2819 Dahlia Street, Klamath Falls, OR 97601. Phone (541) 883-6714. Klamath District Ranger, 1936 California Avenue, Klamath Falls, Oregon 97601. Phone (541) 885-3400. Klamath Department of Tourism, 1451 Main Street, Klamath Falls, OR 97601. Phone (541) 884-0666 or outside Oregon 800-445-6728. Web site: www.KlamathCountyTourism.com.

ROGUE RIVER GORGE AND HISTORIC UNION CREEK

[Fig. 47(3)] In a long patch of pine trees just west of Crater Lake National Park near the junction of OR 230 and OR 62 are two geological oddities; three exceptional campgrounds; several rolling trails, including a beautiful 7-mile segment of Upper Rogue River Trail 1034; and a rustic 70-year-old resort with a reputation for homemade pies and home-style meals.

The attractions are in a 2.5 mile stretch of OR 230, and include the Rogue River Gorge, Natural Bridge, Farewell Bend Campground, and historic Union Creek Resort. They form the recreational center of the Upper Rogue River region.

Directions: On OR 230/62 about 30 miles south of Diamond Lake.

Activities: Geological sightseeing, hiking, camping.

Facilities: Forest Service interpretive areas with paved trails to viewpoints, restrooms, campgrounds at Farewell Bend, Union Creek, and Natural Bridge, private resort with cabins, groceries, and cafe.

Dates: The road and resort are open year-round, but viewpoints and campgrounds are snowbound from Nov. through Apr.

Fees: There are charges for camping, trail park passes, and resort services.

Closest town: Shady Cove is 36 miles southwest on OR 62.

For more information: Rogue River National Forest, 333 W. 8th Street, Medford, OR 97501. Phone (541) 858-2200.

ROGUE RIVER GORGE

[Fig. 47(3)] Rogue River Gorge is a 500-foot-long lava-walled chasm barely 25 feet across, where the 44-degree water in the Rogue River is squeezed into a powerful gush of whitewater roaring through a collapsed lava tube. Wild bouquets of delicate ferns cling to the mist-drenched black walls of the gorge, pine and fir trees canopy the trail and hold in the cool air that drifts upward from the plunging river. A paved path, wheelchair-accessible, runs for .025 mile along the top of the chasm with frequent viewpoints and interpretive signs. Two lava tubes open into the gorge, one is plugged with lava rock and the other appears like a cave opening.

Directions: On OR 62 just south of the junction of OR 230 and the turnoff to the west entrance to Crater Lake National Park.

Activities: Sightseeing.

Facilities: Paved 0.25 mile trail, interpretive signs, and restrooms.

Dates: Open when snow-free.

Fees: None.

NATURAL BRIDGE

[Fig. 47(4)] About 0.5 mile downstream from the thundering Rogue River Gorge the powerful river seems to disappear at Natural Bridge Viewpoint.

What actually happens is that the river plunges into a labyrinth of hollow lava tubes, runs underground beneath a massive basalt outcrop, and reappears on the far side about 50 feet downstream. The outcrop, believed to have been deposited during the last eruption of Mount Mazama, blocks the natural watercourse, and has become a bridge over the underground river. This area is honeycombed with ancient lava tubes that were formed several million years ago when molten lavas burned tunnels through the ground. When the lava quit flowing, the molten flow either drained out or formed a plug at the downhill end of the tube. Left behind were huge carrot-shaped tunnels with walls and floors covered with sheaths of shiny, hard lava. Geologists believe that when the flow of the mighty Rogue was blocked, the river found its way into openings in the lava tubes beneath it.

Directions: See previous directions to Rogue River Gorge.

Activities: Sightseeing, camping.

Facilities: Viewpoint and interpretive signs. USFS Natural Bridge Campground with 16 free campsites and vault toilets is just north of the viewpoint.

Dates: Open year-round.

Fees: None.

FAREWELL BEND CAMPGROUND

[Fig. 47(5)] Although second in size to the 78 campsites offered at nearby Union Creek Campground, Farewell Bend Campground is the most popular overnight site in the Rogue River Gorge-Union Creek area. Located roughly on the Crater Lake pioneer trail, Farewell Bend is one of a half dozen similarly named river crossings where supposedly there was no turning back for the overland wagons.

The bend at this site is wide, carved with deep pools, and while the 44 degree water discourages swimmers, it doesn't stop hundreds of campers from sticking a toe in and hollering in surprise.

Directions: On the west side of OR 62, about 0.5 mile south of Rogue River Gorge or 12 miles north of Prospect Ranger Station.

Activities: Camping, hiking.

Facilities: 61 tent and RV sites, flush toilets, piped water, playground.

Dates: Open mid-May through Sept.

Fees: There is a charge for campsites.

UNION CREEK

[Fig. 47] A Forest Service campground, great ice cream, homemade pies, and rustic 70-year-old Union Creek Resort are about 0.25 mile south of Rogue River Gorge viewpoint. This is the recreational and supply center for the upper Rogue River valley, and a traditional stop for hikers, fishermen, rafters, deer and elk hunters, picnickers, snowmobilers, cross-country skiers, and campers.

Union Creek Resort is open year-round. It's a good place to stock up on groceries, fishing licenses, snow and trail park passes, ice cream cones, and the only place to sample the famous homemade pies that brown in the oven at Beckie's Cafe.

The resort is listed on the National Register of Historic Places, and retains the rustic look of early 1900s.

Union Creek Campground straddles the creek in deep woods, and is a base often used by recreationists. Union Creek, Foster Creek, and the nearby Rogue River provide good fishing for stocked trout.

Directions: See Rogue River Gorge, page 305.

Activities: Camping, hiking, fishing, and sightseeing.

Facilities: Union Creek Campground has 78 tent and RV sites, vault toilets, piped water, stone fireplaces, community kitchen, and campground host. Union Creek Resort has cabins, cafe, store, groceries, fishing licenses, and forest permits.

Dates: Campground is open mid-May to Oct. and resort is open year-round.

Fees: There are charges for camping, and resort services.

Winema National Forest

[Fig. 5, Fig. 47] Patches of 1.1 million-acre Winema National Forest are loosely scattered north of Klamath Falls between spectacular tracts of Crater Lake National Park, Upper Crater Lake National Wildlife Refuge, and pieces of state and Bureau of Land Management ground.

Winema is a Modoc Indian name for a heroine of the Modoc War of 1872. According to accounts, Winema, meaning "Woman of a Brave Heart," lived near Klamath Lakes, and was appointed by the government to act as interpreter between U.S. troops and her native people. Her diplomacy was key to ending the bloody war.

US 97 enters the forest from the north about 4.5 miles south of the junction of OR 58. The southern border lies in a quilt of mixed ownership lands south of Mountain Lakes Wilderness Area (*see* Mountain Lakes Wilderness, page 309). Unlike most National Forests in the Oregon Cascades, much of the Winema is high desert or semiarid plateaus sprinkled with scattered groves of pine trees. Portions of Sky Lakes Wilderness lie within the forest. A pair of unusual volcanic cones within the forest, Goose Neck and Goose Egg, are related to the activities of neighboring Mount Mazama, the ancient volcano that holds Crater Lake.

Other attractions include Devils Garden, a hodgepodge of rock formations; Sand Creek Pinnacles; Ox-Knee Overlook; Pelican Butte, with elevated views of Klamath Lake; Lake of the Woods Visitor Center; and the remoteness of the Mountain Lakes Wilderness.

The forest, which is the newest in Oregon, was created in 1961 from the former Klamath Indian Reservation and portions of adjacent forests. Although young, the Winema has a rich heritage with a blending of Native American prehistory and early exploration and settlement. The habitat diversity in the forest supports a variety of fish and wildlife species, from deer, black bear, mountain lion, bobcat and elk to large populations of water-oriented birds, including eagles, osprey, pelicans and numerous waterfowl.

Recreation opportunities range from the solitude of hiking an isolated trail in one of three wildernesses, Mountain Lakes, Sky Lakes and Mount Thielsen, to family activities in a developed setting at the Lake of the Woods or Miller Lake. The Winema has 82 miles of trails for hiking, mountain biking, and horse packing. The high mountain lakes and streams offer trout fishing, and lakes have warm water species such as largemouth bass, Sacramento and yellow perch, crappie, and catfish.

The Williamson River is a renowned fly fishing stream and serves as spawning grounds for brown trout that migrate from Upper Klamath Lake. There are 190 miles of fish streams and 41 fish producing lakes offering a chance to catch seventeen different species of game fish. Fourmile Lake Campground (*see* Lake Of The Woods Recreation Area, page 298) in the Klamath Ranger District is an excellent place to enjoy water recreation in an alpine lake. Fishing, boating, and swimming are popular. The campground also has horse facilities at the trailhead leading into the Sky Lakes Wilderness Area. There are picnic and 25 tent/trailer sites. Drinking water and restrooms are available at the campground.

The Klamath Basin (*see* Upper Klamath National Wildlife Refuge, page 312) is the largest waterfowl congregating area on the West Coast and has the largest population of wintering and nesting bald eagles in the lower 48 states. Birdwatchers may also see great grey owls (*Stric nebulosa*) at higher elevations. With wingspans of 68 inches, these are the largest owls in North America.

The Winema has seven winter sports sites, 242 miles of snowmobile trails and 39 miles of cross-country ski trails. The major attractions are:

Pelican Butte. The 8,036 foot-elevation summit offers views of Upper Klamath Lake and Sky Lakes Wilderness. Old-growth timber lines the well-marked but narrow, rough

Mountain Lakes Wilderness Area

Mountain Lakes Wilderness is one of the original three Forest Service primitive areas in Washington and Oregon.

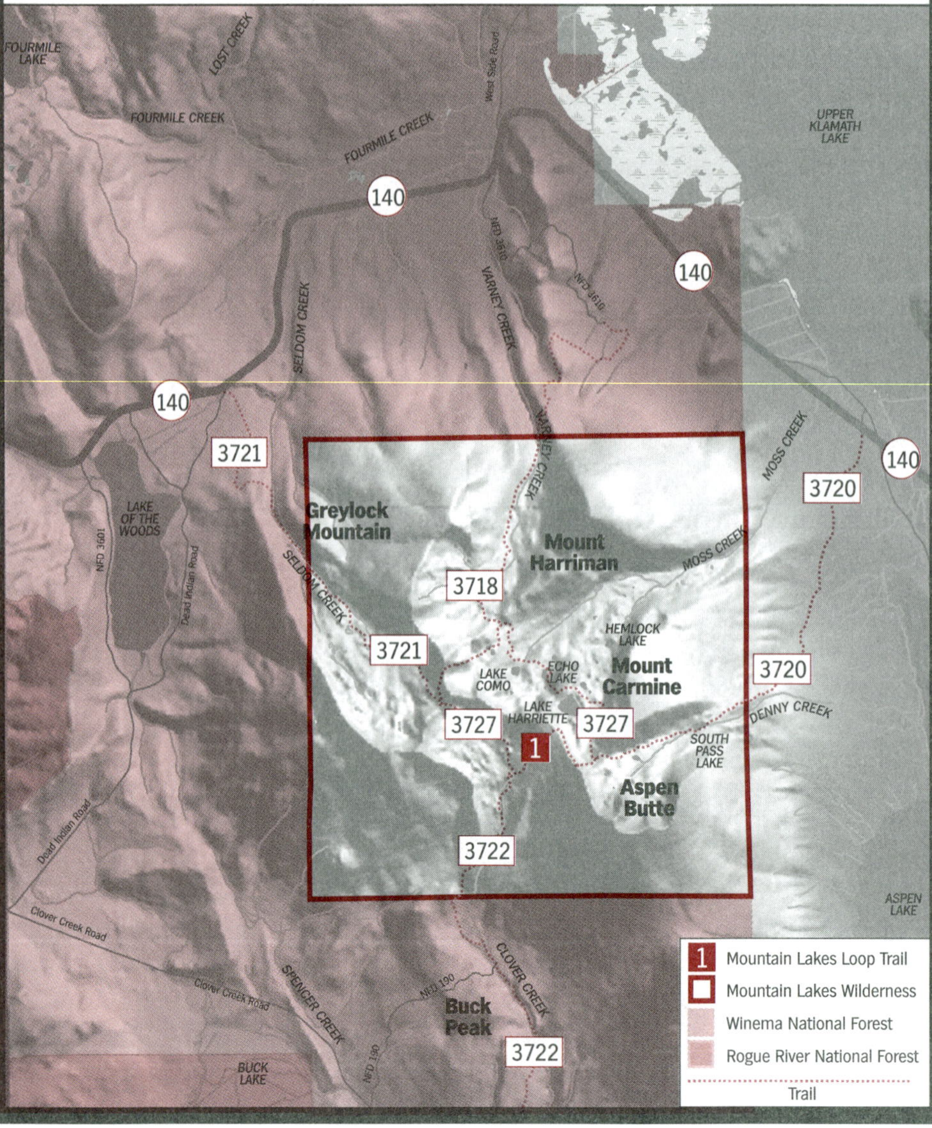

1 Mountain Lakes Loop Trail
Mountain Lakes Wilderness
Winema National Forest
Rogue River National Forest
Trail

road to the top. It is about a one-hour ride to the summit from Klamath Falls.

Calimus Butte. Historic cupola-style lookout built by the Bureau of Indian Affairs in 1920. Overlooks the 48-square mile Lone Pine Fire that occurred in 1992, and the Klamath Marsh and Sprague River Valley.

Ouxkanee Overlook. A short drive off of Highway 97 leads to a picnic area and overlook of the Williamson River Valley. On a clear day you can see Mount Shasta in northern California.

For more information: Winema National Forest Supervisor's Office, 2819 Dahlia Street, Klamath Falls, OR 97601. Phone (541) 883-6714. Chemult District Ranger, PO Box 150, Chemult, OR 97731. Phone (541) 365-7001. Chiloquin District Ranger, 38500 Highway 97 North, Chiloquin, OR 97624. Phone (541) 783-4001. Klamath District Ranger, 1936 California Avenue, Klamath Falls, OR 97601. Phone (541) 885-3400.

MOUNTAIN LAKES WILDERNESS

[Fig. 48] Winema National Forest's Mountain Lakes Wilderness is one of the original three Forest Service primitive areas in Washington and Oregon. Its 23,071 acres are packed 6-miles-wide and 6-miles-deep, making it the only square shaped wilderness in the National Wilderness Preservation System (NWPS). The center of Mountain Lakes occupies a large caldera, a broad craterlike basin left by the explosion or collapse of what was once a 12,000-foot-high volcanic cone southwest of Upper Klamath Lake.

A similar geologic event created Crater Lake, which fills the caldera of Mount Mazama to the north. At Mountain Lakes, however, glaciers scoured out separate drainages inside the caldera, which created a scattering of small lakes instead of one large lake, which is what happened at the national park. Seven named mountains are jammed into an uneven circle at the heart of the wilderness, with peaks rising to 8,208 feet at the summit of Aspen Butte. The peaks roughly outline what was once the rim of the crater.

Mountain Lakes Wilderness is a small wilderness, but rugged, and most trails are strenuous. It can be entered from three directions. The Clover Creek Trail from the south is only 3.6 miles long. The Mountain Lakes Trail from Lake of the Woods entering on the west is 6.5 miles; the Varney Creek Trail from the north is 4.5 miles long. These trails are all connected in the wilderness interior by the 8-mile Mountain Lakes Loop Trail, which climbs from the sparkling blue lakes and winds along the southern caldera rim. Hiking in Mountain Lakes Wilderness varies from easily traversed drainages and lake basins to steep, rugged climbs.

Summer temperatures range from highs in the high 80s to lows of 40-50 degrees Fahrenheit. Thundershowers are a common summer pattern, and it can snow in any month.

Trout are stocked in Mountain Lakes Wilderness lakes every other year. Both brook and rainbow trout are stocked in lakes Harriette, Como, and South Pass. Rainbows only are stocked in Mystic and Paragon Lakes.

Directions: The Varney Creek route is marked from OR 140, which passes between the wilderness and Upper Klamath Lake. Another popular entry spot is on the south side from Clover Creek Road. From OR 140 at Lake of the Woods, turn south onto Forest

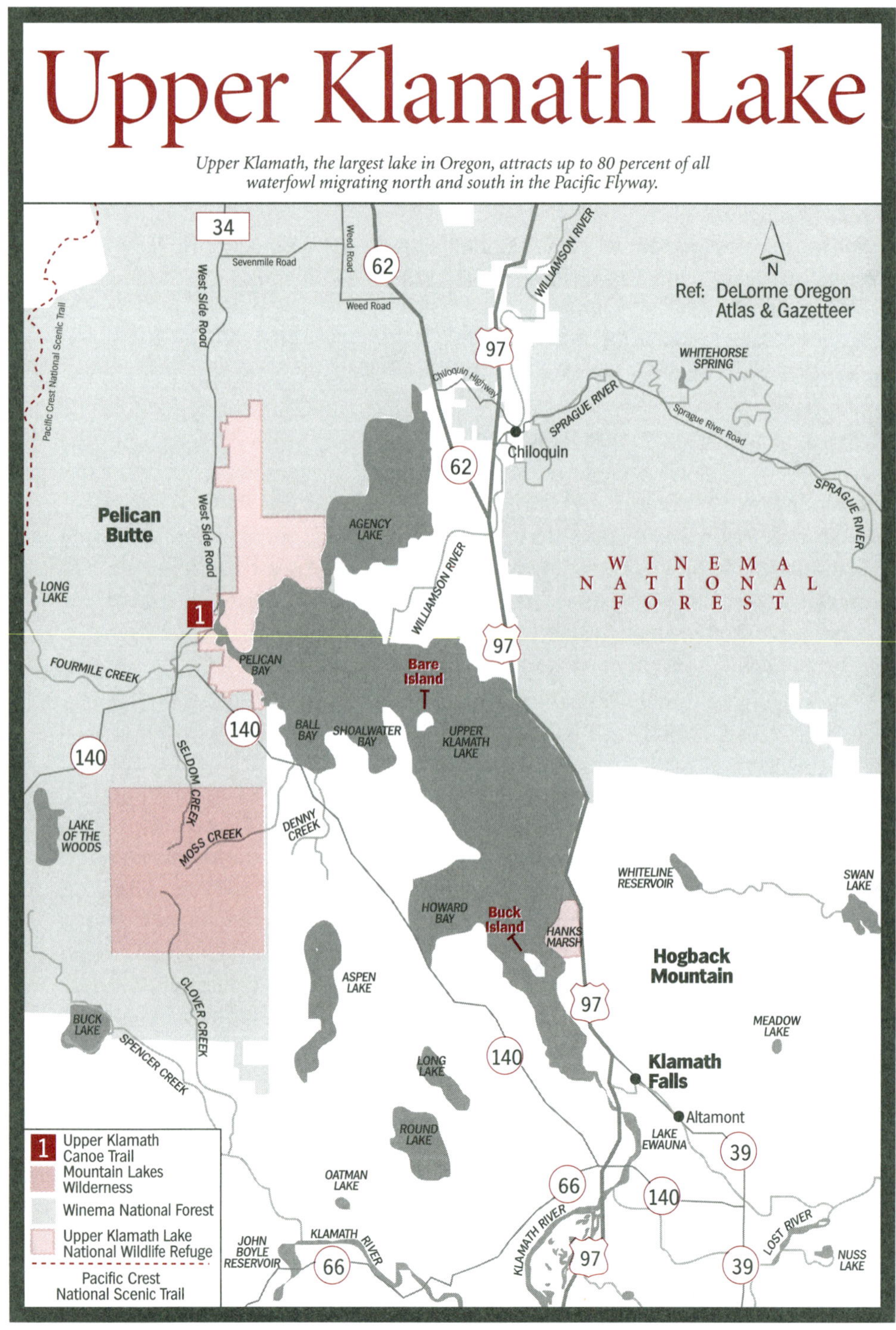
Upper Klamath Lake
Upper Klamath, the largest lake in Oregon, attracts up to 80 percent of all waterfowl migrating north and south in the Pacific Flyway.
Ref: DeLorme Oregon Atlas & Gazetteer
N
34
62
97
140
66
39
Sevenmile Road
Weed Road
West Side Road
Chiloquin Highway
Sprague River Road
Pacific Crest National Scenic Trail
WILLIAMSON RIVER
SPRAGUE RIVER
WHITEHORSE SPRING
Chiloquin
Pelican Butte
AGENCY LAKE
WINEMA NATIONAL FOREST
LONG LAKE
FOURMILE CREEK
PELICAN BAY
Bare Island
BALL BAY
SHOALWATER BAY
UPPER KLAMATH LAKE
SELDOM CREEK
MOSS CREEK
DENNY CREEK
LAKE OF THE WOODS
WHITELINE RESERVOIR
SWAN LAKE
HOWARD BAY
Buck Island
HANKS MARSH
Hogback Mountain
ASPEN LAKE
CLOVER CREEK
BUCK LAKE
SPENCER CREEK
MEADOW LAKE
Klamath Falls
Altamont
LAKE EWAUNA
ROUND LAKE
OATMAN LAKE
JOHN BOYLE RESERVOIR
KLAMATH RIVER
LOST RIVER
NUSS LAKE
1 Upper Klamath Canoe Trail
Mountain Lakes Wilderness
Winema National Forest
Upper Klamath Lake National Wildlife Refuge
Pacific Crest National Scenic Trail

Service 533/Dead Indian Memorial Road. Turn east at the junction of Forest Service 38/ Clover Creek Road. In about 6 miles turn north onto Forest Service 3852 and continue to the trailhead at the end of the road.

Activities: Backpacking, day hiking, camping, fishing.

Facilities: None.

Dates: Open year-round, but snow-free and accessible only from June through mid-Oct.

Fees: None.

Closest town: Klamath Falls.

For more information: Klamath Ranger District, 1936 California Avenue, Klamath Falls, OR 97601. Phone (541) 885-3400.

MOUNTAIN LAKES LOOP TRAIL

[Fig. 48(1)] Alpine lakes, ancient volcanic structures, and spectacular vistas are all part of Mountain Lakes Loop Trail. The popular trail follows an irregular circle route inside the imploded crater of the old volcano that forms Mountain Lakes Wilderness. Hikers will discover sparkling alpine lakes, some stocked with trout, and ridgetop vistas. In places the trail dips into cool forests and rises to ridge tops. Three trails, ranging from 4 to 6 miles long feed into the loop from outside trailheads. A lot of hikers enjoy this trail, and weekend use is heavy.

Directions: Three arterial trails lead from the Winema National Forest into the wilderness area and connect with the loop route. From the south, follow County Road 603 (Clover Creek Road) to Forest Service 3852 and go north to Clover Creek Trail which is 3.6 miles long. The Mountain Lakes Trail from the west at Lake of the Woods is 6.5 miles long; Varney Creek Trail from OR 140 on the north is 4.5 miles long. Turn south at Odessa Transfer Station and follow Forest Service 3637 to 3664 and 2.0 miles to the trail.

Activities: Hiking.

Facilities: None.

Dates: Open year-round, snow covered from Nov. through May.

Fees: None.

Trail: 8 miles, loop.

Elevation: Undulates from about 7,000 to 8,000 feet.

Degree of difficulty: Moderate.

Surface: Dirt and rock.

Upper Klamath Lake

[Fig. 49] The shallow, marshy, algae-filled 64,000 acres of Upper Klamath make it the largest lake in Oregon, and an excellent host for a wildlife refuge that attracts up to 80 percent of all waterfowl migrating north and south in the Pacific Flyway.

Located at the north edge of Klamath Falls, in a watery wedge between the parched hills of central Oregon and the volcanic escarpments below Mount Thielsen, Klamath

Lake is the most important lake at the south end of the East Slope Region.

The lake averages less than 25 feet deep, is subject to howling afternoon winds, and is well-known as a producer of large rainbow trout that often weigh 5 to 10 pounds and sometimes grow to 20 pounds. Fishermen aren't the only ones who love this big lake—thousands of people swarm the lake in late summer to collect an algae (*Aphanizomenon flos aquae*) that grows in dense masses throughout the lake. While the algae interfere with fishing and discourage water sports, many believe that it can provide extraordinary health benefits. Marsh grasses, tules, and cattails extend from the shore hundreds of yards into the lake in many areas, which may explain why most of the shore on this giant lake is undeveloped.

The Upper Klamath National Wildlife Refuge and Canoe Trail occupy 15,000 acres of marsh on the northwest end of the lake.

US 97 follows much of the east shore, and OR 140 traces the west shore. The two highways, and short spur roads, provide lots of access.

The lake is a nesting site for bald eagles and ospreys, and flocks of white pelicans summer here. Nearly 1 million ducks, geese, swans and 250 other species of migratory birds stop at the lake during spring and fall migrations.

Directions: Adjacent to US 97 at Klamath Falls.

Activities: Boating, fishing, canoeing, limited water sports, algae collecting.

Facilities: Public boat ramp at Moore Park in Klamath Falls; along the west shore at Howard Bay Observation Point, Shoalwater Bay Campground, Odessa Creek Campground. Private boat access is at Harriman Springs, Rocky Point and Malone Springs resorts. Public camping is available at Hagelstein Park on US 97 and Odessa Creek on OR 140. The resorts have boat rentals, restaurants, RV and tent sites, and fishing licenses.

Dates: Open year-round.

Fees: None.

Closest town: Klamath Falls.

For more information: Klamath County Department of Tourism, 1451 Main Street, Klamath Falls, OR 97601, phone (541) 884-0666 or (800) 445-6728. Klamath District Ranger, 1936 California Avenue, Klamath Falls, Oregon 97601. Phone (541) 885-3400.

UPPER KLAMATH NATIONAL WILDLIFE REFUGE

[Fig. 49] Occupying 14,400 acres of the northwest corner of Oregon's largest lake, the refuge is a key part of the vast Klamath Basin National Wildlife Refuge, which includes five refuge complexes in southern Oregon and northern California.

In the spring and fall it's a wonderland of migrating birds when 250 species—up to 80 percent of all migrating birds in the Pacific Flyway—land here during their flights. According to ornithologists, it's almost impossible to name a migrating bird in the flyway that's not among the one to five million birds that spend time at Upper Klamath National Wildlife Refuge. The list of birds seen in the refuge is long and includes many varieties of loons, grebes, cormorants, bitterns, herons, cranes, swans, geese, ducks, rails, coots, avocets, stilts, plovers, sandpipers, gulls, terns, owls, swifts, flycatchers, woodpeckers, kingfishers, hawks, eagles, grouse, quail, doves, jays, larks, swallows, wrens, nuthatches, thrushs, kinglets, shrikes, pipits, warblers, grosbeaks, bunts, and sparrows.

White pelicans (*Pelecanus erythrorhynchos*), which have wingspreads up to 50 inches, bald eagles, and ospreys intensely fish the refuge waterways all summer.

The refuge is also the north and west border of Oregon's pronghorn antelope (*Antilocapra americana americana*) range. It's rare but possible to catch a glimpse of these tan-and-white speedsters on the refuge. Jackrabbits, black-tailed (*Lepus californicus*) and white-tailed (*Lepus townsend*), are plentiful, and it's not unusual to see mule deer, beavers, marmots, river otters, and muskrats. The refuge is almost entirely marsh, although the edges sometimes support willow, aspen, and cottonwood trees. The west side tapers into a mountainside of Ponderosa pines, and the east side flows into rich green pastures. Areas of the refuge are channeled for canoes and small boats, and in the fall waterfowl hunting is allowed in specific areas.

Directions: From Klamath Falls, drive west and north on OR 140 to Rocky Point Road. From Rocky Point, drive 2 miles to West Side Road, which continues to the refuge on the north end of the lake. You'll need a boat to really see the refuge.

Activities: Bird-watching, fishing, hunting, canoeing, boating, wildlife photography.

Facilities: None.

Dates: Open year-round.

Fees: None.

Closest town: Klamath Falls.

For more information: Klamath Basin National Wildlife Refuges, Route 1, Box 74, Tulelake, CA 96134. Phone (530) 667-2231. Winema National Forest Supervisor's Office, 2819 Dahlia Street, Klamath Falls, OR 97601. Phone (541) 883-6714.

UPPER KLAMATH CANOE TRAIL

[Fig. 49(1)] Canoeists may paddle quietly down 9.5 miles of trails channeled through the marshes at Upper Klamath Lake at the edge of the national refuge.

The trail has four segments between Pelican Bay on the south and Malone Springs boat launch on Crystal Creek. Shallow Wocus Cut may be dry by late August. The trails are marked with signs.

Directions: The southern end of the trail begins on the northwest side of Upper Klamath Lake at the Rocky Point launch. Malone Springs is the northern put-in.

Activities: Canoeing, fishing, and bird-watching.

Facilities: None. Canoes and motor boats can be rented at Rocky Point Resort.

Dates: Open year-round, and generally ice-free from Apr. through Oct.

Fees: None.

Trail: 9.5 miles

For more information: See Upper Klamath Lake Wildlife Refuge.

WESTERN TANAGER
(*Piranga ludoviciana*)

Crater Lake National Park Area

Crater Lake wasn't discovered until June 12, 1853 and became a National Park in 1902.

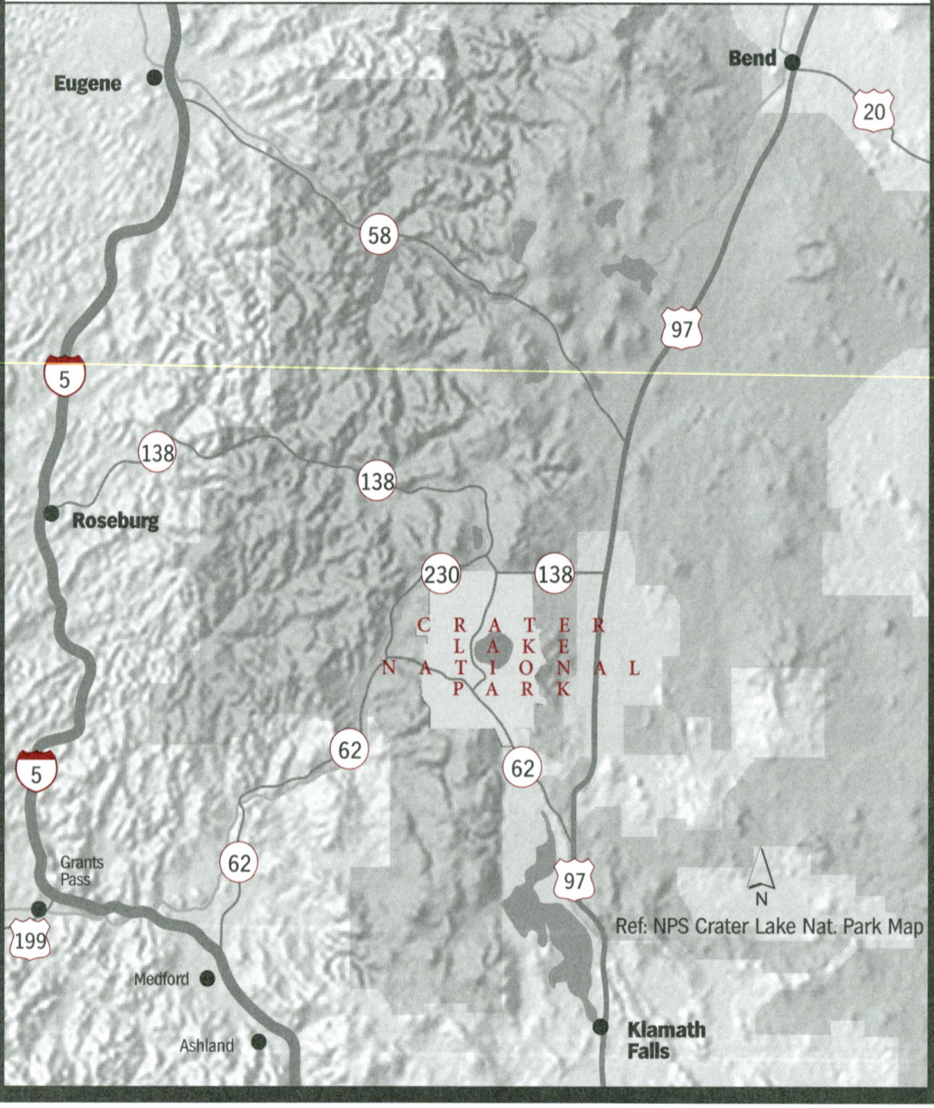

Bend
20
Eugene
58
97
5
138
138
Roseburg
230
138
CRATER LAKE NATIONAL PARK
62
62
5
Grants Pass
62
97
N
199
Ref: NPS Crater Lake Nat. Park Map
Medford
Ashland
Klamath Falls

Crater Lake National Park

In a fiery, incomprehensible burst estimated to have been 50-100 times greater than the 1980 eruption of Mount St. Helens, ancient Mount Mazama lost nearly 1 mile of elevation, buried 350,000 square miles of the Northwest under half-a-foot of pumice, and unleashed walls of molten magma that raced toward southern Oregon valleys at 100 miles an hour and left deposits of lava 300 feet thick.

In its final throes 7,700 years ago, the heart of the volcano, now empty of the magma necessary to support its bulk, collapsed into itself. The caldera that formed is a staggering 6 miles across and 4,000 feet deep. It was framed inside a ragged rim of rock teeth 500 to 2,000 feet high.

The collapse reduced the 12,000-foot-high mountain to 8,000 feet. For the next 4,000 years, steam and pumice dust spurted from vents, and magma continued to push up against the floor of the caldera, eventually forming two cones and sealing

[*Above:* A lava formation in Crater Lake National Park]

Crater Lake National Park

Crater Lake National Park is on the crest of the Cascades northwest of Klamath Falls.

Ref: NPS Crater Lake Nat. Park Map

1 Steel Visitor Center
2 Rim Village Visitor Center
3 Sinnott Memorial Overlook/ Crater Lake Lodge
4 Mazama Campground
5 Lost Creek Campground
6 Mazama Village Motor Inn
7 Rim Drive
8 Annie Creek Trail
9 Godfrey Glen Trail
10 Castle Crest Trail
11 Watchman Peak Trail
12 Sun Notch Viewpoint Trail
13 Cleetwood Cove Trail
14 Mount Scott Trail
15 Pinnacles Overlook

Pacific Crest National Scenic Trail

Trail

the caldera floor with almost 2,000 feet of lava.

In geological terms Mount Mazama is a Pleistocene stratovolcano, and is the largest volcano between Mount Shasta and Three Sisters. It's composed of a cluster of individual stratovolcanoes and shields. The oldest, Mount Scott at an elevation of 8,929 feet, is the highest point in the park, and formed about 400,000 years ago. The youngest stratovolcano is Mount Mazama itself.

Sheet flows of andesite have formed colored bands on the caldera wall that may be seen from the lake tour boat and from some overlooks on Rim Drive. Several areas on the caldera walls and the flanks of Mount Mazama are flecked with small glassy columns and piles of glassy red breccia, a form of lava rock produced by interactions of ice and molten lava.

The bowl-shaped caldera began to fill with seep water, rain, and snow, eventually forming the deepest lake in the United States, second deepest in North America, and the seventh deepest in the world. The events also created the topographical outline of Oregon's only national park, a 183,224-acre rectangle framing a circular-shaped heart of almost indescribable blue water. Only the highest cone, Wizard Island, rises above the surface. The island is actually a rhyolite cone nearly 2,700 feet high. Only 760 feet protrude above the mysteriously blue water of Crater Lake.

Mount Mazama may be dormant but pyroclastic activity is not far away. Scientists have found areas of very high heat flow on the caldera floor, which is evidence of continuing geothermal activity. Temperatures of 66 degrees have been measured 1,400 feet below the surface. Scientists also believe that geothermal fluids continue to seep into the lake. Roads between Mount Mazama and Klamath Falls are built on deposits of pale pumice rock from ash flows. Just north of Klamath Lake is a large fault block now disguised as a lush marsh. Beneath this entire area are unstable fault lines and magma chambers that continue to rumble and reposition.

Crater Lake National Park is on the crest of the Cascades northwest of Klamath Falls. The park is a high-elevation wonderland developed entirely on the remnants of that 7,700-year-old eruption. Monogentic cinder cones, lava fields and small shield volcanoes have formed around Mount Mazama. The highest point in the park is Mount Scott, elevation 8,929 feet, which dominates the skyline east of Crater Lake. There is a hiking trail to the summit.

Indigenous Modoc and Klamath tribes who survived the eruption were traumatized by the cataclysmic event. Klamath legends explain the eruption as a fierce battle between Skell god of the sky and Llao god of the depths, who was angered by a tribal princess' romantic rejection. Some believed that the gods would punish anyone who viewed the beautiful lake that was created during the battle. So firm was that belief for some that they avoided the mountain and didn't mention it to outsiders, including white explorers.

Pioneer-era settlers remained unaware of the huge mountaintop lake until June 12, 1853, when gold prospectors John Wesley Hillman, Isaac Skeeters, and Henry

Winter Recreation

From October to June, Crater Lake National Park is a remote snow-covered wilderness, receiving an average of 533 inches of snow annually, with accumulations of more than 20 feet each year. Entry fees are waived from November to April.

Winter recreation consists primarily of cross-county skiing and sight-seeing, and visitation is light compared with other recreation areas in the Oregon Cascades. A variety of trails and unplowed roads are open for day-trippers and backcountry campers who are prepared to face the challenges of one of the snowiest areas in the entire Northwest.

The only road open during the winter months is the southern entrance road to Rim Village. Steel Information Center is open daily except for Christmas, as is Rim Village, where a cafeteria and gift shop are located. Ranger-led winter ecology walks are held every weekend. Dogs must be kept on a leash at all times and are restricted to parking lot areas. Snowshoeing or walking on any marked ski trail is discouraged. Snowmobile use is only allowed on the North Entrance Road from the park boundary to North Junction (where the entrance road meets Rim Drive).

There are no groomed ski trails in the park, but the most popular trails are marked. The unplowed West Rim Drive and East Rim Drive are popular ski routes.

There is no overnight lodging or roadside camping in the park during the winter months. Backcountry camping is allowed but a free permit is required. Backcountry campers must ski or snowshoe to their campsite.

During winter, the closest gas stations are in Fort Klamath, 20 miles away, and in Prospect and Chiloquin, both about 40 miles from Rim Village and park headquarters.

Klippel, looking for the Lost Cabin mine, rode across the rim and saw what Hillman named "Deep Blue Lake." Not until 1865 was it called Crater Lake, when a newspaper editor saw the cerulean water and accurately speculated that the lake filled the bowl of an ancient volcano. The area became a national park in 1902.

Most of the half million annual visitors find, as Hillman did, that the park's most memorable feature is the striking color of Crater Lake. It's been variously described as azure, cobalt, indigo, ultramarine, cornflower and several dozen other variations of blue that change with the reflection of the sky.

The color is a product of a pristine environment and nearly pure water. Because it is located in a rockbound bowl almost 7,000 feet high inside the top of a lava-sheathed mountain, there is no inlet or outlet to import silts or pollutants. The water, all 46 trillion gallons of it, comes from rain and about 50 feet of snow that falls every year. Evaporation and seepage escaping into cracks in the caldera wall eliminate enough water to keep the lake from filling up and spilling over. Water levels rarely vary more than a foot or two.

The lake's temperature is an almost constant 38 degrees Fahrenheit. Only once has it been known to freeze over.

Because of the high elevation—most of the park is between 5,000 and 7,000 feet high—the snow comes early, stays late, and the tourist season is brief. It usually begins in late June and ends in late September. July and August are peak months, although opportunities for cross-country skiing and snowshoeing are attracting a growing winter crowd.

Almost all of the park's geologic features and service attractions are connected by a web of paved roads and 90 miles of hiking trails, including 33 miles of Pacific Crest National Scenic Trail 2000. Tour boats stop at Wizard Island. Bicycles are restricted to paved roads, and not allowed on trails.

The best way to see the lake and caldera is from Rim Drive, a 33-mile loop around the rim of the caldera with more than 20 overlooks and viewpoints. The two-lane road is usually snow-free from mid-July to September. The only stretch of the Rim Drive that is open during the winter is between Munson Valley and Rim Village.

The only way to get a close-up view of the lake is to hike the popular Cleetwood Trail, which switchbacks 1.1 mile from the caldera rim to tour boats at Cleetwood Cove 700 feet below. Private boats are not allowed on the lake, and Cleetwood Trail is the only permissible entry inside the caldera. Open tour boats leave Cleetwood Cove 9 times daily on 25-mile-long narrated voyages. The tour takes about two hours, including a stop at Wizard Island.

Accommodations are limited, but include a grand circa-1915 lodge with 71 rooms and magnificent fireplaces, and two campgrounds. Two visitor centers operate during the summer, and provide interpretive walks, programs, and a museum. There is little fishing available, but there's always a chance to glimpse wildlife. Deer and elk summer here, and sometimes pronghorn antelope range into the Pumice Desert. One of the Oregon's rarest animals, wolverine (*Gulo gulo*), have been seen here, but sightings are rare. These wilderness-loving members of the weasel family are so rare in Oregon that some biologists doubt they still inhabit the state. Still, park visitors occasionally report a sighting. Pine martens, golden-mantled ground squirrels, Clark's nutcracker, and ravens, however, are plentiful.

Crater Climate

Snow rarely leaves all park roads before July, the month that marks the start of the summer season. July through mid-September is generally mild with little precipitation. Daytime temperatures are in the 70s, dropping into the 30s and 40s at night. Because of the high elevation of the park (6,500 feet at park headquarters and 7,100 feet at Rim Village), weather conditions often change quickly. It can snow every month of the year at this elevation.

From October through June, prepare for extreme weather. Blizzards, high winds, bitter cold, and low visibility are the dominant the weather conditions.

Fish Facts

Crater Lake was originally barren of fish, but from 1888 to 1941, well-meaning angling enthusiasts stocked 1.8 million trout and salmon. The effort was, by any measure, a failure.

The trout found little to eat, their growth was minimal and most of the stocked species died out. Of the species stocked, which included rainbows, browns, cutthroat, steelhead, coho and kokanee salmon, only kokanee salmon (*Oncorhynchus nerka*) and rainbow trout (*Oncorhynchus mykiss*) continue through natural reproduction. No stocking has occurred since 1941.

That they can reproduce here is part of the magic of Crater Lake. In nearly every other area of the Northwest, trout and kokanee spawn in streams and rivers where running water keeps the developing eggs bathed in fresh, well-oxygenated water.

According to biologists, the fish have been reproducing successfully in Crater Lake's water because it is exceptionally clean, cold, and rich in oxygen. The fish are small compared with those found in lower-elevation lakes.

Kokanee are the most abundant species in the lake, recently estimated to number in the hundreds of thousands. These trout-like salmon reach 10-14 inches in length and feed on zooplankton, minute animals that live in open water. Rainbow trout may reach 24 inches in length and feed primarily on large-bodied insects that live or fall into the lake. The largest documented rainbow trout from Crater Lake was 6.5 pounds and 26 inches long.

The introduction of fish undoubtedly changed the ecology of the lake from its natural condition. The magnitude of these changes is affected by the number of fish in the lake. Fish in Crater Lake are relatively few and they are probably here to stay, according to park officials, because all reliable methods of removing them would alter Crater Lake's ecosystem far more than the fish do.

Fish also inhabit many of the small streams within the park's boundary. Unfortunately for fishermen, these little streams are generally not accessible because of the steep canyons surrounding them. According to stocking records, Eastern brook (*Salvelinus fontinalis*) and rainbow trout were planted in park streams.

Eastern brook trout have been found in almost every park stream. Rainbow were originally planted in large numbers throughout the park, but today, it appears that their numbers are few and scattered. Possible rainbow fisheries are Annie, Bybee, Castle, and Munson creeks.

One brown trout (*Salmo trutta*) has been found in Sand Creek, which researchers believe may be the remnant of an unrecorded planting.

Bull trout (*Salvelinus confluentus*) are believed to be the only native fish species within the park. These less competitive fish are threatened and considered rare in the southern Cascades.

Wildflowers abound during the compressed growing season. Some of the best viewing is along Castle Crest Wildflower Trail, a .04-mile loop along a small brook that supports lush plant growth, including pink and blue clusters of spreading phlox (*Phlox diffusa*), tiny blue asters, scarlet spears of Indian paintbrush, white plumes of beargrass, and delicate purple-blue petals of Davidson's penstemon (*Penstemon davidsonii*).

Touring The Lake By Boat

Two-hour narrated boat tours run out of Cleetwood Cove on the north side of Crater Lake from late June to mid-September.

To reach the boats requires hiking 1.1 miles on the Cleetwood Cove trail, which involves a strenuous elevation change of 700 feet from dock to rim. Drinking water is not available at Cleetwood Cove, but toilets are available near the boat dock and at the trailhead.

Tour tickets are purchased at the parking lot before descending the trail.

The boats stop at Wizard Island, and it's permissible to stay on the island and take a later boat back. The island is traditionally a popular fishing spot and anglers often spend the day there.

Two paths wind around the island. Camping is not allowed. A vault toilet is located at the dock area.

Directions: From the north, follow OR 138 east to the park's north entrance. From Bend, follow US 97 south to route 138 then go west to the park's north entrance. The park's north entrance is typically closed for the winter season from mid-Oct. to mid-June.

From the southwest, follow OR 62 north and east to the park's west entrance. From Klamath Falls drive US 97 north to route 62 then north and west to the park's south entrance.

Facilities: Crater Lake Lodge, 71 rooms; Mazama Village Motor Inn, 40 rooms; Lost Creek Campground, 16 sites; Mazama Campground, 200 sites; Steel and Rim Village visitor centers, Cleetwood Cove Tour Boats, bus tours by reservation; gasoline and basic groceries at Mazama Village Store.

Dates: Open year-round. All facilities are open June through Sept. Rim Village Visitor Center is open June through Sept., 8:30-6 daily. Steel Visitor Center is open 9-5 daily. Food Service and Gift Shop at Rim Village are open 8 to 8, and Mazama Village Store, 7 a.m.-10 p.m. From Oct. through May, Steel Visitor Center is open 9-5 every day except Christmas. Rim Drive is passable for passenger cars from July-Sept.

Fees: There are charges for park entry from May-Sept. and for sites at developed campgrounds and tour boats. Free permits are required for backcountry camping.

For more information: Crater Lake National Park, PO Box 7, Crater Lake, OR 97604, phone (541) 594-2211. Visitor information, Ext. 402. Web site: www.nps.gov/crla/home.htm.

Visitor Centers

[Fig. 51(1), Fig. 51(2)] Two visitor centers are open on the south side of the lake during the summer season. Steel Visitor Center at park headquarters, south of Rim Village, is open every day except Christmas from 9 to 5. A park ranger is on duty to assist with information, weather forecasts, backcountry camping permits, ski route advisories, and safety tips. A 20-minute-film, *The Crater Lake Story*, describes the formation of Crater Lake through a story passed down from ancient tribes who witnessed the eruption. Books, maps, posters, postcards, and educational materials are available for purchase. The Steel Center has public restrooms and is wheelchair accessible. A post office is also located in this building. Rim Village Visitor Center is located on the south rim of the caldera, approximately 200 yards west of the Crater Lake Lodge. It is open from 8:30 to 6, June 1 through September 30. General park information and backcountry camping permits are available. Sinnott Memorial Overlook and Crater Lake Lodge have interpretive displays and exhibits that are open to the public in the summer. The Mazama Village complex operates a camper store from June through September, with laundry, showers, and gasoline available. From mid-October until mid-June, the north entrance and Rim Drive are closed because of deep snow and ice buildups along the road. Rim Drive around the east side of the lake can be closed earlier than mid-October and may not open until July.

For more information: Crater Lake National Park, PO Box 7, Crater Lake, OR 97604. Phone (541) 594-2211 ext. 402.

Camping And Lodging

Two developed campgrounds are open during the summer, and two hotels may offer daily room rentals. Room reservations are strongly advised. Reservations at Crater Lake Lodge are accepted up to two years in advance.

The largest campground is Mazama Campground, near the Annie Springs entrance station on OR 62. Much smaller Lost Creek Campground, in the southeast area of the park, is reached by taking East Rim Drive to the Pinnacles Road. Campsites are all first-come, first-served. Reservations are not available.

MAZAMA CAMPGROUND

[Fig. 51(4)] **Facilities:** 200 tent and RV sites, potable water, flush toilets, a dump station, pay showers, fire rings, tables, laundry facilities, and utility hookups.

Dates: Open from late June through early Oct., weather permitting.

Fees: There are charges for campsites.

LOST CREEK CAMPGROUND

[Fig. 51(5)] **Facilities:** 16 tent sites, fire rings, potable water, flush toilets, and tables.

Dates: Normally opens in mid-July and closes in mid-Sept. Check at the park visitor centers for opening and closing dates.

Fees: There are charges for campsites.

CRATER LAKE LODGE

[Fig. 51(3)] The lodge overlooks the south rim of the caldera. The original lodge opened in 1915, and a full renovation was completed in 1995. The distinctive 1920s appearance and atmosphere have been maintained.

Facilities: 71 rooms, dining room, cafeteria, lounge, and gift shop.

Dates: Open from late May to late Oct.

For more information: Phone (541) 830-8700.

MAZAMA VILLAGE MOTOR INN

[Fig. 51(4)] The inn is located at Mazama Village, near the Route 62 junction.

Facilities: 40 rooms; two units are wheelchair accessible; convenience store.

Dates: Open June to early Oct.

For more information: Phone (541) 830-8700.

Hiking Trails

More than 90 miles of trails lead into the backcountry of Crater Lake National Park, and most are snow-free from mid-July to early October. Dogs, other pets, bicycles, and motor vehicles are not allowed on park trails. Although much of the park terrain is reasonably level, nearly all backcountry trails are classed as moderate to strenuous hikes because of the elevations, which range from 6,000 to 9,000 feet. It's not uncommon for lowland residents to experience breathing difficulties in the thin air at these elevations. Free backcountry use permits are required for all overnight stays. Permits and descriptions of restrictions and regulations are available at visitor centers. Firearms, bicycles, and motorized vehicles are not permitted in the backcountry.

Popular trails include:

Annie Creek: [Fig. 51(8)] 1.7 mile loop, descending from Mazama Campground to the bottom of Annie Creek Canyon. **Godfrey Glen:** [Fig. 51(9)] 1 mile forested loop with overlooks of the pinnacles of Annie Creek Canyon. **Castle Crest:** [Fig. 51(10)] 0.4 mile loop through forest, meadows, and stream. **Watchman Peak:** [Fig. 51(11)] 0.8 mile one-way; moderately steep to a fire lookout overlooking Wizard Island. **Sun Notch Viewpoint:** [Fig. 51(12)] .25 mile one-way; moderate difficulty, to an overlook of Crater Lake and Phantom Ship. **Cleetwood Cove:** [Fig. 51(13)] 1.1 miles one-way; steep and strenuous path to the lake boat tours. **Mount Scott:** [Fig. 51(14)] 2.5 miles one-way; moderately steep route to the highest point in the park, a fire lookout at the summit, elevation 8,929 feet.

Appendixes

A. Books and References

Mosses, Lichens & Ferns of Northwest North America, by Vitt, Marsh and Bovey, University of Washington Press, Seattle, WA 1988.
Roadside Geology of Oregon, by David D. Alt and Donald W. Hyndman, Mountain Press Publishing, Missoula, MT, 1998.
Hiking Oregon's Geology, by Ellen Morris Bishop and John Eliot Allen, The Mountaineers, Seattle, WA 1996.
Roadside Wildflowers of the Northwest, by J. E. Underhill, Hancock House, Blaine, WA 1994.
50 Old-Growth Day Hikes, Old Growth Day Hikes Publishing, Eugene, OR 1993.
Roadside History Of Oregon, by Bill Gulick, Mountain Press Publishing, Missoula, MT 1996.
The Columbia, by Tim Palmer, The Mountaineers, Seattle, WA 1998.
Columbia River Gorge, by Philip N. Jones, The Mountaineers, Seattle, WA 1992.
Fishing In Oregon, 8th edition, by Sheehan and Casali, Flying Pencil Publications, Scappoose, OR 1995.
Fishing In Oregon's Cascade Lakes, by Scott Richmond, Flying Pencil Publications, Scappoose, OR 1994.
Fishing Central Oregon 3rd edition, by Hill, Wing, and Snavely, Sun Publishing, Bend, OR 1998.
Hunting Oregon, by Gary Lewis, Sun Publishing, Bend, OR 1999.
Oregon Hunting Guide, by John A. Johnson, Stoneydale Press Publishing, Stevensville, MT 1988.
Oregon Off The Beaten Path, by Myrna Oakley, The Globe Pequot Press, Old Saybrook, CT 1997.
Oregon/Washington Tour Book, American Automobile Association, Heathrow, FL 1998.
Woodall's Camping Guide, Far West Edition, by Barbara Tinucci, Woodall Publications Corp., Lake Forest, IL 1998.
Walks Of The Pacific Northwest, by Gary Ferguson, Prentice Hall Press, New York, NY 1991.
Oregon Handbook, by Warren and Ishikawa, Moon Publications, Chico, CA 1991.
A Waterfall Lover's Guide To The Pacific Northwest, by Gregory Plumb, The Mountaineers, Seattle, WA 1989.
In Search of Western Oregon, by Ralph Friedman, The Caxton Printers, Inc., Caldwell, ID 1990.
Field Guide To The Cascades & Olympics, by Stephen R. Whitney, The Mountaineers, Seattle, WA 1983.
Whitewater Mailmen, by Gary and Gloria Meier, Maverick Publications, Inc., Bend, OR 1991.
The New Savory Wild Mushroom, by Margaret McKenny and Daniel Stuntz, University of Washington, Seattle, WA 1987.
Oregon Geographic Names 5th edition, by Lewis A. McArthur, Press of the Oregon Historical Society, Salem, OR 1982.
Oregon Wildlife Areas, by Bob and Ira Spring, Superior Publishing Co., Seattle, WA 1978.
Exploring Oregon's Central and Southern Cascades, by William L. Mainwaring, Westridge Press, Ltd., Salem, OR 1979.
Pacific Northwest Hiking by Ron C. Judd and Dan A. Nelson, Foghorn Press, Santa Rosa, CA 1999.
Pacific Northwest Camping, by Tom Stienstra, Foghorn Press, Santa Rosa, CA 1998.
Oregon Atlas & Gazetteer, DeLorme Mapping, Freeport, MA 1991.

B. Conservation & Outdoor Organizations

Pacific Crest Trail Association, 1350 Castle Rock Road, Walnut Creek, CA 94598. Phone (510) 939-6111. Parent organization of clubs and hiking groups concerned with the Pacific Crest Trail through Oregon's Cascade Range.

Rocky Mountain Elk Foundation, Oregon, 1265 Hansen Ave. S, Salem, OR 97302. Phone (503) 362-3062. Email rmeftom@teleport.com. Acquires habitat and promotes health and management of elk herds in Oregon.

Mule Deer Foundation, Oregon, 1005 Terminal Way, Suite 140, Reno, NV 89502. Phone (800) 344-Buck. Fax (702) 322-3421 Acquires habitat and promotes health and management of mule and black-tailed deer herds in Oregon.

Trout Unlimited, Oregon Headquarters, 22875 NW Chestnut, Hillsboro, OR 97124. Phone (503) 640-2123. Promotes conservation, habitat, and wise management of trout and salmon in Oregon.

Ducks Unlimited Oregon, Portland Chapter. Phone (503) 629-5986. Promotes conservation, habitat, and management of waterfowl in Oregon.

Oregon Outdoors Association Inc., PO Box 9486, Bend, OR 97708. Phone (541) 382-9758. Email oregon_outdoors@bendnet.com.

Environmental Federation of Oregon, PO Box 40333, Portland, OR 97240. Phone (503) 223-9015. Fax (503) 223-0973. Email efo@teleport.com. A fund-raising and political action coalition of 28 conservation and environmental groups.

1000 Friends Of Oregon, 534 SW Third Ave #300, Portland, OR 97204. Phone (503) 497-1000. Founded in 1978 by Gov. Tom McCall and Henry Richmond to protect places and communities in Oregon.

Audubon Society Of Portland 5151 NW Cornell Road, Portland, OR 97210. Phone (503) 292-6855. Email ikellogg@audubon-pdx.org. Founded in 1902 to promote enjoyment, understanding, and protection of birds, other wildlife, and habitat.

Central Oregon Environmental Center, 16 NW Kansas Street, Bend, OR 97701. Phone (541) 385-6908. Fosters the conservation and appreciation of central Oregon's natural heritage and promotes ecologically sustainable ways of living.

Corvallis Environmental Center, 214 SW Monroe Ave., PO 2189, Corvallis, OR 97339-2189. Phone (541) 753-9211. Committed to the protection and restoration of the Willamette Valley's ecosystems through education, community-based projects, and advocacy.

Forest Service Employees For Environmental Ethics, PO Box 11615, Eugene, OR 97440. Phone (541) 484-2692. Seeks the preservation of ecological values and biological diversity in national forests through education and advocacy for reforms of U.S. Forest Service management practices.

Friends Of The Columbia Gorge, 319 SW Washington, Suite 301, Portland, OR 97204. Phone (503) 241-3762. Vigorously protects the Gorge by support of the Columbia River Gorge National Scenic Act, and promotes new parks and strong land-use planning.

Friends Of Opal Creek, PO Box 318, Mill City, OR 97360. Phone (503) 897-2921. Seeks to further understanding and stewardship of the 35,000-acre Opal Creek forest and old-growth ecosystems through education and scientific study.

Friends Of Trees, 2831 NE Martin Luther King Blvd., Portland, OR 97212. Phone (503) 282-8846. A volunteer-based, nonprofit organization devoted to building community partnerships to plant, care for and preserve urban trees.

Friends Of Bagby Hot Springs, PO Box 15116, Portland, OR 97215. A volunteer group of hot springs enthusiasts who work to maintain and care for the hot spring complex.

Friends of Breitenbush Hot Springs, Box 578, Detroit, OR 97360. Phone (503) 854-3320. A volunteer group of hot springs enthusiasts who work to maintain and care for the hot spring complex.

Headwaters, PO Box 729, Ashland, OR 97520. Phone (541) 482-4459. Works to protect Oregon's forests and watersheds through monitoring and research, citizen advocacy, policy reform, watershed rehabilitation, environmental education, and environmentally sound, socially just economic change.

National Wildlife Federation, 2031 SE Belmont, Portland, OR 97214-2812. Phone (503) 230-0421. The Oregon chapter of the National Wildlife Federation founded in 1934 by people who use the outdoors and want to protect forests and rivers.

Native Plant Society Of Oregon, 2584 NW Savier St., Portland, OR 97210. Phone (503) 245-9242. Dedicated to the enjoyment, conservation and study of Oregon's native vegetation.

The Nature Conservancy Of Oregon, 821 SE 14th Ave., Portland, OR 97214. Phone (503) 230-1221. Email cquinn@tnc.org. Buys and protects habitat for Oregon's native plants and wildlife by working cooperatively with the private sector, public agencies and landowners. Maintains 53 nature preserves in Oregon from the desert to the coast.

Northwest Coalition For Alternatives To Pesticides, PO Box 1393, Eugene, OR 97440. Phone (541) 344-5044. Works to reduce pesticide use by providing people with accurate, credible information to change pesticide use.

Northwest Earth Institute, 921 SW Morrison Suite 532, Portland, OR 97205. Phone (503) 227-2807. Trains and motivates individuals to protect the earth through programs offered in workplaces, schools, churches and homes.

Oregon Environmental Council, 520 SW 6th, Suite 940, Portland, OR 97204. Phone (503) 222-1963. Advances sustainable approaches to reduce human impacts on Oregon's air, land, and water.

Oregon Natural Desert Association, 16 NW Kansas, Bend, OR 97701. Phone (541) 330-2638. Fights to protect and restore Oregon's High Desert, to end public lands grazing and to gain passage of the Oregon High Desert Protection Act.

Oregon Natural Resources Council Fund, 825 N. Greeley, Portland, OR 97217. Phone (503) 283-6343. Aggressively protects and restores Oregon's wild lands, wildlife and waters, including ancient forests, free-flowing rivers and clean drinking water sources.

Oregon Trout, 117 SW Naito Parkway, Portland, OR 97204. Phone (503) 222-9091. Email info@ortrout.org. Protects and restores native wild fish and their ecosystems through policy advocacy, scientific research, demonstration projects in specific watersheds, and environmental education programs.

Ospirg Foundation, 1536 SE 11th Ave., Portland, OR 97214. Phone (503) 231-4181. Focuses on recycling and toxic pollution prevention, combining research with activism to protect Oregon's environment.

Pacific Rivers Council, PO Box 10798, Eugene, OR 97440. Phone (541) 345-0119. Founded in 1988 for the protection and restoration of Oregon's streams and the species that inhabit them.

Recycling Advocates, PO Box 6736, Portland, OR 97228. Phone (503) 591-1454. A grassroots organization with a goal of maximizing waste reduction and recycling by educating the public and influencing government.

River Network, PO BOX 8787, Portland, OR 97207. Phone (503) 241-3506. Supports community-based river groups by helping organize to protect and restore rivers and watersheds; also acquires river lands critical for fish, wildlife and recreation.

The Sierra Club Foundation, 3701 SE Milwaukie Street F, Portland, OR 97202. Phone (503) 238-0442. Oregon office of national group dedicated to preserve wilderness and protect environmental quality through a combination of education, scientific research, publishing, and litigation.

Solar Energy Association Of Oregon, 205 SE Grand Ave., No. 202, Portland, OR 97214. Phone (503) 231-5662. Promotes conservation, solar energy, and other renewable resources.

The Trust For Public Land, 1211 SW 6th Ave, Portland, OR 97204. Phone (503) 228-6620. Protect open space as wilderness, recreation areas, parks, and community gardens.

Tualatin Riverkeepers, 16340 SW Beef Bend Rd., Sherwood, OR 97140. Phone (503) 590-5813. Works to restore and protect Oregon's Tualatin River.

Waterwatch Of Oregon, 213 SW Ash, No. 208, Portland, OR 97204. Phone (503) 295-4039. Works to make sure that Oregon's rivers have enough water flowing in them to meet the needs of the fish and wildlife, recreation, and other public uses.

The Wetlands Conservancy, PO Box 1195, Tualatin, OR 97062. Phone (503) 691-1394. Protects and restores Oregon wetlands and urban stream habitat through wetland acquisition, education, and stewardship.

C. Outfitters and Guides

FLOATING/RAFTING TRIPS

Northwest Rafters Association
PO Box 19008
Portland, OR 97219
(503) 246-0386

Oregon Kayak and Canoe Club
PO Box 692
Portland, OR 97207
(503) 285-0464

Oregon Ocean Paddling Society
PO Box 69641
Portland, OR 97201
(503) 236-6610

The Oregon Paddler
PO Box 1012
Springfield, OR 97478
(541) 741-8661
Email: paddler@rio.com

Ouzel Outfitters
PO Box 827
Bend, OR 97709
(541) 385-5947
Email: ouzel@empnet.com

Lower Columbia Canoe Club
7905 SW Canyon Lane
Portland, OR 97225
(503) 650-0940

Justus Outfitters
Nature Floats
1090 Snell Street
Eugene, OR 97405

Northwest Discoveries, Inc.
Canoe/Snowshoe Trips
11263 SW 81st Avenue
Tigard, OR 97223
(503) 624-4829

HIKING/CLIMBING

Mazamas Mountaineering
909 NW 19th Avenue
Portland, OR 97209
(503) 227-2345

Adventure Out
719 Sherman Street
Hood River, OR 97031
(541) 387-4626
Email: jeremy@gorge.net

Adventure Smith Guides
Rock Climbing
PO Box 2241
Lake Oswego, OR 97035
(503) 293-6727
Email: asg@adventuresmith.com

Ancient Forest Adventures
800 NW 6th Avenue, Suite 201
Portland, OR 97209
800-248-0414
Email: greatnw@teleport.com

Eco Tours of Oregon
1906 SW Iowa Street
Portland, OR 97201
(503) 245-1428

Northwest Eco-Ventures
3556 George Court
Eugene, OR 97401
(541) 686-6789
Email: nwev@een.org

Wild Food Adventures
5036 SE Mitchell Street
Portland, OR 97206
(503) 775-3828
Email: wildfood@teleport.com

BICYCLING

Hood River Trails, Inc.
2149 W. Cascade, Suite 106A-7
Hood River, OR 97031
Email: hrtrails@gorge.net

Pathfinders
PO Box 210
Oakridge, OR 97463
(541) 782-4838
Email: pathfndr@efn.org

FISHING/HUNTING

Oregon Guides and Packers Association
PO Box 10841
Eugene, OR 97440
(503) 683-9552

Lower Columbia Walleye Club
26 NE 108th Avenue
Portland, OR

Oregon Outdoors Association Inc.
PO Box 9486
Bend, OR 97708
(541) 382-9758
Email: oregon_outdoors@bendnet.com

D. Special Events, Fairs, and Festivals

FEBRUARY

Jamaican Days at Mount Hood, snowboard competitions, cardboard box sled races, and music. Phone (503) 287-5438.

20th Annual Bald Eagle Conference at Klamath Falls. Phone (800) 445-6728.

Hoodoo Winter Carnival at Hoodoo Ski Area, competitions, games, snow play. Phone (541) 822-3799.

MARCH

Snowboarding for Native Wildflowers on Mount Hood. Phone (503) 287-5438.

Winter Games of Oregon at Government Camp. Phone (503) 222-2695 and **Meadows Madness,** Mount Hood Meadows. Skiing games, snowboard competition, lots of food. Phone (503) 287-5438.

Fisherman's Breakfast, the third weekend of the month at Leaberg. Phone (503) 896-3330.

High Desert Museum's Homestead Skills Showcase at Bend the first weekend of the month. Phone (541) 382-4754.

APRIL

Bull Bash Bull Riding and Flying U Rodeo at Prineville. Phone (541) 447-6575.

General fishing season opens statewide. Phone (503) 872-5268.

Earth Day Fair in Bend, Phone (541) 385-6904.

Glide Wildflower Show, displays of hundreds of species. Phone (541) 6723-1584.

Medford Pear Blossom Parade and Run. Phone (541) 734-PEAR.

Northwest Cherry Festival in The Dalles. Phone (800) 255-3385.

Blossom Festival at Hood River, including a quilt show and excursion trains through the pear orchards. Phone (800) 366-3530.

MAY

Upper Clackamas Whitewater Festival at Estacada, the second weekend of May. Phone (503) 665-6492.

Pioneer Living Trail and Tales in Oregon City at the end of the Oregon Trail Center. Phone (503) 657-9336.

Tree Planting Festival at Oakridge. Phone (541) 782-4146.

Boatnik Festival on the Rogue River at Grants Pass. Phone (800) 547-5927.

Oregon Festival of American Music at Eugene. Phone (541) 687-6526.

Renaissance Faire in Corvallis. Phone (541) 737-6872.

JUNE

Lebanon Strawberry Festival. Phone (541) 258-7164

Sternwheeler Days in Cascade Locks, last weekend of the month. Phone (541) 374-8619.

Oregon Folklife Festival in Corvallis. Phone (541) 758-3243.

Wheat Festival in Grass Valley. Old-fashioned small town celebration. Phone (541) 333-2181.

Mount Hood Railroad Train Robbery in Hood River. Phone (800) TRAIN-61.

Umpqua Valley Summer Arts Festival at Roseburg. Phone (541) 672-2532.

Sisters/Squaw Creek History Festival at Sisters High School. Phone (541) 549-2111.

Crooked River Rodeo at Prineville. Phone (541) 447-4479 and **Sisters Rodeo and Parade**, Phone (541) 0121.

JULY

Sisters Outdoor Quilt Show, a five-day affair, more than 850 quilts displayed. Phone (541) 549-6061.
World Championship Timber Carnival at Albany. Phone (541) 928-2391.
Western Days Old Fashioned 4th of July at Independence and Monmouth. Phone (503) 838-4268. Stayton, phone (503) 769-3464. Willamina, phone (503) 876-5777.
Marion County Fair at Salem. Phone (503) 585-9998.
Sportsman's Holiday & Sweet Home Rodeo at Sweet Home. Phone (541) 367-6186.
Oregon Country Fair at Veneta. Phone (541) 343-4298.
50th Annual Salem Art Fair & Festival. Phone (503) 581-2228.
Dallas Summerfest. Phone (503) 623-2564.
Santiam Canyon Stampede/Rodeo in Sublimity. Phone (503) 589-2999.
Great Balloon Escape in Albany. Phone (800) 526-2256.
Riddle Sawdust Jubilee. Phone (541) 874-2334.
Living History Days & Country Faire at Fort Klamath. Phone (541) 882-2340.
Bend Summer Festival. Phone (541) 385-6570.
The High Desert Museum Ruggers Rendezvous at Bend. Phone (541) 382-4754.
Jefferson County Fair & Rodeo at Madras. Phone (541) 475-4460.
World Championship Timber Carnival at Albany. Phone (541) 928-2391.
Blackberry Jam in Lowell. Phone (541) 937-2157.

AUGUST

Great Balloon Escape in Albany. Phone (800) 526-2256.
World's 2nd Annual Elephant Garlic Festival at North Plains. Phone (800) 661-1799.
Klamath County Fair & Jefferson Stampede Rodeo. Phone (541) 883-3796.
Canyonville Pioneer Days. Phone (541) 839-4391.
Jedediah Smith Mountain Man Rendezvous in Grants Pass. Phone (541) 476-2040.
High Desert Celtic Celebration in Prineville. Phone (541) 447-3561.
Wasco County Fair in Tygh Valley. Phone (800) 255-3385.
Gravenstein Apple Days at Hood River. Phone (541) 386-2000.
Oregon State Fair in Salem. Phone (503) 378-3247

SEPTEMBER

Forest grouse hunting seasons open statewide. Phone (503) 872-5268.
Jedediah Smith Mountain Man Rendezvous at Grants Pass. Phone (541) 476-2040.
Mt. Hood Railroad Native American Celebration at Hood River. Phone (800) TRAIN-61.
Sisters Folk Festival and Harvest Faire at Sisters. Phone 541-549-4979.
50s Cruise On The Lake at Detroit. Phone (503) 854-3624.

OCTOBER

Most big game, upland bird and waterfowl hunting seasons open. Phone (503) 872-5268.
The High Desert Museum Bat Day at Bend. Phone (541) 382-4754.

NOVEMBER

Festival Of Lights at Ashland. Phone (541) 482-3486. Roseburg, phone (541) 672-3469.
3rd Annual Mountain Mercantile at The Resort at the Mountain in Welches. Phone (503) 272-3403.
Starlight Parade in The Dalles. Phone (800) 255-3385.

DECEMBER

Klamath Falls Snowflake Festival & Parade. Phone (541) 883-5368.
Mt. Hood Railroad Christmas Tree Train at Hood River. Phone (800) TRAIN-61.
The High Desert Museum Winter Wonderfest at Bend. Phone (541) 382-4754.

E. Glossary

Aa—Hawaiian term for broken or fragmented solidified lava rocks.
Algae—Plants that occur in water and contain chlorophyll.
Anadromous fish—Fish that hatch in fresh water, migrate to the sea to mature, then return to breed in the freshwater site where they hatched.
Andesite—Usually gray or brown volcanic rock with a high silica content.
Ashfall—Volcanic ash that rains from the cloud of a volcanic eruption.
Ash flow—Hot gas and ash flowing from a volcanic vent.
Archeology—The scientific study of ancient cultures.
Basalt—A fine-grained, dark, volcanic rock with a heavy content of magnesium and iron.
Bacteria—Unicellular microorganisms that may cause disease in plants or animals.
Caldera—Basin-shaped depression in a volcanic summit, usually filling the crater hole.
Chlorophyll—Green matter that is essential to the photosynthesis process of plants.
Cirque—A circular recess caused by glacial erosion on a mountain.
Clear-cut—The practice of harvesting all the trees in a given area at the same time.
Col—A pass between mountain peaks or in a ridge, often caused by cirques forming on both sides of the ridge.
Conifer—Evergreen, cone-bearing trees and shrubs.
Continental ice flow—A glacier that covers a large area of a continent.
Dacite—A usually light-colored volcanic rock with a high silica content.
Deciduous—Plants that lose their leaves seasonally and are leafless until they grow new leaves.
Ecology—Scientific study of the interrelationship of organisms and their environment.
Environment—The conditions and circumstances that surround organisms or groups of organisms.
Evergreen—Plants with foliage that remains green throughout the year.
Extinct—A plant or animal species that no longer exists or a volcano that no longer is active.
Fauna—Animals of a specific period or region.
Folded—Rock warped or tilted by internal earth forces.
Freestone: A rapidly descending river or stream fed by precipitation or runoff water, with little plant life or nutrients.
Fumarole—A vent in the earth's surface that allows steam or gas to escape into the atmosphere.
Forest canopy—The upper level of trees in a forest.
Fungi—A simple plant that lacks chlorophyll.
Geography—The science that deals with the topography of the earth's surface.
Geology—The science that deals with the origin of the earth's crust and its rocks.
Glacier—A large body of ice formed of compacted snow that is forced to move by its own weight.
Glaciated valley—A valley carved or changed by glacial action.
Gneiss—A metamorphic rock consisting of light and dark bands.
Granite—Coarse igneous rock made up primarily of feldspar and quartz.
Grass—Any of many plants with jointed stems, seed-like fruit, and slender, sheathing sleeves.
Herb—A seed-producing annual that does not develop persistent, woody tissue, but dies down at the end of a growing season.
Igneous—Rock formed when magma solidifies.
Juan de Fuca plate—A small segment of the Pacific Ocean tectonic plate that is being subducted under the Pacific Northwest shore.
Lahars—Volcanic mudflows.
Lava—Magma that has been erupted onto the surface of the earth.
Lichens—Composite organisms formed by the symbiotic union of fungus and algae growing on trees or rocks.
Magma—Molten rock inside the earth.
Mammals—Warm-blooded, vertebrate animals that nourish their young with milk from the females' mammary glands.
Maar—A crater from a volcanic explosion of gas, not lava.
Meadow—An area of land where grasses and other low growing plants predominate.
Metamorphic rock—Rock changed by heat and pressure from the earth's interior or by chemical processes.
Millennia—Periods of 1,000 years.
Moraine—A ridge of fragmented rock left when a glacier recedes.
Mudflow—Rock debris saturated by water flowing downhill as a result of volcanic action.
Nonvascular—Organisms lacking the ability to efficiently circulate-life giving fluids.
Obsidian—A glassy form of rhyolite or dacite lavas.
Old-growth—Refers to trees, usually conifers, at least 32 inches in diameter or 200 years old.
Outcrop—Bedrock that protrudes out of the earth.
Peneplain—A surface area reduced by erosion to a near plain.
Plate Tectonics—A theory that large slabs of the earth's outer shell float on the molten rock beneath and are in constant motion.
Pollination—The transfer of pollen from an anther to a stigma as part of the reproductive process of flowers.
Prevailing wind—Wind that usually blows from the same direction because of atmospheric conditions.
Pumice—Porous, silica-rich volcanic glass, may float on water.
Pyroclastic flow—An avalanche of hot, incandescent rock fragments mixed with hot gas that flows from an erupting volcano.
Rapids—A fast-moving stream caused by a steep descent of the stream bed and often associated with rocks and boulders that impede the flow.
Rush—Grass like, stiff marsh herbs with hollow or pithy stems and small flowers, used to make baskets. Also various similar plants.
Saprophyte—An organism, usually bacterium or fungus, that derives nourishment directly from dead or decaying matter it grows on.
Sedge—Grasslike plants of the family that has solid stems, leaves that grow in three vertical rows and inconspicuous flowers surrounded by scale like bract.
Sedimentary rock—Rock formed of sediment of older rock, or the remains of plants or animals.
Shield volcano—Low-slung volcanoes that erupt mostly basalt, which forms a shield over the crater like a solid puddle.
Shrub—A low, woody plant with multiple stems rising from the base, and lacking a main trunk.
Snowfield—A permanent or semipermanent field of snow that lacks the characteristic movement of glaciers.
Species—A classification of organisms that ranks below genus or subgenus. Members of the same species are capable of interbreeding.
Stratovolcano—A volcano made up of layers of fragmented material and lava flows.
Talus—Broken rock that has fallen from a cliff and accumulated at the bottom.
Timberline—The highest elevaton on a mountain capable of supporting trees, in Oregon between 6,000 and 7,000 feet.
Thundereggs—Roundish, hollow nodules containing chalcedony, a translucent quartz.
Understory—Plant life growing beneath the dominant trees of the forest.
Vascular—Organisms with vessels that circulate life-giving fluids.
Vent—An opening in the earth surface that emits lava, volcanic ash, or gas.
Volcanologist—A geologist who specializes in the study of volcanoes.
Watershed—A geographic area drained by a river and its tributaries.

Index